MOON

D0451381

YELLOWSTONE & GRAND TETON

BECKY LOMAX

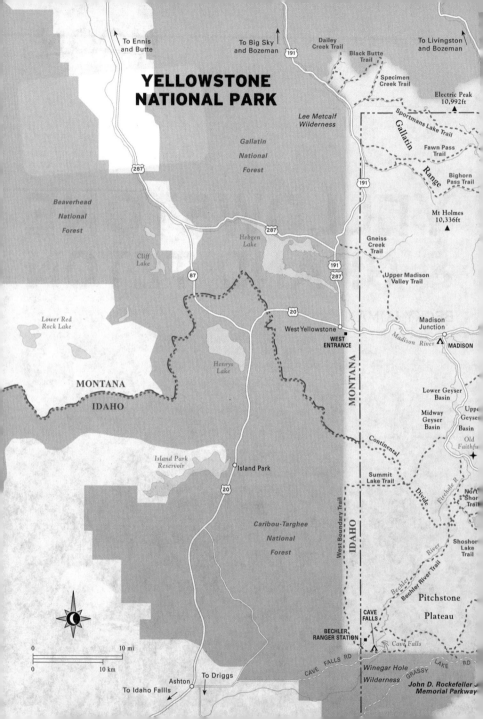

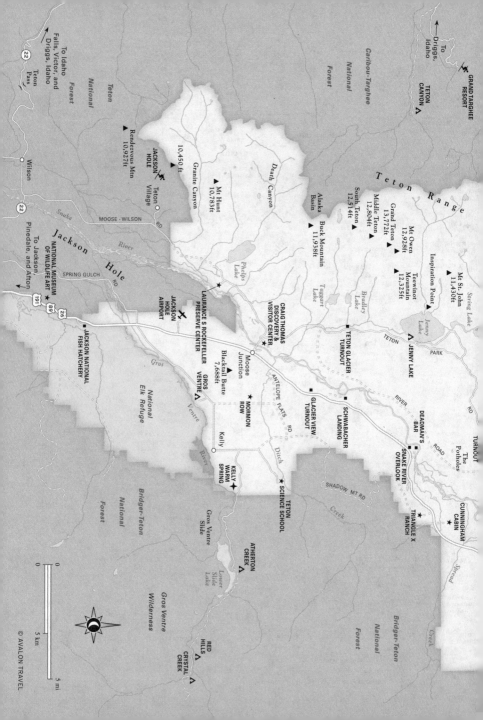

GRAND TETON NATIONAL PARK

Caribou-Targhee National Forest

Jedediah Smith Wilderness

Winegar Hole Wilderness

Moose Mtn 10,054 ft

Survey Peak 9,277 ft

John D Rockefeller Jr Memorial Parkway

To West Thumb and Yellowstone National Park

FLAGG RANCH ★

Moose Basin

Traverse Peak 11,051 ft

Thor Peak 12,028 ft

Bivouac Peak 10,825 ft

Mt Moran 12,605 ft

Eagles Rest Peak 11,258 ft

Ranger Peak 11,355 ft

Waterfalls Canyon

Colter Canyon

Webb Canyon

GRASS LAKE

Snake River

RD

89 191 287

To West Thumb and Yellowstone National Park

Leigh Lake

Jackson Lake

Elk Island

Jackson Lake

LIZARD CREEK

COLTER BAY VISITOR CENTER

COLTER BAY

LEEKS MARINA

Bridger-Teton National Forest

SIGNAL MOUNTAIN

POTHOLES TURNOUT

JACKSON LAKE DAM

Willow Flats

Signal Mountain 7,593 ft

Oxbow Bend

Emma Matilda Lake

Two Ocean Lake

Snake River

Moran Junction

BUFFALO VALLEY RD

To Togwotee Pass and Dubois

26 287

Buffalo River

Pacific Creek

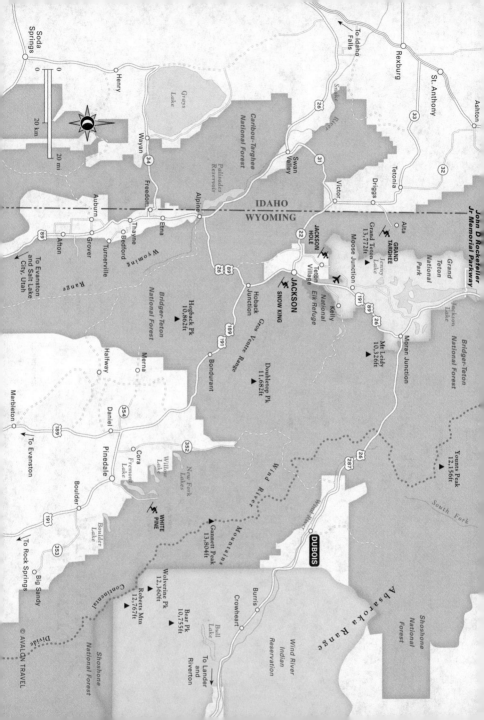

Contents

Yellowstone and Grand Teton

Welcome to the land of fire and ice. The earth's tremendous forces have made Yellowstone and Grand Teton National Parks a volatile landscape. The parks bear the marks of ancient seas, volcanic heat, tectonic upthrusting, and ice scouring. Even today, they shake and roar.

In Yellowstone National Park, rumblings of a supervolcano boil to the surface—spewing, spitting, oozing, and bubbling. Steam rolls from vivid-colored pools, muddy cauldrons burp smelly gases, and blasts of hot water shoot high into the air. The cantankerous landscape gushes with spouters like iconic Old Faithful.

In Grand Teton National Park, toothy spires claw the sky in one of the newest mountain ranges in the Rockies. Glaciers have chewed the terrain, leaving lakes, bowls, and canyons to explore. Towering thousands of feet high to culminate in the Grand Teton, mountains dwarf all that roams across the floor of Jackson Hole.

Clockwise from top left: blooming lupine; Lower Yellowstone Falls; the Gros Ventre Range; trumpeter swans in Hayden Valley; bison in Norris Campground; Punch Bowl in Upper Geyser.

Throughout the Greater Yellowstone area, sagebrush prairies make wildlife easy to spot. Bison, elk, antelope, wolves, and even grizzly bears enchant visitors. Blue-ribbon trout fishing streams, hiking trails, alpine lakes, bicycle paths, white water rivers, and epic ski slopes all create a four-season recreation paradise to explore. The town of Jackson, which anchors the Jackson Hole valley, offers an urban base of operations for the region's myriad recreational bounty.

Come to Yellowstone and Grand Teton National Parks—for the classic experience of the West.

Clockwise from top left: vintage yellow touring sedan; Mormon Row; Great Fountain Geyser; Inspiration Point above Jenny Lake.

Planning Your Trip

Where to Go

North Yellowstone

Staring with the **North Entrance** near **Gardiner** to the **Northeast Entrance** at **Silver Gate** and **Cooke City**, a two-lane park road snakes east across northern Yellowstone. From the travertine terraces at **Mammoth Hot Springs**, the road follows the **Yellowstone River** past sagebrush plateaus to **Tower-Roosevelt**, through the remote **Lamar Valley**, and across the Absaroka Mountains. This is the only park road that remains open year-round, providing **winter access**. The **Mammoth Campground** is also open year-round.

Old Faithful and West Yellowstone

The town of **West Yellowstone** hosts the **busiest park entrance** and the **most services**. As the road enters the park, it follows the Madison and Gibbon Rivers, passing campgrounds at **Madison** and **Norris**. South of Madison, it's geyser paradise: volcanic features include **Fountain Paint Pots**, the **Grand Prismatic Spring**, and the most famous hydrothermal of all—**Old Faithful Geyser**. The Old Faithful area is home to three park lodges, including the architecturally stunning **Old Faithful Inn**.

Canyon and Lake Country

The park hub of **Canyon Village** links Yellowstone's east and west sides. Here, the Yellowstone River cuts deep into the **Grand Canyon of the Yellowstone**. Prominent points and rim-side hikes yield epic views of the plunging waterfalls below. South of Canyon Village, the road follows the Yellowstone River through **Hayden Valley**, prime wildlife habitat. At **Yellowstone Lake**, miles of shoreline host marinas, campgrounds, and lodging at **Fishing Bridge**, **Lake Village**, and **Bridge Bay**.

If You Want...

- **Backpacking:** Plan a route along the Teton Crest Trail in Grand Teton.

- **Bicycling:** Bike to Fairy Falls and Lone Star Geyer in Yellowstone. In Grand Teton, cycle the 30-mile Teton Multi-Use Pathway.

- **Boating:** Boat around Frank Island in Yellowstone Lake or around Elk Island in Jackson Lake.

- **Fishing:** Cast for trout in Yellowstone Lake or Jackson Lake, or aim for Slough Creek, Lamar River, Madison River, or Snake River.

- **Hiking:** Walk to the summit of Mt. Washburn in Yellowstone, or hike Paintbrush Canyon in Grand Teton.

- **Kayaking and Canoeing:** Paddle across Lewis Lake and up the thoroughfare to Shoshone Lake in Yellowstone. In Grand Teton, paddle String Lake or around the islands in Colter Bay on Jackson Lake.

- **Rafting:** Raft the Yellowstone and Gallatin Rivers outside the park. In Grand Teton, float the Snake River.

- **Wildflowers:** Drive Sylvan Pass in Yellowstone for lupine-lined roads, or hike Grand View Point in Grand Teton for pink sticky geranium.

- **Winter Activities:** Take a snowcoach to Old Faithful, or ski at Jackson Hole Mountain Resort.

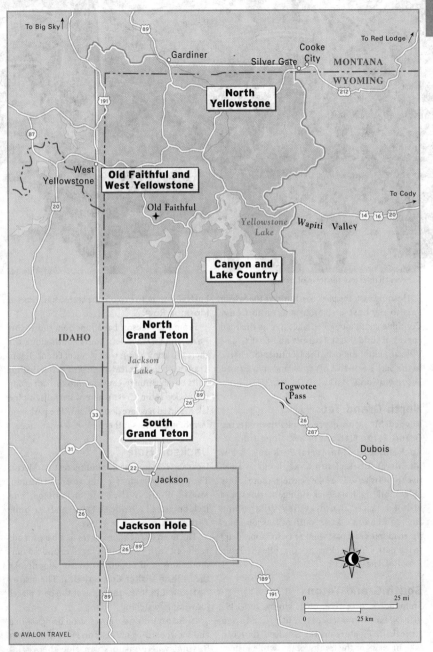

To Big Sky

89

Gardiner

Silver Gate

Cooke City

To Red Lodge

MONTANA

WYOMING

212

North Yellowstone

191

87

West Yellowstone

Old Faithful and West Yellowstone

20

Old Faithful

Yellowstone Lake

Wapiti Valley

To Cody

14 16 20

Canyon and Lake Country

IDAHO

North Grand Teton

Jackson Lake

26 89

Togwotee Pass

26

33

South Grand Teton

287

Dubois

31

22

Jackson

26

Jackson Hole

26 89

189

191

89

0   25 mi

0   25 km

© AVALON TRAVEL

Stagecoach rides tour the town of Jackson.

Heading east, the park road crosses the Sylvan Pass to the **East Entrance** and on to **Cody.** Continue south along the lakeshore as the road curves around **West Thumb** and past **Grant Village,** climbing over the Continental Divide to the park's **South Entrance** and into **Grand Teton National Park.**

North Grand Teton

Rugged Mt. Moran greets visitors entering **Grand Teton National Park** along **John D. Rockefeller, Jr. Memorial Parkway.** Below Mt. Moran sits **Jackson Lake,** home to a native trout fishery. The lake's eastern shore sports lodges, hiking, horseback riding, marinas, and visitor services at **Colter Bay Village** and **Jackson Lake Lodge.** South of Jackson Lake, the road splits east past wildlife-rich Oxbow Bend to the park's **Moran Entrance,** while the Teton Park Road heads south.

South Grand Teton

From the **Moran Entrance,** Highways 26/89/191 offer year-round access south to **Moose Junction.** Floaters on the **Snake River** can take in views of the toothy peaks, while history buffs will want to explore the scenic buildings of **Mormon Row.**

From the Jackson Lake Junction, the **Teton Park Road** (May-Oct.) tours south along the shore of **Jenny Lake,** with views of Grand Teton. Trails such as **Inspiration Point and Hidden Falls** climb through canyons into thin air along the rocky Teton Crest where waterfalls, alpine lakes, and rugged are destinations. The park road terminates at the southern **Moose Entrance.**

Jackson Hole

Jackson Hole is a year-round recreation Mecca. The valley encompasses the towns of Moran, Moose, Kelly, Wilson, Teton Village, and Jackson, as well as **Bridger-Teton** and **Caribou-Targhee National Forests.**

The town of **Jackson** serves as a base for adventures, with year-round services and accommodations, and famous Western saloons like the **Million Dollar Cowboy Bar.** The nearby **National Elk Refuge** is one of the best places for wildlife-watching.

In **Teton Village,** snow season brings skiing and snowboarding to **Jackson Hole Mountain Resort,** where visitors can ride the **Aerial**

Tram to the 10,000-foot summit of Rendezvous Mountain.

West of the Tetons, the **Teton Valley** stretches into Idaho and back, with tiny towns like **Victor** and **Driggs.** The **Grand Targhee Resort** offers fishing, rafting, and biking in summer, and skiing in winter.

Gateways

Big Sky, Montana is the closest gateway to Yellowstone with access to the park's North and West Entrances. **Red Lodge, Montana** serves as the eastern springboard for the scenic Beartooth Highway to Yellowstone's Northeast Entrance. **Cody, Wyoming** offers a Wild West base of operations for Yellowstone's East Entrance. In Wyoming's Wind River Valley, **Lander** and **Dubois** offer dramatic stops on the way to Yellowstone's South Entrance and Grand Teton's Moran Entrance—a route that crosses the Continental Divide at **Togwotee Pass.**

When to Go

High Season
SUMMER (MAY-OCT.)

Summer sees the most visitors, with **July** and **August** luring the biggest crowds. All park **lodges, campgrounds,** and **visitors centers** are open. **June** through **early July** buzzes with mosquitoes, while July through early August brings on rampant wildflowers. **August** also yields the best high-elevation hiking in the Tetons. Most **park roads are open**.

WINTER (DEC.-MID-MAR.)

In winter, deep snows turn the parks white. Alpine skiers gravitate to Jackson Hole while cross-country skiers tackle groomed and untracked trails in both parks. Most **park roads are closed** (Nov.-late Apr.), with the exception of the park road between Yellowstone's North and Northeast Entrances. Touring in Yellowstone is via guided **snowcoach** or **snowmobile,** while lodging is available at **Mammoth Hot Springs** and **Old Faithful.**

Off Season
SPRING (MAR.-MAY)

Mid-April offers **car-free park roads** to cyclists before roads open to vehicles in late April

Baby elk are born in spring.

or May. As the snow melts, fields of yellow glacier lilies emerge. Come in May for bison calving season, or June to spot bighorn sheep ewes with newborn lambs and grizzly bears foraging along Yellowstone Lake. By May, most park roads start to open and visitor services return. Days may be rainy and cold, and some trails remain snow-covered into June.

FALL (SEPT.-NOV.)

Cooler, bug-free days yield pleasant hiking with thinner crowds. Come in late September for the elk rut, when bulls gather harems to prove their dominance and their bugles break the nighttime quiet. Sporadic snowstorms can close park roads temporarily until winter descends in early November. Services are limited as park entrances begin to close.

Before You Go

Park Fees and Passes

The entrance fee for each park is $30 per vehicle ($25 motorcycles, $15 for individuals on foot) and is good for seven days. Visitors planning to enter both parks can buy a joint pass ($50 per vehicle, $40 motorcycles, $20 for individuals on foot).

Other fee options include the Annual Park Pass ($60) for Yellowstone or Grand Teton, and the Interagency Annual Pass ($80), which is good for all national parks and federal fee areas.

Backpackers should reserve a backcountry camping permit in advance (Yellowstone, www.nps.gov/yell, $25, Jan.; Grand Teton, www.recreation.gov, early Jan.-mid-May, $35). Permits are also available first-come, first-served (Yellowstone, 48 hours in advance, $3/person/night; Grand Teton, 24 hours in advance, $25/trip).

Entrance Stations

YELLOWSTONE NATIONAL PARK

Yellowstone has five entrance stations:

- North Entrance (U.S. 89, near Gardiner) is open year-round and provides the closest access to Mammoth Hot Springs.
- Northeast Entrance (Hwy. 212, west of Silver Gate) provides access to Tower-Roosevelt and the Lamar Valley. This road may close temporarily in winter due to snow.
- West Entrance (Hwy. 20, West Yellowstone) is the busiest entrance in the park. This road is

open mid-April to early November and closes in winter.

- East Entrance (U.S. 20) is located between Fishing Bridge and Cody, Wyoming and is open mid-May to early November.
- South Entrance (U.S. 89/191/287) lies on the border between Yellowstone and Grand Teton and is open mid-May to early November.

GRAND TETON NATIONAL PARK

Grand Teton has three entrance stations:

- Moran Entrance (Highway 26/89/191 and Highway 26/287) is open year-round and offers access from the east.
- Granite Canyon Entrance is on the south entrance to the Moose-Wilson Road between Teton Village and Moose. Seasonal access varies.
- Moose Entrance (Teton Park Rd.) is open year-round and provides access to southern region of the park.

Reservations

To guarantee lodging, camping, tours, or dinner reservations for anytime in summer, make reservations at least one year in advance. For winter travel plans, make reservations 6-12 months in advance.

YELLOWSTONE

Xanterra (866/439-7375 or 307/344-7311,

www.yellowstonenationalparklodges.com) operates two winter lodges (Mammoth and Old Faithful Snow Lodge), nine summer lodges (Canyon Lodge, Grant Village, Lake Lodge, Lake Yellowstone Hotel, Mammoth Springs Hotel, Old Faithful Inn, Old Faithful Lodge, Snow Lodge, and Roosevelt Lodge), and five campgrounds (Madison, Grant Village, Canyon, Bridge Bay, and Fishing Bridge RV Park).

GRAND TETON
Grand Teton Lodging Company (800/628-9988 or 307/543-2811, www.gtlc.com) operates four summer lodges (Jackson Lake Lodge, Colter Bay Village, Jenny Lake Lodge, and Headwaters Lodge) and two campgrounds: Headwaters and Colter Bay RV Park.

JACKSON HOLE
For reservations at Jackson Hole Mountain Resort and in the town of Jackson, contact **Jackson Hole Central Reservations** (800/333-7766or 307/733-2292, www.jacksonhole.com) or **Jackson Hole Reservations Company** (800/329-9205 or 307/733-6331, www.jackson-hole.net).

In the Parks

Visitor Centers
YELLOWSTONE
Out of the eight visitor centers, the largest ones are **Old Faithful Visitor Education Center** (307/344-2751, Old Faithful Village) and **Canyon Visitor Education Center** (307/344-2550, Canyon Village).

GRAND TETON
The main visitor center is the **Craig Thomas Discovery & Visitor Center** (307/739-3399) in the South Teton section of the park.

Campgrounds
YELLOWSTONE
Of the 12 campgrounds in Yellowstone, the largest five accept **reservations** (Xanterra,

Snow Lodge at Old Faithful

307/344-7311 or 866/439-7375, www.yellowstone nationalparklodges.com):

- **Madison** (278 sites, early May-mid-Oct.) located at Madison Junction.

- **Canyon** (270 sites, late May-mid-Sept.) in Canyon Village.

- **Fishing Bridge RV Park** (340 sites, early May-late Sept.) in Fishing Bridge.

- **Bridge Bay** (432 sites, late May-early Sept.) in Lake Village.

- **Grant Village** (430 sites, late June-late Sept.) on the West Thumb of Lake Yellowstone.

Campers without reservations should head to the park's **first-come, first-served campgrounds:** Mammoth (85 sites, year-round), Indian Creek (70 sites, mid-June-mid-Sept.), Norris (100 sites, late May-late Sept.), Tower Fall (31 sites, late May-late Sept.), Slough Creek (23 sites, mid-June-early Sept.), Pebble Creek (27 sites, mid-June-late Sept.), or Lewis Lake.

GRAND TETON
Grand Teton's six campgrounds are all

first-come, first-served and include Lizard Creek (60 sites, mid-June-early Sept.), Signal Mountain (81 sites, early May-mid-Oct.), Jenny Lake (49 sites, early May-late Sept.), Gros Ventre (350 sites, early May-early Oct.), and Colter Bay (350 sites, mid-May-late Sept.).

Colter Bay RV Park (Colter Bay Village, 800/628-9988, www.gtlc.com, mid-May-late Sept.) and **Headwaters Campground & RV** (Flagg Ranch, 307/543-2861 or 800/443-2311, www.gtlc.com, late May-Sept.) accept reservations 6-9 months in advance.

Getting Around
YELLOWSTONE
In summer, **you'll need a vehicle** to get around. There is **no park shuttle.** In winter, **Xanterra** (866/439-7375 or 307/344-7311, www.yellowstonenationalparklodges.com) operates snowcoaches into the park.

GRAND TETON
Alltrans (307/733-3135, www.jacksonholealltrans.com) runs a shuttle multiple times daily from Jackson to popular park destinations.

Old Faithful Visitor Education Center

Yellowstone In-Park Lodging

	Location	Price	Season	Amenities
Mammoth Campground	Mammoth Hot Springs	$20	year-round	campsites
Mammoth Hot Springs Hotel	Mammoth Hot Springs	$90-260	May-mid-Oct. and late Dec.-early Mar.	hotel rooms, cabins, restaurant
Tower Fall Campground	Tower-Roosevelt	$15	early June-early Sept.	campsites
Roosevelt Lodge and Cabins	Tower-Roosevelt	$82-140	early June-early Sept.	cabins, restaurant
Slough Creek Campground	Northeast Entrance	$15	mid-June-early Sept.	campsites
Pebble Creek Campground	Northeast Entrance	$15	mid-June-late Sept.	campsites
Madison Campground	Madison	$23	early May-mid-Oct.	campsites
Indian Creek Campground	Mammoth to Norris	$15	mid-June-mid-Sept	campsites
Norris Campground	Norris	$20	late May-late Sept.	campsites
Old Faithful Lodge	Old Faithful	$85-145	mid-May-early Oct.	motel rooms, cabins, restaurant
Snow Lodge	Old Faithful	$110-265	May-mid-Oct. and mid-Dec.-early Mar.	hotel rooms, cabins, restaurants
Old Faithful Inn	Old Faithful	$110-270	early May-mid-Oct.	hotel rooms, restaurants
Canyon Campground	Canyon Village	$26	late May-mid-Sept.	campsites, showers
Canyon Lodge and Cabins	Canyon Village	$195-235	late May-late Sept.	hotel rooms, cabins, restaurants
Fishing Bridge RV Park	Fishing Bridge	$50	early May-late Sept.	RV sites
Bridge Bay Campground	Lake Village	$22	late May-early Sept.	campsites, marina
Lake Lodge Cabins	Lake Village	$85-205	early June-late Sept.	motel rooms, cabins, restaurant
Lake Yellowstone Hotel and Cabins	Lake Village	$155-410	mid-May-early Oct.	hotel rooms, cabins, restaurant
Lewis Lake Campground	West Thumb and Grant Village	$15	mid-June-Oct.	campsites
Grant Village Campground	West Thumb and Grant Village	$26	late June-late Sept.	campsites
Grant Village Lodge	West Thumb and Grant Village	$165-210	late May-late Sept.	hotel rooms, restaurants

Grand Teton In-Park Lodging

	Location	Price	Season	Amenities
Grassy Lake Road	John D. Rockefeller, Jr. Memorial Parkway	free	June-Sept.	primitive campsites
Headwaters Campground & RV	John D. Rockefeller, Jr. Memorial Parkway	$35-70	late May-Sept.	campsites
Headwaters Lodge & Cabins at Flagg Ranch	John D. Rockefeller, Jr. Memorial Parkway	$195-300	June-Sept. and mid-Dec.-early Mar.	motel rooms, cabins, camper cabins, restaurant
Colter Bay Campground	Colter Bay	$25-68	mid-May-late Sept.	campsites
Colter Bay Tent Village	Colter Bay	$65	late May-early Sept.	tent cabins
Colter Bay Cabins	Colter Bay	$90-250	late May-early Oct.	cabins
Lizard Creek	Jackson Lake	$22	mid-June-early Sept.	campsites
Jackson Lake Lodge	Jackson Lake	$290-390	late May-early Oct.	hotel rooms, cottages, restaurant
Signal Mountain Campground	Signal Mountain	$22-45	early May-mid-Oct.	campsites
Signal Mountain Lodge	Signal Mountain	$185-385	early May-mid-Oct.	motel rooms, cabins, restaurants
Jenny Lake Campground	Jenny Lake	$23	early May-late Sept	tent-only campsites
Jenny Lake Lodge	Jenny Lake	$690-960	June-early Oct.	cabins, restaurant
Gros Ventre Campground	Moose	$23	early May-early Oct.	campsites
Dornan's Spur Ranch Cabins	Moose	$200-300	May-Oct. and Dec.-Mar.	cabins, restaurants
Triangle X Ranch	Moose to Moran	rates vary	mid-May-mid-Oct. and late Dec.-mid-Mar.	dude ranch

Headwaters Lodge

The Best of Yellowstone and Grand Teton

Yellowstone and Grand Teton are crammed with unique sights. Opt for three nights in Grand Teton National Park, staying in Jackson Lake Lodge or camping at Signal Mountain or Jenny Lake. Then move to a central location in Yellowstone for the last three nights, overnighting at Old Faithful Inn or Canyon Village. Campers can stay at Canyon or Norris Campground.

Grand Teton

DAY 1

Start in southern Grand Teton National Park. From the **Moose Entrance,** drive south on the **Moose-Wilson Road** to the **Laurance S. Rockefeller Preserve Center,** where exhibits let you explore the sensory importance of nature. At the center, walk to **Phelps Lake** to soak up the sights, sounds, and experiences while sinking into the pace of the natural world. Drive north, watching for **moose** in the beaver ponds, before

continuing onto **Teton Park Road** to the Taggart Lake Trailhead. Hike to **Taggart Lake** for an afternoon swim below **Nez Perce**.

DAY 2

In the early morning, catch views of the **Grand Teton** en route to **Jenny Lake**, an idyllic moraine pool huddling below Teewinot. Long-distance hikers can start at the String Lake Trailhead to hike **Paintbrush-Cascade Loop** over **Paintbrush Divide**. For a shorter hike, hop the shuttle boat across Jenny Lake to climb to **Hidden Point and Inspiration Falls** for an eagle-eye view of the lake. Or opt for a scenic drive to **Mormon Row** for Jackson Hole history. If you have any energy left, take a sunset drive for **wildlife watching.**

DAY 3

After catching the morning sunrise on the **Teton**

the Grand Teton, Teton Glacier, and Mt. Owen

Old Faithful erupts.

Mountains, drive to **Colter Bay.** Take a **horseback ride** to nab views of the lake backed by rugged **Mt. Moran.** In the afternoon, rent a canoe or kayak to paddle **Colter Bay** or take a boat tour on **Jackson Lake.** Head to Jackson Lake Lodge for dinner in the **Mural Room,** where windows look out on the panorama of scenery you experienced during the day.

Yellowstone
DAY 4
Drive north to the **South Entrance** of Yellowstone National Park. Stop at **West Thumb** and walk through the **West Thumb Geyser Basin** to see crystal blue hot pools, cone geysers, and paint pots on the shores of **Yellowstone Lake.** Continue driving north, stopping at picnic areas and pullouts along the lake, particularly **Gull Point Drive.** Stop to take in the historic **Lake Yellowstone Hotel** and again at **Fishing Bridge** to see spawning wild trout in the **Yellowstone River.** Continue north through **Hayden Valley,** where wildlife are prominent. Turn right onto South Rim Drive, just south of Canyon Village, and walk to **Artist Point** for views of the **Grand Canyon of the Yellowstone.**

DAY 5
Today will be spent exploring **Old Faithful.** Stop in at the **Old Faithful Visitor Education Center** to see the exhibits and find out when **Old Faithful Geyser** is scheduled to erupt. Tour the **Upper Geyser Basin** boardwalks and paths while you wait for the famous geyser to blow. Walk to the steam-spewing **Castle Geyser** and take the boardwalk route to **Grotto Geyser,** a fountain geyser. Continue along the paved pathway to see the deep colors of **Morning Glory Pool.** After geyser gazing, stop into **Old Faithful Inn** to admire the historic lodge.

Back on the road, your next stop is in the **Lower Geyser Basin** where you can see all four types of geothermal features at **Fountain Paint Pots.** En route back to Old Faithful, go to **Midway Geyser Basin.** Walk across the **Firehole River** and follow the boardwalk loop to see the giant, colorful **Grand Prismatic Spring.** Return to Canyon Village for your overnight.

DAY 6

Start early in the morning to climb **Mt. Washburn**, just north of Canyon. From the summit, you'll see the entire park and the Tetons in the distance (but be off the summit before afternoon thunderstorms rolls in). After the hike, continue north to **Lamar Valley** for wildlife watching. Use binocular to scan the terrain for bison, antelope, wolves, and grizzlies. Then loop west through **Tower-Fall** to Mammoth to see the **Mammoth Hot Springs** travertine terraces.

DAY 7

From Mammoth, drive south to finish your adventures at the hottest, most dynamic geysers at **Norris Geyser Basin.** Walk the trails and boardwalks to see **Steamboat Geyser**, the tallest geyser in the world, and **Porcelain Basin**, a colorful collection of hot springs and fumaroles. Plan to exit the park via the **West Entrance** to take in a last bit of **wildlife watching** along the **Madison River**.

Best Hikes

Yellowstone National Park
FAIRY FALLS

Traipse **5.8 miles round-trip** through open meadows and a young lodgepole forest to reach the 197-foot **Fairy Falls.** From a narrow slot, the falls plunges into a deep pool. In winter, the falls drape with icicles.

OLD FAITHFUL OBSERVATION POINT

Climb **2.1 miles round-trip** up a couple switchbacks to a point where you can look down on **Old Faithful Geyser.** Crowds below look tiny, and the viewpoint gives a different angle on the erupting geyser. Descend via a different route to complete the loop.

SOUTH RIM TRAIL AND POINT SUBLIME

On the south rim of the **Grand Canyon of the Yellowstone,** this **5.1-mile (round-trip)** trail takes in multiple viewpoints with side trips. **Uncle Tom's Trail** plunges on a steel staircase more than 300 steps to the base of Lower Yellowstone Falls. The route continues to **Artist Point** and on the less-traveled route to **Point Sublime.**

Uncle Tom's Trail

One Day in Yellowstone

If you only have one day to see Yellowstone, concentrate your efforts inside the caldera to see the most geothermal activity. The South Grand Loop will circle mostly within the caldera rim.

From West Yellowstone, drive the Madison River Valley toward National Park Mountain. This wildlife corridor harbors bison and elk. Look for them in the meadows, but be ready to brake as they can be in the road.

At Madison Junction, turn north to follow the Gibbon River, stopping at Gibbon Falls. You'll climb out of the supervolcano caldera en route to Norris Junction, where a right turn continues following the Gibbon River. Within a mile, you'll drop back into the caldera to continue toward Canyon Junction.

At Canyon Junction, stop at the Canyon Visitor Education Center to learn about the volcano's workings. From there, drive Grand Loop Road south to South Rim Drive to reach Artist Point for views of Lower Yellowstone Falls. Then, if you've got gumption, stop at Uncle Tom's Trail to hike the stairway down to stand level with the falls to hear its roaring thunder.

Continue south through Hayden Valley watching for wildlife as you follow the Yellowstone River upstream to Yellowstone Lake, the largest freshwater lake above 7,000 feet in North America. En route, you'll see increasing geothermal activity with fumaroles and mud pots. Stop at the historic Lake Yellowstone Hotel to dine for lunch.

After lunch, follow Yellowstone Lake south to Grant Junction to head west to Old Faithful by crossing the Continental Divide to drop into the Firehole River Valley. Tour the boardwalk loop around Geyser Hill, but check the signs first, so you can catch Old Faithful Geyser erupting. Stop in the Old Faithful Inn to tour the historic log lobby. Then, follow the Firehole River north to Midway Geyser Basin to walk the boardwalk to see Grand Prismatic Spring. Watch for wildlife as you descend the valley past steam vents to return to Madison Junction and back to West Yellowstone.

Artist Point

hikers passing Cascade Lake

MT. WASHBURN

A 5-mile round-trip climb leads to the 10,243-foot summit of Mt. Washburn for 360-degree panoramic views. It's a grunt, but the lookout provides huge rewards.

CHAIN OF LAKES

For fishing and wildflowers, hike 8 miles round-trip to Cascade and Grebe Lakes. With a shuttle and strong route-finding skills, hikers can add on Wolf and Ice Lakes.

Grand Teton National Park

GRAND VIEW POINT

Take in this scenic viewpoint of the Teton Mountains from multiple trailheads. Shorter 3-mile routes go from Jackson Lake Lodge while a 13.2-mile loop takes in the viewpoint plus Two Oceans and Emma Matilda Lakes.

PAINTBRUSH CANYON-CASCADE CANYON

A long day takes hikers up Paintbrush Canyon to the 10,700-foot-high Paintbrush Divide before dropping to Solitude Lake and walking straight toward the Grand Teton. The 20-mile-loop finishes by plunging down Cascade Canyon.

HIDDEN FALLS AND INSPIRATION POINT

The most popular hike in Grand Teton National Park is a 7.2-mile round-trip climb that summits Inspiration Point, a rocky outcrop at 7,200 feet with impressive views of Jackson Hole. Hikers get a bonus of going past Hidden Falls.

SURPRISE AND AMPHITHEATER LAKES

A hefty dose of switchbacks climbs into a subalpine basin below Grand Teton. The 10.2-mile round-trip sun-soaked hike yields rewards of dazzling Surprise and Amphitheater Lakes, the latter of which is in a hanging valley.

HERON POND AND SWAN LAKE

The virtually flat 2.6-mile loop goes to the sheltered Heron Pond, where you can see American pelicans, beaver, and moose.

One Day in Grand Teton and Jackson Hole

Start your day in Jackson at the Jackson Town Square to see the famous antler arches. Before heading north into Grand Teton National Park, stop at pullouts to scan for wildlife at the National Elk Refuge or tour the National Museum of Wildlife Art.

Shortly after entering the park, stop at Sleeping Indian Overlook to take in the view of the famous Gros Ventre Mountain to the east. Then, continue to Moose Junction, watching for wildlife en route: bison, coyote, and bald eagles. Stop at the Craig Thomas Discovery & Visitor Center to learn about the park.

Head north on Teton Park Road, stopping at pullouts for photos of the Teton Mountains and Grand Teton shooting up from the sagebrush meadows of Jackson Hole. Continue past South Jenny Lake to North Jenny Lake before turning left. Stop at the picnic area for lunch and drive the one-way road along Jenny Lake. Talk a stroll on the lakeshore trail for photos of the Cathedral Group. Then, continue north on Teton Park Road to Jackson Lake Junction.

Make a beeline for Jackson Lake Lodge for a break on the back deck to soak up the views overlooking Jackson Lake and Mt. Moran. After touring the historic hotel, drive north to Colter Bay to walk the Colter Bay Lakeshore Trail with more intimate views of the same scenery. If time permits, take a boat tour.

Work your way back south on the Outer Park Road (Hwy. 26/89/191), aiming for Moran Junction. Stop en route at Oxbow Bend Turnout to scan for wildlife. At Moran Junction, turn south to the Snake River Overlook for a photo op that includes the river. Continue south, taking a quick detour to Mormon Row to see the famous historic barn with the Tetons. Then return to your starting point to celebrate the day in the Million Dollar Cowboy Bar in Jackson.

Mormon Row

bison on the road in Hayden Valley

Greater Yellowstone Road Trip

The scenery-laden terrain of the Greater Yellowstone Ecosystem was made for road-tripping. Tackle this journey with a camera and binoculars in hand. Whether camping or staying in lodges (lodge travel can get you on the road faster), reservations are essential in summer. Large RVs will need to make alternate plans for Day 5.

Day 1

With its broad alpine meadows and snow-capped peaks, the **Beartooth Highway** makes a grand entrance to reach the **Northeast Entrance** of **Yellowstone National Park**. After cutting through the Absaroka Mountains, you'll descend into the **Lamar Valley** for wildlife watching. Herds of bison and pronghorn cluster in sagebrush meadows, and raptors fly overhead. Check into the **Roosevelt Lodge** for one night, driving back out at dusk to catch bears, coyotes, and wolves.

Day 2

From Roosevelt, head south on the **Grand Loop Road** and follow the winding road toward Tower. Walk to viewpoints to see **Tower Fall**. After Tower, the road continues with curve after curve, climbing through aspens, conifer forests, and grassy meadows along the side of **Mt. Washburn** to **Dunraven Pass**. Descend into **Canyon Village**, stopping at the **Canyon Visitor Education Center** and then drive the North Rim Road along **Grand Canyon of the Yellowstone**, making stops at **Lookout Point** and **Inspiration Point**. Continue south on Grand Loop Road to explore **Hayden Valley** for wildlife watching before returning to **Canyon Village** to spend the night at **Canyon Lodge**.

Day 3

Today, you'll almost completely circle **Lower Grand Loop Road**, so get an early start. Drive west on the Canyon-Norris Road from Canyon Village toward **Norris**, stopping to tour the **Norris Geyser Basin**. Then follow the Gibbon River south to see **Gibbon Falls**. Continuing south on Grand Loop Road, turn right onto Firehole Canyon Road

Winter Fun

Winter is a time when you can find solitude in the parks with only a handful of people instead of a thousand at Old Faithful Geyser. Most lodges inside both parks close for winter. Only Mammoth Hot Springs Hotel and Snow Lodge stay open in winter.

- **Snowcoach Tours:** Snowcoaches outfitted with special wheels, tracks, or skis take visitors into Yellowstone National Park's interior in winter. They depart from Mammoth, West Yellowstone, and Flagg Ranch for day trips to Old Faithful and Grand Canyon of the Yellowstone. Snowcoaches also convey riders from Mammoth or Flagg Ranch to Snow Lodge at Old Faithful for overnighting.

- **Snowmobiling:** Snowmobile day tours go from West Yellowstone, Mammoth, and Flagg Ranch into Yellowstone's interior to Old Faithful and Grand Canyon of the Yellowstone.

- **Downhill Skiing and Snowboarding:** Four downhill skiing and snowboarding areas are the big places to go in winter. Jackson Hole Mountain Resort and Grand Targhee Resort flank opposite sides of the Teton Mountains, while the smaller Snow King Mountain borders the town of Jackson. Northeast of Yellowstone, Big Sky Resort offers a home base for skiing and exploring Yellowstone.

- **Cross-Country Skiing and Snowshoeing:** Roads and trails in both national parks turn into cross-country ski and snowshoe trails. Rendezvous Trails in West Yellowstone Lone Mountain Ranch in Big Sky and Grand Targhee in Teton Valley groom trails for skate and classic skiing.

- **Wildlife Watching:** Sure, some animals migrate, but many are still out and about in the parks and wintering in areas adjacent to the parks. See bison, elk, wolves, coyote, moose, and raptors. Many animals winter in the Paradise Valley north of Gardiner and Yellowstone, while others go for lower elevations around West Yellowstone. The National Elk Refuge in Jackson Hole is home to thousands of elk in winter, plus other wildlife.

- **Sleigh Rides:** You can bundle up and travel in old fashion style in sleigh rides. Find them in Jackson Hole, Wyoming and Big Sky, Montana in winter.

Skis become a major mode of winter travel in the Tetons.

to gaze at **Firehole Falls**. After rejoining the main road, drive south through **Lower Geyser Basin**. Stop off at Firehole Lake Drive to watch **Grand Geyser** and stretch your legs at **Firehole Lake**.

Back on Grand Loop, walk the **Biscuit Basin** boardwalk to enjoy the clear blue hot pools. For the final geyser stop, pull in to see **Old Faithful Geyser** blow water. Climb eastward where the road crosses the **Continental Divide** twice before descending to West Thumb, where you'll turn south to **Grant Village** to spend the night.

Day 4

This is an easier day spent touring several lakes. Start by driving north along **Yellowstone Lake** toward **Bridge Bay,** stopping to enjoy appealing beaches and the distant Absaroka Mountains. After turning around at Bridge Bay, return south past Grant Village to **Lewis Lake**.

From here, follow the headwaters of the Snake River south through **John D. Rockefeller, Jr. Memorial Parkway** and into **Grand Teton National Park.** At **Jackson Lake**, Mt. Moran dominates the Teton Range. Go as far as **Leek's Marina** for afternoon pizza and drinks on the water. Return north to **Flagg Ranch** to stay in a cabin at **Headwaters Lodge**. Get an early night to prepare for tomorrow's big adventure.

Day 5

Launch west from **Flagg Ranch** where you'll kiss pavement goodbye for several hours on the **Grassy Lake Road**, also known as the Ashton-Flagg Ranch Road. Climb the narrow dirt and cobble road above the Snake River to head west through a slice of **Caribou-Targhee National Forest**.

After reaching Ashton, Idaho, work south through the **Teton Valley** to enjoy the less-traveled bucolic west side of the **Teton Mountains**. At the south end of Teton Valley, climb the 10 percent grade over **Teton Pass,** cresting to

Grassy Lake Road/Ashton-Flagg Ranch Road overlooks the Snake River.

spectacular views of the Tetons, Jackson Hole, and Gros Ventre Mountains. Head to **Jackson** for the night, and celebrate by dining at **Local** across from the **Town Square**.

Day 6

Drive to **Jackson Hole Mountain Resort** to ride the **Aerial Tram** up the 10,927-foot summit of Rendezvous Mountain where you can survey Jackson Hole. After descending, turn north to re-enter Grand Teton National Park at **Granite Canyon** and drive the **Moose-Wilson Road** looking for wildlife. At Moose, tour the **Craig Thomas Discovery and Visitor Center**. From Moose Junction, drive Teton Park Road north, stopping at **Jenny Lake**. At **Signal Mountain,** turn right to ascend Signal Mountain Road to an overlook with a frontal view of the entire Teton Mountain Range.

Exiting the park at **Moran,** head east over **Togwotee Pass**. Glance in your rear view mirror to say goodbye to the Teton Mountains.

Grab the binoculars and spotting scopes. Wildlife-watching is rampant in the Greater Yellowstone Ecosystem.

YELLOWSTONE

Swan Lake Flat: South of Mammoth, Swan Lake Flat in Gardners Hole yields frequent sightings of bears, birds, elk, bison, and wolves.

Lamar Valley: Driving into Lamar Valley catapults visitors back to the days of Lewis and Clark with a seemingly endless herd of bison. Pronghorn antelope feed between the bison, and wolves cruise through looking for the old or infirm. You can also spot bighorn sheep and mountain goats near cliffs on the surrounding mountains.

Madison River: In fall, watch bugling bull elk round up harems of cows. Bison often block traffic on the road. Deer munch grass on the fringes of the meadows, and trumpeter swans float in slow-moving eddies.

Hayden Valley: Spot larger animals in Hayden Valley as well as trumpeter swans. Bison feed next to the Yellowstone River, and grizzly bears and moose use the area, too. Look for harlequin ducks in early summer at LeHardys Rapids.

Tower-Roosevelt: Bighorn sheep cluster in the cliffs for safety from predators around the Tower Fall area.

Mammoth Hot Springs: In the village of Mammoth Hot Springs, elk are easy to spot. They hang out on the lawns.

Fishing Bridge: During spawning season in June and July on the Yellowstone River, stand on the historic Fishing Bridge to see hundreds of wild cutthroat trout, plus bald eagles and grizzly bears as they fish.

Pelican Creek: In spring, Pelican Creek turns into prime bear feeding. Look also for bald eagles and moose.

GRAND TETON

Oxbow Bend: Below Jackson Lake Dam where the Snake River slows into convoluted backwaters, the habitat attracts moose, river otters, muskrats, songbirds, American pelicans, and bald eagles.

Mormon Row-Antelope Flats: Look for bison, pronghorn, coyote, sage grouse, and raptors such as American kestrals and northern harriers.

Teton Park Road: The sage meadows attract elk and bison. Look for raptors overhead.

Moose-Wilson Road: The wetlands on the road are home to beaver and moose while berry bushes and wild fruit trees attract grizzly bears.

JACKSON HOLE

On the **National Elk Refuge,** thousands of elk winter before returning to the mountains. The refuge also is habitat for mountain lions, trumpeter swans, bighorn sheep, and raptors.

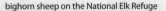
bighorn sheep on the National Elk Refuge

North Yellowstone

Highlights

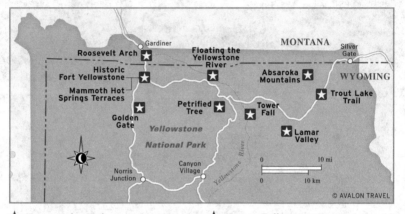

★ **Roosevelt Arch:** Built in 1903, the Roosevelt Arch offers an impressive entrance into Yellowstone National Park (page 41).

★ **Historic Fort Yellowstone:** Tour the stone buildings of this former cavalry outpost while watching resident elk graze on the parade grounds (page 42).

★ **Mammoth Hot Springs Terraces:** Walk the lower formations of these otherworldly travertine terraces and drive through the dormant upper terraces (page 44).

★ **Golden Gate:** The road through Golden Gate climbs 1,500 feet in three miles to crest Kingman Pass, offering views of the amazing landscape (page 45).

★ **Petrified Tree:** Visit a lone petrified tree trunk or view petrified trunks, stumps, leaves, and needles on Specimen Ridge (page 47).

★ **Tower Fall:** This 132-foot-tall waterfall drops through a fantastical collection of rhyolite pinnacles (page 47).

★ **Lamar Valley:** Lamar Valley houses huge bison herds, but you can also spot elk, antelope, bears, wolves, bighorn sheep, and raptors (page 47).

★ **Absaroka Mountains:** Forming the eastern boundary of Yellowstone, these mountains climb higher than 12,000 feet (page 49).

★ **Trout Lake Trail:** This short but steep grunt climbs to an idyllic subalpine lake surrounded by wildflower meadows and forest (page 57).

★ **Floating the Yellowstone River:** Raft through the multicolored rock formations of Yankee Jim Canyon (page 59).

Balancing volcanic features and high mountains, North Yellowstone clings to the park's Montana-Wyoming border.

This is where sagebrush plateaus bisected by the Yellowstone River proliferate with wildlife. Hot water boils to the earth's surface in Mammoth Hot Springs. The ever-changing travertine mixes color and sculpted beauty into a hillside of otherworldly formations.

High mountains rim the northern plateaus and valleys. To the west, the Gallatin Range rises to 10,969-foot Electric Peak. To the northeast, the Absaroka Mountains shoot higher, as a prelude to the Absaroka-Beartooth Wilderness.

Between the mountain ranges, you can watch plenty of wildlife. Elk hang out in Mammoth Hot Springs. Bears and wolves hunt at Swan Lake Flat in Gardners Hole. Vast herds of bison congregate in Lamar Valley. Pronghorn race through sagebrush, bighorn sheep feed on steep slopes, and, higher yet, mountain goats walk the cliffs. Bring binoculars and spotting scopes for watching the action.

Several small communities provide visitor services. Mammoth, a village once known as Fort Yellowstone, houses the visitors center, hotel, and restaurants. Five miles north, Gardiner borders the park's North Entrance, and serves as the capital for rafting, floating, and fishing the Yellowstone River. The tiny mountain outposts of Silver Gate and Cooke City flank the park's Northeast Entrance and anchor the Beartooth Highway.

PLANNING YOUR TIME

The road between Gardiner-Mammoth and Silver Gate-Cooke City remains open all year. In summer, most visitors spend a day or two in the northern section of the park to see Mammoth Hot Springs, raft the Yellowstone River, and watch wildlife. In winter, Gardiner and Mammoth can be a destination for several days of cross-country skiing, snowmobiling, and snowcoach touring to Old Faithful.

Previous: Roosevelt Arch; Mammoth Hot Springs. **Above:** the Yellowstone River

North Yellowstone

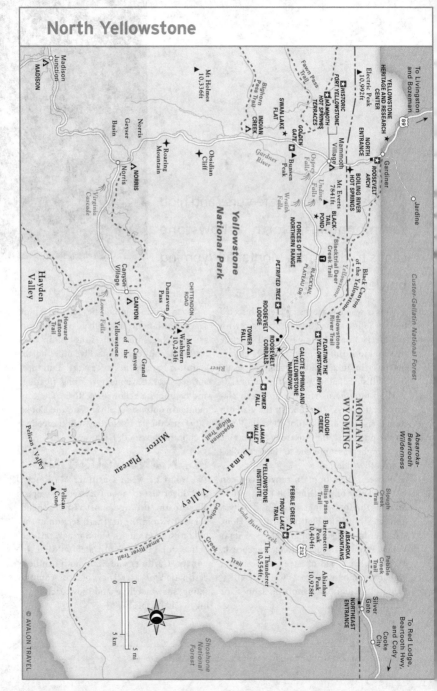

© AVALON TRAVEL

Exploring North Yellowstone

VISITORS CENTERS
Albright Visitor Center
The renovated **Albright Visitor Center** (307/344-2263, 9am-5pm daily year-round) is located in Mammoth Hot Springs, with elk often hanging out on the front lawn. This is one of the historic buildings from the days when the U.S. Cavalry ran the park. The red-tiled roof, brick structure, and large-columned verandah retain the look of Fort Yellowstone, when it served as quarters for bachelor officers. The visitors center has park maps, trail information, brochures, updates, and a **backcountry office** (8am-4:30pm daily June-Aug.), with permits for backcountry camping, boating, and fishing. In 2015, new exhibits on cultural history, wildlife, and the northern area of the park were introduced. The **Yellowstone Association** (406/848-2400, www.yellowstoneassociation.org) operates a small bookstore inside.

Gardiner
The **Gardiner Chamber of Commerce** (216 Park St., Gardiner, 406/848-7971, www.gardinerchamber.com) maintains an information

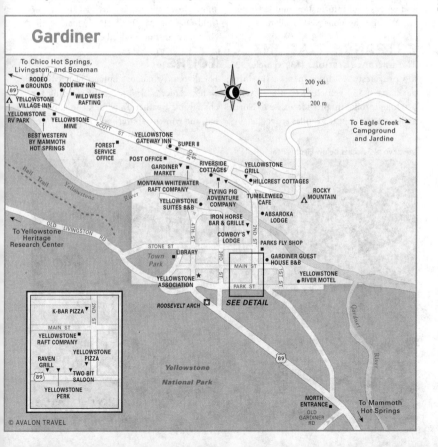

Gardiner

To Chico Hot Springs, Livingston, and Bozeman

RODEO GROUNDS
RODEWAY INN
WILD WEST RAFTING
YELLOWSTONE VILLAGE INN
YELLOWSTONE RV PARK
YELLOWSTONE MINE
SCOTT ST
BEST WESTERN BY MAMMOTH HOT SPRINGS
FOREST SERVICE OFFICE
YELLOWSTONE GATEWAY INN
SUPER 8
POST OFFICE
GARDINER MARKET
RIVERSIDE COTTAGES
YELLOWSTONE GRILL
HILLCREST COTTAGES
MONTANA WHITEWATER RAFT COMPANY
FLYING PIG ADVENTURE COMPANY
TUMBLEWEED CAFE
ROCKY MOUNTAIN
YELLOWSTONE SUITES B&B
ABSAROKA LODGE
IRON HORSE BAR & GRILLE
COWBOY'S LODGE
PARKS FLY SHOP
To Yellowstone Heritage Research Center
OLD LIVINGSTON RD
STONE ST
LIBRARY
Town Park
GARDINER GUEST HOUSE B&B
MAIN ST
YELLOWSTONE RIVER MOTEL
YELLOWSTONE ASSOCIATION
PARK ST
ROOSEVELT ARCH
SEE DETAIL
Rail Trail
Yellowstone River
4TH ST
3RD ST
2ND ST
1ST ST
Gardiner River

To Eagle Creek Campground and Jardine

0   200 yds
0   200 m

K-BAR PIZZA
2ND ST
MAIN ST
YELLOWSTONE RAFT COMPANY
YELLOWSTONE PIZZA
RAVEN GRILL
TWO BIT SALOON
89
YELLOWSTONE PERK

Yellowstone National Park

89

NORTH ENTRANCE
OLD GARDINER RD

To Mammoth Hot Springs

© AVALON TRAVEL

center. While it lacks exhibits, it is a good place to get information on Gardiner, the Custer-Gallatin National Forest, and the Absaroka-Beartooth Wilderness, as well as recreation, lodging, and dining. (It is also one of the few places to find public restrooms in Gardiner.) The **Custer-Gallatin National Forest** (805 Scott St., Gardiner, 406/848-7485, www.fs.usda.gov/gallatin) has a district office in Gardiner, and is the place to go for forest, camping, and trail information and maps.

Cooke City

The **Cooke City Chamber of Commerce** (206 W. Main St., Cooke City, 406/838-2495) runs a tiny visitors center with current conditions on the Beartooth Highway, local outfitters and guides, and information on the Custer-Gallatin and Shoshone National Forests.

ENTRANCE STATIONS

Two **entrance stations** ($30 vehicle, $25 motorcycles, $15 hike-in/bike-in; joint parks pass: $50 vehicle, $40 motorcycles, $20 hike-in/bike-in) provide access to North Yellowstone; they are 52 miles apart.

The **North Entrance** sits on U.S. Highway 89 adjacent to the town of Gardiner, Montana. Smaller vehicles can enter the park through the Roosevelt Arch (RVs and trailers should take the signed shortcut from Park Street to the entrance station.) After passing the pay station, the park hub of Mammoth Hot Springs is only five miles south. The North Entrance is the only park entrance that is **open year-round.**

The **Northeast Entrance** is just west of Silver Gate and Cooke City, Montana, on U.S. Highway 212. From the Northeast Entrance, it is almost 30 miles to the park hub of Tower-Roosevelt. While the park road between the North and Northeast Entrances stays open year-round (except for temporary closures), snow closes the roads east of Cooke City (mid-Oct.-late May), effectively making the Northeast Entrance a dead end in winter.

TOURS

For all tours (winter or summer), plan to bring water, cameras, and layers of clothing for changeable weather. In winter, add gloves, a hat, and winter walking boots to that list. For

the town of Gardiner below Electric Peak

Stagecoach rides depart from the corrals at Roosevelt.

sightseeing tours, bring your own binoculars. Clarify when making reservations for wild-life-watching tours whether binoculars and spotting scopes are available. Most tours do not include lunch (ask to confirm), but do stop at restaurants. Park entrance fees and guide gratuities (15 percent) are not included in the rates. Tour costs and times vary seasonal and may change.

Bus Tours

Departing from Gardiner and Mammoth, the **Yellowstone in a Day** tour (Xanterra, 307/344-7311 or 866/439-7375, www.yel-lowstonenationalparklodges.com, 7:30am-6:30pm daily mid-June-mid-Sept., $111 adults, $56 children 3-11) circles the 142-mile Grand Loop Road to hit the big places: Old Faithful, Yellowstone Lake, and Grand Canyon of the Yellowstone.

Stagecoach Adventure

For a taste of early western travel, take a stage-coach tour with the **Stagecoach Adventure** (Xanterra, 307/344-7311 or 866/439-7375, www.yellowstonenationalparklodges.com, daily early June-early Sept., $14 adults, $7 children 3-11). From the Roosevelt Corrals, the half-hour ride in a replica stagecoach gives a glimpse into the park's history, and authen-ticity comes from the dust. The brave can ride up top.

Wildlife Tours

Historic Yellow Buses depart Mammoth Hot Springs Hotel in summer for dawn and eve-ning **Wildlife Watching Tours** (Xanterra, 307/344-7311 or 866/439-7375, www.yellow-stonenationalparklodges.com, daily late May-mid-Sept., $61-83 adults, kids half price). Each vintage 1930s touring sedan holds 13 passen-gers and has a canvas top that rolls back for easy wildlife-watching in summer. In winter, vans and buses provide tours. Reservations are required.

Wake Up to Wildlife (6:15am-11:30am daily late May-mid-Sept., $83 adults, $41.50 children) departs from either the Mammoth Hotel or the Roosevelt Lodge to explore the Lamar Valley. Juice and muffins are included for breakfast.

Evening Wildlife Encounters (4:15pm-8:30pm daily late May-mid-Aug., 3:45pm-8pm daily mid-Aug.-mid-Sept., $61 adults, $30.50 children) depart from Mammoth on a four-hour tour of Tower-Roosevelt and Lamar Valley.

Wake Up to Winter Wildlife (6:45am-11am daily mid-Dec.-Feb., $50 adults, $25 children) tours the Lamar Valley and includes juice and muffins for breakfast.

Lamar Valley Wildlife Tour (7am-2pm Mon., Thurs., and Sat. mid-Dec.-Feb., $93 adults, $47 children) spends more time in the Lamar Valley and includes juice and muffins for breakfast.

Yellowstone Association Institute (406/848-2400, www.yellowstoneassociation. org) offers expert-led educational tours year-round. Naturalist guides take you to various locations aboard institute buses to watch wild-life. While some programs are high energy, others are more like tours. Private tours, one-day, and multiday programs are available. Locations and rates vary based on program, but are usually held at park hotels, at the institute's Lamar Buffalo Ranch Field Campus, or at the Yellowstone Overlook Field Campus (Gardiner, Montana).

Winter Snowcoach Tours

Mid-December through February, visitors can tour the snow-buried roads of Yellowstone in heated snowcoaches—mostly converted vans or buses with huge tires or tracks. From Mammoth Hot Springs Hotel, Snowcoach Tours (Xanterra, 307/344-7311 or 866/439-7375, www.yellowstonenationalparklodges.com) depart for the Grand Canyon of the Yellowstone and Norris Geyser Basin.

The Grand Canyon Day Tour (8:15am-5pm Tues., Thurs., and Sat. mid-Dec.-Feb., $167 adults, $84 children) departs from Mammoth Hot Springs Hotel and spends two hours at Canyon and Norris, returning to Mammoth by 5pm; bring lunch or order one the night before from the Mammoth Hot Springs Dining Room.

The Norris Geyser Basin Tour (12:30pm-5:30pm Tues., Thurs., and Sat.-Sun. mid-Dec.-Feb., $83 adults, $42 children) visits the geothermal basin south of Mammoth.

Yellowstone Year-Round Safaris (905 Scott St., Gardiner, 406/848-7311 or 800/828-9080, www.yellowstoneyearroundsafaris.com, mid-Dec.-Feb., $180 adults, $90 children under 12) guides full-day snowcoach tours to Old Faithful or the Grand Canyon of the Yellowstone and guided snowmobile tours ($315-350) to Old Faithful or the Grand Canyon of the Yellowstone. Sack lunches are provided.

DRIVING TOURS

While most roads in Yellowstone close in winter, the Gardiner-Mammoth to Cooke City segment stays open year-round. Snowstorms can cause temporary closures in the fall, winter, and spring. For current road conditions, call 307/344-2117. Plan on at least an hour minimum with sightseeing stops to drive 20 miles on any of these tours.

Gardiner to Cooke City
52 MILES

The road between the North Entrance Station at Gardiner and the Northeast Entrance Station at Silver Gate and Cooke City is the only road in Yellowstone open year-round to private cars and RVs. The road is plowed in winter, but check on conditions before driving. Plan 2-3 hours (one way) for this tour.

The 52-mile, two-lane road starts as U.S. Highway 89 in Gardiner, Montana on Park Street. Drive under the Roosevelt Arch (RVs take the signed short cut) in about a half mile, you'll reach the entrance station. The road now climbs five miles south through ancient mudflows, crossing the 45th Parallel at the bridge over the Gardner River in about 2.5 miles, then hitting the Montana/Wyoming state line. The village of Mammoth Hot Springs appears in another 2.5 miles.

At Mammoth Hot Springs, turn east onto the Grand Loop Road to drive 18 miles across the Blacktail Deer Plateau toward Tower-Roosevelt. At Tower Junction, turn left to follow the Northeast Entrance Road for 29 miles across the Yellowstone River and entering the Lamar Valley. The road then swings northeast along Soda Butte Creek into the Absaroka Mountains. After Pebble Creek, the road climbs into narrow Ice Box Canyon, which has frozen waterfalls flanking its sides in winter and early spring. At mile 52, the road exits Yellowstone and enters the tiny blink-and-you-miss-it villages of Silver Gate and Cooke City, located three miles apart. In winter, the route dead-ends at Cooke City due to snowbound roads, but in summer, you can connect with the 68-mile Beartooth Highway.

GARDINER TO JARDINE

From U.S. Highway 89 in Gardiner, turn east on Jardine Road (north of the bridge over the

Yellowstone River). The dirt road climbs six miles north to Jardine, a funky old mining village. While the village has no modern claim to fame, the views on the drive back down make the trip worthwhile. You'll look straight across the Yellowstone River at the park's dramatic landscape with steam rising from Mammoth Hot Springs.

BLACKTAIL PLATEAU DRIVE

Located halfway between Mammoth Hot Springs and Tower Junction, the six-mile Blacktail Plateau Drive (July-early Nov.) offers a place to get away from more crowded roads. This curvy, dirt, one-way road gains territorial views and offers a look at fire succession as well as wildlife such as elk, bears, and bison, before dropping back down to the Grand Loop. No RVs, buses, or trailers are permitted. Plan 30 minutes for the drive, due to slow driving conditions and stops for sightseeing.

Mammoth to Norris
21 MILES

Between Mammoth and Norris, U.S. Highway 89 serves as the park road (mid-Apr.-early Nov.) and offers wildlife-watching and sightseeing. From Mammoth Hot Springs, the road climbs south for about six miles through the Hoodoos, monster travertine boulders formed by a landslide on Terrace Mountain, then along the cliffs of Golden Gate before topping out at Swan Lake Flat, where you can often spot wolves and bison.

Continue south for eight miles to pass Obsidian Cliff, the site of geological, Native American, and historical significance. Stop again at Roaring Mountain in about 3.5 miles to hear the thermal activity and look for trumpeter swans in Twin Lakes. This tour ends in four miles at the Norris Geyser Basin, a hotbed of geothermal activity with a nearby campground. Plan at least one hour for the drive.

Sights

NORTH ENTRANCE

Bordering the national park, Gardiner, Montana, is a small town of about 875 permanent residents that sees 700,000 visitors, mostly in summer. The Yellowstone River runs through the middle of town, making it the rafting capital for those visiting the park. The Roosevelt Arch sits on the south edge of town, marking the historic park entrance.

Yellowstone Heritage and Research Center

Located in Gardiner, the Yellowstone Heritage and Research Center (20 Old Yellowstone Trail, 307/344-2664, 8am-5pm Mon.-Fri.) houses the park archives and library, museum collections, a historian, an archaeology lab, and a herbarium. The lobby rotates small exhibits, but the facility is primarily for research and storage for 5.3 million

archived items. Public tours are available by reservation (307/344-2264, 10am Tues. and Thurs. late May-early Sept., free).

★ Roosevelt Arch

Roosevelt Arch may be one of the best human-built park entrances in the country. The original entrance road crosses under the stone-and-mortar arch dedicated to President Theodore Roosevelt, who laid the cornerstone in 1903. Reconstruction of Park Street, the viewing park and amphitheater, and the arch area in preparation for the 2016 anniversary of the National Park Service has improved access for photographing the arch. The reconstruction also re-opened walkway doors. A signed shortcut road lets large RVs bypass the narrow entrance through the arch, but cars can still drive through it. Park nearby on Park Street to walk around the arch and rebuilt Arch Park.

Roosevelt Arch

45th Parallel

About 2.5 miles south of Gardiner, on U.S. Highway 89 toward Mammoth Hot Springs, the 45th Parallel marks the latitude that is halfway between the North Pole and the equator. A tiny pullout and sign allows for a photo-op.

Boiling River Hot Springs

The natural Boiling River Hot Springs (dawn-dusk midsummer-late spring, free) is the only place in the park to soak in water from a Yellowstone thermal feature. Since the Boiling River water is scalding hot, soaking is at the confluence with the Gardner River. The frigid water of the Gardner River mixes with the thermally heated streams from the Boiling River and the result is an inconsistent mix. To soak, find the line between the heat and cold; usually one side of your body is hot while the other freezes. Exercise caution due to extreme hot and freezing water, slippery rocks, and strong currents. Please respect this thermal site, as you'll see plenty of wear from abuse. Swimsuits are required, and changing facilities are not available; suit up before you go. Bring a towel and water shoes or sandals.

Located about midway between Gardiner and Mammoth, find the unmarked turnoff to the Boiling River Trailhead on the east side of U.S. Highway 89, about 200 feet south of the bridge over the Gardner River. Hike 0.5 mile to two stair-step entrances and the soaking area.

MAMMOTH HOT SPRINGS

Open year-round, Mammoth Village is home to the Albright Visitor Center, Mammoth Hot Springs Hotel, historic Fort Yellowstone, a campground, a picnic area, and other services. But the main attractions are two-fold: the stately elk often lounge on lawns and the fantastical sculptures of the hot springs travertine terraces. However, Mammoth is not a spa, nor does it have developed hot springs for soaking.

★ Historic Fort Yellowstone

The village of Mammoth once was Fort Yellowstone in the pre-National Park Service decades when the U.S. Cavalry managed the park. A self-guided walking tour visits the stone buildings erected by the army between 1891 and 1916. Start at Albright Visitor Center (307/344-2263, 9am-5pm

Mammoth Hot Springs

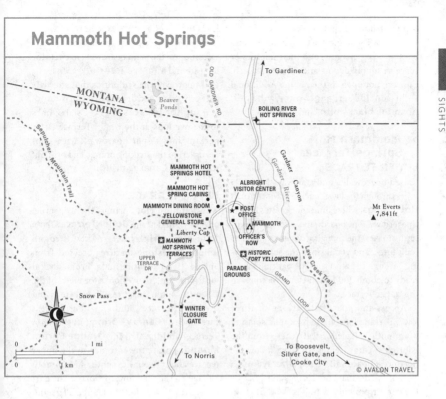

daily year-round), once the Bachelor Officer's Quarters, where you can pick up an interpretive brochure ($1). Across from the visitors center are the **parade grounds** (sometimes called the drill field), now covered with sagebrush and wandering bison or elk. Walk down the row of houses to see the **Captain's Quarters, Field Officer's Quarters,** and

Officer's Quarters at Historic Fort Yellowstone

a row of houses that served as **Officer's Quarters.** Today, most of the buildings house park service personnel and their families or serve as supply depots and offices; as such, they are not open to the public. Additional sights include the **granary, chapel, hospital, blacksmith,** and **stables.**

★ Mammoth Hot Springs Terraces

LOWER TERRACE

Raised boardwalks and stairways loop 1.75 miles through the lower terrace of **Mammoth Hot Springs,** where limestone creates travertine terraces. The boardwalks offers an opportunity to view the changing calcium carbonate sculptures, and you'll smell the sulfur blowing through the air. From the parking lot, be ready to climb 300 feet in elevation to reach the Upper Terrace.

Access the boardwalk at one of three lower parking lots on the park road south of Mammoth Village, or walk there from the Albright Visitor Center. To start, follow the northwest boardwalk to see **Liberty Cap,** a 37-foot-tall dormant hot springs cone. Across the street from Liberty Cap is **Opal Spring,** which adds up to a foot of travertine every year. Past Liberty Cap, a spur on the right leads to the colorful **Palette Spring,** where thermophiles create orange and brown colors. Continue on the main boardwalk to circle the loop around **Minerva Terrace,** known for its striking travertine sculptures that alternate between watery and dry. **Cleopatra, Mound,** and **Jupiter Terraces** flank the stair climbs to the overlook at the Upper Terrace Drive parking lot. A spur boardwalk with steps heads left to the striking orange and brilliant white sinter **Canary Spring.**

UPPER TERRACE

At Mammoth Hot Springs, the 0.75-mile, one-way, single-lane **Upper Terrace Drive** (mid-May-early Nov.) snakes through unique limestone features created from once-active hydrothermals. From several locations, walk to overlooks for views of the Gallatin Mountains, the village below, and the lower terraces, and view thermal features such as **Canary Spring** (off the Main Terrace) and the striking **Orange Spring Mound.** Locate the entrance to the upper terrace about two miles south of Mammoth Village on the road toward Norris. The narrow road curves close to Douglas firs and junipers, prohibiting trailers or vehicles longer than 25 feet.

Boardwalks tour the Mammoth Hot Springs Terraces.

Golden Gate with its pillar

MAMMOTH TO NORRIS

Between Mammoth and Norris, U.S. Highway 89 serves as the park road (mid-Apr.-early Nov.). From Mammoth, the road travels 21 miles south to the campground and geyser basin at Norris.

Orange Spring Mound on Upper Terrace Drive

★ Golden Gate

Driving south from Mammoth toward Norris, the curvy road climbs 1,500 feet in three miles on a cliff-clinging viaduct to reach Kingman Pass. The passage through Glen Creek Canyon is known as the **Golden Gate,** named for the vivid color of yellow lichens on the rhyolite cliffs. While the road has been rebuilt several times, its first incarnation in 1884 was a rickety wooden trestle bridge. A unique **rock pillar,** which was moved with each reconstruction of the road, sits at the bottom of the climb, while at the top, **Rustic Falls** sprays down 47 feet of natural stair-step stones. You'll also view **Bunsen Peak,** a cone volcano. An overlook on the east side of the road between the rock pillar and falls allows you to enjoy both.

Swan Lake Flat

Wildlife frequents **Swan Lake Flat,** and so do wildlife-watchers. Bring the binoculars, cameras, and telephoto lenses. Located on the Grand Loop Road about five miles south of Mammoth (look for a small parking lot), the sagebrush prairie of Swan Lake Flat in Gardners Hole offers a great chance to see wildlife: gray wolves, grizzly bears, and elk. Tiny Swan Lake, which once filled the entire

flat, often houses trumpeter swans in summer. The vast, open, high-elevation valley makes for a broad arena, where almost any movement is visible. You can hear the sounds of birds and waterfowl. In winter, look for bison.

Obsidian Cliff

Located between Mammoth and Norris on the east side of Grand Loop Road, the half-mile-long Obsidian Cliff, a National Historic Landmark and archaeological site, resulted from a 180,000-year-old rhyolite lava flow that crystallized. Look closely to see the shiny black volcanic glass bits of obsidian in the layers, but do so with binoculars or from a car as the site is closed to exploring. Early natives in the area quarried the sharp obsidian for making knives, arrowheads, and other tools. North of the cliff on the west side of the road, the Obsidian Cliff interpretive kiosk is one of the first interpretive exhibits created by the National Park Service.

Roaring Mountain

Five miles north of Norris Geyser Basin, the seemingly barren hillside of Roaring Mountain is riddled with fumaroles. Steam billows from multiple vents across the hillside. While the sound has lessened considerably in the past century, you can still hear the hissing roar when you get out of your vehicle at the interpretive site, which was revamped in 2015. Excessive tree-killing heat and gases combined with billowing steam make the hillside look like the aftermath of a fire. Despite the geothermal activity, some thermophiles survive in this toxic environment. Steam is more visible in early morning, evening, or winter.

MAMMOTH TO TOWER-ROOSEVELT

From Mammoth Village, the Grand Loop Road heads east for 19 miles across the Blacktail Deer Plateau to Tower Junction. Bison jams are common along this road, and traffic may be congested.

Undine Falls

Drive four miles east on the Grand Loop Road and look for a pullout for Undine Falls on the north side of the road. Lava Creek drops over a lava cliff formed about 700,000 years ago; Undine Falls, named for water spirits in German mythology, cascades 60 feet down three shelves.

Blacktail Pond

Blacktail Pond offers an opportunity for wildlife-watching, particularly for sandhill cranes, Canada geese, waterfowl, and bald eagles in spring; you can also spot pronghorn and bison. Look for a pullout on the north side of the road about six miles east of Mammoth.

Forces of the Northern Range

About two miles east of Blacktail Pond and eight miles east of Mammoth, look for an interpretive boardwalk on the north side of Grand Loop Road. This easy 0.5-mile boardwalk loop tours the Northern Range through an open sagebrush plateau, aspens, and younger lodgepole pines. The self-guided interpretive loop is one of the best ways to learn about northern Yellowstone's wildlife, wildflowers, trees, geology, landscape, and scenery.

Yellowstone River

The Yellowstone River tumbles 132 feet through a series of cascades in the Narrows of the Yellowstone, slicing between the Buffalo and Blacktail Deer Plateaus before plunging through the Black Canyon of the Yellowstone and exiting the park at Gardiner. From Gardiner, the river froths into white water for rafters and kayakers before settling into calmer waters in the Paradise Valley that lure anglers for wild trout.

The best viewpoints are at the Calcite Springs Overlook (between Tower Junction and Tower Fall), the trail heading north at the Yellowstone River Picnic Area along the Grand Loop Road, and in the town of Gardiner. Strong hikers can enjoy all the moods of the river along the trail through the **Black Canyon of the Yellowstone.**

TOWER-ROOSEVELT
★ Petrified Tree

Tucked off a side road about 0.8 mile west of Tower Junction, a lone **Petrified Tree** trunk stands on a steep hillside. Once a giant ancient redwood, the now-petrified tree is a clue to the wetter forests that covered the area prior to the supervolcano eruption. A 0.25-mile path leads to the solidified tree. (Ravaged by souvenir seekers, this specimen is now fenced off for protection.) To the east in Lamar Valley, **Specimen Ridge** has the largest collection of petrified trees in the world, accessible via a steep 1.5-mile trail.

★ Tower Fall

Tower Fall plunges 132 feet from its brink between rhyolite spires, dropping from a hanging valley into a ribbon that spews in a long freefall. An overlook, located 0.1 mile from the Tower Fall parking lot, offers the best view. Due to a washout in 2004, the viewing

Tower Fall

platform and trail to the base of the falls are closed.

Calcite Spring

The **Calcite Spring** loop connects 0.2 mile of boardwalk trails with platforms. From the overlook above the Narrows of the Yellowstone River, you can see basalt columns from lava across the gorge, the springs at the river level, and the Yellowstone River about 500 feet below. The calcite spring itself emits minerals that color the slope white and yellow. A parking lot is located 0.75 mile north of Tower Fall (1.6 miles south of Tower Junction).

NORTHEAST ENTRANCE
Slough Creek

Slough Creek is often packed with wildlife-watchers sporting scopes. The dirt Slough Creek Road has a few pullouts that offer a vast territorial view where you can spy bears, bighorn sheep, bison, and pronghorn. Bring binoculars, but you may be able to sneak a peek through someone else's scope. Most wildlife-watchers enjoy sharing what they are seeing. To get there from Tower Junction, drive 5.8 miles east on the Northeast Entrance Road and turn left onto Slough Creek Road.

★ Lamar Valley

Park guides often refer to the massive **Lamar Valley** as America's Serengeti due to its hefty supply of wildlife. The Lamar River flows through the sagebrush valley where immense herds of bison feed. In between herds, look for pronghorn, bighorn sheep, elk, bears, coyotes, and wolves. The valley also provides rich hunting grounds for predators. In late fall, listen for bighorn sheep crash-butting heads or elk bugling as displays of dominance. The **Yellowstone Association Institute's** Lamar Buffalo Ranch Field Campus is also located in this valley. (Access is via registered programs only at www.yellowstoneassociation.org).

From Tower Junction, follow the Northeast Entrance Road east past the turnoff for Slough Creek. Multiple pullouts along the road allow

The Yellowstone River

The Yellowstone River carries rafters through Yankee Jim Canyon.

The 692-mile Yellowstone River drains some of the highest mountains in the northern Rocky Mountains. It starts in the remote elevations of the Absaroka Mountains of Wyoming before cruising northward through Yellowstone National Park. It pools into Yellowstone Lake and then gushes through the **Grand Canyon of the Yellowstone** before squeezing through the Narrows just south of **Yellowstone River Picnic Area.** It then crosses from Wyoming into Montana.

As the river departs the north portion of Yellowstone National Park, it flows through the **Black Canyon of the Yellowstone,** accessible only by hiking. From Gardiner, it wends north through Montana's Paradise Valley, gathering more water from the Gallatin and Absaroka Mountains, before curving eastward toward North Dakota, where it finishes its journey by dumping into the Missouri River.

For Native Americans, the river served as a travel route between wintering grounds in lower-elevation valleys and summering grounds inside Yellowstone. Early park expeditions followed it to scope out Yellowstone's volcanic features and wildlife.

In Montana, the bulk of the river has been classified as **blue-ribbon trout fishing**, the highest rating for the state's fisheries. Starting in the park, the river runs free. The lack of dams aids in promoting movement of trout from the upper to lower elevations. Among the trout, anglers can catch native Yellowstone cutthroat. Inside the park, anglers don waders for fishing or cast from the shore in the reaches around the bridge east of Tower Junction or outside the park west of Gardiner.

Inside the park, no floating is permitted on the river. But outside the park, Class I-IV white water attracts rafters and kayakers. **Yankee Jim Canyon** provides four river miles of rugged scenery and splashy fun. Below the canyon, anglers fly-fish the **Paradise Valley** via rafts or dories. River accesses run by the State of Montana (http://fwp.mt.gov/fishing) accommodate launching, floating downstream, and taking out. **Gardiner** has five rafting companies that get people on the river for scenic floats or white-water paddling.

The Yellowstone River has several notable features. In the course of its tour through the national park, it is the park's longest river. More importantly, it is the last free-flowing major river in the Lower 48.

herds of bison in Lamar Valley

for observation. Wildlife is most active at dawn and dusk; bring spotting scopes, cameras, and binoculars.

Soda Butte Creek

As the Northeast Entrance Road swings north from the Lamar Valley, it follows **Soda Butte Creek,** a popular fly-fishing stream for

Soda Butte Creek in the Absaroka Mountains

its ease of access and productive trout fishery. The creek is named for the extinct **Soda Butte Geyser** that left a large white cone. Look for the interpretive sign and pullout on the east side of the Northeast Entrance Road.

★ Absaroka Mountains

In Yellowstone's northeast corner, the **Absaroka Mountains** (pronounced Ab-zor-ka) stretch into high rugged peaks more than 11,000 feet high. From Soda Butte Geyser, drive northwest for 14 miles on the Northeast Entrance Road to tour the mountains. As the road climbs past Pebble Creek and swings east, it squeezes through **Ice Box Canyon,** where Soda Butte Creek has carved a narrow passageway. In winter and early spring, the canyon displays frozen walls from water seeps. Past the canyon, the road climbs a high-elevation, forested valley tucked below **Amphitheater Mountain** and **Barronette Peak.** The precipitous terrain harbors bighorn sheep, mountain goats, and grizzly bears. With few visitors, this region of the park offers solitude.

To further explore this area, plan to camp at Slough Creek or Pebble Creek. Most hiking trails, such as Bliss Pass, are backpacking trips, but **Trout Lake** offers a short, idyllic destination.

Recreation

DAY HIKES

National Park Service rangers lead free, guided hikes (www.nps.gov/yell, daily or several times weekly, early June-early Sept.) that tour the Mammoth Hot Springs Terraces and Wraith Falls, providing interpretive, educational details on the natural history of the travertine terraces at the hot springs and the ecology of the Wraith Falls environment. Check in at the Albright Visitor Center for a current schedule and location of where to meet.

Guided Hikes

Expert-led educational hikes are also available through Yellowstone Association Institute (406/848-2400, www.yellowstone-association.org, year-round). Private tours, one-day, and multiday programs are available with varied rates. Hiking programs include day hikes and backpacking trips. Some of the hiking programs operate out of the institute's cabin complex in Lamar Valley.

Operating out of Gardiner, Yellowstone YearRound Adventures (406/585-9041, www.yellowstoneyearround.com, from $455 for 1-4 people) guides hikes for families and private small groups. Rates include the licensed guide, transportation to the trailhead from Gardiner, lunch, and snacks.

Mammoth to Norris
BEAVER POND LOOP

Distance: 5 miles one-way
Duration: 2.5 hours
Elevation change: 380 feet
Effort: moderate
Trailhead: in Mammoth Hot Springs between Liberty Cap and the stone house (see map p. 43)

Blooming with arrowleaf balsamroot, bluebells, and larkspur in June, Beaver Pond Loop is a good early-season hike when higher country still has snow. The route's meadows offer broad vistas of Bunsen Peak, Gardiner, and the Absaroka Mountains. Start with a one-mile climb up Clematis Creek. At the signed junction, turn right; the trail alternates between rolling, flat, or downhill terrain. About halfway, the trail waltzes along the shoreline of an old beaver pond split by a dam and then descends through open sagebrush meadows, Douglas fir forests, and aspen groves. The route ends on the Old Gardiner Road behind the Mammoth Hotel.

BUNSEN PEAK AND OSPREY FALLS

Distance: 4.2 miles round-trip or 11.6-mile loop
Duration: 3-7 hours
Elevation change: 1,278-2,058 feet
Effort: strenuous
Trailhead: Old Bunsen Peak Road Trailhead, 4.8 miles south of Mammoth on the east side of Grand Loop Road

The peak, a volcanic cone named for Robert Bunsen, who invented the Bunsen Burner, contains a summit weather station with the building and connecting power lines posing a minor disruption to the wilderness feel. Start early in summer to nab a parking spot at the popular trailhead.

Starting in a sagebrush meadow, this popular trail climbs through steep forests, meadows, and 1988 burns to the 8,564-foot summit. Shortly after starting the climb, spot the Golden Gate from above along with Glen Creek Canyon hoodoos. The trail winds back and forth around the mountain, passing Cathedral Rock at 1.4 miles, where views plunge to Mammoth Hot Springs. Steep switchbacks then lead across talus slopes to the summit. The reward is the view of Electric Peak in the Gallatin Range and Gardners Hole. For the shortest hike, retrace your route back down. Or, for an alternative, drop eastward 1.4 steep miles through a burn zone to the Old Bunsen Peak Road, turning right to circle three gentle miles (shared by bikers)

North Yellowstone Hikes

Trail	Effort	Distance	Duration
Wraith Falls	Easy	0.8 mi rt	45 min
Trout Lake Trail	Easy	1.2 mi rt	1 hr
Lost Lake Loop	Moderate	4 mi rt	2.5 hr
Narrows of the Yellowstone River	Moderate	4 mi rt	2.5 hr
Slough Creek	Moderate	4 mi rt	3 hr
Grizzly Lake	Moderate	4.2 mi rt	3 hr
Beaver Pond Loop	Moderate	5 mi one-way	2.5 hr
Hellroaring Creek	Moderately Strenuous	4 mi rt	3 hr
Specimen Ridge	Strenuous	3 mi rt	4 hr
Bunsen Peak and Osprey Falls	Strenuous	4.2-11.6 mi rt	3-7 hr
Blacktail Deer Creek	Strenuous	7.4 mi rt	4-5 hr
Sepulcher Mountain	Strenuous	12.5 mi rt	7 hr
Black Canyon of the Yellowstone	Strenuous	13.5-16.9 mi rt	7-9 hr

around the south of **Bunsen Peak** (6.6 miles total).

Strong hikers can lengthen the loop with a descent and return climb to see 150-foot **Osprey Falls** on the Gardner River. Descend eastward from the peak to the Old Bunsen Peak Road, then turn left to find the Osprey Falls Trailhead. From the trailhead, a 1.4-mile trail traverses the edge of Sheepeater Canyon with the basalt-columned Sheepeater Cliffs visible on the opposite side. Drop down steep, narrow, sunny switchbacks into the ravine below the falls. After climbing the 780 feet back up, follow the old road south around Bunsen Peak to return to your vehicle. Those wanting to avoid the Bunsen Peak climb can hike out and back on the old road to see Osprey Falls (8.8 miles, 780 feet elevation gain).

SEPULCHER MOUNTAIN

Distance: 12.5-mile loop
Duration: 7 hours
Elevation change: 2,366 feet

Effort: strenuous
Trailhead: Glen Creek Trailhead opposite Old Bunsen Peak Road Trailhead, 4.8 miles south of Mammoth (see map p. 43)

Selpulcher Mountain attracts hikers out for big views without the crowds of Bunsen Peak. But since the trail uses the same crowded parking lot at Bunsen Peak, you'll need to get an early start. The trail begins with a gentle 1.8-mile walk through sagebrush meadows below **Terrace Mountain,** home to bighorn sheep. Continue through several junctions where trails turn off to Fawn Pass, Snow Pass, and Sportsman Lake Trail. After the third turnoff, begin climbing the switchbacks up an open mountainside with views of Electric Peak. With less than 0.5 mile to go, the trail enters a forest before popping out on the summit for views of the Absaroka Mountains. A jaunt along the 9,652-foot **summit** yields more views, including the Yellowstone River and Gardiner far below.

Continue the loop by following the cliff edge and then descending through pines and meadows overlooking Mammoth Hot Springs. At the junction with the Clagett Butte Trail, turn right to climb uphill to the **Snow Pass Trail**. Turn right again for one mile to cross Snow Pass. Turn left to return back to Glen Creek Trailhead.

As an alternate descent for a point-to-point hike, the route connects with trails to Mammoth Hot Springs. The Snow Pass Trail ends at the Upper Terrace, and the Clagett Butte Trail links to the trailhead adjacent to Liberty Cap.

GRIZZLY LAKE

Distance: 4.2 miles round-trip
Duration: 3 hours
Elevation change: 725 feet
Effort: moderate
Trailhead: a pullout on the west side of Grand Loop Road, 16 miles south of Mammoth

Start by crossing **Obsidian Creek** on a footbridge, one of many log bridges in the first 0.5 mile through this boggy marsh. Leaving the meadows, the trail climbs through a 1988 fire zone. Turn around for views of the valley you just crossed. On the ascent, the trail breaks into a meadow before reentering the burn with regrowing lodgepoles. The trail then descends to **Grizzly Lake**, where anglers can fish for brook trout and yellow lilies grow along the shores.

Mammoth to Tower-Roosevelt
WRAITH FALLS

Distance: 0.8 mile round-trip
Duration: 45 minutes
Elevation change: 74 feet
Effort: easy
Trailhead: a pullout on the south side of Grand Loop Road, 0.5 mile east of Lava Creek Picnic Area east of Mammoth

Launch onto this trail by walking through a sagebrush-scented meadow blooming with columbine and buckwheat in early summer. An intermittent **boardwalk** crosses small streams and marshes. The route tucks in between coniferous tree islands, crosses Lupine Creek, and climbs one switchback to reach the viewing platform. The 79-foot **Wraith Falls** cascades down a wide-angled rock face squeezed into a canyon. In June, the water fills the full width, but by September, the water thins in the middle making the falls look like two parallel falls.

BLACKTAIL DEER CREEK

Distance: 7.4 miles round-trip
Duration: 4-5 hours

A hiker enjoys the view of Wraith Falls.

Elevation change: 1,340 feet
Effort: strenuous
Trailhead: Blacktail Deer Creek Trailhead on Grand Loop Road, 6.7 miles east of Mammoth (see map p. 54)

From the trailhead on the east end of **Blacktail Pond,** the route plunges to the Yellowstone River and the Black Canyon of the Yellowstone. On summer days, the treeless trail can be hot, especially on the return climb back up to the trailhead.

After crossing the Blacktail Pond valley, the trail climbs 130 feet in elevation over a sagebrush hill before dropping northward, passing the **Rescue Creek Trail** junction at 0.7 mile. The trail parallels **Blacktail Deer Creek** in its descent down the ravine to reach the suspension bridge at the **Yellowstone River.** The return climb is 1,210 feet in elevation back up. You can also add on another 0.5-mile round-trip to see **Crevice Lake.**

HELLROARING CREEK

Distance: 4 miles round-trip
Duration: 3 hours
Elevation change: 643 feet
Effort: moderately strenuous
Trailhead: Hellroaring Trailhead on Grand Loop Road, 3.5 miles west of Tower Junction (see map p. 54)

The trail takes a steep drop to the Yellowstone River and crosses the Buffalo Plateau to reach Hellroaring Creek, a prized angler destination. It requires a hefty climb on a hot, dusty, dry trail to return to the trailhead. The trail is popular with horseback riders, so be ready for manure and flies.

A one-mile plunge through a semi-forested hillside passes the **Garnet Hill Loop** junction before reaching the **suspension bridge** over the Yellowstone River. Cross the river and continue across the open, sagebrush Buffalo Plateau for 1.1 miles, passing a junction with the **Buffalo Plateau** and **Coyote Creek Trail.** Above **Hellroaring Creek,** the trail reaches the east-west path where you can go either direction. Go left and then take the first spur right for the fastest access to the creek.

BLACK CANYON OF THE YELLOWSTONE

Distance: 13.5-16.9 miles round-trip
Duration: 7-9 hours
Elevation change: 2,036 feet
Effort: strenuous
Trailhead: Hellroaring Trailhead on Grand Loop Road, 3.5 miles west of Tower Junction (see map p. 54)

This point-to-point hike used to go to Gardiner, but that trailhead is now closed. Most hikers combine the **Hellroaring Creek Trail** and the **Yellowstone River Trail** through the Black Canyon, and climb out via **Blacktail Deer Creek.** You'll need two cars to set up a shuttle as the trailheads are eight miles apart. Carry plenty of water, be prepared for heat and dust, and take a map to aid with route-finding due to multiple side trails.

To connect the two trails when you reach **Hellroaring Creek,** you have two options. In late season when the water is low, drop to the river, ford it, and climb to the trail heading downstream to reach the Yellowstone River. In early summer when the water is too high, turn east instead to hike 3.7 miles northeast, crossing the river via **Hellroaring Creek Bridge** to reconnect with the trail on the opposite side. At the junction, head straight north for the **Yellowstone River Trail** through the Black Canyon, climbing and dropping multiple times above the river. In 6.9 miles, take the **Blacktail Deer Creek Trail** junction for 0.8 mile to reach the suspension bridge to cross back over the Yellowstone River and climb to the **Blacktail Deer Creek Trailhead.**

Tower-Roosevelt
LOST LAKE LOOP

Distance: 4 miles round-trip
Duration: 2.5 hours
Elevation change: 608 feet
Effort: moderate
Trailhead: behind Roosevelt Lodge, the Petrified Tree parking lot, or Tower Fall Campground (see map p. 55)

Hikers can start this trail from a variety of trailheads, and it has plenty of things to see:

Black Canyon of the Yellowstone

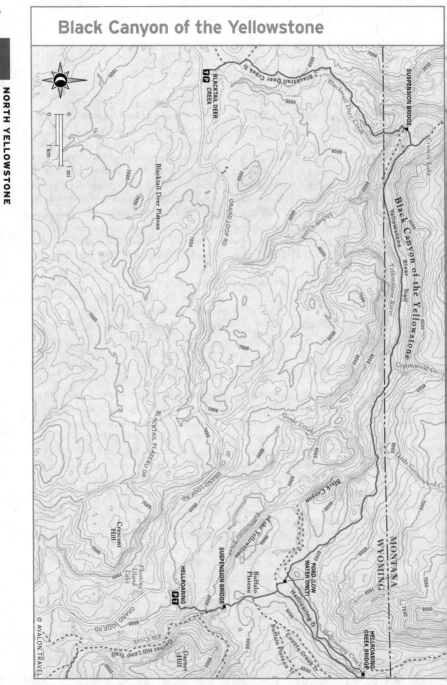

© AVALON TRAVEL

Lost Lake Loop

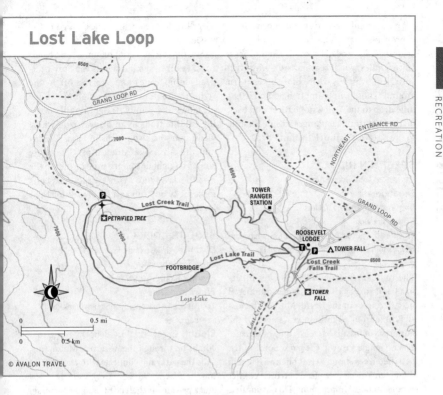

a waterfall, the small lake, Petrified Tree, and views of the Absaroka Mountains. The trail is also used by horses, which means you'll encounter manure and flies. If you run into horses, step to the downhill side of the trail unless the wrangler instructs otherwise. Remain still until they have passed.

From behind Roosevelt Lodge, take the left spur to the **Lost Creek Falls Trail** that climbs up a pine-shaded ravine to the 40-foot falls. Return to the junction to continue up the **Lost Lake Trail.** Switchbacks head up the steep hill to reach the small bridge at the lake's outlet. The trail rims the lake until it heads west through another ravine to **Petrified Tree.** From the Petrified Tree parking lot, the trail mounts a hill east to a sagebrush meadow before dropping to swing behind **Tower Ranger Station** and then around to Roosevelt Lodge.

Northeast Entrance
NARROWS OF THE YELLOWSTONE RIVER

Distance: 4 miles round-trip
Duration: 2.5 hours
Elevation change: 393 feet
Effort: moderate
Trailhead: Yellowstone River Picnic Area Trailhead, 1.2 miles east of Tower Junction on the Northeast Entrance Road

A steep grunt uphill through sagebrush meadows with pink sticky geranium and arrowleaf balsamroot leads to the east rim of the Narrows of the Yellowstone River. The trail saunters along the rim above the deep canyon with several viewpoints. In one mile, the trail overlooks **Calcite Springs.** As it traverses a ridge 500 feet above the Yellowstone River, the route affords spectacular views of the narrows, sculpted minarets, and columnar basalt.

It's also a good place to spot bighorn sheep, osprey, and peregrine falcons. Pronghorn cross the ridge, and marmots live in the rocks. In two miles, you'll reach a **four-way trail junction**, which is where most hikers turn around. Those with gumption add on a 0.8-mile drop to the Yellowstone River and back on the spur trail that plunges steeply 0.4 mile to the historic **Bannock Indian Ford.**

SPECIMEN RIDGE

Distance: 3 miles round-trip
Duration: 4 hours
Elevation change: 1,024 feet
Effort: strenuous
Trailhead: a pullout 4.5 miles east of Tower Junction on the south side of the Northeast Entrance Road (see map p. 36)

The route up Specimen Ridge takes hikers to a fossil zone, part of the largest number of petrified trees in the world. Most of the fossils come from 50 million years ago. Of the hundreds of fossilized trees, some of the species no longer grow in the park. Some of the petrified trees stand 20 feet tall and 8 feet in diameter. You can also find petrified conifer needles and leaf impressions. Do not confuse this hike on this unmaintained route with the Specimen Ridge Trail from Yellowstone

River Picnic Area, which does not go to the fossils.

Starting off as a trail on an **abandoned road** (a hiker-symbol sign is the only trail-head designation) and veering off to the right, the route tromps through open sage meadows and grunts straight uphill, crossing wildlife trails to an **open ridge** where views span the bison herds in Lamar Valley and the Absaroka Mountains. The route climbs straight up about a mile farther to the **petrified redwood tree trunks** area. Look for a rocky outcrop as a landmark for their location.

SLOUGH CREEK

Distance: 4 miles round-trip
Duration: 3 hours
Elevation change: 597 feet
Effort: moderate
Trailhead: 1.8 miles north on Slough Creek Road (see map p. 36)

Slough Creek Trail is a lengthy route that climbs up through the Absaroka Mountains, exits the park, and connects with trails entering the **Absaroka-Beartooth Wilderness** and a private ranch. It attracts anglers, horseback riders, and backpackers. To reach the first meadow of the outstanding fishing

the trail circling Trout Lake

stream, climb 423 feet up through the open Douglas fir forest and small meadows until the trail drops to a **patrol cabin** on a giant meadow surrounding Slough Creek. The return hike climbs 174 feet over the hill back to the trailhead.

★ TROUT LAKE TRAIL

Distance: 1.2 miles round-trip
Duration: 1 hour
Elevation change: 220 feet
Effort: easy
Trailhead: a small pullout with limited parking on the Northeast Entrance Road, 3 miles north of Soda Butte Trailhead and 1.5 miles south of Pebble Creek Campground (see map p. 36)

An idyllic little lake sitting at about 7,000 feet in elevation, **Trout Lake** is actually the largest of three small lakes tucked near the Northeast Entrance Road in the **Absaroka Mountains.** From the trailhead, the path catapults vertically through a Douglas fir forest to the lake. About 0.3 mile up the trail, the **route splits** to circle the lake. Go either way. The trail circles the shoreline, which is semi-forested on the east shore and open meadows on the west shore. In early summer, phlox blankets the hillsides, cutthroat trout spawn in the inlet stream, and osprey hang around to fish. Short unmaintained trails connect with Shrimp and Buck Lakes.

BACKPACKING

Backpackers must obtain **permits** ($3/person, children 8 and younger free) for assigned backcountry campsites. Permits are available in person 48 hours in advance from the backcountry offices. For more information, see the *Essentials* chapter.

Mt. Holmes
21.2 MILES

The Gallatin Mountains have the best backpacking in the northern part of the park. Until July, snow can clog the upper elevations of the 21.2-mile round-trip route to climb 10,336-foot **Mt. Holmes** in the Gallatin Range. After that, the route is usually accessible. Camp for

two nights at **Winter Creek** (campsite 1C4 or 1C5), near the junction for Trilobite Lake. The next day, climb to the unstaffed lookout on the summit for immense views.

Black Canyon of the Yellowstone
16.5 MILES

Since the closure of the west end of the Black Canyon of the Yellowstone Trail at Gardiner, point-to-point backpacking trips in the canyon go from **Hellroaring Creek Trailhead** to **Blacktail Creek Trailhead.** Plan three days for the 16.5-mile trip, and mentally prepare for the ascent up on the last day. Choose from 19 **campsites** on the route, but the best flank the Yellowstone River (1R1, 1R2, 1Y6, and 1Y8) about three miles apart where anglers can fish. Due to the short mileage on the middle day, there's time to explore the Black Canyon trail running west down the Yellowstone.

BIKING

Around Mammoth Hot Springs, old roadbeds work for riding mountain bikes; otherwise, bikes are not permitted on trails. Bring your own bike, as rentals are not available.

Just inside the park boundary at Gardiner, cyclists can ride the **old rail trail** (5 miles one-way, Apr.-mid-Nov.) that parallels the Yellowstone River running downstream to Reese Creek. It's gentle enough for kids, but can be hot in summer. The trailhead is located 0.1 mile west of the Yellowstone Heritage and Research Center (20 Old Yellowstone Trail).

Old Gardiner Road (5 miles one-way, late Apr.-early Nov.) offers a downhill route to Gardiner, but a huge climb back up. Biking is permitted in both directions, but vehicle traffic is downhill only. Road access is behind Mammoth Hot Springs Hotel or at the park entrance station south of Gardiner. South of Mammoth, two short rides depart from the top of the Golden Gate. **Bunsen Peak Loop** (6 miles one-way, May-early Nov.) partially circles Bunsen Peak on an old road. Leave a shuttle at the Old Bunsen Peak Trailhead (5.8

Yellowstone's roads have minimal shoulders for cycling.

miles south of Mammoth), then circle the old road around Bunsen Peak. You'll wind through employee housing before joining the main road (between the Upper and Lower Terraces) back to Mammoth. Bicyclists can also ride the service road from Golden Gate to Joffe Lake (1.5 miles one-way, May-early Nov.).

On the Grand Loop Road, Blacktail Plateau Drive (6 miles one-way, mid-July-early Nov.) is a rolling higher-elevation tour with broad views and wildlife. Biking is permitted in both directions, but vehicle traffic is eastbound only. Access the drive 8.7 miles west of Tower Junction (9.5 miles east of Mammoth).

HORSEBACK RIDING
Inside the Park
Wranglers lead Saddle Up (Xanterra, 307/344-7311 or 866/439-7375, www.yellowstonenationalparklodges.com, daily early June-early Sept.) tours departing from the Roosevelt Corrals. The one-hour ride (hours vary daily, $40-55) tours sagebrush flats, while the two-hour ride (12:15pm daily, $58-70) makes Lost Lake a destination. Reservations are required.

Yellowstone Wilderness Outfitters (406/223-3300, www.yellowstone.ws, daily June-Sept.) guides half-day ($100-125), full-day ($200-225), and overnight ($1,800-3,000) pack trips to a variety of northern destinations. Guides with degrees in wildlife biology lead trips to places with superb wildlife-watching, such as Swan Lake Flat. The outfitter also partners with a rafting company for a saddle-paddle trip ($80-150) with horseback portions inside the park.

Outside the Park
Outfitters guide trail rides outside the park. Near Gardiner, Hell's A-Roaring Outfitters (164 Crevice Rd., Jardine, 406/848-7578, www.hellsaroarinoutfitters.com, daily May-Sept., $40-220) kicks off the annual season on Memorial Day weekend, when ranch staff ride their 100 horses through the town streets. From the Johnson ranch, located about six miles north of Gardiner, wranglers lead one-hour, two-hour, half-day, and full-day horseback rides through high sagebrush and grass plains surrounded by Custer-Gallatin National Forest with views into Yellowstone. Overnight rides reach into the Absaroka-Beartooth Wilderness. Make reservations by phone or email only.

Book trips online through their partner,

Trail rides depart from the Roosevelt Corrals.

Flying Pig Adventure Company (511 Scott St., Gardiner, 866/264-8448, www.flyingpi-grafting.com), who also offer paddle-saddle trips. **Wild West Rafting** (114 Main St., Gardiner, 406/848-2252, www.wildwestraft-ing.com, $40-195) also offers a full lineup of trail rides with online booking.

Trail rides from Cooke City tour the Absaroka Mountains and are available through **Skyline Guest Ranch** (31 Kersey Lake Rd., Cooke City, 406/838-2380 or 877-238-8885, www.flyfishyellowstone.com, Mon.-Sat. June-early Sept., $30-130) lead horseback trail rides for one, two, or three hours; the half-day ride to Rock Island Lake includes lunch. Make reservations three days in advance.

WATER SPORTS

Rafting and kayaking are not permitted inside the park, so all Yellowstone River floats take place outside the park in Gardiner.

★ Floating the Yellowstone River

The **Yellowstone River** (Class I-IV) flows through Gardiner and on to Yankee Jim Canyon, where wave trains throw up a roll-ing kick for white-water rafting. Below the canyon, the river settles into a calmer pace, better for scenic floats. While floating the Yellowstone, you have an excellent chance of seeing wildlife from the river. Most of the shorter white-water trips are intermediate—good for families looking for some thrills and splashing, but not a frightening ride.

There are no raft or kayak rentals available in Gardiner, but if you have your own raft or kayak, you can float the Yellowstone River. No permits are needed. Put-in is near Gardiner, at Queen of the Waters Fishing Access; from there, you can float through Yankee Jim Canyon to the Tom Miner Bridge take-out, a distance of 7.2 miles. Below the bridge, river access sites lie every few miles en route to Livingston.

GUIDES

There are five rafting companies in Gardiner that guide trips **May-September** on the Yellowstone River. Most offer scenic floats, half-day and full-day white-water trips, and paddle-saddle combinations. Half-day white-water trips cover eight miles in 2-3 hours and depart multiple times daily. Full-day white-water trips combine rafting and floating with lunch, while covering about 18 miles of river. Life jackets are supplied. In cooler shoulder seasons, companies provide wetsuits, booties, and splash tops. Professional photographers shoot photos of your raft bouncing through white water; the photos are then available for purchase.

Rates are comparable between companies, but clarify whether taxes are included. Rafting and scenic float trips cost $40-45 for a half day, $80-90 for a full day ($80-95 for paddle-saddle combos). Smaller boats that hold 4-6 paddlers and inflatable kayaks are also available ($10-20 more per person). Rates for children 12 and younger are about $10-20 less. Reservations are suggested, and most companies accept online booking. Some trips and companies may have weight or minimum age restrictions. Plan to tip your river guide 15 percent.

Flying Pig Adventure Company (511 Scott St., 888/687-1276, www.flyingpigrafting. com) launches from behind their camp store in Gardiner. Overnight trips run $300 per person; a three-day trip runs $550 per person.

Montana Whitewater (603 Scott St., 800/799-4465, www.montanawhitewater. com) takes out specialty day trips: small boats that fit 4-6 paddlers plus the guide and inflatable kayak trips. The company also runs the ziplines in Gardiner, and they offer a raft and zipline package ($90/person).

Wild West Rafting (906 Scott St. W., 406/848-2252 or 800/862-0557, www.wild-westrafting.com) runs special small-boat trips in June high water for extra bounce and splash, as well as inflatable kayak trips. Overnight trips cost $300 per person.

Two other companies include **Yellowstone Raft Company** (111 2nd St., 406/848-7777 or 800/858-7781, www.yellowstoneraft.com) and **Paradise Rafting** (120 E. Park St., 406/333-7183 or 888/722-6505, www.paradiserafting.com).

Fishing
INSIDE THE PARK

In the northern region of the park, multiple rivers harbor wild trout. The **Gardner River, Slough Creek, Soda Butte Creek,** and **Lamar River** offer iconic places to fish. The deeper, wider, and bigger Yellowstone River is better fished during July and early August. Inside the park, you'll need to wade-fish or cast from shore. In the northeast, the Trout Lake inlet stream is permanently closed to fishing.

To help native trout conservation, kill all nonnative fish including brook and rainbow trout in the Lamar River drainage above the Lamar River Bridge and Slough

Soda Butte Creek attracts anglers for fly-fishing.

Creek drainage above the campground. The Gardner River also has fine fly-fishing. Anglers who hike can find trout fishing with less pressure on Blacktail Deer Creek and Hellroaring Creek. Most of the rivers clear of runoff by July.

For kids, smaller creeks work best for fishing. Take them to the picnic areas at the Gardner River or Lava Creek, or near the campgrounds of Slough, Indian, or Pebble Creeks. Joffe and Trout Lakes are smaller lakes where kids can have fun fishing, too.

Inside Yellowstone, a **fishing permit** is required for anglers 16 years and older ($18 for three days, $25 seven days, $40 season). For permit information and regulations, see the *Essentials* chapter.

OUTSIDE THE PARK

Outside Yellowstone, you'll need a **Montana fishing license** (http://fwp.mt.gov, $13-26 for residents, $25-70 for nonresidents). For fishing east of Cooke City, you'll need a **Wyoming fishing license** (residents: $3 youth, $6 adults daily, $24 adults annual; nonresidents: $15 youth, $14 adults daily, $92 adults annual). For information, see the *Essentials* chapter.

Two of Gardner's fly shops have permits for guiding inside Yellowstone and outside the park in Montana waters. Guided trips inside the park are walking with wade-fishing; guided raft, drift boat fishing, and powerboat fishing are only outside the park. Trips for 1-2 people cost $350-400 for a half day and $450-500 for a full day. Trips are for beginners through experts; beginners can get lessons. **Parks' Fly Shop** (202 S. 2nd St., Gardiner, 406/848-7314, www.parksflyshop.com, 8am-6pm daily) has flies, tackle, and gear and sells Montana fishing licenses. They also guide wade-fishing, float, and powerboat fishing trips. **Flying Pig Store and Fly Shop** (204 Park St., Gardiner, 888/792-9193, www.flyingpigrafting.com, 8am-9pm daily May-mid-Oct., shorter hours in fall) carries flies, tackle, gear, rents rods and waders, and sells Yellowstone fishing permits. They also guide wade-fishing, float, and horseback angling trips. The **Town Sinclair Station** (126 Park St., Gardiner) sells Montana fishing licenses. The **Cooke City Store** (101 Main St., Cooke City, 406/838-2234, http://cookecitystore.com, 8am-8pm daily May-Sept.) sells tackle and Yellowstone, Montana, and Wyoming fishing licenses.

THRILL SPORTS

At Yellowstone Ranch, **Yellowstone Zip** (603 Scott St., Gardiner, 800/799-4465, www.yellowstonezip.com, June-Aug., $60-95 adults, $50-85 kids) has zipline tours whizzing through the forest and tiptoeing along sky bridges. The longest lines fly 1,200 feet and the highest is 200 feet. Rates include the shuttle from the meeting location at Montana Whitewater to the historic ranch outside Gardiner. The company also packages a half day of rafting with ziplining.

WINTER SPORTS
Cross-Country Skiing and Snowshoeing

Winter transforms Yellowstone into a prime cross-country ski and snowshoe locale. All unplowed roads become trails, which allows for experiencing them differently than in summer. With the exception of the plowed road between Gardiner, Mammoth, and Cooke City, all other roads closed to wheeled vehicles are open for skiing. Some have snowcoach and snowmobile traffic. Winter trail maps are located online (www.nps.gov/yell) and at Albright Visitor Center.

In Mammoth, **Upper Terrace Loop** and **Bunsen Peak Trail** are groomed for cross-country skiing. Other trails for skiers are the **Snow Pass, Sheepeater,** and the **Indian Creek-Bighorn Loop** trails. Warming huts sit at the Indian Creek and Upper Terrace Trailheads. Parking to access all trails is at Upper Terrace Loop and the lower Bunsen Peak Trailhead. The **Old Gardiner Road Trail,** located behind the hotel, and Upper Terrace Loop provide good snowshoeing.

In the Roosevelt area, the **Blacktail**

Plateau Trail is groomed. By parking at Petrified Tree or the Tower Junction, skiers and snowshoers can tour the Lost Lake Trail or ski 2.3 miles up Grand Loop Road to Tower Fall.

In the northeast corner of Yellowstone, unplowed roads and snow-buried trails provide touring routes. The Barronette and Bannock Trails parallel Soda Butte Creek, the latter trail connected with an unplowed road that runs between Silver Gate and Cooke City.

GUIDES AND RENTALS

Cross-country ski, snowshoe, and winter gear rentals are available in the Bear Den Ski Shop (7:30am-5pm daily late Dec.-early Mar.), adjacent to the Mammoth Hot Springs Hotel. You can rent gear for a half day, full day, or three days for $2-22 per item: snowshoes, gaiters, touring skis, poles, ski boots, sleds, and Yaktrax. A full-day ski package costs $25. The shop offers repairs, wax, and lessons. Parks' Fly Shop (202 S. 2nd St., Gardiner, 406/848-7314, www.parksflyshop. com, $10-15 per day) rents cross-country ski and snowshoe packages.

SHUTTLES AND TOURS

Shuttles (Xanterra, 307/344-7311 or 866/439-7375, www.yellowstonenationalparklodges. com, daily late Dec.-early Mar., $21-32 adults each way, $10-12 kids) operate for skiers from Mammoth. Each week, snowcoaches go to Indian Creek on four days and shuttle buses go to Tower Junction on three days.

The park service guides a two-hour snowshoe tour (Sun. late Dec.-Feb., free) around Upper Terrace Drive in winter. Yellowstone Association Institute (406/848-2400, www.yellowstoneassocia-tion.org) offers expert-led educational ski and snowshoe trips starting from Gardiner, Mammoth, or Lamar Valley. Private tours, one-day, and multiday programs are available with varied rates.

Snowmobiling

The snowmobile season in Yellowstone runs

Guided snowmobile tours launch from Mammoth Hot Springs.

mid-December-early March. You can go with a commercially guided group or enter the permit lottery (www.recreation.gov, early Sept.-early Oct.). If you miss the lottery, you can pick up remaining or cancelled permits in November. Snowmobiles must stick to roadways in Yellowstone.

From Mammoth, the most popular route departs from the snowmobile staging area at the Upper Terrace Trailhead and travels the Grand Loop Road south to Old Faithful, Canyon, and Lake Yellowstone. From Cooke City, routes follow roads outside the park closed by snow for winter, particularly the Beartooth Highway (U.S. Hwy. 212). Snowmobiling in the Custer-Gallatin and Shoshone National Forests is not restricted to roadways. In Cooke City, rent snowmobiles from Crown Butte Rentals (203 Eaton St., 406/838-2231, www.cookecity-motorsports.com, $200-230/day, including snowsuits and helmets).

TOURS

From Mammoth, full-day **snowmobile tours** (late Dec.-early Mar., $315-350 per machine, includes helmets, snowmobile suits, gloves, and shuttles) go out multiple days per week to Old Faithful and Grand Canyon of the Yellowstone; fees do not include park entrance. **Yellowstone Year-Round Safaris** (905 Scott St., 406/848-7311 or 800/828-9080, www.yellowstoneyearroundsafaris.com) operates the only snowmobile concession in the Gardiner-Mammoth area. Rentals ($200-230/ day, including snowsuits and helmets) usually have age limits and license requirements. Avalanche gear (beacons, probes, shovels, and airbags) usually costs $50.

Entertainment and Shopping

INSIDE THE PARK
Ranger Programs

The amphitheater at **Mammoth Campground** (8pm-9:30pm daily early June-mid-Sept.) hosts free rotating evening programs. The 45-minute presentations illustrate Yellowstone wildlife, cultural history, flora, and natural history. In winter, naturalist talks take place in the **Mammoth Hot Springs Hotel** (8pm Thurs.-Sat. late Dec.-late Feb.) in the map room.

Shopping

Inside the park, shopping is limited to gift shops in the lodges and the **Yellowstone General Stores** (406/586-7593, www.yellowstonegift.com, 7:30am-9:30pm daily) located in **Mammoth Hot Springs** (year-round) and adjacent to **Roosevelt Lodge** (June-Aug.). A **Yellowstone Association** (406/848-2400, www.yellowstoneassociation.org) park store is located in the Albright Visitor Center at Mammoth.

GARDINER

While people hunker down in Mammoth for the night, the action kicks up at a couple of western saloons in Gardiner. You can dance to live music at the **Two Bit Saloon** (107 2nd St. S., 406/848-7743, www.twobitsaloon.com, 9am-2am daily) on select nights.

Gardiner's annual **rodeo** (100 U.S. 89 S., www.northernrodeo.com, late June) is held over two days at the Jim Duffy Arena. A parade kicks off the events, which include calf roping, barrel racing, and bareback bronco riding. Sponsored by the Northern Rodeo Association and Gardiner Rodeo Club, the competitions run Friday and Saturday evenings and are open to the public.

Gardiner has a handful of shops concentrated on Park Street adjacent to the Roosevelt Arch. Art and photography galleries contain western works, and bookstores feature local and regional authors. You'll also find gift, jewelry, and clothing shops. **Yellowstone Association** (308 Park St., 406/848-2400, www.yellowstoneassociation.org) runs an outlet that sells books on history, geology, wildlife, science, flora, and photography, plus field guides and recreation guidebooks.

COOKE CITY

The **Cooke City Store** (101 Main St., 406/838-2234, http://cookecitystore.com, 8am-8pm daily May-Sept.) is listed on the National Register of Historic Places due to its start in 1886. Today, it serves as a general mercantile carrying groceries, sporting goods, maps, books, hardware, and gifts.

Accommodations

Park accommodations include historical, budget, family, moderate, and pricey options, but upscale lodging is limited to nonexistent. In-park lodging fills up first—and fast. For amenities such as TVs, wireless Internet, and air-conditioning, book a stay in Gardiner. Those planning to drive the Beartooth Highway and explore more remote sections of Yellowstone's northeast corner should look for lodging in Silver Gate or Cooke City.

INSIDE THE PARK
Reservations

Xanterra (307/344-7311 or 866/439-7375, www.yellowstonenationalparklodges.com) runs all the lodges inside Yellowstone. Reservations are recommended one year in advance for summer and holidays in winter (especially if you want a room with an en suite bath). Last-minute bookings may be available due to cancellations, but with limited choices.

In keeping with the historical ambience, most in-park rooms and cabins lack televisions, radios, telephones, and air-conditioning. If you are a light sleeper, bring earplugs; if you are traveling during midsummer heat, you may want to bring a fan with an extension cord (very few are available from the front desks). ADA rooms are limited. Lodging rates listed are for two people; add $15-18 per each additional person. Some of the cabins permit pets for an added fee of $25. When staying inside the park, expect utility fees and taxes to add about 14 percent to the rates.

Mammoth Hot Springs
MAMMOTH HOT SPRINGS HOTEL

In the busiest tourist center in the park's north end, ★ Mammoth Hot Springs Hotel (1 Grand Loop Rd., May-mid-Oct. and late Dec.-early Mar., $90-260 rooms and cabins, $480 suites) is a large complex with almost 100 hotel rooms and 125 cabins. The U.S. Cavalry built the north wing of the four-story hotel in 1911; the main lobby and remainder of the hotel were erected in 1936. True to their roots, rooms have old push-button light switches, thin walls, and minimal electrical outlets. The historic attraction off the lobby is the Map Room, containing a large wooden U.S. map constructed in 1937 from 2,544 pieces of 15 different kinds of wood from nine countries. Look closely for one error: The capital of Maryland is not Baltimore but Annapolis. The hotel is within walking distance from the Albright Visitor Center, travertine terrace boardwalks, trailheads, a gift shop, post office, and two restaurants. Xanterra charges about $5 per hour, $12 per day, or $25 for three days for Internet access, available only in the map room. In winter, Mammoth is the only hotel in the park accessible by private vehicles on plowed roads. The park service and Xanterra aim to operate Mammoth year-round by 2017.

In summer, the hotel has seven types of accommodations: hotel rooms (with or without baths), two-room suites, one- or two-room rustic cabins with sinks, cabins with baths, and hot tub cabins. Hotel rooms and rustic cabins without baths have access to shared baths down the hall or community bathhouses in the cabin complex. Rustic cabins have one queen or one queen and two doubles. Shower stalls throughout the hotel and cabins tend to be small. Hotel rooms and larger cabins have two queens. An elevator accesses the upper floors of the hotel. The two high-end suites have a bedroom with two queen beds plus a sitting room with a couch, chairs, trundle bed, television, and telephone. Four cabins have the added perk of fenced private hot tubs. In winter, only hotel rooms, the two suites, and the hot tub cabins are available.

Tower-Roosevelt
ROOSEVELT LODGE AND CABINS

At Tower Junction on Grand Loop Road, **Roosevelt Lodge and Cabins** (Grand Loop Rd. at junction with Northeast Entrance Rd., early June-early Sept., $82-140) sits near the Roosevelt Corrals, Tower Fall, Petrified Tree, and Lamar Valley. The 1920s lodge derives its name from a nearby campsite used by President Theodore Roosevelt, and the locale is perfect for dawn and dusk wildlife-watching drives. The lodge has a gift shop, dining room, and a lineup of cane rockers on the front porch that overlooks the dusty parking lot. Two types of small bucolic cabins surround the lodge. Spartan **Roughrider cabins** contain one or two double beds and wood-burning stoves for heat (two Presto Logs included), but require walking to the nearby community toilet-and-shower house. **Frontier cabins** come with an en suite toilet, shower, sink, and usually two double beds. Walk to the neighboring corral for trail rides, wagon rides, and Old West Dinner Cookouts. With no Internet, the western atmosphere has more backwoods authenticity.

OUTSIDE THE PARK
Gardiner

Flanking the park boundary and the Yellowstone River, Gardiner bustles in summer with tourists. Most of Gardiner's lodging properties rim the highway through town on the north side of the bridge over the Yellowstone River. Located only five miles from Mammoth, the town makes a good alternative for lodging while exploring the north end of Yellowstone. Staying in Gardiner offers easy access to shopping, art galleries, rafting, fly-fishing, and multiple restaurants and bars.

Most rooms in Gardiner have televisions, wireless Internet (although perhaps not strong enough for major streaming or downloading), phones, and air-conditioning. Rates are highest June-September, then lower in fall, winter, and spring. Add on a 7 percent Montana bed tax year-round; for June-September stays, add on 3 percent more for the Gardiner Resort Tax. For summer or winter holiday lodging, make reservations 9-12 months in advance.

HOSTEL
North Yellowstone Lodge and Hostel (1083 U.S. Hwy. 89, 406/823-9683, www.northyellowstonehostel.com, May-Sept.) sits 10 miles north of Gardiner on acreage

Roosevelt Lodge has lodging in rustic cabins.

with a quiet apple orchard and beach on the Yellowstone River. Accommodations are in shared dorm rooms with bunk beds ($35/person) and private rooms for 2-4 people ($90-140) with a queen bed and set of bunks. Shared bath facilities are down the hall. Private rooms come with linens, but you'll need a sleeping bag for the dorm beds (or $5 for linens). The lodge has a communal kitchen, dining room, living room, and recreation room.

MOTELS

Gardiner has several national chain motels. Year-round options include **Super 8** (702 Scott St. W., 406/848-7401 or 800/800-8000, www.yellowstonesuper8.com, $65-245) and **Best Western by Mammoth Hot Springs** (905 A Scott St. W., 406/848-7311 or 800/828-9080, www.bestwestern.com, $100-255), which has one building of rooms overlooking the Yellowstone River. The newest chain motel is the **Rodeway Inn & Suites** (109 Hellroaring St., 406/848-7520, mid-Apr.-Oct., $120-240), an adjunct to the **Comfort Inn** (107 Hellroaring St., 406/848-7536, www.comfortinn.com, $120-240).

Several independent motels are open year-round. ★ **Yellowstone Gateway Inn** (103 Bigelow Ln., 406/848-7100, http://

yellowstonegatewayinn.com, $80-375) has 16 suites with full kitchens, 1-2 bedrooms, a living room, framed wildlife photographs, and access to communal barbecue grills. Each unit sleeps 2-8 people. The master bedroom has a king bed, while the second bedroom has a queen. One or two sofa beds, with specially made, comfortable mattresses, are in the living room. The ground-level suites include a few steps up to the door, and each unit has a tiny outdoor patio with seating; some have views of Electric Peak. A grocery store is across the street for stocking the kitchen.

Overlooking the Yellowstone River, the three-story **Absaroka Lodge** (310 Scott St., 406/848-7414 or 800/755-7414, www.yellowstonemotel.com, $60-190) has rooms with private decks to enjoy the river and views of the park's peaks. Chain hotel-type rooms include two queen beds, mini-fridges, and microwaves; some have kitchenettes. Located adjacent to the bridge across the river, the lodge is well situated for walking to restaurants and shopping on either side of the river. With no elevator, be prepared to carry your luggage.

Other independent motels are open only spring through fall. Located on the west end of town, the two-story **Yellowstone Village Inn and Suites** (1102 Scott St., 406/848-7417,

Yellowstone Gateway Inn

www.yellowstoneinn.com, mid-Apr.-Oct., $140-240) offers simple hotel rooms and suites with 1-3 bedrooms, full kitchens, and living rooms. Hotel rooms and suites contain one king or queen bed, two queens, or one of each. The inn has an indoor pool, basketball court, and free continental breakfast.

Adjacent to the Yellowstone River, the **Yellowstone River Motel** (14 Park St., 406/848-7303 or 888/797-4837, www.yellowstonerivermotel.com, Apr.-Oct., $65-165) is a two-story, 38-room, no-frills property with an additional three-bedroom unit with a full kitchen. Rooms in the older wing have small but revamped bathrooms. The newer wing has larger rooms at higher rates. Communal outdoor areas include a patio overlooking the river, a charcoal grill, and picnic tables.

CABINS

On the Yellowstone River, the **Riverside Cottages** (521 Scott St. W., 406/848-7719 or 877/774-2836, www.riversidecottages.com, year-round, $70-260) include several different options. Cottages and balcony suites have full kitchens; balcony suites are newer, while some of the tiny vintage cabins have thin walls. Efficiency rooms feature microwaves and mini-fridges. A large wooden deck with tables and chairs overlooks the river and the park's peaks, as does the hot tub, and a wooden stairway drops to the shore.

Hillcrest Cottages (400 Scott St. W., 406/848-7353 or 800/970-7353, http://hillcrestcottages.weebly.com, early May-mid-Oct., $85-170) sleep 2-8 people each in their 15 cottages. The tiny rooms have varied configurations with queen and single beds. Smaller cottages include microwaves, mini-fridges, and coffeemakers, while larger cottages have full kitchens.

BED-AND-BREAKFASTS

Two Gardiner B&Bs are within walking distance to restaurants and shops. The ★ **Gardiner Guest House B&B** (112 Main St. E., 406/848-9414, www.gardinerguesthouse.com, year-round, $70-150) offers three

rooms in a 1903 Victorian house, plus a backyard cabin, with en suite or shared bathrooms. Most rooms have one queen bed, except for Room 2, which has an antique double bed. Room 3 features an additional single bed. Amenities include full breakfasts and late-night snacks.

The **Yellowstone Suites Bed and Breakfast** (506 4th St. S., 406/848-7937 or 800/948-7937, www.yellowstonesuites.com, Feb.-Oct., $85-175) sits three blocks from the Roosevelt Arch in a restored 1904 stone home with a covered porch that allows guests to enjoy the garden. Located on the 2nd and 3rd floors, two guest rooms have one queen bed each with shared baths, while two other rooms feature queen beds and private baths. The Roosevelt Room has an additional single bed. There is no elevator.

Located four miles north of Gardiner, ★ **Yellowstone Basin Inn** (4 Maiden Basin Dr., 406/848-7080, http://yellowstonebasininn.com, May-mid-Oct., $100-445) has 11 rooms or suites, each one unique and themed after the Montana outdoors. Studios and three-bedroom apartments with full kitchens and king and queen beds sleep 2-5 people each. Amenities include an outdoor hot tub, home-cooked hot breakfasts, and to-go lunches in summer. With advance notice, the owners can accommodate dietary preferences.

Silver Gate and Cooke City

Located within three miles of each other, and just outside the Northeast Entrance to Yellowstone, Silver Gate and Cooke City offer a more backwoods, bucolic ambience than Gardiner, with an emphasis on outdoor recreation rather than shopping. Because the towns sit at 7,600 feet in elevation, the altitude may bother some people with labored breathing or fitful sleeping. While the two villages pack out in summer, winter is another high season due to snowmobiling and winter sports.

MOTELS

Basic motels are along the main drag of U.S. Highway 212 in Cooke City. Most are open year-round. **Super 8** (303 E. Main St., Cooke City, 406/838-2070 or 877/338-2070, www.super8.com, $90-150) is the only chain motel in town. **Alpine Motel** (105 E. Main St., Cooke City, 406/838-2262 or 888/838-1190, www.cookecityalpine.com, $80-150) offers rooms with one or two queen beds, plus a microwave and mini-fridge, or two-bedroom suites with full kitchens. **High Country Motel** (113 W. Main St., Cooke City, 406/838-2272, www.highcountrymotelandcabins.com, $90-150) has 11 motel rooms and four 1950s log cabins with microwaves and mini-fridges or kitchens, as well as a communal hot tub. Most units have one or two queen beds. **Soda Butte Lodge** (209 Hwy. 212, Cooke City, 406/838-2251, www.cookecity.com, $90-150) features 32 motel rooms in a two- and three-story building with no elevator. Room choices include a king bed, two queen beds, and family rooms with three queen beds. A restaurant and saloon are part of the complex.

High Country Motel in Cooke City

Open late spring-mid-fall, **Elk Horn Lodge** (103 Main St., Cooke City, 406/838-2332, www.elkhornlodgemt.com, May-mid-Oct., $90-150) includes motel rooms with two beds, microwaves, and mini-fridges plus two additional cabins. A communal hot tub is on-site.

CABINS

Pine Edge Cabins (107 and 109 U.S. Hwy. 212, Silver Gate, 406/838-2371, www.pineedgecabins.com, year-round, $125-170) is a collection of 29 log cabins, five motel rooms, and a general store that rents spotting scopes for wildlife-watching. Three different cabin styles are available, most with full kitchens. At the upper price range, the newer Silver Gate Cabins have kitchens and one or two queen beds (some with additional bunk beds or sofa beds). At mid-range prices, the Pine Edge Cabins mostly include one or two double beds, with some additional bunks. At the lowest price range, most of the older Whispering Pines Cabins have one or two double beds and access to a wood-fired sauna. Motel rooms include one queen bed.

For a breakfast with cabin stay, the **Log Cabin Café Bed & Breakfast** (106 Hwy. 212, Silver Gate, 406/838-2367 or 800/863-0807, www.thelogcabincafe.com, May-Oct., $100) has two small log cabins with two double beds each. Bathroom facilities are in a separate shower house, and breakfast is made to order in the café.

Antler's Lodge (311 Main St. E., Cooke City, 406/838-2432 or 866/738-2432, www.cookecityantlerslodge.com, year-round, $85-170) has 12 single or duplex cabins plus motel rooms on a historic property. Bed configurations vary between units with queens, single beds, and bunks. The lodge restaurant (mid-Dec.-Mar.) serves breakfast and dinner.

GUEST RANCH

In a quiet three-story log lodge set amid firs, **Skyline Guest Ranch** (31 Kersey Lake Rd., Cooke City, 406/838-2380 or 877-238-8885, www.flyfishyellowstone.com, year-round, $120-170) operates a bed-and-breakfast along with an outfitting service for horseback riding, hunting, fishing, and snowmobiling. Six guest rooms include private bathrooms and one or two queen beds. Communal areas include a hot tub, picnic tables, outdoor grill, living room, and dining room. In winter, the ranch is only accessible via snowmobile.

Camping

INSIDE THE PARK

This region of Yellowstone has smaller campgrounds than elsewhere in the park. With the exception of Mammoth Campground, each offers a quiet place to get away from crowds. Reservations are not accepted; all campgrounds are **first-come, first-served.** Amenities include potable water, picnic tables, bear boxes for food storage, fire rings with grills, and flush or vault toilets, but no showers. Accessible sites are available at Mammoth and Indian Creek Campgrounds. It is possible to check online (www.nps.gov/yell) to see whether campsites have filled.

Mammoth Hot Springs

At 6,200 feet, **Mammoth Campground** (year-round, $20) clusters its 85 campsites on an open sagebrush hillside with scattered trees. This is the only campground in the northern region of the park with flush toilets and where generators are permitted (8am-8pm).

Most campsites have pull-through parking to accommodate RVs (some can fit combinations up to 75 feet), and 51 sites have tent pads. Campers can walk to trailheads, Mammoth Hot Springs Terraces, restaurants, and shops. Though it can be windy or hot in midsummer, most campsites get broad scenery of Gardner River Canyon. The access road to Mammoth Hot Springs circles the campground, which makes daytime traffic noise a factor. In midsummer, plan to claim a site by 9am.

Mammoth to Norris

At 7,300 feet, **Indian Creek Campground** (mid-June-mid-Sept., $15) has 70 sites, vault toilets, and a quiet ambience with views of Electric Peak in the Gallatin Range. This is a place to hear the haunting hoot of owls or bugling elk in fall. Most campsites are tucked into the forest with parking pads (35 feet or less). The campground offers quick access to Swan Lake Flat for wildlife-watching,

Mammoth Campground

the trailhead to Bighorn Pass, Bunsen Peak Bike Trail, Sheepeater Cliff, and fishing. The campground is located eight miles south of Mammoth Hot Springs on the Grand Loop Road and often fills by noon in summer.

Tower-Roosevelt

Set on a steep hillside above Tower Fall, Tower Fall Campground (late May-late Sept., $15) has 31 campsites with parking pads (30 feet or shorter), plus a hairpin turn to negotiate. Some sites sit in the open while others tuck under large pines. At 6,600 feet in elevation, hiking up or down the hill to vault toilets or to the hand-cranked water pump may have you huffing and puffing. A trail drops from the campground to the Tower Fall observation area, but be prepared to climb back uphill. Horseback trail rides and a restaurant are two miles north at Roosevelt Lodge. The amphitheater has evening naturalist talks. The campground often fills by noon in summer.

Northeast Entrance

★ Slough Creek Campground (mid-June-early Sept., $15) is prized for its remoteness, solitude, wildlife-watching, and fishing. Lined up along Slough Creek at 6,250 feet in elevation, the 23 campsites vary from open sagebrush meadows to shady conifers. Prime campsites include creek frontage within sound of the water. All sites have less than 30-foot parking pads; amenities include hand pumps for water and vault toilets. This primitive campground is accessed via the dirt Slough Creek Road, five miles east of Tower Junction on the Northeast Entrance Road.

North of Lamar Valley at 6,900 feet elevation, Pebble Creek Campground (mid-June-late Sept., $15) loops through forest-flanked wildflower meadows. Some of the 27 campsites are open with views of the surrounding Absaroka Mountains, and a few are walk-in tent-only sites. Facilities include a hand pump for water and vault toilets. Nearby, you can access the trailhead to Trout Lake, fishing in Soda Butte Creek, wildlife-watching in Lamar Valley, or Silver Gate and Cooke City. The campground

is located along the Northeast Entrance Road, 13 miles past Slough Creek Road.

OUTSIDE THE PARK
Gardiner

Two private campgrounds sit in the town of Gardiner with hookups for sewer, water, and electricity. Facilities include picnic tables, wireless Internet, cable TV, laundries, flush toilets, and showers. Add on a 10 percent tax to the rates.

Rocky Mountain Campground (14 Jardine Rd., 406/848-7251 or 877/534-6931, www.rockymountainrvpark.com, May-Sept., $43-62) perches on a bluff in downtown Gardiner, within walking distance to shopping, restaurants, a ranger station, visitors centers, art galleries, groceries, and the Roosevelt Arch. With 71 RV campsites, the sunny campground commands views of the town, the Yellowstone River, and north slopes of the park. A few campsites tuck under the shade of large trees, but all stack up in parking-lot fashion and lack privacy. RVs are limited to 45 feet. Facilities include a community campfire area, miniature golf, and a disposal station.

Yellowstone RV Park (117 Hwy. 89 S., 406/848-7496, www.ventureswestinc.com/YellowstoneRVPark.htm, May-Oct., $45-60) sits farther from the main action of town, but overlooks the Yellowstone River. Two rows of 46 RV sites line up like a parking lot. The campsites are open, sunny, and speckled with a few low trees, and have views across the canyon to sagebrush hills. Expect to hear both the river and the highway; winds also frequently blow through the canyon. The campground can accommodate a few tents and RVs up to 70 feet.

FOREST SERVICE CAMPGROUNDS
Custer-Gallatin National Forest (Gardiner Ranger District, 406/848-7375, www.fs.usda.gov/gallatin) operates several campgrounds around Yellowstone that work for overflow camping in a pinch or places to stay before heading into the park.

Three miles north of Gardiner along Jardine Road, Eagle Creek Campground (first-come, first-served, year-round, $7 first vehicle, $3 additional car) has commanding views across the valley into Yellowstone. Set on an open hillside, the 16 campsites have no shade or privacy, and many sites are sloped. Eagle Creek runs along the west side of the campground, surrounded by brush, aspens, and willows. RVs are limited to 40 feet, and there is a corral adjacent to the campground.

About 15 miles north of Gardiner along U.S. Highway 89, **Canyon Campground** (first-come, first-served, year-round, $7 first vehicle, $3 additional car) has 17 arid campsites in Yankee Jim Canyon set amid huge clustered boulders and junipers. Sites 3, 4, and 6 tuck back into mini-canyons for more privacy. This campground is best for tents and small RVs (up to 48 feet), as navigation requires squeezing between boulders. Watch for rattlesnakes. Sites at each campground have picnic tables, fire rings with grills, bear boxes, and vault toilets. There is no drinking water, so be prepared to filter creek water or bring your own.

North of Jardine, primitive dispersed campgrounds include **Timber Camp** and **Bear Creek Campgrounds.** Both are open mid-June-October, and there is no fee or services. For more information, contact the Gardiner Ranger Station.

Cooke City

Along U.S. Highway 212 east of Cooke City are three **Custer-Gallatin National Forest** (Gardiner Ranger District, 406/848-7375, www.fs.usda.gov/gallatin) campgrounds, each set at around 8,000 feet in elevation and within 4-7 miles of the Northeast Entrance to Yellowstone.

Overlooking burbling Soda Butte Creek, **Soda Butte Campground** (first-come, first-served, July-Sept., $9 first vehicle, $3 additional car) has 27 campsites for hard-sided RVs (no tents) up to 48 feet. Surrounded by pink sticky geranium and white cow parsnip, the campground is six miles from the Northeast Entrance and one mile east of Cooke City on U.S. Highway 212.

Just east of Soda Butte, on the north side of U.S. Highway 212, is neighboring **Colter Campground** (first-come, first-served, July-Sept., $9 first vehicle, $3 additional car) with 18 campsites for hard-sided RVs (no tents) up to 48 feet. Set in new-growth forest and meadows with views of the Absaroka Mountains, the campground is seven miles from the Northeast Entrance and two miles east of Cooke City on U.S. Highway 212.

Chief Joseph Campground (first-come, first-served, July-Sept., $8) is named after the

Chief Joseph Campground sits on the route of the Flight of the Nez Perce.

Nez Perce chief who led his people across Idaho, Wyoming, and Montana while being chased by the U.S. Army. Camping is for hard-sided RVs only (no tents), with six sites tucked into mature lodgepole pines and spruce. Across the road from the campground are interpretive sites for the Nez Perce National Historic Trail, a wildlife nature trail, and the Flume Interpretive Trail and Picnic Area, which has a fishing pier, a wheelchair-accessible trail, a giant rushing waterfall, historical mining artifacts, a view of Granite Peak (Montana's highest peak), and access to the Russell Creek Trail. The campground is nine miles from the Northeast Entrance and four miles east of Cooke City on U.S. Highway 212.

Facilities at each campground include picnic tables, fire rings with grills, bear boxes, vault toilets, and drinking water. The forest canopy has thinned out due to bark beetle infestations, opening up the campgrounds to sunlight and views.

Food

INSIDE THE PARK

Xanterra (307/344-7311 or 866/439-7375, www.yellowstonenationalparklodges.com) operates the park lodge restaurants, grills, and cookouts. **Delaware North Company** (406/586-7593, www.visityellowstonepark. com) runs the lunch counters and cafés in the Yellowstone General Stores. In winter, dinner **reservations** are accepted at **Mammoth Hotel Dining Room;** in summer, reservations are mandatory for the **Old West Dinner Cookout.** In all park restaurants, casual dress is common. No dresses, heels, or ties needed.

Mammoth Hot Springs

Located across from the Mammoth Hot Spring Hotel in a separate building, the **Mammoth Hotel Dining Room** (307/344-7311 or 866/439-7375, www.yellowstonenationalparklodges.com, breakfast 6:30am-10am, lunch 11:30am-2:30pm daily early May-early Oct. and late Dec.-early Mar., dinner 5pm-10pm daily early May-early Oct., 5:30pm-8pm or 9pm daily late Dec.-early Mar., $9-29) overlooks the parade grounds where wildlife often adds entertainment. This certified-green restaurant changes up menus between winter and summer, but both seasons offer a variety of lighter, healthy, small-plate, vegan, gluten-free, and select topping options alongside classic full meals. Kids have their own menu. Breakfast is from the menu or, in summer, from the large all-you-can-eat buffet ($13 adults, $7 kids). Lunches feature soup, salad, sandwiches, and burgers. Local specialties include wild-game chili and bison tacos or burgers. In summer, dinner is first-come, first-served; in winter, make reservations through Xanterra. Fish, pastas, and Montana farm-raised meats comprise the dinner menu. Beer, wine, and cocktails are also served, and the restaurant makes to-go breakfasts or lunches.

At the opposite end of the dining room building, **Mammoth Terrace Grill** (307/344-7311 or 866/439-7375, www.yellowstonenationalparklodges.com, 7am-9pm daily late Apr.-mid-Oct., hours vary seasonally, $3-9) serves breakfast, lunch, dinner, light snacks, ice cream, sandwiches, burgers, and kiddie meals. Breakfast choices narrow to continental selections in spring or fall; in summer, expect hot meals. Prices are inexpensive, but à la carte items add up.

Mammoth General Store (1 Mammoth Upper Loop Rd., 406/586-7593, www.visityellowstonepark.com, 7:30am-9:30pm daily in summer, shorter hours in winter) has a small cafeteria and serves hot dogs, snacks, and Montana-made Wilcoxson's ice cream.

Tower-Roosevelt

With a cowboy-friendly menu and a lobby bar, dining at Roosevelt Lodge just feels western.

Mammoth Terrace Grill

vegetarian options can replace the steak.) Check-in times at the Roosevelt Corral range between 2:45pm-4:45pm (hours vary seasonally). Horseback rides take 1-2 hours to reach the site; the wagon ride takes 30-45 minutes. All return rides take 30 minutes. Reservations are required.

Located adjacent to the Roosevelt Lodge, the **Roosevelt Store** (1 Roosevelt Lodge Rd., 7:30am-9:30pm daily early June-Aug.) has a small grocery.

If you get hungry while driving the Grand Loop between Canyon Village and Tower Junction, **Tower Fall General Store** (7:30am-9:30pm daily late May-mid-Sept.) has a snack bar that sells hot dogs, chips, drinks, and limited groceries. Outdoor picnic tables are available.

OUTSIDE THE PARK
Gardiner

Due to limited dining inside the park, many people drive 15 minutes from Mammoth to Gardiner for dinner. Most restaurants shorten their hours or days in winter, so call ahead to confirm when they are open. Summer visitors pay a 3 percent resort tax added to meals.

CAFES

Yellowstone Perk (208 Park St., 406/848-9430, 7am-10pm daily in summer, shorter hours in winter) is a small store that also serves as a pharmacy, selling espresso drinks and Livingston-made Wilcoxson's ice cream in homemade waffle cones. Internet access is also available.

Part bookstore and part eatery, the **Tumbleweed Cafe** (501 Scott St., 406/848-2225, http://tumbleweedbooksandcafe.weebly.com, 7am-9pm daily May-Oct., 9am-6pm daily Nov.-Apr., $4-11) serves light homemade meals for breakfast, lunch, and dinner; choose from cereal, breakfast burritos, wraps, paninis, salads, soups, and espresso. You can also find gluten-free, vegan, and vegetarian options, as well as baked goodies and to-go items, such as a sack lunch ($11) to take into the park.

Lauded by many locals as the best food in the park, ★ **Roosevelt Lodge Dining Room** (307/344-7311 or 866/439-7375, www.yellowstonenationalparklodges.com, 7am-10am and 11:30am-9:30pm daily early June-Sept., $10-26) designs menu items for flexibility with plenty of size, toppings, sides, and gluten-free choices. Breakfast skillets, Tex-Mex, wild game, and smoked barbecue ribs are house specialties. At 4:30pm, the menu expands with additional western-style dinner options. Seating is first-come, first-served, and a kiddie menu is available. You can also order to-go lunches ($13).

The **Old West Dinner Cookout** (307/344-7311 or 866/439-7375, www.yellowstonenationalparklodges.com, rides start at dusk daily early June-mid-Sept., $60-88 adults, $49-81 children 8-11) is adventure dining. Guests saddle up or ride a wagon from the Roosevelt Corrals to Yancy's Hole. At the cookout, wranglers grill up steaks to order and serve up traditional cookout sides along with coffee cooked on a fire. (With advance notice,

Adjacent to the Best Western Hotel, the family-owned **Yellowstone Mine** (905 Scott St. W., 406/848-7336, 7am-10pm Tues.-Sun. year-round, $10-30) is decked out with old mining implements. Breakfast (served until 11am) can be ordered off the menu, or enjoy the buffet spread, which includes waffles, cereal, eggs, sides, and fruit. The lunch and dinner menu is available the rest of the day and features old-school meat-and-potatoes meals, such as prime rib, rib eye, burgers, salmon, trout, and other fish.

BARBECUE

With owners from southern Georgia, **Cowboy's Lodge and Grille** (208 Stone St., 406/848-9175, http://cowboyslodge.com, 11am-9pm daily year-round, $10-28) dishes up southern barbecue in a small and rustic log cabin restaurant that houses a stuffed mountain lion perched in the rafters ready to swipe at patrons. The lunch and dinner menu specializes in medium portions (rather than huge cowboy-type meals) with barbecued meat, chicken, brisket, or ribs served with traditional sides; opt for the combo platter to taste different sauces. Also on the menu are hand-cut fries, including sweet potato fries, and chicken pot pie, bean stew, beer, and wine.

MEXICAN

A small café, ★ **Yellowstone Grill** (404 Scott St., 406/848-9433, 7am-2pm Tues.-Sun. summer, 7am-2pm Wed.-Sun. winter, $8-15) is a combo bakery-grill-Mexican food restaurant that serves fresh breakfast and lunch. South-of-the-border fare includes burritos, quesadillas, and tacos, though you can also choose from omelets, hash, blueberry pancakes, soups, salads, wraps, burgers, and espresso. The baked goods specialty is caramel cinnamon rolls.

PIZZA

For a small town, Gardiner has multiple pizza options. Visitors can pair up a pie with a local microbrew or wine, or grab a pizza to go. Open since 1953, **KBar Pizza** (202 Main St., 406/848-9995, www.kbarpizza.com, 11am-11pm daily summer, 4pm-9pm Fri.-Sun. winter, $10-25) bakes pizzas in a vintage deck oven with wheat or gluten-free crusts. Their Crazy Woman pizza has a kicky spice. **Yellowstone Pizza Company** (210 Park St., 406/848-9991, http://yellowstonepizza-company.com, 11am-10pm daily May-Oct., $10-20) dishes up 12-inch pizzas cooked in a brick oven with regular or gluten-free crust. Elk or bison pizza is the house specialty. You can also get salads or pasta-of-the-day. In summer, outdoor dining on the upstairs deck yields views of the Roosevelt Arch.

PUBS

With a large outside deck overlooking the Yellowstone River, the **Iron Horse Bar & Grille** (200 Spring St., 406/848-7666, 11am-midnight daily May-Sept., $8-26) allows viewing of the river and peaks while dining. Specialties include elk tacos, bison burgers, grilled bison meatloaf, bison shepherd's pie, trout, fries, local microbrews, and huckleberry margaritas. Lunch usually runs until 4pm, while dinner is served until 9pm. Bar food is available until midnight. There is also indoor seating, pool tables in the pub, and takeout available.

The **Two Bit Saloon & Grill** (107 2nd St., 406/848-7743, www.twobitsaloon.com, 9am-2am daily year-round, $6-17) serves western food: biscuits and gravy, eggs, burgers, sandwiches, and a few Tex-Mex dishes. This longtime Gardiner staple is the place to go for an elk burger and a regional Montana microbrew, or start the day with a pick-me-up cocktail. Breakfast is served until 11:30am, followed by a lunch and dinner menu that lasts until 9pm; families are welcome until 10pm. The saloon also has slot machines and billiards, plus occasional live music.

FINE DINING

The tiny ★ **Raven Grill** (220 W. Park St., 406/848-7600, 5pm-10pm daily mid-Apr.-mid-Oct., $17-40) sits right outside the park entrance in view of the Roosevelt Arch and

Lighthouse Restaurant

ranch with views of Yellowstone across the valley. The cowboy steak cookout takes place around a campfire and is accompanied by potatoes, salad, cornbread, dessert, beverages, and marshmallow roasting. You can also combine a one-hour horseback ride with dinner ($88 adults, $70 children). Since the ranch only accepts reservations by phone or email, make cookout reservations online via their partner, **Flying Pig Adventure Company** (www.flyingpigrafting.com).

Corwin Springs

Located seven miles north of Gardiner in Corwin Springs, the ★ **Lighthouse Restaurant** (752 Hwy. 89 S., 406/848-2138, www.lrmts.com, 5:30pm-11pm Wed.-Mon. late May-late Sept., $12-26) may have the appearance outside of a ramshackle dive, but inside is food of a much higher caliber. Choose from locally sourced, organic, and fresh-made options such as burgers (beef, bison, crab cake, lamb) or pasta with chicken or shrimp added. Eclectic house specialties are big on flavor with Asian twists and unique sauces.

Silver Gate and Cooke City

Two small stores carry limited groceries, beer, and wine: **Cooke City Store** (101 Main St., Cooke City, 406/838-2234, http://cookecitystore.com, 8am-8pm daily May-Sept.) and **Silver Gate General Store** (109 U.S. Hwy 212, Silver City, 406/838-2371, www.pineedgecabins.com, 8am-10pm daily May-Oct.). Stop in at the ★ **Bearclaw Bakery** (303 E. Main, Cooke City, 406/838-2040, 5am-11am Tues.-Sun. late May-Sept., hours vary in winter, $4-9) for breakfast burritos, eggs with sides, biscuits and gravy, cinnamon rolls, bear claws, blueberry scones, cookies, and breads. The house specialty is Bearclaw French toast. Go early or you may not get a seat in the tiny restaurant, which also serves as the front room for an automobile and snowmobile repair shop. You can also order a breakfast sammie to go, as well as espresso and ice cream.

Housed in a 1940s log cabin, the **Beartooth Café** (14 Main St., Cooke City,

Electric Peak. The restaurant is crammed with minimal diner-style seating and a few outdoor tables, making reservations a good idea. Though primarily a steakhouse with grilled meats (beef, bison, elk rib eye, chicken, seafood) and elk burgers, it also serves wild-game pastas and small plates.

GROCERIES

While you won't find big box grocers, the **Gardiner Market** (701 Scott St., 406/848-7524, www.gardinermarket.com, 7am-11pm daily in summer, 7am-8pm daily winter) sells fresh produce and meat, frozen and baked goods, convenience food, deli items, and beer and wine. It also has a Montana State Liquor Store for the stronger stuff. The closest full-size supermarket is Albertson's in Livingston.

Jardine

Hell's A-Roaring (164 Crevice Rd., 406/848-7578, www.hellsaroarinoutfitters.com, Sun.-Fri. late May-mid-Aug., $48 adults, $30 children) hosts an evening cookout at their

406/838-2475, www.beartoothcafe.com, 11am-10pm daily late May-late Sept., $8-28) is a Cooke City institution run by a fourth-generation family. Meals are made from scratch, including appetizers and desserts, and served al fresco on a deck filled with flowers and umbrella tables. Lunch (served until 5pm) includes sandwiches and burgers, while dinner (served after 5pm) rolls out burgers, steaks, prime rib, dinner salads, and pasta. Wine or an extensive selection of 120 beers can accompany your meal. A kiddie menu and vegetarian choices are also available.

In a log cabin more than 75 years old, the

Log Cabin Café (106 Hwy. 212, Silver Gate, 406/838-2367, www.thelogcabincafe.com, 7am-10pm daily May-Oct. $8-28) serves breakfast, lunch, and dinner. Find fresh-ground organic coffee, homemade hash browns, and grilled pumpkin bread with Montana honey for breakfast followed by soups, salads, burgers, and wraps for lunch. Pies, desserts, baked goods, and soups are homemade. Fresh produce is mostly organic, and grass-fed, free-range beef is sourced locally for dinner steaks. Trout is also served for breakfast and dinner. Beer and wine is available.

Transportation and Services

DRIVING

Gardiner is located on U.S. Highway 89, which becomes Park Street approaching the North Entrance to Yellowstone. From Gardiner, the **North Entrance Road** (U.S. 89, open year-round) runs five miles south to Mammoth Village.

From Mammoth Village, the two-lane **Grand Loop Road** travel east for 19 miles across the Blacktail Deer Plateau to Tower Junction and the park hub of Roosevelt. At Tower Junction, the **Northeast Entrance Road** continues 30 miles east to the Northeast Entrance. These roads are open year-round, and are the only park roads accessible by private cars and RVs in winter.

Snowstorms can cause temporary closures during fall, winter, and spring. Call for current **road conditions** (307/344-2117). In winter, plowing terminates just east of Cooke City where snow closes Highways 212 and 296. While this stretch of road offers prime wildlife-watching, the two-lane road is often clogged with "bison jams" (bison herds crossing the road), as well as traffic from stopped vehicles and dazed tourists taking photos. The drive from Mammoth to Tower Junction

can take one hour or more in summer; the Northeast Entrance Road can take also take up to one hour.

Find **parking** streetside in towns and villages or in parking lots at trailheads, lodges, picnic areas, and campgrounds in Yellowstone. Covered parking is not available at motels in Gardiner, Mammoth, Roosevelt, or Cooke City.

SHUTTLES

There is no public transportation between Gardiner, Mammoth Village, and Cooke City. **Karst Stage** (800/287-4759, www.karststage.com) provides shuttle services to and from the Bozeman, Montana airport and to Gardiner or Mammoth Village.

EMERGENCY SERVICES

Inside the park, medical emergencies can be treated at the **Mammoth Clinic** (Mammoth Village, 307/344-7965). You can also get help at the ranger stations located at Tower Junction and at the park entrance at Gardiner. Neither Gardiner nor Cooke City has a medical clinic, but they do have emergency medical services (dial 911).

Where Can I Find . . .?

- **Banks and ATMs:** An ATM is available in Mammoth Village and in Gardiner at First Interstate Bank (903 Scott St. W., 406/848-7474).

- **Cell Service:** Verizon service is available in the village of Mammoth Hot Springs. Tower-Roosevelt does not have cell service. Outside the park, service is available in Gardiner, but not in Cooke City.

- **Day Care:** Little People's Learning Center (330 Lower Mammoth, 307/344-9011, http://little-peopleslearningcenter.blogspot.com, 6:45am-5:45pm Mon.-Fri. summer, hours vary seasonally, $6-10/hour, $42-70/day) offers drop-in day care for ages six weeks-school age with 24-hour advance notice and immunization records.

- **Gas and Garage Services:** Gas stations (406/848-7548) are located at Mammoth (mid-May-mid-Oct.) and Tower Junction (June-Sept.). You can pay at the pump 24 hours a day with a credit card; in summer, you can also pay with cash. Outside the park, Gardiner and Cooke City have gas stations; head to Gardiner for auto repairs.

- **Internet Service:** Internet is available at the Mammoth Hot Springs Hotel lounge ($4.75/hour). Outside the park, Cooke City's visitors center has wireless Internet.

- **Laundry:** The closest laundry services are at Gardiner Laundry (111 E. Main St., Gardiner, 406/223-9936) and North Entrance Washtub (209 Main St., Gardiner, 406/848-9870), which also has public showers.

- **Pet-Friendly Lodging:** Available in Mammoth Hot Springs Hotel and Roosevelt Lodge.

- **Post Office:** A year-round post office (8:30am-5pm Mon.-Fri.) is located in Mammoth Village next to the Albright Visitor Center. There is also a post office in Gardiner (707 Scott St. W., 406/848-7579).

- **Showers:** Pay showers are located in the Mammoth Hot Springs Hotel (May-Oct.) and at the Roosevelt Lodge (June-Sept.) at Tower Junction.

The nearest hospital to Gardiner is **Livingston HealthCare Hospital** (32 Alpenglow Ln., Livingston, MT, 406/823-6262, www.livingstonhealthcare.org), 54 miles north along U.S. Highway 89, or head to their **Livingston HealthCare Urgent Care** (104 Centennial Dr., Ste. 103, 406/222-0030, 11am-10pm Mon.-Fri., 9am-5pm Sat.-Sun.).

The nearest hospital to Cooke City is **West Park Hospital** (07 Sheridan Ave., Cody, WY, 307/527-7501, www.westparkhospital.org), located 78 miles long and winding miles south in Cody. However, road closures can prevent access in winter, in which case you must drive 112 miles north to Livingston instead.

Old Faithful and West Yellowstone

The western arc of Yellowstone's supervolcano houses a string of geyser basins that contain some of the world's most active hydrothermal features.

Paint pots simmer with colorful microscopic creatures. Mud pots bubble like witches' cauldrons. Fumaroles blow off steam, and geysers spout scalding water. Rumbling with geothermal gusto, Upper Geyser Basin has the largest concentration of geysers. Old Faithful draws crowds for its regular eruptions, and hot pools yield mesmerizing colors. Midway Geyser Basin houses two of Yellowstone's largest geothermal features: Grand Prismatic Spring and Excelsior Geyser. Lower Geyser Basin spreads across the largest piece of landscape, almost 11 square miles of steaming portals from the earth's bowels. Norris Geyser Basin harbors the hottest hydrothermals and Steamboat Geyser, the world's tallest geyser.

For those exploring this bubbling landscape, Old Faithful and West Yellowstone house visitor services, restaurants, and lodging; Madison and Norris have the camping. Between them, fishing abounds, particularly in the trout-rich waters of the Firehole, Madison, and Gallatin Rivers.

Wildlife is easy to spot, even in winter. Bison wander through the geyser basins, and elk herds gather along the Madison River with the bulls bugling in fall. Carnivores follow the herds. Raptors fly overhead.

This supervolcano arc is one of the most active geothermal zones in Yellowstone; it is also the most popular. Old Faithful and West Yellowstone buzz with throngs of visitors in summer. But nowhere else in the world will you see such utter uniqueness.

PLANNING YOUR TIME

Wildlife-watching and geothermal activity go on year-round in Yellowstone. What alters is access and crowds. **High season is July-August**. June and September are still busy, but with smaller hordes. To avoid crowds, go in spring or late fall. **Park roads close** to private vehicles **November-mid-April**. During **winter high season (mid-Dec.-mid-Mar.)** only snowmobiles and snowcoaches are permitted on the roads into Old Faithful. West Yellowstone is open

---

Previous: bicycling Fountain Flats Road; visitors ski to Fairy Falls. **Above:** Great Fountain Geyser.

Look for ★ to find recommended
sights, activities, dining, and lodging.

Highlights

★ **Old Faithful Visitor Education Center:** Learn how geothermal features work and what scientists are discovering (page 83).

★ **Winter Snowcoach Tours:** See the volcanic landscape of the park in winter for a clash of heat and ice (page 84).

★ **Wildlife Watching:** Elk and bison dominate the region between Old Faithful and the Madison River (page 87).

★ **Fountain Paint Pots:** This 0.5-mile interpretive boardwalk loop visits all four of Yellowstone's different volcanic features (page 87).

★ **Great Fountain Geyser:** The only predictable eruption in Lower Geyser Basin blows for one hour to heights of 75-220 feet (page 87).

★ **Grand Prismatic Spring:** Vivid blue water surrounded by radiating browns and oranges comprise the largest hot springs in the United States (page 88).

★ **Old Faithful Inn:** The log lobby of this 1904 masterpiece holds an 85-foot-tall stone fireplace, the centerpiece of one of the first "parkitecture" inns (page 90).

★ **Old Faithful Geyser:** This geyser spews hot water 145 feet into the air every 65-90 minutes (page 90).

★ **Norris Geyser Basin:** Walk through the

hottest and most changeable geothermal basin in the park (page 94).

★ **Fairy Falls Trail:** Hike to this 197-foot-tall waterfall as it plummets over a cliff and sprays down rock steps to collect in a cold pool (page 98).

year-round, but Old Faithful (mid-Apr.-early Nov. and mid-Dec.-mid-Mar.) is a seasonal destination.

No matter where you start, go early, heading first on the lower loop to see the Lower, Middle, and Upper Geyser Basins before the crowds thicken midday. For the best touring experience, pack a picnic lunch. Then you won't be pressed by starvation to forgo sightseeing in favor of finding a restaurant. Most visitors who drive the Grand Loop in one day do so because they have limited time. You'll find exploring the route more enjoyable with multiple days of touring

Summer

For geothermal activity, you'll want to schedule visiting some sights based on when geysers erupt. Stop at visitors centers or use the park's geyser app to check eruption schedules, then plan excursions based on the predicted eruptions. For Old Faithful, crowds gather 30 minutes before eruptions to claim front-row viewing.

In July and August, get an early start. When parking lots max out (10am-4pm), you may have to circle around to find a parking spot, or go elsewhere and come back. Restrooms will have long waiting lines.

For Old Faithful lodging, make reservations a year in advance (starting May 1) to guarantee getting your preferred room. For West Yellowstone lodging, book 6-12 months in advance for July-August. You can find last-minute lodging in summer, but may have limited options.

Winter

In winter, when park roads are closed for driving, West Yellowstone serves as the biggest hub to access Old Faithful. Make reservations six months in advance for snowcoach and snowmobile tours.

At Old Faithful, only the Snow Lodge is open for about 10 weeks in winter. Book at least six months in advance or as early as March 15 for winter holidays. While the lodge may have rooms available, limited snowcoaches hamper accessibility. Make reservations for travel into Old Faithful at the same time you make lodging reservations. As of 2015, snowcoach transportation to overnight at the Snow Lodge originates only from Mammoth Hot Springs or Flagg Ranch (outside the South Entrance).

Spring and Fall

A less hectic time to travel, spring and fall may be hampered by snow squalls. Late March-mid-April and early November offers a few weeks when cyclists can ride the plowed road without cars.

Exploring Old Faithful and West Yellowstone

VISITORS CENTERS
West Yellowstone Visitor Information Center

The West Yellowstone Visitor Information Center (30 Yellowstone Ave., West Yellowstone, 307/344-2876, www.nps.gov/yell, 8am-8pm daily late Apr.-early Nov., 8am-4pm daily mid-Dec.-late Apr., hours vary in spring and fall) is located in West Yellowstone (outside the park) at the corner of Canyon Street and the park entrance road. Inside is the West Yellowstone Chamber of Commerce (406/646-7701, www.destinationyellowstone.com) and a National Park Service desk. At the park service desk, you can get maps, ranger programs, and naturalist-led tour schedules, as well as information on campgrounds, backcountry permits (8am-4:30pm daily June-Aug.), wildlife, and geothermal hot spots. Restrooms are also available.

Old Faithful and West Yellowstone

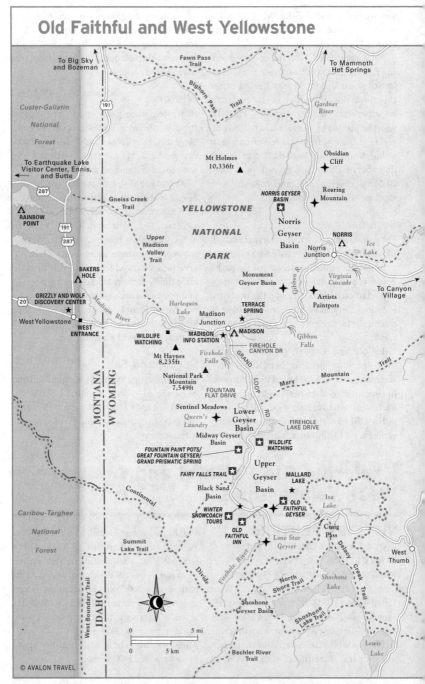

© AVALON TRAVEL

Madison Information Station

A National Historic Landmark, the small Madison Information Station (307/244-2876, www.nps.gov/yell, 9am-6pm daily late May-early Sept.) is housed in a historic cabin overlooking the Madison River near Madison Junction. Also known as the Madison Junior Ranger Station, this is where naturalists put on short presentations about wildlife and ecology for families. Visitors can get maps and information, and there is a tiny bookstore in one corner. In winter, a wood-sided trailer in the adjacent parking lot serves as the information station (and sells hot chocolate).

Norris Geyser Basin Museum & Information Station

Located at the entrance to Norris Geyser Basin, the Norris Geyser Basin Museum & Information Station (307/344-2812, www. nps.gov/yell, 9am-6pm daily late May-Sept.) houses exhibits on geothermal features and offers information on naturalist-led tours, camping, sightseeing, and wildlife. Rangers lead several programs, including walks into the geyser basin. Completed in 1930, the log-and-stone building is a National Historic Landmark. A Yellowstone Association bookstore (406/848-2400, www.yellowstoneassociation.org) is housed in an adjacent building.

★ Old Faithful Visitor Education Center

The Old Faithful Visitor Education Center (307/344-2751, www.nps.gov/yell, 8am-8pm daily late Apr.-early Nov., 9am-5pm daily mid-Dec.-Feb., hours vary in spring and fall), located adjacent to Old Faithful Geyser, is the place to learn about geysers, hot springs, mud pots, fumaroles, and other geothermal features. Visitors can get maps, park information, and schedules for naturalist-led tours, including tours of the facility; short films rotate daily in the on-site theater. Current research exhibits reveal what scientists are discovering, while a special kids' room takes a hands-on approach for young scientists.

Kids can get Junior Ranger booklets ($3) and are sworn in after completion and receive a patch. Naturalists post geyser eruption predictions, also available by phone (304/344-2751), Twitter (@Twitter.com/GeyserNPS), or a mobile app. The Yellowstone Association (406/848-2400, www.yellowstoneassociation.org) runs a bookstore inside.

ENTRANCE STATION

Located on U.S. Highway 20 near the town of West Yellowstone, Montana, the West Entrance ($30/vehicle, $25 motorcycles, $15 hike-in/bike-in; joint parks pass: $50/vehicle, $40 motorcycles, $20 hike-in/bike-in) is the busiest entrance in the park. From the West Entrance, the park hub of Madison lies 14 miles east; the Old Faithful area is 16 miles farther south. The West Entrance is open to cars and RVs mid-April-early November; in winter (mid-Dec.-mid-Mar.), the road closes and is accessible only to snowmobiles and snowcoaches.

In summer, the West Entrance sees more than 100,000 visitors each month; in July, more than 4,000 visitors enter each *day* (that's more than double some of the other park entrance stations). These high numbers are due to the volume of lodging available in West Yellowstone and the entrance's close proximity to Old Faithful. If visiting in summer (especially July), stop at the West Yellowstone Visitor Information Center in West Yellowstone first and buy your park entrance pass there. This will allow you to enter the (shorter) entrance line for vehicles with passes (usually the left lane). Plan to enter the park either before 10am or after 2pm in summer; wait times as long as 30 minutes can clog the four entrance lanes.

TOURS

Summer and winter tours in Yellowstone require reservations—the earlier, the better. For July, August, or winter, aim for 6-12 months ahead. Make them when you book your lodging. But you can also call a day ahead to pick up spare seats. Generally, rates for trips do not include entrance fees into the park, lunch, or tips for guides (15 percent). Take along layers for warmth, a water bottle, and snacks.

Bus Tours

Several tours depart from Old Faithful Inn. **Reservations** (Xanterra, 307/344-7311 or 866/439-7375, www.yellowstonenationalparklodges.com) are required for all tours.

Geyser Gazers (1.5 hours, 4:15pm daily June-early Oct., $26 adults, $13 children) visits Midway Geyser Basin and Firehole Lake Drive. Passengers travel in historic yellow buses from the 1930s with rollback canvas tops that allow for stand-up viewing when stopped.

Other tours are in vans or buses. The evening **Twilight on the Firehole** (two hours, daily June-mid-Sept., $34 adults, $17 children) offers a way to see steamy thermal features around sunset. The **Yellowstone in a Day** tour (8:15am-6pm daily mid-June-mid-Sept., $105 adults, $53 children 3-11) departs from Old Faithful Inn to circle the 142-mile Grand Loop Road with stops at Yellowstone Lake, Grand Canyon of the Yellowstone, and Mammoth Hot Springs.

Departing from West Yellowstone, **Buffalo Bus Touring Company** (415 Yellowstone Ave., West Yellowstone, 406/646-9564 or 800/426-7669, www.yellowstonevacations. com, daily late Apr.-early Nov., $70-135 adults, $55-115 kids 15 and younger) offers full-day tours in big yellow buses with large windows. The daily tour circles Lower Grand Loop Road around Old Faithful, Yellowstone Lake, and Grand Canyon of the Yellowstone. The Monday, Wednesday, Friday tour loops the Lower and Upper Grand Loop Road, which adds on Tower Fall, Mammoth Hot Springs, and Norris Geyser Basin.

Wildlife Tours

The best wildlife-watching is in early morning or evening, and safari tours accommodate that to provide optimum chances of seeing bison, elk, bears, moose, and wolves. **Yellowstone Alpen Guides** (555 Yellowstone Ave., West

Yellowstone, 406/646-9591 or 800/858-3502, www.yellowstoneguides.com, 1pm-9pm late May-early Sept., $88) runs an evening wildlife tour several times weekly. With a picnic dinner en route, the van safari loops up through Mammoth Hot Springs and Lamar Valley.

★ Winter Snowcoach Tours

When snow covers the geyser basins, every pore in the landscape emits copious steam, creating an otherworldly peek at nature. Due to colder winter temperatures, the scenes take on more drama than in summer. Snowcoach tours are the only way to experience Old Faithful in winter, with only a handful of people in the usually crowded geyser basins

WEST YELLOWSTONE TO OLD FAITHFUL

Several companies run snowcoach tours mid-December-mid-March. Designed for snow travel, snowcoaches are heated sightseeing buses or vans equipped with tracks, skis, or huge wheels. Bombardiers are a very loud, but fun nostalgic ride; the vans on tracks sway and bounce, especially for backseat riders. Most of the tours from West Yellowstone depart at 8am-9am and take 8-9 hours to reach Old Faithful and return. Led by interpretive guides, coaches stop at sights where visitors can photograph geysers or wildlife. Bring your park entrance pass, lunch, a water bottle, an optional thermos with hot drinks, a camera, and binoculars, and wear warm layers of winter clothing and boots for walking in snow. Tours range $115-135 for adults and $95-120 for kids. Some companies offer discounts for seniors.

- **Backcounty Adventure** (224 N. Electric St., West Yellowstone, 406/646-9317 or 800/924-7669, www.backcountry-adventures.com) uses converted vans for their tours.

- **Buffalo Bus Touring Company** (415 Yellowstone Ave., West Yellowstone, 406/646-9564 or 800/426-7669, www.yellowstonevacations.com) operates a fleet of six-passenger Chevy Suburbans and 30-passenger sightseeing coaches.

- See Yellowstone Tours (217 Yellowstone Ave., West Yellowstone, 800/221-1151, www.seeyellowstone.com) drives vans and sightseeing coaches with large windows (without tinting) for easy photography.
- Yellowstone Alpen Guides (555 Yellowstone Ave., West Yellowstone, 406/646-9591 or 800/858-3502, www.yellowstoneguides.com) drive revamped historic Bombardiers with pop-open top hatches for viewing and a lower profile for easy boarding. All 10 passengers have window seats (the windows are smaller than those on a van or bus and the ride is more intimate).

OLD FAITHFUL TO CANYON

From the Old Faithful Snow Lodge, the Grand Canyon Day Tour (Xanterra, 307/344-7311 or 866/439-7375, www.yellowstonenationalparklodges.com, 8:15am Mon., Wed., and Fri.-Sun. mid-Dec.-Feb., $235 adults, $118 children 3-11) provides a narrated snowcoach tour to the Grand Canyon of the Yellowstone. The eight-hour tour spends two hours at the Grand Canyon of the Yellowstone. A box lunch option (advance reservations required) is available. A Ski Tour (7:45am-6pm Tues., Thurs. and Sun. mid-Dec.-Feb., $194 adults, $97 children) and Snowshoe Tour (7:45am-6pm Wed. and Sat. mid-Dec.-Feb., $194 adults, $97 children) also depart from the Snow Lodge. Make reservations 6-9 months in advance.

DRIVING TOURS
West Entrance Road
14 MILES

For an evening wildlife-watching drive, take the West Entrance Road (mid-Apr.-early Nov.) from West Yellowstone to Madison Junction. The road parallels the Madison River, with sprawling meadows that are often full of bison in summer and elk herds in fall. Pullouts allow places to watch, but don't be so enamored by the megafauna that you miss eagles in the trees.

Madison Junction to Old Faithful
16 MILES

From Madison Junction, the Grand Loop Road (mid-Apr.-early Nov.) climbs south along the Firehole River to Old Faithful. Three short spur roads allow scenic tours. The road passes through the Lower Geyser Basin housing Fountain Paint Pots, Firehole Lake, and Grand Geyser before passing Midway Geyser Basin. The road then enters Upper Geyser Basin, reaching Biscuit Basin first, then Black Sand Basin, before the Old Faithful Complex. Steam plumes from most of the basins are visible from Grand Loop Road.

FIREHOLE CANYON DRIVE

At 0.5-mile south of Madison Junction, Firehole Canyon Drive (2 miles, mid-Apr.-early Nov., no RVs or trailers) cuts off on the west side of the Grand Loop Road. This one-way, steep, and narrow road offers a scenic overlook of the 40-foot-tall Firehole Falls and 800-foot-thick lava flows; however, there are minimal places to pull over for photos. It also accesses a swimming hole reached by steps. Plan 15 minutes for this tour if you just want to see the falls.

FOUNTAIN FLAT DRIVE

Find the Fountain Flat Drive (1 mile, late May.-early Nov.) on the west side of the Grand Loop Road about 10.4 miles south of Madison Junction and 3.5 miles north of Old Faithful. The short drive is a good place for wildlife-watching, particularly elk and bison in June; it has the Nez Perce Picnic Area at its start and several pullouts en route. When the two-way drive dead-ends, bicycles and foot traffic can continue until the route reconnects with the Grand Loop. Bear activity keeps it closed in spring.

FIREHOLE LAKE DRIVE

Located about 9.3 miles south of Madison Junction and 6.8 miles north of Old Faithful, the one-way Firehole Lake Drive (3.3. miles, late May.-early Nov., no RVs or trailers) is accessed off the east side of the Grand Loop Road. The drive passes eight thermal features, including the brown **Firehole Lake,** the largest hot springs on the road, and the **Great Fountain Geyser,** which erupts every 10-14 hours—it blows up to 220 feet high with some eruptions lasting an hour. The nearby **White Dome Geyser** erupts up to 30 feet high, but at more frequent 15- to 30-minute intervals. Plan 30 minutes for this drive with roadside stops; longer if you wait for geysers to shoot off. The *Fountain Paint Pot Trail Guide* ($1, available at visitors centers) includes interpretive information on Firehole Lake Drive. Bear activity keeps it closed in spring.

Norris to Madison Junction
14 MILES

The Grand Loop Road (mid-Apr.-early Nov.) from **Norris** to **Madison Junction** parallels the **Gibbon River.** From Norris, the road tours **Gibbon Meadows** where you can see bison and elk. After passing **Artists' Paintpots,** the road sidles by **Beryl Springs** (pullover available) and begins the descent into the ancient caldera. The road curves through a canyon housing **Gibbon Falls** with a turnoff and interpretive viewpoints. Just before reaching Madison Junction, pull off to tour **Terrace Springs.**

Sights

WEST ENTRANCE

West Yellowstone is the largest tourist town on Yellowstone's boundary. Part of the town retains its mom-and-pop souvenir shops, which crowd in summer with scads of visitors. In winter, it serves as a cross-country ski, snowmobile, and snowcoach tour headquarters. It is home to Rendezvous Ski Trails, Grizzly and Wolf Discovery Center, and Yellowstone Nature Connection. For the park's history, the **Yellowstone Historic Center** (104 Yellowstone Ave., 406/646-1100, www.yellowstonehistoriccenter.org, 9am-6pm daily mid-May-mid-Oct., closes at 9pm in summer, $2-6) has hands-on exhibits on stagecoaches, railroads, and early pioneers. The museum also runs walking tours, ranger talks, films, and a children's program.

The **Grizzly and Wolf Discovery Center** (201 S. Canyon St., West Yellowstone, 406/646-7001 or 800/257-2570, www.grizzlydiscoveryctr.com, 8:30am-8:30pm daily mid-May-early Sept., hours vary in fall, winter, and spring, $12 adults, $11 seniors, $7 kids, free for children under 4) provides a place to watch wildlife up close and learn about grizzly bear, wolf, and raptor behaviors. (The grizzlies don't hibernate because they are fed.) Admission is good for two consecutive days, so you can see the animals multiple times. Sometimes a discount coupon is available online.

MADISON

The campground at Madison lies 14 miles east of the West Entrance and 16 miles north of Old Faithful. From this junction, the Norris Geyser Basin is 14 miles farther northeast. Allow at least 45 minutes for the drive from Madison Junction to Old Faithful. Bison herds frequent the area; prepare for stopped traffic.

Firehole River and Falls

An outstanding trout fishery, the **Firehole River** gets its name from the adjacent geyser basins pouring in scalding water; the resulting steam makes it looks like the land is on fire. The 21-mile Firehole River ends at the confluence with the Gibbon River to form the Madison River at Madison Junction. Along the way, the river drops through three waterfalls, most notably the 40-foot-high frothy-white **Firehole Falls.** Traveling south on the park road toward Old Faithful allows views of the river in the Upper, Midway, and Lower Geyser Basins and of Firehole Falls from Firehole Canyon Drive.

★ Wildlife Watching

Wildlife-watching is equally as captivating as watching geysers blow. Along the **Madison River** and the **West Entrance Road,** pull-outs permit viewing for bison, elk, and raptors. The **Madison Junior Ranger Station** (access via the Madison Picnic Area parking lot) is another good vantage point. In fall, bull elk often round up harems along the river, with the bulls' bugling echoing across the valley.

Maintain a safe distance (at least 75-100 feet) from all wildlife and give them plenty of room The animals may look tame, but gorings continue to occur when people get too close—especially while trying to take selfies or photos of others posed with bison.

bull elk

LOWER GEYSER BASIN
★ Fountain Paint Pots

Eight miles south of Madison Junction (or north of Old Faithful), the **Fountain Paint Pots** is a 0.5-mile interpretive boardwalk loop that includes all four hydrothermal features in the park: geysers, mud pots, hot springs, and fumaroles. Pick up the *Fountain Paint Pot Trail Guide* ($1) at the start of the trail.

At the boardwalk junction, look left into the blue **Celestine Pool** or right for the colorful bacterial mats of thermophiles formed in the runoff from the silica-rich, turquoise **Silex Spring** straight ahead. The trail then divides around pink and gray **Fountain Paint Pot,** bubbling more in the liquid clay of early summer, but thicker by fall. (Its clay was used to paint the former hotel across the road.) The trail splits to circle **Red Spouter,** named for the red clay that acts like a mud pot, hot springs, or steam vent based on changing water amounts throughout the year. As the boardwalk continues west downhill, several geysers spurt and fume. When **Fountain Geyser** erupts, it can shoot water 20-50 feet in the air for longer than 20 minutes. The smaller neighboring **Clepsydra Geyser,** which sputters nonstop from several vents, can pause when Fountain erupts.

★ Great Fountain Geyser

Great Fountain Geyser shoots 75-220 feet high every 10-14 hours. Contrary to Old Faithful's short durations, Great Fountain Geyser eruptions last about an hour, with short bursts of water interspersed between quiet periods. The geyser ushers in a long, dramatic prelude to erupting. Water floods the vent, and bubbles appear about 30 minutes later. As the water boils into giant three-foot bubbles followed by one big large burp, the eruption begins.

Great Fountain Geyser is located on the one-way Firehole Lake Drive. The entrance is 9.3 miles south of Madison Junction and 6.8 miles north of Old Faithful.

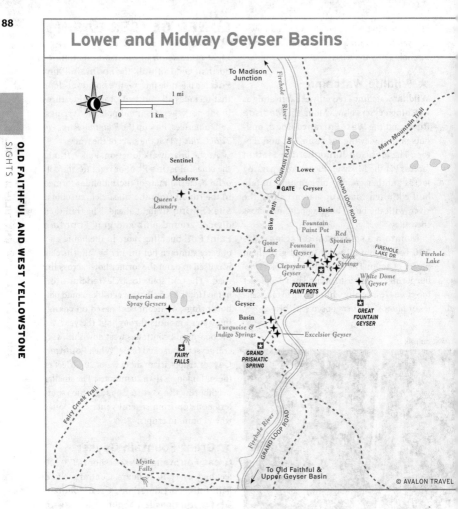

Lower and Midway Geyser Basins

To Madison Junction

Firehole River

FOUNTAIN FLAT DR

Mary Mountain Trail

Sentinel
Meadows

Lower

GATE

Geyser

Basin

GRAND LOOP ROAD

Bike Path

Queen's
Laundry

*Fountain
Paint Pot*

*Red
Spouter*

*Goose
Lake*

*Fountain
Geyser*

*Silex
Springs*

*FIREHOLE
LAKE DR*

*Firehole
Lake*

*Clepsydra
Geyser*

**FOUNTAIN
PAINT POTS**

*White Dome
Geyser*

Midway
Geyser
Basin

Imperial and
Spray Geysers

**GREAT
FOUNTAIN
GEYSER**

*Turquoise &
Indigo Springs*

Excelsior Geyser

**FAIRY
FALLS**

**GRAND
PRISMATIC
SPRING**

Fairy Creek Trail

Firehole River

GRAND LOOP ROAD

*Mystic
Falls*

*To Old Faithful &
Upper Geyser Basin*

© AVALON TRAVEL

0   1 mi
0   1 km

MIDWAY GEYSER BASIN

Midway Geyser Basin is located 6.5 miles north of Old Faithful and about 10 miles south of Madison. The basin only has four thermal features—but they are huge. Two are the largest hot springs in Yellowstone.

From the parking area (on the west side of the Grand Loop Road), head south to walk over the bridge across the Firehole River. Start the 0.7-mile loop, admiring the thermophile colors in the stream pouring into the river. After climbing up a boardwalk switchback, go south along the dormant **Excelsior Geyser.**

Excelsior is now a stunning turquoise hot pool spilling 4,050 gallons of water per minute into the Firehole River. Beyond the Excelsior crater, steam pours from the larger **Grand Prismatic Spring,** which commands the high point of the loop. Turn north to finish the loop, passing the clear blue pools of smaller **Turquoise** and **Indigo Springs.**

★ Grand Prismatic Spring

At 370 feet across and 121 feet deep, **Grand Prismatic Spring** is the largest hot spring in Yellowstone and the third-largest in the world.

Great Fountain Geyser

Sit on the surrounding benches to enjoy the glorious hues: fiery arms of orange, gold, and brown that radiate in a full circle from the yellow-rimmed, blue hot pool. Its 160-degree water discharges in all directions at 560 gallons per minute.

UPPER GEYSER BASIN

The Upper Geyser Basin is the most popular hydrothermal basin, drawing thousands of visitors each day in summer but few in winter. It contains a maze of four miles of boardwalk, dirt, and paved interpretive loops through the largest concentration of geysers in the world. Walkers, bikers, and wheelchairs share the paved portion; in winter, the snow-covered pavement is groomed for cross-country skiing. Often herds of buffalo or elk feed in the meadows in between geothermal features. Signs at trail junctions have maps to assist

Grand Prismatic Spring

Beat the Geyser Basin Crowds

Old Faithful and the geyser basins attract visitors by the thousands in summer, when huge parking lots fill to maximum capacity. Here are some tips to beat the crowds:

- Visit in June or September, while kids are still in school. Crowds thin in comparison to midsummer.

- Avoid July, which has the heaviest visitation for the park, with clogged parking lots and the thickest numbers on trails and boardwalks.

- Try May or October. May offers a chance to watch newborn bison calves prance around geyser basins. October brings on fall colors and active bears in hyperphasia.

- Go in winter. Enjoy the beauty of the icy landscape and prolific steam in the geyser basins due to the colder temperatures. You may even have Old Faithful to yourself.

- Avoid midday hours (10am-4pm), when most of the crowds are out in force. Utilize the early morning and late afternoon-evening hours instead. Hit Midway and the Lower Geyser Basins in the early morning en route to Norris Geyser Basin by 10am. Visit the Upper Geyser Basin (Old Faithful, Black Sands, Biscuit) in the evening.

- Visit Old Faithful at sunrise. In summer, sunrise occurs 5am-6:30am. While most people are still rubbing sleep from their eyes, you can check the eruption predictions and score front-row seats in time for Old Faithful to blow.

- Tour in the evening. After an early dinner, explore the geyser basins until sunset occurs, which is 8pm-9:30pm in summer. You'll encounter far fewer people on the boardwalks and will have several hours for exploring hot pools, fumaroles, mud pots, and geysers.

- Park early. Trailhead parking lots at popular paths fill up by late morning. Plan to be at your trailhead by 8am-9am or earlier.

- Stop at picnic areas for restroom breaks, as the popular geyser basins usually have lengthy restroom lines.

with route-finding. The Old Faithful Visitor Education Center and a mobile phone geyser app predict eruption times for five geysers: Old Faithful, Castle, Grand, Grand, Daisy, and Riverside. Pick up the interpretative *Old Faithful Trail Guide* ($1) at the visitors center.

★ Old Faithful Inn

Built in 1903-1904 from surrounding logs, tree limbs, and rhyolite stone, Old Faithful Inn is worthy of wows. With a steep-pitched roof and gabled dormers, the lobby vaults five stories high and is centered around an 85-foot-tall stone fireplace and handcrafted clock built from wood, copper, and iron. Today, this National Historic Landmark houses 327 guest rooms in two wings. Walk around the lobby balcony to take in all the

historical intricacies. Daily tours (hours vary daily May-mid-Oct., free) are available.

★ Old Faithful Geyser

Old Faithful Geyser anchors the Upper Geyser Basin. When Old Faithful erupts, it shoots up to 8,400 gallons of hot water as high as 185 feet. It's not the tallest geyser in the park, but it is one of the most regular, erupting about every 90 minutes for 1.5-5 minutes. Often, the geyser sputters for up to 20 minutes before the eruption. A quiet interval between eruptions correlates to the length of the previous eruption. Expect massive crowds of people in summer, with benches surrounding the geyser filling 30 minutes in advance. Winter eruptions see only a handful of people. Old Faithful is located behind the Old Faithful

Visitor Education Center, which posts eruption times. A 0.7-mile boardwalk loop circles the famous geyser.

GEYSER HILL LOOP

From the Old Faithful viewing area, head east across the Firehole River to climb the boardwalk and stairs that ring **Geyser Hill,** which is sprinkled with several active geysers. Geyser Hill is a 1.3-mile walk from the visitors center, and a boardwalk connects it with the Firehole River Loops.

On the south section of this loop, turn left to view **Beehive Geyser,** which can shoot up 200 feet, but has an irregular schedule. The smaller nearby **Anenome** and **Plume Geysers** erupt regularly, the first about every 10 minutes and the second hourly. Continue north past Beehive to find the clear blue **Heart Spring** near the cones of the interconnected **Lion Group,** a family of geysers called Little Cub, Big Cub, Lioness, and Lion, the latter of which heralds eruptions by a roar. Turn right to access the upper part of this loop. Admire the radiant color and ledges of **Doublet Pool.** From here, a spur trail heads north to **Solitary Geyser,** which surges with short, six-foot bursts every 4-8 minutes.

FIREHOLE RIVER LOOP

Northwest of Geyser Hill, the bigger Firehole River Loop crosses two bridges to take in the famous hot pools of the Upper Geyser Basin, plus more geysers, fumaroles, and springs.

At the southern start of this loop is **Castle Geyser,** a cone geyser built into the largest sinter formation in the world. About every 14 hours, Castle Geyser erupts for 20 minutes and then pumps out copious steam. Continue north and turn right to cross the Firehole River and reach **Grand Geyser,** a predictable fountain geyser that throws water 200 feet skyward in several short bursts. To the north sit a pair of interconnected hot springs, **Beauty Pool** and **Chromatic Pool.** When the water level rises in one, it drops in the other.

As the boardwalk crosses the river again, you might get to see the erratic **Giant Geyser** throw water up 300 feet. At the junction with the paved trail, **Grotto Geyser** squirts water from its odd-shaped cone for sometimes up to 24 hours. Continue north on the paved trail to **Riverside Geyser,** which shoots an arc of water at six-hour intervals over the Firehole for about 20 minutes. The striking green, orange, and yellow **Morning Glory Pool** marks the turnaround point.

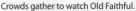

Crowds gather to watch Old Faithful.

Upper Geyser Basin

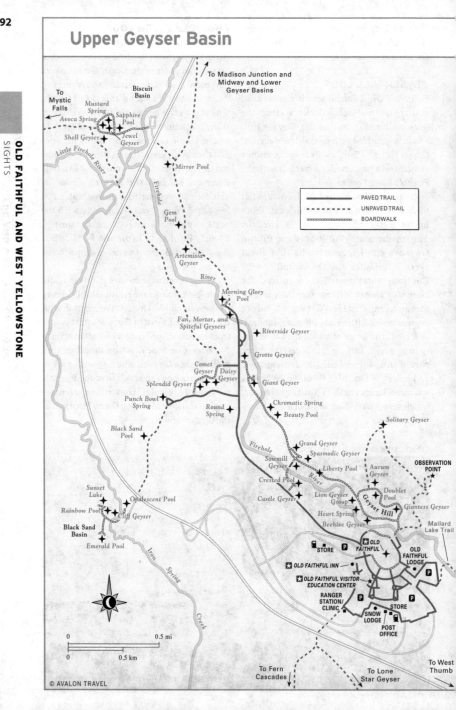

DAISY GEYSER BASIN LOOP

From the paved trail on the west side of the Firehole River, the Daisy Geyser Basin loops through smaller, but unique features. Daisy Geyser erupts every 2-3 hours with water spewing out to 75 feet. As the paved trail turns west, Punch Bowl boils in its 12-foot-diameter sinter bowl.

Biscuit Basin

One of several hydrothermal basins in Upper Geyser Basin, Biscuit Basin holds a collection of smaller geothermal features, accessed by a 0.7-mile boardwalk that ascends into the basin to circle hot pools, geysers, and fumaroles. After crossing the Firehole River on a footbridge, the boardwalk tours past Black Opal Pool, Wall Pool, and Sapphire Pool. The latter is the most commanding feature, a hot pool of crystal clear 200-degree blue water that once used to be a geyser. At the junction, go either way to circle the basin. Highlights on the upper loop include the yellow Mustard Spring and Jewel Geyser, which shoots water up to 20 feet in the air about every 10 minutes, a short enough time to wait to see it.

Biscuit Basin is located on the park road, two miles north of the Old Faithful turnoff and south of the Midway Geyser Basin. From the Old Faithful Visitor Education Center, it is a 5.9-mile round-trip hike to the basin. From the paved trail, take the Daisy Geyser Loop junction and turn west. At the next junction, turn north to reach Grand Loop Road. A trail continues on the opposite side to reach the back of the geyser basin. (Bikes must turn right onto the road to reach the parking lot.)

Black Sand Basin

In the Upper Geyser Basin, Black Sand Basin has a 0.6-mile boardwalk across Iron Spring Creek with two short spurs that tour past small geysers and colorful hot pools. The basin acquired its name from the bits of obsidian that speckle the area. On the creek's edge, Cliff Geyser blows water up to 40 feet from a small crater. Eruptions last 0.5-3 hours, with copious steam spewing out. At the boardwalk junction, turn right to see Sunset Lake, named for its yellow-orange rim, and left to see Emerald Pool, colored from its algae. Before hopping back in the car, walk a tiny spur off the north corner of the parking lot to see Opalescent Pool, fed by the almost constantly erupting Spouter Geyser, which flooded an area of lodgepoles. The dead trees are now known as Bobby sox trees due to the white socks around their silica-soaked trunk bases.

Reach Black Sand Basin by driving 0.5 mile northwest of Old Faithful. It's also possible to hike there (4.4 miles round-trip) from Old Faithful Visitor Education Center. From the paved trail, turn left to take the Daisy Geyser Loop cutoff. After touring past the basin geysers and pools, cross Grand Loop Road to reach Black Sand Basin.

MADISON TO NORRIS
Gibbon Falls

On the road between Madison Junction and Norris, Gibbon Falls plunges 84 feet into the Gibbon River. The cascade-type falls froths from every rock ledge. The falls used to be a barrier for migrating fish, but now introduced species such as arctic grayling and rainbow trout populate the upper reaches of the Gibbon River and Grebe Lake at its headwaters. From the signed large parking area on the east side of the road, walk to the interpretive viewpoints to see the falls.

Artists' Paintpots

Located 3.7 miles south of Norris Junction, Artists' Paintpots gets its name from its bubbling gray mud pots. A sunny gravel, dirt, boardwalk, and stair-step trail (one mile) starts by cutting through lodgepoles recovering from the 1988 fire. The path tours past small geysers, fumaroles, light blue pools, and red crusts. Thermophiles, organisms that proliferate in hot water, add the bright colors. Stinky hydrogen sulfide gas leaks from underground, and the mud pots burp and spurt.

At the junction, turn in either direction; the remainder of the trail loops around the side of **Paintpot Hill.** The base of the hill holds bubbling hot springs, clear hot pools, and streams with thermophiles. Geothermal features at the bottom of the loop have more water, while the famous paint pots at the top are formed of thicker clay; they emit gasses, which scent the air. By late summer, the mud pots thicken or dry up when less water feeds them.

NORRIS

Located 14 miles north of Madison Junction and 30 miles north of Old Faithful, Norris houses a large double geyser basin with boardwalks, two museums, and a campground.

The **Norris Geyser Basin Museum & Information Station** (307/344-2812, 9am-6pm daily late May-Sept.) and a **Yellowstone Association bookstore** (406/848-2400, www.yellowstoneassociation.org) anchor the visitor services.

★ Norris Geyser Basin

Of Yellowstone's thermal basins, **Norris** Geyser Basin is the hottest, measuring 459°F at 1,087 feet below the surface. With features 115,000 years old, it is the oldest geothermal basin. Most vigorous of the park's geyser basins, Norris has some features that change daily, many due to earthquakes. It also contains rare acidic geysers; you'll smell the rotten egg stench.

Interpretive boardwalks and paths tour two hydrothermal basins, Back Basin and Porcelain Basin. The *Norris Geyser Basin Trail Guide* ($1, available at visitors centers) can aid in touring the site. Explore the boardwalks and trails in three ways: self-guided, with a ranger-led walk, or on a one-mile trail from Norris Campground. Due to the changing nature of the basin, boardwalks can be closed for reconstruction.

BACK BASIN

The thinly forested **Back Basin** double-loop (1.5 miles) houses two geysers that each hold world records: the tallest geyser and the largest acidic geyser. Heading south from

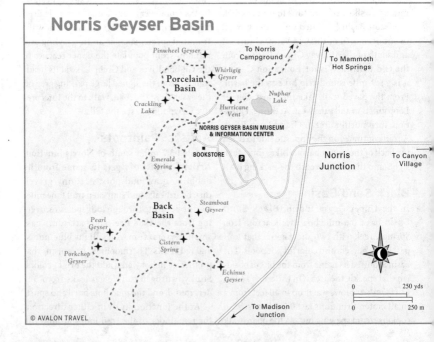

the museum, the boardwalk first reaches **Emerald Spring** with its striking color created from the yellow sulfur minerals, blue near-boiling water, and colorful thermophiles. Continue south to unpredictable **Steamboat Geyser,** which shoots small bursts of water up to 40 feet in the air (its world-record eruptions of 300-400 feet happen infrequently). The geyser links underground to the blue-green **Cistern Spring,** which puts out so much sinter that pipes often clog and force water to the surface in new pools. Turn left to stay on this outer loop as it winds past the red-orange rimmed pool of **Echinus Geyser.** With unpredictable eruptions, it's the world's largest acidic geyser—on par with vinegar. After passing several fumaroles, geysers, hot springs, and mud pots, **Porkchop Geyser** roils turquoise water but is more like a hot spring (it hasn't erupted since 1989). Due to superheating in this evolving basin, the park service rerouted the boardwalk to **Pearl Geyser** to avoid the 200-degree ground.

This outer loop completes at the junction near **Palpitator Spring.** Continue north through the Back Basin, past **Minute** and **Monarch Geyers,** to return to the museum junction and connect with the Porcelain Basin.

PORCELAIN BASIN

The wide-open **Porcelain Basin** is named for its color. Two loops of the 0.5-mile boardwalk cross the acidic basin that contains the park's highest concentration of silica; thermophiles add brilliant splashes of green or red. From the museum junction, turn left past turquoise **Crackling Lake,** a hot pool that bubbles along the edges of the basin. The loop brings you to the defunct **Pinwheel Geyser** and active **Whirligig Geyser,** which spills into a runoff stream full of orange iron oxide and green thermophiles. A smaller boardwalk loop heads left past roaring **Hurricane Vent** and colorful **Porcelain Springs,** a changeable hot pool that waffles from water action to dry. Complete the loop and return to the museum by heading south, or follow the trail from Porcelain Springs to the Museum of the National Park Ranger.

Museum of the National Park Ranger

Tiny **Museum of the National Park Ranger** (307/344-7353, www.nps.gov/yell, 9am-5pm daily late May-Sept., free) in located in an 1886 historic log cabin near the Norris Campground. Staffed by volunteer retired rangers, the museum houses a small collection of photos that show the evolution of the park ranger profession. A small auditorium runs a movie on the National Park Service, which celebrates its centennial in 2016.

Recreation

DAY HIKES

Short, easy hikes dominate the Old Faithful area, but several elements conspire to turn them challenging for some. The high elevation can cause labored breathing with huffing and puffing on short uphills. Pace yourself and drink plenty of water to combat headaches from dehydration. There is minimal shade; wear a hat and sunglasses, and slather on the sunscreen (the altitude or winter snow can intensify the sun's glare).

Boardwalks are designed to protect the fragile geyser ecosystems and prevent people from falling into scalding water. In **summer,** they are crowded, but in the off-season and winter, you can often have them to yourself. In **winter,** when many trails convert to snowshoe and cross-country ski routes, skiers should remove skis on boardwalks, as

Volcanic Facts

GEYSERS

Geysers are all about plumbing—clogged plumbing, that is. Similar to hot springs, geysers have underground pipes that let boiling water bubble up to the surface. But in the case of geysers, the pipes constrict, producing a backup of water and bubbles pushing up. When the pressure becomes too great, the explosion occurs. (Hot springs don't have constrictions, therefore allowing water to move freely upwards.) Yellowstone has more than 450 active geysers.

There are two types of geyser eruption patterns. Cone geysers shoot water into the air in a narrow stream. Fountain geysers spray water in multiple directions, usually from a pool. Park rangers predict eruption schedules (available at visitors centers) for six geysers: Old Faithful, Castle, Great Fountain, Riverside, Grand, and Daisy.

MAGMA

Take solid rock and add searing heat. The result? Pockets of rock melt into magma. The stove that heats Yellowstone is actually a magma chamber on top of a huge magma reservoir. This magma chamber lurks 3-9 miles below the earth's surface in the upper and lower crust. It is 2,500 cubic miles in size, or roughly 19 miles wide by 55 miles long. The chamber draws heat from the reservoir below it in the earth's lower crust; the reservoir is 11,200 cubic miles, swelling to 16 miles thick, 30 miles wide and 44 miles long. The chamber and reservoir have enough magma to fill the Grand Canyon 14 times.

Beneath the magma chamber, magma reservoir, and the earth's crust layers sits the Yellowstone hotspot plume that once heated the Snake River Plain in Idaho. The crust, with its magma chamber and reservoir, have shifted, thus putting the hotspot under Yellowstone today. This is the source of the heat that produces magma.

COLORS

Many of Yellowstone's geothermal features show the artistry of colors from heat-loving organisms, acidic thrivers, and minerals. One of the most vivid displays is at Grand Prismatic Spring in Midway Geyser Basin.

Thermophiles are microscopic organisms that thrive on extreme heat, seeking out the water

they can get slick with ice. For winter walkers, boot cleats help; rent them at the Bear's Den (307/344-7311 or 866/439-7375, daily mid-Dec.-early Mar., $3-5) in the Snow Lodge.

Guided Hikes

Hikers in the west geyser basin arc have little need of guides. Most hikes are short, interpretive trails that are signed at the start and major junctions. However, private, park-licensed guides (www.nps.gov/yell) are available for hikes beyond the geyser boardwalks.

Yellowstone's naturalist rangers lead free daily interpretive hikes in the Old Faithful area. Walks usually meet at Old Faithful Visitor Education Center or the trailhead. In summer, guided walks explore Mystic Falls, Geyser Hill in the Upper Geyser Basin, Black Sand Basin, and Old Faithful Geyser Loop. In winter, rangers lead snowshoe hikes in the Old Faithful area and West Yellowstone. Check the visitors centers for schedules.

Madison

HARLEQUIN LAKE

Distance: 0.6 mile round-trip
Duration: 1 hour
Elevation change: 102 feet
Effort: easy
Trailhead: On the West Entrance Road, 1.9 miles

colorful thermophiles

of hot pools and runoff streams. Some prefer hot water up to 174 degrees, and photosynthetic capabilities allow others to show pigments. Thermophiles can be bacteria, viruses, and Eukarya such as flies, spiders, algae, fungi, or microscopic organisms. Look for thermophiles in the green, brown, orange, and red mats in the Lower, Midway, and Upper **Geyser Basins.**

Archea are single-celled creatures (also called extremophiles) that thrive in hot, acidic waters. See the green or colorless archea at **Norris Geyser Basin.** Many hydrothermal features gain color from minerals. The orange-red iron deposits in **Norris Geyser Basin** and the pink and gray iron oxides in **Fountain Paint Pots** are examples of mineral coloration.

Some hot pools have changed color due to the amount of coins, trinkets, and trash thrown inside by visitors; the garbage clogs the plumbing systems and alters the temperature. For example, **Morning Glory Pool** has changed from brilliant blue to green.

west of Madison Junction. Park in the pullout on the south side of the road opposite the trailhead (see map p. 82).

This easy trail is popular with families and campers staying at **Madison Campground.** It's more of a scenic walk with possible **wildlife sightings** (elk in June and fall), as there's no water play or fishing. A short ascent through the lodgepole corridor climbs north up a hill to swing west and reach the south shore of **Harlequin Lake.** Copious yellow pond lilies, water rushes, and cattails rim the shallow 10-acre lake by late summer. The lake is named after harlequin ducks, but they don't use the lake, as they prefer swift streams.

There are active beavers, as evidenced by chewed trees and the lodge across the lake.

Upper and Lower Geyser Basins
SENTINEL MEADOWS AND QUEENS LAUNDRY

Distance: 3.8 miles round-trip
Duration: 2 hours
Elevation change: 45 feet
Effort: easy to moderate
Trailhead: Fountain Flat Drive parking lot, south of Madison (see map p. 100)

From the trailhead, head south on the old road to the bridge over the Firehole River. To the

Old Faithful and West Yellowstone Hikes

Trail	Effort	Distance	Duration
Ice Lake	Easy	0.6 mi rt	30 min
Harlequin Lake	Easy	0.6 mi rt	1 hr
Lone Star Geyser	Easy	4.8-8.2 mi rt	3-5 hr
Fairy Falls Trail	Easy	5.8-9 mi rt	3-5 hr
Sentinel Meadows and Queens Laundry	Easy to moderate	3.8 mi rt	2 hr
Howard Eaton	Easy to strenuous	7-18.2 mi	4-10 hr
Old Faithful Observation Point	Moderate	2.1 mi rt	1 hr
Mystic Falls and Biscuit Basin Overlook	Moderate	2.4-8 mi rt	1-4 hr
Spring Creek	Moderate	2-12.4 mi rt	1.5-6 hr
Mallard Lake	Moderate	7-8.4 mi rt	4 hr
Divide Overlook	Strenuous	2.6 mi rt	1.5 hr
Monument Geyser Basin	Strenuous	2.8 mi rt	2.5 hr

west, the riverside Ojo Caliente hot spring pours water down yellow sulfur runoff channels. Cross the bridge to find the trail junction on the right. Turn west to walk through grasslands, crossing Fairy and Sentinel Creeks. At **Sentinel Meadows,** thermal features come into view; the first is **Mound Spring,** which is also the largest. Several smaller cones spread around the meadows. (Use caution in exploring the basin, as thermal features can be dangerous.) Follow the trail south between the forest and the multiple smaller cones. The next major thermal is **Queens Laundry Geyser,** at 1.9 miles. On top of the sinter mound is an old, roofless log structure that was built in 1881; it served as the bathhouse for soaking in the hot spring. (To protect the spring, soaking is not recommended.)

While you can hike out and back on this trail, you can also tie on extensions to **Imperial Geyser** and **Fairy Falls.** Since the route is a spur off the **Fountain Flat Drive** that permits bicycles, many hikers bike to trail junctions and lock up bikes to walk to their destinations. Due to bear activity, this trail is closed in spring until Memorial Day weekend.

★ FAIRY FALLS TRAIL

Distance: 5.8-9 miles round-trip
Duration: 3-5 hours
Elevation change: 52-129 feet
Effort: easy
Trailheads: Fairy Falls parking area off Grand Loop Road; an alternate trailhead is located at the Fountain Flat Drive parking lot (see map p. 100)
Directions: The Fairy Falls parking area is located off the Grand Loop Road, 11.5 miles south of Madison Junction or 4.5 miles north of Old Faithful. The Fountain Flat Drive trailhead is 5.5 miles south of Madison Junction or 10.5 miles north of Old Faithful. On Fountain Flat Drive, continue south 0.8 mile to the trailhead parking lot.

At 197 feet, Fairy Falls is the park's fourth-highest waterfall, and it provides a scenic destination year-round. Hikers, bikers, and skiers on this route frequently encounter bison. Due

Fairy Falls

your own bike lock), as bikes are not permitted farther. Plan five hours for the **nine-mile round-trip** hike from Old Faithful.

MYSTIC FALLS AND BISCUIT BASIN OVERLOOK

Distance: 2.4-8 miles round-trip
Duration: 1-4 hours
Elevation change: 135-545 feet
Effort: moderate
Trailheads: Biscuit Basin parking area, 2 miles northwest of Old Faithful, or access from Old Faithful Visitor Education Center (see map p. 100)

At Biscuit Basin, a short boardwalk loop provides hiking access to Mystic Falls and the overlook trail. Due to bear management closures, the trail opens for hiking in **late May.** The route can be hot in summer with sparse shade.

From the Biscuit Basin parking area, follow the **boardwalk trail** 0.3 mile west to the trailhead for Mystic Falls. Turn right and hike 0.4 mile through young lodgepoles and meadows to a junction. Take the left fork and ascend 0.5 mile into the canyon along the Little Firehole River to **Mystic Falls**, a 70-foot waterfall that feeds a series of cascades. To make this a **2.4-mile hike,** retrace your steps to Biscuit Basin.

Continue west from the falls on the 1.5-mile loop trail to the Biscuit Basin Overlook. Climb the south-facing switchbacks to reach another junction at the forested 7,827-foot summit. Turn right to reach **Biscuit Basin Overlook** (a left turn heads to Fairy Falls). As the trail crosses the ridge and descends, you'll get multiple views of Biscuit Basin, the Firehole River valley, and steam rising across the Upper Geyser Basin. Continuing down the trail, take the left fork to return to Biscuit Basin in **3.9 miles.**

It is also possible to hike to Biscuit Basin from Old Faithful Visitor Education Center. The **8-mile round-trip** hike follows the trail system through the Upper Geyser Basin to connect to Biscuit Basin across the Grand Loop Road.

to bear management, this trail opens in late May.

From the **Fairy Falls Trailhead,** cross the Firehole River and hike 1.4 miles northwest, passing the steaming cauldron of **Grand Prismatic Spring** in the Midway Geyser Basin. At the junction with the **Fairy Falls Trail,** turn west and hike 1.5 miles through the young lodgepole forest to the base of the falls. In summer, the falls plunge ribbonlike into a pool; in winter, ice sculptures flank the falls. Plan three hours for the **5.8-mile round-trip** to the falls. In winter, cross-country skiers can catch a snowcoach shuttle from Old Faithful to ski from the Fairy Falls parking area.

Reaching Fairy Falls from the alternate **Fountain Flat Drive trailhead** requires hiking, biking, or skiing the old road, which is closed to vehicles. From the Fountain Flat Trailhead, hike three miles south through open terrain, crossing the Firehole River and passing **Goose Lakes.** At the turnoff to the **Fairy Falls Trail,** there is a bike rack (bring

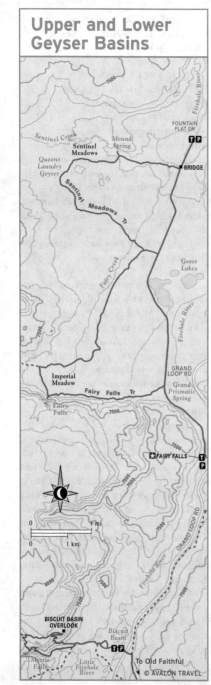

Upper and Lower Geyser Basins

© AVALON TRAVEL

Old Faithful

OLD FAITHFUL OBSERVATION POINT

Distance: 2.1 miles round-trip
Duration: 1 hour
Elevation change: 237 feet
Effort: moderate
Trailhead: Old Faithful Visitor Education Center (see map p. 92)

Most hikers coordinate the walk up to Observation Point with an eruption of Old Faithful Geyser. From the overlook, you can look down on the masses of people surrounding the geyser and watch it blow, but the steam plume sometimes occludes the water spouting, depending on wind direction. In winter, when the ground is snow covered, wear snowshoes or boot cleats (available from the Bear's Den in the Snow Lodge). While hiking time is short, waiting for Old Faithful to erupt may be long.

From the Old Faithful Visitor Education Center, circle the east side of Old Faithful Geyser heading toward **Geyser Hill** and cross the Firehole River. After crossing the bridge, turn right at the sign for **Observation Point.** The trail switchbacks uphill for 0.5 mile, making a small loop at the top. At the point, claim your spot in the trees to watch Old Faithful erupt. In winter, you may be the only one there, but in summer, you'll join a crowd. To descend, walk down the loop then continue westward on the trail through the forest to **Solitary Geyser.** From the geyser, a dirt trail connects south with the boardwalk on Geyser Hill near Aurum Geyser. Follow the boardwalk east to retrace your route across the Firehole River and back to Old Faithful.

MALLARD LAKE

Distance: 7-8.4 miles round-trip
Duration: 4 hours
Elevation change: 867-945 feet
Effort: moderate
Trailhead: Behind the employee cabins of Old Faithful Lodge, or 3.8 miles north of Old Faithful at Mallard Creek Trailhead (see map p. 92)

Mystic Falls

Mallard Lake is a small, 34-acre lake set in the forest at 8,037 feet in elevation. Located on the edge of the Central Plateau, it is one of the few places to get away from the crowds around the geyser basins. It serves as a hiking destination, and anglers won't find fish in its sterile waters. Wildlife sightings can include bison, elk, bears, and osprey. While lupine, harebells, and paintbrush can line the trail in early summer, the air also fills with copious mosquitoes. In winter, the route serves as a cross-country ski trail.

The out-and-back trail starts from either **Old Faithful** (7 miles) or the Mallard Creek Trailhead (8.4 miles). The easiest route is from Old Faithful. Head east, crossing the **Firehole River.** You'll tromp through lodgepole regrowth from the 1988 fire and a rocky ravine with lichen-covered volcanic boulders. Newer, thicker lodgepoles create long green corridors, but high points offer peek-a-boo views of the Upper Geyser Basin. About 0.2 mile before reaching **Mallard Lake** is the junction with the **Mallard Creek Trail,** where the route

drops to the forested shoreline. With a shuttle, a point-to-point hike (7.3 miles) to the Mallard Creek Trailhead is possible.

HOWARD EATON

Distance: 7-18.2 miles round-trip
Duration: 4-10 hours
Elevation change: 250-583 feet
Effort: easy to strenuous
Trailhead: On Grand Loop Road across from Old Faithful. Pick up a connecting trail south of the Snow Lodge (see map p. 102)

While this hot, dusty, forested walk has little to recommend it, the route is part of the historic 157-mile Howard Eaton loop trail through Yellowstone, dedicated in 1923. With the exception of a few sections (including this one), much of the trail today parallels the Grand Loop Road and is unmaintained with brush and downed trees. You'll find far less people on this trail than elsewhere around Old Faithful.

From Old Faithful, the 7-mile round-trip route goes southeast to climb 250 feet then drop to a junction. At the junction, turn left for 0.3 mile to reach **Lone Star Geyser.**

The longer, 18.2-mile route leads to **Shoshone Geyser Basin,** the largest backcountry geyser basin. After reaching the Lone Star Geyser junction, follow the trail southeast through loose forest broken by intermittent meadows and streams. The trail grunts 350 feet over the **Continental Divide** at 8,050-foot **Grant's Pass,** then drops to the west end of Shoshone Lake. This basin area holds 110 hydrothermal features, including hot pools and geysers. The main attraction, **Minute Man Geyser** spouts 10-40 feet high every 1-3 minutes during active phases. There are no boardwalks touring the geyser basin, so use caution. Savvy hikers start from Lone Star Geyser Trailhead instead of Old Faithful, or ride bikes to Lone Star Geyser to chop the hiking down to 13.4 miles.

LONE STAR GEYSER

Distance: 4.8-8.2 miles round-trip
Duration: 3-5 hours

Elevation change: 65-243 feet

Effort: easy

Trailhead: Lone Star Geyser Trailhead or the adjacent Kepler Cascades parking area (park at either), 2.5 miles east of Old Faithful or Old Faithful Lodge (see map p. 102)

From the Lone Star Geyser Trailhead, walk south along the old **asphalt service road** through conifers along the meandering Firehole River. The trail passes a large meadow (scout for wildlife) before ascending a gentle hill to the geyser basin. **Lone Star Geyser,** a 12-foot-tall pink and gray sinter cone, sits tucked away, hidden from the hubbub of the Upper Geyser Basin. Spouting up to 40 feet in the air, the geyser erupts about every three hours with spurts lasting 30 minutes. If you see the geyser go off, add the date and time to the logbook in the old interpretive stand.

Hiking the trail **from Old Faithful Lodge** almost doubles the mileage. From the southeast corner of the Old Faithful cabin complex, hop onto the **Mallard Lake Trail.** After crossing the Firehole River, turn right to follow the signage to **Kepler Cascades.** The trail climbs through forest and meadows until it parallels Grand Loop Road, then crosses to the Kepler Cascades parking lot. Locate the Lone Star Geyser Trailhead just south of the cascades. For an alternate return, take the Howard Eaton Trail 2.9 miles north back to Old Faithful.

SPRING CREEK

Distance: 2-12.4 miles round-trip

Duration: 1.5-6 hours

Elevation change: 750 feet

Effort: moderate

Trailheads: Spring Creek Picnic Area or Lone Star Geyser Trailhead (see map p. 102)

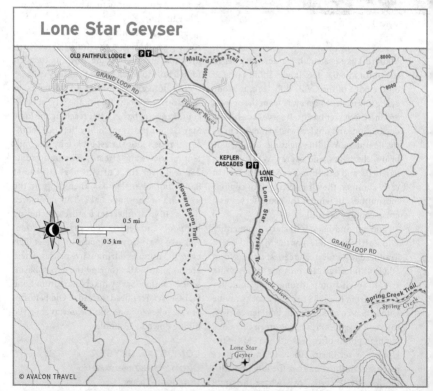

Lone Star Geyser

© AVALON TRAVEL

Lone Star Geyser

Creek Trail sign and cross the Firehole River just below the confluence of Spring Creek. The trail climbs gently, interrupted with a few short, steep grunts to the picnic area. Turn around at Spring Creek Picnic Area.

DIVIDE OVERLOOK

Distance: 2.6 miles round-trip
Duration: 1.5 hours
Elevation change: 546 feet
Effort: strenuous
Trailhead: Divide Trailhead on Grand Loop Road, about 7 miles east of Old Faithful (see map p. 103)

From the trailhead, a short climb up a forested ravine leads to an overlook that once housed a fire lookout. At the junction with the **Spring Creek Trail,** turn left to hike to **Divide,** a pass named for the Continental Divide. Views from the 8,590-foot summit include Shoshone Lake to the south. In winter, cross-country skiers can hop a snowcoach

Directions: From Old Faithful, drive 5.6 miles east on the Grand Loop Road to the Spring Creek Picnic Area; or drive 2.5 miles to the Lone Start Geyser Trailhead.

The Spring Creek Trail tours a dramatic forested canyon flanked with immense rhyolite boulders, spires, and cliffs that make hikers feel minuscule. Cold-water springs feed the creek. The trail used to be a stagecoach route, although parts of the route seem impassable. With a shuttle, you can hike Spring Creek as a point-to-point trail, even linking with other trails to return to Old Faithful.

For a short scenic walk along the creek, start at **Spring Creek Picnic Area** and head westward downhill. The trail crosses back and forth over the creek on small wooden bridges. A descent of about one mile reaches some of the rock features. Retrace your steps back up to the picnic area.

For an out-and-back hike, start from the **Lone Star Geyser Trailhead.** This route is for enjoyment of the canyon, rather than the picnic area. Start by walking 2.7 miles on the Lone Star Geyser Trail. Turn left at the Spring

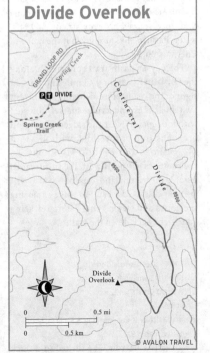

Divide Overlook

GRAND LOOP RD

Spring Creek

P T DIVIDE

Spring Creek Trail

Continental

Divide

8500

8500

Divide Overlook ▲

0   0.5 mi

0   0.5 km

© AVALON TRAVEL

shuttle to the trailhead to ski to Divide and then continue back toward Old Faithful via Spring Creek, Lone Star Geyser, and Kepler Cascades Trails.

Norris
MONUMENT GEYSER BASIN

Distance: 2.8 miles round-trip
Duration: 2.5 hours
Elevation change: 637 feet
Effort: strenuous, but short
Trailhead: On Grand Loop Road 4.7 miles south of Norris Junction and 8.7 miles northeast of Madison Junction. Parking lot sits on the west side of the road at the south end of the bridge over the Gibbon River (see map p. 104).

Monument Geyser Basin takes more effort than the popular hydrothermal basins, but the reward is fewer people and a boardwalk-free basin that has a more natural look. At almost 8,000 feet in elevation, the basin features multiple cylindrical sinter cones created from now-defunct geysers. The basin's namesake **Monument Geyser** is a 10-foot-tall cone that once spewed a steady stream of 194°F water. Its shape has also given it the name of Thermos Bottle.

The geyser basin trail runs north along the **Gibbon River** for 0.45 mile and stays in sight of the road before swinging southwest. Switchbacks ascend a ridge sparsely forested with lodgepoles. Near the ridgetop, the trail broadens into an overlook with views of **Mt. Holmes** and **Gibbon Meadows.** As the route travels northwest, the sulfur smell heralds the barren landscape of **Monument Geyser Basin.** Use caution while exploring the cones and steam vents before retracing your steps back down the trail.

ICE LAKE

Distance: 0.6 mile round-trip
Duration: 30 minutes
Elevation change: 22 feet
Effort: easy
Trailhead: Norris-Canyon Road, 3.5 miles east of Norris (see map p. 92)

Ice Lake is a narrow lake tucked in a thick

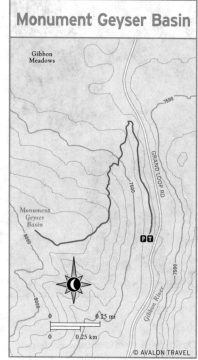

Monument Geyser Basin

Gibbon Meadows

Monument Geyser Basin

GRAND LOOP RD

Gibbon River

P T

7600

7500

7500

8000

8000

0   0.25 mi

0   0.25 km

© AVALON TRAVEL

lodgepole pine forest regrowth after the 1988 fires. The lake is less than a mile long and rimmed with downed timber and regrowth; there are only a couple of beach areas.

From the trailhead, hike 0.2 mile up the trail to a **junction.** Take the right fork for the quickest access. The left fork heads farther to the northwest corner of the lake and at 0.5 mile reaches a junction with the **Howard Eaton Trail.** The trail westward reaches **Norris Campground** in 4.1 miles, an alternate trailhead. The trail right goes along the north shore of **Ice Lake** to **Wolf Lake, Grebe Lake,** and **Cascade Lake.**

BACKPACKING

Backpackers must obtain **permits** ($3/person, children 8 and younger free) for assigned backcountry campsites. Permits are available in person 48 hours in advance from the backcountry offices. For more information, see the *Essentials* chapter.

Mallard Lake
3-5 MILES

For one-night backpacking with young kids, Mallard Lake (campsite OB2-4) works as a short destination with 3-4 miles of hiking. You can swim in the lake, which holds no fish.

Bechler River Trail
30 MILES

The king of Yellowstone backpacking trips gets you farther away from day hiker hordes. The Bechler River Trail descends into Bechler River Canyon and the land of waterfalls. While you can backpack the 30-mile trail in 3-5 days point-to-point from the Lone Star Geyser Trailhead to the Bechler Ranger Station, you'll need eight hours to set up the shuttle. To avoid the shuttle, you can hike to Collonade Falls in the canyon and back in 5-6 days (40 miles). While overnighting at a campsite en route is necessary, aim your daily mileage allowance for the core canyon campsites (9B4-9B9), especially Ouzel, Collonade, and Albright Falls. Due to snow and water levels, permit reservations are only available from July 15 onward. While elevation gain is minimal (980 feet), crossing the Continental Divide twice, fording multiple streams and the river adds difficulty.

BIKING
Inside the Park

Yellowstone park roads offer prime road cycling with rolling terrain along the Madison River, a big climb from Madison to Norris, and a slightly lesser grade to Old Faithful and the Continental Divide.

The park road from West Yellowstone to Madison (14 miles) and then north from Madison to Mammoth Hot Springs (35 miles) is plowed late March-mid-April. During this time, this stretch of the park road opens to cyclists yet remains closed to vehicles. Confirm the road status online (www.nps.gov/yell) and plan to carry all supplies (including pepper spray for bears), as no services are open. After traffic thins in fall, riding from West Yellowstone to Old Faithful is a prime time to hear elk bugling.

Mountain bikes are only permitted on three level routes in the Old Faithful area; most are wide level remnants of old asphalt roadbeds and are good places for family biking (they are open to hikers, too, so use caution). Fountain Flats Road (4 miles, late May-early Nov.) links the Fountain Flat Drive parking lot with the Fairy Falls Trailhead (park at either end). En route between Goose Lake and Grand Prismatic Spring, stop and park your bike in the rack to walk to Fairy Falls. Due to bear activity, the Fountain Flat Drive is closed in spring until Memorial Day weekend.

A round-trip ride connects Old Faithful Inn with Biscuit Basin (5 miles). Start in front of Hamilton's Store and ride the paved path along the south side of the Firehole River for 1.2 miles. Turn left into the second Daisy Geyser Loop entrance, then turn right onto a single-track trail that leads to Grand Loop Road near Biscuit Basin.

The Lone Star Geyser Trail (4.8 miles round-trip) offers a pleasant forest ride along the Firehole River to Lone Star Geyser. Parking is at the Lone Star Geyser Trailhead or Kepler Cascades.

In Old Faithful, the Snow Lodge (866/439-7375 or 307/344-7311, www.yellowstonenationalparklodges.com, daily late May-early Oct.) rents bikes for adults and children, including helmets, and kiddie trailers. Bike rentals cost $6-10 for one hour, $15-30 for four hours, and $25-35 for one day.

Outside the Park

In West Yellowstone, mountain bikers have two trail systems. Rendezvous Ski Trails (www.rendezvousskitrails.com, mid-June-mid-Oct.) becomes biking and hiking trails when snow melts in June. About 15 miles of gently rolling, easy-to-intermediate trails loop through meadows and forests. Mountain bikers can also ride the Riverside Trail (2.8 miles round-trip) along the Madison River into the park. Locate the trailhead across from the Dude Motel (3 Madison Ave., West Yellowstone).

Freeheel and Wheel (33 Yellowstone Ave., West Yellowstone, 406/646-7744, www.freeheelandwheel.com, 9am-6pm daily year-round) rents road bikes and front suspension mountain bikes for $8-10 per hour or $35-40 per day. Helmets and kiddie trailers are available, too.

HORSEBACK RIDING

There are no horseback riding operations in the Old Faithful area. Just outside the park, West Yellowstone has several ranches with trail rides (mid-May-Sept.), though you'll need to drive a few minutes out of town to the ranches. Make reservations at least one day in advance; ask about weight and age restrictions and wear fitted long pants and sturdy shoes, hiking boots, or cowboy boots.

The closest ranch, **Creekside Trail Rides** (175 Oldroyd Rd., 406/560-6913, www.creeksidetrailrides.com, 10am-6:30pm Mon.-Sat.), is 6.5 miles west of town. Reservations are not required for the guided one-hour ride ($35) through the ranch's forests and meadows. June-August, Rodeo Ride ($45) packages are available, departing at 6:30pm to return in time to watch the Wild West Yellowstone Rodeo. Reservations are required. Arena riding lessons and wagon rides are also available.

Trail rides are also available at **Diamond P Ranch** (2865 Targhee Pass Hwy., 406/646-0606, www.thediamondpranch.com, hours vary daily, $70-90), about six miles west of West Yellowstone.

WATER SPORTS
Boating

Outside the park, 15-mile-long **Hebgen Lake** offers opportunities for boating, lake angling or paddling, sailing, and waterskiing. Located 8.5 miles northwest of West Yellowstone, the dammed lake has several long arms, which make for good paddling and bird-watching. Winds tend to kick up in the afternoon. (The lake is also the site of the 1959 earthquake that shook Yellowstone and created Quake Lake to the west.) The nearest boat launch is at **Rainbow Point Campground**

(Custer-Gallatin National Forest, 406/823-6961, www.fs.usda.gov/gallatin, mid-May-mid-Sept.), which has a cement boat ramp, docks, and trailer parking. To reach Rainbow Point from West Yellowstone, drive five miles north on U.S. Highway 191. Turn west onto Rainbow Point Road (Forest Rd. 6954) and drive 1.7 miles to the boat launch.

Montana has amped up control efforts for aquatic invasive species (AIS). If you are bringing a boat to Hebgen Lake, you will most likely pass a boat check station; boaters are required to stop for an AIS check. Wash your boat completely before bringing it to Montana.

GUIDES AND RENTALS

Two companies in West Yellowstone rent kayaks and guide tours on Hebgen Lake. Both companies include life jackets, paddles, and transport equipment (foam pads and straps) to carry the boats on your vehicle.

Yellowstone Alpen Guides (555 Yellowstone Ave., West Yellowstone, 406/646-9591 or 800/858-3502, www.yellowstone-guides.com, mid-May-mid-Oct.) rents single and tandem kayaks ($40-60 half day, $50-70 full day). They also guide three-hour morning, evening, and daytime tours (adults $55, kids $45) on Hebgen Lake. Note that tours start from West Yellowstone and do not enter the park.

The **Madison Arm Resort Marina** (5475 Madison Arm Rd., West Yellowstone, 406/646-9328, www.madisonarmresort.com, $30-35/hour) is located on Hebgen Lake and rents small, motorized aluminum and pontoon boats.

Fishing
INSIDE THE PARK

The western region of Yellowstone serves as headwaters for Montana's blue-ribbon trout streams. Inside the park, the **Firehole, Madison,** and lower **Gibbon Rivers** offer prime fly-fishing for rainbow and brown trout. Riffles and slow ambling stretches alternate with deep pools. Most of the rivers begin to clear of runoff sediments by early July, when the real fishing begins. Most anglers wade in to fish.

For kids, two waterways near Norris, the **Gibbon River** at Virginia Meadows and **Solfatara Creek,** offer good places to gain fishing skills. Near Madison Junction, take the kids to the large meadows that flank the Madison River. For lake fishing near Old Faithful, try Goose Lake.

Only fly-fishing is permitted on the Firehole, Madison, and lower Gibbon Rivers. If you don't have a fly rod, that's okay, just attach a fly on a casting rod. Three waterways are closed to fishing: the Firehole River upstream of Old Faithful to Biscuit Basin, the Midway Foot Bridge area, and the Seven Mile Bridge area of the Madison.

Fishing **permits** are required for anglers 16 years and older ($18 for three days, $25 seven days, $40 season). For permit information and regulations, see the *Essentials* chapter.

OUTSIDE THE PARK

Northwest of West Yellowstone, **Hebgen Lake** harbors several sportfish species, especially brown trout in May and June before the streams clear up. The Madison River has classic fly-fishing. You'll need a **Montana fishing license** (http://fwp.mt.gov, residents: $13-26; nonresidents: $25-70) available at West Yellowstone fly shops.

West Yellowstone houses fishing outfitters that guide trips inside and outside the park. Trips inside the park are wade-fishing, but outside the park, guides offer float-fishing on certain rivers. Rates run $300-350 for a half day and $500-600 full day for 1-3 people. Fees usually include the guide, lunch, and gear, but clarify that when you make reservations. Park entrance fees, fishing licenses, and guide tips (15-20 percent) are not included in the rates. In West Yellowstone, call the fly-fishing outfitters at **Arrick's Fly Shop** (37 Canyon St., 406/646-7290, www.arricks.com), **Bud Lilly's Trout Shop** (39 Madison Ave. W., 406/646-7801 or 800-854-9559, www.budlillys.com), or **Madison River Outfitters** (117 N. Canyon St., 406/646-9644 or 800-646-9644, www.madisonriveroutfitters.com).

Swimming

Geothermal features can scald, thus swimming is not permitted in any of the hot pools

fishing on the Madison

in the geyser basins. A swimming hole on the **Firehole River** opens up once the high water abates in early July. From Madison, drive south a short distance on the park road and turn right onto Firehole Canyon Drive (one-way). Park near the outhouses and descend a set of stairs to the river. There is no lifeguard; swim at your own risk. Outside the park at Hebgen Lake, you can swim at **Rainbow Point Campground.**

THRILL SPORTS

In West Yellowstone, **Yellowstone Aerial Adventures** (105 S. Faithful St., 406/646-5171, http://yellowstoneparkzipline.com, 9am-8pm daily late May-late Sept., hours shorten in late summer, weekends only after Labor Day, $45-50) strings an aerial park through the treetops. Start easy and work up in difficulty through more than 50 challenges on swinging ropes, ziplines, climbing walls, nets, and aerial bridges. Multiple-visit and multiple-day passes are sold, too, and online reservations are a good idea.

WINTER SPORTS
Cross-Country Skiing and Snowshoeing

Winter turns Old Faithful into an otherworldly landscape of snow broken by steam and melt-outs from geothermal activity. Park roads between West Yellowstone and Old Faithful are closed to wheeled vehicles, but open for skiing and snowshoeing.

The park service grooms several roads around **Old Faithful** for skate and classic skiing or snowshoeing. A groomed ski trail ascends a gentle grade to **Lone Star Geyser,** while a less-traveled loop tours through the cabins of **Old Faithful Lodge** with views of the Firehole River. The park service also grooms a trail from **Old Faithful Inn to the Morning Glory Pool,** but geothermal hot spots cause melt-outs; visitors may have to remove their skis in order to walk or cross the trail on fake grass carpets.

All summer hiking trails turn into winter ski and snowshoe trails, including Biscuit Basin, Fairy Falls, Spring Creek, Divide Overlook, and trails around the geyser basins. Kick off the skis at boardwalks, as some get icy. **Snowcoach shuttles** (by reservation only from Snow Lodge, $21 adults, $10-12 kids) help whittle down mileages. Skiers at the Snow Lodge can save a few dollars with **Nordic ski packages** (Xanterra, 307/344-7311 or 866/439-7375, www.yellowstonenationalparklodges.com) that bundle lodging, breakfast, shuttle drops, snowcoach transportation to and from Old Faithful, and ski rentals.

GUIDES AND RENTALS

At Old Faithful, the **Bear's Den** (Snow Lodge, 307/344-7311 or 866/439-7375, www.yellowstonenationalparklodges.com, daily mid-Dec.-early Mar.) rents cross-country ski packages that include skis, boots, and poles ($16 half day, $25 full day), as well as snowshoes ($13 half day, $22 full day) and boot cleats for walking on ice. Multiday rates are lower, as are rentals with a lesson package. The shop also waxes skis and repairs gear, and guides ski and snowshoe trips around Old Faithful ($30, snowshoe only) and to Lone Star Geyser ($55) or Grand Canyon of the Yellowstone ($185). Reservations are required.

Other guides lead tours mid-December-mid-March. Park naturalists guide a two-hour **snowshoe tour** (Sun., free) at Old Faithful. From West Yellowstone, **Yellowstone Alpen Guides** (555 Yellowstone Ave., 406/646-9591 or 800/858-3502, www.yellowstoneguides.com) can shuttle skiers to Biscuit Basin to ski to Old Faithful for pick up.

OUTSIDE THE PARK

West Yellowstone serves as a regional destination for Nordic skiing November-March. With a reputation for stellar grooming, consistent snowpack, and a long season, **Rendezvous Ski Trails** (www.rendezvousskitrails.com) offers groomed skate and classic ski trails in Custer-Gallatin National Forest. Find the 35 kilometers of rolling trails at the log arch at the south end of Geyser Street. The trails loop around 6,800 feet elevation through meadows and forests. Purchase trail passes ($8) at the self-service, cash-only kiosk at the trailhead near the arch, or at the chamber of commerce, Forest Service office, or Freeheel and Wheel. The ski area launches the season with the annual Yellowstone Ski Festival at the end of November and wraps up the racing season with the annual Yellowstone Rendezvous marathon races in early March.

Because West Yellowstone sits on the park boundary, skiers and snowshoers can also tour the Riverside Trail along the Madison River inside the park. The nine-mile trail has three loops, but skiing only one loop or so shortens the distance. Sometimes you can see bison, bald eagles, trumpeter swans, and foxes.

Freeheel and Wheel (33 Yellowstone Ave., West Yellowstone, 406/646-7744, www.freeheelandwheel.com, 9am-6pm daily year-round) rents cross-country skis ($8/hour, $20-30/day), snowshoes, pull sleds for tots, and touring, racing, and performance skate and classic skis. Call ahead to reserve equipment. The shop also repairs and waxes skis, teaches lessons, and gives guided tours (by reservation).

Snowmobiling

The snowmobile season in Yellowstone runs mid-December-early March. You can go with a commercially guided group or enter the annual lottery for a permit to go with your own group. Rentals ($200-300/day) are only available in West Yellowstone. Snowsuits, gloves, boots, and helmets rent for $10-20. Avalanche gear (beacons, probes, shovels, and airbags) cost $50.

TOURS

Guided full-day snowmobile tours travel roads inside Yellowstone daily on the new quieter, less stinky machines required by the park. To reach Old Faithful, tours stage from Mammoth, Flagg Ranch, and mostly from West Yellowstone. Tours from West Yellowstone also go to Grand Canyon of the Yellowstone.

From West Yellowstone, the tour to Old Faithful is 65 miles round-trip. You'll have time to get off the snowmobile to tour geyser basins and walk around Old Faithful. The Grand Canyon of the Yellowstone tour is a 90-mile round-trip. Snowmobiles can take one or two riders, and because the roads are groomed daily, you don't need to have previous experience. Tours into the park are limited to 10 snowmobiles and usually launch at 8am for the eight-hour ride. Rates for tours run $300-375 per day per machine. Insulated snowmobile suits, helmets, mittens, and boots rent for $15-20; higher-priced tours usually include gear in the rates. Rates do not include park entrance fees, meals, taxes, or 15 percent guide gratuities.

Snowmobile tours launch from West Yellowstone through Yellowstone Vacations (415 Yellowstone Ave., 406/646-9564 or 800/426-7669, www.yellowstonevacations.com) and Backcountry Adventures (224 N. Electric St., 406/646-9317 or 800/924-7669, www.backcountry-adventures.com). Make reservations 6-9 months ahead for holidays.

For alternate staging locations to Old Faithful, Yellowstone Year-Round Safaris (905 Scott St., Gardiner, 406/838-7311 or 800/828-9080, www.yellowstoneyearround-safaris.com) leads tours from Mammoth, and Old Faithful Snowmobile Tours (Jackson, WY, 307/733-9767 or 800/253-7130, www.snowmobilingtours.com) leads trips from Flagg Ranch.

In West Yellowstone, a Montana snowmobile capital, street-legal snow machines are parked in front of bars, stores, and hotels on all but the main drag and highways. Guides lead snowmobile tours outside the park on more than 200 miles of groomed trails in Custer-Gallatin National Forest. The most popular route travels the 28-mile Two Top Trail, a National Recreational Snowmobile Trail that climbs 2,000 feet to views of the Teton Mountains.

Entertainment and Shopping

INSIDE THE PARK
Ranger Programs

Free ranger naturalist programs are held at several locations. Program schedules are available at visitors centers, on campground bulletin boards, in park hotels, and online (www.nps. gov/yell). Daily daytime programs cover volcanic activity, geology, wildlife, natural history, and cultural history. **Old Faithful Visitor Education Center** (307/344-2751, www.nps. gov/yell, 8am-8pm daily mid-Apr.-Sept., 9am-5pm daily mid-Dec.-Feb., shorter hours spring and fall) hosts a short 10-minute ranger talk on geysers every half hour in the afternoon near Old Faithful Geyser. The center also shows a rotating lineup of films on the park all day. In addition to education about geysers, wildlife, park history, and ecology, many have stunning photography. The daily film schedule is posted outside the theater. Inside the **Old Faithful Theater** (7pm daily late May-Sept., 7:30pm Fri.-Sun. late Dec.-early Mar.), naturalists give evening presentations on geysers, wildlife, and current science. At the **Madison Junior Ranger Station,** 30-minute programs run several times daily in summer and are designed for kids and their families.

Evening programs run nightly in summer at Madison Campground, Norris Campground, and Old Faithful Visitor Education Center. In early summer, don bug spray for mosquitoes at the campground outdoor amphitheaters. Topics for the 45-minute presentations vary nightly. The **Madison Campground Amphitheater** (late May-early Sept.) holds evening presentations at 9:30pm in early summer (9pm in late July). At the **Norris Campground Amphitheater** (7:30pm early June-early Sept.), rangers conduct periodic programs on night sky observations and stargazing on moonless nights.

Shopping

Old Faithful has two **Yellowstone General Stores** (406/586-7593, www.visityellowstonepark.com, 7:30am-9:30pm daily) in historic buildings. Built in 1897, the **Old Faithful Basin Store** (2 Old Faithful Loop, late May-late Sept.) is located in the historic Hamilton's Store near Old Faithful Inn. The shop sells clothing and gifts, as well as food service.

Old Faithful General Store (1 Old Faithful Loop, May-mid-Oct.), located south of the visitors center, is a 1920s building with a large fireplace and log beams. The shop sells gifts and offers photos and food service.

Yellowstone Association park stores (406/848-2400, www.yellowstoneassociation.org) are located at Old Faithful Visitor Education Center, Norris, and Madison Information Station and sell a plethora of park-themed items, from books and maps to souvenirs.

Gift shops (Xanterra, 307/344-7311 or 866/439-7375, www.yellowstonenationalparklodges.com) operate in Old Faithful Inn, Old Faithful Lodge, and the Snow Lodge when the hotels are open.

WEST YELLOWSTONE

West Yellowstone nightlife heats up in western saloons and lounges. Some have live music, and the dancing rocks until 2am. Bands vary from western to rock and mountain. Find them by walking the strip to check out the scene.

Ranger Programs

The **West Yellowstone Visitor Information Center** (30 Yellowstone Ave., 307/344-2876) presents free naturalist and ranger programs in summer. Families can enjoy wildlife talks (20 min., 9am and 3:30pm daily late May-early Sept) and ranger introductions to Yellowstone (30 min., 9:30am daily late May-early Sept). Evening presentations (45 min., 7pm Tues. and Fri., early June-Aug.) cover a variety of unique features in the park.

Off-site afternoon programs (30 min., 2pm daily late May-early Sept.) alternate locations between the Yellowstone Historic Center Museum (Sun.-Mon., Wed., and Fri.) and the Grizzly and Wolf Discovery Center (Tues., Thurs., and Sat.).

Entertainment

With three or more shows per day in rotation, the **Yellowstone Giant Screen Theater** (101 S. Canyon St., 888/854-5862, www.yellowstonegiantscreen.com, daily in summer, Mon.-Sat. in winter, closed in spring, $8-10) gives huge visuals. The screen is six stories tall and 80 feet wide with a six-track audio system. Catch 40-minute educational films on Yellowstone, Lewis and Clark, and the ice ages hourly and Hollywood family flicks in the evening. You can also see movies at **Bears Den Cinema** (15 N. Electric St., 406/646-7777, http://yellowstonemovies.com).

The **Playmill Theatre** (29 Madison Ave., 406/646-7757, Mon.-Sat. late May-early Sept., box office open 10am-9pm, $20-24) is a small, long-running theater that imports its cast and crew every summer for plays like *Singin' in the Rain* or *Mary Poppins*. Three plays run in repertory, usually family musicals and comedies. Shows are at 6pm and 8:30pm, with a 2pm show on Saturday. Discounted tickets for seniors and children are available Monday-Thursday.

Events

In true cowboy fashion, the **Yellowstone Rodeo** (175 Oldroyd Rd., 406/560-6913, www.yellowstonerodeo.com, 8pm Thurs.-Sat. June, 8pm Wed.-Sat. July-Aug., $12-15 adults, $6-8 kids), located 6.5 miles west of town, stages cowpoke competitions during the summer. Rodeo events include bareback bronc riding, barrel racing, bull riding, team roping, breakaway roping, saddle bronc riding, and a calf scramble for kids. You can purchase tickets at the gate, but to guarantee seating on sellout shows, buy tickets in advance online.

The annual **West Yellowstone Old Faithful Cycle Tour** (www.cycleyellowstone. com, Sept.), a one-day, 60-mile round-trip ride to raise funds for the Yellowstone Park Foundation and other organizations, happens on the third weekend of September with registration open mid-June. Entry is limited to 350 riders.

West Yellowstone is also home to the annual **World Snowmobile Expo** (http://snowmobileexpo.com, Mar.), held for three days every March. The town packs out for high-flying snowmobile stunts, races, drags, demos, exhibits, bands, and outdoor concerts.

Shopping

Outside the park, West Yellowstone has streets full of shops. During summer high season, shops and galleries stay open in the evening along Canyon Street, which has several blocks of independent gift shops, candy outlets, cowboy hat and boot stores, fly shops, galleries, and eclectic stores. Most galleries specialize in western art with wildlife, mountain scenes, and geothermal landscapes. Some shops close during fall and spring off-seasons; in winter, many shops shorten business hours.

Built in 1927, the **Eagle's Store** (3 N. Canyon St., 406/646-9300, www.eagles-store.com, 8am-8pm daily) sells a gaggle of souvenirs, western and outdoor clothing, Native American crafts, and tackle. It is listed on the National Register of Historic Places and also houses an old-fashioned soda fountain. For outdoor gear, check out the small **Freeheel and Wheel** (33 Yellowstone Ave., 406/646-7744, www.freeheelandwheel.com, 9am-6pm daily), which specializes in reputable bicycle, snowshoe, cross-country ski gear, and lattes. Along with fly-fishing gear, **Madison River Outfitters** (117 N. Canyon St., 406/646-9644 or 800-646-9644, www.madisonriveroutfitters.com, 8am-6pm daily) carries tents, sleeping bags, and packs as well as outdoor clothing, wildlife-watching binoculars and scopes, and camping, backpacking, and hiking gear. Visitors can take home coffee beans locally roasted by **Morning Glory Coffee and Tea** (129 Dunraven St., 406/646-7061, www.morningglorycoffee.net, 7am-3pm Mon.-Sat.).

Accommodations

INSIDE THE PARK
Reservations

Competition for reservations (Xanterra, 307/344-7311 or 866/439-7375, www.yellowstonenationalparklodges.com, May-Oct., Snow Lodge mid-Dec.-early Mar.) at Old Faithful is fierce. Plan ahead and book one year in advance for summer stays and winter holidays. Though you may be able to pick up last-minute reservations due to cancellations, there may not be many choices for room types.

Old Faithful has three lodging options, with 557 rooms total, all within a five-minute walk from the visitors center and Old Faithful Geyser. None of the lodges have televisions, radios, or air-conditioning. Most rooms do not have telephones, but they do have cell phone reception. Only Snow Lodge has wireless Internet. Bathrooms come in four types: tub-shower combo, shower only (shower stalls are small), shared baths down the hall, or communal toilets and showers in a separate cabin. Clarify your needs when reserving a room; a few ADA rooms and cabins are available. Rates listed are for two people; add on 14 percent tax and $16-18 per each additional person.

Old Faithful
OLD FAITHFUL INN

The most-requested lodge in the park, ★ Old Faithful Inn (early May-mid-Oct., $110-270 rooms, $480-530 suites) is a National Historic Landmark. The Old House, or the main log lodge, was built in 1903-1904 with the east wing added in 1913-1914 and west wing in 1927-1928. As such, room styles, sizes, and ambience are a throwback to the last century. It is reputed to be the largest log building in the world, with distinctive log architecture. The Old House contains the immense lobby, dining room, lounge, snack bar, gift shop, and old-style rooms, while the two wings are more modern.

The 327-room inn has nine styles of rooms, some overlooking Upper Geyser Basin and Old Faithful Geyser. Historic rooms in the Old House have fixtures with minimal outlets for charging electronics, 1-3 queen beds, and either private baths with clawfoot tubs or shared marble-and-tile baths with showers down the hall. No elevators access the upper floors of the Old House. The two more modern wings (but still dated) are 3-4 stories tall with elevators. Most of the hotel rooms have 1-3 queen beds with private baths. The east wing has rooms facing Old Faithful Geyser, although trees may block the view. Upper-end suites have sitting rooms, bedrooms with two queen beds, and private baths.

OLD FAITHFUL LODGE

Old Faithful Lodge (mid-May-early Oct., $85-145) is close to Old Faithful Geyser, but away from the hubbub around the visitors center, which makes the location quieter. You can sit on the lodge deck or in the lobby to watch the geyser blow. Inside, the huge stone-and-log lodge has a snack shop and a food court cafeteria.

Between the lodge and the Firehole River, accommodations are in 96 simple rustic cabins with small motel-style rooms in duplexes or four-plexes. Cabins have tiny windows and no porches. From cabins 112-116 and 200-203, you can step right out the door to watch Old Faithful. Cabins 22-25 and 31-35 overlook the Firehole River. The bare-bones cabins have two double beds or one double and one single. Some have private baths; others are more like camping with a bed and roof where you walk to a nearby communal bathroom and shower cabin.

West Yellowstone

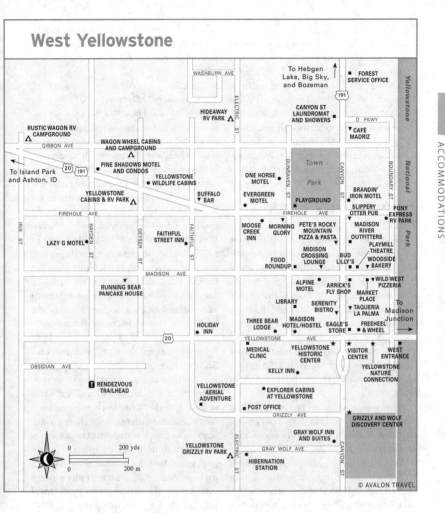

SNOW LODGE AND CABINS

Built in 1989-1999 with modern western architecture, ★ **Snow Lodge** (May-mid-Oct. and mid-Dec.-early Mar., $110-265) sits behind the visitors center with no views of the geyser basin and partially surrounded by parking lots. Snow Lodge is the most modern hotel at Old Faithful. The 134 rooms are larger and have modern-style bathrooms and furnishings. Cabins are located a few-minute walk from the lodge; you might encounter wildlife en route to breakfast. Wireless Internet is available in the lobby and main lodge ($5/hour, $12/day, $25/three days). The lodge has a restaurant, grill café, lounge, gift shop, and winter ice rink.

Hotel-style rooms with one king or two queen beds and log furnishings are in the three-story main lodge. Motel-style rooms cluster in plain duplex or quad buildings. Larger cabins have two queen beds per room with some rooms adjoining, while smaller cabins have one or two double beds. In winter, slide your bags to your room on plastic sleds, or use the bell service.

In winter, the park road to Old Faithful is closed. Snowcoach transportation from Mammoth to the Snow Lodge is available via Xantera (866/429-7375 or 307/344-7311, http://www.yellowstonenationalparklodges.com, $117 adults, $59 children, mid-Dec.-Feb.). Snowcoaches depart daily at 7:45am arriving at noon; return trips depart at 1:45pm arriving at 6pm.

OUTSIDE THE PARK
West Yellowstone

On the western boundary of the park, West Yellowstone houses a mix of circa 1950 mom-and-pop motels interspersed with three-story modern hotels. More than 50 lodging properties cram into the town and sprawl throughout surrounding ranchland. Most motels have satellite television, phones, wireless Internet, air-conditioning, refrigerators, and microwaves. Due to limited lodging at Old Faithful, many visitors choose to stay in West Yellowstone, as the drive between the two places is only 30 miles.

Some motels are open year-round while many are summer season only. Reservations are recommended six months in advance for summer, when the town packs out. Summer and winter see the highest prices, with rates $100-200 higher than in off-season. Spring and fall have the lowest rates. Rates listed reflect the lowest and highest seasonal prices.

HOSTEL

Built in 1912, the Madison Hotel Motel and Hostel (139 Yellowstone Ave., 406/646-7745 or 800/838-7745, www.madisonhotelmotel.com, mid-May-early Oct., $38) is listed on the National Register of Historic Places. The hostel has small, gender-separated 2nd-floor dorm rooms with bunks and shared bathroom-shower facilities down the hall. The lobby has the common lounge, computers for Internet catching-up, a small refrigerator and microwave, but no kitchen for cooking. Hotel and motel rooms ($73-150) are also available, with varied combinations of queen, double, and single beds.

MOTELS

The three-story Kelly Inn (104 S. Canyon St., 406/646-4544 or 800/635-3559, www.yellowstonekellyinn.com, year-round, $103-345) has carved bears climbing up outside railings to stare in windows. Rooms, which have a king or two queens, feature log furniture, and rates include a breakfast bar. Some suites have wet bars and whirlpool tubs. The inn has an indoor pool, hot tub, sauna, outdoor patio with gas fire pit, laundry, pet walk, and play areas. DNC Parks and Resorts (406/586-7593 or 877/600-4308, www.visityellowstonepark.com) runs several properties, including the Holiday Inn and Explorer Cabins, with seasonal packages that bundle up activities in Yellowstone with their lodging. Most of them have rooms that will take pets for an additional fee. Opposite the Grizzly and Wolf Discovery Center, the Gray Wolf Inn and Suites (250 S. Canyon St., year-round, $120-305) has three stories of rooms: one- or two-bedroom family suites with full kitchens, smaller suites with full kitchens, king hotel rooms, and standard two-queen hotel rooms. Some units have full kitchens. The inn serves a free continental breakfast and has an indoor pool, sauna, hot tub, and underground heated parking. Built in 2007 on the quiet western side of town, the Yellowstone Park Hotel (201 Grizzly Ave., mid-Apr.-early Oct. $120-330) is a three-story hotel with 66 standard hotel rooms, free continental breakfast, indoor heated swimming pool, hot tub, and coin-op laundry.

Two longtime West Yellowstone staples sit on or near the Canyon Street activity. The Brandin' Iron Inn (201 Canyon St., 406/646-9411 or 800/217-4613, www.hotelyellowstone.com, year-round, $85-190) has 80 remodeled rooms with one queen or king, two queens, three queens, or suites with kitchens. Amenities include indoor hot tubs, complimentary hot breakfast, a ski wax room, and laundry services. The inn also has packages that bundle up rooms, sightseeing tours, and activities, including snowmobiling in winter. The **Stage Coach Inn** (209 Madison Ave., 406/646-7381 or 800/842-2882, www.yellowstoneinn.com, year-round, $93-295) has rooms with two queens or one king. Historic rooms are smaller; the new-addition rooms are bigger. The two-story knotty pine lobby has a sweeping wood-railed staircase and a display of local wildlife mounts. An elevator accesses 2nd-story rooms. Amenities include a guest laundry, free continental breakfast, underground parking, and, new in 2015, an indoor heated pool, sauna, and fitness room.

West Yellowstone abounds with relic motels from the 1950s or earlier. Some offer good places to stay for those on a budget. The ★ **Alpine Motel** (120 Madison Ave., 406/646-7544, May-Oct., $65-175) has small rooms with one queen or king and rooms with two queens. Bathrooms are small, and the walls are thin. It has a reputation for friendly owners and cleanliness. A renovated motel from 1931, the **Evergreen Motel** (229 Firehole Ave., 406/646-7655, www.theevergreenmotel.com, year-round, $68-195) is a small single-story motel with 17 rooms that have a king, queen, or two queen log beds. A laundry is available, and a few rooms have kitchens or kitchenettes. Tiny **Pine Shadows Motel** (229 N. Hayden St., 406/646-7541 or 800/624-5291, www.pineshadowsmotel.com, year-round, $63-135) also has a reputation for cleanliness. The motel has four king rooms and four double-queen rooms. The complex also has an on-site laundry, outdoor picnic table with gas barbecues, and condos with 2-3 bedrooms. One mile from the park entrance, **Lazy G Motel** (123 Hayden St., 406/646-7586, http://lazygmotel.com, year-round, $92-135) has pine-walled single rooms, two-bedroom units, and kitchenettes (add $20/day) in single-story and two-story wings. Picnic tables with a gas grill are outdoors. Four blocks from the park, **One Horse Motel** (216 Dunraven St., 406/646-7677 or 800/488-2750, www.onehorsemotel.com, mid-May-Oct., $58-148) is a simple single-story motel with a homespun look to rooms. Laundry facilities are available.

CABINS

Cabins are common in West Yellowstone, from older minimalist log cabins to modern with frills. Instead of an out-in-the-woods ambience, the town cabins are clustered close together with views of streets. Cabins listed here are open year-round. Several of the campgrounds also have cabins in summer: Yellowstone Grizzly RV Park, Wagon Wheel RV Campground, Rustic Wagon RV Campground, and Yellowstone Cabins and RV Park.

The ★ **Explorer Cabins at Yellowstone** (DNC Parks and Resorts, 201 Grizzly Ave., 406/586-7593 or 877/600-4308, www.visityellowstonepark.com, $120-400) has 50 modern cabins with kitchenettes. Front porches have seating, although most view the road. Community fire pits provide places to roast the s'mores supplied at check-in. Different cabin configurations include king, queen, and bunk beds.

★ **Faithful Street Inn** (120 Faithful St., 406/646-1010, www.faithfulstreetinn.com, $135-700) has nine cabins, townhomes, and houses of different configurations with 2-8 bedrooms and full kitchens. Set on a less-traveled street, they sleep 2-18 people and have clean, well-kept, updated interiors, some with knotty pine walls. A minimum of 3-7 nights is required.

Yellowstone Wildlife Cabins (225 Geyser St., 406/646-7675, www.yellowstonewildlifecabins.com, $148-340) has six cabins with one or two bedrooms, full kitchens, and washers and dryers. A three-night minimum is required. A few of the cabins are manufactured homes.

Hibernation Station (212 Gray Wolf Ave., 406/646-4200 or 800/580-3557, www.hibernationstation.com, $112-325) tucks 50 modern single and duplex log cabins around a 27-foot-long bronze dueling bull elk statue and a 30-foot waterfall with bronze mountain goats and bighorn sheep. Nine styles of cabins come with varied combinations of doubles, queens, kings, and bunks. Some cabins have jet tubs, fireplaces, and kitchenettes. In winter, a four-night minimum is required, and minimal services are available.

With 1950s-style log cabins, **Moose Creek Inn** (220 Firehole Ave. for the cabins, 119 Electric St. for the inn and check-in, 406/646-9546, www.moosecreekinn.com, $78-225) has a mix of lodging. Four 450-square-foot log and knotty pine-walled cabins have one bath, two queen beds in separate rooms, and refrigerators and microwaves rather than kitchens. The two-story inn has a variety of hotel rooms including king, queen, two queens, two doubles, and three queens.

BED-AND-BREAKFAST

Located four miles outside town, **West Yellowstone Bed and Breakfast** (20 Crane Ln., 406/646-7754, www.westyellowstone-bandb.com, year-round, $138-185) has three rooms, each with fireplace and log furniture. Two rooms are for 3-4 people. Rates are for two people, with each extra person at $20. Hot breakfast is served from a menu, with special diets accommodated.

LODGE

With the original lodge dating from 1932 and several rebuilds from fires, **Three Bear Lodge** (217 Yellowstone Ave, 406/646-7353 or 800/646-7353, www.threebearlodge.com, year-round, $160-280) is a survivor. Exhibits in the lodge detail the history and use of reclaimed wood and local rocks in the remodels. Large lodge rooms, including two-room Goldilocks suites for families, have mountain west decor and handcrafted reclaimed wood furnishings. More economical rooms (king, two queens, or two-room suites) are in the older single-story motel. Amenities include an outdoor heated pool (summer only), hot tubs, business center, theater, and restaurant.

GUEST RANCHES

Guest ranches are one of the hallmarks of Montana. These two are located 6-18 miles outside of West Yellowstone, with breathing room and places to ride horses. On a 200-acre ranch, the **Bar N Ranch** (890 Buttermilk Rd., 406/646-0300, www.bar-n-ranch.com, mid-May-mid-Oct., $145-550) has accommodations in the 9,000-square-foot main log lodge or in cabins. On-site amenities include an outdoor heated pool, hot tub, and restaurant. The lodge has seven rooms, each with different bed configurations, decor, and jetted tubs. The log cabins have one or two bedrooms, wood-burning fireplaces, baths, and personal outdoor hot tubs. On an old homestead, **Parade Rest Guest Ranch** (1279 Grayling Rd., 406/646-7217 or 800/753-5934, http://paraderestranch.com, mid-May-Sept., $280/day adults, $95-225 children 5-11) is an all-inclusive program with lodging, three meals per day, horseback riding, fly-fishing, and western cookouts. Lodging is in 15 unique cabins with 1-4 bedrooms and private baths. The dining room serves meals made from scratch.

Camping

INSIDE THE PARK

Two campgrounds sit on the west side of Yellowstone. Madison is the closest to Old Faithful while Norris is closer to Mammoth and Grand Canyon of the Yellowstone. Both campgrounds have flush toilets, potable water, picnic tables, fire rings with grills, food storage boxes, tent pads (at some sites), firewood and ice sales, evening ranger programs (mid-June-mid-Sept.), accessible sites, and shared biker and hiker campsites ($7/person). No hookups are available. Reservations are accepted for Madison only.

Madison

At Madison Junction, below National Park Mountain, **Madison Campground** (307/344-7311 or 866/439-7375 for advance reservations, 307/344-7901 for same-day reservations, www.yellowstonenationalpark-lodges.com, early May-mid-Oct., $23) has 278 sites spread around 10 loops on a flat plain. For July-August, make reservations 6-9 months in advance. The Madison River flowing past the campground attracts anglers for iconic fly-fishing, and wildlife-watchers often spot bison and elk. In fall, you can hear elk bugling through the campground. At the campground's west end, G and H loops have 65 sunny sites for tents only. Some campsites can fit RVs up to 40 feet.

Norris

Across from Norris Geyser Basin at 7,555 feet elevation on Upper Grand Loop's southwest corner, **Norris Campground** (first-come, first-served, late May-late Sept., $20) has 100 sites spread around a steep hillside. Sites are limited for RVs over 30 feet. Loop A campsites are flatter and have views of surrounding meadows that often contain elk, bears, moose, or sandhill cranes. Bison often walk through campsites and bed down in the loop, too. Prime walk-in tent sites line up along

Solfatara Creek. Arrive by 9am in summer to claim a campsite. At the campground, the Museum of the National Park Ranger contains exhibits about early rangers. Hiking trails depart from the campground to Norris Geyser Basin, Ice Lake, and north along Solfatara Creek.

OUTSIDE THE PARK

For those requiring RV hookups, head to West Yellowstone, where private campgrounds have flush toilets, showers, potable water, wireless Internet, and hookups for water, electricity, sewer, and cable TV; most also have laundries. Reservations are a must for July-August.

West Yellowstone

Private campgrounds in West Yellowstone are surrounded by residential and commercial properties. From most, you can walk to restaurants, shopping, attractions, trailheads, fishing, the visitors center, and park entrance. Rates are for two people. Add $3-6 for each additional person.

The largest campground, **Yellowstone Grizzly RV** (210 S. Electric St., 406/646-4466, www.grizzlyrv.com, May-Oct., RVs $58-68, tents $43, extra people cost $5-10) has 261 RV campsites (limited to 80 feet) and 16 tent campsites. Bordered on two sides by Montana's Custer-Gallatin National Forest, the campground has landscaped gardens and lawns with aspens and lodgepole pines providing partial shade. The RV sites, with paved back-in or pull-through parking pads, cement walkways, and patios, are positioned right next to each other, but they are roomy enough for slide-outs and awnings. The tent campsites ring a grassy area across from the playground and clubhouse, which has outdoor kitchen sinks. Facilities include picnic tables, barbecue grills (bring your own charcoal), dog walk, game room, playground, convenience store, launderette, accessible facilities, and horseshoes. Between Rustic Wagon RV Campground (637 Hwy. 20, 406/646-7387, www.rusticwagonrv.com) and Wagon Wheel RV Campground (408 Gibbon Ave., 406/646-7872, www.wagonwheelrv.com), which sit two blocks apart, the campgrounds have 81 RV campsites and 25 tent sites (mid-May-Sept., RVs $48-53, tents $40). Located on the northwest corner of town, they are removed from the busy crowds and quieter. Cramped campsites tuck close together under spruce and pine trees that give some seclusion. Tents have grassy sites. Hideaway RV Park (320 Electric St., 406/646-9049, www.hideawayrv.com, early May-Sept., RVs $40-45, tents $28) has 14 RV campsites that can fit rigs up to 45 feet and one tent campsite.

Three campgrounds are for RVs only. The Pony Express RV Park (4 Firehole Ave., 406/646-9411 or 800/217-4613, www.yellowstonevacations.com, Apr.-Nov. full hookups, winter dry camping, $30-40) sits across the street from Yellowstone National Park with the West Entrance gate five blocks away. The 16 RV campsites squeeze close together in an open lot with a handful of trees dotting the campground with minimal shade. Located one mile from the park entrance, Yellowstone Cabins and RV Park (504 Hwy. 20, 406/646-9350 or 866/646-9350, www.yellowstonecabinsandrv.com, May-mid-Oct., $40) has seven gravel and grass campsites for RVs up to 38 feet. Conifers shade this campground, which is connected to a small cabin and motel complex. Buffalo Crossing RV Park (101B S. Canyon St., 406/646-4300, www.buffalocrossingrvpark.com, May-Oct., $35-55) tucks behind the Yellowstone Giant Screen Theater and Yellowstone Trading Post. The campground is a large gravel parking lot with a few small trees, with full hookups, showers, flush toilets, laundry, and a tiny pet walk area.

In the Vicinity

Several private campgrounds located outside West Yellowstone offer a quieter alternative to the bustle of town. Rates are for two people; add $4-6 for each additional person. In addition to full hookups, flush toilets, and wireless Internet, the campsites have picnic tables and some fire rings.

Seven miles outside town near the rodeo and trail rides, two large campgrounds are KOAs (late May-Sept., RVs $35-75, tents $25-41). Set in shady pine forests and sunny mowed lawns, the campgrounds have 343 RV campsites that can fit the largest rigs and 104 tent campsites, a few with electricity. The main campground, Yellowstone KOA (3305 Targhee Pass Hwy., 406/646-7606 or 800/562-7591, www.yellowstonekoa.com) has an indoor pool, hot tub, camping kitchen, pancake breakfasts, nightly barbecue dinners, espresso kiosk, mini-golf, playground, basketball, dog walk, game room, and surrey bike rentals. Located behind the Super 8, the Yellowstone KOA Mountainside (1545 Targhee Pass Hwy., 406/646-7662 or 800/562-5640, www.yellowstonekoamountainside.com) has grills, convenience store, playground, dog park, camping kitchen, and disposal station. Denny Creek flows past the back of the campground, with bridges accessing nature trails and constructed fishing ponds.

On the south shore of the Madison Arm of Hebgen Lake, 8.5 miles outside West Yellowstone, Madison Arm Resort (5475 Madison Arm Rd., 406/646-9328, www.madisonarmresort.com, mid-May-Sept., RVs $40-48, tents $30) has 22 tent and 52 RV campsites overlooking a sandy beach, buoyed swimming area, and marina tucked into a small bay. For boating, paddling, fishing, waterskiing, and sailing, this is the place to camp. The resort rents canoes, paddleboats, kayaks, water-bikes, and 14-foot aluminum boats with 8-horsepower motors.

In a broad field on Bar N Ranch, about six miles north of West Yellowstone, Yellowstone Under Canvas (890 Buttermilk Creek Rd., 406/219-0441, www.mtundercanvas.com, late May-early Sept., $95-425) has luxury camping in safari tents, tepees, and cabin-style luxury canvas tents. Standard tents have cots and floors; luxury tents include beds, furniture, and heat. Baths with hot water, showers, and flush toilets are in separate private facilities. Some bathrooms and showers are in tepees; others are individual rooms in trailers.

Forest Service Campgrounds

Three **Custer-Gallatin National Forest campgrounds** (Hebgen Lake Ranger District, 330 Gallatin Rd., West Yellowstone, 406/823-6961, www.fs.usda.gov/gallatin, mid-May-mid-Sept., $14-22 plus $6 extra vehicle) are near West Yellowstone. These work as backups when town campgrounds are full, and with their locations and recreation, they might be preferable. The campgrounds have picnic tables, fire rings with grills, vault and pit toilets, drinking water, bear boxes, firewood for sale, accessible campsites, and campground hosts.

Flanking the Madison River, **Baker's Hole Campground** sits three miles north of West Yellowstone, where the trout-fishing river slows to a crawl in convoluted oxbows through willow wetlands that provide habitat for moose, birds, and mosquitoes. It has 73 first-come, first-served campsites (33 with electrical hookups, 75-foot RV limit), some with river frontage.

Two campgrounds sit on Hebgen Lake, located about 10 miles from West Yellowstone. The campgrounds are equipped with boat launches, and the lake is popular for swimming, paddling, waterskiing, boating, and fishing. Both campgrounds take **reservations** (877/444-6777, www.recreation.gov). **Rainbow Point Campground** sits on an east arm of Hebgen Lake. Four loops contain 85 quiet campsites (15 with electrical hookups, 40-foot RV limit) tucked back from the lake in a thick shady forest of tall lodgepole pines. Big, flat spaces for tents are available. **Lonesomehurst Campground** sits on the South Fork Arm. Conifers dot the sunny, quiet campground with 27 campsites (five with electrical hookups, 45-foot RV limit) surrounded by arid grass and sagebrush meadows. Campsites along the east side of the one campground loop overlook the lake, and all campsites have territorial views of the Madison Range.

Food

INSIDE THE PARK

At Old Faithful, three lodges (Xanterra, 307/344-7311 or 866/439-7375, www.yellowstonenationalparklodges.com) contain restaurants. Their seasons of business coincide with when the lodges are open: all are open in summer, but only the Snow Lodge is open in winter. All lodges sell box lunches ($13), and casual attire is appropriate.

The two full-service restaurants are the dining room at Old Faithful Inn and Obsidian Room in the Snow Lodge. Both serve beer, wine, and cocktails. Varied menus can pacify light eaters, as well as those who want multi-course meals, and include vegan, vegetarian, and gluten-free options. Entrées incorporate local and regional sources, along with select fresh organic ingredients.

Egg whites instead of whole eggs are also available.

Old Faithful
OLD FAITHFUL INN

In the historic hotel, the ★ **Old Faithful Inn Dining Room** (daily mid-May-mid-Oct.) is an experience of ambience. The log dining room with its immense fireplace and woven twig chairs harkens back to another era. Breakfast (6:30am-10am, $6-11) serves up traditional egg and griddle dishes. You can custom-design several entrées, such as oatmeal and omelets, with toppings, fillings, and sides. Lunch (11:30am-2:30pm, $10-19) serves burgers, sandwiches, and salads. While breakfast and lunch are first-come, first-served, dinner requires reservations.

Without, one hour or longer waits for tables are common. Make reservations by phone or online up to a year in advance when booking lodging at the inn. Those not staying at the inn can make reservations 60 days in advance. The dinner menu (5pm-10pm, starts at 4:30pm summer, $10-30) mixes lighter options with heavier specialties such as bison pot roast, steak, pork osso bucco, pasta, fish, and quail. For faster meals that avoid the sometimes slow service, buffets are available at all three meals (breakfast and lunch $13-16 adults, $7-8 kids; dinner $29 adults, $11 kids). Lunch features a western buffet with trout, pulled pork, and barbecue-style sides, and dinner rolls out the prime rib.

The inn also has two other alternatives for lighter meals. You can get bison burgers, pub-style meals, and appetizers in the Bear Pit Lounge (11:30am-11pm). The Bear Paw Deli (6:30am-6pm) serves continental breakfast, salads, sandwiches, ice cream, and to-go items for hiking. Espresso is served on the 2nd-floor balcony overlooking the lobby.

The Old Faithful Basin Store (7:30am-8:30pm daily mid-May-late Sept., $6-10) is located in the historic Hamilton's Store, built in 1897 near Old Faithful Inn. The shop still retains its original marble fountain counter and serves ice cream. The café serves breakfast, lunch, and dinner with diner-style foods and kids' options, too.

OLD FAITHFUL LODGE

With its cafeteria and deck looking out at its namesake geyser, the Old Faithful Lodge (daily mid-May-early Oct.) is the place to go for light, quick meals, especially if you are waiting for Old Faithful to blow. You can even grab to-go sandwiches and claim your seat on the benches surrounding the geyser. The cafeteria (11am-9pm, closes at 8pm in fall, $8-14) serves hot or cold sub sandwiches, pasta, chili, and full dinners of meatloaf, trout, turkey, or chicken. The Bake Shop (6:30am-10pm, closes at 8pm in fall) serves snacks, beverages, and grab-and-go foods. The Ice Cream Shop serves ice cream spring-fall.

SNOW LODGE

The Snow Lodge (daily early May-mid-Oct. and mid-Dec.-early Mar.) has two places to eat and is the only option in winter. A more modern facility, the Obsidian Dining Room is decorated as a contemporary lodge with gas fireplaces and trendy western chandeliers. In summer, the restaurant serves only breakfast and dinner, but in winter, it serves all three meals. Breakfast (6:30am-10:30am, until 10am in winter, $6-13) has a specialty of smoked salmon eggs Benedict. A faster alternative, the breakfast buffet ($13 adults, $7 kids) is served in summer, and in winter only when the lodge reaches a certain capacity. Lunch (11:30am-3pm winter only, $10-15) has salads, burgers, sandwiches, and a few pasta entrées. For dinner (5pm-10:30pm, until 9:30pm in winter, $15-33), you can go lighter with salads and burgers, or with full entrées that include trout, prime rib, and a polenta fritter stacked with grilled vegetables and portobello mushrooms. For all meals, be prepared for leisurely dining as service is frequently slow. For lighter meals, the Geyser Grill (8am-9pm summer, shorter hours in shoulder seasons, 10:30am-3:30pm winter, $4-9) has burgers, sandwiches, soups and chili, fries, beer, and wine. Breakfast is served only in summer.

Old Faithful General Store (7:30am-8:30pm daily early May-mid-Oct., $4-10), located east of the Snow Lodge in a circa 1920 building with a large fireplace and log beams, has seated food service: personal pizzas, soups and chili, hot and cold sandwiches, salads, and ice cream.

Groceries

For picking up a forgotten item or two and putting together lunches for hiking, you can get a few supplies at the two stores in Old Faithful (DNC Parks and Resorts, 406/586-7593, www.visityellowstonepark.com): Old Faithful Basin Store (7:30am-9:30pm mid-May-late Sept.), located in the historic Hamilton's Store, and Old Faithful General Store (7:30am-9:30pm daily early May-mid-Oct.), located east of the Snow Lodge. For a full-size grocery, head to West Yellowstone.

Picnicking

Between West Yellowstone, Old Faithful, and Norris, plenty of picnic areas offer places to eat an alfresco meal. Most are equipped with picnic tables and accessible restroom facilities that are sometimes vault toilets rather than flushers. Find picnic areas at the Madison River and Madison Junction, along the West Entrance Road. On Grand Loop Road between Norris and Madison Junctions, picnic spots are at Norris Meadows, Virginia Cascade, Gibbon Meadows, Caldera Rim, Iron Spring, Gibbon Falls, and Tuff Cliff. Between Madison and the Continental Divide east of Old Faithful, look for them at Firehole River, Nez Perce, Whiskey Flat, East Lot, Spring Creek, and DeLacy Creek. The only picnic areas that permit fires are Nez Perce, Whiskey Flat, Spring Creek, and Norris Meadows.

OUTSIDE THE PARK
West Yellowstone

For a small town, West Yellowstone packs in nearly 40 restaurants with mainstays being pizza, burger, and barbecue joints. It is also a tourist town that sees huge crowds in summer, so expect waiting lines at restaurants. About half the restaurants close in winter; those that stay open shorten hours in the off-seasons, and some take a few weeks off in early spring and early December. Many restaurants sell to-go lunches ($10).

CAFES

Woodside Bakery (17 Madison Ave., 406/646-7779, www.woodsidebakery.net, 7am-4pm Mon.-Sat. mid-May-Sept., $3-10) is a place to grab fresh-baked breakfast goodies to snack on while driving into the park or to-go sandwiches for hiking. You can also dine in. The roundup of fresh-from-the-oven sweets includes cookies, cupcakes, breads, cinnamon rolls, brownies, and pies. Espresso West (10 Canyon St., 406/646-0829, 7am-9pm daily early May-late Sept.) does it all: lattes, mochas, cappuccinos, iced drinks, ice cream, and milkshakes.

AMERICAN

A family restaurant now run by the second generation, Running Bear Pancake House (538 Madison Ave., 406/646-7703, http://runningbearph.com, 6am-2pm daily year-round, $7-12) keeps the griddle going with pancakes, either buttermilk or buckwheat, and omelets. Specialty French toast is made from apple-pecan and other sweet breads. The lunch menu (11am-2pm) includes burgers, sandwiches, salads. Espresso with that breakfast? You bet. Beartooth Barbecue (111 N. Canyon St., 406/646-0227, 11am-10pm daily year-round, $11-30) has draft local beers, pulled pork sammies, brisket, ribs, cheese grits, fried pickles, jalapeño poppers with huckleberry sauce, and traditional barbecue sides.

LATIN

Bringing Spain to Montana, the small ★ Café Madriz (311 N. Canyon St., 406/646-9245, 11am-2pm and 5pm-9pm Mon.-Sat. May-Sept, $10-22) serves lunches and dinners of made-from-scratch Spanish foods including the house sangria from chef-owner Elena deDiego. Have bocadillos for lunch in or to go for a picnic. Dinners feature hot and cold tapas, paella, and Chorizo al Inferno. For a local fave, squeeze into the Taco Bus for authentic Mexican food from Taqueria Las Palmas (21 N. Canyon St., 406/640-1822, 10:30am-10:30pm daily Apr.-Oct., $8-12). Eat at the old white-painted school bus with seating mostly outside on picnic tables, or get takeout to go back to your motel or campsite. The huge menu has traditional choices of meat or vegetarian standards of tacos, enchiladas, quesadillas, carne asada, fajitas, and burritos.

PIZZA

★ Wild West Pizzeria and Saloon (14 Madison Ave., 406/646-4400 or 406/646-7259, http://wildwestpizza.com, 11am-midnight daily year-round, $12-24) relies on Wheat Montana flour for its pizza dough and fresh ingredients for toppings. Pizzas come in menu-recommended combinations, or create your own. Pasta and sandwiches also are available, as well as wine and beer. They deliver, too. The saloon has gambling machines and frequent live music with dancing. Music starts around 8pm with a $3 cover charge. **Pete's Rocky Mountain Pizza and Pasta Company** (112 Canyon St., 406/646-7820, http://petespizzapasta.com, 11am-10pm daily year-round, $11-26) serves up create-your-own-style pizzas or Pete's designs. Lunch adds pasta and sandwiches. Dinner expands the pasta menu with lasagna, elk sausage spaghetti, and bison ravioli. Beer, wine, and Italian sodas are available. After 5pm, you can get pizza delivered to your campsite or motel.

SALOONS

After seeing bison in the park, head to the ★ **Buffalo Bar** (335 Hwy. 20, 406/646-1176, http://thebuffalobar.com, 10am-2pm daily year-round, $10-33), where the broad menu dishes up bison in many forms: nachos, tacos, burritos, burgers, chili, and meatloaf. You can also get western appetizers such as Rocky Mountain oysters and wild game sausage. The bar has Montana craft beers, wine, and cocktails. It serves breakfast until 4pm. Portions are big. It also has outdoor seating in summer, live poker on weekends, sports on big-screen TVs, pool, and a little casino action. On the main drag, the **Slippery Otter Pub** (139 Canyon St., 406/646-7050, 11:30am-9pm daily year-round, $10-30) serves pizza, salads, burgers, beer-battered cod and chips, and, on Friday and Saturday nights, prime rib. The elk burger can be prepped with a gluten-free bun. The pub has a broad beer and wine selection and kids' menu, too.

FINE DINING

With a cozy dining room, ★ **Serenity Bistro** (38 N. Canyon St., 406/646-7660, www.serenitybistro.com, 11am-3pm and 5pm-10pm daily year-round, $13-38) expands with patio seating in summer. Soups, salads, sandwiches, burgers, and wraps make up the lunch menu. Dinner plates Montana cuisine: rib eye,

elk tenderloin, quail, and pasta with suggested wine pairings. The menu has gluten-free and vegetarian options with vegan possible with prior notice. With extensive tapas, the menu is more conducive to ordering multiple small plates. You'll need to drive about six miles north of town to reach the **Bar N Ranch** (890 Buttermilk Creek Rd., 406/646/9445, www.bar-n-ranch.com, 5pm-10pm daily mid-May-Sept., $24-42) to dine in its upscale stone-and-log ranch house with mountain west decor and wildlife mounts. The restaurant specializes in steaks, bison, wild game, and fish accompanied by a worldwide wine list, Montana microbrews, and traditional cocktails. Located in the old first grade classroom of the 1918 West Yellowstone school, the **Madison Crossing Lounge** (121 Madison Ave., 406/646/7621, www.madisoncrossinglounge.com, 5pm-10pm daily May-Oct. and mid-Dec.-mid Mar., $13-26) serves up contemporary steaks, fish, burgers, chicken, and pasta. Regional microbrews, worldwide wines, whiskey, and specialty cocktails add to the ambience. Appetizers include bison nachos.

DESSERT

The log **Eagle's Store** (3 N. Canyon St., 406/646-9300, www.eagles-store.com), built in 1927 and listed on the National Register of Historic Places, serves ice cream from its old-fashioned soda fountain with some of the original leather stools and historical tiled counter and back bar. **City Creamery** (105 N. Canyon St., 406/843-5515) has homemade ice cream with rotating flavors, including huckleberry.

GROCERIES

West Yellowstone has two grocery stores for stocking up RVs or just putting a cooler together. Prices may be a little higher than your local big city market. The **Market Place** (22 Madison Ave., 406/646-9600, 7am-10pm daily year-round) has takeout foods, a deli, produce, meats, and a liquor store, too. The **Food Roundup Supermarket** (107 Dunraven St., 406/646-7501, 7am-10pm daily year-round) is a little larger grocery.

Transportation and Services

DRIVING

Only two-lane roads tour this area of Montana and Wyoming. Inside and outside the park, roads cut through wildlife habitat. Be on the lookout for deer, antelope, elk, and other wildlife wandering out onto the road.

The West Entrance is 14 miles from Madison Junction. The road from Madison Junction to Norris Junction is 14 miles northwest. From Madison Junction to Old Faithful, the drive is 16 miles south. Driving each of these roads can take 35-45 minutes due to wildlife jams and traffic. These roads close early November to mid-April.

Parking

At many of the geyser basins, parking lots restrict entry of RVs, buses, and trailers. This is due to small, tight parking spaces, sharp corners, and lack of turnaround area. You may need to park elsewhere and hike to access the geyser basin.

OLD FAITHFUL

Driving into Old Faithful can be confusing, as one-way roads enter and depart the complex. Look for signage at junctions. For overnight visitors staying at lodges, check in first and park where the front desk directs. For day visitors, two giant parking lots are available, both equal distance from Old Faithful Geyser. They pack out in summer; row signs will help you remember where you parked. The smaller parking lot is southwest of the visitors center in between Snow Lodge and Old Faithful Inn. The other parking lot is southwest of Old Faithful Lodge. To see Old Faithful Geyser, you must walk about five minutes or so from the parking lots, as no road passes by it. RVs are not permitted to park overnight in the lots.

WEST YELLOWSTONE

Streetside parking in West Yellowstone is crowded in summer. Rather than drive from your West Yellowstone lodging to the shopping and restaurant streets, plan to walk from your lodging or campground. RVs can find parking along Boundary Street and at the West Yellowstone Visitor Information Center on the corner of Yellowstone Avenue and Canyon Street. Hidden in the middle of four blocks are parking lots. They are difficult to see because they are surrounded by commercial businesses. Find the entrances to these parking lots on Boundary, Canyon, and Dunraven Streets between Firehole, Madison, and Yellowstone Avenues. In winter, be aware that snowmobiles are street legal on all streets except Canyon and the highways.

Car Rental

Rent cars in West Yellowstone from Big Sky Car Rentals (415 Yellowstone Ave., 406/646-9564 or 800/426-7669, http://yellowstonevacations.com). Budget Car Rental (406/646-5156, www.budget.com) has a desk in the Yellowstone Airport and an office in West Yellowstone (131 Dunraven St., 406/646-7882 or 800/231-5991, http://budget-yellowstone.com).

AIR

The Yellowstone Airport (WYS, 607 Airport Rd., West Yellowstone, 406/646-7631, www.yellowstoneairport.org) operates just outside of West Yellowstone in summer only. You can fly in and be at Old Faithful within a couple of hours. The airport is serviced only by Delta Air Lines from Salt Lake City (two flights daily weekdays, three flights daily weekends June-Sept.).

SHUTTLES

Based in West Yellowstone, Yellowstone Road Runner (406/640-0631, http://yellowstoneroadrunner.com) operates a year-round taxi and van service to airports (West Yellowstone, Bozeman, Jackson Hole, and

Where Can I Find . . .?

- **Banks and ATMs:** ATMs are available in park lodges and at First Security Bank (106 S. Electric St., West Yellowstone, 406/646-7646).

- **Cell Service:** Verizon service is available in Old Faithful and West Yellowstone. There is no cell service in Madison or Norris.

- **Gas and Garage Services:** A gas station is located at Old Faithful (late Apr.-late Oct.). You can pay at the pump 24 hours with a credit card. West Yellowstone has gas auto services.

- **Internet Service:** In the park, Wi-Fi is available for hotel guests only at Snow Lodge at Old Faithful.

- **Laundry:** A coin-op laundry is available in Snow Lodge (May-Oct.). In West Yellowstone, coin-op machines are available at Swan Cleaners and Laundromat (520 Madison Ave., 406/646-7892) and Canyon Street Laundromat (312 N. Canyon St., 406/646-7220).

- **Post Office:** A post office is located at Old Faithful (1000 Old Faithful, 307/545-7252, 8:30am-12:30pm and 1:30pm-5pm Mon.-Fri. early May-late Oct.) and in West Yellowstone (209 Grizzly Ave., 406/646-7704, 8:30am-5pm Mon.-Fri.).

- **Showers:** Pay showers are available at Old Faithful Inn (May-Oct.) and at Canyon Street Laundromat (312 N. Canyon St., 406/646-7220).

Idaho Falls), campgrounds, and trailheads in Yellowstone. Their vehicles have bike racks.

EMERGENCY SERVICES

In an emergency, stop at the ranger station at Old Faithful (staffed daily). In West Yellowstone, the **Hebgen Lake Ranger District Station** (330 Gallatin Rd., 406/823-6961) is staffed weekdays only. For medical emergencies, drop in to the **Old Faithful Clinic** (Old Faithful Ranger Station, 307/545-7325, 7am-7pm summer).

Until the West Yellowstone Medical Center is constructed, the **West Yellowstone Clinic** (11 S. Electric St., 406/646-9441, Tues.-Fri., call for hours) provides the only medical service. The nearest hospitals are about 100 miles away: **Bozeman Deaconess Hospital** (915 Highland Blvd., Bozeman, MT, 406/585-5000, www.bozemandeaconess.org) and **Eastern Idaho Regional Medical Center** (3100 Channing Way, Idaho Falls, ID, 208/529-6111, http://eirmc.com).

Canyon and Lake Country

Highlights

★ **Canyon Visitor Education Center:**
See murals, computer-generated exhibits, films,
and a huge relief model of the park illustrating
the geologic history of Yellowstone's supervolcano (page 129).

★ **Grand Canyon of the Yellowstone:**
From Artist Point, view the thunderous Upper
and Lower Falls as they plummet through the
colorful canyon (page 133).

★ **Fishing Bridge:** Watch cutthroat trout
spawn and perhaps see bears fishing from the
shore (page 136).

★ **Yellowstone Lake:** The largest freshwater lake above 7,000 feet in North America is an
immense body of water (page 136).

★ **West Thumb Geyser Basin:** This geyser
basin contains steaming hot pools and yields
views across Yellowstone Lake to the Absaroka
Mountains (page 138).

★ **Lewis Lake:** Yellowstone's third-largest
lake is a favorite for boaters, paddlers, and
anglers, with access to remote Shoshone Lake
(page 138).

★ **Mt. Washburn:** Topping out at 10,243
feet, Mt. Washburn is one of the highest peaks in
Yellowstone (page 141).

★ **South Rim Trail to Point Sublime:** Get
ready for more than 300 stair steps, the closest

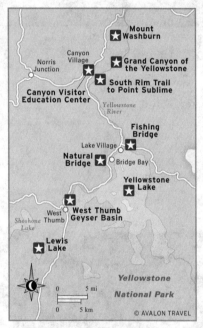

view of the Lower Falls, and unique canyon views
(page 147).

★ **Natural Bridge:** This 1.3-mile forested trail
leads to a natural rhyolite bridge of rock spanning
a canyon (page 150).

S culpted by a glacier, water, earth-quakes, and wind, the Grand Canyon of the Yellowstone is one of the park's most striking features.

Prominent points allow visitors to gape down to the Yellowstone River far below and the Upper and Lower Falls plunging over their precipices. Trails with steep stairways climb down to platforms for viewing. At Brink of the Lower Falls, you can feel the pounding of the water.

Upstream at 7,732 feet, Yellowstone Lake is the largest freshwater, high-elevation lake in North America. Rimmed with a handful of steaming thermals, the lake holds islands and remote bays that offer boaters, canoers, and kayakers plenty of places for solitude. Native cutthroat and introduced lake trout appeal to sport anglers. Miles and miles of shoreline give visitors scenic drives and places to enjoy the water, but be prepared for frigid temperatures.

In addition to the canyon and lake, the area contains several other remarkable ecosystems. Mt. Washburn, one of the highest mountains in the park, is flanked with trails for hikers. For wildlife-watchers, Hayden Valley proliferates with bison, elk, trumpeter swans, and grizzly bears. Lewis Lake offers a quiet trout fishery and paddler paradise to reach Shoshone Lake.

Most of the visitor services concentrate in Canyon, Fishing Bridge, Bridge Bay, Lake, and Grant Villages, with additional campgrounds sprinkled throughout the area. Visitors to canyon and lake country get to discover a diverse landscape shaped by the powers of the earth.

PLANNING YOUR TIME

Starting the third week in April, you can drive into Canyon via Norris, West Yellowstone, and Mammoth. In early May, East and South Entrance roads open for access to Canyon and Yellowstone Lake. Dunraven Pass and Craig Pass open in late May, with heavy snow years sometimes posing delays. In summer, Canyon overlook parking lots crowd with cars and tour buses between 10am and 4pm, and parking lot restrooms will have long waiting lines.

All visitor facilities, including visitors centers, restaurants, lodges, and campgrounds,

---

Previous: Yellowstone Lake from Lake Butte; Lower Falls in the Grand Canyon of the Yellowstone.
Above: Gull Point.

Canyon and Lake Country

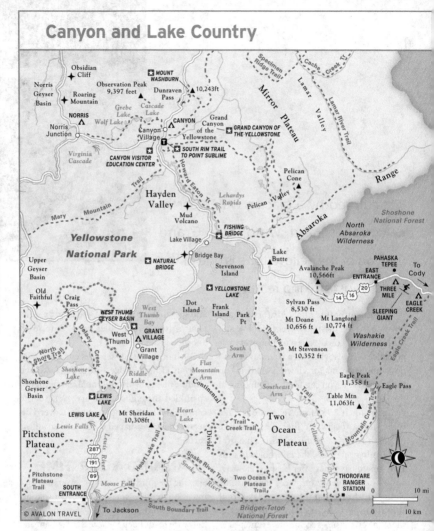

are fully operational **June-early September.** A handful start the summer season in mid-May and linger into **early October.** In fall, Dunraven Pass closes in mid-October for the winter. All other roads close for the season in **early November.**

In winter, no lodging, restaurants, or facilities are open at Canyon or Yellowstone Lake.

Mid-December-mid-March, visitors can tour the region on snowcoach, snowmobile, or skis. Warming huts with minimal services are in the Canyon Visitor Education Center lobby, Fishing Bridge, and West Thumb. Tours originate in Mammoth, West Yellowstone, Old Faithful, or Flagg Ranch/Headwaters.

Exploring Canyon and Lake Country

VISITORS CENTERS
★ Canyon Visitor Education Center

The **Canyon Visitor Education Center** (307/344-2550, www.nps.gov/yell, 8am-8pm daily late May-mid-Oct., shorter hours in fall) is located in Canyon Village. Interactive exhibits explore the powerful geologic forces of fire and ice that created Yellowstone's supervolcano, with films, murals, and photos that bring it to life. Other exhibits include a huge relief model of the park that traces its geologic history, a 9,000-pound rotating kugel ball that shows volcanic hotspots around the globe, and one of the world's largest lava lamps to show how magma works. You can even check the strength of the current earthquakes resounding underground. The visitors center also contains a **backcountry office** (8am-4:30pm daily June-Aug.). A **Yellowstone Association Bookstore** (406/848-2400, www.yellowstoneassociation.org) sells books, field guides, and maps.

Fishing Bridge Museum and Visitor Center

Located on the north end of Yellowstone Lake, the log-and-stone **Fishing Bridge Museum and Visitor Center** (307/344-2450, www.nps.gov/yell, 8am-7pm daily late May-Sept.) tucks into the trees on the East Entrance Road, less than one mile from the historic Fishing Bridge. Built in 1931, the small museum is now a National Historic Landmark and contains bird and waterfowl specimens as well as other wildlife. There is an outdoor amphitheater for naturalist presentations and a **Yellowstone Association Bookstore** (406/848-2400, www.yellowstoneassociation.org) on-site.

West Thumb Information Center

Located on the west thumb of Yellowstone Lake, the **West Thumb Information Center** (307/344-2650, www.nps.gov/yell, 8am-5pm daily late May-Sept.) is a log

Canyon Visitor Education Center

building with exhibits on the West Thumb Geyser Basin. This is where you can ask about the 100-foot-high bulge growing on the floor of Yellowstone Lake due to activity from faults and hot springs. A **Yellowstone Association Bookstore** (406/848-2400, www.yellowstoneassociation.org) is on-site.

Grant Visitor Center

Just south of West Thumb in Grant Village, the **Grant Visitor Center** (307/344-2650, www.nps.gov/yell, 8am-7pm daily late May-Sept.) is the place for information about the 1988 Yellowstone fires, the largest in the park's history. Exhibits and a movie detail the role of fire in the park. A **Yellowstone Association Bookstore** (406/848-2400, www.yellowstoneassociation.org) is on-site.

ENTRANCE STATIONS

Two **entrance stations** ($30/vehicle, $25 motorcycles, $15 hike-in/bike-in; joint parks pass: $50/vehicle, $40 motorcycles, $20 hike-in/bike-in) provide access to the Lake Yellowstone region; they are 70 miles apart. The entrance roads into the park are generally open spring-fall; winter access (mid-Dec.-early Mar.) is only via snowmobile at both entrances or by snowcoach from the south at Flagg Ranch outside the park boundary.

The **South Entrance** (mid-May-early Nov.) is located on U.S. Highway 89/191/287 south of Lewis Lake at the boundary between Yellowstone and Grand Teton National Parks. If entering the park from Grand Teton, you will drive through this entrance. The closest park hub is West Thumb, 22 miles north; the Old Faithful area is 17 miles farther west. The road is closed to vehicles November -mid-May.

The **East Entrance** (late May-early Nov.) sits on the east side of Sylvan Pass on U.S. Highway 20, the road between Fishing Bridge and Cody, Wyoming (53 miles away). From the East Entrance, it is 27 miles to Lake Yellowstone and Fishing Bridge.

TOURS

A variety of tours launch from Canyon Village and Yellowstone Lake locales. Some departure and return times vary seasonally based on daylight hours. **Reservations** (Xanterra, 307/344-7311 or 866/439-7375, www.yellowstonenationalparklodges.com, daily late May-late Sept.) can be made while booking accommodations.

Bus Tours

Rebuilt 1930s yellow touring sedans help visitors cruise the park in historic style. The evening **Yellowstone Lake Butte Sunset Tour** (two hours, daily June-mid-Sept., $35 adults, $18 children) departs from Lake Hotel and Fishing Bridge RV Park to watch the sunset from the 8,348-foot summit of Lake Butte.

Other tours travel via vans or sightseeing buses. The full-day **Circle of Fire** (eight hours, daily mid-June-early Sept., $75 adults, $38 children) tour cruises the lower loop of Grand Loop Road to take in the biggies: Old Faithful, Yellowstone Lake, Hayden Valley, Grand Canyon of the Yellowstone, and Fountain Paint Pots. Tours pick up from Canyon Village, Fishing Bridge RV Park, Lake Hotel, Bridge Bay Campground, and Grant Village.

Picture Perfect Photo Safaris (five hours, daily mid-May-Sept., $90 adults, $45 children) depart around sunrise from Lake Hotel to tour Hayden Valley and the Grand Canyon of the Yellowstone. The tour helps amateur and professional photographers get the cool shots, and instruction is offered for beginning photographers.

Boat Tours

One of the best ways to experience Yellowstone Lake is on the water. The **Yellowstone Lake Scenic Cruise** (one hour, several times daily mid-June-mid-Sept., $15 adults, $10 children) departs from Bridge Bay Marina on the *Lake Queen* to circle Stevenson Island. The interpretive tour fills you in on the lake's history, geology, and natural history, and you may see osprey, eagles, ducks, herons, and other shorebirds. The enclosed boat also shelters passengers from the strong afternoon lake winds. Reservations are not required but can be made in advance online and are highly recommended midsummer. Guests should arrive at the marina at least 15 minutes prior to departure.

Wildlife Tours

Two tours use historic yellow touring sedans for wildlife watching. The **Wake Up to Wildlife** (6:15am-11:30am daily late May-mid-Sept., $83 adults, $42 children) tour departs from Canyon Village to explore the Lamar Valley. **Evening Wildlife Encounters** (four hours, daily June-mid-Sept., $61 adults, $31 children) departs from Canyon Village in the late afternoon for a ride to Dunraven Pass, Tower Fall, and the Tower Junction sagebrush flats for wildlife-watching.

The **Lamar Valley Wildlife Excursion** (one hour, times vary daily June-Aug.) vans or sightseeing buses depart in the afternoon from Canyon ($44 adults, $22 children) or from Fishing Bridge RV Park, Lake Hotel, and Bridge Bay Campground ($70 adults, $35 children) in the Lake Yellowstone area for an evening in Lamar Valley.

Winter Snowcoach Tours

Winter Snowcoach Tours (Xanterra, 307/344-7311 or 866/439-7375, www.yellowstonenationalparklodges.com, mid-Dec.-Feb., $167-300 adults, $84-150 children 3-11) of the Grand Canyon of the Yellowstone depart from the Old Faithful Snow Lodge and from Mammoth Hot Springs. Ski and snowshoe tours depart from Old Faithful.

DRIVING TOURS
South Entrance Road
22 MILES

The **South Entrance Road** (mid-May-early Nov.) travels from West Thumb to the South Entrance of Yellowstone. The road climbs to **Lewis Lake** and **Lewis Falls** to follow the **Lewis River** to its confluence with the Snake River at the park border.

East Entrance Road
27 MILES

The **East Entrance Road** (late-May-early Nov.) tours along the north shore of **Yellowstone Lake** between Fishing Bridge and the East Entrance Station. At Sedge Bay, the road passes **Steamboat Point,** a collection of steaming, noisy fumaroles. On a paved side spur, the one-mile **Lake Butte Road** (no RVs or trailers) climbs through the 2002 forest fire zone to **Lake Butte Overlook** at 8,348 feet, where you can look down on Steamboat Point and Yellowstone Lake, and view the Teton Mountains in the distance. Thick lupine flanks the road as it climbs past **Sylvan and Eleanor Lakes** to the rocky **Sylvan Pass** at 8,530 feet. From there, it plummets to the East Entrance Station (use second gear to avoid burning your brakes).

West Thumb to Old Faithful
17 MILES

From West Thumb, the Grand Loop Road heads west to take you twice over the **Continental Divide,** the highest point at 8,391 feet. The route continues west through lodgepole pine and spruce forests. **Isa Lake,** located at **Craig Pass,** has the unique status of flowing toward both the Pacific Ocean and Gulf of Mexico. After Craig Pass, the road descends before descending into the **Upper Geyser Basin.**

West Thumb to Lake Village
21 MILES

From West Thumb, the Grand Loop Road tours north along **Yellowstone Lake.** South of Bridge Bay on Yellowstone Lake, look for a spur for **Gull Point Drive** (2.1 miles), a scenic drive through conifers to the **Gull Point Picnic Area** on the lake. A long sandbar extends out into the lake at Gull Point, accessible from the picnic area; however, high water can close the drive in late May and June. Continuing north, the road passes the trailhead to **Natural Bridge** and the campground at Bridge Bay just before hitting the park hub at Lake Village. There are plenty of **picnic** areas and pullouts that offer places to enjoy the lake, but be prepared for wind.

Lake Village to Canyon Village
17 MILES

The Grand Loop Road travels north from Lake Village to tour the ultra-scenic **Hayden Valley** with the meandering **Yellowstone River** and the smelly, volcanic features of **Mud Volcano** and **Sulphur Cauldron.** The valley usually has scads of **wildlife:** bison, elk, deer, and sometimes bears or wolves. (For the best chance at seeing wildlife, drive Hayden Valley in early morning or at dusk.) The park hub of **Canyon Village** appears to the right; to the left, a junction offers access to Norris and the west side of the park.

Canyon Village to Tower Junction
19 MILES

North of Canyon Village, the Grand Loop Road climbs five miles to **Dunraven Pass,** where you can get territorial views off either side of the pass. South of the pass, you'll nab a view of the lookout on the summit of **Mt. Washburn.** (The descent from the pass is a 6-7 percent grade; shift into second gear to avoid burning your brakes.) North of the pass, the road descends to **Tower Fall, Calcite Springs,** and **Tower Junction.**

Grand Canyon of the Yellowstone

Two short drives off Grand Loop Road offer unique views of Grand Canyon of the Yellowstone, plus access to trailheads. For the scenery, you must get out of the car to walk to viewpoints, as the canyon is not visible from the road. Expect crowds, traffic congestion, and restroom lines in summer.

The **North Rim Drive** (2.1 miles) turns east 1.2 miles south of Canyon Junction to

glacial boulder on the road to Inspiration Point

reach overlooks at **Lookout Point, Grand View,** and **Inspiration Point.** Longer paved switchback trails and stairs lead to close-up viewpoints from **Brink of the Lower Falls** and **Red Rock Point.** To find **Inspiration Point,** turn right at 1.3 miles onto a two-way spur that passes **Glacial Boulder,** an erratic deposited by giant glaciers from the Beartooth Mountains.

Find **South Rim Drive** (1.7 miles) 1.1 miles south of the North Rim Drive turn-off. On this two-way road, the first left turn goes to overlooks of **Upper Falls** and **Uncle Tom's Point,** plus **Uncle Tom's Trail,** which drops 500 feet on steep steel steps to see the Lower Falls. The less strenuous overlook at **Artist Point** sits at the road's terminus.

Sights

CANYON VILLAGE

Located at the junction of park roads connecting the east and west sides of Yellowstone is the park hub of Canyon Village. Canyon is 19 miles south of Tower Junction and 16 miles north of Yellowstone Lake (a 45-minute drive each way). Expect slow going through Hayden Valley, where frequent wildlife jams stall traffic. From Canyon, the Norris-Canyon Road leads west for 12 miles (about 30 minutes) to the Norris area.

Dunraven Pass and Mt. Washburn

Located on the Grand Loop Road between Tower-Roosevelt and Canyon Village, 8,859-foot **Dunraven Pass** is the highest drive-to point in Yellowstone. Those coming from sea level will feel sluggish and short of breath just stepping a few feet from the car at scenic pullouts. The pass crosses the Washburn Range right at the base of **Mt. Washburn.** But to reach the 10,243-foot summit of Mt. Washburn and the lookout, you must climb. You can walk three miles up the old roadbed on the south side of the peak from Dunraven Pass Picnic Area or drive up Chittenden Road to the trailhead to attack the 2.7-mile ascent via bike or foot to the summit. From the lookout, you might see the Tetons on a clear day.

★ Grand Canyon of the Yellowstone

The iconic, 20-mile-long **Grand Canyon of the Yellowstone** has been made famous in paintings and photographs. The **Yellowstone River** cuts a colorful swath 1,000 feet deep and 0.75-mile wide through the landscape. The river plunges over the 109-foot **Upper Falls** before thundering down the 308-foot **Lower Falls,** the tallest falls in the park and the most famous. Trails with multiple overlooks flank the North and South Rims, as do roads.

Be aware: You are at 8,000 feet in elevation. While most stops have overlooks with short and easy paved routes, all descents to these overlooks require strenuous climbs back up. Prepare for crowds, as tour buses disgorge swarms of visitors. Go in the early morning or evening for fewer people, as parking lots are congested in summer 10am-5pm. Pick up a trail guide ($1) at visitors centers.

NORTH RIM

From the North Rim, trails descend to the brinks of both falls, where you can feel the pounding of the water in your feet. Access the **Brink of the Upper Falls** from the signed road off Grand View Loop; the turnoff is on the east side of the road 0.4 mile south of the turnoff for North Rim Drive. The overlook has a wheelchair-accessible portion, plus stairs that descend to the actual brink.

The first stop after turning east onto **North Rim Drive** (one-way) is the **Brink of the Lower Falls,** which thunders with almost 40,000 gallons of water per second. A paved switchback trail descends 600 feet to the lip, where you'll feel the pounding water underfoot. Back on the drive, a second signed stop leads to **Lookout Point,** a short 25-foot ascent to where you can view the Lower Falls, the canyon, and an osprey nest. Rangers sometimes set up a spotting scope to watch the nest in early summer. From this stop, the trail drops slightly west to **Red Rock Point,** a 0.4-mile switchback-and-boardwalk stair descent of 500 feet to a perch facing Lower Falls. The third signed stop on North Rim Drive is for **Grand View,** with a 150-foot paved descent to the overlook. Near the end of North Rim Drive, turn right onto the two-lane road to reach **Inspiration Point** for the more distant, but striking view of the canyon and Lower Falls.

SOUTH RIM

From the South Rim, two main parking areas have viewpoints; the South Rim Trail runs

Grand Canyon of the Yellowstone

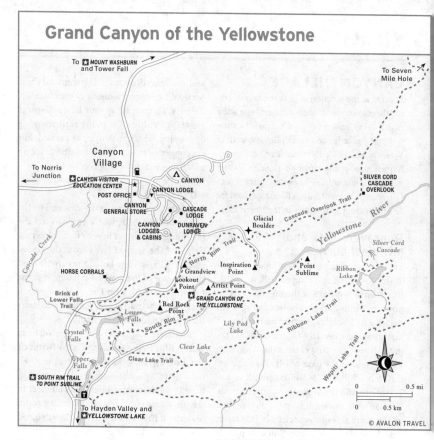

To ★ MOUNT WASHBURN
and Tower Fall

To Seven
Mile Hole

To Norris
Junction

Canyon
Village

★ CANYON VISITOR
EDUCATION CENTER

POST OFFICE

CANYON
GENERAL STORE

CANYON
LODGES
& CABINS

HORSE CORRALS

Brink of
Lower Falls
Trail

Crystal
Falls

Upper
Falls

★ SOUTH RIM TRAIL
TO POINT SUBLIME

To Hayden Valley and
★ YELLOWSTONE LAKE

CANYON

CANYON LODGE

CASCADE
LODGE

DUNRAVEN
LODGE

North Rim Trail

Grandview
Point

Lookout
Point

Artist Point

Red Rock
Point

Lower
Falls

South Rim Tr.

Clear Lake Trail

Clear Lake

Lily Pad
Lake

Inspiration
Point

★ GRAND CANYON OF
THE YELLOWSTONE

Glacial
Boulder

Cascade Overlook Trail

Yellowstone River

SILVER CORD
CASCADE
OVERLOOK

Silver Cord
Cascade

Point
Sublime

Ribbon
Lake

Ribbon Lake Trail

Wapiti Lake Trail

Cascade Creek

0   0.5 mi

0   0.5 km

© AVALON TRAVEL

between them and adds on other viewpoints of the Yellowstone River and canyon.

From the Grand Loop Road, turn east onto South Rim Drive and cross the Chittenden Bridge. The first stop is **Uncle Tom's Point,** on the left. Park and follow the easy walk to the **Upper Falls viewpoint.** The most difficult walk, **Uncle Tom's Trail,** drops 500 feet on paved switchbacks and 328 metal stairs to a platform directly in front of the Lower Falls for the closest overlook. The South Rim road terminates at the parking lot for **Artist Point,** with an easy, paved walk to the classic view of the canyon and Lower Falls. Those looking to broaden their canyon experience can add on a hike to **Point Sublime,** a trail with multiple exposed viewpoints of the ultra-colorful section of the canyon.

HAYDEN VALLEY

The park road south from Canyon to Yellowstone Lake runs 16 scenic miles through **Hayden Valley.** Occupying almost 50 square miles, Hayden Valley once held an arm of Yellowstone Lake. Today, it contains prime **wildlife-watching** between Yellowstone Lake and Grand Canyon of the Yellowstone, where bison jams are common. Look for coyotes, moose, bison, elk, raptors, grizzly bears, trumpeter swans, wolves, and hordes of Canada geese. The **Yellowstone River** meanders through the sagebrush and grass valley, giving it a bucolic feel. No off-trail travel is allowed, and most waterways are closed to fishing in order to protect the sensitive area.

Red Rock Point

Mud Volcano

Before you see Mud Volcano, you'll smell the rotten-egg scent of hydrogen sulfide gas billowing from the earth. A 0.7-mile boardwalk and trail tours several thermal features; the two most prominent ones are on the lower and shorter boardwalk loop. **Mud Volcano** is a 17-foot-deep burbling pot of watery clay that especially amuses kids when they can stand the stench. Nearby, hot steam from 170-degree water belches from **Dragon's Mouth Spring.**

At the high end of the larger paved and stair-step boardwalk loop, **Black Dragon's Cauldron** stretches nearly 200 feet across, bubbling up from a crack with the dark color created from iron sulfides. Across the road to the north is one of the park's most acidic hot springs. On par with battery acid, **Sulphur Cauldron** boils with yellow color created from sulphur and bacteria. Pick up a trail guide ($1) at Mud Volcano.

LeHardys Rapids

South of Mud Volcano and three miles north of Fishing Bridge, **LeHardys Rapids** drops in a cascade on the Yellowstone River; boardwalk

LeHardys Rapids

platforms allow for viewing. In early summer, cutthroat trout wriggle up the rapids to reach Fishing Bridge for annual spawning, and colorful harlequin ducks surf the white water. The viewing boardwalk closes during mating season for their protection.

FISHING BRIDGE

The park hub of Fishing Bridge lies on the north shore of Yellowstone Lake, at the junction with the Grand Loop Road and the East Entrance Road. A small caldera, **Mary Bay,** flanks the north shore of Yellowstone Lake, while the **Steamboat Springs** fumaroles fester on **Steamboat Point.** As the East Entrance Road climbs through a hillside of charred trees, **Lake Butte** offers a higher-elevation overlook that takes in the entire lake, including the southern arms, islands, and West Thumb.

The Fishing Bridge Historic District is home to the 1931 **Fishing Bridge Museum and Visitor Center** (307/344-2450, www.nps.gov/yell, 8am-7pm daily late May-Sept.). Now a National Historic Landmark, the building's other facilities include Fishing Bridge RV Park, a store, and a gas station. Backcountry and boating permits are available at the **Lake Ranger Station.**

★ Fishing Bridge

The original log **Fishing Bridge** was erected over the Yellowstone River in 1902. The current bridge replaced it in 1937 with walkways on both sides to accommodate the hoards of anglers. The attraction: spawning cutthroat trout. Due to threats to the trout population from lake trout and overfishing, angling is no longer allowed on the bridge, but visitors can still watch spawning trout in June and early July.

Pelican Creek

Pelican Creek, located on the East Entrance Road, offers prime wildlife-watching. Early mornings or evenings are best for spotting waterfowl, bald eagles, elk, moose, or bears. The creek twists and turns in slow eddies through

a two-mile-long wetland that stretches 0.3 mile wide. Pullouts on the east end of the bridge over the creek offer the best place to scan the terrain with binoculars.

Sylvan Pass

From Fishing Bridge, the East Entrance Road climbs about 18 miles to **Sylvan Pass.** Flanked on the west by Sylvan and Eleanor Lakes, Sylvan Pass cuts through an 8,524-foot-high rocky slot in the Absaroka Mountains. Small pullouts at the lakes allow photo ops; a pullout on the east side overlooks the canyon descending into Middle Creek. A small parking lot at the summit offers a place to stop and scan the hillsides for bighorn sheep and peruse long, thin waterfalls while listening to the wind howl. The pass, famed for rockslides, is open for driving **early May-early November.** Snowmobiles can tour it in winter (mid-Dec.-mid-Mar.).

LAKE VILLAGE

From Fishing Bridge, the Grand Loop Road continues to Lake Village, a cluster of visitor services rather than an actual village. But it houses the **Lake Yellowstone Hotel,** a National Historic Landmark built in 1891. Stop at the large yellow colonial lakeside hotel to stay, dine, or sit in the sunroom. Drive along the beach road, stopping at the overlook in front of the hotel and the octagonal cedar **Yellowstone General Store,** built in 1919 and displaying historical photos. Backcountry and boating permits for kayaks or canoes are available at the **Lake Ranger Station.**

★ Yellowstone Lake

At 7,733 feet, the natural **Yellowstone Lake** is the largest water body in Yellowstone National Park; it is also the largest freshwater lake in North America above 7,000 feet. From the shoreline, look for trumpeter swans, pelicans, ducks, eagles, herons, and other shorebirds; you can also spot **Frank Island,** the largest of the lake's islands.

The lake's average temperature in summer is about 45°F, although it can be warmer

Lake Village

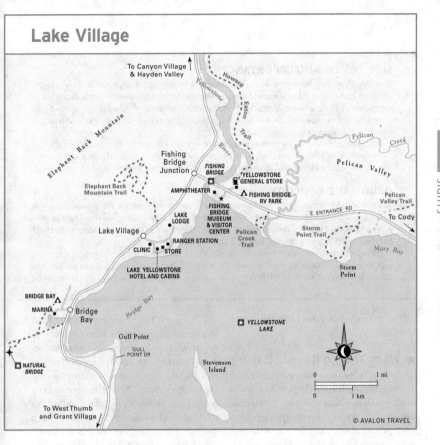

near thermal features; swimmers only enter the water on the hottest days. Beach access is available in multiple locations along the roadsides on the north and west shores. **Bridge Bay Marina** rents boats to experience being on the lake. Anglers fish for trout, while boaters tour the shoreline, and paddlers head to the three southern arms for remote getaways. Backcountry and boating permits are available at **Bridge Bay Ranger Station**. Afternoon winds frequently whip the lake into whitecaps. The *Lake Queen* offers boat tours around Stevenson Island.

Gull Point Drive provides a side tour to Gull Point, a windswept point for fishing, swimming, and beachcombing. From the point, you can see Stevenson Island, Lake Hotel, and the Absaroka Mountains.

GRANT VILLAGE AND WEST THUMB

The adjoining villages of West Thumb and Grant Village provide the most southern services in the park. About 21 miles south of Fishing Bridge is the West Thumb Junction, where the Grand Loop Road connects west to Old Faithful in 17 miles. From the junction, the South Entrance Road leads 22 miles south to the South Entrance.

In West Thumb, the **West Thumb Geyser Basin** burbles and steams with hydrothermal features. The **Grant Village Marina** offers

Yellowstone Lake

SIZE, DEPTH, AND IMPORTANCE

In the bigger picture, Yellowstone Lake drains into the Yellowstone River, which flows northward and then eastward into the Missouri River and then the Mississippi River. With the exception of thermal areas, the lake freezes over with three feet of ice in winter and often doesn't melt out until early June. Fed by snowmelt, the lake's size fluctuates—bigger in June as the water level rises and smaller as it sinks to its lowest level in fall.

The lake is 20 miles long by 15 miles wide, has six islands, and covers 136 square miles. It has an average depth of 139 feet, but dives to its deepest spot at 410 feet. With an irregular shape, the lake has more than 141 miles of shoreline for boaters and paddlers to explore.

ORIGIN AND GEOLOGY

Half inside and half outside the Yellowstone Caldera, the northern part of the lake has its origins in volcanic activity and lava flows while the southern part formed from glaciation The lake once extended bigger than its current shoreline, encompassing Hayden Valley. The lakeshore and floor has thermal activity with geysers, fumaroles, and hot springs.

In the 1990s, two vents were found that rose and fell year-to-year, but overall gained about one inch annually. In 2004, scientists discovered that a 2,000-foot-long vent at the lake bottom had started to bulge up, swelling 100 feet high. In addition, the lake basin is rising on the north end

boat access to Yellowstone Lake and visitor services.

★ West Thumb Geyser Basin

Located on Yellowstone Lake at West Thumb Bay, the **West Thumb Geyser Basin** is a smaller caldera within the larger Yellowstone Caldera. The geyser basin dumps more than 3,100 gallons of hot water daily into the lake and contains three geysers, 11 hot springs, fumaroles, and mud pots. Two loops (0.8 mile) guide visitors around the thermal features; most on the larger boardwalk loop near the lake.

Early park visitors cooked fish in **Fishing Cone.** The striking turquoise and emerald **Abyss Pool** may be one of the deepest in the park at 53 feet. **Twin Geyser** has two vents that shoot water as high as 75 feet. Many of the hot pools are colorful, their hues derived from heat-happy thermophiles. Pick up a trail guide ($1) on the boardwalk.

★ Lewis Lake

Named for Meriwether Lewis (of the Lewis and Clark Corps of Discovery expedition), **Lewis Lake** is Yellowstone's third-largest lake at 2,716 acres. Fed by the Lewis River from Shoshone Lake, the lake is a favorite for boaters, paddlers, and campers. A few hot springs empty into the lake, and anglers go after several species of trout that weren't originally in the fishless waters. The lake also serves as an access point for Shoshone Lake. Paddlers can work up the slow-moving inlet river to reach the bigger lake. Lewis Lake feeds the **Lewis River,** which tumbles over Lewis Falls and continues until it runs into the Snake River and eventually to the Pacific Ocean. Lewis Lake is located on the South Entrance Road, about 10 miles south of West Thumb.

Lewis Falls

After the Lewis River departs Lewis Lake, it tumbles down the 30-foot-high **Lewis Falls,** which roars at its fullest in June with high water. The falls are viewable from the South Entrance Road, just a short distance from Lewis Lake, or from an overlook at the end of a short climb. South of the falls, the river slices through the **Lewis River Canyon,** but only a few tiny pullouts afford places to peer into the ravine.

due to Sour Creek Dome north of Fishing Bridge. That makes the lake basin tilt southward, creating larger sandy beaches on the north shore and more flood zones in the southern arms.

SCIENTIFIC DISCOVERIES

Little was known about the floor of Yellowstone Lake until recently when scientists found strange features on the floor of Bridge Bay. Sonar images followed by photo images revealed spires created from hydrothermal vents putting up silica sinter that formed vertical spires as they solidified. Freshwater algae and sponges then gained a foothold on the spires, creating underwater gardens. One spire studied turned out to be 11,000 years old, but younger than the last glacial age.

INVASION OF LAKE TROUT

Fish-stocking programs introduced rainbow trout, mountain whitefish, and Atlantic salmon between 1890-1910. But none survived. Native Yellowstone cutthroat now populate the lake along with redside shiners, longnose suckers, longnose dace, and lake chubs. In the 1990s, lake trout were discovered, most likely introduced accidentally or intentionally. Their growing populations have caused a decline in native cutthroat trout due to predation and food source competition. The park service has embarked on a program to reduce lake trout numbers. Anglers should kill all lake trout and release all cutthroat trout. Anglers can fish the lake mid-June-early November.

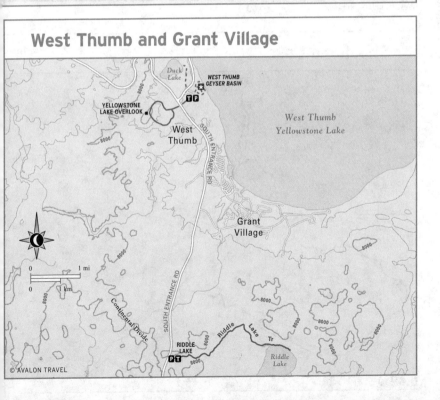

West Thumb and Grant Village

© AVALON TRAVEL

West Thumb Geyser Basin

Shoshone Lake

Map labels:

GRAND LOOP RD

DELACY CREEK

Divide Overlook ▲

Delacy Creek

DeLacy Trail

GRAND LOOP RD

West Thumb

West Thumb

Pocket Lake

Continental Divide

DeLacy Trail

Grant Village

0 2 mi
0 2 km

Cement Hills

Shoshone Lake

Shoshone Geyser Basin

Riddle Lake

SOUTH ENTRANCE RD

Shoshone Lake Trail

Lewis Channel Tr.

Dogshead Trail

SHOSHONE DOGSHEAD

Lewis Lake

© AVALON TRAVEL

Shoshone Lake

Remote, 8,050-acre **Shoshone Lake** is the second-largest lake in Yellowstone. The lake is only accessible by paddlers (no motorboats) or hikers; there are no roads. The **DeLacy Creek Trailhead** on Grand Loop Road (8.8 miles west of the West Thumb junction) provides the best hiking access, while paddlers must navigate three miles of the **Lewis Lake** river channel. About 20 backcountry campsites rim the lake.

At the lake's southwestern corner sits **Shoshone Geyser Basin** with one of the highest concentrations of geysers in the world. More than 80 hot springs and mud pots cram into the geyser basin.

CONTINENTAL DIVIDE

The **Continental Divide** splits the water flow between the Gulf of Mexico and the Pacific Ocean. Between Old Faithful and West Thumb, the Grand Loop crosses the Continental Divide twice. Tiny, lily-pad-filled **Isa Lake,** which straddles the divide at 8,262-foot **Craig Pass,** is unique because it drains to both the Gulf and Pacific, but it does so in a roundabout manner. The lake's east-side outlet stream curls around southward into the Lewis River, which eventually joins the Snake River westward to the Pacific. The lake's west side drains into the Firehole River, which flows into the Madison River and northward to the Missouri River, where it circles to the Mississippi River and the Gulf of Mexico. An interpretive site sits on the east end of the lake.

Recreation

DAY HIKES

Hikes vary from short pops to scenic viewpoints to long treks up river drainages. Mountainous terrain makes some trails steep. Combine that with the high elevation, and those from sea level may find themselves breathing hard. Take your time and drink lots of fluids. The elevation and arid climate can dehydrate hikers, which can lead to headaches and altitude sickness.

Some trails remain **closed until July 1** in order to minimize conflicts with grizzlies and black bears (especially during seasons when bears concentrate on food sources). Conditions such as bear activity, high water, snow, and fires can close trails at any time. For information about seasonal closures, contact the ranger stations and visitors centers, or check trails online (www.nps.gov/yell). A small booth near the visitors center at Canyon Village rents **pepper spray** ($10/day, $28/week).

Guided Hikes

Naturalist rangers lead **free walks and hikes** (daily and weekly June-Sept.) in Canyon, West Thumb, and Fishing Bridge. Some walks run daily while others are offered weekly. Schedules are available in park newspapers. Popular short hikes include **Storm Point, Yellowstone Lake Overlook,** and **canyon rim** trails. Yellowstone also permits multiple concessionaires (www.nps.gov/yell) to guide day hikes.

Canyon Village
★ MT. WASHBURN

Distance: 5.4-6.4 miles round-trip
Duration: 4 hours
Elevation change: 1,400-1,483 feet
Effort: easy grade, but strenuous by elevation
Trailheads: For the south trail: Dunraven Pass Trailhead parking area on the east side of Grand Loop Road, 5.4 miles north of Canyon Junction. For the north trail: 10.3 miles north of Canyon Junction, drive 1.3 miles up Chittenden Road to reach the parking area (see map p. 143).

At 10,243 feet, the Mt. Washburn Lookout yields a 360-degree panorama with big views. On a clear day, hikers can see the Grand

Canyon and Lake Country Hikes

Trail	Effort	Distance	Duration
Duck Lake	Easy	1 mi	30 min
Pelican Creek Nature Trail	Easy	1.3 mi rt	1 hr
Storm Point	Easy	2.3 mi rt	1.5 hr
Clear Lake and Ribbon Lake	Easy	2.2-7.3 mi rt	1.5-4 hr
Natural Bridge	Easy	2.6 mi rt	2 hr
Riddle Lake	Easy	4.8 mi rt	3 hr
South Rim Trail to Point Sublime	Easy	5.1 mi rt	3 hr
Shoshone Lake via DeLacy Creek	Easy	5.8 mi rt	3-4 hr
Grebe Lake	Easy	6.6 mi rt	3-4 hr
North Rim of Grand Canyon of the Yellowstone	Easy to Strenuous	3.8 mi one-way	3-4 hr
Cascade Lake and Observation Peak	Easy to Strenuous	4.4-9.6 mi rt	2.5-5 hr
Mt. Washburn	Easy to Strenuous	5.4-6.4 mi rt	4 hr
Yellowstone Lake Overlook	Moderate	2 mi rt	1.5 hr
Elephant Back Mountain	Moderate	3.6 mi rt	2.5 hr
Chain of Lakes	Moderate	10.7 mi one-way	5-6 hr
Shoshone Lake via Dogshead Trail	Moderate	10.8 mi rt	5-6 hr
Heart Lake	Moderately Strenuous	15 mi rt	7-8 hr
Avalanche Peak	Strenuous	5 mi rt	4 hr

Canyon of the Yellowstone, Yellowstone Lake, and even the Tetons. The Chittenden Trail is steeper and has a bit more elevation gain that the Dunraven Pass Trail, but both trails climb up switchbacks in a steady plod on former roads at high elevation.

The Dunraven Pass Trail (6.4 miles, hikers only) traverses across a southern slope before swinging north at 9,100 feet around a ridge. It then makes four switchbacks up the west slope to crest the ridge for a long, scenic 360-degree circle to the Mt. Washburn Lookout. In the upper elevations, look for bighorn sheep in the cliffs and meadows.

The steeper Chittenden Trail (5.4 miles, bicycles allowed) ascends just below a ridge with a few switchbacks thrown in to work up the slope. On the final ridge, the trail swings east and then switchbacks west for the last steps to the summit of Mt. Washburn.

At the summit, the Mt. Washburn Lookout is an ugly three-story cement block covered in radio equipment. Visitors can access only two levels: an observation room

summit thrill on top of Yellowstone's highest peak

still be snow-covered in June, so many hikers wait until the end of July to hike this trail. But June and July usually bring on bluebells, prairie smoke, and elephant's head lousewort in the meadows en route to **Cascade Lake** (4.4 miles). The trail to Cascade Lake also sees copious mosquitoes; pack the bug juice until September.

From the trailhead, a relatively flat route crosses through large meadows made marshy by myriad streams, especially near the lake. (Some streams have footbridges, while others don't.) At 1.3 miles, the trail reaches the junction at Cascade Lake, the easternmost lake in the Chain of Lakes. The scenic lake sits in a basin surrounded by meadows and is covered by lily pads on its southwest end. Look for trumpeter swans.

At the junction, turn north, passing the lake and heading toward the rocky, 9,415-foot summit of **Observation Peak** (9.6

with windows on three sides, interpretive displays, and a viewing scope; and a deck above. Restrooms are available.

Slopes may be **snow-covered in June,** but burst with rampant alpine wildflowers by July. Due to afternoon thunderstorms, plan to **descend before early afternoon.** Even though the treeless trail looks hot, **bring warm clothing;** the alpine tundra summit is often windy and cold. Due to the trail's popularity, you'll meet plenty of people at the lookout.

CASCADE LAKE AND OBSERVATION PEAK

Distance: 4.4-9.6 miles round-trip
Duration: 2.5-5 hours
Elevation change: 60-1,389 feet
Effort: easy to strenuous
Trailhead: Cascade Picnic Area on Grand Loop Road, 1.3 miles north of Canyon Junction (see map p. 146)

Spring snowmelt can make the lower elevations of this trail muddy in marshy areas around the stream. Observation Peak can

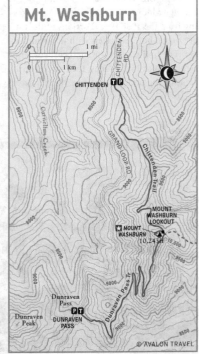

Mt. Washburn

miles). Climbing 2.6 miles at a steady clip, the trail crosses a broad ridge for a long walk through the 1988 burn area. Views stretch out for miles. From the summit, you can see Grebe Lake below and Hayden Valley spread out to the south. An old wood and stone fire lookout perches at the summit.

GREBE LAKE

Distance: 6.6 miles round-trip
Duration: 3-4 hours
Elevation change: 350 feet
Effort: easy
Trailhead: Grebe Lake Trailhead on Grand Loop Road, 3.8 miles west of Canyon Junction (see map p. 146)

This hike to Grebe Lake, the largest of the Chain of Lakes, requires a minimal climb over a low gentle hump. Prepare for swarms of mosquitoes throughout most of the summer, though. For anglers, the 156-acre lake holds rainbow trout and arctic grayling.

From the trailhead, hike northward through a lodgepole forest that is fast regrowing from the 1988 fires. Portions of the trail are dusty, hot, and open with downed timber. The trail reaches the southeast corner of Grebe Lake in 3.3 miles, then circles north around the lake to continue farther west.

Meadows and marshes surround the scenic lake. When high water abates after June, beaches appear on the north shore.

You can also reach Grebe Lake from Cascade Lake. From Cascade Lake, the trail heads west for two miles with a 100-foot gain in elevation. The round-trip distance from the Cascade Lake Trailhead to Grebe Lake and back is eight miles.

CHAIN OF LAKES

Distance: 10.7 miles one-way
Duration: 5-6 hours
Elevation change: 950 feet
Effort: moderate
Trailhead: Cascade Picnic Area on Grand Loop Road, 1.3 miles north of Canyon Junction (see map p. 146)

The Chain of Lakes are a string of lakes on the upper Solfatara Plateau. While hikers can reach each lake individually from separate trailheads, this trail connects all four lakes: Cascade, Grebe, Wolf, and Ice. Hiking this trail one-way requires setting up a car shuttle at the Ice Lake Trailhead. It's a mosquito-infested walk most of the summer, due to scads of potholes, streams, and marshes. If you're an angler, bring a rod for fishing.

From the Cascade Picnic Area, hike two miles west to Cascade Lake, then continue

Grebe Lake

two more miles west to **Grebe Lake,** following signed trail junctions. From the north shore of Grebe Lake, continue 1.4 miles west to **Wolf Lake.** West of Wolf Lake, you'll have to ford the Gibbon River to continue over rolling lodgepole hills for two miles to a junction. Go west at this junction toward **Ice Lake,** reaching it in another mile. After passing Ice Lake on the north side, turn left at the next junction and continue 0.5 mile west to reach the **Ice Lake Trailhead.** (You can also hike the trail in reverse.)

For those who just want to hike point-to-point to Cascade and Grebe Lake (7.5 miles), the route starts at the **Cascade Lake Trailhead** north of Canyon Junction and exits at the **Grebe Lake Trailhead.**

NORTH RIM OF GRAND CANYON OF THE YELLOWSTONE
Distance: 3.8 miles one-way

Duration: 3-4 hours
Elevation change: 250-850 feet
Effort: easy to strenuous
Trailheads: Wapiti Lake Trailhead on South Rim Drive, on the west side of the bridge over the Yellowstone River (see map p. 134)
Directions: Park at Wapiti Picnic Area on the east side of the South Rim Drive bridge over the Yellowstone River. Walk back across the bridge to find the trailhead heading north.

This trail is not about backcountry solitude, but rather tremendous views of the Grand Canyon of the Yellowstone. A combination of paved and dirt trails link together multiple overlooks; some include steel stairways and boardwalks down to overlook platforms. You can start at either the north or south end to hike the entire trail, or shorten the distance by driving some segments. (In several places, the trail pops out to cross parking lots on North Rim Drive.) At each overlook, spur

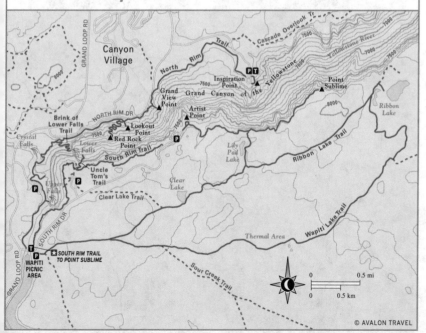

Grand Canyon of the Yellowstone Trails

© AVALON TRAVEL

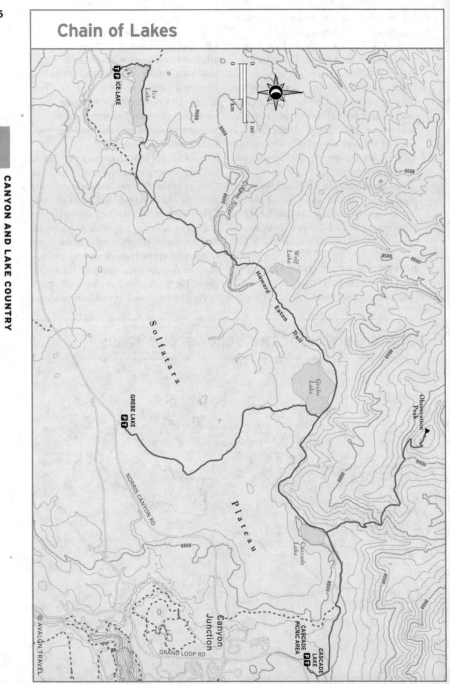

Chain of Lakes

Point Sublime yields plummeting views of the Grand Canyon of the Yellowstone.

to **Red Rock Point.** Returning to the North Rim Trail, continue north to **Grand View Point,** where a short paved trail drops about 150 feet to the viewpoint. Past Grand View Point, the trail curls northeast about 1.3 miles to the **Inspiration Point** parking lot. Walk through the parking lot and descend 50 feet in elevation in 0.1 mile to the classic viewpoint.

It's also possible to park at the Inspiration Point parking lot (the north end) and hike this trail in reverse. For the 3.8-mile one-way hike, leave a car shuttle at either the Inspiration Point or Wapiti Picnic Area parking lots. Or return the way you came for a 7.6-mile out-and-back hike.

★ SOUTH RIM TRAIL TO POINT SUBLIME

Distance: 5.1 miles round-trip
Duration: 3 hours
Elevation change: 55 feet
Effort: easy
Trailheads: South trailhead: Wapiti Picnic Area on South Rim Drive, on the east side of the bridge over the Yellowstone River. North Trailhead: Artist Point parking lot where South Rim drive ends (see map p. 134).

The South Rim Trail has multiple overlooks of the Grand Canyon of the Yellowstone. From the Wapiti Picnic Area, a 0.4-mile forested walk heads north following the Yellowstone River to the first viewpoint at the **Upper Falls.** A spur trail drops 15 feet to the viewpoint. Continue north to circle the bluff for snippets of views as the trail continues north to **Uncle Tom's Trail,** a 500-foot descent down paved switchbacks and 328 metal stair steps (that you have to climb back up) to an overlook. Past Uncle Tom's Trail, the route continues east through the forest with several viewpoints along the canyon rim until reaching the Artist Point parking lot. Walk northeast through the length of the parking lot to reach the **Artist Point Trailhead** and continue 0.1 mile to the scenic point. From Artist Point, the dirt trail continues east 0.75 mile to **Point Sublime.** On this section, exposed overlooks (without railings) require caution as you take in the depth of the canyon. The

trails drop down switchbacks and steep stairways to viewing platforms—all require climbing back up. Completing all the spurs adds a climb of nearly 1,500 feet in elevation and two more miles.

Start the North Rim Trail at the **south end** of the trail by crossing South Rim Drive to follow the Yellowstone River downstream (heading north). In 0.4 mile, the trail reaches the first viewpoint at **Brink of the Upper Falls.** A spur trail drops 42 feet to an overlook of the 109-foot falls. Continue north, passing the parking lot for Brink of the Upper Falls, to the 130-foot **Crystal Falls** as it spews from a slot in the North Rim cliffs. Heading northeast now, the 308-foot **Lower Falls** comes into view; follow the trail to a junction where a spur plummets 600 feet down switchbacks and stairs to the **Brink of the Lower Falls.** Climb back up the spur and continue east to the **Lookout Point Trailhead,** where a short trail climbs up 25 feet to **Lookout Point.** Just west, a longer trail plunges 500 feet in 0.4 mile down switchbacks and steep stairs

Lower Falls drops out of view, but the canyon walls and hoodoos become far more colorful with smears of reds and pinks above the frothy blue water. The trail dead-ends at Point Sublime at a log railing where the forest claims the canyon.

CLEAR LAKE AND RIBBON LAKE

Distance: 2.2-7.3 miles round-trip
Duration: 1.5-4 hours
Elevation change: 950 feet
Effort: easy
Trailhead: Wapiti Picnic Area on South Rim Drive (see map p. 134)

This trail climbs gently to tour three small lakes, each one strikingly different. From the south end of the Wapiti Picnic Area parking lot, head east to ascend the hillside trail. The open meadows afford expansive views of Mt. Washburn and Hayden Valley. In 0.5 mile, turn left at the fork.

The Ribbon Trail ascends a little over one mile east through the forest to Clear Lake, a shallow lake with a sand and rock bottom (hikers can turn around here for a 2.2-mile round-trip hike). In another 0.7 mile, the trail reaches a junction. Turn north for the short job to narrow Lily Pad Lake (3.6 miles round-trip), where lily pads can grow so thick the water is barely visible. Return to the main trail and continue east for 1.2 miles to Ribbon Lake. This third lake sits amid scenic meadows and forest. Follow the trail farther north to see the lake, then backtrack to the trail junction. To complete the loop, follow the trail south from Ribbon Lake to the junction with the Wapiti Lake Trail and turn right. This trail wanders through thermal areas, so stay on the trail for safety. At 6.3 miles, the trail breaks out of the forest onto the hillside to descend to the original fork and return to the parking lot in 0.5 mile.

Other trailheads on South Rim Drive offer alternatives to hiking to these lakes. Across the road from the parking lot at Uncle Tom's Point, the Clear Lake Trail climbs 0.7 mile to meet the Clear Lake-Ribbon Lake Trail. On the trail from Artist Point to Point Sublime, a trail junction leads 0.25 mile southeast past Lily Pad Lake. From that junction, it is 0.7 mile southwest to Clear Lake.

Fishing Bridge
PELICAN CREEK NATURE TRAIL

Distance: 1.3 miles round-trip
Duration: 1 hour
Elevation change: negligible
Effort: easy
Trailhead: the west end of Pelican Creek Bridge on the East Entrance Road, 0.9 mile east of Fishing Bridge (see map p. 137)

Starting at Pelican Creek Bridge, the trail cuts through the old-growth forest to the north shore of Yellowstone Lake. The trail then follows Pelican Creek, crossing to a marshy island on a boardwalk, and emerges from the forest onto a sandy obsidian beach. In early summer, the boardwalk and marsh traverse may be too wet, so stick to the forest trail. Watch for wildlife: otters, birds, ducks, pelicans, and bison. In spring, grizzly bears feed in the area.

STORM POINT

Distance: 2.3 miles round-trip
Duration: 1.5 hours
Elevation change: 40 feet
Effort: easy
Trailhead: Indian Pond pullout on the East Entrance Road, 3 miles east of Fishing Bridge (see map p. 137)

This loop hike offers wildlife-watching from an impressive point on the north shore of Yellowstone Lake. Grizzlies frequent the area, which can sometimes close the trail (check trail status at Fishing Bridge Ranger Station). Look for waterfowl at Indian Pond, marmots at Storm Point, and bison in the meadows. Winds can rage across the point, so bring an extra layer.

From the pullout at Indian Pond, the trail cuts across a sagebrush meadow for 0.2 mile to a fork. The left fork heads straight toward Mary Bay, an ancient caldera on Yellowstone Lake, before swinging into the forest to reach the rocky Storm Point that juts out into the lake (and takes the brunt of

Storm Point

winds from the south). From Storm Point, you can see Stevenson Island and Mt. Sheridan in the distance. The trail continues west along broken rock and sandy bluffs reminiscent of an ocean coast with sandy beaches and driftwood. Clusters of yellow arrowleaf balsamroot flank the trail as it cuts back into the woods, where winds make the conifers clatter and creak. The trail returns to the fork in the meadow and the pullout.

AVALANCHE PEAK

Distance: 5 miles round-trip
Duration: 4 hours
Elevation change: 2,094 feet
Effort: strenuous
Trailhead: On the East Entrance Road, 17 miles east of the Fishing Bridge junction. Park on the south side of the road at the west end of Eleanor Lake and find the trailhead across the road (see map p. 128).

Get an early start on this trail in order to avoid regular afternoon lightning and rain squalls, and prepare for strong winds at the summit by packing along warm layers. This trail often remains covered in snow until July; avoid hiking in September and October due to bear activity.

Cross the East Entrance Road to find the trail catapulting straight up the mountain with minimal switchbacks—it packs in steepness as if someone was on a mission to get to the summit in a hurry. The trail starts out in thick forest, climbing 2,000 feet in about one mile until breaking out of the trees across a scree slope to a **false summit.** Trails diverge around the false summit, created by hikers trying to shortcut or walk around snowfields.

The route crawls left onto an open, narrow ridge where the in-your-face views of the surrounding Absaroka peaks are the lure to continue onward. The **0.4-mile ridge** traverse leads in a stunning conclusion to the 10,566-foot summit of **Avalanche Peak.** From the summit, you'll have an impressive panorama to soak up, from the foreground Yellowstone Lake to the backbone of the Absaroka-Beartooth Wilderness and distant Grand Tetons. On the descent, be cautious on scree; the small rocks feel like walking on marbles.

ELEPHANT BACK MOUNTAIN

Distance: 3.6 miles round-trip
Duration: 2.5 hours
Elevation change: 710 feet
Effort: moderate
Trailhead: Elephant Back Trailhead on the west side of Grand Loop Road, 1 mile south of the Fishing Bridge junction (see map p. 137)

From the Grand Loop Road, this trail climbs up through a sparse lodgepole forest for 0.8 mile to a **junction.** Take the left fork to steadily ascend to the summit in a more direct line. An **overlook,** a small clearing in the trees, provides outstanding views. At the 8,618-foot **summit,** wooden benches offer spots to absorb the scenery, as views from the summit stretch across Yellowstone Lake to the Absaroka Mountains. In the foreground are Lake Village and the Lake Yellowstone Hotel; off-shore is Stevenson Island. The summit loop returns to the trail junction in 1.9 miles. Descend 0.8 mile to return to the trailhead.

Lake Village
★ NATURAL BRIDGE

Distance: 2.6 miles round-trip
Duration: 2 hours
Elevation change: 181 feet
Effort: easy
Trailhead: Bridge Bay Marina parking lot near the entrance to the campground (see map p. 137)

This scenic loop tours Natural Bridge, a 51-foot-high sculpture of rhyolite rock that has been eroded through by Bridge Creek. The bridge is impressive, although much smaller than Utah's famed arches. Note that this trail is **closed late spring-early summer** due to grizzlies feeding on spawning trout in Bridge Creek. A bicycle route also begins south of the bridge from a separate trailhead.

From the parking lot, the trail cuts west through the forest for 0.7 mile before joining an old **paved road.** The route continues working westward for 0.4 mile, turning right at all junctions to reach an **interpretive exhibit** at the base of the loop trail. From the exhibit, a short, steep path switchbacks 0.2 mile up to the top of **Natural Bridge;** cross the creek behind the bridge to loop back down the other side. (The top the bridge is closed in order to protect the fragile rock, but you'll see marmots run across it.)

West Thumb and Grant Village
DUCK LAKE

Distance: 1 mile round-trip
Duration: 30 minutes
Elevation change: 200 feet
Effort: easy
Trailhead: Duck Lake Trailhead at the north end of the West Thumb Geyser Basin parking lot (see map p. 139)

A short hike through a loose forest leads to 0.3-mile long **Duck Lake,** a good destination for families with young kids. From the trailhead, the path crosses the road and climbs uphill. At the top of the hill, the trail crosses a power line before dropping down to the lake in 0.4 mile. The eastern lakeshore has a long **beach** with room to spread out. Duck Lake waters are often warmer and more wind-protected for **swimming** than Yellowstone Lake.

YELLOWSTONE LAKE OVERLOOK

Distance: 2 miles round-trip
Duration: 1.5 hours
Elevation change: 194 feet
Effort: moderate
Trailhead: west side of the West Thumb Geyser Basin parking lot (see map p. 139)

The Lake Overlook Trail climbs from the start, beginning in a meadow and entering a forest. In 0.3 mile, the trail crosses the **South Entrance Road** and reaches a **fork.** Turn left and continue hiking south up to a meadow with red paintbrush and yellow buckwheat in early summer; the panoramic views of the Yellowstone Lake and the Absaroka Mountains unfolds. Look for a **bench** to enjoy the view; a **short spur** behind the bench climbs up about 30 feet for a peekaboo view of the Tetons. Complete the loop in 1.1 miles and return to the parking lot.

RIDDLE LAKE

Distance: 4.8 miles round-trip
Duration: 3 hours
Elevation change: 100 feet
Effort: easy
Trailhead: Riddle Lake Trailhead on the east side of the South Entrance Road, 2.3 miles south of Grant Village (see map p. 139)

The 275-acre Riddle Lake gets its name from the mystery of whether it fed two oceans due to its placement on the Continental Divide. The mystery was solved when more accurate mapping placed the lake and its outlet on the east side of the divide.

From the trailhead, the **Riddle Lake Trail** heads east. Even though this trail is fairly level, it crosses the **Continental Divide.** The route swaps between forest and marshy meadows to reach Riddle Lake's north shore in 2.4 miles. Find a sandy beach at the northeast corner of the lake to sit and enjoy the view of Mt. Sheridan and the Red Mountains. Anglers fish the lake for cutthroat trout, but much of the shoreline has marsh and lily pads.

Due to bear management, the trail is **closed every spring** (Apr. 30-July 15). Tree trunks on the trail sport claw scratches, a testament to the population of bears that inhabit the area. Closures can extend later into July if trumpeter swans are nesting; check with a ranger station or visitors center for trail status.

SHOSHONE LAKE VIA DELACY CREEK

Distance: 5.8 miles round-trip
Duration: 3-4 hours
Elevation change: 280 feet
Effort: easy
Trailhead: DeLacy Creek Trailhead on Grand Loop Road, 8.8 miles west of the West Thumb junction (see map p. 140)

Shoshone Lake is the largest backcountry lake in Yellowstone. Trails reach the lake from several directions, but the **DeLacy Trail** is the shortest and easiest with a gentle uphill return. From the trailhead, the route heads 2.9 miles south to follow **DeLacy Creek,** a stream that twists through a giant meadow where anglers can find good fly-fishing for brook trout. As the trail alternates between forest and meadows along the creek, look for moose in the prime habitat. At **Shoshone Lake,** enjoy a pebble beach of volcanic rock. It's a scenic picnic location and a good place to wade or swim in the lake.

SHOSHONE LAKE VIA DOGSHEAD TRAIL

Distance: 10.8 miles round-trip
Duration: 5-6 hours
Elevation change: negligible
Effort: moderate
Trailhead: Shoshone Dogshead Trailhead on the west side of the South Entrance Road, 5.3 miles south of Grant Village (see map p. 140)

When combined with the Lewis Channel Trail, the Dogshead Trail offers a loop hike to Shoshone Lake. The 4.6-mile Dogshead Trail takes a direct, hence shorter, route to the lake. The more scenic, 6.2-mile Lewis Channel follows the convolutions of the north shore of the Lewis River. Anglers head to the channel

to fish for brown trout. A portion of the trail goes through burned areas from the 1988 fires.

From the **Dogshead Trail,** the route cuts 4.6 miles north through marshy zones and lodgepole forest in a fairly straight route to **Shoshone Lake.** Just before reaching the lake, the trail connects with the **Lewis Channel Trail** and the **DeLacy Creek Trail** along the east shore. Follow the trail southward toward the lake and look for a lunch spot on the pebble beach. Return south on the **Lewis Channel Trail** for 6.2 miles; the trail requires fording one creek.

HEART LAKE

Distance: 15 miles round-trip
Duration: 7-8 hours
Elevation change: 869 feet
Effort: moderately strenuous
Trailhead: Heart Lake Trailhead on the east side of the South Entrance Road, 5.4 miles south of Grant Village (see map p. 128)

Heart Lake is the fourth-largest lake in the park, a place where anglers go after cutthroat trout. Bear management closes the Heart Lake Trail every spring until **July 1.**

Part of the 3,300-mile Continental Divide Trail, Heart Lake Trail passes through thick stands of lodgepoles and small wetland meadows to cross the Continental Divide at 8,154 feet. Climb 187 feet in elevation and descend 682 feet to the lake on the way in, then climb 682 feet on the return trip. From the trailhead, hike four miles southeast. The landscape opens up with views, thermal areas with hot springs along **Witch Creek,** and the 10,305-foot **Mt. Sheridan** rising from the west shore of the lake. A seasonal **backcountry ranger station** sits 250 feet from the shore, but may not be staffed. The north shore of the lake offers plenty of pebbly beaches for scenic lunch spots, lake enjoyment, and seeing **Rustic Geyser.** Ten backcountry campsites surround the lake.

BACKPACKING

Backpackers must obtain **permits** ($3/person, children 8 and younger free) for assigned backcountry campsites. Permits are available in person 48 hours in advance from the backcountry offices. For more information, see the *Essentials* chapter.

Chain of Lakes
10.7 MILES

Families with young kids, anglers, and beginning backpackers should try the 10.7-mile **Chain of Lakes Trail** (2-3 days), which has five campsites within two miles of the trailhead. With multiple starting, ending, and point-to-point options, backpackers can keep the mileage short or tour all four lakes on the Solfatara Plateau: Cascade, Grebe, Wolf, and Ice. Camp at 4E2 on **Cascade Lake** to take a side trip up Observation Peak. **Grebe Lake** spreads four campsites (4G2, 4G3, 4G4, 4G5) around its shore. At **Wolf Lake,** campsite 4G6 and 4G7 offer more solitude than the other popular day-hike lakes. Campsite 4D3 at **Ice Lake** is reserved for campers in wheelchairs and with special needs.

Heart Lake
21 MILES

Competition for permits is keen for Heart Lake, which is closed until July 1 due to it being prime grizzly habitat. For a 21-mile round-trip, spend two nights at **Heart Lake** and climb the steep 2,700-foot vertical trail up **Mt. Sheridan** on the second day. Campsites 8H1 is the most secluded; campsites 8H5 and 8H6 are closest to the Mt. Sheridan Trail. This route also extends to Yellowstone Lake's South and Southeast Arms or the South Entrance Station via the Snake River.

Shoshone Lake
21.4 MILES

Competition is high for multiday backpacking trips to Shoshone Lake. A level trail, accessible from several trailheads, circles 21.4 miles around Shoshone Lake and takes in the remote **Shoshone Geyser Basin,** the biggest backcountry hydrothermal basin in the park. Access the loop via the 4.6-mile **Dogshead Trail,** 6.2-mile **Lewis Channel Trail,** or the 2.9-mile **DeLacy Creek Trail.** Only nine

campsites are accessible by trail, including Bluff Top (8R2), Cove (8R3), and Basin Bay Point (8R5); the latter is the closest to the geyser basin.

BIKING

During spring (late Mar.-early Apr.), the **South Entrance Road to West Thumb** (22 miles) and the **East Entrance Road to Sylvan Pass** (six miles) are open to bicycles after plowing, but remain closed to vehicles until May. The roads reopen for bicycling in November, after the annual closure for winter. Bikers can ride until snow covers the road. Guided bicycle trips (www.nps.gov/yell) are also available.

Mountain bikes are only permitted in a few locations, mostly on old roadbeds; they are not allowed on trails. The most challenging mountain bike ride is to the **Mt. Washburn Lookout.** From the Chittenden Road parking lot, bikers can grunt 2.7 miles up to the lookout. The difficulty level is compounded by the 10,243-foot summit elevation, but the return trip sails downhill. (The Dunraven Pass route is not open to bikers.)

Mountain bikers can explore shorter routes that are especially good for kids. At **Lake Village,** a one-mile slice of road runs from Lake Hotel to Grand Loop Road south of Lake Junction. Although short, the level ride is scenic along the waterfront of Yellowstone Lake. At Bridge Bay, mountain bikers can ride an old one-mile road from the south of the marina bridge opposite Gull Point Drive to **Natural Bridge.** (Bikes are not allowed on the hiking trail to the site.)

HORSEBACK RIDING

From the **Canyon Corrals** (Xanterra, 307/344-7311 or 866/439-7375, www.yellowstonenationalparklodges.com, daily late June-Aug., $45-70), wranglers lead one-hour rides (8-9 times daily) through meadows and pine forests along Cascade Creek. Two-hour rides depart at 8:30am and extend to the rim of Cascade Canyon. Riders must be at least eight years old and weigh less than 240 pounds. The corral is located one mile south of Canyon Junction, on the west side of Grand Loop Road.

Yellowstone Wilderness Outfitters (406/223-3300, www.yellowstone.ws, June-Sept., $1,800-2,700) guides overnight pack trips on one of the most remote routes in the park: an 81-mile, six-day trip down the Thorofare Trail to the Yellowstone River headwaters and looping past Heart Lake. Guides with degrees in wildlife biology can expand your understanding of fishing, photography, wildlife-watching, and bear safety. They also guide pack trips to other locations and can put together custom trips. Rates include the horses and saddles, guides, meals, tents, and pack mules.

WATER SPORTS

Yellowstone Lake attracts boaters for sightseeing, cruising, angling, sailing, and paddling. (Jet Skiing, parasailing, wakeboarding, waterskiing, and boats over 40 feet long are not permitted.) Motorized boats are only allowed on Lewis Lake and Yellowstone Lake, with the exception of nonmotorized zones in the South and Southeast Arms of Yellowstone Lake. Complete boating regulations, along with permit requirements, licenses, and hazard maps are available online (www.nps.gov/yell).

Permits are required for all boats, motorized and nonmotorized, after successfully passing an Aquatic Invasive Species inspection. Boaters planning to fish or overnight will need additional permits. Those who want to overnight on Yellowstone Lake or Shoshone Lake will need a backcountry camping permit.

Boating
YELLOWSTONE LAKE
Yellowstone Lake is huge and offers expansive water for boating, angling, island touring, and 110 miles of rocky shoreline to explore. **Boating closures** are enforced around thermal areas, hotel beaches, and Yellowstone Lake outlet. Some of the islands also have restrictions: **Stevenson** and **Frank Islands** are closed mid-May-mid-August to protect

nesting birds, although you can still dock or beach at certain locations and tour the waters around the islands. No-wake zones marked by buoys reduce travel speeds in the northern sections of South and Southeast Arms. Touring the east shore of the lake is best in the morning, as afternoon winds can push heavy onto the shore. For day stops, keep an eye on wind upcrops.

Four docks allow places to tie up: at the south end of Frank Island, Wolf Point, Eagle Bay, and Plover Point. Priority for tying up is for overnighters with permits; day-use visitors must be accommodating.

Motorized boats can access 32 primitive **campsites** for overnighting; some are anchoring sites for sleeping aboard. There are 10 primitive campsites in the nonmotorized zone of the South and Southeast Arms.

Two marinas tuck into sheltered bays on Yellowstone Lake. **Bridge Bay Marina** (Xanterra, 307/344-7311 or 866/439-7375, www.yellowstonenationalparklodges.com, late May-Oct.) has a boat launch with cement ramp and docks, moorage, rentals, store, boat gas, charter boat tours, and scenic cruises. The marina rents 16-foot rowboats and 18-foot boats with 40-horsepower outboard motors (first-come, first-served mid-June-early Sept., daily, $10-50/hour). They also run a charter service (daily mid-June-early Sept., $88/hour) available for two hours to a full day on a boat that fits six people. Reservations are required. Watch where you park at the marina, as separate parking zones are designated for day-use and overnighters. Located on the West Thumb, **Grant Village Marina** (mid-June-Oct.) has a boat launch with a cement ramp, docks, and boat slips, but no services.

Sailboats will need to check into launch sites for keel and mast requirements. Sailboats may encounter difficulties at Bridge Bay; you may need to lower the mast in order to go under a bridge to reach the lake. Grant Village provides an easier launch with no obstructions for sailboats; however, in late summer the lake levels may not be high enough to accommodate keels.

Getting Out on the Lake

If you are going to launch anything on a lake in Yellowstone, a **permit** (Backcountry Office, 307-344-2160, www.nps.gov/yell) is required. All watercraft must first be inspected by park rangers for Aquatic Invasive Species (AIS) before a permit can be issued. Boats that may have AIS must be decontaminated before a permit will be issued. If your boat has a **motor,** the permit cost is $10 for seven days or $20 for the season. **Nonmotorized** boat permits (kayaks, canoes, paddleboards, windsurfers, and float-tubes) cost $5 for seven days, $10 for the season. Jet Skiing, parasailing, wakeboarding, waterskiing, and boats more than 40 feet long are banned.

Permit locations include:

· **South Entrance** (U.S. 89/191/287)

· **Grant Village Backcountry Office** (307/344-2609, June-Sept.)

· **Bridge Bay Ranger Station** (307/242-2413, mid-May-Sept.)

Backcountry Camping

Spending the night on your boat or on shore requires a **backcountry camping permit** ($3/person, children under 8 free, $15 maximum/night/party). Permits are first-come, first-served and are assigned 48 hours before departure for specific anchoring locations or shoreline campsites on Yellowstone Lake and Shoshone Lake.

Each campsite (and therefore each permit) holds 6-12 people, depending on location. On-land campsites have pit toilets and bear boxes or food-hanging bars. Where fires are permitted, fire rings are available. Bring your own water or filter lake water. **Reservation requests** (www.nps.gov/yell/planyourvisit, $25/trip) for backcountry campsites can be made starting January 1 using an online application; confirmations are delivered in April. A reservation just guarantees your campsite; you must pick up the actual permit within 48 hours before departure and pay the nightly permit fees.

Fishing

Anglers will need a Yellowstone National Park **fishing permit** ($18 for three days, $25 seven days, $40 season). Permits are required for anglers ages 16 years and older. Kids under age 16 can fish on their parent's permit or get their own permit (free) signed by a parent or guardian. Kids must be supervised fishing under a parental license, but can fish by themselves with the free permit.

Safety

Be prepared before you get out on the water and consult weather predictions at marinas, visitors centers, or ranger stations before launching.

Frigid waters, which can be in the 30s after June, melt out to only the upper 50s in August and may pose a threat of hypothermia should the boat capsize.

Afternoons are known for heavy winds from the west or southwest. Some raise waves beyond a chop to giant whitecaps of four feet. Morning and evening boating can bring calmer waters (but not always). Plan your boating day accordingly. When overnighting, completely beach boats to avoid trashing them with heavy wave action or losing them.

Afternoon thunderstorms can accompany winds, adding squalls and lightning to the mix. For safety, avoid open-water crossings and stay closer to shore. Keep an eye on incoming storms, usually from the west or southwest.

LEWIS LAKE

Lewis Lake is prized for its beauty, quiet ambience, and fishing for brown trout. The lake connects with the larger Shoshone Lake via the Lewis Channel; however, only nonmotorized boats are allowed up the three-mile-long channel into Shoshone Lake. Boaters with outboard motors can detach the motor and chain it up with a lock onshore at the channel entrance to row upstream. A sign marks where the closure begins.

A **boat launch** is located adjacent to the Lewis Lake Campground, accessed from a well-signed turnoff on the South Entrance Road. A cement ramp and dock are at the launch site. Designated parking areas are for day-use and overnight boaters. Even though Lewis Lake is smaller than Yellowstone Lake,

Kayakers paddle Lewis Lake and the Lewis Channel to Shoshone Lake.

Park. Bring your own, or rent from companies in Jackson.

YELLOWSTONE LAKE

Paddlers can launch from multiple locations to tour the shoreline of Yellowstone Lake. To launch from developed boat ramps, go to Bridge Bay Marina or Grant Village Marina. But you can carry your boat or paddleboard to launch from the north shore of Yellowstone Lake at Sedge Bay or any of the picnic areas along the west shore between Lake Village and West Thumb. You can also launch from parking areas on Gull Point Drive. Be aware of restrictions for paddling around thermal areas, hotel beaches, and wildlife preserves. All boating regulations are available online (www.nps. gov/yell). In the Southeast Arm nonmotorized zone, the Molly Islands are a bird sanctuary; beaching boats is prohibited. Travel at least a half mile out to protect this wild zone.

For prized overnight paddle trips, **campsites** are strung around the lake, with 10 coveted sites in the quiet nonmotorized zones of South and Southeast Arms. These bays with paddler-accessible campsites have abundant wildlife and birds. You can also overnight in Flat Mountain Bay and the smaller Wolf and Eagle Bays, but these also may have motorboaters with no limits on speed. With early-morning launches to beat the onshore winds, many overnighters launch at Sedge Bay to paddle the eastern shoreline to Southeast Arm. To avoid paddling the long distance to the southern arms, you can shuttle from Bridge Bay Marina with your boat to reach them instead. **Shuttles** (Xanterra, 307/344-7311 or 866/439-7375, www.yellowstonenationalparklodges.com, mid-June–mid-Sept., base rate $180 one-way) can take a maximum of six people with gear and a few canoes or kayaks. The shuttle can also be arranged to pick you up on a scheduled day at a predetermined time and location. Call the **backcountry shuttle office** (307/242-3893) to make reservations and inquire about additional fees for shuttles longer than two hours, including loading and unloading time.

it still churns up waves with afternoon winds often from the west or southwest; more sheltered boating is along the west shore.

Canoeing and Kayaking

Paddlesports allow boaters to access some of the most scenic waterways in Yellowstone, particularly Shoshone Lake and the South and Southeast Arms of Yellowstone Lake. The quiet plop of the paddle into the water offers a chance to hear the cry of an eagle in the trees or the snap of twigs from a bear walking along shore. While the solitude and scenery can be profound, take safety precautions. Bring along a paddling jacket and pants or wetsuit—the waters can be frigid. Shoreline paddles are safer rather than crossing open water, as winds can crop up huge whitecaps fast. (Wait for winds to subside; don't attempt to paddle in them). Western shorelines are more sheltered than the eastern shorelines battered by onshore winds.

No kayak, canoe, or paddleboards rentals are available inside Yellowstone National

LEWIS LAKE

Higher than Yellowstone Lake, the much smaller Lewis Lake sits at 7,830 feet. While it offers pleasant paddling for day tours, most paddlers use it as a waterway to access the Lewis Channel and Shoshone Lake, both quiet nonmotorized zones. For paddling Lewis Lake, the trees along the western shore provide a little shelter from the afternoon winds, while the eastern shore takes the brunt of the winds pushing toward it. Unless the lake is dead calm, take the shoreline route rather than crossing open water. On many days, winds can start up at 10am.

Find the **boat launch** with a cement ramp and dock at the south end of Lewis Lake adjacent to the campground. Be sure to park in the appropriate zone for day-use or overnight parking. A second, but more difficult launch due to onshore winds, is along the northeast shore of the lake at a parking pullout that has a short pebble beach access. Find the pullout about 1.6 miles north of the boat launch.

SHOSHONE LAKE

Shoshone Lake is on every serious paddler's bucket list. With no road access and no motorized boats permitted, it is a paddler paradise. It has seclusion, wildlife, a geyser basin, and access via a river channel. With the entrance on the northwest corner of Lewis Lake, the channel is about three miles long as the crow flies, but convolutions in the river make the route actually longer. You can paddle up the slow-moving stream for the first two miles, but then encounter the challenge: You will need to wade the last mile due to the water moving too fast to paddle upstream or being too shallow to paddle.

Wading the upper portion of the Lewis Channel is easier if you bring a 15-foot rope to use to pull your boat. Summer paddlers into early July will need a wetsuit or drysuit to sustain the cold, deep runoff of the high water season. The water can get up to four feet deep in places. If that sounds too challenging, wait until later in summer when the water warms and lowers in depth. Then, with a sturdy pair of water shoes that can protect your feet on rocks, you can wade the last mile in calf-deep water.

Shoshone Lake is divided into two sections by **the Narrows,** a pinch in the shoreline squeezing the lake to a half mile across. The Narrows provides the best place to cross open water, if you must do so. The southeast shore is the safest travel route; winds hammer the east shore with waves up to three feet. To visit **Shoshone Geyser Basin,** with 80 active geysers, beach boats at the landing area denoted with an orange marker. Find the area in a small bay in the northwest corner of the lake where a trail connects to the geyser basin. Sixteen boating **campsites** rim the north and south shores of the lake.

GUIDES

Based out of Jackson, Wyoming, **Geyser Kayak** (307/413-6177, www.geyserkayak.com, daily mid-May-Oct.) leads day or overnight paddle trips in sea kayaks in Yellowstone. On Yellowstone Lake, the day trips tour West Thumb, including thermal features, and the shorter sunset tour brings on the colorful sky ($125-175 adults, $75-125 kids under 12). Rates include kayaks, life jackets, lunch, and guides. The company also guides overnight trips and custom tours. Yellowstone Lake trips are scheduled multiple times each summer for 4-6 days ($1,000-1,300) into the Southeast Arm. The shorter version uses a boat shuttle to reach the arm, while the longer version paddles the eastern shore. The company also leads two-, three-, and four-day trips ($450-1,000) on Lewis and Shoshone Lakes at various times during the summer. Rates include kayaks, life jackets, meals, and guides. Tents and sleeping bags can be provided for a fee. Plan to tip 15 percent.

Windsurfing

With strong afternoon winds, a few diehard windsurfers take to Yellowstone Lake, but most opt for warmer lakes elsewhere. Due to the cold and potential gale-force winds, the lake is not a place for beginners, only experts.

Winds can go from zero to extreme in a few minutes, and the frigid water requires wearing a wetsuit or drysuit. No rentals are available, so bring your own gear. Be prepared to self-rescue. Windsurfers need boating permits.

Fishing

Large lakes and blue-ribbon trout streams dominate the fishing scene. The attraction is the native Yellowstone cutthroat trout, recognized by its red slash. Unfortunately, fishing pressure and competition from lake trout have reduced the population of cutthroat to a point where its future is threatened. Catch-and-release fishing helps protect the species. Inside Yellowstone, a **fishing permit** is required for anglers 16 years and older ($18 for three days, $25 seven days, $40 season). For permit information and regulations, see the *Essentials* chapter.

Yellowstone Lake and **Lewis Lake** are both accessible for shoreline, float-tube fishing, spin-casting, or fly-fishing. Both lakes have monster lake trout, but while Yellowstone Lake also has cutthroat trout, Lewis Lake holds brown trout instead. Both lakes can also be fished from motorized boats. On Yellowstone Lake, the stretch of shoreline between Bridge Bay and Gull Point often sees a lineup of anglers, perhaps due to its ease of access and reputation for fishing. But other areas have less fishing pressure. On the East Entrance Road, **Sylvan Lake** is also worth fishing. From hiking destinations, you can pull cutthroat trout from **Heart** and **Riddle Lakes.** (Check with rangers before hiking to lakes or streams, as some waterways are barren.)

Two areas on Yellowstone Lake are permanently closed to fishing: the shoreline between West Thumb Geyser Basin and Little Thumb Creek, and the marinas, harbors, and waterways to Yellowstone Lake from Bridge Bay and Grant Village. The lower two miles of Pelican Creek is also closed.

While portions of the **Yellowstone River** are closed to fishing, the remainder is an outstanding trout fly-fishery with parts accessible from Grand Loop Road. Along the South Entrance Road, the **Lewis River** offers easy access as it meanders through high meadows. Here it has a reputation for 20-inch brown trout.

Yellowstone River closures include the 1.9-mile Fishing Bridge zone, LeHardys Rapids area, and the Hayden Valley including tributaries. With the exception of permanent

shore angler at Yellowstone

closures, the Yellowstone River opens for fishing usually in mid-July.

Those with kids should head to the shoreline of Lewis Lake near the boat launch and campground to find some protected places to drop in a line. To fish the shore on the larger Yellowstone Lake, take the kids to Gull Point Drive or Sand Point.

GUIDES

The **Bridge Bay Marina** (Xanterra, 307/344-7311 or 866/439-7375, www.yellowstonenationalparklodges.com, daily mid-June-early Sept., $88/hour) runs a fishing charter service on Yellowstone Lake ranging from two hours to all day. Boats can accommodate up to six people, but only three can fish at a time. Rates include fishing rods and tackle, and a guide captain who can take you to where the fish are biting. Reservations are required; tip guides 15 percent (20 percent if you catch lots of fish).

Swimming

While swimming is permitted, Yellowstone Lake does not have designated swimming areas or lifeguards; swimming is at your own risk. The water is a bone-chilling 35 degrees in June. In August, temperatures in some areas may reach the low 60s; however, it is illegal to swim near thermal features. If you take the kids swimming, watch for signs of hypothermia, off-shore winds, sudden whitecaps, and thunderstorms. North of West Thumb, water behind a sand bar may be a few degrees warmer and the sand bar cuts the waves. A pullout with beach access is 6.8 miles north of the West Thumb Junction.

WINTER SPORTS
Cross-Country Skiing and Snowshoeing

At **Grand Canyon of the Yellowstone,** you can tour from the snowy canyon rim trails to overlooks and enjoy the frozen splendor of the giant chasm; all snow-covered roads become winter ski and snowshoe routes in winter. Bring your own cross-country skis and snowshoes; rentals are only available at Old Faithful, Mammoth Hot Springs, West Yellowstone, and Jackson. Winter trail maps and guides are available online (www.nps.gov/yell) and at visitors centers. Snowcoaches are required to reach many trails, so most skiers and snowshoers tour the area with guides.

GUIDES

Cross-country ski and snowshoe tours of the Grand Canyon of the Yellowstone depart from the **Old Faithful Snow Lodge** (Xanterra, 307/344-7311 or 866/439-7375, www.yellowstonenationalparklodges.com, mid-Dec.-Feb., $185 adults, $93 kids) several mornings weekly. Tours start with a two-hour snowcoach ride to the canyon, where a guide leads groups along the canyon rim to see the Upper and Lower Falls. Ski tours cover about six miles; snowshoe tours travel three miles. Advanced beginners can handle the easy routes. Lunch is included; reservations are required.

Yellowstone Expeditions (536 Firehole Ave., West Yellowstone, 406/646-9333 or 800/728-9333, http://yellowstoneexpeditions.com, late Dec.-early Mar., $1,050-1,750/person double occupancy) leads cross-country ski and snowshoe tours from their yurt camp located at 8,000 feet in a meadow about half a mile from Grand Canyon of the Yellowstone. The camp has private heated sleeping huts surrounding two large communal huts for dining and socializing, a heated shower, and a cedar sauna. All-inclusive packages (four, five, or eight days) include snowcoach transportation to and from the camp, lodging, sleeping bags and sheets, all meals, and guide service. Guides lead daily ski tours from the camp (or after a short shuttle). January rates cost a bit less than the rest of the winter season; full moon trips fill first. Plan a 15-20 percent gratuity for guides and camp staff. The yurt camp is the only overnight winter facility on the east side of the park.

Snowmobiling

The Yellowstone snowmobile season runs

mid-December-early March. Several companies guide snowmobile tours (www.nps/gov/yell) to Grand Canyon of the Yellowstone, launching from West Yellowstone, Gardiner, Mammoth Hot Springs, and outside the park at Flagg Ranch. You can launch on your own with a permit (www.recreation.gov, early Sept.-early Oct.) from the annual lottery and an approved BAT (Best Available Technology) snowmobile. Snowmobiles rentals are only available in West Yellowstone and Gardiner in Montana, and Jackson in Wyoming.

Entertainment and Shopping

RANGER PROGRAMS

In summer (Memorial Day-Labor Day), naturalist programs take place daily at Canyon, Fishing Bridge, Lake Village, Grant Village, and West Thumb. Meeting locations vary. The free programs last 15-45 minutes and explore wildlife, geology, history, and ecology. Some programs are specifically designed for families with young kids. Fall programs are offered daily in September. There are no winter programs on the east side of the park, as facilities are closed.

Evening outdoor programs are held at the Canyon, Bridge Bay, Fishing Bridge, and Grant Village campground amphitheaters,

and the amphitheater at Fishing Bridge Museum and Visitor Center. Programs usually start at 9pm or 9:30pm; prepare for mosquitoes.

A complete list of ranger programs is printed in the seasonal park newspaper and available online (www.nps.gov/yell).

SHOPPING

Yellowstone General Stores (Delaware North Company, 406/586-7593, www.visityellowstonepark.com, 7:30am-9:30pm daily May-Sept.) are available at Canyon Village, Fishing Bridge, Lake Village, Bridge Bay, and Grant Village. Two historic shops are worth seeing even if you don't like shopping: The Fishing Bridge General Store (1 East Entrance Rd.) store is a relic from 1931, while the Lake General Store (1 Lake Loop Rd.) is a cedar octagon constructed in 1919 that looks more like a visitors center. Most stores sell the same gifts and souvenirs, as well as outdoor supplies, books, and limited groceries.

For specialty outdoor gear, Yellowstone Adventures (1 Canyon Village Loop Rd., mid-Apr.-early Nov.) sells hiking, camping, photography, and fishing supplies. Bridge Bay Marina Store (1 Bridge Bay Marina, late May-early Sept.) carries boating, angling, and camping supplies.

Canyon Lodge, the Lake Yellowstone Hotel, Lake Lodge, and Grant Village Lodge have gift shops (Xanterra, 307/344-7311 or 866/439-7375, www.yellowstonenationalparklodges.com) operated by the same concessionaire.

the Yellowstone General Store in Lake Village

Accommodations

INSIDE THE PARK
Reservations

There are four in-park lodging options open in summer only. Lake Yellowstone Hotel is the most requested of the three for its location, architecture, and historical ambience. Reservations (Xanterra, 307/344-7311 or 866/439-7375, www.yellowstonenational-parklodges.com) are a must and should be booked one year in advance for summer.

Park lodges and cabins do not have televisions, radios, or air-conditioning; a few have mini-fridges. Rooms have private bathrooms in two styles: a tub-shower combination or shower only. When booking, clarify your room needs and confirm whether there is an elevator; a few ADA rooms and cabins are available. Cell phone reception is usually available at the lodge or nearby. Internet access ($5/hour, $12/day, or $25 for three days) may be available.

Rates listed are for two people; add on 14 percent tax plus $16-18 per additional person.

Canyon Village

With more than 500 rooms in a huge complex, ★ Canyon Lodge and Cabins (late May-late Sept., $195-235 rooms and cabins, $485 suites) has hotel rooms in multistory lodges or motel rooms in cabins. It is the largest facility in the park and has the newest accommodations. Five new three-story, stone-and-wood lodge buildings were added in 2015-2016 to replace low-end cabins. With attention to the environment, these lodges have recycled glass bathroom counters, electric car charging stations, and keycard-accessed lights. Two other lodges, Cascade and Dunraven, were built in the 1990s. Rooms typically have 1-2 doubles or queens, and two-bedroom suites have a king room, queen room, and sofa-sleeper in a sitting room. Some rooms have refrigerators. All the lodges, except Cascade, have elevators to access the upper floors. The cabins in the four- or six-unit buildings have motel-style rooms with two queens. The complex includes several restaurants, gift shops, and wireless Internet.

Lake Village

Built in 1891 and named a National Historic Landmark in 2015, ★ Lake Yellowstone Hotel and Cabins (mid-May-early Oct., $155-410 rooms and cabins, $550-665 suites) in Lake Village is a striking colonial building with tall Ionic columns, bright yellow exterior, and entrance facing the lake. The three-story hotel sports 15 fake balconies added in 1903 for looks rather than usability, and later additions of the portico, dining room, and sunroom gave the hotel more distinction. Listed on the National Register of Historic Places, it is the oldest operating hotel in Yellowstone. Interior renovations completed in 2014 revamped the dining room, bar, deli, and guest rooms, and added a business center and wired Internet to hotel rooms. The complex has three types of accommodations: hotel rooms in the historic lodge, hotel rooms in an older lodge, and cabins. Historic hotel rooms include a king or 1-2 queen beds. Superior rooms face the lake, while standard rooms face the parking lot, kitchen, buildings, or trees. Two high-end suites have multiple rooms. Behind the hotel are economical options with no lake views. The two-story Sandpiper Lodge has hotel rooms with 1-2 double beds. The yellow 1920s duplex cabins have two double beds and small showers.

Despite renovations, Lake Hotel is not a luxury resort, but a historical experience. Expect sound to travel between rooms, minimal amenities, history, and a delightful location. Make dinner reservations when you book your lodging, as the dining room packs out with waiting lines. The sunroom is the place to lounge with views of the lake, sometimes with quartet music. Nearby, a gated old roadway offers one mile of walking along the shore.

Set back from the shore of Yellowstone Lake, Lake Lodge Cabins (early June-late Sept., $85-205) is a complex of rustic buildings. The single-floor, log Lake Lodge has a large porch with old-style cane-and-wood rockers where you can look across a meadow to Yellowstone Lake. The classic log-raftered interior houses a lobby with two stonework fireplaces, cafeteria with wireless Internet, bar, and gift shop. Behind the lodge, 186 heated cabins come in three styles, all with private baths. Set in wild grasses and conifers, the Western Cabins have 4-6 large, modern motel rooms with two queen beds. Built in the 1920s, the renovated small duplex Frontier Cabins and the tiny, basic Pioneer Cabins have 1-2 double beds. Their small baths have narrow shower stalls and no tubs, and sounds carry between rooms. Take a flashlight for walking after dark to and from the lodge.

Grant Village

Located at Grant Village at the southern end of West Thumb on Yellowstone Lake, Grant Village Lodge (late May-late Sept., $165-210) is a collection of six buildings with hotel rooms. Built in 1984, each two-story building contains 50 rooms that come in two styles, both with private baths and wireless Internet. Premium rooms, which have two double beds and a refrigerator, were remodeled in 2015. Standard rooms have a queen bed or two doubles. Trees growing up around the buildings cut off views of the lake. The complex includes two restaurants, a bar, and Yellowstone General Stores. A 5- to 10-minute walk drops to the beach and mostly empty marina, and a 10-minute walk connects to the restaurants, visitors center, lake, and outdoor amphitheater, which has evening ranger talks.

Camping

INSIDE THE PARK
Reservations
Of the five campgrounds on the park's east side, four accept reservations (Xanterra, 307/344-7311 or 866/439-7375, www.yellowstonenationalparklodges.com). For July and August, reservations should be made 9-12 months in advance, although last-minute cancellations can open up. Camping fees cover six people or one family; taxes and utility fees are added on. For RVs, only a few campsites fit rigs or combos of 40 feet or more. The only campground with full hookups for RVs is Fishing Bridge. All campgrounds have flush toilets, cold running water, potable water, coin-op ice machines, and evening amphitheater programs. With the exception of Fishing Bridge, they also have picnic tables, fire rings, firewood for sale, dishwashing stations, bear boxes, tent pads, and shared campsites for hikers and bikers ($7/person).

Canyon Village
At Canyon Village, Canyon Campground (late May-mid-Sept., $26) is one of the most requested campgrounds due to its central location. In a hillside forest of conifers, the 270 campsites squeeze into tight quarters in a dozen loops at 7,944 feet. Some of the sites are sloped. Campsites are designated for RVs, tents, or RV and tent combos. Some pull-through and back-in sites can fit RVs up to 40 feet. The campground check-in building has pay showers (two per night included), coin-op

laundry, and an RV dump station, although when temperatures freeze, it shuts down. Within 0.25 mile are stores, restaurants, Grand Canyon Visitor Education Center, a post office, and a gas station with repair service; Grand Canyon of the Yellowstone is one mile away.

Fishing Bridge

Just east of Fishing Bridge on Yellowstone Lake's north end, Fishing Bridge RV Park (early May-late Sept., $50) is the closest campground to the East Entrance Station. At 7,751 feet, it is the only campground in the park with electrical, water, and sewer hookups for RVs. All of the 340 sites are double-wide back-ins. If you don't have huge slide-outs, you can fit a towed RV and a vehicle side-by-side. Hardsided units are required; pop-up tent trailers are not allowed here. Surrounded by a forest, the campground stacks RVs close together like a parking lot, with a few pine trees separating some of the sites. Amenities include pay showers (two per night included), coin-op laundry, store, and an RV dump station. Nearby are a gas station with vehicle repair service, a general store that carries camping supplies and groceries, and the Fishing Bridge Museum and Visitor Center.

Lake Village

Just north of Bridge Bay Marina at 7,784 feet, ★ Bridge Bay Campground (late May-early Sept., $22) flanks a hillside across the road from Yellowstone Lake. With 432 campsites in 12 loops swooping through meadows and forests, the campground is the largest in the park. The five huge front loops sit on a large, sunny, sloped meadow with some views of the water, the Absaroka Mountains in the distance, and neighboring campers. The meadows are green in June, brown in August. The back loops circle through conifers with more shady sites. Bridge Bay Marina has a boat launch, rentals, scenic cruises, store, RV dump station, and ranger station. Separate trails for bikers and hikers lead one mile to Natural Bridge, a rock arch above Bridge Creek.

A shuttle boat service (Xanterra, 307/242-3893, mid-June-mid-Sept., $190 base rate) travels from Bridge Bay Marina to the southern arms of Yellowstone Lake for backcountry campers. The shuttle boat can take up to six people per trip and a few canoes, kayaks, and gear. Extra fees ($50-95) may apply for canoes, rowboats, kayaks, or additional hours or passengers.

West Thumb and Grant Village

In a wooded setting at 7,733 feet, Grant Village Campground (late June-late Sept., $26) sits on West Thumb Bay of Yellowstone Lake. Through a lodgepole forest, a paved road with paved parking pads loops through this giant campground of 430 campsites with a midsummer population larger than some Wyoming towns. A lack of understory gives views of neighboring campers. Trails lead to a large pebble and sand beach for sunbathing or swimming in chilly water even in August. Local streams with spawning trout attract bears in spring, keeping the campground closed until June 25. If bears are still hanging around spawning areas, the nearby campground loops stay closed until bear concentrations dissipate. Within a half mile, Grant Village has stores, restaurants, pay showers, coin-op laundry, visitors center, post office, RV dump station, and a marina that has cement boat launch ramps, docks, slips, and trailer parking. West Thumb Geyser Basin sits about three miles north of Grant Village. Of the lake campgrounds, this is the closest one to Old Faithful, 17 miles west over the Continental Divide.

At 7,830 feet, ★ Lewis Lake Campground (307/344-7381, www.nps.gov/yell, mid-June-Oct., $15/site, $5/person for shared biker-hiker sites) sits on the third-largest lake in the park, a favorite of motorboaters, anglers, and paddlers. The quieter, less-visited campground is the closest to the South Entrance, hence the first campground for those heading north from Grand Teton National Park and Jackson Hole. The campground flanks a forested hillside with 85 campsites—some sunny, some shaded. This campground is the one of the last to fill in the park, but in peak season, all the sites can be claimed by noon. Check the previous day's fill time online. RVs are limited to 25 feet, and no generators are allowed. Facilities include picnic tables, fire rings with grills, vault toilets, drinking water, garbage service, bear boxes, boat launch, boat dock, and trailer parking. Paddlers can also tour up the Lewis Channel to Shoshone Lake. From the lake's north end, trails lead to Shoshone Lake and, across the highway, to Heart Lake. Lewis Falls sits one mile south on the road.

OUTSIDE THE PARK

Shoshone National Forest (Wapiti Ranger District, 307/527-6921, www.fs.usda.gov/

shoshone) flanks the eastern boundary of Yellowstone. When Yellowstone Lake campgrounds fill up, you can drive out the East Entrance Station to reach a few Forest Service campgrounds usually open mid-May-late September.

Within the 3-7 miles east of the park entrance, **Threemile** and **Eagle Creek Campgrounds** ($15) have 20 campsites each for hard-sided RVs only. No tents are permitted due to the prevalence of bears. Both have picnic tables, fire rings with grills, drinking water, bear boxes, and wheelchair-accessible vault toilets. These also make good campgrounds to use en route into the park. Threemile takes **reservations** (877/444-6777, www.recreation.gov), but Eagle Creek does not.

Food

INSIDE THE PARK

Dining in Canyon Village or around Yellowstone Lake is limited to restaurants and cafés operated by two companies, Xanterra and Delaware North Company. As such, similar menus are in each of their respective venues. In summer, mid-June-early September, plan on long waiting lines at some of the restaurants, especially in lodges, where the wait might be an hour or two for a table. Only the Lake Hotel Dining Room and Grant Village Dining Room take **reservations.** In all the park restaurants, including the lodges, casual dress is common for dining.

Canyon Village

Canyon Lodge (Xanterra, 307/344-7311 or 866/439-7375, www.yellowstonenationalpark-lodges.com, daily late May-late Sept.) has the lodge dining room, a cafeteria, and a deli; all three are first-come, first-served seating. The concessionaire is slated to redesign Canyon Lodge meal facilities starting in fall 2016 to offer other food services, local and sustainable

meals, and take the interior appearance back to its 1960s color schemes and appearance.

Canyon Lodge Dining Room has a few flexible options if you are trying to speed out the door. Go for table service only if you have leisure time. Breakfast (7am-10am, $5-13) can either be ordered off the menu if you want it hot or off the buffet, which is faster if you are trying to hit a trail. Lunch (11:30am-2:30pm, $10-16) features burgers, sandwiches, and salads, but the soup and salad bar is speedier. Dinner (5pm-10pm, $10-30) includes the lighter lunch menu with the addition of prime rib, trout, and wild game meatloaf entrées. Wine, beer, and cocktails are served. Order lunches to go for $13.

Canyon Lodge Cafeteria serves breakfast, lunch, and dinner until early September when it serves only breakfast and dinner with shorter hours. For breakfast (6:30am-10:30am, $2-6), create your own combinations of entrées and sides with à la carte items. Lunch (11:30am-3pm, $9-10) has sandwiches, rice bowls, wraps, and salads. Dinner

(4:30pm-9:30pm, $9-20) serves the lunch menu plus a trout meal. Beer and wine are available.

Canyon Lodge Deli (7:30am-9:30pm, $4-8) serves deli and breakfast sandwiches, hot dogs, chili, salads, snacks, beverages, beer, wine, ice cream, and espresso. You can get sandwiches to go for hiking or touring. Hours shorten in May and September.

Part of the ★ **Canyon General Store** (Delaware North Company, 2 Canyon Village Loop Rd., 406/586-7593, www.visityellowstonepark.com, 7:30am-8:30pm daily mid-May-late Sept., $5-10) has a large soda fountain diner with red stools around four huge peninsula counters. Music from the 1950s adds a retro feel. The diner serves breakfast until 10:30am followed by lunch and dinner of burgers, sandwiches, fries, salads, soda fountain ice cream treats made from Wilcoxson's from Montana, and Junior Ranger meals for kids.

The small grocery carries produce, meats, camping supplies, snacks, beer, wine, frozen foods, and premade sandwiches for hiking. If you need large brand selection or specialty items, you'll need to head to Cody or Jackson.

Yellowstone Adventures (1 Canyon Village Loop Rd., 7:30am-9:30pm daily) serves frozen yogurt and coffee (but no espresso).

Fishing Bridge

At Fishing Bridge, the circa 1931 **Fishing Bridge General Store** (Delaware North Company, 1 East Entrance Rd., 406/586-7593, www.visityellowstonepark.com, 7:30am-8:30pm daily mid-May-late Sept., $5-10) has seated food service in a small diner area with breakfast until 10:30am followed by the lunch and dinner menu of sandwiches, burgers, and salads. Old-fashioned ice cream soda fountain treats headline the desserts, and kids can get Junior Ranger meals. The store also serves espresso.

Lake Village

Lake Yellowstone Hotel and **Lake Lodge** (Xanterra, 307/344-7311 or 866/439-7375, www.yellowstonenationalparklodges.com) provide dining options.

Surrounded on three sides by large windows with peekaboo water views on the lake side, the ★ **Lake Yellowstone Hotel Dining Room** (daily mid-May-early Oct.) clusters tables around white columns that echo the outside architecture of the colonial building. Breakfast (6:30am-10:30am, $6-15) can either be ordered off the menu or off the buffet, which is faster if you are trying to get out the door to hike. Breakfast specialties include eggs Benedict on crab cakes and a design-your-own omelet that can be made with whole eggs or egg whites. Lunch (11:30am-2:30pm, $10-17) features burgers, wraps, sandwiches, entrée salads, a soup and salad bar, and plated entrées with sides. Dinner (5pm-10pm, $10-35) has multiple courses with appetizers, soups, salads, and plated entrées of fresh fish, steak, and wild game, but you can also go lighter with entrée salads or a Wyoming burger. Vegetarian, vegan, gluten-free, and children's menu options are available, too. No reservations are taken for breakfast or lunch, but you should make advance reservations for dinner by phone or online when booking your lodging. If you are not staying in Lake Yellowstone Hotel, you can make reservations 60 days out. The **deli** (6:30am-9pm, $4-13) serves breakfast, lunch, dinner, and desserts. Breakfast can be continental or entrées such as quiche or breakfast croissants. Lunch and dinner choices include soups, salads, sandwiches, and wraps. Some are fish specialties. Sandwiches can be made to go. Drinks include espresso, beer, and wine. Hours shorten and no breakfast is served in the shoulder season.

At Lake Lodge, the **Lake Lodge Cafeteria** (6:30am-10pm daily mid-June-late Sept., $6-20) rotates specials each day that include trout, chicken, pasta, and pot roast, but prime rib and roast turkey are served daily. Order breakfast entrées and burritos until 10am or continental breakfast items until 11:30am when sandwiches, paninis, and chili come on the menu. Sandwiches can be made to go. In September, only breakfast and lunch are served with shortened hours.

At **Lake General Store** (Delaware North Company, 1 Lake Loop Rd., 406/586-7593, www.visityellowstonepark.com, 7:30am-8:30pm daily mid-May-mid-Sept., $5-10), diners could take advantage of the million-dollar view if the restaurant had big windows, but you can get food to take outside to enjoy the lake. The menu features breakfast, hot sandwiches, burgers, chili, wraps, salads, and Junior Ranger meals for kids. The old-fashioned soda fountain serves ice cream, malts, milkshakes, and sundaes.

West Thumb and Grant Village

Grant Village (Xanterra, 307/344-7311 or 866/439-7375, www.yellowstonenational-parklodges.com, daily late May-late Sept.) has two restaurants. With views overlooking Yellowstone Lake from the defunct marina on West Thumb Bay, **Grant Village Lake House Restaurant** has prime window tables for relishing sunrise or sunset colors glowing on the lake. Breakfast (6:30am-10:30am, $6-13) is a basic buffet or à la carte. For dinner (5pm-9:30pm, $9-15), in 2015 the restaurant swapped out their pub-style menu in favor of salads and noodle bowls, which didn't go over so well. Local beers are on tap, and wine is served. Order your food in line, and servers deliver it to your table. Hours shorten in shoulder seasons.

Tucked in the forest, ★ **Grant Village Dining Room** is in a vaulted room with a warm wood ceiling and large-paned windows overlooking the lake. Breakfast (6:30am-10am, $5-13) can be ordered from the menu, or for a quicker meal, choose the breakfast buffet. Lunch (11:30am-2:30pm, $10-15) includes salads, burgers, and sandwiches. Vegetarians can get black bean burgers or frittatas. Dinner (5pm-10pm, $13-30) serves up fresh fish including trout, prime rib, and stuffed eggplant. Specialties for lunch and dinner revolve around wild game: elk sliders, bison and elk meatloaf, and bison. The restaurant serves vegetarian, vegan, gluten-free, and children's menu options, plus beer, cocktails, and wine from a worldwide wine list. No reservations

are taken for breakfast or lunch, but you should make advance reservations for dinner by phone or online when booking your lodging. If you are not staying in Grant Village Lodge, you can make reservations 60 days out.

In the Grant General Store, the **Grant Village Grill** (Delaware North Company, 2 Grant Village Loop Rd., 406/586-7593, www.visityellowstonepark.com, 7:30am-8:30pm daily late May-mid-Sept., $5-12) serves a small menu of fast-food-style burgers, fries, salads, and ice cream, milkshakes, and floats. Breakfast is served until 10:30am.

Groceries

Yellowstone General Stores (Delaware North Company, 406/586-7593, www.visityellowstonepark.com, 7:30am-9:30pm daily generally mid-May-late Sept.) are more like large convenience marts with limited fresh produce, frozen and packaged foods, and wine and beer. They also have sundaes, root beer floats, milkshakes, malts, and ice cream cones, several served from old-style soda fountains. Stores are located at **Canyon Village, Fishing Bridge, Lake Village,** and **Grant Village** (general store and a mini-mart). For larger grocery needs, you'll need to drive to Cody or Jackson to find the supermarkets.

Picnicking

Find tables for picnicking north of Canyon Village at **Dunraven Pass** or **Cascade,** the only one with fire rings. Along the Yellowstone River, picnic at **Chittenden Bridge/Wapiti Lake** or **Nez Perce Ford.**

Thirteen picnic areas rim Yellowstone Lake, offering places to enjoy the water, but hold onto the plates, as afternoons are frequently windy. All the picnic areas have tables; half have vault toilets. Picnic areas at Grant Village and Bridge Bay have fire rings. On the west shore, **Sand Point** and **Gull Point** each flank a long spit that creates a shallow pool with warmer, protected water for swimming. On the north shore, **Sedge Bay,** a blustery driftwood beach with waves crashing on shore, is best on calm days.

Transportation and Services

DRIVING

Two-lane roads are the standard in Yellowstone. Throw in curves, wildlife, and scenery, and drivers need to pay attention. Use pullouts for sightseeing or wildlife-watching rather than stopping in the middle of the road. Traffic gets extremely congested on summer afternoons on North Rim and South Rim Drives at Grand Canyon of the Yellowstone. To avoid the mayhem, visit earlier or later in the day, and stop at picnic areas to use toilets.

Parking lots cram full between 10am and 5pm (restroom lines are long, too). RVs will find limited parking. At trailheads such as Dunraven Pass and all trailheads around Grand Canyon of the Yellowstone, claim a spot before 10am.

EMERGENCY SERVICES

Ranger stations are available at Bridge Bay and the South Entrance Station. For medical emergencies, **Lake Clinic** (307/242-7241, 8am-5pm daily mid-May-mid-Sept.), in Lake Village, is a small facility that can handle most medical issues. For major medical emergencies, hospitals are 60-120 miles away. Head south to Jackson to **St. John's Medical Center** (625 E. Broadway, 307/733-3636, www.teton-hospital.org) or east to Cody to **West Park Hospital** (707 Sheridan Ave., 307/527-7501, www.westparkhospital.org).

Where Can I Find . . .?

- **Banks and ATMS:** ATMs are in all park lodges and Yellowstone General Stores.

- **Cell Service:** Verizon service is available in Canyon Village. Verizon and AT&T service may be available around Yellowstone Lake lodges.

- **Gas and Garage Services:** Gas stations (406/848-7548) are located at Canyon Village (early May-late Oct.) and Fishing Bridge and Grant Village (mid-May-late Sept.). You can pay at the pump 24 hours a day with a credit card.

- **Internet Service:** Wireless Internet is available at Canyon Lodge and Grant Village lodges (fee); wired service is in hotel rooms at Lake Hotel. Internet is not available at the visitors centers.

- **Laundry:** Coin-op laundries are located at Canyon Campground (late May-mid-Sept.), Grant Village Campground (late June-mid-Sept.), Lake Lodge (mid-June-late Sept.), and Fishing Bridge RV Park (late June-mid-Sept.).

- **Post Office:** Post offices are at Lake Village (mid-May-mid-Oct.), Grant Village (mid-May-mid-Sept.), and Canyon Village (late May-mid-Sept.).

- **Showers:** Pay showers are located at Canyon Campground (late May-mid-Sept.), Grant Village Campground (late June-mid-Sept.), and Fishing Bridge RV Park (late June-mid-Sept.).

North Grand Teton

Look for ★ to find recommended sights, activities, dining, and lodging.

Highlights

★ **Mt. Moran:** This 12,605-foot peak towers over Jackson Lake, with almost half its height exposed above the shore (page 175).

★ **Jackson Lake:** Backdropped by the Teton parapets, this is a unique spot for boating, paddling, fishing, or scenic cruising (page 176).

★ **Jackson Lake Lodge:** This National Historic Landmark commands a prime spot overlooking the lake (page 177).

★ **Oxbow Bend:** Watch wildlife congregate at this wetland backdropped by the Tetons (page 177).

★ **Signal Mountain:** At 7,720 feet, Signal Mountain's location yields big views (page 179).

★ **Colter Bay Lakeshore Trail:** This virtually flat trail wraps around the forested Colter Peninsula, linking rocky beaches on Jackson Lake (page 182).

★ **Grand View Point:** Climb the trail to this 7,823-foot point for a panorama of the entire valley of Jackson Hole and the Teton Mountains (page 184).

★ **Horseback Riding:** Colter Bay trail rides come with stunning views of Jackson Lake flanked by the Grand Tetons (page 188).

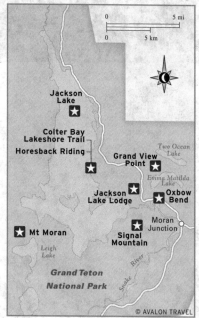

The Tetons rise like no other, commanding attention from almost every location in the park.

Showing the results of colossal earth forces, the peaks contain ancient sea layers metamorphosed under pressure, height from upthrusting, and a jagged appearance from glaciation.

Mt. Moran at 12,605 feet in elevation looms over the other peaks in the northern half of the Tetons. Its massive east face is flanked with several small active glaciers, and its trailless access is forbidding even to climbers. It plummets 6,000 feet from its summit to the shores of Jackson Lake, where it reflects in glassy water.

Once a smaller natural lake, Jackson Lake increased in size with a dam on its east side. More than 15 islands dot the lake, which serves as a foreground for the North Tetons. Marinas, campgrounds, and trails allow visitors to enjoy the shoreline. Boaters ply the waters for sightseeing, and anglers go after trout. Campgrounds and lodges rim the lake's eastern shore.

Fueling Jackson Lake, the Snake River gathers its first waters to begin its lengthy journey to the Columbia River as the 13th-largest river in the United States. The river curls through Jackson Hole, where anglers and recreational rafters float the water.

A slice of John D. Rockefeller, Jr. Memorial Parkway connects the Tetons to Yellowstone. The swath extends west with one of the most remote roads in the region, the rugged gravel Grassy Lake Road. Only those with the gumption for a several-hour backwoods adventure head here.

PLANNING YOUR TIME

Summer is the time when all visitors centers, campgrounds, lodges, marinas, and services are open. No wonder: That's when the weather is the warmest and the best. Most roads open in May, and lower-elevation trails are snow-free in June. But June is the wettest month, followed by July as the driest.

Jackson Lake is at its best in summer, with the ice melting out between early May and early June. Shoreline trout fishing in the shallows during June's high water gives way to lower lake levels in August with bigger beaches, less-frigid water temperatures, and fishing in deeper waters.

When visitor services close for winter, Grand Teton becomes a place of winter fun. Cold temperatures reign along with winds,

Previous: wildflower meadows to Grand View Point; Colter Bay and the Grand Teton. **Above:** an osprey at Oxbow Bend.

North Grand Teton

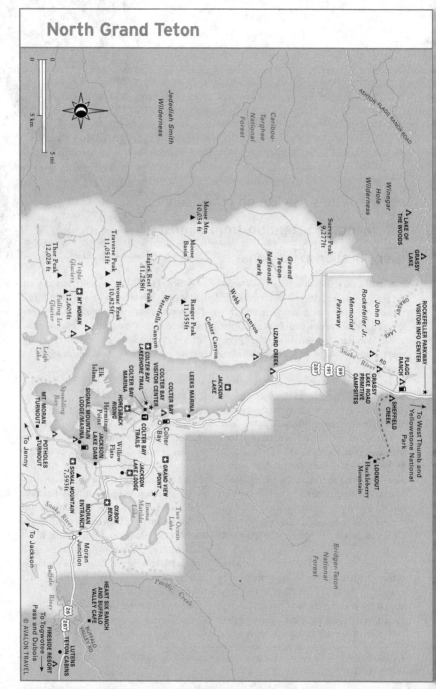

0 5 km

0 5 mi

Jedediah Smith Wilderness

Caribou-Targhee National Forest

Winegar Hole Wilderness

ASHTON-FLAGG RANCH ROAD

LAKE OF THE WOODS ▲

GRASSY ▲ LAKE

Moose Mtn 10,054 ft ▲

Survey Peak 9,277 ft ▲

Grand Teton National Park

John D. Rockefeller Jr. Memorial Parkway

GRASSY LAKE RD

ROCKEFELLER PARKWAY VISITOR INFO CENTER

To West Thumb and Yellowstone National Park →

Traverse Peak 11,051 ft ▲

Eagles Rest Peak 11,258ft ▲

Moose Basin

Thor Peak 12,028 ft ▲

Triple Glaciers ▲ 12,605ft

▲ MT MORAN

Bivouac Peak 10,825ft ▲

Ranger Peak 11,355 ft ▲

Waterfalls Canyon

Webb Canyon

Colter Canyon

LIZARD CREEK △

Snake River

287 191 89

FLAGG RANCH ■

GRASSY LAKE ROAD PRIMITIVE CAMPSITES

SHEFFIELD △ CREEK

Falling Ice Glacier

Leigh Lake

Spaulding Bay

MT MORAN TURNOUT ■

Elk Island

COLTER BAY LAKESHORE TRAIL ○

COLTER BAY VISITOR CENTER ¡

JACKSON LAKE

LEEKS MARINA ●

COLTER BAY MARINA ⚓

Hermitage Point

HORESBACK RIDING

COLTER BAY TRAILS

COLTER BAY △

Colter Bay

LOOKOUT ■ Huckleberry Mountain

SIGNAL MOUNTAIN LODGE/MARINA ●

JACKSON LAKE DAM

Willow Flats

GRAND VIEW POINT ▲

SIGNAL MOUNTAIN 7,593ft △

POTHOLES TURNOUT ■

JACKSON LAKE LODGE ●

To Jenny →

MORAN ENTRANCE ■

OXBOW BEND

Emma Matilda Lake

Jackson Lake

Two Ocean Lake

Bridger-Teton National Forest

Snake River

To Jackson →

Moran Junction

Buffalo River

Pacific Creek

HEART SIX RANCH AND BUFFALO VALLEY CAFE ■

BUFFALO VALLEY RD

To Togwotee Pass and Dubois →

26 287

FIRESIDE RESORT △

To Teton Pass and Victor →

LUTENS ▲ TETON CABINS

© AVALON TRAVEL

which plunge the windchill. The main highway up the park's east boundary from Jackson to Flagg Ranch is open year-round, offering wildlife-watching and views of the Tetons. November-April, Teton Park Road closes from Signal Mountain Lodge south, turning into a scenery-laden cross-country ski and snowshoe route.

Snowmobiles can tour the Grassy Lake Road and South Entrance Road into Yellowstone. They can also access frozen Jackson Lake for ice fishing.

Exploring North Grand Teton

VISITORS CENTERS
Rockefeller Parkway Visitor Information Center

North of Jackson Lake at Flagg Ranch in John D. Rockefeller, Jr. Memorial Parkway, Rockefeller Parkway Visitor Information Center (U.S. 89/191/287, 307/543-2372, 9am-4pm daily early June-early Sept.) is a one-room log cabin north of Headwaters Lodge with a small exhibit on John D. Rockefeller, Jr., who donated the land for the parkway. You can get information on trail conditions, road conditions, and weather, and obtain maps for both Grand Teton and Yellowstone National Parks. Anyone planning to drive the Ashton-Flagg Ranch Road (Grassy Lake Road) should get road condition updates here. The station sells a few books from Grand Teton Association (307/739-3606, www.grandtetonpark.org).

Colter Bay Visitor Center

Located in Colter Bay Village at the marina, the Colter Bay Visitor Center (307/739-3594, 8am-7pm daily early June-early Sept., closes at 5pm spring and fall) has maps and information on hiking, boating, weather, backcountry permits, and activities. The small center has an auditorium that runs documentaries on Grand Teton National Park during the day. In summer, you can participate in interpretive programs, see craft demonstrations, and go on tours of the tiny Indian Arts Museum, which features intricate beadwork among other artifacts from the David T. Vernon collection. Forty-six restored pieces of the 1,416-piece collection were added during summer 2013, including clothing, jewelry, tools, and weapons. A Grand Teton Association store (307/739-3606, www.grandtetonpark.org) carries books on wildlife, wildflowers, hiking, history, geology, and natural history.

ENTRANCE STATIONS

Moran Entrance ($30 vehicle, $25 motorcycles, $15 hike-in/bike-in; joint parks pass: $50 vehicle, $40 motorcycles, $20 hike-in/bike-in), just west of Moran Junction, is open year-round and provides access to North Grand Teton along with the connecting Highways 26/89/191/287. The Moran Entrance

Rockefeller Parkway Visitor Information Center

is 29 miles southeast of Yellowstone's South Entrance and 30 miles north of Jackson, Wyoming. John D. Rockefeller, Jr. Memorial Parkway (driving south from Yellowstone) has no entrance station.

TOURS
Bus Tours

Scenic bus tours (Grand Teton Lodging Company, 307/543-2811, www.gtlc.com, late May-early Oct.) offer guided narration to the sights in Grand Teton and Yellowstone National Parks. Tours depart at 8:30am from Jackson Lake Lodge. The half-day tour of **Grand Teton** (Mon., Wed., and Fri., $65 adults, $30 kids) takes in views of the Tetons, Jenny Lake Overlook, Chapel of Transfiguration, and Oxbow Bend. The full-day tour of **Yellowstone National Park** (Tues., Thurs., and Sat., $100 adults, $60 kids) circles the lower Grand Loop with stops at Old Faithful, Grand Prismatic Spring, Grand Canyon of the Yellowstone, West Thumb, and Yellowstone Lake. Reservations are required for all tours. When making reservations, ask how current road construction may impact tour stops, and check discounts for both tours.

Boat Tours

From the marina at Colter Bay, catch a **Jackson Lake boat tour** (Grand Teton Lodging Company, 307/543-2811, www.gtlc. com, daily late May-mid-Sept., $30-65 adults, $14-37 kids) to get out on the water and soak up the lustrous views of Mt. Moran. Scenic daytime cruises (10:15am, 1:15pm, and 3:15pm daily, additional departure 6:15pm Thurs.) accommodate 36 and 40 passengers for a 1.5-hour scenic tour. Breakfast (7:15am Fri.-Wed.), lunch (12:15pm (Mon., Wed., and Fri.-Sat.), and dinner (5:15pm Fri.-Wed.) cruises combine a tour with an outdoor meal around the campfire on Elk Island. Reservations are required for all tours.

Wildlife Tours

The **Teton Science School** (700 Coyote Canyon Rd., Jackson, 877/404-6626, www. tetonscience.org, daily year-round) leads half-day, full-day, and multiday wildlife expeditions in Grand Teton and Yellowstone. Taught by biologists and naturalists, the programs offer ways to see wolves, bears, bison, elk, antelope, moose, and birds. Binoculars and spotting scopes are provided; guests ride in safari-style rigs with top hatches for standing up to view animals. Most programs pick up in Jackson or Teton Village; for an additional fee, pickup can be arranged at Jackson Lake Lodge or Signal Lake Lodge. Half-day expeditions ($130 adults, $100 kids) go out for sunrise or sunset, the best time for viewing wildlife. Full-day programs ($210-300 adults, $150-250 kids) depart early in the morning to catch animals feeding. The school also has wildlife-watching float, hiking, or specialty seasonal trips.

DRIVING TOURS
Grassy Lake Road/ Ashton-Flagg Ranch Road
52 MILES

A narrow dirt and cobble road winds west from Flagg Ranch through John D. Rockefeller, Jr. Memorial Parkway and Caribou-Targhee National Forest. Called the **Grassy Lake Road,** or the **Ashton-Flagg Ranch Road,** it looks like a shortcut to reach the west side of the Tetons, but it's not. The 52-mile road will take about 3-4 hours one-way to drive at top speeds of 15 or 20 mph, due to bumps, ruts, potholes, dust, and washboards. New gravel in 2014 improved the parkway section, but after that, high-clearance and four-wheel-drive vehicles are best. It has scenic primitive campsites, solitude and quiet, minimal traffic, fishing, trailheads to hot springs, and wildlife, such as trumpeter swans, bears, and moose. It eventually reaches pavement 12 miles before Ashton, Idaho, and is a route to connect with the Bechler Trailhead, Cave Falls Campground, and waterfalls in the southwest corner of Yellowstone.

Do not attempt to drive the complete road in large RVs or with big trailers, as turnarounds are few and far between, and many places squeeze into one lane with nowhere to pass. Small RVs and truck-camper combinations can handle the road most of the time, but you must be comfortable backing up. The road is usually snow-free for driving **June-October,** but a late-melting snowpack can flood the road in places. Before driving, get current conditions at the Rockefeller Parkway Visitor Information Center at Flagg Ranch. In winter, the road is a snowmobile route.

Yellowstone to Moran Junction
29 MILES

A year-round, two-lane highway runs along the entire eastern flank of Grand Teton National Park. From the South Entrance of Yellowstone to Moran Junction, **Highway 89/191/287** crosses eight miles through John D. Rockefeller, Jr. Memorial Parkway before traveling 16 miles down Jackson Lake to Jackson Lake Junction. The forested **John D. Rockefeller, Jr. Memorial Parkway** pales in comparison to the spectacular views along Jackson Lake. In the parkway, Flagg Ranch is really a pit stop with food, lodging, camping, and an information center, but it does allow access to the scenic **Snake River.** Along Jackson Lake, you can stop to picnic at three designated spots, the first two with trails that drop to the shore. Between the northern two picnic areas, **Jackson Lake Overlook** affords a dramatic view southward of the lake flanked by the massive Tetons. Of the two marinas on this road, **Colter Bay** offers the better sightseeing stop because of the visitors center and the miles of scenic walking trails around Colter Bay. A stop at **Jackson Lake Lodge** lets you peruse this National Historic Landmark. South of the lodge, **Willow Flats Overlook** gives another viewpoint of the Teton Mountains with Jackson Lake in the distance past the marshy willows. At Jackson Lake Junction, head east to stop at **Oxbow Bend Turnout,** a good place for watching birds and wildlife.

Inside Road/ Outside Road Loop
43 MILES

The **Inside Road** (Teton Park Rd., May-Oct.) and **Outside Road** (Hwy. 26/89/191, year-round) form a large 43-mile loop with huge changing views of the Teton Mountains.

Willow Flats offers a good viewpoint for wildlife.

Continental Divide

The Continental Divide is the division between giant watersheds. It sends water in two different directions—to the Pacific Ocean and the Atlantic Ocean. Since the Continental Divide separates watersheds, one could surmise that it should be the tallest thing around. Yet it's a confusing land feature because it avoids the highest peaks.

The Grand Teton stands at 13,770 feet in elevation, yet the Continental Divide runs through the lower Absaroka Mountains east of Jackson Lake. Despite the higher height of the Tetons on the west side of the park, Jackson Lake and the Snake River drain toward the Pacific via a southward arc around the Teton Range. The divide's location east of Grand Teton National Park has more to do with how ancient glaciers carved out river valleys rather than which peaks are the highest.

To drive over the Continental Divide, go to 9,658-foot Togwotee Pass, 25 miles east of Moran. One of the defining peaks there is Two Ocean Mountain, appropriately named for where its waters flow. The return descent, best in morning or sunset, faces the splendor of the Teton Mountains.

Two Ocean is a vast plateau stretching from Yellowstone Lake south into the Bridger-Teton National Forest. The plateau sheds water toward the two continental oceans, and Two Ocean Pass drains through Atlantic Creek and Pacific Creek, which denote their eventual destinations. Pacific Creek tumbles into Grand Teton National Park to join the Snake River. But here's the oddity: Two Ocean Lake in the Pacific Creek drainage is a bit of a misnomer, as the lake drains only to one ocean, the Pacific.

Sometimes the peaks loom so close that they fill the front windshield of the vehicle. Starting at Jackson Lake Junction, take the two-lane Inside Road 12 miles south. En route, it crosses the Snake River at Jackson Lake Dam and passes Chapel of the Sacred Heart, Signal Mountain Lodge, Signal Mountain Summit Road, and several scenic pullouts before reaching Moose Junction to shift the direction back northward on the two-lane Outside Road. At Moran Junction, turn west for five miles to return to Jackson Lake Junction. Watch for bison, elk, moose, and pronghorn on this loop, especially when driving at dusk. The speed limit reduces on the Outside Road to 45 mph sunset-sunrise.

Signal Mountain Summit Road
5 MILES

For a short driving tour, the narrow, paved five-mile Signal Mountain Summit Road (May-Oct.) climbs 800 feet in elevation to two overlooks near the 7,720-summit of Signal Mountain. The lower viewpoint looks south to Jackson Hole, Jackson Lake, and the southern Tetons, while the upper overlook faces the Absaroka Mountains. When driving up, be cautious of bikers enjoying the flying descent. Tiny parking areas do not have room or turnaround space for large RVs and trailers, but you can leave trailers in the base parking lot.

Pacific Creek Road
8 MILES

Just west of Moran Junction, you can explore an eight-mile Forest Service road usually open May-early November. Pacific Creek Road affords wildlife-watching, especially at dawn or dusk, and views of the Tetons on your return. Turn northeast onto pavement, which ends at the park boundary and turns into a wide gravel road. The road terminates at Pacific Creek Campground in Bridger-Teton National Forest. A 2.4-mile side spur also reaches Two Ocean Lake inside the park.

Sights

COLTER BAY

Colter Bay is one of those do-everything places where you can settle in for several days without moving the car. Stay in a log cabin, tent cabin, RV park, or the campground while you picnic, swim, hike, paddle, and boat. The bay and offshore islands offer protected places on the water for paddling and boating. You can rent kayaks, canoes, or boats from the marina to tour around the islands. A maze of hiking trails loop peninsulas, passing tiny lakes named for water birds, such as Cygnet, Swan, and Heron. You can also go horseback riding. The **Colter Bay Visitor Center** (307/739-3594, 8am-7pm daily early June-early Sept., closes at 5pm spring and fall) houses a small collection of Native American artifacts, and the amphitheater offers evening programs. Don't forget the scenery, with Jackson Lake reflecting Mt. Moran and the Teton Mountains.

★ Mt. Moran

Despite the higher Grand Teton to the south, **Mt. Moran** dominates the scenery in the north end of Grand Teton National Park. Its 12,605-foot summit looms over Jackson Lake. Visitors coming from Yellowstone often mistake Mt. Moran's prominence for the Grand Teton. The peak acquired its name from Thomas Moran, famous for his western landscape paintings. For climbers, the peak poses multiple technical routes pioneered after the first 1922 ascent. For sightseers to appreciate its intricacies, use binoculars to look for the **Black Dike** west below the summit. The 150-foot-wide vertical dike, an intrusion of magma from 775 million years ago, runs unseen behind the peak westward for 6-7 miles. You can also spot a tiny cap of beige marine Flathead Sandstone on the top, evidence of the ancient sea that covered the Teton rocks before uplifting and glaciation changed them into their current shape. Look closely below the summit mound to see two of the peak's five tiny glaciers. **Falling Ice Glacier** wedges in the lower Black Dike zone, while **Skillet**

Recognize Mt. Moran by its vertical black dike and two glaciers, Falling Ice and Skillet.

Colter Bay and Jackson Lake

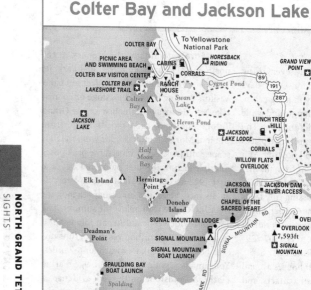

Glacier sits lower down on the north side. They are easier to distinguish from snow in late summer.

So where's the best views of Mt. Moran? Hike Heron Pond at Colter Bay to enjoy reflections of Mt. Moran in the water. Drive up Signal Mountain to gaze across Jackson Lake. Dine at Signal Mountain Lodge or Jackson Lake Lodge to enjoy its backdrop at dinner.

JACKSON LAKE
★ Jackson Lake

At 40 square miles, Jackson Lake is huge. Its 15-mile length runs from the Snake River in the north to Spalding Bay in the south. Lake water exits via the Jackson Lake Dam into the Snake River. Today, the water is about 438 feet deep, the natural lake deepened for Idaho farm irrigation by the dam. Fifteen islands inhabit the lake, including Elk Island, the largest. You can explore the lake on a cruise, paddle its islands, dine at Signal

Mountain Lodge overlooking the lake, hike portions of its shoreline around Colter Bay, picnic on the shore at its northern end, and camp on its shore at Lizard Creek or by boat at 15 primitive backcountry campsites that rim the lake. It has two marinas that rent boats and four launch sites. Kayaking and canoeing is best in the protected islands surrounding Colter Bay. Anglers go after nonnative brown and lake trout year-round, with ice fishing in winter. But the real prizes are native Snake River fine-spotted cutthroat trout and mountain whitefish. Expect chilly waters for swimming, as the lake usually warms only to the high 50s in summer, and afternoon winds are common.

ELK ISLAND

Of the 15 islands in Jackson Lake, Elk Island is the largest and is visited by the Colter Bay cruise boat. Most of the islands sit off the eastern shore, making them accessible from the

Jackson Lake flanks the lower Teton Mountains.

three marinas. To avoid open-water crossings, several of the protected islands make good kayaking and canoeing destinations, especially the sheltered islands between Colter Bay and Half Moon Bay. Rent canoes, kayaks, and boats at Colter Bay Marina and Signal Mountain Marina. Motorboats can tour around all the islands, and primitive campsites offer places to camp.

★ Jackson Lake Lodge

With views of Mt. Moran and Jackson Lake, **Jackson Lake Lodge** (800/628-9988, www.gtlc.com, late May-early Oct.) is a National Historic Landmark. Windows in the Mural Dining Room framing the Teton Mountains compete for attention with the 10 Rendezvous Murals by Carl Roters, a late 20th-century American artist. The *Trappers Bride* mural by western heritage artist Charles Banks Wilson also decorates the wall in the Blue Heron Lounge. John D. Rockefeller Jr. hand-selected the location on **Lunch Tree Hill** for

its unobstructed mountain views. It was also the site where Rockefeller and Yellowstone Park superintendent Horace Albright hatched the plans to buy the mountain-front swath in Jackson Hole to preserve it from development. Commissioned by Rockefeller and built in 1955, the three-story lodge uses the modern international architecture of its era blended with artful takes on western and Native American elements. It houses a small selection of the 1,416-piece David T. Vernon collection of Native American artifacts including pottery, baskets, beadwork, weavings, and arrowheads from tribes of the Northern Rockies.

Two Ocean and Emma Matilda Lakes

This pair of glacially carved lakes are located one mile apart in a mix of forest and meadows on the 6,800-foot flanks of the Absaroka Mountains. Both lakes are about 2.7 miles long and a half mile wide. A maze of hiking trails circle the lakes, cuts between them, and links to Jackson Lake Lodge. With an 800-foot-climb, the 7,586-foot **Grand View Point** between the west ends of both lakes gets the best views of the Tetons and Jackson Lake, but you'll get to see the distant peaks from the north shores of both lakes, too. While you can only reach **Emma Matilda** via hiking trails, vehicles can drive to **Two Ocean Lake** via the dirt Two Ocean Road. From there, you can launch nonmotorized boats such as kayaks and canoes for placid shoreline paddling. Both lakes offer fishing.

★ Oxbow Bend

The slow-moving convolutions of water through **Oxbow Bend** yield outstanding wildlife habitat. Located one mile east of Jackson Lake Junction, Oxbow Bend provides a place for wildlife and bird-watching. Bring binoculars or spotting scopes to aid in viewing from the pullout above the bend. Look for river otters, beavers, or muskrats in the water, or moose foraging on willows. Squawking and grunting American pelicans add to the cacophony from songbirds, and osprey and bald eagles hunt for fish. Opt for the prime viewing at dawn or dusk, but be cautious of large animals such as bears and moose that might be using the road as a travel corridor.

Snake River

Legend says that the **Snake River** derived its name from the S-shaped gesture for salmon used by the Shoshone tribe and was mistaken for the shape of the river by early explorers. While the Snake River starts in Yellowstone National Park from three streams descending from Two Ocean Plateau, the 1,078-mile river really gets going in Grand Teton

National Park. It flows south through John D. Rockefeller, Jr. Memorial Parkway to enter Jackson Lake and then departs the lake through the dam. With its first 50 miles cutting through Jackson Hole, it eventually becomes the largest tributary for the Columbia River and the 13th-longest river in the United States.

To enjoy the river, camp in one of the **primitive campsites** on Grassy Lake Road. In its reaches above and below Jackson Lake, you can raft, float, fish, or watch birds and wildlife. River accesses are located near **Flagg Ranch**, at **Cattleman's Bridge Site** east of Jackson Lake Junction, and west of **Moran**

Finding Solitude

Plenty of places offer solitude in a wilderness experience, and you don't have to climb one of the Tetons to get away from the hordes. These softer off-the-beaten-path adventures yield gorgeous scenery, wildlife-watching, hiking, and fishing with more serenity than you may find along the main park roads.

JACKSON LAKE

Jackson Lake is one of Grand Teton National Park's most-loved places. If you hang out in a boat along the eastern shore of Jackson Lake near the islands, you're bound see fellow boaters, especially around the marinas. But paddlers and boaters can find private beaches to call their own by heading to the western shore, which sees far less boating traffic. To experience the best of the lake's remoteness, pick up a backcountry permit to camp overnight at **Wilcox Point, Warm Springs, Little Grassy Island,** or **Deadmans Point Island.**

GRASSY LAKE ROAD

The 52-mile Grassy Lake Road (also called Ashton-Flagg Ranch Rd.) puts you on a historic travel route used by Native Americans and wagons. The route snuggles between Grand Teton National Park and Yellowstone National Park in the John D. Rockefeller, Jr. Memorial Parkway and Caribou-Targhee National Forest. The rugged dirt road connects with **Grassy Lake** and **Lake of the Woods** for fishing, paddling, and motorboating (small ones only). Primitive **campsites** offer places to experience silence and perhaps hear the sound of a wolf howl at night.

CAVE FALLS

The southwest corner of Yellowstone National Park is known as the land of waterfalls. Reach this remote, uncrowded spot via the **Grassy Lake Road** (Ashton-Flagg Ranch Rd.). Located on the Fall River, Cave Falls is only 20 feet tall, but it spans 250 feet across. Trails lead to more falls in the area, and the Fall and Bechler Rivers deliver trout fishing. Camp two miles away just outside the park in Caribou-Targhee National Forest at **Cave Falls Campground** (June-mid-Sept., $10, $5 extra vehicle, RVs limited to 24 feet). The campground lines up most of its 22 campsites overlooking the river. Getting there requires first a 3-4-hour drive on Grassy Lake Road. From Flagg Ranch,

Junction. The waterway is prime habitat for elk, bison, deer, moose, bald eagles, and great blue herons.

SIGNAL MOUNTAIN
Chapel of the Sacred Heart

A log chapel located off Teton Park Road about a half mile north of Signal Mountain Lodge is an attraction for weddings, although some visitors enjoy just stopping by for the scenery of the lake a short walk from the chapel. Owned by Our Lady of the Mountains parish in Jackson, the **Chapel of the Sacred Heart** (307/733-2516, www.olmcatholic.org) schedules Mass on weekends in summer, the

only time it is open. Check online for the current schedule.

★ Signal Mountain

At only 7,720 feet high, **Signal Mountain** cowers below the massive Tetons. Formed in part from ash falling from the Yellowstone supervolcano and a glacier leaving it as moraine, Signal Mountain rises above the valley of Jackson Hole with the closest peaks 10 miles away. The result is big views. Two forested routes climb 800 feet to reach the summit. Drive or bike the five-mile paved road, or hike the 6.8-mile trail from Signal Mountain Lodge. The summit has two overlooks,

Cave Falls in remote southwest Yellowstone

drive the 52-mile rugged, narrow dirt road to five miles north of Ashton and turn east on **Cave Falls Road** (Greentimber Rd./Forest Rd. 582) for 18 miles.

BUFFALO RIVER VALLEY

Just outside Grand Teton National Park near Moran, a scenic dirt road circles through Buffalo River Valley. For a tour, drive it east to west for the best views of the distant Tetons. The valley has small **campgrounds,** fishing on the Buffalo River, dude ranches with horseback riding, and groomed cross-country skiing in winter.

Jackson Point Overlook on the south with majestic Teton Mountain views and Emma Matilda Overlook on the north facing the Absarokas.

Signal Mountain Lodge

Located on Teton Park Road, the area around Signal Mountain Lodge offers views straight across Jackson Lake to Mt. Moran.

While the lodge doesn't make "must-see" lists, the views from the lodge restaurants, marina, beach, parts of the campground, and the boat launch are spectacular. You can spend the night, rent a boat, walk along the beach, or camp overlooking the lake to enjoy the scenery. Donoho Point Island sits offshore, a good destination for boaters and paddlers.

Recreation

DAY HIKES

Hiking trails in the north half of Grand Teton National Park are all about getting different angles to see the Teton Mountains. Their jagged pinnacles dominate the scenery. You'll appreciate the views more if you learn what peaks you are seeing, and their distinctive shapes help in identifying them. Use the cheat sheet diagram of the Tetons in the park newspaper.

Several trail complexes offer chances to design routes based on conditions, available time, season, and interest. The park service produces non-topographical maps of two complexes that can aid in sorting out the mazes. One is available for the Two Ocean Lake-Emma Matilda Lake-Grand View Point complex; the other is for Colter Bay-Hermitage Point trails. Pick up copies of these at visitors centers or online (www.nps.gov/grte).

Most trails are snow-free late May-early

North Grand Teton Hikes

Trail	Effort	Distance	Duration
Colter Bay Lakeshore Trail	Easy	2 mi rt	1.5 hr
Polecat Creek Loop	Easy	2.5 mi rt	2 hr
Heron Pond and Swan Lake	Easy	2.6 mi rt	2 hr
Flagg Canyon	Easy	5 mi rt	3 hr
Two Ocean Lake	Easy	6.4 mi rt	3 hr
Grand View Point	Moderate	2.2-8.8 mi	3-5 hr
Hermitage Point	Moderate	9.2 mi rt	5 hr
Emma Matilda Lake	Moderate	9.9-10.7 mi rt	5 hr
Signal Mountain	Moderately Strenuous	13.4 mi rt	6.5 hr
Huckleberry Mountain Lookout	Strenuous	11 mi rt	6 hr

Flagg Ranch Trails

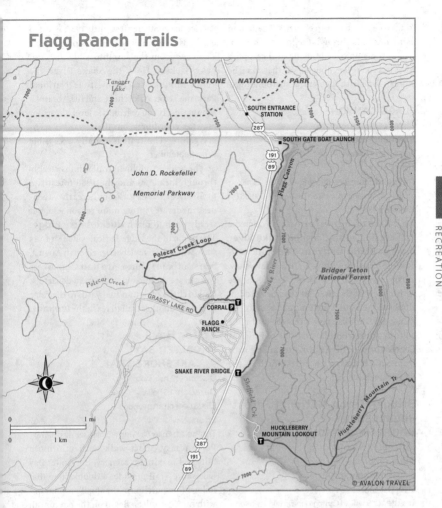

November. Be aware of your own abilities and conditioning. Elevation, wind, and sun can conspire to lead to fast cases of dehydration and altitude sickness.

Guided Hikes

In summer, rangers lead naturalist hikes daily to **Swan Lake.** Usually the hikes meet at 1pm at the flagpole in front of the Colter Bay Visitor Center for the three-mile easy walk. Plan about three hours with lots of stops to learn about wildlife, wetland communities, and flora.

John D. Rockefeller, Jr. Memorial Parkway
POLECAT CREEK LOOP

Distance: 2.5-mile loop
Duration: 2 hours
Elevation change: 25 feet
Effort: easy
Trailhead: Flagg Ranch corral (see map p. 181)

This short loop yields an option for wildlife-watching, especially in early morning or evening. The marsh can house moose and birds, but make noise for bears. Start by heading west to reach **Polecat Creek,** where the trail fringes the forest with creek views. The second half loops back through the forest. The trail circles the employee housing and camping zone, but you're far enough away that you'll be more in tune with the natural surroundings.

FLAGG CANYON

Distance: 5 miles round-trip
Duration: 3 hours
Elevation change: 71 feet
Effort: easy
Trailhead: Snake River Bridge River Access 0.5 mile south of Flagg Ranch turnoff on Highway 89/191/287 (see map p. 181)

Walk across the highway eastward to catch the trail heading north along the **Snake River** through **Flagg Canyon.** The trail wanders upstream through an ancient lava flow, grassy meadows, and forest. Segments are within view of the river. At the north end, it climbs to the **South Gate Boat Launch** and Picnic Area. You can also access the trail at the halfway point from the east side of **Polecat Creek Loop** or hike downstream and back from **South Gate,** 1.6 miles north of the Flagg Ranch turnoff.

Bridger-Teton National Forest
HUCKLEBERRY MOUNTAIN LOOKOUT

Distance: 11 miles round-trip
Duration: 6 hours
Elevation change: 2,703 feet
Effort: strenuous
Trailhead: Sheffield Campground in Bridger-Teton National Forest (see map p. 181)
Directions: From Highway 89/191/287, 0.6 mile south of Flagg Ranch, turn east onto the Sheffield Creek Road. Drive 0.7 mile to the trailhead. En route, the dirt road passes through a creek, which may be impassable in early summer.

While this hike is outside Grand Teton National Park, you'll get views of the entire park and more. **Sheffield Creek Trail** (#027) climbs from the **Sheffield Campground** to **Huckleberry Lookout,** perched at 9,638 feet. The lookout, built in 1938 by the Civilian Conservation Corps and used by the Forest

Service for spotting fires until 1957, is listed on the National Register of Historic Places. The view from the summit is big: Jackson Lake, Jackson Hole, the Snake River, the Teton Mountains, Yellowstone National Park, the Teton Wilderness, and the Absaroka Mountains. If you're from sea level, the grunt may tax your lungs, but the reward is scenery galore. The trail is usually accessible June-September.

The arid, windblown trail climbs steeply through meadows and the 1988 forest fire to **Sheffield Creek.** From here, the steepness moderates into a more reasonable, but steady pitch to reach **Huckleberry Ridge.** The name of the ridge indicates its flora. As such, when the huckleberries ripen in August, bears can be in the area. At a **trail sign,** where you can see the lookout to the west, depart the trail to climb a few hundred yards to the ridge to pick up another trail to reach the **lookout.**

Colter Bay
★ COLTER BAY LAKESHORE TRAIL

Distance: 2-mile loop
Duration: 1.5 hours
Elevation change: none
Effort: easy
Trailhead: Colter Bay Visitor Center (see map p. 176)

For an easy, short walk with minimum hills and maximum scenery, the Colter Bay Lakeshore Trail provides a double loop that follows the shoreline of the small promontory with multiple inlets. Begin on the paved trail that rims the north shore of the **marina** to tour a breakwater spit. After walking the spit, head west on the trail toward a tiny **isthmus** of rocks that connects the two parts of the peninsula. Once across the isthmus, go either way to circle the **1.1-mile loop.** Side trails reach beaches that yield views across Jackson Lake to the Teton Mountains. Upon returning to the causeway, follow your original tracks back to the visitors center, or take the other **spur trail** northeast toward the swimming beach and then return to the visitors centers on a trail paralleling the road.

Colter Bay Lakeshore Trail

HERON POND AND SWAN LAKE

Distance: 2.6-mile loop
Duration: 2 hours
Elevation change: 115 feet
Effort: easy
Trailhead: Swan, Heron, and Hermitage Point Trailhead at Colter Bay Village (see map p. 176)

A series of three ponds named for birds flanks the hillside east of Colter Bay Village. All three ponds have significant growths of yellow pond lilies, leaving little visible water, but they make prime habitat for a variety of wildlife: sandhill cranes, trumpeter swans, osprey, muskrats, river otters, and great blue herons. Depending on which ponds you want to see, hike a **2.6-mile loop** to the larger **Swan Lake** and **Heron Pond,** or extend to a **6.8-mile loop** (3.5 hours) to include the smaller **Cygnet Pond,** the least scenic water. Views from the trail pick up Mt. Moran and Rockchuck Peak in the Teton Mountains, best seen from Heron Pond. You'll pass multiple junctions, all well signed on this forest and meadow trail. A map from the visitors center can help in navigating the junctions. Be

ready for mosquitoes. Hikers can also access this loop from Jackson Lake Lodge, which will add 10 miles round-trip.

The trail starts on an **old service road** that curves around the south edge of Colter Bay. After leaving the bay, climb over a loosely forested hill to **Heron Pond,** where the trail follows the northeastern shore with several ultra-scenic viewpoints. At the southeast corner of the pond, turn left at the trail junction to reach **Swan Lake.** After following the shore northward, the trail returns to a junction where going straight will curve around **Jackson Lake Overlook** back to the trailhead.

HERMITAGE POINT

Distance: 9.2-mile loop
Duration: 5 hours
Elevation change: 380 feet
Effort: moderate
Trailhead: Hermitage Point Trailhead at Colter Bay Village (see map p. 176)

The hike out to Hermitage Point can take in Jackson Lake Overlook, Heron Pond, and Swan Lake, too. Hermitage Point sits on the end of a long forest and meadow peninsula. The rocky beach at the point offers a scenic place for lunch on Jackson Lake with views of several islands, Mt. Moran, and the Teton Mountains. But be prepared for winds on this treeless point, mosquitoes in early summer, and shadeless heat in midsummer. With plenty of wetlands on this trail, you'll see tracks: moose, bears, and deer. While the main trail junctions are well signed, plenty of unmarked spur trails head off to viewpoints and explorations. Pick up a map at the visitors center to aid with navigation.

For the quickest route to the point, start on the **old service road** at the trailhead. At every junction, **turn right** to reach Hermitage Point via the west side of the peninsula. The route will take you past **Jackson Lake Overlook** and **Heron Pond.** The trail goes through a lodgepole forest broken by sagebrush and wildflower meadows with lupine, paintbrush, and harebells until it emerges at

Grand View Trails

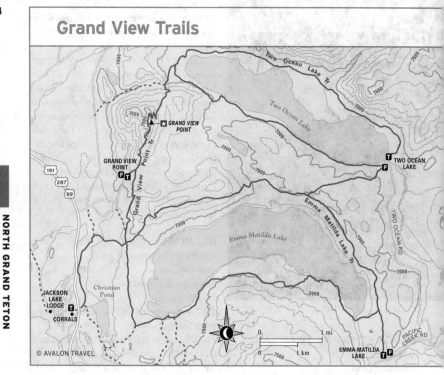

Hermitage Point. From the point, continue up the east side of the peninsula. When you reach a broad meadow, the view eastward spans Willow Flats, Jackson Lake Lodge a few miles away, the Absaroka Mountains, and the Teton Wilderness. At the next trail junction, **go left** to return to your previous trail and back to the trailhead via Heron Pond or Swan Lake.

Jackson Lake
★ GRAND VIEW POINT

Distance: 2.2-8.8 miles round-trip
Duration: 3-5 hours
Elevation change: 550-800 feet
Effort: moderate
Trailhead: Grand View Point (see map p. 184)
Directions: Drive 0.9 mile north of Jackson Lake Lodge on Highway 89/191/287. Take the unmarked, rough, narrow dirt road east, veering right at 0.1 mile and climbing 0.7 mile farther to the trailhead.

Multiple trailheads lead to Grand View Point,

an aptly named 7,286-foot summit with huge panoramic views of Jackson Lake and the Tetons. The large hillside rocky bluff of west of Grand View Point gives the full picture of the jagged peaks of Mt. Moran and the Cathedral group of Grand Teton, Mt. Owen, and Teewinot Mountain. From the signed Grand View summit, you overlook Two Ocean and Emma Matilda Lakes.

The shortest route, a **2.2-mile** out-and-back with only 550 feet of climbing, goes from the **Grand View Point** parking area to the viewpoint. From the trailhead, hike up a steep 0.2-mile connector trail to reach the **Grand View Point Trail.** The trail ascends steeply through meadows and forest.

From **Jackson Lake Lodge,** the trail is **6.1 miles** round-trip with 790 feet elevation gain. From the trailhead near the corrals, cross under the highway and gently ascend across sagebrush meadows. At **Christian Pond** (mostly grown in with greenery), take the left

the trail to Grand View Point

junction toward Grand View Point. En route to the point, you'll pass several trail junctions. At the **four-way junction,** turn left and continue straight, climbing into the forest and meadows of pink sticky geranium. Most of the elevation gain packs into the last mile.

The longest route at **8.8 miles** and 800 feet elevation gain goes from **Two Ocean Lake Trailhead.** Since Grand View Point sits above the head of the lake, hikers can loop around the lake, adding in an ascent of Grand View Point. From the trailhead, circle the north side of **Two Ocean Trail** through meadows and forest to the junction at the head of the lake. Turn right for 0.3 mile to another junction, where ascending straight up the ridge leads to Grand View summit and then the overlook. Return to the head-of-the-lake trail junction and turn right to circle back around the forested south side of Two Ocean Lake.

TWO OCEAN LAKE
Distance: 6.4-mile loop
Duration: 3 hours

Elevation change: 150 feet
Effort: easy
Trailhead: Two Ocean Lake Trailhead (see map p. 184)
Directions: From Highway 89/191/287 one mile north of Jackson Lake Junction, take the paved Pacific Creek Road 2 miles to a junction with Two Ocean Road. Turn left and drive 2.4 miles on dirt road to the trailhead at Two Ocean Lake.

The flat trail loops around Two Ocean Lake, a trough gouged from the Pacific Creek glacial lobe. Two Ocean Plateau, which straddles the Continental Divide, sheds water to the Pacific and Atlantic Oceans, hence the name. However, the misnamed Two Ocean Lake only drains to the Pacific. The trail travels through forests and meadows, with more open meadows on the north shore and denser forest on the south shore. In June, yellow arrowleaf balsamroot dominates the meadows, while in fall, golden aspens light up the hillside. Distant views of the Tetons line the horizon. The lake is home to trumpeter swans, waterfowl, and moose. Bears move in for food sources: cow parsnip in early summer and patches of huckleberries and thimbleberries in midsummer.

From the trailhead, start on the **south-shore** or **north-shore trail.** To head to the bigger views first on the more meadowed north side, the trail circles 3.4 miles with a short climb and descent to a **junction** at the head of the lake. From the junction, a steep trail grunts up to **Grand View Point.** If you tack on the point up and back, it will add 2.2 miles to your total. To continue around the lake from the junction, turn left to return three miles along the more forested south side to the trailhead.

Many hikers opt to combine Two Ocean Lake with **Emma Matilda Lake** and **Grand View Point.** The distance ranges 9.3-13.2 depending on the routes chosen around the lakes.

EMMA MATILDA LAKE
Distance: 9.9-10.7 miles round-trip
Duration: 5 hours

Signal Mountain

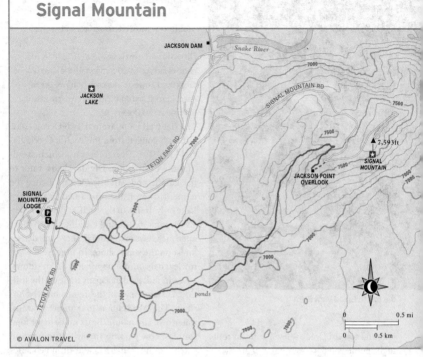

Elevation change: 600 feet

Effort: moderate

Trailhead: Emma Matilda Trailhead on Pacific Creek Road or Two Ocean Lake Trailhead at Two Ocean Lake (see map p. 184)

Directions: From Highway 89/191/287 one mile north of Jackson Lake Junction, take the paved Pacific Creek Road 1.5 miles to the Emma Matilda Trailhead for the shorter loop. For the longer loop, drive 0.5 mile farther to Two Ocean Road. Turn left and drive 2.4 miles on dirt road to the trailhead at Two Ocean Lake.

Two different trailheads access Emma Matilda Lake. From the **Emma Matilda Trailhead** on Pacific Creek Road, hike **0.6 mile** to the lake. From **Two Ocean Lake Trailhead**, hike **1 mile** to the lake. Once there, the trail loops **8.7 miles** around Emma Matilda Lake. Circling the lake will take you through two lightning fire zones from burns in 1994 and 1998 where new growth is changing the flora.

On the north shore of the lake, the trail climbs about 400 feet up a ridge that yields views of the lake backed by the Teton Mountains. A loose Douglas fir forest covers the ridge, and you can see Jackson Lake Lodge in the distance. Near the trail junction that goes to Jackson Lake Lodge, a **spur trail** cuts to **Lookout Rock** for views of the lake. From the junction, bear left to circle the south shore of the lake, where the trail tours closer to the shoreline but travels through a dense forest of spruce and fir.

From Jackson Lake Lodge, trails link into the Emma Matilda Loop. Total distance of the loop is **10.7 miles**, but elevation gain is about 750 feet. As another alternative, many hikers opt to combine Two Ocean Lake with Emma Matilda Lake and Grand View Point. From the Two Ocean Lake Trailhead, the distance ranges 9.3-13.2 depending on the routes chosen around the lakes.

SIGNAL MOUNTAIN

Distance: 13.4-mile loop
Duration: 6.5 hours
Elevation change: 920 feet
Effort: moderately strenuous
Trailhead: At Signal Mountain Lodge, park in the main lot and walk uphill opposite employee housing to the trailhead (see map p. 186).

Although you can drive to viewpoints on Signal Mountain, a trail also climbs to Jackson Point Overlook near the summit. Because of the mountain's island-like perch in the middle of Jackson Hole, it offers tremendous views of Jackson Lake, Jackson Hole, and the Teton Mountains despite its diminutive size in comparison to surrounding peaks. In its first mile, the trail crosses **Teton Park Road** and **Signal Mountain Road.** Once past those, you'll feel more in the wilderness.

At the **signed junction,** opt for ascending via the right fork to the ponds. This portion loops through meadows, wetlands, ponds, aspens, and conifers, a good mix of habitat for wildlife. At a second junction, the climb to the summit begins. The final ascent to **Jackson Point Overlook** is steep, gaining 600 feet in one mile. Intermittent Douglas fir and aspen offer bits of shade on a hot day, and the sagebrush meadows yield bursts of wildflowers in early summer including cinquefoil and pink sticky geranium. At Jackson Point Overlook, the view is huge. Lower forested ridges below are glacial moraines from 15,000 years ago, with glacial kettles or potholes to the southeast. These features often get lost below the sweeping panorama of the Teton Mountains, Jackson Lake, Jackson Hole, and the Snake River.

BIKING

Mountain biking is not permitted on trails in Grand Teton National Park, but you can still ride several scenic dirt roads just outside the national park. Be ready for sucking dust from passing cars. Bring your own bikes, as the nearest rentals are at the south end of Jackson Hole at Moose, Teton Village, and Jackson.

Inside the Park

Road cycling has its lure with the big views of the Teton Mountains. Though the main roads have paved shoulders, most drivers are gawking at the scenery or wildlife; wear a helmet and bright colors for safety. If riding with friends, travel single file. Cyclists should be comfortable with large RVs whizzing past at their elbows, but children and families should stick to riding campground loops. One popular ride climbs 800 feet in elevation up the paved **Signal Mountain Road** (10 miles round-trip); two different overlooks at the top offer excellent views. On the way down, let the descent do the work. Cyclists can camp in shared biker and hiker campsites ($5-7/person) at Headwaters, Lizard Creek, Colter Bay, and Signal Mountain Campgrounds.

Outside the Park

Eight miles east of Moran Junction, **Flagstaff Road** offers a long, scenic mountain bike ride on a dirt road through Bridger-Teton National Forest with outstanding vistas of the Tetons. **Buffalo River Valley Road** also has scenic riding past ranches and along the Buffalo River. For information and road conditions, contact **Bridger-Teton National Forest** (Blackrock Ranger District, Moran, 307/543-2386, www.fs.usda.gov/btnf).

An epic mountain bike ride over cobble and potholes, the 52-mile **Grassy Lake Road** (Ashton-Flagg Ranch Road) is an old Native American travel route that squeezes between Yellowstone and Grand Teton National Parks. On a backwoods trek through the Rockefeller Parkway and Caribou-Targhee National Forest, the route starts from Flagg Ranch to ride west, climbing past primitive campsites overlooking the Snake River before assuming a rolling grade. Take pepper spray for bears, and check on conditions at the Rockefeller Parkway Visitor Information Center at Flagg Ranch. The road usually is muddy in June, and August brings copious dust.

Teton Mountain Bike Tours (545 N. Cache St., Jackson, 307/733-0712 or

800/733-0788, www.tetonmtbike.com) guides half-day, full-day, and multiday mountain bike tours. One of their tours bikes the dirt road of the Buffalo River Valley outside Moran.

★ HORSEBACK RIDING
Inside the Park

Grand Teton Lodging Company (800/628-9988, www.gtlc.com) operates three corrals at Colter Bay, Jackson Lake Lodge, and Flagg Ranch. Reservations are a good idea, but you can also just show up 30 minutes in advance. Daily rides cost $40-48 for one hour or $65-75 for two hours; $5 pony rides are offered at all three corrals. One-hour trail rides depart **Flagg Ranch corrals** (John D. Rockefeller, Jr. Memorial Parkway, 307/543-2861 or 800/443-2311, June-Aug.) hourly to tour through forests.

From the **Colter Bay Village corrals** (307/543-3100 or 800/628-9988, early June-early Sept.), trail rides go through lodgepole forests to Jackson Lake Overlook and Heron Pond with views of the Teton Mountains. Breakfast and dinner wagon and trail rides (by reservation only, Mon.-Sat. mid-June-late Aug., $72-75 adults, $56-57 kids) tour through Willow Flats to a picnic site with views of the

Grassy Lake Road/Ashton-Flagg Ranch Road

Grand Tetons. The three-hour breakfast tours depart at 7:15am. The four-hour dinner tours depart at 4:15pm. Kids can ride ponies at the corral 8:45am-10:15am or 1:45pm-2:15pm. Horseback riders must be at least eight years

Horseback rides depart from the Colter Bay Village corrals.

old. Vegetarian options are available with advance request.

Horseback trail rides from **Jackson Lake Lodge corrals** (307/543-3100 or 800/628-9988, mid-June-late Aug.) always seem to get views of the Tetons. The most scenic ride is two hours (departs at 7:30am and 11:45am) and climbs to meadows above Christian Pond to reach Emma Matilda Lake with a stop at Oxbow Bend Overlook before returning to the lodge. One hour rides (3pm) follow a shorter version of the excursion. Kids can get pony rides at the corral 8am-10am or 12:30pm-2:30pm.

Outside the Park

Several dude ranches outside the park lead horseback trail rides through private lands and Bridger-Teton National Forest. Most ranches package trail rides with all-inclusive overnight stays. **Yellowstone Outfitters** (23590 Buffalo Valley Rd., Moran, 307/886-5421 or 307/543-2418 or 800/447-4711, http://yellowstoneoutfitters.com, daily Memorial Day-mid-Sept., $50 for two hours, $85 half day) guides trail rides from its Turpin Meadows Base Camp near Box Creek into the national forest. Reservations are required.

WATER SPORTS

Jackson Lake offers prime boating, sailing, and windsurfing, and the Teton Mountains provide a backdrop worthy of scenic drama. Due to elevation, weather, and topography, both Jackson Lake and the Snake River can be unforgiving. Frigid waters are common in spring (35-45 degrees). In summer, Jackson Lake rarely warms up to 60 degrees. Afternoons frequently bring winds that can raise huge whitecaps on Jackson Lake; floaters on the Snake River often encounter headwinds. Morning and evening boating can bring calmer lake waters, but not always. In addition, afternoon thunderstorms can roll in unannounced. For safety on lakes, avoid open-water crossings and stay closer to shore.

You'll need multiple permits for boating or paddling excursions. Sailboats and windsurfers require all the same **permits** as boats. Bring your own sailboats, boards, and gear; rentals are not available. Hand-propelled boats (except sailboats and windsurfers) are permitted at **Emma Matilda** and **Two Ocean Lakes.**

Boating
JACKSON LAKE

Jackson Lake is the place to boat. In general, motorboats, nonmotorized boats, sailboats, windsurfing, and waterskiing are allowed on Jackson Lake. Jet Skis and motorized personal watercraft are not. Filling a trough scooped out by an ice-age glacier, Jackson Lake is so big that it takes multiple days to explore all of its nooks and crannies. Fifteen islands, several peninsulas, and numerous bays provide places to get away from crowds and enjoy the solitude of your own beach. The west shore runs from Steamboat Mountain in the north to the base of Mt. Moran in the south. At full pool, the lake is 15 miles long, 7 miles wide, and more than 400 feet deep. By August, the lake level drops, which enlarges beaches.

While the image of cutting lazy turns in glassy water below the sun-drenched Teton Mountains sounds idyllic, the reality is quite different. Due to chilly water, most water-skiers wear wetsuits or drysuits, and afternoons often see big waves crop up. Waterskiing and wakeboarding are allowed on Jackson Lake from sunrise to sunset. Water-skiers must be out on open water, not in channels or within 500 feet of marinas, docks, swimming beaches, and moored boats in bays.

MARINAS AND BOAT LAUNCHES

You can launch boats at four locations on Jackson Lake: Leek's Marina, Colter Bay Marina, Signal Mountain boat launch, and Spalding Bay boat ramp. If you have a small hand-carried watercraft, you can launch it on any beach where you can haul it. But be sure you are parking in an appropriate location before lugging your boat to the water.

Leek's Marina, Colter Bay Marina, and Signal Mountain boat launch have cement

Navigating the Permit Maze

Boating, floating, or paddling in Grand Teton National Park requires a lengthy list of permits. These are not available in one location, so you may have to do a bit of running around. With prior planning, you can take care of some of them in advance.

Wyoming Permits

All boaters must purchase a Wyoming Aquatic Invasive Species (AIS) sticker and pass a boat inspection prior to launching. Permits are available in the park, or in advance online through the Wyoming Game and Fish Department (307/777-4638, https://wgfd.wyo.gov), but allow several weeks. Boat inspection locations are found on roads entering Wyoming.

- Fees: If you have a motor of any type, pay the motorized fee ($10 Wyoming residents, $30 nonresidents). If you have a kayak, canoe, rowboat, or rubber raft longer than 10 feet, pay the nonmotorized fee ($5 Wyoming residents, $15 nonresidents). If you have an inflatable craft smaller than 10 feet, a paddleboard, windsurfer, or fishing float tube, you are exempt from the AIS sticker fee.

- Permit locations: Colter Bay Marina (307/543-3100 or 800/628-9988, www.gtlc.com, daily late May-late Sept.), Signal Mountain Lodge (307/543-2831, www.signalmountainlodge.com, daily mid-May-mid-Sept.), and Headwaters Lodge at Flagg Ranch (800/443-2311, www.gtlc.com, daily early June-early July).

- Boat inspection locations: Rendezvous River Sports (945 W Broadway, Jackson, 307/733-2471, www.jacksonholekayak.com, 9am-6pm Mon.-Sat. Apr. 1-Oct. 30), for nonmotorized watercraft only; regional offices in Jackson (420 N. Cache St., Jackson, 307/733-2321, 8am-5pm Mon.-Fri. year-round, call for appointment) and Lander (260 Buena Vista, Lander, 8am-5pm Mon.-Fri. year-round, call for appointment); and along I-80 and I-90.

Boating Permits

Once you have a Wyoming AIS sticker, you can get the Grand Teton National Park boating permit (for inside-park waters only).

- Fees: Motorized boats ($40) include boats with any type of motor, including rafts using motors between Flagg Ranch-Lizard Creek. Nonmotorized boats ($10) include canoes, kayaks, rowboats, paddleboards, windsurfers, rafts, drift boats, dories, and fishing float tubes.

ramps, docks, and trailer parking. Leek's Marina and Signal Mountain Lodge Marina are operated by the same concessionaire (307/543-2831, www.signalmountainlodge.com, daily late May-late Sept.), while Colter Bay Marina (307/543-3100 or 800/628-9988, www.gtlc.com, daily late May-late Sept.) is operated by Grand Teton Lodging Company. All three marinas have restaurants, boater services, boat gas, buoy rentals, and some boating supplies. All three marinas have designated trailer parking for day-use, overnight, and long-term parking. Most are signed, but if you are confused, ask in the marina offices. Water levels can affect the season ending dates.

Spalding Bay requires a parking permit due to limited space. It only allows boat trailers that have single axles. The permit (available first-come, first-served 24 hours in advance) can be picked up at Colter Bay Visitor Center. You can only park for one day at Spalding Bay. No overnight parking is allowed.

RENTALS

Two marinas on Jackson Lake rent boats, sea kayaks, and canoes. Signal Mountain Lodge Marina (307/543-2831, www.signalmountainlodge.com, daily mid-May-mid-Sept.) rents deck cruisers, pontoon boats, runabouts, fishing boats, canoes, and kayaks.

- Permit location: **Colter Bay Visitor Center** (307/739-3594, 8am-7pm daily early June-early Sept., closes at 5pm spring and fall).

- If you want to launch at **Spalding Bay** on Jackson Lake, you'll need a **parking permit** (free) for the day (no overnight parking allowed). Permits are available 24 hours in advance from the Colter Bay Visitor Center and are given to the first people to pick them up.

Backcountry Camping

Spending the night at a lake-accessed campsite requires a **backcountry camping permit** (fee is $25/trip, not/person, three-night limit). Permits are assigned for specific primitive shoreline campsites that have fire rings and bear boxes; a few have tent platforms. Bring your own water or filter lake water, and pack out solid human waste.

- Advance **reservations** (307/739-3309, www.recreation.gov, early Jan.-mid-May, $35) will guarantee your campsite choice, but you must still pick up the physical permit.

- Permits are available **first-come, first-served** within 24 hours before departure. During July and August, competition for overnight camping permits on Jackson Lake has boaters lining up an hour before the backcountry office opens at 8am.

- Pick up the physical permit at **Colter Bay Visitor Center** (307/739-3594, 8am-7pm daily early June-early Sept., closes at 5pm spring and fall) by 10am on the day of your departure.

- Jackson Lake has 10 individual **campsites** (for up to six people) and five group campsites (for 7-12 people), all in prime lakefront locations accessible only by boat, kayak, or canoe. Five of the campsites are on islands. Coveted northwest shore campsites at Wilcox Point and Warm Springs are closest to Leek's Marina. Grassy Island, Deadman Point, Spalding Bay, South Landing, and Hermitage Point are closest to Signal Mountain Marina and boat launch. Elk Island and Little Mackinaw Bay are closest to Colter Bay Marina and boat launch. Group campsites are at Warm Springs, South Landing, Hermitage Point, and Elk Island.

- If you want to build a fire on shore, you'll need a **fire permit** (free, available from Colter Bay Visitor Center). Fires are not allowed on the east shore, from Spalding Bay to Lizard Creek Campground.

Canoes, one-person kayaks ($19-25/hour), and two-person kayaks ($79-99) are available first-come, first-served. Larger cruiser and pontoon boats can hold 8-10 people; the smaller runabouts and fishing boats can fit up to five people. **Reservations** (307/543-2831) are accepted for cruisers, pontoon boats, and runabouts ($62-129/hour, $299-675/day). Fishing boats are first-come, first-served ($42/hour, $185/day).

Colter Bay Marina (307/543-2811 or 307/543-3100, www.gtlc.com, daily late May-late Sept.) rents motorboats ($42/hour, two-hour minimum, $175/day) and canoes and kayaks ($19-21/hour, two-hour minimum). Reservations are not accepted.

TOURS

Three-hour guided kayak tours go out from **Colter Bay Marina** (307/543-2811 or 307/543-3100, www.gtlc.com, late May-late Sept., $83-90/boat) three days each week in the afternoon on single or tandem boats. Reservations are required 24 hours in advance. **Jackson Lake Kayaking Tours** (800/346-6277, www.oars.com) guides multiple trips on Jackson Lake mid-June-mid-September. Some are suitable for families and first-time kayakers. Two-night sea kayak trips go out to camp overnight on Grassy Island. Other trips pair up paddling on Jackson Lake with rafting on the Snake River or combined tours of Jackson Lake and Yellowstone Lake in Yellowstone National Park.

Boat tour, rafting, and horseback adventures can be paired up with alfresco dining adventures. Make reservations through **Grand Teton Lodging Company** (307/543-2811 or 800/628-9988, www.gtlc.com). From Colter Bay Marina, **Jackson Lake boat cruises** (early June-mid-Sept., $43-65 adults, $20-37 kids) combine scenic boat tours with outdoor picnics around a campfire on Elk Island. Meal cruises, which last 2.5 hours, are offered for breakfast (7:15am and 8am Fri.-Wed.), lunch (12:15pm Mon., Wed., and Fri.-Sat.), and dinner (5:15pm Fri.-Wed.).

Canoeing and Kayaking
JACKSON LAKE
Paddlers can find fun cubbyholes to explore on **Jackson Lake,** with islands and protected bays the best places for touring. Due to big winds that can arise on Jackson Lake, avoid open-water paddles; take shoreline routes rather than out where winds can turn a placid glassy-lake paddle into whitecaps threatening to swamp boats. The most sheltered paddles are from Colter Bay Marina. Between Colter Bay and Half Moon Bay, a series of channels weaves through a collection of islands.

To paddle to Elk Island, you can launch from Signal Mountain instead, but will encounter longer stretches of open water, so aim for Donoho Point and Hermitage Point to reach Elk Island. To paddle to east-shore locations, use Spalding Bay boat launch (permit required) for paddling at the base of Mt. Moran or launch from Lizard Creek Campground (minimal parking) for northwest shore paddling. Jackson Lake has 15 lake-accessed **campsites** (permit required) for overnighting, some located on islands.

EMMA MATILDA AND TWO OCEAN LAKES
Paddlers can access two smaller glacial lakes that don't permit motorboats: **Emma Matilda** and **Two Ocean Lakes**. These lakes offer quiet venues for shoreline paddles, wildlife-watching, and distant scenery of the Teton Mountains. Trumpeter swans inhabit the waters, and autumn paddles yield spectacular gold hillsides of aspens. Drive to the parking lot at Two Ocean Lake's east shore to launch. The lake, at 6,896 in elevation, has no boat ramp, so you'll need to carry your boat down a steep embankment

paddling the islands at Colter Bay

to the shore. The lake is less than a half mile wide, but about 2.5 miles long. To paddle Emma Matilda Lake requires a portage of a mile on a trail to launch. Most paddlers who go to Emma Matilda carry in ultra-lightweight boats or inflatables. The Emma Matilda shoreline is brushier and more difficult for launching, but you'll be guaranteed solitude on the water.

SNAKE RIVER

For river paddlers, the **Snake River** above and below Jackson Lake has Class II water from Flagg Ranch to Lizard Creek (10 miles) and from Jackson Lake Dam past Cattleman's Bridge to Pacific Creek (10 miles) north of Moran Junction. While they are calmer waters, paddlers need to be skilled in maneuvering around snags and debris. Scout the swift current at the Pacific Creek take-out before launching.

Rafting

In rafts, dories, canoes, or river kayaks, boaters can float two different sections of the **Wild and Scenic Snake River** in Grand Teton National Park: one 13-mile section runs from the border of Yellowstone National Park to Jackson Lake, and the other 25-mile stretch starts below Jackson Lake Dam. Both sections of the river yield scenery and wildlife sightings, but the Snake River below the lake adds grand views of the Teton Mountains. Watch for great blue herons, bald eagles, and osprey fishing the river; to protect the birds, avoid stopping near nests.

Starting in John D. Rockefeller, Jr. Memorial Parkway, the **13-mile** section above the lake sees high water in **late May-June.** Floating from South Gate through Flagg Canyon to Flagg Ranch Landing at the Snake River Bridge takes about one hour. At higher water levels, standing waves can be Class III-IV through Flagg Canyon's white water. Floating the entire route from South Gate to Lizard Creek Landing takes five hours, and the float ends with four miles of flat-water paddling through Jackson Lake. Water levels

drop too low for rafting by mid-July, with exposed mudflats and gravel bars.

Below Jackson Lake Dam, the Snake River is **open April-mid-December.** Class I-II dam-controlled flows produce more consistent water. Floating the five miles from Jackson Lake Dam past Cattleman's Bridge to Pacific Creek (north of Moran Junction) takes about two hours. From Pacific Creek Landing to Deadmans Bar, the 10-mile stretch of river poses a more challenging 2-3 hour float due to braiding, channels, islands, logjams, and strong currents.

Floating either section of the Snake River requires some river knowledge and is not for discount store blowup rafts (inner tubes and air mattresses are not allowed). Parts of the river require advanced rafting skills. Beginners should aim for the Jackson Lake Dam-Pacific Creek segment. Elsewhere, you'll need river savvy to navigate around logjams and maneuver in strong currents. Be ready for afternoon winds that seem to unleash an upriver gale, forcing rowing against the breeze. Spring water is cold, fast, and unforgiving.

Before launching for do-it-yourself floating, check on water levels through USGS monitors (800/658-5771, http://waterdata.usgs.gov) and call (307/733-5452) for information on water flow. For the Snake River above Jackson Lake, accesses are located at **South Gate Launch, Flagg Ranch Landing,** and **Lizard Creek Campground.** In the stretch below Jackson Lake, accesses are at **Jackson Lake Dam, Cattleman's Bridge, Pacific Creek Landing,** and **Deadmans Bar.** Floating regulations and descriptions of different sections of the river are available in the Grand Teton National Park floating brochure (ww.nps.gov/grte).

GUIDES

From Jackson Lake Lodge, four-hour scenic Snake River **rafting trips** (9am and 11:30am daily, $76 adults, $53 kids) include a lunch of burgers or hot dogs, or dinner (Tues., Thurs., and Sat., 4:30pm, $82 adults, $57 kids) of steak or trout at a scenic overlook.

Floating on the upper section of the Snake River above Jackson Lake is available through **Headwaters Lodge at Flagg Ranch** (Grand Teton Lodging Company, 800/443-2311, www.gtlc.com, daily early June-early July, $70 adults, $47 kids). The 10-mile float only runs for a limited time in early summer due to water levels on the river dropping too low. A motor gets the raft through the flat water of Jackson Lake. Tip your guide 15 percent, depending on expertise.

Guided floating on the Snake River below Jackson Lake Dam usually goes from Pacific Creek or Deadmans Bar to Moose in the south portion of Grand Teton National Park. The guide does the rowing; you sit back and enjoy the view. **Float trips** ($70 adults, $47 kids, tip 15 percent) take about 3.5 hours and include transportation to and from the river; the actual float time is about two hours to cover 10 miles of river. **Signal Mountain Lodge** (307/543-2831, www.signalmountainlodge.com) books trips. Multiple trips daily go out from **Jackson Lake Lodge** (Grand Teton Lodging Company, 307/543-2811 or 307/543-3100, www.gtlc.com), plus float trips combined with lunch or dinner at a scenic overlook.

Fishing

A good day of fishing in Grand Teton National Park yields the sun glinting off a wild trout on the line. But even if the fish aren't biting, the experience is worth it as the mountainous scenery provides such an inspirational environment for angling. In general, anglers can fish year-round in the park, with some areas having closures during part of the year. Fishing regulations for closures, creel limits, and specific lure and bait requirements are available in the fishing regulations brochure (www.nps.gov/grte).

Immense **Jackson Lake** flanks the North Tetons with deep, cold water and several species of native and nonnative trout. Shore fishing is best in May when fish move to shallower water to feed. June-September offer better lake fishing from a boat. The lake is closed to fishing in October. In midwinter, anglers can ice fish on frozen portions of the lake. For ultra-remote fishing, drive the Grassy Lake Road (Ashton-Flagg Ranch Road) west from Flagg Ranch to **Grassy Lake** for cutthroat trout, rainbow, and lake trout and **Lake of the Woods** for mostly rainbows. For kids, **Two Ocean Lake** is a good place to start fishing for cutthroat trout. Portions of the shoreline are free from brush, and early summer produces the most action.

The **Snake River** feeds Jackson Lake's north end and exits the lake at the dam, providing two different stretches for fishing. Above the lake, fishing is accessed via river sites at Southgate and Flagg Ranch. Below the lake, anglers can access the river for fishing right below Jackson Lake Dam. Anglers float drift boats or rafts to fish from the dam to Cattleman's Bridge or Pacific Creek. From the Buffalo Fork confluence to Menors Ferry, the Snake River closes annually mid-December-April.

To fish in Grand Teton National Park or the John D. Rockefeller, Jr. Memorial Parkway requires a **Wyoming state fishing license** (residents: $3 youth annual, $6 adults daily, $24 adults annual; nonresident: $15 youth annual, $14 adults daily, $92 adults annual). When supervised, kids under 14 can fish for free under a parent's license or purchase a license to fish on their own. Buy licenses at Signal Mountain Marina, Colter Bay Marina, and Headwaters Lodge at Flagg Ranch. Float tubes also need boat permits.

GUIDES

Guides take anglers fishing on Jackson Lake and the Snake River. Be sure to use only guides licensed through the national park. During late season, dropping water levels may shut down guided fishing trips, and severe weather can cancel trips, too. Rates do not include fishing licenses or tips. Plan to tip your guide 15 percent (if you catch lots of fish, tip 20 percent).

For guided fishing on Jackson Lake, make

reservations through two marinas. A minimum of two hours is needed for fishing the lake, but you can fish up to eight hours if you have the stamina. Rates run $92-98 per hour for 1-2 people. Each additional person costs $20-25 per hour. You can charter a guided fishing boat from **Colter Bay Marina** (307/543-3174 ext. 1097, www.gtlc.com, daily late May-late Sept.) or **Signal Mountain Lodge Marina** (307/543-2831, www.signalmountainlodge.com, daily mid-May-mid-Sept.). The marina also offers a four-hour trip ($290 for 1-2 people, $90 each additional person).

Book fishing trips on the lower Snake River through the lodges when you make your reservation: **Signal Mountain Lodge** (307/543-2831, www.signalmountainlodge.com), **Jackson Lake Lodge** (Grand Teton Lodging Company, 307/543-2811 or 307/543-3100, www.gtlc.com), and **Headwaters Lodge** (800/443-2311, www.gtlc.com). Each raft, drift boat, or dory can take 1-2 anglers, plus the guide. Four-hour trips usually cost around $450-475; full-day trips with lunch run $575-600. Transportation to the put-in is usually included.

Swimming

Jackson Lake has plenty of beaches for swimming, but there are no lifeguards and the water is frigid; even in August, the water may not hit 60°F. Frequent afternoon winds can raise big waves. While you can swim anywhere in Jackson Lake except for marinas, **Colter Bay swimming beach,** adjacent to the picnic area, has a buoy-marked swimming zone for families.

WINTER SPORTS
Cross-Country Skiing and Snowshoeing

When snow settles on Grand Teton National Park, winter gear comes out. Snow-buried roads and trails turn into cross-country ski and snowshoe routes; with the snow, you can go anywhere. Trails are not marked in winter, so you're on your own for route-finding—don't assume the previous ski tracks go where you want to go. Even roadways become backcountry in winter. Bring a map, GPS or compass, and know how to navigate.

Follow proper etiquette, and take along enough gear to survive an emergency or self-rescue. Snowshoers should travel parallel to ski tracks, but not on them. If skiing or snowshoeing where snowmobiles travel, stay to the right. If you are touring on closed roads, you won't encounter much avalanche danger, but check conditions at **Jackson Hole Avalanche Forecast** (307/733-2664, www.jhavalanche.org) to understand the snow surface.

Grand Teton has a brochure (www.nps.gov/grte) that shows popular ski and snowshoe routes, where to park vehicles, and winter wildlife closure zones. The nearest rentals and guides for cross-country skiing and snowshoeing are in Jackson.

INSIDE THE PARK

From Signal Mountain Lodge, climb six miles and 800 feet in elevation on **Signal Mountain Road** to the summit of Signal Mountain for views of the Tetons. This intermediate tour requires the ability to ski downhill on the return trip; when the conditions are right, gravity does all the work. From the Colter Bay Visitor Center, the **Swan Lake and Heron Pond Loop** (2.6 miles round-trip) is more suitable for beginners. At Flagg Ranch, the **Polecat Creek Loop** (2.5 miles round-trip) and **South Flagg Canyon Trail** (5 miles round-trip) are easy routes with minimal climbing. You can also tour the **Grassy Lake Road/Ashton-Flagg Ranch Road** or the road into Yellowstone National Park, but you will encounter snowmobiles.

OUTSIDE THE PARK

Outside the park east of Moran Junction, **Turpin Meadow Ranch** (24505 Buffalo Valley Rd., 307/543-2000, 9am-5pm Tues.-Sun. winter, $15 adults, $5 kids) grooms 15 kilometers of trails for skate and classic skiing. Rentals run $10-30 per day.

Snowmobiling

Grand Teton National Park does not permit snowmobiling on snow-buried roads, but it does allow machines on Jackson Lake when it is frozen. All snow machines in the park must be BAT (Best Available Technology)-approved. Grassy Lake Road/Ashton-Flagg Ranch Road is a popular backcountry snowmobile route in winter. You don't need a guide to snowmobile on Jackson Lake or Grassy Lake Road.

GUIDES AND RENTALS

Grand Teton National Park has no companies licensed to guide snowmobile trips in the park. However, snowmobiles are available to rent in Jackson to take out on your own. Headwaters Lodge at Flagg Ranch (800/443-2311, www. gtlc.com, daily mid-Dec.-mid-Mar., $275-325 driver, $175 extra rider) serves as a jumping-off point for touring Yellowstone National Park by snowmobile in winter. Tours go to Old Faithful or Grand Canyon of the Yellowstone. Both rides demand stamina, as they last 8-12 hours. While you will stop for sightseeing, you'll be straddling the machine for much of the day. Rates include snowmobiles, helmets, boots, winter suits, breakfast, lunch, and snacks. Park entrance fees are extra. Plan to tip your guide 15 percent.

Entertainment and Shopping

RANGER PROGRAMS

Informative naturalist programs take place throughout the day at various locations around Jackson Lake. Check schedules of activities in the park newspaper (www.nps. gov/grte). At Colter Bay Visitor Center, the park service offers talks on the back deck, tepee demonstrations, bear safety presentations, and family-friendly programs. Grand Teton Lodging Company (800/628-9988, www.gtlc.com) has special programs at two of their locations. At Jackson Lake Lodge, visitors can join raptor presentations, grizzly bear talks, Lunch Tree Hill walks, and property tours. At Colter Bay Village, a walking tour explores the historic Colter Bay Cabins that used to be Jackson Hole ranch houses.

At Colter Bay, evening ranger-led activities (daily mid-June-early Sept.) take place at the outdoor amphitheater, with 45-minute evening presentations start at 7pm. In the visitors center auditorium, photo talks or park films start at 9pm. Stargazing and solar-gazing programs are available, too.

SHOPPING

There are small gift shops at Headwaters Lodge at Flagg Ranch, the marina and general store in Colter Bay Village, and Signal Mountain Lodge. Jackson Lake Lodge has a few gift shops that specialize in high-end clothing and jewelry, art and sculptures, and logo wear.

Accommodations

INSIDE THE PARK

All the in-park lodges are open in summer; only Headwaters Lodge opens in winter for the snowmobile season. For midsummer stays, make reservations a year in advance, especially for Jackson Lake Lodge, the most popular location. You can still get last-minute reservations in summer, but you may not have much in the way of choices. At all lodges, expect rusticity without televisions, radios, or air-conditioning; only a few units at Signal Mountain Lodge offer air-conditioning. Cell phone service is available at all lodges. Rates are for double occupancy; add on $6-15 per additional person. Taxes run about 9 percent.

John D. Rockefeller, Jr. Memorial Parkway

Located between Grand Teton and Yellowstone National Parks, **Headwaters Lodge & Cabins at Flagg Ranch** (307/543-2861 or 800/443-2311, www.gtlc.com, June-Sept. and mid-Dec.-early Mar., $195-300) sits at Flagg Ranch. The river rock-and-log lodge houses the front desk, restaurant, bar, gift shop, and convenience store. Horseback rides depart from the corrals, hiking trails are nearby, and you can walk to the Snake River to fish. You can get all-day Yellowstone summer bus tours, winter snowmobile tours to Old Faithful or Grand Canyon of the Yellowstone, and winter packages that include breakfast or snowmobiling. For winter cross-country skiing and snowshoeing, bring your own gear. Parking is in one large lot on the north side of all the cabins, which are accessible by paved walkways; roll your gear to your cabin on the provided carts. Each cabin is actually a row of motel rooms. Standard, deluxe, and premium rooms have 1-2 queens, en suite baths, and shared front porches with rocking chairs. The standard cabins permit pets for a fee. Upper-end rooms have microwaves, mini-fridges, and newer fixtures and furniture.

In the adjacent campground, also run by Headwaters Lodge, tiny **camper cabins** (no electricity, $80) help those on a budget. The cabins are a wooden box with roof, walls, and windows that provide shelter from the elements and two sets of bunk beds with thin mattress pads. Bunks are doubles or a double with a twin on top. Outside, you can roast marshmallows in the fire pit and eat dinner on the picnic table. Bring your own sleeping bags or bedding, and walk to shared bathroom and shower facilities.

Colter Bay

Colter Bay Village (307/543-3100 or 800/628-9988, www.gtlc.com) has a visitors center, Indian arts museum, general store and grocery, two restaurants, bar, marina, corral, laundry, showers, swimming beach, boat launch, and amphitheater for naturalist ranger talks.

The 166 **Colter Bay Cabins** (late May-early Oct., $90-250) are really motel rooms without kitchens or lake views. The small, rustic-worn cabins—relocated historic log Jackson Hole homestead buildings—have

Colter Bay Cabins

1-2 rooms surrounded by a loose pine forest, where you can walk five minutes to the marina. These are the most popular cabins in the park due to their location. Choose from three styles. For budget travelers, tiny semi-private cabins have two twins or one double with shared bath facilities accessed through a hall or in a separate building. Private one-room cabins have their own bathrooms with a shower and bed configurations (doubles and twins) that sleep 2-5 guests. Private two-room cabins have two bedrooms with different combos of double and twin beds and one bathroom.

For an experience reminiscent of summer camp, **Colter Bay Tent Village** (late May-early Sept., $65) have two log walls, a wood floor, and the remaining two walls and ceiling made from canvas. Each tent cabin can sleep a family of six between pull-down bunks and two cots with thin mattresses. You stoke a fire in an old-fashioned potbelly stove to heat the interior. The outside covered patio has a picnic table, fire pit with grill, and bear box. Bring your own sleeping bags or rent bedding. Communal bathrooms a short walk away are part of the deal.

Jackson Lake

The crown of Grand Teton National Park lodging, ★ **Jackson Lake Lodge** (800/628-9988, www.gtlc.com, late May-early Oct., $290-390 rooms and cottages, $730-830 suites) is a National Historic Landmark built in 1955 with a dining room commanding a panoramic view of the Tetons. The modern international architecture features 60-foot-tall lobby windows and an outdoor patio designed to soak up the Tetons. Many visitors assume the lodge sits on the shore of Jackson Lake, but it sits about 1.5 miles as the bird flies from the water, and the closest access to lake activities is Colter Bay Marina. The lodge overlooks Willow Flats, which allow for unobstructed views of the mountains. The property includes several restaurants, a lounge, gift shops, Native American artifacts, playground, and a heated outdoor swimming pool (late

May-Aug.). The 25-yard pool, snack cabana, and kiddie pool are located behind the lodge parking lot as an afterthought to the property. Concierges aid in setting up fly-fishing, river float, and park tour trips, and horseback rides from the on-site corral.

Jackson Lake Lodge has 385 rooms in the hotel and surrounding cottages; all have private baths and wireless Internet. Rooms come with or without views of the Teton Mountains and Jackson Lake; non-view rooms look out on conifers or buildings. Rooms are in three locations: the main lodge, separate two-story lodges, or cottages. On the 3rd floor of the main lodge, rooms have two queens. Those facing the Tetons do not have balconies. Separate from the main lodge, three two-story buildings have rooms facing the Tetons with patios or balconies. In the forest, cottages line up multiple motel rooms in single-story buildings. Rooms have a king, two queens, or two doubles. Mountain View Suite cottages add on an indoor sitting area to soak up the scenery. Some rooms have mini-fridges, and some require a two- or three-night minimum.

Signal Mountain

Sitting on Jackson Lake, ★ **Signal Mountain Lodge** (1 Inner Park Rd., 307/543-2831, www.signalmountainlodge.com, early May-mid-Oct., $185-385) overlooks blue water backed by Mt. Moran and the Teton Mountains. Because it overlooks the lake, the lodge is so popular that it takes reservations 16 months out. The complex has two restaurants, a bar, marina, motorboat rentals, canoe and kayak rentals, laundry and showers, gift shops, campground, camp store, and wireless Internet. Guided fishing trips and white-water rafting are available. From the lodge, you can drive, mountain bike, or hike to the top of Signal Mountain.

The lodge has a variety of different room options with wireless Internet and with or without views. Rooms have various combinations of king, queens, doubles, twins, and sofa beds. Some of the units have extra amenities such as gas fireplaces, jetted tubs, microwaves, mini-fridges, and sitting areas. Older rustic log cabins can sleep 2-6 people. Motel-style rooms can sleep 2-4 people. Premier Western Rooms have wood furnishings, granite and slate bathrooms, and air-conditioning. Lakefront units have kitchenettes, balconies or shared patios, and views of Jackson Lake and the Tetons. If you want to stay right on the lake overlooking the water, these lakefront units are the only options on Jackson Lake, hence their appeal.

OUTSIDE THE PARK
Moran

Outside Grand Teton National Park, Moran has a couple of lodging options, good alternatives when in-park lodging books out or in winter. Some people prefer them for the amenities. Five miles east of the park entrance at Moran, **Lutens Teton Cabins** (24000 Gun Barrel Flats Rd., 307/543-2966 or 855/248-2489, www.tetoncabins.com, early May-Oct., $238-448) has two- or three-room cabins. Located on the highway, **Hatchet Resort** (19980 E. Hwy. 287, 307/543-2413 or 877/543-2413, www.hatchetresort.com, May-Oct., $90-500) centers around an older revamped log lodge with a restaurant. Rooms in the historic wing (built in 1954) were renovated in 2014, and the complex has cabins, budget rooms with shared baths, a collection of suites, and a house.

Buffalo Valley

Several small dude ranches sit in Buffalo Valley. With views of the Teton Mountains from the ranches, they offer horseback riding and fishing. **Heart Six Guest Ranch** (16985 Buffalo Valley Rd., 307/543-2477 or 888/543-2477, http://heartsix.com, mid-June-mid-Aug., mid-Sept.-Oct., mid-Dec.-mid-Mar., and May, $1,100-2,200 adults, $900-1,800 kids) has 19 guest rooms with 3-6-night all-inclusive packages. At 13 miles east of the entrance to Grand Teton, **Turpin Meadow Ranch** (24505 Buffalo Valley Rd., 307/543-2000, June-Oct. and winter, $265-600) has one- and two-room log cabins flanking the Buffalo River with groomed cross-country ski trails in winter.

Camping

INSIDE THE PARK

Only Colter Bay RV Park and Headwaters Campground take reservations. Make **reservations 6-9 months in advance.** All other campgrounds are first-come, first-served. All campsites, except in Colter Bay RV Park, include picnic tables, fire rings, drinking water, flush toilets, and bear boxes for food storage. ADA campsites and toilets are available. Bikers and hikers can share designated campsites for $5-11 per person.

John D Rockefeller, Jr. Memorial Parkway

Located at Flagg Ranch, **Headwaters Campground & RV** (reserve at 307/543-2861 or 800/443-2311, www.gtlc.com, late May-Sept., $70 RVs with hookups, $35 tents, $5 extra person over double occupancy) sits between Yellowstone National Park and Grand Teton National Park. Close to the Snake River, the large tourist center (lodge, restaurant, grocery, and gas station) offers guided fly-fishing, horseback riding, rafting trips, and interpretive programs. From the campground, you can fish the river, mountain bike Grassy Lake Road, and hike Polecat Loop Trail.

The forested campground with 175 campsites sits adjacent to the Snake River. Campsites vary from fully shaded under large spruces and firs to partly sunny with mountain views. RV campsites have gravel pull-throughs wide enough for slide-outs and awnings. The lack of understory yields little privacy. The eastern loops sit closest to the highway, but traffic dwindles at night.

Facilities include RV hookups for sewer, water, and electricity, plus a disposal station, showers, and laundry. RV combinations are limited to 60 feet.

In the first 10 miles of the primitive Grassy Lake Road (Ashton-Flagg Ranch Road), **Grassy Lake Road campsites** (first-come, first-served, 307/739-3300, www.nps.gov/grte, June-Sept., free) spread out along the old Native American and wagon route. Fourteen primitive campsites are separated along the road in eight tiny camps rather than clustered together in one campground. Camps 1-4 command outstanding views of the Snake River and Teton Wilderness peaks, but all are prized for privacy and solitude. Facilities include picnic tables, vault toilets, bear boxes, and large spaces for tents. No drinking water is available, so you'll need to bring your own. Some sites are suitable for small RVs. You can fish for trout from several campsites, and mountain bike the road. Improvements were made to parts of the road in 2014, making access to the primitive campsites in the parkway section accessible by any rig, but parking at the campsites is limited.

Jackson Lake

At an ultra-scenic location, **Lizard Creek** (first-come, first-served, 307/543-2831, www.signalmountainlodge.com, www.nps.gov/grte, mid-June-early Sept., $22) sits right on the north end of Jackson Lake. As an old-school campground, it still has some prime campsites overlooking the water and Teton Mountains plus walk-in campsites right on the shoreline. In early summer, fishing, launching canoes or kayaks, and swimming from the campground is prime. In late summer when lake levels drop low, huge mudflats surround the campground rather than rocky beaches. The campground has 43 RV or tent campsites and 17 walk-in tent campsites on a partly sunny hillside of spruce and lodgepole. An amphitheater has evening interpretive programs, and campground hosts are on-site. Many of the generator-free lower loop campsites overlook the lake and the Tetons. Claim a campsite by 11am midsummer. RVs are limited to 30 feet.

Colter Bay

Located at Jackson Lake in a lodgepole forest, ★ **Colter Bay Campground** (Colter Bay Village, 800/628-9988, www.gtlc.com, mid-May-late Sept., $58-68 RVs, $25 tents) is built in two sections on a bluff above the lake. The **RV park** (reservations accepted) has 112 pull-through campsites with hookups for

Lizard Creek campground

water, sewer, and electricity. No tents or fires are permitted in the RV park, but you can use your own gas or charcoal grills. RV length, including rigs and trailers, is limited to 45 feet. The larger **campground** (first-come, first-served) contains 350 non-hookup, nine walk-in tent, 11 group, and 13 electrical hookup ADA campsites for tents and RVs of any type. Some loops are generator-free zones. Sites are assigned at the staffed check-in station. The campground rarely fills—but it can. If you arrive after the station closes, a whiteboard lists the available sites. Reservations are available for group campsites only. **Winter camping** (Dec.-mid-Apr., $5) is possible at Colter Bay in the plowed parking lot.

Colter Bay Village houses a visitors center, amphitheater for evening naturalist programs, general store, two restaurants, coin-op laundry and showers, gas, disposal station, boat launch, swimming beach, and a marina with motorboat, canoe, and kayak rentals.

Signal Mountain

On a bluff adjacent to Signal Mountain Lodge, ★ **Signal Mountain Campground** (first-come, first-served, 307/543-2831, www.signalmountainlodge.com, early May-mid-Oct., $22 campsite, $45 electrical hookup) commands one of the best panoramic views of the Teton Mountains from its perch on the west shore of Jackson Lake. The campground loops around a hillside, where some of the campsites yield outstanding views of the lake and the Tetons. It has 81 RV or tent campsites, four tent-only campsites, and an ADA site with electricity. A mix of fir and spruce provides some shade, but most of the campsites are sunny in midday. The campsites are small, with low brush creating partial privacy along with the trees. The narrow campground road and narrow parking pads can pose challenges for RV drivers unskilled in squeezing into tight spots, and RVs are limited to 30 feet. Loop 3 is generator-free. Because of its location and scenery, plan on arriving before 10am to claim a campsite.

Adjacent to the campground, Signal Mountain Lodge houses a restaurant, convenience store, gas station, and marina with guided fishing and rentals of canoes, kayaks, and motorboats.

OUTSIDE THE PARK

When in-park campgrounds fill up, national forest and private campgrounds can work as a backup. Find these campgrounds surrounding North Grand Teton and east of Moran. If you need hookups, go to the private campground, as Forest Service campgrounds have amenities limited to vault or pit toilets, picnic tables, bear boxes, fire rings, and potable water only where noted.

Private Campground

A campground for convenience located 5.6 miles west of Moran Junction, **Fireside Resort** (17800 Hwy. 287, Moran, 307/733-1980 or 800/563-6469, www.yellowstonerv.com., year-round, $70-100 hookups, $30-50 tents, $8/person over four people) is a sunny highway campground, but with views that give it appeal. From many campsites, the entire Teton Mountain range is visible across the horizon to the west. Buffalo Fork, good for fishing or paddling, circles around this older ex-KOA campground. The campground has 14 tent campsites and 160 RV campsites with hookups for sewer, water, and electricity. Facilities include flush toilets, showers, laundry, store, and wireless Internet.

National Forest Campgrounds

In **Bridger-Teton National Forest** (Blackrock Ranger District, 307/543-2386, www.fs.usda.gov/btnf, late May-Sept.), two quiet campgrounds sit outside the east boundary of Grand Teton National Park. Due to grizzly bears feeding, they may close temporarily to tents, tent campers, and tent trailers, allowing **only hard-sided RVs.** If weather permits, the campgrounds remain open later in fall, but without services. RVs are limited to 30 feet.

With the turnoff located one mile south of Flagg Ranch, **Sheffield Creek Campground** ($5) cuddles below the

9,615-foot Huckleberry Mountain in the Teton Wilderness. From the campground, a trail climbs to Huckleberry Lookout. The campground has five sunny campsites with huge territorial views of the surrounding mountains, Jackson Hole, and the Tetons. Check on access: The narrow road requires driving through a creek that may have too much water to cross in June. With eight camp-sites, **Pacific Creek Campground** ($10), lo-cated eight miles up Pacific Creek Road, has campsites under cottonwoods with expansive views of the surrounding mountains on the edge of the Teton Wilderness. Pacific Creek offers fly-fishing for trout, and a trail leads eight miles to Gravel Lake, tucked on the side of Pinyon Peak.

Outside Moran at the east entrance to Grand Teton National Park, two camp-grounds (late May-Sept., $10) have water.

Located 0.2 mile west of the Blackrock Ranger Station (formerly Buffalo), which is eight miles east of Moran, **Hatchet Campground** is a not-so-scenic roadside camp. In addition, the adjacent dirt Forest Road 30160 climbs in a scenic drive up to viewpoints of the Teton Mountains, and a few primitive free camp-sites with outstanding views are on it. Off the main highway on Buffalo Valley Road, **Turpin Meadow Campground** sprawls 18 pastoral campsites in sunny loops between lodgepole stands and sagebrush meadows.

In **Caribou-Targhee National Forest** (Island Park Ranger District, 208/558-7301, www.fs.usda.gov/ctnf), free primitive camp-sites line Grassy Lake Road (Ashton-Flagg Ranch Road). The best campsites are at **Grassy Lake** and **Lake of the Woods** due to opportunities for fishing, paddling, and solitude.

Food

INSIDE THE PARK
John D. Rockefeller, Jr. Memorial Parkway

In Headwaters Lodge, **Sheffields Restaurant & Bar** (307/543-2861 or 800/443-2311, www.gtlc.com, daily June-Sept. and mid-Dec.-early Mar.) serves breakfast, lunch, and dinner in summer and only lunch with a short menu in winter. Breakfast (6:30am-10am, $6-11) includes traditional griddle and egg entrées and baked goods plus non-tradi-tional breakfast goodies such as quinoa, trout, burritos, and tofu. The breakfast buffet (7am-10am, $14) can get you out the door faster. Lunch (11am-2:30pm, $7-28) serves salads, sandwiches, burgers, and a couple of plated full meals with bison prepared in various ways. Dinner (5:30pm-9:30pm, $10-35) runs the gamut from prime rib and trout to pasta, salads, burgers, and smaller plates. The lodge has other dining options adjacent to the din-ing room. The **Bistro** (6:30am-11pm) serves up quick light meals. The **bar** (2:30pm-10pm),

a western-style saloon that carries local beers and drinks, has sandwiches and burgers.

Colter Bay

Colter Bay Village has two restaurants, both run by **Grand Teton Lodging Company** (307/543-2811 or 800/628-9988, www.gtlc. com). The **John Colter Café Court** (11am-10pm daily late May-early Sept., $3-10) has order-at-the-counter meals of American and Tex-Mex fare, sandwiches, salads, burgers, and ice cream. Kids have their own menu, and beer and wine are served. Some items are pre-made grab-and-go, while others are made-to-order for dining at the cafeteria. To-go lunches and meals work for the trail or your campsite. Café Court serves up hard ice cream, as does the general store.

★ **Ranch House** (daily late May-Sept.) serves up comfort-type foods with a western flair. You can eat in rustic booths while taking in historical park photos or dine in the bar to see brands representing area ranches burned

Leek's Marina

into the countertop. The restaurant serves local bison (from outside the national park), all natural beef, sustainable seafood, and some locally sourced produce. A kids' menu, vegetarian options, and beer, wine, and cocktails are available. Breakfast (6:30am-10:30am, $7-15) features a buffet, or you can order from the menu that includes traditional griddle and egg entrées. Lunch (11:30am-1:30pm, $9-18) includes burgers, sandwiches, soup, salad, and comfort entrées such as mac 'n cheese or roasted chicken. For dinner (5:30pm-9pm, $9-30), go lighter with entrée salads or order a full entrée such as prime rib, ribs, beef, trout, and pasta. The small bar (11:30am-10:30pm, $7-14) menu has burgers, sandwiches, chili, and appetizers.

With indoor and outdoor picnic tables, **Leek's Pizzeria** (Leek's Marina, 307/543-2494, www.signalmountainlodge.com, 11am-10pm daily late May-mid-Sept., $9-25), operated by Signal Mountain Lodge, has partial views of Jackson Lake and the Teton Mountains from its deck. With pizza, pasta,

and a kids' menu, it attracts families. You can also drop in after hiking for a cold brew and pizza by the slice. Build your own pizzas, or order specialty pizzas or calzones prepared with house-made organic flour dough. They also serve Italian sandwiches, salads, pasta, beer, and wine. Leek's hand-scoops ice cream into cones, too.

Jackson Lake

Jackson Lake Lodge has three distinctly different restaurants for dining, plus outdoor dining at the pool. **Grand Teton Lodging Company** (307/543-3100 or 800/628-9988, www.gtlc.com, daily mid-May-early Oct.) operates all the food concessions at the lodge. All facilities offer a few vegetarian options and kids' menus.

Dining in the ★ **Mural Room** is an experience for the panoramic views of the Grand Tetons outside and the murals depicting western Native American and Wyoming trapper life inside. Waiting lines in summer attest to its popularity; make **reservations** (www.opentable.com) to avoid the wait and ask for a window table. For breakfast (7am-9:30am daily, $7-14, buffet $17 adults, $10 kids), partake of the buffet or order light meals or full entrées from the menu. The buffet's Belgian waffle iron puts a moose imprint on the waffle, and pastries, breads, and cinnamon rolls are baked on-site. Lunch (11:30am-1:30pm daily, $10-20) serves up sandwiches, burgers, salads, small plates, and full entrées such as trout, chicken pot pie, and wild-game sausage frittata. For dinner (5:30pm-9:30pm daily, $21-44), appetizers, soups, and salads lead into main courses of prime rib, elk loin, trout, duck, and salmon. Vegetarian, gluten-free, vegan, and low-fat options are available.

Located across the mezzanine, the **Blue Heron Lounge** (11am-midnight daily, $5-10) has indoor and outdoor seating on the deck. Small plates, appetizers, sandwiches, and salads are served, as are a variety of Wyoming, Montana, and Idaho regional beers.

Reminiscent of a 1950s soda fountain, the **Pioneer Grill** serves breakfast, lunch, and dinner. Breakfast (6am-11am daily, $3-11) can be light with yogurt and muffins or full egg or griddle entrées. Lunch and dinner menus (11am-10:30pm daily, $8-25) have salads that can be customized with chicken or salmon, sandwiches, burgers, and full dinners of trout, meatloaf, and pasta. The soda fountain serves up homemade ice cream milkshakes, specialty desserts, and huckleberry ice cream.

The **Pool Side Café** (11am-5pm daily July-Aug., $5-10) serves salads, pizza, cold or grilled sandwiches, and ice cream bars. In the evening, the café turns into the **Pool Barbecue** (307/543-3463, 5pm-9pm daily July-Aug., $23 adults, $12 kids, reservations recommended). Hot dogs, burgers, beef brisket, and barbecue chicken come with traditional barbecue sides and dessert. Add on s'mores ($5) to roast by the fire and listen to live music.

The **Lobby Coffee Cart** (7am-4pm daily) at Jackson Lake Lodge is the only place to get espresso.

Sargeants Bay Picnic Area

Signal Mountain

At the **Signal Mountain Lodge** complex (307/543-2831 or 800/672-6012, www.signalmountainlodge.com, daily early May-mid-Oct.), two restaurants have big menus, kids' menus, beer, wine, cocktails, and outstanding views. Windows look out at Jackson Lake, Mt. Moran, and the Tetons.

Peaks Dining Room (5:30pm-10pm daily, closes early in shoulder seasons, $10-33) serves dinners of small plates or upscale western bistro entrées of trout, salmon, beef, bison, and elk. Many have gluten-free variations. Specialty sides include whipped maple-bourbon sweet potatoes in addition to traditional potatoes or rice. The roasted garlic soup warms on cooler days.

With a deck in addition to windows, ★ **Trapper Grill** (7am-10pm daily early May-mid-Oct.) has large menus with many choices that include organic, sustainable, vegetarian, heart healthy, egg substitute, and gluten-free options. Breakfast (until 11am, $8-15) specialties include eggs Benedict, skillets, and

omelets. The lunch and dinner menu ($10-18) is available in the restaurant and bar and includes salads, sandwiches, burgers, ribs, and Tex-Mex entrées. The attached Deadman's Bar serves local brews, wine, and cocktails, including a blackberry margarita. Giant nachos are a post-hiking favorite here.

Groceries

Located in Colter Bay Village, **Colter Bay General Store** (307/543-3100 or 800/628-9988, www.gtlc.com, 7:30am-9pm daily late May-late Sept.) is a small grocery with a deli where you can get sandwiches for hiking and soups-to-go, fresh fruits and veggies, free-range meat and poultry, and fresh pastries come from the bakery. Camping supplies, including firewood, ice, snacks, beer, and wine are available.

In summer, **Headwaters Lodge at Flagg Ranch** and **Signal Mountain Lodge** carry convenience-type items with a few limited groceries; only Headwaters is open in winter (mid-Dec.-mid-Mar.).

Picnicking

Colter Bay has the only picnic area with fire rings with grills (bring your own wood). Between Lizard Creek Campground and Leek's Marina (on Hwy. 89/191/287), three picnic areas line the road. **Lakeview** is the most popular due to its water views and lake access for water play, but the rough parking lot fits only small RVs. South of Lakeview, **Arizona Island** and **Sargeants Bay Picnic Areas** have parking that can fit large RVs, but no water access. **Two Ocean Lake** also has a small picnic area on the lake.

OUTSIDE THE PARK
Moran

Limited restaurants sit outside the park around Moran. Off the beaten path, **Buffalo Valley Café** (Heart Six Guest Ranch, 16945 Buffalo Valley Rd., 307/543-2062, http://heartsix.com, 7am-8pm daily May-Sept., $7-14) is a homey cowboy café. Breakfast is served until 11am, followed by lunch and dinner. Beer and wine are served, too. **Hatchet Resort** (19980 E. Hwy. 287, 877/543-2413, http://hatchetresort.com, 7am-8:30pm daily May-Oct., $8-36) has a café and restaurant that serve breakfast, lunch, and dinner.

Transportation and Services

DRIVING

From the South Entrance of Yellowstone to Moran Junction, **U.S. Highway 89/191/287** (open year-round) crosses eight miles south through John D. Rockefeller, Jr. Memorial Parkway before traveling 16 miles down Jackson Lake to Jackson Lake Junction. At Jackson Lake Junction, head five miles east to exit the park at Moran Junction, or continue south from Moran on the "Outside Road" for 15 miles to Moose.

From Jackson Lake Junction, the Teton Park Road (closed in winter) continues south to Jenny Lake.

Wildlife Precautions

Driving in Grand Teton National Park is on two-lane roads, some with no shoulders. Speed limits vary between 25 and 55 mph; nighttime speed limit is 45 mph in order to protect wildlife. U.S. Highway 26/89/191 has been the "local speedway" for getting from Jackson Lake to Jackson, often making the road a wildlife slaughterhouse. Wildlife crossing areas are rarely signed, and lighting at dusk and dawn make spotting animals more difficult. Drive slowly at night as wildlife can be difficult to see.

SHUTTLES

Shuttles in Grand Teton are run by **Alltrans** (307/733-3135 or 800/443-6133, www.alltransparkshuttle.com, daily late May-early Oct., $15/person/day) and travel between Jackson, Moose, Jenny Lake Visitor Center, Jenny Lake Lodge, Signal Mountain Lodge, Jackson Lake Lodge, Colter Bay Village, and Headwaters Lodge at Flagg Ranch. Shuttles run several times north and south each day. Departure times are available at the visitors centers. The one-day fee lets you get on and off the shuttle as many times as you want and wherever you want. No reservations are needed; pay with cash, Visa, or Mastercard when you board. Alltrans also provides shuttles from the Jackson Hole Airport (www.jacksonholealltrans.com) to lodges in the park.

EMERGENCY SERVICES

In an emergency, ranger stations are at Colter Bay Village, Moran Entrance Station, and Yellowstone's South Entrance Station. These stations are not staffed like visitors centers, but they can help in emergencies. For emergencies in the Bridger-Teton National Forest, contact **Blackrock Ranger District** (Hwy

Where Can I Find?

- **Banks and ATMs:** Find ATMs at Colter Bay General Store in Colter Bay Village and at Jackson Lake Lodge.

- **Cell Service:** Moran and the Jackson Lake area get limited cell phone reception, although it is best for those with Verizon. You can get cell reception at Flagg Ranch, Colter Bay, Jackson Lake Lodge, and Signal Mountain Lodge.

- **Gas and Garage Services:** In summer, gas stations operate at Flagg Ranch, Colter Bay Village, Jackson Lake Lodge, Signal Mountain Lodge, and Moran. Flagg Ranch operates in winter (mid-Dec.-mid-Mar.), and Moran is open year-round. Boat gasoline is sold at Leek's Marina, Colter Bay Marina, and Signal Mountain Lodge.

- **Internet Access:** Wi-Fi is available at Jackson Lake Lodge and Signal Mountain Lodge. Colter Bay Village has Wi-Fi available in public locations such as restaurants, launderettes, and lodging check-in lobbies.

- **Laundry:** Coin-op laundries are at Headwaters Campground at Flagg Ranch, Colter Bay, and Signal Mountain Lodge.

- **Post Office:** A post office is located in Moran (1 Central St., 8:30am-1pm and 1:30pm-4:30pm Mon.-Fri., 10am-11:30am Sat.), outside the east entrance of Grand Teton National Park.

- **Showers:** Showers ($5-7) are at Headwaters Campground at Flagg Ranch, Colter Bay, and Signal Mountain Lodge. The Signal Mountain Lodge shower house has large individual shower rooms.

26/287, Moran, WY, 307/543-2386, www.fs.usda.gov/btnf). For help on the Ashton-Flagg Ranch Road in Caribou-Targhee National Forest, contact **Ashton/Island Park Ranger District** (46 S. Hwy. 20, Ashton, ID, 208/652-7442, www.fs.usda.gov/ctnf).

Grand Teton Medical Clinic (Jackson Lake Lodge, 307/543-2514, after hours 307/733-8002, http://grandtetonmedicalclinic.com, 9am-5pm daily late May-early Oct.) can take care of most situations except severe emergencies. The closest hospital, **St. John's Medical Center** (625 E. Broadway, Jackson, WY, 307/733-3636, www.tetonhospital.org), is about 30 miles south of Moran Junction.

South Grand Teton

Look for ★ to find recommended
sights, activities, dining, and lodging.

Highlights

★ **Craig Thomas Discovery & Visitor Center:** Art and technology provide an introduction to Grand Teton National Park (page 211).

★ **Laurance S. Rockefeller Preserve Center:** Unique conservation exhibits connect you with nature through the senses (page 212).

★ **Teton Park Road:** This scenic Inner Road tours the west side of Jackson Hole, right under the Teton Mountains (page 213).

★ **Moose-Wilson Road:** This narrow road weaves through beaver, porcupine, and moose habitat (page 215).

★ **Grand Teton:** At 13,770 feet, the Grand tops all other peaks in the Teton Mountains (page 216).

★ **Jenny Lake:** Jenny Lake is flush with hiking trails and pristine water for paddling and fishing (page 217).

★ **Snake River Overlook:** The Wild and Scenic Snake River offers wildlife-watching and views laden with scenery (page 220).

★ **Mormon Row:** The scenic old barns and buildings of this historic community claim expansive views of the Teton Mountains (page 221).

★ **Hidden Falls and Inspiration Point:** Hike to a rocky outcrop at 7,200 feet with views of

Jackson Hole and the blue waters of Jenny Lake (page 225).

★ **Paintbrush-Cascade Loop:** Hikers place this 19.2-mile loop, topping out at 10,720-foot Paintbrush Divide, on their bucket lists (page 225).

The Grand Teton crowns the Teton Mountains, towering as the zenith for minions of toothy peaks spreading north and south, forming the youngest range in the Rocky Mountains.

From the flat sagebrush plains of Jackson Hole, the Grand shoots 7,000 feet into the sky. Along with its skirts of peaks, it lures mountain climbers, hikers, photographers, artists, and those who seek inspiration to get up close and personal.

Visitors have two options: experience the peaks from the floor of Jackson Hole or hike into the mountainous canyons. Snuggled at the base of the peaks, small lakes string along the valley floor offering picturesque places to fish, paddle, and hike, backdropped by sky-scraping grandeur. High up, glacier-scoured basins house idyllic alpine lakes rimmed with meadows of wildflowers, moraines from alpine glaciers, giant rock-slab ledges topped by vertical spires, and high passes on the Teton Crest.

Cutting through Jackson Hole, the Wild and Scenic Snake River zigzags with changing views of the colossal peaks. Families relax on the river in rubber rafts, and anglers fly-fish for trout.

Wildlife abounds in the southern Tetons. Bison, elk, moose, pronghorn, and deer populate the fields of Jackson Hole. Bald eagles and great blue herons fish the Snake River, also home to river otters and muskrats. Grizzly bears roam the forests, and shrieking pikas inhabit high-elevation talus slopes.

PLANNING YOUR TIME

Summer packs out Jenny Lake with visitors. Parking gets tight, tent campers must claim sites early, boat tours book out, and low-elevation trails crowd with hikers. But as you climb up canyons into the Teton Mountains, the number of hikers thins. **June-early September,** all visitor services, visitors centers, lodges, and restaurants are open, and all park service and concessionaire activities run full programs. **June** brings out wildflowers around the moraine lakes along the base of the Tetons with fields of purple lupine and yellow balsamroot. By **August,** lush sagebrush

---

Previous: Taggart Lake Trail; lupine bloom against a summer sky. **Above:** bison.

South Grand Teton

To Driggs, Idaho

GRAND TARGHEE RESORT

TETON CANYON

Teton National Forest

Caribou-Targhee National Forest

Fox Creek Pass

Teton Range

Solitude Lake

Thor Peak 12,028ft

Paintbrush Canyon

Leigh Lake

10,450 ft

JACKSON HOLE

Granite Canyon

Death Canyon

Holly Lake

Mt St. John 11,430ft

Mt Hunt 10,783ft

Phelps Lake

Alaska Basin

Middle Teton 12,804ft

GRAND TETON 13,772ft

Mt Owen 12,928ft

Teewinot Mountain 12,325ft

HIDDEN FALLS AND INSPIRATION POINT

CASCADE LOOP

PAINTBRUSH CANYON

Cascade Canyon

North Jenny Lake

Holly Jenny Lake

South Teton 12,514ft

Buck Mountain 11,938ft

Rendezvous Mtn 10,927ft

Teton Village

To Wilson and Jackson

MOOSE - WILSON RD

MOOSE-WILSON ROAD

Snake River

Jackson Hole

GRANITE CANYON ENTRANCE STATION

WINTER CLOSURE GATE

JACKSON HOLE AIRPORT

LAURANCE S. ROCKEFELLER PRESERVE CENTER

CRAIG THOMAS DISCOVERY & VISITOR CENTER

WINTER CLOSURE GATE

Taggart Lake

Bradley Lake

CHAPEL OF THE TRANSFIGURATION

MENOR'S FERRY

Moose Junction

JENNY LAKE

South Jenny Lake Junction

JENNY LAKE

String Lake

North Jenny Lake Junction

Grand Teton National Park

WINTER CLOSURE GATE

TETON GLACIER TURNOUT

TETON PARK ROAD

SCHWABACHER LANDING

MT MORAN TURNOUT

To Jackson

JACKSON NATIONAL FISH HATCHERY

To Wilson and Jackson

89 26 191

Multi-Use Pathway

Gros Ventre

GROS VENTRE

Blacktail Butte 7,688ft

MORMON ROW

BLACKTAIL PONDS OVERLOOK

GLACIER VIEW TURNOUT

ANTELOPE FLATS RD

National Elk Refuge

Kelly

Gros Ventre River

KELLY WARM SPRING

Gros Ventre Slide

TETON SCIENCE SCHOOL

SHADOW MT RD

Ditch Creek

RIVER RD

Snake River

SNAKE RIVER OVERLOOK

DEADMAN'S BAR RIVER ACCESS

The Potholes

MOOSE HEAD RANCH

POTHOLES TURNOUT

CUNNINGHAM CABIN

LOST CREEK RANCH

TRIANGLE X RANCH

89 26 191

To Moran Junction

To Buffalo River

Spread Creek

Bridger-Teton National Forest

Gros Ventre Wilderness

ATHERTON CREEK

Lower Slide Lake

Bridger-Teton National Forest

RED HILLS

CRYSTAL CREEK

0   5 km

0   5 mi

© AVALON TRAVEL

grassland greens give way to golden browns, and copious early summer mosquitoes disappear as ponds dry up. In the canyons of the Tetons, waterfalls gush as snows melt, but access to high snow-buried passes may not be possible until mid-July or early August.

To avoid the crowds of summer, spring and fall offer quieter times to visit, although weather can be erratic. If your goal is to climb the Grand Teton or hike to the Teton Crest, snow may impede travel in upper elevations. If lower-elevation hiking and sightseeing is on your agenda, the shoulder seasons are the perfect time, and the snow-clad peaks stand out dramatically against a blue sky. All roads are open, and wildlife is active. **Spring** brings the chance to see bison and pronghorn newborns, and during fall, the air fills with the sound of elk bugling. **Fall** also brings outstanding hiking with warm bug-free days and cool nights. During early spring or late fall, you may need to stay in Jackson or Teton Village when in-park facilities are closed.

When **winter** descends on Grand Teton National Park, so does the snow. **Teton Park Road,** along with several lesser roads, **closes November-April.** Only **U.S. Highway 26/89/191** remains **open year-round.** While the park bans snowmobiles on roads, the snow-buried routes work for cross-country skiing and snowshoeing. A small section is even machine-groomed. Winter offers a chance for exquisite scenery: trees rimmed with frost, wind-sculpted snow, and icicles. Barring periodic blizzards, the park fills with utter quiet.

Most in-park **facilities are closed,** but just outside the national park, **Jackson** and **Teton Village** offer lodging, restaurants, and amenities. While bears hibernate, wildlife such as raptors, bison, deer, and wolves move through the valley. Rangers guide snowshoe walks in winter to look for tracks, and concessionaires lead wildlife-watching tours.

Exploring South Grand Teton

VISITORS CENTERS
Jenny Lake Visitor Center

The small **Jenny Lake Visitor Center** (307/739-3392, www.nps.gov/grte, 8am-7pm daily mid-May-late Sept., 8am-5pm daily Oct.-mid-May) is located at South Jenny Lake. Stop here to pick up activity schedules, ranger program information, and maps. The center has a relief map of the park and geology exhibits, and houses a small bookstore run by **Grand Teton Association** (307/739-3606, www.grandtetonpark.org) that sells field guides and books on natural history, human history, and geology. Also located in the complex is the **Jenny Lake Ranger Station** (307/739-3343, 8am-5pm daily early June-early Sept.), which contains climbing displays. Go to the ranger station for backcountry camping and boating permits, and information on mountain climbing routes and conditions.

★ Craig Thomas Discovery & Visitor Center

The **Craig Thomas Discovery & Visitor Center** (307/739-3399, www.nps.gov/grte, 8am-7pm daily early Mar.-Nov. 1, 8am-5pm daily in shoulder seasons, limited winter hours), called the Moose Visitor Center by locals, was built in 2007 with large windows that take advantage of the Teton Mountains. Built with a combination of public and private funding, the $22 million, 22,000-square-foot building has exhibits on the natural history of the park and mountaineering, large bronze wildlife sculptures, a 30-foot climbing wall, in-floor videos, kids' exhibits, and a topographic map with laser technology that shows wildlife migration and glacier progression. The theater also shows a documentary on the park, and Native Americans crafts are displayed on select days. The information desk has maps, schedules of ranger programs and hikes,

Craig Thomas Discovery & Visitor Center

current weather data from park monitors, and permits for backcountry camping and boating. A large **Grand Teton Association bookstore** (307/739-3606, www.grandteton-park.org) sells field guides and books on wildlife, human history, and geology.

★ Laurance S. Rockefeller Preserve Center

The **Laurance S. Rockefeller Preserve Center** (307/739-3654, www.nps.gov/grte, 9am-5pm daily late May-late Sept.) is a different type of visitors center. Located on a 1,000-acre preserve that was once a ranch owned by the Rockefeller family. The preserve's LEED-certified building contains exhibits that appeal to the senses: visual, tactile, and auditory. Watch high-definition nature videos, view an ultra-large Phelps Lake photograph made from one-inch nature photos, and listen to natural soundscapes. Rangers lead daily programs, talks, hikes, sunrise strolls, and evening walks. Kids can check out a backpack for a journaling experience while hiking the preserve's eight miles of trails, including a loop around Phelps Lake. The parking lot is limited

to 50 cars and usually fills up 10am-3pm; plan your visit early in the morning or late afternoon. In May and October, visitors can drive to the center and hike, even when the building is closed. In winter, cross-country skiers and snowshoers tour trails at the preserve.

ENTRANCE STATIONS

South Grand Teton has two entrance stations ($30 vehicle, $25 motorcycles, $15 hike-in/bike-in; joint parks pass: $50 vehicle, $40 motorcycles, $20 hike-in/bike-in); both are open year-round. The **Granite Canyon Entrance Station** (no RVs or trailers) sits just north of Teton Village on the south entrance to the Moose-Wilson Road. In winter, the road is only open for cars for about a half mile for ski and snowshoe trailhead access. The **Moose Entrance Station** sits on Teton Park Road on the east side of the Snake River. U.S. Highway 26/89/191 (open year-round) has no entrance stations.

TOURS

Most scenic tours (May-mid-Oct., $195-200 adults, $100-150 kids) are with companies based in the town of Jackson and via small vans or buses. **Buffalo Roam Park Tours** (307/413-0954, www.buffaloroamtours.com) guides full-day van tours that include the Craig Thomas Discovery & Visitor Center, a boat ride on Jenny Lake, wildlife-watching, and other sites around the park. **VIP Adventure Travel** (307/699-1077, www.vipadventuretravel.com) takes in sightseeing in luxury SUVs.

Boat Tours

Cruise around Jenny Lake to see the Teton Mountains from a different perspective; bring your camera for the views. From the dock at South Jenny Lake, **Jenny Lake Boating** (307/734-9227, www.jennylakeboating.com, daily mid-May-late Sept., no tours July 4, $19 adults, $17 seniors, $11 kids) guides one-hour interpretive tours of the lake on boats that hold 44 people. Guides cover tidbits about geology, history, plants, and wildlife during the shoreline loop tour. Early June-early September, three tours launch daily: 11am, 2pm, and 5pm. In spring and fall, two tours depart each day at noon and 3pm. Reservations by credit card are highly recommended.

Wildlife Tours

Safari-style wildlife tours get you out with expert naturalists to watch animals in their natural habitats. Guides supply binoculars, spotting scopes, and field books. **Teton Science School** (700 Coyote Canyon Rd., Jackson, 877/404-6626, www.tetonscience.org, year-round) leads half-day ($130 adults, $99 kids under 7), full-day ($210 adults, $150 kids under 7), and multiday wildlife expeditions that use customized vans with roof hatches for stand-up viewing. Tours pick up in Jackson and Teton Village; pickups at park lodges cost extra. Full-day expeditions include lunch—a picnic in summer or a restaurant in winter. Departure times vary based on sunrise, an active time for wildlife.

Based in Jackson, **Ecotour Adventures** (307/690-9533, www.jhecotouradventures.com, year-round) runs four-hour sunrise and sunset wildlife tours ($130 adults, $95 kids). Eight-hour tours ($225 adults, $190 kids) include lunch at one of the park lodges. Departure times vary depending on daylight hours. Tours are limited to seven participants so that each person gets a window seat; roof hatches allow everyone to stand up to view and photograph wildlife. Most of the company's rigs run on biodiesel to protect air quality around wildlife.

DRIVING TOURS
★ Teton Park Road
20 MILES

From Jackson Lake Junction in the north to Moose in the south, the **Teton Park Road** (20 miles, May-Oct.) gives up-close views of the Teton Mountains. The road (called the Inside Road by locals) has wildlife-watching, but **closes in winter** from Signal Mountain Lodge to Taggart Lake Trailhead. From the Craig Thomas Discovery & Visitor Center at Moose, start by driving north on Teton Park Road. Just past the Moose Entrance Station, turn right to see the **Menors Ferry Historic District** and the small log **Chapel of the Transfiguration.** Continuing north for 3.7 miles leads to a turnoff where you can look straight up at the small **Middle Teton Glacier.** In about three miles, stop at **South Jenny Lake** to walk from the visitors center to the lake. Continuing north on Teton Park Road, stop at the **Mt. Moran turnout** to examine the black dike and two small glaciers in its upper cliffs.

Inside-Outside Loop
43 MILES

The Inside and Outside Roads (Teton Park Rd. and U.S. Hwy. 26/89/191) link together in a 43-mile scenic loop, a four-hour-tour with stops. Begin at the **Craig Thomas Discovery & Visitor Center** to drive the Inside Road, stopping for wildlife and sightseeing. At Jackson Lake Junction, turn east for one mile to the **Oxbow Bend Turnout.** Use binoculars to help in spotting animals and birds in this wildlife-rich wetlands. Continue east to Moran Junction and turn south onto the Outside

Road. About 5.5 miles south, turn right to see the **Cunningham Cabin Historic Site.** Stop next at the **Snake River Overlook** to see the riffles of the 13th-largest river in the country and at **Blacktail Ponds Overlook** for wildlife-watching along with alternate views of the Tetons. At Moose Junction, turn right to return to the visitors center.

Jenny Lake Road
4 MILES

The tour of **Jenny Lake Road** (four miles, May-Oct.) starts at North Jenny Lake. After the String Lake Junction, Jenny Lake Road becomes one-way as it passes **Jenny Lake Lodge** before reaching the only turnout at **Jenny Lake Overlook** for a spectacular view of Grand Teton, Mt. Owen, and Teewinot Mountain. When the lake is glassy, the viewpoint yields stunning photos of the water reflecting the Cathedral Group. The drive loops back to Teton Park Road north of South Jenny Lake in about 15 minutes.

River Road (4WD)
9.2 MILES

For four-wheel-drive vehicles only, the **River Road** (RKO Rd., 9.2 miles, May-Oct.) runs along the Snake River. Locate it from the Teton Park Road north of Cottonwood Creek Picnic Area or south of the Potholes Turnout. Surrounded by sagebrush grasslands, the rolling, narrow dirt road is rough in places with washboards, and in rain it can mutate to muck. But it does afford ultra-close-up views of the Snake River, access for anglers to fish, and wildlife-watching.

Antelope Flats
10 MILES

Through a flat, sagebrush plain, a loop on dirt and paved roads tours **Antelope Flats** (10 miles), a place of park history with wildlife-watching especially around sunrise or dusk. Late 1800s ranches and homesteads left irrigation ditches, old buildings, and barns in **Mormon Row,** where you can take a self-guided tour. The southeast corner of the loop goes through the small burg of **Kelly,** with a population of 130 residents. Access the loop from the Gros Ventre River Road or Antelope Flats Road, both turnoffs from U.S. Highway 26/89/191. In spring, see newborn bison calves and pronghorn fawns, and in fall, watch large herds of elk cross into the National Elk Refuge to the south. Mormon Row and Antelope Flats

Teton Park Road

a moose cow and calf on the Moose-Wilson Road

Roads close November-April, but Gros Ventre River Road stays open year-round.

★ Moose-Wilson Road
8 MILES

Moose-Wilson Road (eight miles, www.nps. gov/grte, May-Oct.) snuggles into the southern base of the Teton Mountains between the Granite Canyon Entrance Station and the Craig Thomas Discovery & Visitor Center in Moose. The skinny, shoulderless road (paved and dirt) packs in curves and shrinks to almost one lane in places (no vehicles over 23 feet long or trailers). Spot moose and birds, especially at **Sawmill Ponds.** The **Laurance S. Rockefeller Preserve** is in the road's central stretch. On busy days, the road sees about 1,000 vehicles. The park service has proposed limiting the road to 200 cars at a time during peak days in July and August. Check at visitors centers for updates that may affect use. Drive slowly; collisions happen far too often. This road also serves as a summer shortcut between Teton Village and Jenny Lake.

Sights

TETON PARK ROAD
The Teton Range

The Teton Mountains run north-south parallel to the valley of Jackson Hole. The mountains are dominated by the highest peaks, called the **Cathedral Group: Grand Teton, Mt. Owen, Teewinot, Middle Teton,** and **South Teton.** At 13,770 feet, the **Grand Teton** is the tallest peak in the range. **Mt. Moran,** at 12,605, is the most prominent peak north of the Cathedral Group. About 40 miles long, the range is the newest of the Rocky Mountains. Eight of the mountains require technical climbs to reach their summits.

Enjoy the range by learning a few of its bigger landmarks; the park newspaper supplies a panorama of the peaks and identifies their summits. In summer, use binoculars to view the peaks from the **Mt. Moran Turnout** (north of North Jenny Lake), **Cathedral Group Turnout** (on North Jenny Lake Rd.), or the **Teton Glacier Turnout** on Teton Park Road. You will see tiny glaciers, black vertical dikes, and myriad toothy spires. In winter,

Teton Facts

While glaciers helped carve the dramatic spires, freeze-thawing water and winds continue to shape the pinnacles. But if that's all there was, they would be like many other high peaks in the Rocky Mountains. Part of what makes the Tetons so spectacular is their prominence, or the amount of land jutting above the valley floor. It's close to 7,000 feet. When the Teton fault started shoving the peaks up in elevation, instead of creating foothills, the easternmost layer of rock fell, forming a gigantic valley, or hole, known today as Jackson Hole. The distance in elevation between Jackson Hole and the serrated summits of the Tetons lets visitors take in the full majesty of the mountain range. On the western side of the Tetons, the prominence is much less, with rounded foothills descending to the Teton Valley. More facts:

- The proper name for the mountain range is the Teton Mountains or Tetons rather than the Grand Tetons. The Grand Teton refers to the highest peak in the range.

- The highest peak in the Teton Mountains is the Grand Teton at 13,770 feet.

- Twelve peaks in the Teton Range stretch up to 12,000 feet or more.

- Ten glaciers that formed during the Little Ice Age still cling to the Teton Mountains. (See the 53-acre Teton Glacier from Teton Glacier Turnout on Teton Park Road.)

- Seven moraine lakes tuck at the base of the Teton Range, and the mountains cradle more than 100 alpine lakes.

- More than 200 miles of trails wander through the Teton Mountains.

CLIMBING

Climbing the Grand Teton involves 14 miles of hiking and 6,545 feet of climbing and descent. Most climbers take an ultra-long day from the valley floor; however, for climbing the peak itself, the fastest time for climbing and descending, at 2:53, was set in 2012 by a climbing ranger. Although controversy surrounds the first ascent, documentation points to a team of four summiting first in 1898 and a team of two earlier in 1873, although the latter may have summited The Enclosure instead. Either way, archaeological evidence indicates that Native Americans most likely reached the summit before both groups.

More than 35 climbing routes lead to the summit with countless variations, and climbers pioneer new routes almost every year. The most popular and famous route for climbing the Grand Teton is the exposed Upper Exum Ridge, considered a classic in mountaineering. Since 1971, ski and snowboard descents have been added to the record books.

stop at the **Glacier View** or **Teton Point Turnouts** (Hwy. 26/89/191). For photographers, sunrise photos will light up the peaks, while sunset colors will backlight their shadows. **Cascade Canyon** (to Hurricane Pass) or **Death Canyon** (to Fox Creek Pass) hikes climb into the backbone of the mountain range along the Teton Crest Trail.

★ GRAND TETON

Like the Matterhorn, the **Grand Teton** spirals up into a pinnacle. You can spot its 13,770-foot pointed summit from almost everywhere in Jackson Hole. Carved by erosion from ice, water, and wind, the spire commands the highest point in the Teton Mountains. A lure for climbers, the Grand serves as a notch in the belts of mountaineers who summit its vertical cliffs. Most people, however, won't attempt climbing the peak, but you can check out what it's like to ascend via a virtual climb (www.nps.gov/grte). Other than climbing, the best ways to enjoy the peak are hiking the **Paintbrush Canyon-Cascade**

Grand Teton

Canyon Loop, catching the sunrise glow on camera from Jenny Lake, and eyeballing its crags through binoculars at the **Teton Glacier Turnout** on Teton Park Road.

The Potholes

Best seen from Teton Park Road, **The Potholes** (Potholes Pullout north of Jenny Lake, road closed in winter) are glacial kettles that are evidence of a huge 2,000-foot-deep glacier that once covered Jackson Hole. (Kettles are large depressions or potholes in the landscape.) As the glacier melted, pieces broke off, and where those chunks melted, they created kettles; some are filled with trees, like the one at the pullout. The Potholes Pullout is located on the south side of the road, between Signal Mountain and North Jenny Lake.

★ Jenny Lake

Tucked below the Grand Teton, **Jenny Lake** is a placid place of beauty. The two-mile-long lake was created in the glacial depression left behind a moraine and is about 250 feet deep.

The lake beckons photographers and artists to capture its grandeur, but it's also a place where visitors can lodge or camp and spend days outdoors hiking, biking, boating, paddling, fishing, swimming, climbing, backpacking, and wildlife-watching. Jenny Lake trails range from short, easy jaunts to long, uphill grunts with immense views. South Jenny Lake houses a visitors center, ranger station, store, scenic boat tours, and campground. **Jenny Lake Historic District** contains a homestead cabin that serves as the ranger station. **Jenny Lake Lodge** is reached from North Jenny Lake.

Teton Glacier

Peek at **Teton Glacier** below the north face of **Grand Teton** at the Teton Glacier Turnout on Teton Park Road (2.8 miles south of Jenny Lake and 4 miles north of Moose). The ice field is the park's largest remaining glacier and one of 12 that are named. Less than 53 acres in size, it is shrinking annually. Its terminal moraine is visible below the glacier, marking the original size where it deposited rock debris. By mid-summer, when the

Jenny Lake Area

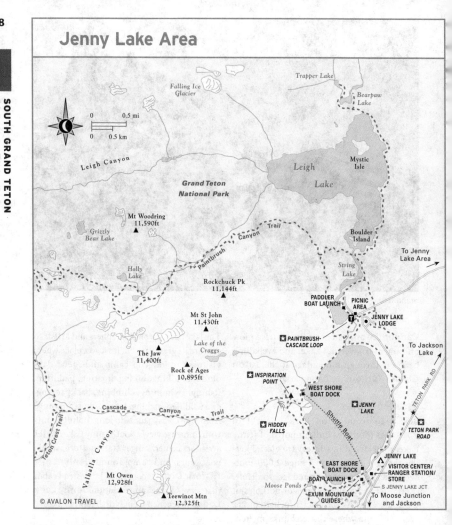

blanket of the past winter's snow melts, its crevasses are visible.

MOOSE
Menor's Ferry

Located on a spur road north of the Moose Entrance Station, **Menor's Ferry Historic District** preserves buildings from the 1890s. Its location at a narrowing of the Snake River allowed for a ferry to cart people back and forth. In summer, rangers guide 45-minute walks through the district each afternoon,

usually meeting at 2:30pm at the ferry dock. You can also do a self-guided tour of the cabins, barns, a smokehouse, farm implements, wagons, a replica ferry (rideable in late summer), and a **general store** (operated by Grand Teton Association, 307/739-3606, www.grandtetonpark.org, 9am-4:30pm daily late May-late Sept.). The **Maud Noble Cabin** hosted some of the 1923 talks to create Grand Teton National Park. Menor's Ferry Historic District has coverage for free cell phone tours of the area.

Moose Area

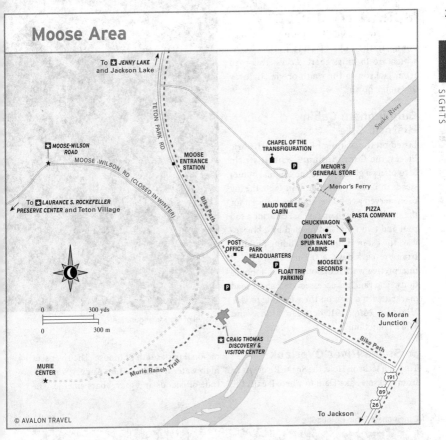

To ⭐ JENNY LAKE
and Jackson Lake

TETON PARK RD

⭐ MOOSE-WILSON
ROAD

MOOSE -WILSON RD (CLOSED IN WINTER)

MOOSE
ENTRANCE
STATION

To ⭐ LAURANCE S. ROCKEFELLER
PRESERVE CENTER and Teton Village

Bike Path

Snake River

CHAPEL OF THE
TRANSFIGURATION

P

MENOR'S
GENERAL STORE

Menor's Ferry

MAUD NOBLE
CABIN

PIZZA
PASTA COMPANY

CHUCKWAGON

DORNAN'S
SPUR RANCH
CABINS

POST
OFFICE
PARK
HEADQUARTERS

MOOSELY
SECONDS

FLOAT TRIP
PARKING

P

0   300 yds
0   300 m

CRAIG THOMAS
DISCOVERY &
VISITOR CENTER

To Moran
Junction

Bike Path

MURIE
CENTER

Murie Ranch Trail

191

89

26

To Jackson

© AVALON TRAVEL

Chapel of the Transfiguration

On the road to Menor's Ferry, a small log chapel was built to frame a view of the Cathedral Group of the Teton Mountains. Built in 1925 to serve homesteaders in Jackson Hole, the 50-foot-long **Chapel of the Transfiguration** substituted one of its stained-glass windows for a clear window over the altar that looks squarely at the Grand Teton. **St. John's Episcopal Church** (http://stjohnsjackson.diowy.org) in Jackson owns the building, which is listed on the National Register of Historic Places. Services are held Sunday mornings in summer. The chapel is open for visiting, but please be respectful of those using it for worship.

Murie Center

Located at the north end of Moose-Wilson Road, the **Murie Center** (1 Murie Ranch Rd., Moose, 307/739-2246, www.muriecenter.org, 9am-5pm Mon.-Fri. summer, free) is a National Historic Landmark where the Murie family had their 77-acre ranch. The Muries, a family of four conservationists, sought to protect nature for its importance to the human spirit. Today, the center serves as a place to foster the preservation of wilderness and nature with conservation programs. Visitors can tour one of the ranch cabins with docents and walk the self-guided one-mile trail on the ranch. In 2015, the Murie Center became part of the Teton Science School.

MORAN TO MOOSE

U.S. Highway 26/89/191 (open year-round) connects the hubs of Moran and Moose, which are 18 miles apart. Access this road from Jackson in the south or via Highway 287 in the north.

Cunningham Cabin Historic Site

Listed on the National Register of Historic Places, the **Cunningham Cabin Historic Site** offers a glimpse into the original homesteads in Jackson Hole. Built in 1888, the log cabin served as a home, smithy, and barn for the small Cunningham ranch. Featuring a sod roof and two rooms connected by a breezeway, the cabin is the only standing building from pre-park days. A 0.3-mile self-guided interpretive walk tours other ranch foundations. The ranch is accessed via a short road marked with a sign on the west side of U.S. Highway 26/89/191, between Moose and Moran Junctions.

Chapel of the Transfiguration

★ Snake River Overlook

Through Jackson Hole, the Snake River winds from Jackson Lake Dam to where it exits the national park south of Moose. The river sees high water in June, but by August, a multitude of islands and gravel bars emerge. The

Cunningham Cabin Historic Site

Mormon Row

river corridor provides prime habitat for songbirds, bald eagles, great blue herons, raptors, bears, bison, and ungulates. From the **Snake River Overlook** on U.S. Highway 26/89/191 between Moose and Moran Junctions, you can walk along the bluff to snap photos of the winding river channel below the Teton Mountains. Find the lighting on the Tetons best in morning.

Blacktail Ponds Overlook

Stop at **Blacktail Ponds Overlook** with a pair of binoculars or spotting scope for wildlife-watching (best in early morning or late evening). Moose often feed in the ponds, and the habitat is good for osprey, waterfowl, and songbirds. Active beavers maintain the dams, which keep the ponds in water. The overlook is located on the west side of U.S. Highway 26/89/191, about 1.3 miles north of Moose Junction.

Antelope Flats Road

Antelope Flats actually refers to the entire plateau (not just the road) and offers outstanding wildlife-watching for bison, pronghorn, moose, coyote, and raptors such as northern harriers or American kestrals. Due to its location near the National Elk Refuge, elk migrate through in spring and fall. It's also a good area in spring to spot bison and pronghorn newborns. The best wildlife-watching is in the early morning or late evening. The road also provides access to scenic Mormon Row.

★ MORMON ROW

Located in the southeast corner of the park, **Mormon Row** is a treat for history buffs, photographers, and wildlife fans. The tract was originally a Mormon ranch settlement that started in the 1890s and grew to 27 homesteads. Today, the Mormon Road is on the National Register of Historic Places. It retains six clusters of buildings, one ruin, and the famous Moulton barn that appears in the foreground of so many photos of the Grand Teton. Even amateur photographers can capture impressive images of historic buildings backdropped by the Teton Range.

Recreation

DAY HIKES

Hiking in the Teton Mountains yields a mix of canyons, alpine basins, and high passes. With the exception of paths that circle the moraine lakes along the base, all trails climb up—seriously up! Visitors coming from sea level will feel the altitude and experience heavy breathing. Slow your hiking pace to adjust to a steady rhythm, rather than stopping every 10 feet to catch your breath. Drink plenty of water (more than you would at home), as hydration helps ward off headaches and nausea from altitude sickness.

Most lower-elevation trails along the base of the Tetons are snow-free by late May, but trails that crest high passes above 9,000 feet may be buried in snow until late July. Until then, ice axes are necessary for safe travel. Accidents and fatalities in the Tetons are due to improper use (or no use) of ice axes when traversing steep snowfields. Weather conditions for high-elevation hikes are usually best mid-July-August, but expect afternoon thundershowers and snow by late August.

For Jenny Lake area hikes, you can trim mileage with a boat shuttle (307/734-9227, www.jennylakeboating.com, 7am-7pm daily mid-May-Sept., shorter hours in shoulder seasons, $15 adults, $8 kids round-trip; $9 adults, $6 kids one-way). Reservations are not required; just show up at the east- or west-side dock. Shuttles run every 10-15 minutes.

South Grand Teton Hikes

Trail	Effort	Distance	Duration
String and Leigh Lakes	Easy	3.7 mi rt	2 hr
Taggart and Bradley Lakes	Easy to Moderate	3-5.9 mi rt	2-4 hr
Phelps Lake	Easy to Moderate	1.8-7.9 mi	2-5 hr
Jenny Lake	Moderate	7.1 mi rt	3.5 hr
Hidden Falls and Inspiration Point	Moderately Strenuous	7.2 mi rt	4 hr
Surprise and Amphitheater Lakes	Strenuous	10.1 mi rt	6 hr
Granite Canyon and Marion Lake	Strenuous	11.8-18.5 mi rt	7-10 hr
Cascade Canyon, Hurricane Pass, and Lake Solitude	Strenuous	13.6-23 mi rt	7-13 hr
Paintbrush-Cascade Loop	Very Strenuous	13-19.2 mi rt	7-13 hr
Death Canyon, Static Peak Divide, and Fox Creek Pass	Very Strenuous	16.3-18.4 mi rt	9-12 hr

Fun for Kids

JUNIOR RANGERS

Kids can learn about Grand Teton National Park and earn a Junior Ranger patch or badge. Stop by a visitors center to pick up *The Grand Adventure*, the Junior Ranger activity guide. To receive the patch or badge, kids need to complete the activities in the guide geared toward their age group, attend a ranger-led program, and go on a hike. (A second ranger-led program can take the place of the hike.) Once completed, kids bring the guide to a visitors center to receive their patch or badge and be sworn in as Junior Rangers. During summer, park rangers also lead Junior Ranger programs for kids (they need one adult with them) for walking and outdoor learning adventures at **Jenny Lake Visitor Center** and **Colter Bay Visitor Center.** Check with visitors centers or online (www.nps.gov/grte) for schedules.

CAMPS AND PROGRAMS

The **Teton Science School** (700 Coyote Canyon Rd., Jackson, WY, 877/404-6626, www.teton-science.org, year-round) offers multiday summer camps and single-day programs for kids. Kids from kindergarten through grade 12 can participate in summer camps that take place on the campus north of Kelly or at various locations in the park. Some programs use hiking, canoeing, and camping as vehicles for learning about the science of the Tetons and wildlife. Programs are hands-on and experiential rather than classroom based; some emphasize outdoor skills. The school also runs family adventures based on seasonal wildlife activity.

KID-FRIENDLY HIKES

For successful hiking trips with kids, take water and snacks, even if the hike is short. Kids also should carry their own packs as soon as possible, even if it only holds a windbreaker. Rewards of ice cream after a good hike are always welcome, as is swimming in lakes on a hot day. While kids often don't care about scenery, they do love water, wildlife, and spotting animal tracks. Plenty of short trails offer good destinations for kids. For kids ages 3-6, walk **String Lake Loop** and **Hidden Falls** at Jenny Lake, Taggart Lake, or Phelps Lake. For kids ages 7-12, bump up the mileage and difficulty with the Jenny Lake Loop, Bradley-Taggart Lakes Loop, and Phelps Lake Loop.

YOUNG NATURALISTS

At the **Laurance S. Rockefeller Preserve Center,** kids ages 6-12 can check out a Nature Explorer's Backpack for journaling while exploring trails at the center. Families can also check out naturalist backpacks from the **Craig Thomas Discovery & Visitor Center** for kids' activities while outdoors.

Designed for 8-12-year-olds (but other kids can join in, too) and one parent, the **Jenny Lake Young Naturalist program** (early June-late Aug.) takes kids on a one-mile hike with a ranger to learn about natural wonders. The 90-minute program takes place three times per week. Find the schedule at visitors centers or in the park newspaper, and make reservations at the Jenny Lake Visitor Center or Craig Thomas Discovery & Visitor Center.

Guided Hikes

Grand Teton National Park does not permit guided hikes led by concessionaires, but **naturalist rangers** lead short hikes (2-3 hours, 2-4 miles, daily in summer, free) to various scenic destinations along the base of the Teton Mountains. These hikes are loaded with interpretive stops and are great for families. Current schedules are listed in the park newspaper available at entrance stations and visitors centers.

Reservations are not needed, except for the hike to Hidden Falls and Inspiration Point. The hike to Hidden Falls and Inspiration Point is limited to 25 participants and requires the boat shuttle (one-way, fee). Reservations can be made at Jenny Lake Visitor Center.

Teton Park Road
JENNY LAKE

Distance: 7.1-mile loop
Duration: 3.5 hours
Elevation change: 456 feet
Effort: moderate
Trailhead: String Lake Trailhead or Jenny Lake Village. Plan to arrive early to claim a parking spot at the popular trailheads (see map p. 218).

This trail loops completely around Jenny Lake; part of the path is paved near the visitors center, but most of the trail is dirt. Unless you hike early in the morning or late in the evening, expect to meet crowds in midsummer. All trail junctions are well signed; unsigned spur trails cut to the lakeshore for views or fishing.

From the **Jenny Lake Visitor Center**, follow signs toward the boat dock. At the first junction, take either fork to reach the lake where a right turn begins the counter-clockwise route. Head northeast on the trail, passing a short **spur trail** (for those staying at Jenny Lake Campground). Heading north, the trail cuts 3 miles between the water and Jenny Lake Scenic Drive with views of the Teton Mountains to reach the String Lake Trailhead. **Jenny Lake Overlook** provides one of the best reflections of Teewinot Mountain when the water is glassy, best in morning light.

From the **String Lake Trailhead,** head 0.3-mile west, crossing a bridge over the String Lake outlet stream. At the junction, head left for 1.7 miles above the north shore of Jenny Lake through the remains of the 1999 Alder Fire. You'll pass large boulders (erratics) before reaching the maze of junctions around the west **boat dock.** Continue straight as three trails junction to **Inspiration Point** and **Cascade Canyon,** the boat dock (2 trails), and **Hidden Falls.** After crossing Cascade Creek on a **wooden bridge,** you'll reach a fourth junction. Continue straight toward the lakeshore route running 1.5 miles south along the west shore of Jenny Lake. Once the route reconnects with your trail, it reaches a junction with the **Moose Pond Loop.** Stay left for

0.9 mile, passing one more Moose Pond Loop junction and the boat launch before reaching a **bridge** crossing Jenny Lake outlet into Cottonwood Creek at the tour boat dock. Follow the signs on the paved path back to the visitor center.

STRING AND LEIGH LAKES

Distance: 3.7-miles round-trip
Duration: 2 hours
Elevation change: 325 feet
Effort: easy
Trailhead: String Lake Trailhead from North Jenny Lake (see map p. 218)

This trail circles String Lake and takes in the southern tip of Leigh Lake, a less-crowded loop than Jenny Lake. While you can go either way on the loop, hiking counterclockwise will produce big views down the western side of the loop.

Start from the **String Lake Trailhead** and hike 1.4 mile north along the forested eastern shore of String Lake. Stop frequently along the shallow sand-bottom lake to look for moose and waterfowl. To the north, Mt. Moran rises into view while Teewinot Mountain pokes above the trees southward. At the south end of Leigh Lake, a trail junction splits right and continues up the east side of Leigh Lake to Bearpaw Lake. Stay straight instead to follow a **short spur** to the edge of the deeper **Leigh Lake** for the views.

Return to the junction and head west to cross the **bridge** at the rocky outlet of Leigh Lake. Enjoy the view of Boulder Island from the bridge, then continue westward as the trail climbs 0.7 mile through a lodgepole forest to a second **junction.** Turn left to break out of the woods and onto the open slopes of **Rockchuck Peak** and Mt. St. John with views of Teewinot Mountain. The trail gradually descends 1.6 miles to the foot of String Lake where it meets the **Jenny Lake Trail.** Turn left and cross the **bridge** at the outlet of String Lake to return to the String Lake Trailhead.

Hikers have two alternatives on this trail: a round-trip walk to Leigh Lake (1.8 miles), or

hikers on the trail to Inspiration Point

going past Leigh Lake to Bearpaw Lake (eight miles round-trip).

★ HIDDEN FALLS AND INSPIRATION POINT

Distance: 7.2 miles round-trip
Duration: 4 hours
Elevation change: 1,250 feet
Effort: moderately strenuous
Trailhead: Jenny Lake Visitor Center (see map p. 218)

Hidden Falls, a 200-foot tumbler in Cascade Canyon, and Inspiration Point, a rocky knoll at 7,257 feet, squeeze between Mt. Teewinot and Mt. St. John. Given the point's perch, the scope of views from the summit lives up to its name. You'll look straight down on the blue waters of Jenny Lake, up to the peaks on both sides, and across Jackson Hole to the Gros Ventre Mountains. Hordes of hikers clog this trail, except in early morning or late in the day.

From the **visitor center,** head west toward the **boat dock** and cross the **bridge** at the outlet of Jenny Lake at Cottonwood Creek.

Continue 0.9 mile west along the south shore of Jenny Lake. You'll pass the boat launch and two junctions for **Moose Pond Loop.** At the second Moose Pond Loop junction, take either the upper or lower trails to reach Hidden Falls; the lower trail walks 1.5 mile along the scenic lakeshore. Before reaching the lower bridge over Cascade Creek, you'll come to a junction for **Hidden Falls.** Turn left and then right immediately at the next junction, climbing 0.35 mile to the base of Hidden Falls. Hikers wanting to skip Inspiration Point can loop across Cascade Creek on the upper bridge to descend via the north side to link back in with the lower bridge and the return trail.

To continue to Inspiration Point, cross the **bridge** below the falls, then climb four south-facing switchbacks to **Inspiration Point.** (The slope can get hot in mid-summer; mornings are best for hiking to the point.) At Inspiration Point, plenty of other trails cut off to various viewpoints and places for lunch. From the point, retrace your steps back to the visitor center or loop west to connect with the **Cascade Canyon Horse Trail** and descend the north side of the canyon toward Jenny Lake. After reaching the **Jenny Lake Trail,** turn south passing two boat dock junctions and crossing the lower bridge over Cascade Creek. Immediately after crossing the bridge, you'll reach the junction for the lakeshore trail back to the visitor center. Retrace your earlier steps.

The boat shuttle (fee) reduces this hike to a 2.4-mile loop from the west boat dock.

★ PAINTBRUSH-CASCADE LOOP

Distance: 13 miles round-trip to Holly Lake; 17 miles round-trip to Paintbrush Divide; 19.2 miles round-trip for Paintbrush-Cascade Loop.
Duration: 7-13 hours
Elevation change: 4,350 feet
Effort: very strenuous
Trailhead: String Lake Trailhead at North Jenny Lake (see map p. 218)

The Paintbrush-Cascade Loop is a trail for long-distance hikers and backpackers. Spectacular scenery, wildlife, and in-your-face views of the Grand Teton are only a few of its rewards. Crossing through multiple ecosystems, the grueling route climbs Paintbrush Canyon to Holly Lake, then crests the 10,720-foot Paintbrush Divide to drop to Lake Solitude before connecting with Cascade Canyon for the descent back to the trailhead. Until late July, you may need an ice ax for crossing the divide. For those who only want to explore part of the route, Holly Lake (13 miles, 2,600 vertical feet) and Paintbrush Divide (17 miles round-trip, 4,350 vertical feet) make outstanding destinations in their own right. For hiking the full loop, plan to depart at dawn for maximum daylight.

From the trailhead, follow the path up the east side of **String Lake.** At the junction at **Leigh Lake,** turn left and cross the rocky stream. At the next junction, turn right to circle around the north side of Rockchuck Peak and climb into **Paintbrush Canyon.** The trail goes through conifer forests interrupted by giant talus fields and avalanche paths before switchbacking up through wildflower meadows and boulders to crest into a hanging valley. Listen for the "eeep" of pikas that live around the boulders. At the next trail junction, go right to **Holly Lake** or straight for a more direct route to Paintbrush Divide.

The trail to Holly Lake ascends through broken meadows to reach the idyllic alpine lake that tucks into a tight cirque filled with wildflower meadows and talus slopes. A small point on the southwest shore offers a place to relax and enjoy the scenery. From the lake, an **unmarked path** heads directly up to join the route to **Paintbrush Divide.** The trail climbs steadily 1.7 miles upward, leaving the small pockets of trees behind and entering alpine scree slopes, where steep snow can linger late into summer. After passing the junction to **Grizzly Bear Lake,** the trail swings north across the slope to switchback steeply under a cliff face and pop out at the summit of Paintbrush Divide. The trail walks along the pass, soaking up views in both directions.

To continue on the full loop to Cascade Canyon, follow the trail as it descends 2.4 miles of switchbacks to **Lake Solitude**, a larger turquoise lake flanked by wildflower meadows in August. The Grand Teton comes into view to the south. From the lake, the trail heads 2.4 miles through meadows straight toward the Grand before dropping into the forest to reach the fork in **Cascade Canyon.** From the fork, descend 6.8 miles and 1,950 feet via **Cascade Canyon Trail,** turning

hikers climb Paintbrush Divide

north at the base to skirt Jenny Lake back to the String Lake parking lot.

CASCADE CANYON, HURRICANE PASS, AND LAKE SOLITUDE

Distance: 13.6 miles round-trip to Fork of Cascade Canyon; 18.4 miles round-trip to Lake Solitude; 23.8 miles round-trip to Hurricane Pass

Duration: 7-13 hours

Elevation change: 1,950-4,200 feet

Effort: strenuous to extremely strenuous

Trailhead: Jenny Lake Visitor Center or String Lake parking lot (see map p. 218)

Cascade Canyon Trail ascends a U-shaped glaciated canyon on the north side of the Grand Teton. During the ascent, perspective changes on the Cathedral Group (Teewinot, Grand Teton, Mt. Owen), and lower-elevation cliffs and spires often occlude their summits. Most hikers go to the Fork of Cascade Canyon (6.8 miles) and turn around. While the fork is not a summit or lake destination, the trail is nonetheless scenic. From the fork, Cascade Creek splits in **two directions:** Take the north fork to Lake Solitude (2.4 miles) or take the south fork to Hurricane Pass (5.1 miles). Starting at the String Lake parking lot instead of the Jenny Lake Visitor Center drops about 0.3 mile each way.

To ascend Cascade Canyon from either trailhead, circle around **Jenny Lake** to the west side. Start climbing via **Hidden Lake and Inspiration Point** or take the horse trail up the north side of the canyon. Once in the canyon, the number of hikers thins on the climb through wildflower meadows and forest to reach the fork. During the ascent, the trail contacts Cascade Creek at various points; look for harlequin ducks or moose in early summer. The trail also traverses countless avalanche paths where bears feed.

To go to **Lake Solitude**, take the **North Fork of Cascade Creek** 2.4 miles through conifers and avalanche slopes until the trail breaks out into meadows. Meadows and broken forests flank the U-shaped, glacially carved valley that cradles the lake at 9,035 feet. Views southward stare straight at the Grand Teton. The total elevation gain to the lake is 2,955 feet.

To reach **Hurricane Pass** at 10,400 feet on the Teton Crest, follow the **South Fork of Cascade Creek** to climb through broken conifer forests as the trail circles west of the Grand Teton. Toward the head of the drainage, the trail leaves tree line in favor of scree fields, wildflower meadows, and glacial moraine between Middle Teton and Table Mountain. The

Lake Solitude

Surprise and Amphitheater Lakes

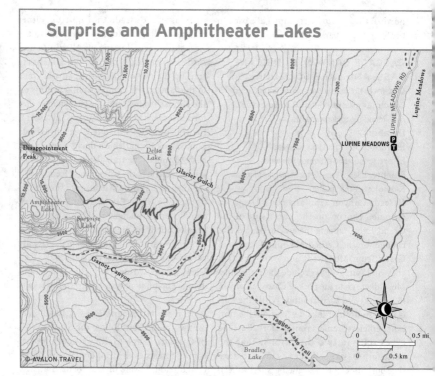

© AVALON TRAVEL

trail swings along the north side of a turquoise lake filled with glacial flour and ascends to the pass with views of Schoolroom Glacier, a total climb of 4,200 feet.

SURPRISE AND AMPHITHEATER LAKES

Distance: 10.1 miles round-trip
Duration: 6 hours
Elevation change: 2,966 feet
Effort: strenuous
Trailhead: Lupine Meadows Trailhead off Teton Park Road south of Jenny Lake (see map p. 228)

At 9,714 feet, Surprise and Amphitheater Lakes cluster 0.2 mile apart in a high, narrow subalpine basin on an eastern ridge extending from the Grand Teton. Since the trail provides access for many technical climbing routes, you may see people loaded with ropes, helmets, and gear. Start early, as the sun-soaked climb can be hot midday.

Begin by hiking 1.7 miles on a flat trail

that ascends a moraine ridge to the junction with the **Taggart Lake Trail.** At the **junction,** turn right and follow switchbacks that climb steeply on the open, east-facing slope. Views of Jackson Hole get bigger the higher you go; **Bradley Lake** is below to the south. After the fourth switchback, a climber trail cuts left into Garnet Canyon—ignore that trail and stay on the switchbacks. After four more switchbacks, the trail heads more directly toward the Middle Teton. At **Surprise Lake,** descend to the shore and enjoy the lake, or climb the rough trail up the south pinnacle for bigger views. The main trail passes above the north side of Surprise Lake to climb into the small hanging valley housing **Amphitheater Lake,** tucked at the base of Disappointment Peak. After the lake, a rough trail climbs north 0.2 mile to grab a partial view of Teton Glacier and the Grand Teton. Retrace your route to return to the trailhead.

Taggart and Bradley Lakes

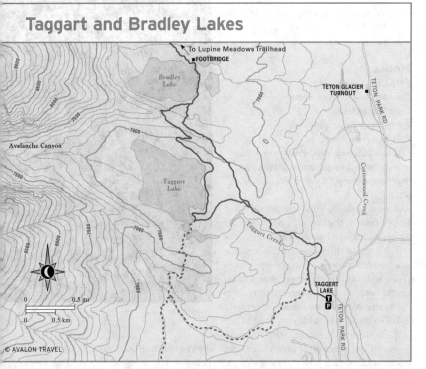

TAGGART AND BRADLEY LAKES

Distance: 3-5.9 miles round-trip
Duration: 2-4 hours
Elevation change: 400-900 feet
Effort: easy to moderate
Trailhead: Taggart Lake Trailhead off Teton Park Road between Jenny Lake and Moose (see map p. 229)

Two lower-elevation lakes cower around 7,000 feet at the base of Avalanche and Garnet Canyons. Those who want a shorter hike can go three miles to Taggart Lake and back. A loop adds on Bradley Lake for 5.9 miles. Get an early start in order to claim a parking spot at this popular trailhead. Hikers can also reach Bradley and Taggart Lakes from the Lupine Meadows Trailhead for a 6-8.8-mile trip. On hot days, both lakes make good swimming holes.

From the trailhead, walk through open meadows for less than 0.2 mile to a **junction.** The left trail circles on a longer route to Taggart Lake, while the right trail goes more directly to the lake. After turning right at the junction, the trail wanders past a tumbling stream, through meadows and conifers, and over glacial moraines for 1.1 miles to the **next junction.** If you are planning to hike both lakes, you will return to this junction via the right trail. To reach **Taggart,** turn left to hike 0.5 mile to the lake. At Taggart, explore the small peninsula to the north for a place to enjoy the water and views.

To continue the loop to **Bradley Lake,** walk north around the shore of Taggart Lake. On the lake's north side, the trail climbs two switchbacks to crest a glacial moraine before descending toward Bradley Lake. At the **junction,** turn left to visit Bradley Lake. A **0.3-mile walk** circles to the north side of the lake to a footbridge, beaches (in later summer), fishing, and wading. After the lake, retrace your steps back to the last junction. To continue the loop, take the fork heading left to climb over the moraine again and reach the Taggart Lake junction in 0.9 mile. From there, head back to the trailhead.

Moose
PHELPS LAKE
Distance: 1.8-7.9 miles round-trip
Duration: 2-5 hours
Elevation change: 350-975 feet
Effort: easy to moderate
Trailhead: Laurance S. Rockefeller Preserve Center or Death Canyon Trailhead, located on Moose-Wilson Road north of Granite Canyon Entrance (see map p. 231).

A maze of trails surrounds the low-elevation Phelps Lake in the Laurance S. Rockefeller Preserve, a special area where hiking the trails is more about the experience than reaching destinations. Visiting the preserve's center adds to the hiking experience. The access to both trailheads requires entry from the Moose-Wilson Road (no RVs or trailers). Trails circle the lake, which sits at 6,645 feet at the bottom of Open and Death Canyons. From various viewpoints around the lake, hikers are rewarded with stunning views of the Teton Mountains. The lake provides a year-round destination, although you'll need skis or snowshoes in winter.

Phelps Lake

Most hikers opt to park at the **Laurance S. Rockefeller Preserve Center.** Arrive before 10am to claim a parking spot in the small 50-car lot that is designed to limit crowds and create a climate of solitude. If it's full, you'll need to hike via the Death Canyon Trailhead. From the center, you can design your own route through the maze of trails. Junctions are well signed to help in selecting routes. The shortest and easiest route to Phelps Lake is the **Lake Creek-Woodland Trail Loop** (3.1 miles). The loop tours forests and meadows on both sides of a creek, offering opportunities to watch moose. At the lake, enjoy contemplation from several different constructed rock-slab overlooks. The **Aspen Ridge-Boulder Ridge Loop** (5.8 miles) climbs through large talus fields and aspens that shimmer gold in fall to reach Phelps Lake. The longest hike, the **Phelps Lake Loop** (6.6 miles) climbs via Lake Creek to reach the lake and then loops around the lake for a changing perspective on the Teton Mountains.

From **Death Canyon Trailhead,** hike south on the steep trail that climbs about 400 feet in 0.9 mile to Phelps Lake Overlook. You can just appreciate the view from here, or drop down the switchbacks for the lake loop, but you'll need to climb 575 feet in elevation back up to the overlook to return to the trailhead. To descend to the lake, continue west from the overlook to a trail junction. Take the left fork to descend to the lake for the 4.5-mile loop around it. The overlook and lake loop tally 7.9 miles with 975 feet total elevation gain.

DEATH CANYON, STATIC PEAK DIVIDE, AND FOX CREEK PASS
Distance: 16.3-18.4 miles round-trip
Duration: 9-12 hours
Elevation change: 2,800-5,250 feet
Effort: very strenuous
Trailhead: Death Canyon Trailhead off

Phelps Lake and Death Canyon

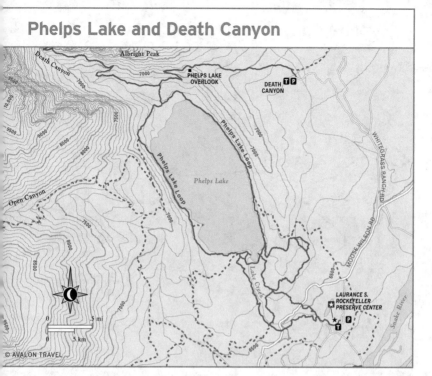

© AVALON TRAVEL

Moose-Wilson Road north of Granite Canyon Entrance (see map p. 231).

With the exception of hiking to Phelps Lake Overlook and Phelps Lake, Death Canyon is a place to go to get away from hordes of people. However, the destinations require long hikes, some with excessive elevation gain. Rewards are huge with views of glaciated canyons, alpine wonderlands, and peaks of the Tetons. The two main destinations sit on the Teton Crest: Static Peak Divide with more than 5,000 feet of elevation gain, and Fox Creek Pass with nine miles of hiking. On the knee-pounding returns, distance adds up. Many people opt for backpacking for these hikes, although strong in-shape hikers can do them in a day. You may need ice axes for steep snowfield that linger well into August in the upper elevations.

The climb begins by heading up to **Phelps Lake Overlook** and dropping three switchbacks to reach a **junction.** From here, head west along the base of **Albright Peak.** The trail ascends through open avalanche swaths and talus fields alternating with coniferous forests to reach a trail junction at 7.9 miles at a **patrol cabin.** For Static Peak, take the north fork up the steep trail that climbs to the rocky scree and cliff ridge of **Static Peak** to reach the divide and look down into Alaska Basin. For **Fox Creek Pass,** take the south fork to follow the less steep trail through meadows and sparse trees along Death Canyon Creek to reach the **Teton Crest** and the pass, where you'll see the Death Canyon Shelf.

GRANITE CANYON AND MARION LAKE

Distance: 11.8-18.5 miles round-trip
Duration: 7-10 hours
Elevation change: 3,000-4,100 feet
Effort: strenuous
Trailhead: Granite Canyon Trailhead on Moose-Wilson Road; or at Jackson Hole Mountain Resort (see map p. 232).

Granite Canyon and Marion Lake

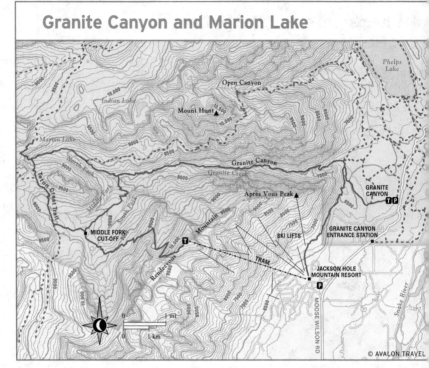

© AVALON TRAVEL

You can hike 18.5 miles round-trip up Granite Canyon with 3,700 feet of elevation gain to reach Marion Lake on the Teton Crest, or do as locals do and hike this canyon by riding the tram outside the park at Jackson Hole Mountain Resort to chop off miles. After riding the tram to the 10,450-foot summit of Rendezvous Mountain, you can hike out to Marion Lake and back, reducing the round-trip distance to 11.8 miles. You can also use the tram for hiking about 12 miles one-way, either up or down 4,100 feet, through Granite Canyon. A fee is charged to ride the tram. Upper elevations can hold snow late into July; an ice ax may be necessary.

From the summit of **Rendezvous Mountain,** start the descent by hiking left along the ridge followed by a service road to reach the boundary of Grand Teton National Park. Switchback down Rendezvous Mountain to reach the first junction at 3.9 miles. To go to **Marion Lake,** turn left on

the **Middle Fork Cutoff** to connect with the **Teton Crest Trail.** The route has steep ups and downs through alpine wildflower meadows to reach Marion Lake sitting at 9,200 feet, snuggled up against a limestone wall. To descend into **Granite Canyon** instead, go right to a second junction at 5.6 miles. Turn right again to plunge into the lower-elevation forest, where you'll hit a four-way junction at 10.3 miles. Turn sharp right for 2.4 miles to return to Jackson Hole Mountain Resort or head 1.6 miles down Granite Creek to the Granite Canyon Trailhead if you set up a car shuttle.

BACKPACKING

Backcountry camping **permits** (www.recreation.gov, apply early Jan.-mid-May, $35/trip) are required and are available in advance. Walk-in permits ($25/trip) are available first-come, first-served in person 24 hours before departure. Competition for walk-in permits is high in July and August; a waiting line usually forms at the Jenny Lake Ranger Station one hour before opening at 8am. Permits are also available at the Craig Thomas Discovery & Visitor Center in Moose. Bear-proof canisters are required for food storage; the permit office has loaners.

Paintbrush Canyon-Cascade Canyon
19 MILES
The entire Paintbrush-Cascade Loop (19.2 miles) can be done as a 2-3-day backpacking trip, with outstanding scenery, a high pass, and Lake Solitude. Camping is at Upper Paintbrush and North Fork Cascade. From the String Lake Trailhead, no shuttle is needed as you end at the same spot.

Teton Crest Trail
39 MILES
The king of backpacking trips is the Teton Crest Trail (39 miles) from Cascade Canyon to Granite Canyon, crossing Hurricane, Mt. Meek, and Fox Creek Passes at 9,600-10,400 feet. The route begins at String Lake Trailhead and finishes at Granite Canyon Trailhead. Camping zones are at South Fork Cascade, Death Canyon Shelf, and Upper Granite. An additional night in Alaska Basin in Caribou-Targhee National Forest in between Mt. Meek Pass and Hurricane Pass is usually necessary. With steep climbs and drops over passes, backpacking on the crest may require fewer miles per day than you usually travel; you'll need 4-5 days for the trip.

CLIMBING
Technical climbing skills are required to reach the summits of the Tetons. If you do not possess the skills, do not attempt to summit peaks; hire a guide service instead. Climbing permits are not required, but a backcountry camping permit is required if you plan to camp overnight in the backcountry. Most of the prominent peaks seen from Jackson Hole can be climbed in one day, albeit an extremely long day.

Weather is a consideration. Spring is rainy, accompanied by thawing ice and snow that produce copious rockfall and wet slab avalanches. Mid-July-August offers the best weather, but you must be ready to cope with sporadic afternoon rains and potential lightning. Snow usually starts to appear at high elevations by late August and continues to accumulate throughout fall. Winter brings heavy snow, frigid temperatures, high winds, and avalanches.

Due to rockfall year-round, wear a helmet. Until late July, ice axes (and the skill to use them correctly) may be necessary in high elevations on steep snowfields to access rock routes. Be prepared with the appropriate gear, as even summer can snap into extremes with cold, snow, wind, and rain.

Self-Guided Climbing
Jenny Lake Ranger Station (307/739-3343, 8am-5pm June-mid-Sept.) is the only place to go for current climbing conditions and information. The rangers are actual climbers who know the area, risks, difficulties, routes, and what type of experience you need for different climbs. To help you plan climbs, the ranger station has guidebooks, maps, and photographs of peaks with routes. The climbing rangers also update conditions and mountaineering scene information online (www.tetonclimbing.blogspot.com). The ranger station has a voluntary climbing register, too. Check current conditions for fall, winter, or spring climbs (307/739-3309). Above all, be prepared to self-rescue.

Mountaineering routes in the Tetons can be snow, ice, or rock, or a mix of all three. Two guidebooks are worth consulting: *Teton Classics: 50 Selected Climbs in Grand Teton National Park* by Richard Rossiter, and *A Climber's Guide to the Teton Range* by Leigh N. Ortenburger and Reynold G. Jackson. Both are available through Grand Teton Association (307/739-3606, www.grandtetonpark.org) online or at association bookstores in the park, including at Jenny Lake.

Guides and Schools

Two companies guide climbs and ski mountaineering trips year-round in Grand Teton National Park; the main climbing camps, school, and guided climbs happen in summer. Each leads climbs up the Grand Teton, as well as most of the other technical peaks. In most cases, the companies will supply all the technical climbing gear.

Launched in 1931 by Glen Exum (who solo-pioneered the most famous and common route up Grand Teton) and Paul Petzoldt (who started NOLS), **Exum Mountain Guides** (307/733-2297, http://exumguides.com) leads climbs for individuals, groups, families, and kids. Their office at South Jenny Lake provides climbing instruction, camps, and kids' camps. Private guides can go one-on-one with you to the summit of Grand Teton, or with a group (after successfully passing prerequisites). Programs are available for everyone from first-timers to experts.

Based in Jackson, **Jackson Hole Mountain Guides** (307/733-4979, www.jhmg.com) leads multiday trips up Grand Teton, even for beginners. Single-day climbs summit other peaks such as Middle Teton, South Teton, and Teewinot.

BIKING

While cyclists can ride all the park roads, prepare to ride on shoulders with giant RVs whizzing by at 55 mph. (On the road, ride single file to allow room for large RVs to pass.) Summer offers the best cycling weather, but prepare for potential dousing from afternoon thundershowers and strong winds. Plan rides early in the morning or late afternoon to avoid peak midday traffic. For safety and visibility, wear a helmet and bright colors (most drivers are gawking at the peaks or wildlife rather than the road).

The most popular road ride is the **Inside-Outside Loop** (43 miles) starting from Moose, which connects Teton Park Road, Jackson Lake Junction, Moran Junction, and U.S. Highway 26/89/191; most of the route has paved shoulders. **Jenny Lake Scenic Drive**

The Multi-Use Pathway parallels Teton Park Road.

(three miles) offers a family-friendly ride with a marked bike lane. Even though the road is one-way for vehicles, bicyclists can ride both directions.

Mountain bikers are relegated to dirt roads or the paved Multi-Use Pathway; no bikes are permitted on the trails. Summer is best for mountain biking, but dirt roads churn up mounds of dust from passing vehicles, and afternoon rains can turn them muddy.

Antelope Flats Road works for mountain biking, but prepare for winds due to the wide-open plain. Extensions include touring the historic Mormon Row or Shadow Mountain in Bridger-Teton National Forest, which has single-track trails. Consult with Dornan's **Adventure Sports** (12170 Dornan Rd., Moose, 307/733-3307, http://dornans.com, 8am-6pm daily early May-late Sept.) for route conditions and details.

One of the early season prized rides is the **Moose-Wilson Road** (14.6 miles round-trip). Park at the Granite Canyon Trailhead, north of the Granite Canyon Entrance Station, or at the Craig Thomas Discovery and Visitor Center in Moose. Then ride out and back between the two locations. In some springs, the road opens to cycling before it opens for vehicles.

Multi-Use Pathway

The Multi-Use Pathway (29 miles, open dawn-dusk May-Oct.) is a paved bicycling and walking pathway that parallels roads between Jenny Lake, Moose, and Jackson. In 2015, a paved spur was added to connect Moose with Antelope Flats Road. The mostly level pathway is perfect for families with kids and cyclists who don't want to bike roads with RV traffic. Use caution, as wildlife (including bison) can be on the trail. The most scenic section is the 7.75-mile stretch between Jenny Lake Visitor Center and Craig Thomas Discovery and Visitor Center in Moose. The southern section from Jackson to Gros Ventre Junction is closed November-April for wildlife.

River Road

The unpaved River Road (9.2 miles), also known as the RKO Road, parallels the west bank of the Snake River. Near South Jenny Lake, the Bar B C Road connects to River Road, and on the south end the Cottonwood Creek Road makes the connection. The ride on a shelf above the river offers scenery: the river, Teton Mountains, and often wildlife. Prepare for coping with plenty of rocks in the dirt. Using the Multi-Use Pathway between South Jenny Lake and Cottonwood Creek Picnic Area, you can turn the ride into a loop.

Guides and Rentals

From family-friendly to challenging tours, Teton Mountain Bike Tours (307/733-0712 or 800/733-0788, www.tetonmtnbike.com, year-round) guides half-day, full-day, and multiday bike tours—even winter tours on fat tires. Half-day family rides through Antelope Flats ($65/person) and full-day Teton Tours ($100/person) cruise paved and dirt roads. Dornan's Adventure Sports (12170 Dornan Rd., Moose, 307/733-3307, http://dornans.

com, 8am-6pm daily early May-late Sept., $29-65 adults, $22-29 kids) rents road bikes and mountain bikes by the hour, half day, full day, multiday, and weekly; rates include helmets. You can also rent Trailalongs and Burleys for towing kids, or bike racks for hauling gear to ride elsewhere. A paved pathway connects with the Multi-Use Pathway.

WATER SPORTS

Two permits (Wyoming Game and Fish, 307/777-4638, https://wgfd.wyo.gov, Wyoming residents: $10 motorized, $5 nonmotorized; nonresidents: $30 motorized, $15 nonmotorized) are required for boating. Boaters must pick up a State of Wyoming Aquatic Invasive Species (AIS) sticker and pass a boat inspection prior to launching. Inflatable watercraft smaller than 10 feet and paddleboards are exempt. For Grand Teton National Park boat permits (motorized $40, nonmotorized $10), go to Jenny Lake Ranger Station or any visitors center.

Boating

Boating on Jenny Lake is a quiet experience, as only motorboats with 10 horsepower or less are permitted, plus any hand-propelled boats. Besides Jackson Lake, it's the only lake that permits motorized watercraft. However, sailboats, windsurfers, waterskiing, and Jet Skis are not allowed on Jenny Lake. The boat launch is located on Lupine Meadows Road. After crossing the bridge over Cottonwood Creek, turn right to reach the dirt ramp and small loop for trailer parking.

Canoeing and Kayaking

Paddlers have access to idyllic lakes tucked up against the base of the Teton Mountains. While Jenny Lake permits small-horsepower motorboats, all other lakes are limited to hand-propelled watercraft, making them perfect for paddlers of the silent sports. From melt-out in late May-October, visitors can paddle these lakes. North of Jenny Lake, String Lake connects via a portage to Leigh Lake. Phelps, Taggart, Bradley, and **Bearpaw Lakes** are also open to paddlers, but require portaging boats a distance to reach the water. Mornings offer a calmer time to paddle, with the best days yielding smooth, glassy reflections. Afternoons often bring winds and sometimes thundershowers.

To reach the dirt Jenny Lake boat launch, turn right from Teton Park Road onto Lupine Meadows Road and immediately right again after the bridge over Cottonwood Creek. String Lake has a canoe and kayak launch site, located in the second parking lot on the left on the String Lake Picnic Area road north of Jenny Lake Road. All other lakes require carrying boats from trailhead parking lots.

Paddlers with skills on moving water can tackle 10 miles of the **Snake River** from the put-in at Deadmans Bar to Moose, a section with outstanding scenery and wildlife. Strong currents, braided channels, and logjams require advanced river savvy.

LEIGH LAKE

North of Jenny Lake, String Lake connects via a 600-foot portage through a rocky, shallow stream to **Leigh Lake,** where paddlers can overnight in solitude at eight prime **campsites.** Those on the eastern shore can capture dramatic mountain reflections on the water; sites on the western shore do not have trail access, thus guaranteeing more privacy. A **backcountry camping permit** is required (www.recreation.gov, early Jan.-mid-May, $35/trip); walk-in permits from the Jenny Lake Ranger Station or the Craig Thomas Discovery & Visitor Center are released 24 hours prior to departure ($25/trip).

RENTALS

Jenny Lake Boating (Jenny Lake boathouse, 307/734-9227, www.jennylakeboating.com, 7am-7pm daily early-June-late Sept., shorter hours in shoulder seasons) rents two-person kayaks and canoes that can carry three people ($20/hour, $75/day, children under 5 not permitted). Reservations are not accepted. Rates include life jackets and paddles.

Dornan's **Adventure Sports** (12170 Dornan Rd., Moose, 307/733-3307, http://dornans.com, 8am-6pm daily early May-late Sept.) rents canoes, one- and two-person kayaks, and paddleboards ($22-25/hour, $50/day). Rates include life jackets, paddles, and pads and straps for carrying boats on your vehicle. The shop also rents boat trailers.

Rafting

Boaters can float the **Wild and Scenic Snake**

Jenny Lake Boating

River in rafts, dories, canoes, or river kayaks. Starting below Jackson Lake Dam, the river runs 25 miles to Moose Landing and yields scenery, including grand views of the Teton Mountains. Wildlife is also attracted to the water; watch for great blue herons, bald eagles, and osprey fishing the river (to protect the birds, avoid stopping in the eagle nest closure area). On shore, you can also spot bison, deer, elk, and bears.

While rafts can float spring, summer, and fall, the shoulder seasons are cold, rainy, and snowy. Summer offers the best time for floating, with the highest water in June, when the water is swift and cold. From Jackson Lake Dam to Menor's Ferry, the river closes annually (Dec. 15-Apr. 1) to floating. Before launching, check water levels at river landings, permit offices, and through USGS monitors (800/658-5771, http://waterdata.usgs.gov). The Grand Teton National Park floating brochure is available in visitors centers and online (www.nps.gov/grte).

River access is at Pacific Creek, Deadmans Bar, Schwarachers Landing, and Moose Landing. Most floats put in at Pacific Creek Landing or Deadmans Bar and take out at Moose Landing (10 miles, two hours). The Class II water requires some river savvy to deal with strong currents, a few waves, and logjams. The river braids into multiple channels with islands; the Maze below Schwarachers Landing breaks into many small streams. Braided channels change during summer and require knowledge of safer routes; strong upriver winds seem to crop up every afternoon. You can also continue rafting beyond the park boundary to the Wilson Bridge.

GUIDES

Most companies guide multiple float trips (daily mid-May-Sept., some run longer seasons, $70-75 adults, $50-65 kids) on the Snake River. The guide does all the rowing and maneuvering; you get to sit back to absorb the views of the peaks and look for wildlife. From Moose, transportation is via bus or van to Deadmans Bar for launching; trips end back in Moose. With shuttles, the total trip takes about three hours with two hours on a raft that holds 10-12 people. Some companies offer lunch or dinner floats; most have a minimum age limit. Rates include life jackets and transportation to and from the river. Reservations are required; plan to tip your guide 15 percent.

Barker-Ewing Scenic Float Trips (307/733-1800 or 800/365-1800, www.

Guided float trips go down the Snake River through Jackson Hole.

barkerewing.com) has a reservations desk in the grocery at Dornan's in Moose. **Triangle X-National Park Float Trips** (307/733-5500, www.trianglex.com) meets guests in Moose or at their ranch and offers specialty sunset and sunrise trips. Based in Jackson, **Solitude Float Trips** (307/733-2871 or 888/704-2800, www.grand-teton-scenic-floats.com) meets guests in Moose and also offers sunrise trips. Park lodges can book rafting trips for guests.

Fishing

Grand Teton National Park is one of those places that combines stunning scenery with exceptional fishing. While spin-casting works, fly-fishing is the iconic method. Waters swim with native cutthroat and introduced brown, rainbow, and lake trout. Only artificial flies and lures are allowed for fishing in the southern section of Grand Teton. Fishing regulations for closures, creel limits, and lure and bait requirements are available online (www.nps.gov/grte).

The **Snake River** flows southward through the park, providing plenty of locations for fishing along its 25 miles from Jackson Lake Dam to Moose Landing. While you can fish from shore or wade into the river to fish, the best way to fish is from a drift boat or raft. The river is the place to fish for the unique indigenous Snake River fine-spotted cutthroat trout; however, conscientious anglers catch-and-release only. Most anglers use dry-flies to attract the wild trout that can get up to 18 inches.

On the river, runoff usually hits mid-May-June. In deep snowpack years, with long cool springs, runoff can last through July and even nip into August. After runoff, when the river clears, the fishing gets good. Many anglers consider **September** to be the best month for fishing. Trout fishing season on the Snake runs **April-October** (catch-and-release only Nov.-Mar.). Tributaries to the Snake River also offer fishing. **Cottonwood Creek** and **Ditch Creek** open August-October for fishing. Most other streams plunging through

the canyons of the Teton Mountains are open April-October.

In the south end of Grand Teton, seven moraine lakes tuck up against the base of the Teton Mountains and offer fishing. Fishing pressure is pretty hefty on **Jenny** and **String Lakes,** due to their drive-up access and number of visitors. **Leigh, Bradley, Taggart,** and **Phelps Lakes** offer fishing at the end of short hikes, although you may need to work around shoreline brush to good sites. Take the kids to **Jenny Lake** to learn to fish. Hiking up to alpine lakes in the Teton Mountains can also yield rewarding fishing. However, you'll most likely reach the lakes midday; morning and evening fishing are usually better, and some lakes are barren.

Fishing in Grand Teton National Park requires a **Wyoming state fishing license** (residents: $3 youth annual, $6 adults daily, $24 adults annual; nonresident: $15 youth annual, $14 adults daily, $92 adults annual), available for sale at Dornan's in Moose. For float tubes, pick up a Grand Teton National Park **boating permit** ($10) at visitors centers.

GUIDES

Only licensed guides are allowed to lead fishing trips in Grand Teton. Since the better fishing is on the Snake River, that's where most of the guided trips go. Many of the guide companies are based in Jackson but meet clients at Moose or elsewhere in the park. One or two anglers and a guide can go in a drift boat, dory, or raft. Companies provide transportation to and from the river; full-day trips usually include lunch. Plan to tip your guide 15 percent (or 20 percent if you catch lots of fish). The **Snake River** works for beginners or experts; guides will coach beginners in mastering where to cast and technique. Boats, life jackets, waders, reels, and rods are provided, but you will need to purchase your fishing license and sometimes flies and leader. Reservations are required.

Snake River Angler (10 Moose St., Moose, 307/733-3699, www.snakeriverangler.com, $475-575) guides half- and full-day

Ski to Jenny Lake in winter.

backcountry skiing, cross-country skiing, and snowshoeing. Snowmobiling on snow-buried roads is not permitted, and as of 2015 snowbikes are not allowed. The park closes several zones in winter to protect wildlife, including the Snake River bottom. Check on **park closures** online (www.nps.gov/grte) or in the winter edition of the park's official newspaper. A good resource for snow conditions all over the park is compiled and updated periodically by the **Jenny Lake climbing rangers** (http://tetonclimbing.blogspot.com).

Venturing into Grand Teton National Park in winter demands preparedness and attention to weather and snowpack. While most park roads convert to touring trails and are not in avalanche zones, they can see whiteouts, high winds, and frigid temperatures. Prepare accordingly to prevent exposure and hypothermia. Traveling into mountain canyons or skinning up peaks to ski down will increase exposure to avalanches. Take the appropriate survival and avalanche gear along and be prepared to self-rescue. Check for avalanche conditions updated daily through the **Jackson Hole Avalanche Center** (307/733-2664, www.jhavalanche.org).

fishing trips on the Snake River. **National Park Float Trips** (307/733-5500, http://nationalparkfloattrips.com, $425-550) also guides half- and full-day trips.

Swimming

Swimming is allowed in all park waters; however, most are chilly. **String Lake** is shallow, so waters tend to heat up a little warmer there than elsewhere, making it more pleasant. Swimming access is from the picnic area. Due to strong currents and logjams, the park service discourages swimming in the Snake River. **Kelly Warm Springs** (Gros Ventre Rd.) is a soaking spot surrounded by marsh; the tepid pool sometimes fills with water plants and algae. The draw is the view of the Tetons while soaking. A restroom and parking area are on the north side of the road with a soaking zone across the road.

WINTER SPORTS

In southern Grand Teton National Park, winter sports consist of the silent sports:

Cross-Country Skiing and Snowshoeing

November-April some roads in the national park close to vehicles, which means they turn into cross-country ski and snowshoe routes. From the Taggart Lake Trailhead to Signal Mountain Lodge, **Teton Park Road** (14 miles) becomes a winter ski and snowshoe trail; it's the way to ski to frozen Jenny Lake. The road is groomed twice a week mid-December-mid-March (call 307/739-3682 for current grooming conditions). Hit the trail on Friday and Monday for fresh-buffed tracks. Follow protocol on the groomed trail: Snowshoers should walk on the smooth grooming, not the tracks cut for skiing.

In winter, closed **Moose-Wilson Road** offers a road tour through a forest, but the road is not groomed. Be ready to break your own trail or follow previous tracks from skiers and snowshoers. From the Granite Canyon Trailhead, you can tour the road north to the Laurance S. Rockefeller Preserve Center (closed in winter) and circle Phelps Lake on trails. Park at the Death Canyon junction to tour south on the road. **Antelope Flats Road** also offers winter touring, although its wide-open plain can kick with wind. **Taggart and Bradley Lakes** make good trail destinations for those who want to get off the roads. Because it is one of the few trailheads that drivers can access in winter, the lakes are a popular destination.

Backcountry skiers and snowboarders can access Grand Teton National Park from the valley floor along Teton Park Road and the Moose-Wilson Road or from neighboring Jackson Hole Mountain Resort.

GUIDES AND RENTALS

Several companies are licensed to guide winter tours in the national park and even instruct avalanche courses. Most trips are scheduled on demand (consider pairing up with other visitors to reduce rates). **Hole Hiking Experience** (866/733-4453, www.holehike. com) offers 2-6-hour cross-country ski and snowshoe trips, some in tandem with wildlife-watching, sleigh rides, or dogsledding. **Teton Backcountry Guides** (307/353-2900, http:// tetonbackcountryguides.com) leads full-day backcountry skiing, cross-country skiing, or snowshoe tours. **Exum Mountain Guides** (307/733-2297, www.exumguides.com) leads one-day backcountry ski trips, ski mountaineering excursions, and ski camps. **Jackson Hole Mountain Guides** (307/733-4979, www.jhmg.com) also leads one-day backcountry ski trips, ski mountaineering expeditions, and ice climbing in Death Canyon.

Dornan's Trading Post (12170 Dornan Rd., Moose, 307/733-3307 or 307/733-2415, ext. 302, http://dornans.com, 9am-5pm daily Dec.-Mar., $18/day) rents cross-country skis and snowshoes by the day or week. You can also rent backcountry skis, cross-country skis, and snowshoes for adults and kids in Jackson and Teton Village.

Entertainment and Shopping

RANGER PROGRAMS

Rangers lead programs at visitors centers and other locations; check current schedules in the park newspaper or online (www.nps. gov/grte). Shorter programs last 20 minutes; longer ones run 30-45 minutes. All visitors centers have bear safety programs. **Craig Thomas Discovery & Visitor Center** hosts map chats and nature presentations. **Jenny Lake Visitor Center** presents lakeshore conversations. **Laurance S. Rockefeller Preserve Center** hosts critter chats. **Gros Ventre Campground Amphitheater** holds a Twilight Talk for families with kids a few evenings in summer.

In winter, rangers guide interpretive **snowshoe walks** (307/739-3399, www.nps. gov/grte, late Dec.-mid-Mar., free). The two-hour tours meet at the Taggart Lake Trailhead;

look for tracks, play with snow science, and examine the ecology of winter. Dress in layers, bring water and a pack, and wear snow boots or sturdy hiking boots. Reservations are required starting in early December. Snowshoes are available for rent ($5 adults, $2 kids).

SHOPPING

A handful of gift shops dot the southern portion of the national park at Jenny Lake, Dornan's at Moose, and the Menor's Ferry General Store. **Grand Teton Association** (307/739-3606, www.grandtetonpark.org) bookstores are located in visitors centers and the Menor's Ferry General Store. Located at Dornan's, **Moosely Mountaineering** (12170 Dornan Rd., 307/739-1801, 9am-8pm daily mid-May-Sept.) sells camping, hiking, and mountaineering gear from the Jackson staple Skinny Skis.

Accommodations

INSIDE THE PARK

Lodging inside the south end of Grand Teton National Park is limited to a few cabin complexes, ranches, and campgrounds. They fill up fast, especially in midsummer. **Advance reservations are a must;** book a year ahead for mid-June-mid-September stays. Just south of the park boundaries, a full slate of lodging options are available in Jackson and Teton Village. Visitors seeking more amenities opt for Jackson or Teton Village lodging while exploring the southern section of the Tetons.

In general, inside park lodging is rustic with minimal amenities. Televisions, air-conditioning, mini-fridges, microwaves, and wireless Internet are not available, unless specified.

Jenny Lake

Secluded in the woods at North Jenny Lake, ★ **Jenny Lake Lodge** (400 Jenny Lake Loop, 307/733-4647 and 800/628-9988, www.gtlc.com, June-early Oct., $690-960 d, $165 each extra person) offers a slice of old-style rustic luxury and the highest priced lodging inside Grand Teton National Park. Breakfast, lunch, and activities are included in the price, but you can stay for less without the meals and activities when cabins are available. The 37 log cabins, built in 1920, have been revamped to an upscale historical feel, but still have old-fashioned rockers on porches for soaking up views. Twice-a-day housekeeping includes water and ice delivery. Visitors often mistakenly assume the lodge sits right on the lake; it does not. But from many of the cabin decks or windows, the tops of the Tetons poke up above the tall pines. The complex includes a dining room that specializes in gourmet and multi-course meals. Hiking trails depart from the lodge, and South Jenny Lake offers scenic cruises, kayak and canoe rentals, a visitors center, stores, the Multi-Use Pathway for bicycling, and horseback riding. The lodge has cruiser-style bicycles and horseback riding for guests.

Lodging is in **three types of log cabins:** freestanding cabins, duplex cabins that share a common porch, and cabin suites. All the cabins have western furnishings, private

Jenny Lake Lodge

bathrooms, wireless Internet, handmade quilts, and down comforters. Rooms are single-story, motel-style with mini-fridges (no kitchens). Freestanding cabins have a king or two queens. Duplex cabins have a queen and twin bed. Suites have one bedroom with a king or two queens and a sitting room with a sofa bed and wood-burning stove. One suite has a jetted tub.

Three miles south of Jenny Lake on Teton Park Road, the American Alpine Club has the concessionaire contract to operate the **American Alpine Club Climber's Ranch** (307/733-7271, http://americanalpineclub.org, 8am-8pm daily early June-mid-Sept., $16 ACC members, $25 nonmembers), which was originally built in 1924 as the Double Diamond Dude Ranch and has its dining hall listed on the National Register of Historic Places. You don't have to be a climber to stay here, but you must supply your own sleeping bag, pad, cook gear, food, towels, and other personal gear. Facilities include small co-ed log cabins that sleep 4-6 people each on wooden bunks dorm-style, separate bathroom and shower houses for women and men, an outdoor cook shelter with dishwashing sinks and picnic tables, and a lounge with a hard-wired computer for Internet. Ice is for sale, and coolers are provided for food storage. You may be sharing a cabin with a climber rustling around in the middle of the night to pound down trail miles before sunrise, or with a family that has kids.

Moose

Located at Moose, the multi-generational family-owned and operated **Dornan's Spur Ranch Cabins** (307/733-2522, www.dornans.com, May-Oct. and Dec.-Mar., $200-300 summer, $150-180 off-season) can sleep 4-6 people. The 12 one- and two-bedroom cabins built in 1992, some as duplexes, have full kitchens, and most have covered decks with barbecue grills and views of the Tetons, which light up at sunrise. Beds come with down comforters, and furniture is hand-crafted. They are part of a 10-acre complex that includes a grocery, deli with ice cream

and espresso, gift shop, wine shop, gas station, two restaurants, and a bar. Their Adventure Sports center rents bikes, canoes, kayaks, paddleboards, cross-country skis, and snowshoes in the appropriate seasons, and fly-fishing and rafting trips are available on-site. A paved path connects to the Multi-Use Pathway to ride bikes to the Craig Thomas Discovery & Visitor Center or Moose Landing river access across the river.

Moose to Moran

Several guest ranches line the national park. Most inholdings are private properties owned prior to the creation of the national park. Find these on U.S. Highway 26/89/191 between Moose and Moran Junction. From all of these ranches, the views of the Teton Mountains provide an exquisite backdrop for horseback riding, which is one of the main reasons to stay at a ranch. Rates are all-inclusive with lodging, meals, and activities, but the duration for the packages vary.

The ★ **Triangle X Ranch** (2 Triangle X Ranch Rd., 307/733-2183, http://trianglex.com, mid-May-mid-Oct. and late Dec.-mid-Mar.) is a dude ranch operated for four generations by the Turner family. Lodging is in one-, two-, or three-bedroom log cabins with private bathrooms. Early June-late August is peak season for the ranch, when seven-night stays, Sunday to Sunday, are the program ($1,820-2,520/person/week). Outside of peak season, four-night stays are available (mid-May-early June and Sept.-Oct., $260-283/person/day). Winter season ($140-150/person/night) has cross-country skiing, snowshoeing, snowmobiling, and wildlife-watching.

North of the Cunningham Cabin, ★ **Moose Head Ranch** (21255 N. Hwy. 89, 307/733-3141, www.mooseheadranch.com, early June-mid-Aug., $410/person/night, five-night minimum) is a 1925 family-run homestead and dude ranch. Log cabins for guests surround the main lodge, where gourmet breakfasts and lunches are served buffet-style and dinner dresses up plated fish and game entrées. Sunday nights have cookouts. The ranch has fishing and swimming ponds.

Five cabins in a historic and ultra-scenic location are at the ★ **Moulton Ranch Cabins** (202 Mormon Row Rd., Kelly, 307/733-3749, www.moultonranchcabins. com, late May-Sept., $110-290). Located amid the historic buildings on Mormon Row with views of the Tetons, the rustic cabins can sleep two, four, or six people; most have kitchenettes. Three of the cabins have en suite bathrooms, while two have private bathrooms in separate buildings. The cabins have combos of queen, double, sofa, and twin beds. The owners request a three-night minimum stay. Minus dining and horseback riding, these ranch cabins are for overnighting only.

OUTSIDE THE PARK

Opposite the Snake River Overlook, ★ **Lost Creek Ranch and Spa** (1 Old Ranch Rd., Moose, 307/733-3435, http://lostcreek.com, late May-mid-Sept., $5,250-13,500/week) pairs up dude ranch activities with a spa. Lodging is in two-bedroom cabins with living rooms, one-bedroom duplex cabins, and king suites, and the ranch has tennis courts, a hot tub, a heated swimming pool, kids' programs, yoga classes, and meals served family-style in the dining room. Cabins sleep up to eight people. Activities such as the spa, fly-fishing, and golf are available for an additional fee.

Camping

INSIDE THE PARK

Two campgrounds at the south end of the national park offer very diverse experiences. Facilities include picnic tables, fire rings with grills, bear boxes, drinking water, garbage service, firewood for sale, and ADA campsites. No hookups are available. All campsites are **first-come, first served;** reservations (307/739-3300 or 800/628-9988, www.nps. gov/grte) are available for large group campsites at Gros Ventre. Shared hiker and biker campsites cost $7-8 per person.

Jenny Lake

The most-coveted campground in the park, **Jenny Lake Campground** (early May-late Sept., $23) has front-row seating with exceptional scenery right below the Teton Mountains. Trails lead to Hidden Falls, Inspiration Point, Leigh Lake, Cascade Canyon, and Paintbrush Canyon, plus peaks for climbing. Jenny Lake also has scenic cruises, kayak and canoe rentals, fishing, paddling, and the paved Multi-Use Pathway running south to Moose and Jackson.

In a hilly, loose pine forest with big boulders, the campground has 49 tent campsites including several walk-in sites. RVs, pop-ups, trailers, truck campers, and generators are prohibited, and vehicles must be smaller than 8 feet wide and 14 feet long. Each site allows a maximum of two tents, one vehicle or two motorcycles, and six people. Bathroom facilities are vault toilets. Locate the campground by turning from Teton Park Road into the north entrance at South Jenny Lake and veering right. The campground fills by 9am midsummer, but you may need to start trolling for a site around 7am.

Moose

On the Gros Ventre River along the southeast national park boundary, **Gros Ventre Campground** (early May-early Oct., $23) sits opposite the National Elk Refuge. Unfortunately, the Gros Ventre River often becomes a barren riverbed mid-July-September because of water diverted for irrigation. Gros Ventre Road makes for mellow bicycling where you might see bison and elk, and Black Butte blocks most of the view of the Teton Mountains. Because the campground sits 12

Jenny Lake Campground

miles from Jackson, you can pop into town for dinner and watch wildlife on the return trip. Gros Ventre is often the last campground to fill in the park, usually by dinnertime. Stop at the office to get a campsite.

As the largest campground in Grand Teton, Gros Ventre has 350 RV and tent campsites plus five group campsites. It has flush toilets, a dump station, and an amphitheater for evening interpretive programs. For RVs and trailers, the campground can accommodate large combos in a limited number of sites, and certain loops are designated for generator use. Each campsite can fit two vehicles, two tents, and six people. Seven huge loops circle the flat, sagebrush plateau under large cottonwood trees that lack understory for privacy. Make **reservations** (307/543-3100 or 800/628-9988) for large group campsites through Grand Teton Lodge Company.

Food

Casual attire is standard for all restaurants, with the exception of dressing for dinner at Jenny Lake Lodge. With limited dining options inside the park, many visitors drive to Jackson or Teton Village for dinner. Evening drives back to lodging or campsites often add on wildlife-watching or catching the sunset over the Tetons.

INSIDE THE PARK
Jenny Lake
At ★ **Jenny Lake Lodge** (400 Jenny Lake Loop, 307/733-4647 and 800/628-9988, www.gtlc.com, daily June-early Oct.), the dining room is an experience by itself. The log lodge hosts an intimate restaurant with views of the Teton peaks for a romantic setting. Breakfast (7:30am-9am, $27) is gourmet with a prix fixe menu from which you can select all options to go with your entrée. Brunch (noon-1:30pm, $13-18) features burgers, sandwiches, salads, and entrées such as trout. Dinner (6pm-8:45pm, $90) is a five-course prix fixe affair with menus rotating on a five-night schedule. Vegetarian, gluten-free, vegan, organic, all-natural, and low-fat options are available. Local and Wyoming food sources are used, and the wine list spans the world. **Reservations** (3047/543-3351) are required;

jackets, slacks, and dress attire are recommended for dinner.

At South Jenny Lake, the **general store** (307/543-2811, www.gtlc.com, 8am-7pm daily mid-May-mid-Sept.) carries a few convenience foods and minimal camping supplies. The closest supermarkets are in Jackson.

Moose

At Moose, Dornan's (307/733-2522) has two restaurants in their complex: one Italian and one western. **Pizza Pasta Company** (307/733-2415, ext. 204, www.dornans.com, 11:30am-9:30pm daily year-round, closed Nov. and Apr., shorter hours in winter, $8-26) serves pasta, pizza, calzones, hot subs, paninis, soups, and salads. Sandwich breads are fresh-baked in their bakery, and pastas and pizza dough (gluten-free is available) are fresh. Lasagna specials and 10 different pasta dishes give hefty Italian choices. Rooftop seating, patio dining, and indoor seating have outstanding views of the Tetons. Order at the counter, which frequently has a waiting line, and the staff delivers to the table. Seating is sometimes crowded and noisy indoors. Kids have their own menu. Order beer, wine, and cocktails separately from the **Spur Bar,** backed by a window framing

the Tetons. As an alternative, the **deli** in the Trading Post has a few tables for dining on huge sandwiches.

Summers bring on the old-time ★ **Chuckwagon** (307/733-2415, ext. 203, daily mid-June-Labor Day) for cowboy fare in a covered outdoor pavilion with picnic tables. You can even eat in a tepee. Breakfast (7am-11am, $10) serves biscuits and gravy, French toast, or all-you-can-eat sourdough pancakes. Lunch (noon-3pm, $8-13) offers sandwiches on breads baked fresh in the bakery, soups, and salads. Dinner (5pm-8pm Sun.-Thurs., $10-32) has all-you-can-eat western barbecue sides plus choices of an entrée: Wyoming beef short ribs cooked in a Dutch oven over a wood fire, barbecue chicken, baby back pork ribs, or blackened Idaho red trout. On Sundays, strip steak and prime rib are added to the menu. Beer and wine are served. Options for kids are available at all three meals. Mondays have free hootenannies, and concerts are scheduled periodically.

The small **Moose Trading Post & Deli** (307/733-2415, www.dornans.com, 9am-5pm daily winter, 8am-8pm daily summer, closed Nov. and Apr.), run by Dornan's, sells groceries, deli sandwiches (summer only), freeze-dried meals, trail mix, cheeses, and

Dornans serves up meals at their Chuckwagon in summer.

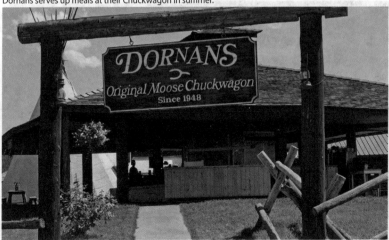

baked goods. A wine shop is also on-site, and espresso and ice cream are sold June-August.

Picnicking

Teton Park Road has two picnic areas. Between the Moose Entrance Station and Jenny Lake, the **Cottonwood Creek Picnic** **Area** sits roadside on Cottonwood Creek opposite the Taggart Lake Trailhead. The more scenic picnic area is at **String Lake,** accessed via North Jenny Lake. Both have picnic tables and vault toilets; String Lake also has fire rings with grills.

Transportation and Services

DRIVING

Two-lane paved roads are the norm in Grand Teton National Park. While they are relatively straight compared to some of the curvy roads in portions of Yellowstone, they still require attention when driving. Animals travel in road corridors and can jump out unexpectedly in front of cars. Even though speed limits range 25-55 mph in the park, speed limits drop to 45 mph after dark to protect bison, bears, wolves, and other wildlife. Several secondary roads are dirt: Moose-Wilson and Mormon Row, for example. In **winter,** most of the Teton Park Road and Moose-Wilson Road close to vehicles; U.S. Highway 26/89/191 is plowed and remains open. Weather can make for whiteouts, and roads can be icy. Check conditions for park roads (307/739-3682).

During July and August, **parking** lots at trailheads pack out. Off the Moose-Wilson Road, the Death Canyon and Granite Canyon parking lots fill up early, as do the Jenny Lake parking lots at South Jenny Lake, String Lake Trailhead, and Lupine Meadows Trailhead. Arrive early (before 9am) to claim a spot. The Laurance S. Rockefeller Preserve Center limits parking to 50 cars.

SHUTTLES

Shuttles are run by **Alltrans, Inc.** (800/443-6133 or 307/733-3135, www.alltransparkshuttle.com, daily late May-late Sept., $14/person/

Shuttle boats run every 15 minutes for hikers on Jenny Lake.

Where Can I Find . . .?

- **Banks and ATMs:** ATMs are located at Dornan's in Moose and outside the park in Teton Village and Jackson.

- **Cell Service:** Verizon has the widest coverage across Jackson Hole, including Jenny Lake and Moose.

- **Gas and Garage Services:** At Moose, Dornan's has gas available year-round. Pumps are open 24 hours a day with a credit card. Other gas stations are in Jackson and Wilson.

- **Internet Access:** Wireless Internet is available at the Craig Thomas Discovery & Visitor Center at Moose.

- **Post Office:** Post offices are in Moose (3 Teton Park Rd., 307/733-3336, 9am-1pm and 1:30pm-5pm Mon.-Fri., 10am-11:30am Sat.) and in Kelly (4486 Lower Gros Ventre Rd., 10am-2pm Mon.-Fri., 10am-noon Sat.), near Mormon Row.

- **Showers:** The nearest public showers and laundry are at Signal Mountain Lodge or outside the park in Jackson.

day) between Jackson, Moose, Jenny Lake Visitor Center, Jenny Lake Lodge, Signal Mountain Lodge, Jackson Lake Lodge, Colter Bay Village, and Headwaters Lodge at Flagg Ranch. Shuttles run several times north and south each day, but do not travel on Moose-Wilson Road. Departure times are available online or at visitors centers. A one-day fee lets you get on and off the shuttle as many times as you want and wherever you want. Reservations are not accepted; pay with cash, Visa, or Mastercard when you board. Alltrans also provides shuttles from the Jackson Hole Airport (www.jacksonholealltrans.com).

Jenny Lake Boating (307/734-9227, www.jennylakeboating.com, 7am-7pm daily early June-early Sept., 10am-4pm daily mid-May-early June and mid-late Sept., $15 adults, $12 seniors, $8 kids round-trip; $9 adults, $6 kids one-way) runs shuttles from the boat dock on Jenny Lake near the visitors center. Boats travel to the base of Mt. Teewinot to connect with multiple hiking trails around Jenny Lake and to Hidden Falls, Inspiration Point, and Cascade Canyon. Shuttles run every 10-15 minutes throughout the day. The last boat leaves the dock at the posted closing time. Reservations are not required.

EMERGENCY SERVICES
If you have an emergency, contact **Jenny Lake Ranger Station** (307/739-3343, 8am-5pm early June-early Sept.). The closest medical facility is **St. John's Medical Center** (625 E. Broadway, Jackson, 307/733-3636, www.tetonhospital.org).

Jackson Hole

Jackson Hole is a year-round playground, with the best mountain recreation: camping, hiking, fishing, rafting, biking, and skiing.

At Jackson Hole's south end, the town of Jackson is the main southern portal for exploring Grand Teton and Yellowstone National Parks. From its antler arches in the Jackson Town Square to the iconic Million Dollar Cowboy Bar, the town melds the Old West with modern places to stay and dine. Local breweries, galleries, shops, music, theater, and coffee shops let you explore the culture, while a trip to the National Elk Refuge in winter lets you count up hundreds of elk.

On the west side of Jackson Hole, Teton Village snuggles just outside Grand Teton National Park. The village is home to upscale hotels and restaurants that cluster at the base of Jackson Hole Mountain Resort. In winter, the resort's steep 4,139-foot vertical lures skiers and snowboarders. In summer, the tram whisks sightseers and hikers to the summit of Rendezvous Mountain for stunning views of Jackson Hole and the Tetons.

Caribou-Targhee National Forest and neighboring Teton Valley act as a back door into the Teton Mountains. Quiet and less crowded than Jackson Hole, the small town of Driggs serves as the gateway to the Tetons for four seasons of recreation. Grand Targhee Resort has the uncrowded slopes for skiing and snowboarding in winter that convert in summer into a mountain biking mecca and home for long-running summer music festivals.

PLANNING YOUR TIME

Swarms of visitors descend on Jackson in summer when the national parks are in full swing, hiking trails dry out, rivers offer white-water rafting and fishing, and the thermometer hangs around 70-80°F. Lodging properties have the highest prices of the year in summer. To guarantee what you want, book flights and lodging 6-12 months in advance.

To avoid the big crowds and take advantage of lower lodging prices, travel in April-May or September-October. While the weather may be more schizophrenic, wildlife-watching is often prime during migrations, mating,

---

Previous: hiking through Alaska Basin; Jackson's elk antler arches. **Above:** the Million Dollar Cowboy Bar.

Look for ★ to find recommended
sights, activities, dining, and lodging.

Highlights

★ **Jackson Town Square:** The town square is famous for its four antler archways, stagecoach rides, and shootouts on summer evenings (page 254).

★ **Million Dollar Cowboy Bar:** Walk into this historic bar and you've suddenly entered the Old West (page 254).

★ **National Museum of Wildlife Art:** This museum houses a collection of art that matches the natural environment (page 256).

★ **National Elk Refuge:** The refuge provides a winter home for elk, plus bighorn sheep, pronghorn, wolves, and trumpeter swans (page 256).

★ **Aerial Tram:** The tram whips skiers, snowboarders, hikers, and sightseers up 10,450-foot Rendezvous Mountain (page 259).

★ **Jackson Hole Mountain Resort:** This world-class resort attracts expert skiers and snowboarders (page 267).

★ **Teton Pass:** Relish the steep 10 percent grade as the road climbs to 8,432 feet, squeezing over the Teton Crest (page 288).

★ **Alaska Basin:** Backpackers come here for prolific wildflower displays, mountaintop views, and sparkling lakes (page 291).

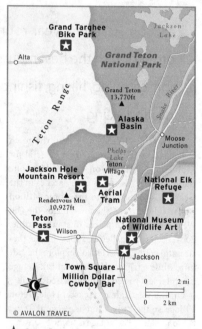

★ **Grand Targhee Bike Park:** It's the place to go for mountain biking in summer, with lift-accessed trails (page 292).

Jackson Hole

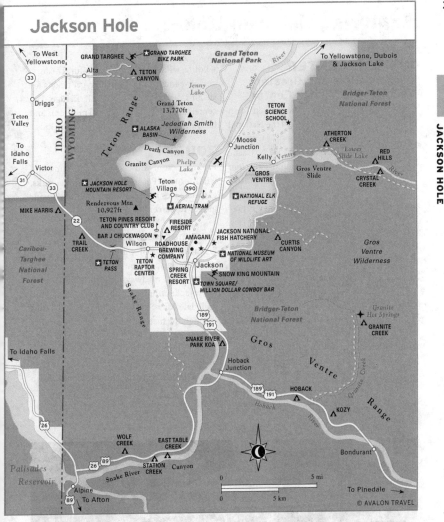

and birthing. Temperatures range 50-70°F, but sometimes cold winds can turn rain into snow, and the mercury plunges to 30°F. Fall delivers brilliant colors with aspens turning gold.

Winter brings on skiing, snowboarding, snowmobiling, ice climbing, cross-country skiing, and snowshoeing. While the winter season runs **Thanksgiving-early April**, high season includes all holidays and school vacations: Christmas, New Year's, Martin Luther King weekend, President's Day week, and school spring breaks. Prices go up for those holiday periods. To avoid the crowds, **plan midweek trips** outside of the holidays. **January** and **February** usually bring the coldest weather, while **March** often delivers big dumps of snow.

High temperatures in Jackson Hole hang mostly in the 20s and 30s, but drop lower at night and lower at higher elevations in the mountains. Ice and snow can impinge driving, especially over Teton Pass.

Exploring Jackson Hole

VISITOR CENTER

Jackson Hole and Greater Yellowstone Visitor Center

Located a half mile north of the Jackson Town Square at the southeast corner of the National Elk Refuge, the **Jackson Hole and Greater Yellowstone Visitor Center** (532 N. Cache St., 307/733-3316, daily year-round, 8am-7pm summer, 9am-5pm winter) has interpretive displays on the elk refuge and information for visitors. The interagency center represents the **National Elk Refuge** (www.fws.gov/refuge/National_Elk_Refuge), **Grand Teton National Park** (www.nps.gov/grte), **Bridger-Teton National Forest** (www.fs.usda.gov/btnf), and **Jackson Chamber of Commerce** (www.jacksonholechamber.com). Information is available on camping, lodging, wildlife-watching, activities, events, and road conditions for all four agencies. You can pick up maps and permits; the center also rents bear canisters and panniers. **Grand Teton Association** (307/739-3606, www.grandtetonpark.org) operates a bookstore in the visitors center selling books on wildlife, wildflowers, history, natural history, geology, and hiking. In winter, get tickets for sleigh rides on the National Elk Refuge. The center also puts on educational programs and has Junior Ranger activity booklets for kids.

TOURS

From Jackson, you can get sightseeing and wildlife tours. For trips that go into the parks, entrance fees are additional. Plan to tip your guides 15 percent.

Summer Tours

From the Stage Stop building on the south side of the Jackson Town Square, **stagecoach rides** (25 E. Broadway, Jackson, 307/733-3316, www.jacksonholechamber.com, 9am-9pm daily late May-Sept., $6 adults, $4 kids) tour through the historic part of town. Two mules pull the authentic red stagecoach that departs every 15 minutes. You'll get an authentic feel on the bench seats during the 10-minute ride. Proceeds help fund the shootout in the Town Square.

Companies that lead summer bus or van

Stagecoach rides tour through Jackson in summer.

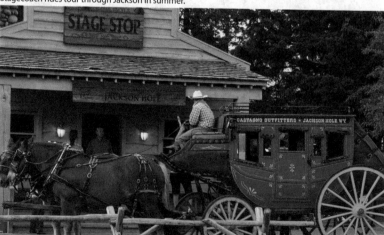

Geography 101

Jackson Hole: Visitors often get confused about Jackson Hole. A hole is an older term for a valley. Jackson Hole refers to the 80-mile-long by 15-mile-wide valley paralleling the Teton Mountains. It includes Jackson Lake, portions of Grand Teton National Park, and the towns of Moran, Moose, Kelly, Wilson, Teton Village, and Jackson.

Jackson: The town of Jackson, the largest town in Jackson Hole, sits at the south end of Jackson Hole.

Jackson Hole Mountain Resort: Jackson Hole Mountain Resort sits in Teton Village, which is one of the towns located in Jackson Hole. It is 12 miles from the town of Jackson and one mile from Grand Teton National Park.

Teton Valley: Teton Valley is on the less-traveled west side of the Teton Mountains, with tiny towns like Victor and Driggs in Idaho. Teton Valley accesses wilderness areas and Caribou-Targhee National Forest, which flanks the west side of the Teton Mountains and Grand Teton National Park.

Teton Pass: While Teton Pass is in the Teton Mountains, it is not in Grand Teton National Park. In fact, the pass sits seven air miles south of the park. Teton Pass connects Jackson Hole to the Teton Valley.

Gros Ventre Mountains: Named for the Gros Ventre Indians and French for "big belly," the Gros Ventre Mountains flank the eastern side of Jackson Hole and run southeast from the town of Jackson. Far older than the younger Tetons, the more eroded rounded peaks hold Bridger-Teton National Forest and the Gros Ventre Wilderness.

Greater Yellowstone Ecosystem: This geographic term arose from the fact that national park boundaries are artificial. They do not define the ecosystem, especially as used by wildlife. Wildlife wander across boundaries to find seasonal habitat in more hospitable places. The Greater Yellowstone Ecosystem includes Yellowstone National Park, Grand Teton National Park, Jackson Hole, John D. Rockefeller, Jr. Memorial Parkway, National Elk Refuge, four national forests (Custer-Gallatin, Caribou-Targhee, Bridger-Teton, and Shoshone), Jackson Hole, and Teton Valley.

---

sightseeing tours (mid-May-mid-Oct., $195-200 adults, $100-150 kids) in Grand Teton and Yellowstone National Parks are based in Jackson. Some offer pickups at your hotel. **Buffalo Roam Park Tours** (307/413-0954, www.buffaloroamtours.com) guides van tours. **VIP Adventure Travel** (307/699-1077, www.vipadventuretravel.com) offers sightseeing in luxury SUVs.

Wildlife Tours

Most of the tour companies in Jackson guide wildlife tours year-round. Tour routes vary depending on the season based on where wildlife congregates, but take in the National Elk Refuge, national forests, Grand Teton National Park, and Yellowstone National Park. Tour companies bring the spotting scopes and binoculars. Most will pick you up at your hotel. Half-day, full-day, and specialty tours are available every day. Rates run

$100-300 per person. Three reputable companies are **Eco Tour Adventures** (307/690-9533, www.jacksonholewildlifetours.com), **Jackson Hole Wildlife Safaris** (307/690-6402, http://jacksonholewildlifesafaris.com), and **Grizzly Country Wildlife Adventures** (307/413-4389, http://grizzlycountrywildlifeadventures.com).

Winter Sleigh Rides

For winter sleigh rides, wear warm clothing layers including hat, gloves, and snow boots. At the National Elk Refuge, you can take a one-hour winter tour on a **horse-drawn sleigh** (Double H Bar, Inc., 307/733-0277 or 800/772-5386, www.bar5.com, 10am-4pm, daily mid-Dec.-early Apr., $20 adults, $15 kids). The sleigh rides tour among the elk herd, offering opportunities for watching the stately ungulates and photography. Participants pick up tickets at the Jackson

Hole and Greater Yellowstone Visitor Center (532 N. Cache St., 307/733-3316) and meet at the visitors center for the free shuttle to the sleigh ride area.

Scenic Flights

Fly Jackson Hole (1250 E. Jackson Hole Airport Rd., Jackson, 844/359-5499, www.flyjacksonhole.com, $300-750) has 60- to 90-minute flights over the Tetons, as well as family and alpenglow flights.

DRIVING TOURS
National Elk Refuge
3.5 MILES

Driving the 3.5-mile Refuge Road on the **National Elk Refuge** (675 E. Broadway, 307/733-9212, www.fws.gov/refuge/National_Elk_Refuge, Dec.-Apr.) offers wildlife-watching when bison, bighorn sheep, pronghorn, and thousands of elk winter on the refuge. Drivers are not allowed to stop on the narrow road with no shoulders, but can use five pullouts for wildlife-watching and photography. The road can be covered in ice or snowdrifts, and visibility may be limited by blowing snow or fog. Find the road at the east end of Broadway.

Southern Jackson Hole Loop
33 MILES

A 33-mile loop circles the southern portion of Jackson Hole, connecting Jackson, Moose, and Teton Village. Starting from Jackson or Teton Village, you can drive the loop clockwise or counterclockwise May-October. Counterclockwise yields impressive views of Jackson Hole backdropped by the Teton Mountains. The route cuts through Grand Teton National Park. From Jackson, the loop starts up U.S. Highway 26/89/191, passing the **National Wildlife Refuge.** At Moose Junction, turn left to cross the Snake River. After passing the Craig Thomas Discovery & Visitor Center, turn left onto the paved and dirt **Moose-Wilson Road** (no RVs or trailers), which is closed in winter. After exiting the national park and passing **Teton Village,** continue south on the Moose-Wilson Road to Highway 22. Turn left to return to Jackson.

Sights

JACKSON
★ Jackson Town Square

In downtown Jackson, the **Jackson Town Square** is a year-round attraction. Four antler arches, each made from 2,000 tightly intertwined elk antlers, flank the four corners of the park. In summer, their sun-bleached white is striking. In winter, holiday lights wrap the arches in glitter. Each May, the Boy Scouts hold their **annual elk antler auction** (http://elkfest.org/auction) in the park, selling off shed antlers collected each year from the National Elk Refuge. Horse-drawn **stagecoaches** (daily Memorial Day-Labor Day) give tours from the park. In summer, a free **gunfight reenactment** is staged at 6:15pm Monday-Saturday (www.jacksonholechamber.com). Crowds show up to watch the event put on by the Jackson Hole Playhouse, a tradition since 1956. The Jackson Town Square sits between Broadway and Deloney Avenues and Cache and Center Streets.

★ Million Dollar Cowboy Bar

A landmark in downtown Jackson since 1937, but in a building that dates to the 1890s, the **Million Dollar Cowboy Bar** (25 N. Cache St., 307/733-2207, www.milliondollarcowboybar.com, 11am-1am or 2am daily year-round) can be recognized by its neon sign of a cowboy on a horse. Knobbled pine trims out the bar, and saddles with saddle blankets serve as stools. Cowboy murals, wildlife mounts, ranch gear, and western artifacts make the bar look more like a museum than a watering hole.

Jackson

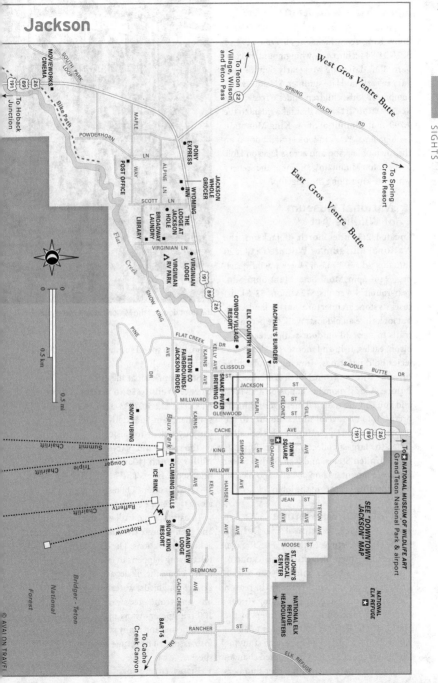

To Teton
Village, Wilson,
and Teton Pass 22

West Gros Ventre Butte

SPRING GULCH RD

To Spring
Creek Resort

East Gros Ventre Butte

MOVIEWORKS CINEMA

SOUTH PARK LOOP

191 89 26

To Hoback
Junction

Bike Path

POWDERHORN

MAPLE

PONY EXPRESS

LN

WAY

ALPINE LN

LN

POST OFFICE

SCOTT LN

JACKSON WHOLE GROCER

WYOMING INN

THE LODGE AT JACKSON HOLE

BROADWAY LAUNDRY

LIBRARY

VIRGINIAN LN

VIRGINIAN LODGE

VIRGINIAN RV PARK

Flat Creek

SNOW KING

191 89 26

COWBOY VILLAGE RESORT

MACPHAIL'S BURGERS

ELK COUNTRY INN

SADDLE BUTTE DR

FLAT CREEK DR

PINE DR

KARNS AVE

KELLY AVE

CLISSOLD ST

JACKSON ST

ST

PEARL

DELONEY

GILL

TETON CO FAIRGROUNDS/ JACKSON RODEO

SNAKE RIVER BREWING CO

MILLWARD

GLENWOOD

KARNS

CACHE

AVE

Beaux Park

SNOW TUBING

KING

SIMPSON

ST

Broadway

TOWN SQUARE

191 89 26

To ★ NATIONAL MUSEUM OF WILDLIFE ART
Grand Teton National Park & airport

Summit Chairlift

Cougar Triple Chairlift

Rafferty Chairlift

Ropetow

CLIMBING WALLS

ICE RINK

SNOW KING RESORT

WILLOW

AVE

KELLY

HANSEN

JEAN

TETON AVE

ST

AVE

MOOSE

ST

SEE "DOWNTOWN JACKSON" MAP

GRAND VIEW LODGE

REDMOND

ST

ST. JOHN'S MEDICAL CENTER

NATIONAL ELK REFUGE

Bridger - Teton

National

Forest

CACHE CREEK

AVE

RANCHER

BAR T-5

To Cache
Creek Canyon

NATIONAL ELK REFUGE HEADQUARTERS

ELK REFUGE

0   0.5 km

0   0.5 mi

Snow King Mountain

In summer, **Snow King Mountain** (100 E. Snow King Ave., Jackson, 307/734-3194 or 307/734-9442, http://snowkingmountain.com, 9am-8pm daily late May-early Sept., hours vary in early and late summer, $17 adults, $12 seniors, $8 kids, children under 6 free) offers **scenic chairlift rides** that take riders to the 7,799-foot summit of Snow King Mountain for big views. You can look straight down on the town of Jackson and across Jackson Hole to the Teton Mountains, and enjoy the scenery while walking along the ridgetop.

★ National Museum of Wildlife Art

Located 2.5 miles north of Jackson, the **National Museum of Wildlife Art** (2820 Rungius Rd., 307/733-5771, www.wildlifeart. org, 9am-5pm Mon.-Sat., 11am-5pm Sun. year-round, $14 adults, $12 seniors, $2-6 kids) fuses its stone architecture into the landscape, but looks like an old fort. Walk the perimeter trails to view 30 outdoor sculptures of elk, bison, eagles, fish, and moose. Inside, 14 galleries hold paintings, drawings, and sculptures of wildlife from North America and Europe. A kids' room has hands-on activities, and you can use a digital messager for interpretive info on several works. Be sure to see Robert Bateman's painting of a bison called *Chief*, the largest collection of Carl Rungius in the United States, and Ken Bunn's *Silent Pursuit*, a mountain lion poised to pounce on unsuspecting visitors in the lobby.

★ National Elk Refuge

The 27,500-acre **National Elk Refuge** (www.fws.gov/refuge/National_Elk_Refuge) borders the town of Jackson and is one of the best places to see wildlife year-round. Preserving the elk herd is the main reason the refuge was established. About 70 percent of the Jackson elk herd winters at the National Elk Refuge; that equates to about 7,000 elk. Biologists who have been studying the elk for about 35 years have noted changes in migratory patterns, with larger numbers

the front doors of the Million Dollar Cowboy Bar

choosing to spend summers within 6.2 miles of the refuge.

Start your visit at the **Jackson Hole and Greater Yellowstone Visitor Center** (532 N. Cache St., 307/733-3316, 8am-7pm daily summer, 9am-5pm daily winter), where you can buy tickets for a sleigh ride (in winter) on the refuge and plan a visit to the historic **Miller Ranch** (10am-4pm daily late May-mid-Sept., free). The **Multi-Use Pathway** (May-Oct.) offers a bike-friendly way to tour along the refuge border and look for wildlife.

In early spring, **bull elk** shed their antlers and then migrate from the refuge to summer at higher elevations. The elk return in late fall. Elk calving happens in late spring (April and May). While the elk depart, **migrating birds** arrive: songbirds, waterfowl, great blue herons, and trumpeter swans. (In winter, about 100 trumpeter swans make the refuge wetlands home, and many stick around in spring for nesting.) The refuge has about 175 avian species.

Bison, pronghorn, and **deer** also make

the National Museum of Wildlife Art

the refuge home. A drive on the refuge road past Miller Butte will often yield views of bighorn sheep, pronghorn, and mule deer. The Pinnacle Peak Pack of **wolves** has also found the refuge a sustainable habitat, and they are thriving, which is why they have been removed from the Endangered Species List. Refuge biologists have radio-collared several of the canines to study their movements and assess their impacts on the elk herd.

Winter is the best season for watching wildlife in Jackson Hole. In winter, many animals migrate to lower elevations on the valley floor that sees around 65 inches of snow, instead of up in the mountains where snowfall can top 500 inches.

The refuge also has annual bison and elk hunts to manage the herd populations. Hunters with Wyoming permits can apply for a permit to hunt bison or elk on the refuge.

Wildlife often crosses the National Elk Refuge road.

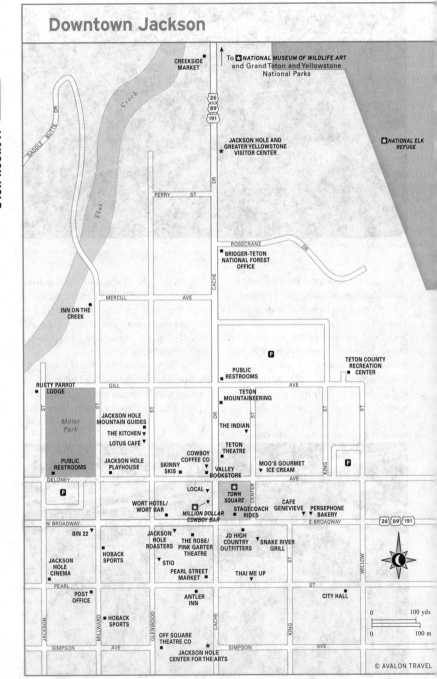

Downtown Jackson

CREEKSIDE MARKET

To ★ NATIONAL MUSEUM OF WILDLIFE ART and Grand Teton and Yellowstone National Parks

26 89 191

SADDLE BUTTE DR

Creek

Flat

JACKSON HOLE AND GREATER YELLOWSTONE VISITOR CENTER

★ NATIONAL ELK REFUGE

PERRY ST

CACHE DR

ROSECRANZ DR

BRIDGER-TETON NATIONAL FOREST OFFICE

MERCILL AVE

INN ON THE CREEK

P

TETON COUNTY RECREATION CENTER

RUSTY PARROT LODGE

GILL ST

PUBLIC RESTROOMS

AVE

TETON MOUNTAINEERING

Miller Park

JACKSON HOLE MOUNTAIN GUIDES

THE KITCHEN ▼

LOTUS CAFÉ ▼

CACHE DR

THE INDIAN ▼

TETON THEATRE

PUBLIC RESTROOMS

JACKSON HOLE PLAYHOUSE

COWBOY COFFEE CO ▼

SKINNY SKIS ■

MOO'S GOURMET ▼ ICE CREAM

P

KING ST

ST

VALLEY BOOKSTORE

DELONEY

P

LOCAL ▼

★ TOWN SQUARE

CAFE GENEVIEVE ▼

PERSEPHONE ▼ BAKERY

WORT HOTEL/ WORT BAR ●

★ MILLION DOLLAR COWBOY BAR

CENTER ST

STAGECOACH RIDES

AVE

W BROADWAY

BIN 22 ▼

JACKSON ▼ HOLE ROASTERS

THE ROSE/ PINK GARTER THEATRE

JD HIGH COUNTRY OUTFITTERS

▼ SNAKE RIVER GRILL

E BROADWAY

26 89 191

HOBACK SPORTS

▼ STIO

JACKSON HOLE CINEMA

PEARL STREET MARKET ■

THAI ME UP ▼

WILLOW ST

PEARL ST

ST

POST OFFICE ■

ANTLER INN

CITY HALL ■

JACKSON ST

MILLWARD

■ HOBACK SPORTS

GLENWOOD ST

CACHE

KING ST

0   100 yds

0   100 m

SIMPSON

OFF SQUARE THEATRE CO ★

JACKSON HOLE CENTER FOR THE ARTS ★

SIMPSON AVE

© AVALON TRAVEL

Details on the seasons and application process are available online.

Two roads tour the refuge year-round. From Jackson, U.S. Highway 26/89/191 parallels the western boundary of the refuge; a pullover for wildlife watching is just north of the Jackson Hole and Greater Yellowstone Visitor Center, and another is 4.3 miles north. From the east end of Broadway Street, follow the 3.5-mile dirt refuge road.

WILSON
Teton Raptor Center

Injured raptors in Jackson Hole are taken for rehabilitation to the Teton Raptor Center (5450 W. Hwy. 22, Wilson, 307/203-2551, http://tetonraptorcenter.org, $12 adults, $10 kids and seniors) on the historic Hardeman Ranch. The center puts on one-hour outdoor programs where you can meet the resident birds of prey and learn about raptors in Greater Yellowstone. Programs take place at noon and 2pm in summer (Tues.-Thurs. June-Sept.) and winter (Tues.-Wed. Oct.-May). Reservations are required.

TETON VILLAGE
★ Aerial Tram

At Jackson Hole Mountain Resort, the Aerial Tram (3265 W. Village Dr., Teton Village, 307/733-2292 or 888/333-7766, www.jackson-hole.com, 9am-6pm daily late May-early Oct., 9am-5pm in shoulder seasons, $37 adults, $29 seniors, $22 juniors, children 5 and under free) is the easiest way to get on top of a mountain in the Teton Range. The tram goes to the 10,450-foot summit of Rendezvous Mountain at the south end of the Tetons and right outside Grand Teton National Park. The tram saves you climbing 4,139 vertical feet to reach the summit. At the summit, most people feel sluggish or lightheaded from the elevation, but the view makes you forget any discomfort. You'll stare down at Jackson Hole and north across the Teton summits to the Grand. You can take photos, walk to viewpoints, eat waffles at the tiny Corbet's Cabin,

hike trails into Grand Teton National Park, or hike down to the base. Get discounted tickets online.

BRIDGER-TETON NATIONAL FOREST

Bridger-Teton National Forest (www.fs.usda.gov/btnf) surrounds Jackson Hole. The forest offers hiking, mountain biking, rafting, horseback riding, and camping. In the Gros Ventre Mountains, Lower Slide Lake is the place to go for boating, windsurfing, sailing, waterskiing, kayaking, canoeing, and paddleboarding. Granite Hot Springs, a pool built in the 1930s by the Civilian Conservation Corps, is open for soaking in summer and winter. The Snake River kicks up with white-water rafting and kayaking through Hoback Canyon. Drivers crossing Teton Pass drive through the Bridger-Teton National Forest on the east side.

Gros Ventre Mountains

Often ignored because of the higher, more jagged Teton Mountains, the Gros Ventre Mountains flank the eastern slopes of Jackson Hole. The older, more rounded and eroded mountains hold several high peaks taller than 11,000 feet. One of the most prominent peaks seen from the floor of Jackson Hole is Sheep Mountain. Its upper cliffs have gained the name "Sleeping Indian" due to the shape that looks like the profile of a person sleeping. View the Sleeping Indian from an overlook about one mile north of Jackson Hole Airport. To explore the Gros Ventre Mountains, drive to see where the 1927 landslide formed Lower Slide Lake or tour up Granite Creek Road to Granite Hot Springs.

LOWER SLIDE LAKE

Located east of the park, Slide Lake Overlook is a must-see for geology buffs. Rough pavement on Gros Ventre Road accesses the overlook to see the Gros Ventre Landslide of 1925 that created Lower Slide Lake. Two years later in 1925, the

the Gros Ventre Range

impoundment failed and flooded Jackson Hole from Kelly to Wilson. **Lower Slide Lake** offers boating, paddling, windsurfing, sailing, waterskiing, and camping. After leaving the park boundary, the road is rough, even the paved portion.

From Gros Ventre Junction north of Jackson and the National Elk Refuge, turn right onto Gros Ventre Road until it passes Kelly, swings north, and then turns right to climb into the mountains. Ascend the curvy, bumpy paved road over a summit to an interpretive overlook above Lower Slide Lake and below orange rocky hillsides. Pavement ends at Atherton Creek Campground. From there, the dirt road continues to follow the headwaters of the Gros Ventre River downstream with aspen groves, sagebrush meadows, and coniferous forests flanking the forested road.

GRANITE HOT SPRINGS
Granite Hot Springs (end of Granite Creek Rd., Forest Rd. 30500, 307/690-6323, www.fs.usda.gov/btnf, 10am-6pm daily late May-Oct., 10am-5pm daily early Dec.-early Apr., $6) requires a bumpy dirt-road drive, but with the reward of soaking beneath rocky outcrops in a cement pool built by the Civilian Conservation Corps in the 1930s. The hot springs heat to 93°F in summer (when rain and snowmelt dilute the hot water) and to 112°F in winter. Primitive hot pools also sit below Granite Falls. The facility has changing rooms (no lockers) and pit toilets, and there is a Forest Service campground nearby. In winter, access is only via snowmobiling, skiing, dogsledding, or fat-tire bikes. The site is in Bridger-Teton National Forest, 11 miles off U.S. Highway 189/191 (34 miles from Jackson).

From Jackson, drive U.S. Highway 26/89/189/191 south 13 miles to Hoback Junction. About halfway, the road begins to parallel the Snake River where the scenic canyon constricts the water from its ambling pace into frothy rapids. At Hoback Junction, turn left to follow U.S. Highway 189/191 eastward for 15 miles. Turn left onto the gravel two-lane Granite Creek Road (Forest Rd. 30500) and enjoy a leisurely 11-mile tour through aspen-rimmed meadows along the creek to Granite Hot Springs.

Recreation

DAY HIKES

Trails run up mountains in the Bridger-Teton National Forest (www.fs.usda.gov/btnf). For hiking maps, stop by the **Jackson Hole and Greater Yellowstone Visitor Center** (532 N. Cache St., Jackson, 307/733-3316, 8am-7pm daily summer, 9am-5pm daily winter).

Guides and Equipment

Jackson Hole Mountain Resort (3265 W. Village Dr., Teton Village, 307/733-2292 or 888/333-7766, www.jacksonhole.com) guides day hikes by reservation and overnight hikes 2.5 miles to the Rock Springs Yurt ($500). The yurt sleeps eight guests, and the yurtmeister cooks dinner and breakfast. It's poshy backpacking, and all gear is included.

Based in Jackson, **Hole Hiking Experience** (866/733-4453, www.holehike.com, year-round) guides day hikes, combination programs mixing hiking with rafting or other activities, and customized backpacking trips for 2-5 days. Led by seasoned naturalists, the hikes are in Bridger-Teton and Caribou-Targhee National Forests. Day hike lengths vary from four, six, or eight hours with rates at $230-435 for 1-2 people or $86-170 per person for three or more hikers (reduced rates for kids). Transportation to trailheads, snacks, and lunch for longer trips are included.

To rent hiking gear, go to **Teton Mountaineering** (170 N. Cache Dr., Jackson, 307/733-3595, www.tetonmtn.com, $3-20/item/day). They rent day packs, backpacks, ice axes, crampons, kid carriers, bear canisters, trekking poles, boots, tents, sleeping bags, and sleeping pads. Weeklong gear rentals are priced for five days.

Jackson
SNOW KING MOUNTAIN
Distance: 3.6 miles round-trip
Duration: 3-4 hours
Elevation change: 1,500 feet
Effort: strenuous, but short
Trailhead: at the corner of Snow King Avenue and Cache Street

Hiking up Snow King Mountain in Bridger-Teton National Forest is something locals do for exercise, but it's also a worthy climb for the views of the Tetons, National Elk Refuge, Gros Ventre Mountains, Sleeping Indian, and the town of Jackson. Prepare for a grunt and carry water as the route climbs to gain the views. For those who only want to hike one-way (either up or down), take the scenic chairlift ride from **Snow King Mountain** (100 E. Snow King Ave., 307/734-3194 or 307/734-9442, http://snowkingmountain.com, 9am-8pm daily late May-early Sept., $17 adults, $12 seniors, $8 kids, kids under 6 free, $5 for summit to base ride).

From the base area, find the **Snow King Summit Trail** above the ticket office at the chairlift. The trail is a combination of trail and service roads. Climb 0.7 mile up three switchbacks on the lower slope of **Snow King Ski Area,** passing the Sink or Swim Trail, to a signed **junction** with a mountain road. Turn west and traverse 0.3 mile across the slope to the end of a switchback, where the steep work begins. You'll climb 0.75 mile up three more switchbacks on the dirt road. The switchbacks crest out on the summit ridge, where the dirt road reaches the **summit** and the top of the chairlift in less than 0.2 mile.

Teton Village
RENDEZVOUS MOUNTAIN
Distance: 13.4 miles round-trip
Duration: 5-10 hours
Elevation change: 4,139 feet
Effort: strenuous
Trailhead: Jackson Hole Mountain Resort in Teton Village

It's one long ascent to climb the 10,450-foot Rendezvous Mountain at Jackson Hole Mountain Resort in Bridger-Teton National

Forest. Prepare for exposure to sun, heat, wind, snow, and thunderstorms. To whittle the mileage down, most people hike 6.7 miles to the summit and take the **Aerial Tram** (9am-6pm daily late May-early Oct.) back down; the tram ride down is free for those who reach the summit on foot. Other hikers take the tram up ($22-37) and do the 6.7-mile knee-pounding descent instead. At the top, hikers can reward themselves with waffles at **Corbet's Cabin** (9am-4pm daily late May-early Oct. and late Nov.-early Apr., $7).

From the base of the **Bridger Gondola,** climb 0.1 mile up a wide road, swinging southwest when at a T-junction with a dirt road. Continue uphill on the dirt road for 0.2 mile to reach a fork. Veer west and continue uphill for 0.3 mile to the top of the **Union Pass chairlift** (does not operate in summer). On the uphill side of the top terminal, catch the **Lower Faces Trail** heading north. (This is a real trail, not a service road.) In 0.1 mile, take the uphill fork. Ascend switchbacks 1.2 miles up the ski run to intersect with the **Summit Trail** above the Casper Lodge (closed in summer). The remaining trail to the summit is on service roads.

Turn west onto the Summit Trail and climb 0.7 mile to a three-way **junction.** Turn north

and continue 0.3 mile to the next junction; stay straight through this second junction for 0.4 mile to another junction. Ignore the spur road that heads north; swing west instead and hike 0.75 mile uphill below steep cliffs to a junction with a spur road that traverses north across the slope to the Couloir Restaurant and **top of Bridger Gondola** (both open in summer). Swing west again to climb through cliffs; stay on the service road for 2.7 miles to reach the summit of **Rendezvous Mountain** and the top of the tram. Views span Jackson Hole, with the Snake River and Gros Ventre Mountains to the east. You'll see the Grand Teton, plus 360-degree views of Grand Teton National Park, the national forest, and Jackson Hole. Snow can cover parts of the trail into July. Descend via foot or tram.

ROCK SPRINGS LOOP

Distance: 4.3 miles round-trip
Duration: 3 hours
Elevation change: 1,000 feet
Effort: strenuous due to elevation
Trailhead: summit of Rendezvous Mountain at Jackson Hole Mountain Resort

For a hike with giant views, take the Aerial Tram up Rendezvous Mountain at **Jackson Hole Mountain Resort** (3265 W. Village

the view from Rendezvous Mountain

Dr., Teton Village, 307/733-2292 or 888/333-7766, www.jacksonhole.com, 9am-6pm daily late May-early Oct., closes at 5pm in shoulder seasons, $37 adults, $29 seniors, $22 juniors, kids 5 and under free). Since the tram whisks you to 10,450 feet, you may feel short of breath at the altitude. Drink lots of water and take your time hiking, especially on the ascent. The signed route uses a combination of service roads and trails to take in views of Jackson Hole, the Gros Ventre Mountains, and the Tetons.

Begin by taking the Top of the World Loop along the ridge southward. At the junction, continue downhill to a second junction, where the loop begins. Turn right here, bypassing the Granite Canyon and Marion Lake turnoff. After you drop off the ridge, you'll reach a short spur to Rock Springs Overlook, worth the view. Continue to descend into Cody Bowl through wildflower meadows broken by talus and a few trees. Snow can linger in this boulder-filled bowl well into July. A second spur leads to Cody Bowl Overlook. At the junction after the overlook, turn left to switchback down, across a bench, and then head back up. The Rock Springs Loop Trail connects with the Summit Trail, a summer maintenance road, to switchback up to the tram.

Bridger-Teton National Forest
GOODWIN LAKE

Distance: 6 miles round-trip
Duration: 4 hours
Elevation change: 1,393 feet
Effort: moderate
Trailhead: Goodwin Lake Trailhead
Directions: From the east end of Broadway Street in Jackson, drive northeast on the Elk Refuge Road for 3.7 miles. Turn north and drive one mile, then turn east onto Curtis Canyon. Turn right for 4.3 miles, switchbacking past the campground. At Sheep Creek Junction, stay right for 0.2 mile, then veer left onto Forest Road 30440 for 0.8 mile to reach the trailhead. High-clearance rigs are best on the washboard and pothole road.

At 9,516 feet, Goodwin Lake sits below Jackson Peak in the Gros Ventre Wilderness. The well-traveled trail is mostly snow-free by the end of June and busy in midsummer (get an early start to claim a parking spot at the trailhead). For anglers, the lake holds brook trout.

Starting in a loose forest, the trail breaks out to climb a sagebrush hillside in 0.5 mile. Be sure to look back over your shoulder to see the Tetons. The trail travels south through forest on a steep ascent. After crossing into the wilderness, the route reaches a rocky slope at 2.3 miles and climbs through talus breaks. After crossing a dry creek at 2.8 miles, the trail reaches west shore of Goodwin Lake.

For bigger views, add on another four miles round-trip (1,225 feet vertical) to summit 10,741-foot Jackson Peak. From the lake, take the trail southward; at the rock cairn, follow the unmaintained trail to the top for impressive 360-degree views.

BACKPACKING
Teton Crest Trail
45 MILES

While many backpackers limit Teton Crest Trail routes to the national park section, the full route encompasses more of the crest south of the park. The 45-mile (4-5-day) trek starts near Teton Pass at Phillips Pass Trailhead and finishes at String Lake Trailhead. It combines trails from Bridger-Teton and Caribou-Targhee National Forests with trails in Grand Teton National Park. Permits (www.nps.gov/grte) are not needed for the national forests, but are required for camping in the national park sections. Bear canisters are required in the national park, but thick bear populations also inhabit the national forests in the Tetons; even if you don't plan on camping inside the park, take a canister.

BIKING

Although Highway 22 has no bike lane to ascend Teton Pass, it's the prime ride for cyclists who like climbing. Most riders start the day early to avoid heavy midday traffic and heat.

Road cyclists have a chance to get off the narrow, no-shoulder highways onto paved pathways that parallel roads. About 56 miles of the Jackson Hole Pathway (www.friendsofpathways.org) system connects Jackson with Teton Village, National Elk Refuge, and Moose and Jenny Lake in Grand Teton National Park; maps are available online. The pathway along the elk refuge is usually closed in winter for wildlife protection, and only a few roads are plowed in winter. The pathways are multiuse, so there will be some walkers and, in places, equestrians.

Single-track trails abound in the Bridger-Teton National Forest surrounding Jackson. The closest riding complex is the Snow King Trails, where mountain bikers can ride to the summit of Snow King or loop the mountain on the 20-mile Cache-Game Trails. Teton Pass also has several routes, including Old Pass Road, for those who want to climb to the pass. Some trails are for downhill mountain biking only, while others are multiuse or closed to mountain biking. Maps (available from www.friendsofpathways.org) specify which trails are open to specific user groups.

Jackson Hole Mountain Resort (3265 W. Village Dr., Teton Village, 307/739-2687, www.jacksonhole.com, mid-June-late Sept.) has lift-accessed mountain biking via the five-minute Teewinot Lift. Six trails include jump tracks, banked corners, and skills features for beginners through advanced riders. Lift tickets and rentals are available through Jackson Hole Sports, located in the Bridger Center. Mountain bike tours, lessons, and rentals ($35-70 half day, $50-80 full day) include lift tickets and helmets; downhill protective pads are also rented.

Rentals and Guides

Hoback Sports (520 W. Broadway Ave. #3, Jackson, 307/733-5335, http://hobacksports.com, 10am-6pm daily) rents hybrids, demos, hardtails, and full-suspension mountain bikes ($33-75/day). They also rent kids' bikes, kiddie trailers, and bike racks. Rentals come with helmets and bike locks. The shop also does tuning and repairs.

Teton Mountain Bike Tours (545 N. Cache St., Jackson, 307/733-0712 or 800/733-0788, www.tetonmountainbike.com, year-round, $65 half day, $100-150 full day) guides half-day and full-day mountain bike tours. In winter, they guide fat-tire bike tours. Tour routes go into the national parks and national forests, and the company offers rental bikes and tours for different skill levels, including family-friendly or challenging single-track rides.

HORSEBACK RIDING

In Jackson, the most convenient trail rides are operated by Jackson Hole Trail Rides (330 E. Snow King Ave., 307/733-6992, www.jhtrailrides.com, daily in summer, $38-40 one hour, $58-60 two hours). The rides tour trails on Snow King Mountain overlooking the town. One-hour rides depart six times daily; two-hour rides go out four times. Wranglers also lead kids younger than eight around the corral on a horse ($20). Due to their location near the Snow King Mountain ski area, you can walk from downtown.

In Teton Village, horseback trail rides go out from Teton Village Trail Rides (307/733-2674, www.tetonvillagetrailrides.com, daily in summer, $38-40 one hour, $58-60 two hours), across the street from Snake River Lodge. The rides tour trails on the private, historic Snake River Ranch. Starting at 8am, one-hour rides depart every hour; two-hour rides depart every two hours. Wranglers lead four-hour rides (8:15am or 1pm, $100, reservation only) on Munger Mountain, located about 10 miles south of Teton Village.

You don't have to be a guest at the upscale Spring Creek Ranch (1800 Spirit Dance Rd., 307/733-9209, www.springcreekranch.com) to participate in their trail rides on East Gros Ventre Butte. Rides are 1-4 hours long, and the location offers 360-degree views of Jackson Hole. The ranch offers horseback rides and corral dinner combos on Tuesday and Thursday nights at 5pm ($78 adults, $68 kids).

WATER SPORTS

Boaters need to have current **registration** (Wyoming Game and Fish, https://wgfd.wyo. gov, Wyoming residents: $10 motorized, $5 nonmotorized; nonresidents: $30 motorized, $15 nonmotorized). In addition, you'll need an Aquatic Invasive Species (AIS) sticker. The only exemption is for inflatable boats shorter than 10 feet, paddleboards, and windsurfers. Forest Service permits are not needed for rafting day trips (unless you have a large group), but you will need a Wyoming AIS sticker.

Rendezvous River Sports (945 W. Broadway, Jackson, 307/733-2471, www.jacksonholekayak.com, 8am-7pm daily) rents touring kayaks, canoes, tandems, and stand-up paddleboards ($40-65/day) as well as river kayaks, inflatable kayaks, play boats, river runners, rafts, surfboards, and trailers ($20-100/day). The company also rents wetsuits, paddle jackets, dry tops, booties, spray skirts, helmets, throw bags, pumps, and PFDs. You can get lessons in kayaking or paddleboarding or guided tours in inflatable kayaks.

Boating

One of the most popular lakes outside Grand Teton National Park is **Lower Slide Lake** in the Gros Ventre Mountains. The five-mile-long lake formed from a 1925 natural landslide. The lake has a boat launch with a dock and trailer parking on the east end adjacent to Atherton Campground. It is usually calm in the morning for paddling and fishing, but in the afternoon winds crop up, making it a favorite with windsurfers and small sailboats. Use caution: The lake has standing dead trees due to the forest that once grew where the lake now sits. To get there, turn right on Gros Ventre Road north of Jackson to reach the lake.

River Rafting and Kayaking

The Snake River is a prime waterway for floating, rafting, and kayaking. The stretch from Grand Teton Park to Hoback Junction provides meandering Class I-II floating with river accesses at Moose, Wilson Bridge, and South Park Bridge. South of Jackson, a trail for kayakers accesses King's Wave for surfing.

Skilled kayakers and rafters hit some of the tributaries, such as the **Gros Ventre River** (May-July). From Lower Slide Lake in Bridger-Teton National Forest to Kelly, the river hops through a boulder field with Class III-IV white water. Those who want a calmer float can put in upriver at the Warden Bridge to float eight miles of the Gros Ventre River to the boat launch at Lower Slide Lake.

SNAKE RIVER CANYON

With easy access along U.S. Highway 89, 25 miles south of Jackson, the Class III+ Snake River jounces through steep-walled **Snake River Canyon** (also called Hoback or Alpine Canyon). It's one of the classic day trips for white water, but don't expect wilderness; its popularity can line the river length with boats and crowd parking areas at put-ins and take-outs. From the put-in at West Table southwest of Hoback Junction, the white-water section runs 7.4 miles to the Sheep Gulch take-out. You'll hit rapids such as Double D, Haircut Rock, Blind Canyon, and Big Kahuna. Several surf waves provide play boat places for kayakers, but there are also several rapids where rafts frequently flip the unskilled and unwary. A trail above Big Kahuna allows faster access to the big waves for play boating and river surfing. Spring high water can increase the difficulty of this classic rafting river; the river is usually runnable May-September. Easier float sections are upriver from West Table.

A detailed description of the rapids is available from **American Whitewater** (www. americanwhitewater.org), with information on put-ins, take-outs, and river permits from Bridger-Teton National Forest (www.fs.usda. gov/btnf). For diehard boaters who want repeated days, several Forest Service campgrounds are in the canyon.

GUIDES

Whitewater trips (eight miles, mid-May-late Sept., $72-88 adults, $60-84 kids 6 and older) through Snake River Canyon take four hours round-trip from Jackson. Smaller rafts (6-8 people) give more splash, while large rafts can fit up to 10-16 people; small rafts are at the upper end of the rate scale. Forest Service fees may not be included in the rates; inquire before booking. Most companies have 4-5 departures daily for white-water trips; full-day trips start with floating and end with the white water. Scenic floats and trips with meals (breakfast, lunch, or dinner) are also available. Photographers are stationed on the river and can provide photos (for a fee).

Bridger-Teton National Forest licenses all the commercial trips on the Snake River. All rafting companies run the same trips. Four companies operate out of Jackson: **Barker-Ewing Whitewater** (945 W. Broadway, 307/733-1000 or 800/448-4202, www.barker-ewing.com), **Mad River Boat Trips** (1255 S. Hwy. 89, 307/733-6203 or 800/458-7238, http://mad-river.com), **Dave Hansen Whitewater** (225 W. Broadway, 307/733-6295 or 800/732-6295, www.davehansenwhitewater.com), and **Jackson Hole Whitewater** (650 W. Broadway, 307/733-1007 or 888/700-7238, http://jhww.com).

Fishing

Fly-fishing anglers gravitate to Jackson Hole for trout fishing, especially for fine-spotted cutthroat trout in the **Snake River** (year-round), south of Grand Teton National Park. Dry-fly fishing is best in early spring and after the waters clear in mid-July. Anglers must use catch-and-release tactics. Fishing in the **Gros Ventre River** comes on in early July and runs through August above Lower Slide Lake. In late summer, the river dries up below Kelly.

Anglers must buy a Wyoming state **fishing license** (https://wgfd.wyo.gov, residents: $3 youth annual, $6 adults daily, $24 adults annual; nonresident: $15 youth annual, $14 adults daily, $92 adults annual).

GUIDES AND EQUIPMENT

For beginners, **Jackson Hole Fly Fishing School** (445 Wister Ave., Jackson, 307/699-3440, www.jhflyfishingschool.com) can teach the basics of casting, mending, and reeling in fish. They offer a 90-minute introductory class ($90 adults, $70 kids), a half-day floating school ($140 adults, $100 kids), and half-day stream fishing ($425 for two people). They also have a two-day Orvis school.

In Jackson, you can stop in the shops of multiple anglers to book trips: **Reel Deal Anglers** (2070 Cedar Loop, 307/739-7020, www.reeldealanglers.com), **Snake River Angler** (185 Center St., 307/733-3699, http://snakeriverangler.com), **Jackson Hole Anglers** (90 Montana Rd., 307/690-5717, http://jacksonholeanglers.com), and **Fish the Fly** (7255 N. Spring Gulch, 307/690-1139, www.fishthefly.com).

Grand Fishing Adventures (Teton Village, 307/734-9684, www.grandfishing.com, $450 half day, $575 full day) offers guided fishing trips, floats, and lessons in Jackson Hole and runs a fly shop out of Teton Village Sports.

Fishing **guides** (daily May-Oct., $425-450 half day, $525-550 full day for two people) abound in Jackson Hole for wade-fishing or float-fishing. Float trips can take a maximum of two anglers per boat and guide. Full-day trips often include lunch.

Swimming

The **Teton County Recreation Center** (155 E. Gill St., Jackson, 307/739-9025, www.tetonparksandrec.org, 6am-8pm Mon.-Fri., noon-8pm Sat., noon-7pm Sun. year-round, $7 adults, $5-6 kids and seniors) has a swimming pool with a waterslide and waterfall, fitness facilities, and locker rooms with showers. Call to confirm hours for lap swimming or open swim.

THRILL SPORTS

In summer, **Snow King Mountain** (330 E. Snow King Ave., Jackson, 307/733-5200, http://snowkingmountain.com, daily late May-early

Sept.) turns into a play zone for families. The miniature golf course has 18 holes with fun obstacles. A pair of parallel alpine slides offers families the opportunity to race each other down the mountain (although the slides must close during rainstorms), and the mountain coaster offers a descent on a track. A bungee trampoline gets kids airborne, and the Treetop Adventure Park gives aerial thrills. **Baux Park** (10 E. Snow King Ave., Jackson) has climbing walls.

Jackson Hole Mountain Resort (3265 W. Village Dr., Teton Village, 307/739-2779 or 307/739-2654, www.jacksonhole.com, daily late May-early Oct.) also caters to families with thrill sports. The Aerial Adventure Course drapes trees with a maze of ziplines, cargo nets, balance beams, and different levels of challenges. A bungee trampoline offers flying thrills, and the family can play a nine-hole, 3,150-foot-long disc golf course, or climb on the climbing tower. Buy tickets in the Bridger Center.

GOLF AND TENNIS

North of the National Elk Refuge, **Jackson Hole Golf and Tennis Club** (5000 Spring Gulch Rd., Jackson, 307/733-3111, www.jhgtc.com, daily early May-mid-Oct., $65-185) is an 18-hole course redesigned by Robert Trent Jones, Jr. It's a semi-private club, but guests can book tee times 10am-11:50am and any time after noon (book one month in advance by phone or online). Club rentals are $50, and lessons are available through the pro shop.

Teton Pines Resort and Country Club (3450 N. Clubhouse Dr., Wilson, 307/733-1005, www.tetonpines.com, daily May-mid-Oct., $65-160) is the closest golf and tennis club to Teton Village. The 18-hole semi-private golf course was designed by Arnold Palmer and Ed Seay. Nonmembers can make tee times for noon or later; a few tee times are available online, but you may have better luck by phone. Club rentals cost $50, and lessons are available from the pro shop; carts are included with fees. Tennis (307/733-9248, 8:30am-7:30pm Mon.-Thurs., 8:30am-6pm

Fri.-Sun., $13-26/person, by reservation only) aficionados can play indoors or outdoors on six hard courts and two clay courts.

WINTER SPORTS
Skiing and Snowboarding
Snow King Mountain (100 E. Snow King Ave., Jackson, 307/734-3194, http://snowkingmountain.com, early Dec.-Mar., lift tickets $48 adults, $30 juniors and seniors) is not usually a choice for diehard destination skiers and snowboarders, but families like its smaller size (400 acres), night skiing for kids, tubing, and cheaper rates.

★ JACKSON HOLE MOUNTAIN RESORT
With big vertical, steep chutes, and a reputation as a big, bad experts-only ski area, **Jackson Hole Mountain Resort** (3265 W. Village Dr., Teton Village, 307/733-2292, www.jacksonhole.com, late Nov.-early Apr., lift tickets $121 adults, $75 juniors, $98 seniors) has only 50 percent of its terrain devoted to advanced skiers and snowboarders. The rest is rolling groomers for beginners and intermediates. The resort's 4,139 vertical feet has 19 lifts spread across 2,500 acres, including the Aerial Tram that goes to the 10,450-foot summit of Rendezvous Mountain. The average year delivers 450 inches of snowfall. Lift tickets are pricey, but you often can get cheaper rates with lodging packages or online. The resort has several terrain parks, on-mountain and base area restaurants, rental shops, and lessons. The resort does not own lodging properties, but Teton Village has accommodations ranging from a hostel to luxury lodging.

Heli- and Snowcat Skiing
Heli- and snowcat skiing can rack up 12,000-15,000 vertical feet in places where you have elbow room in big bowls, glades, and steeps. **High Mountain Heli-Skiing** (Teton Village, 307/733-3274, www.heliskijackson.com, mid-Dec.-Mar., $1,200/person) has access to five mountain ranges surrounding Jackson

Hole. A trip usually gets in six runs per day. Reservations are required; sometimes you can get packages that combine a trip with lodging.

Backcountry Skiing

The Tetons are a backcountry ski mecca. Slap on a pair of skins and grab the transceiver, beacon, and probe to head out for skiing. Teton Pass, Jackson Hole Mountain Resort side country, and hike-to terrain beyond the boundaries of Grand Targhee Resort are the most popular places to go. Consult with experts at **Teton Mountaineering** (170 N. Cache Dr., Jackson, 307/733-3595, http://tetonmountaineering.com) when renting gear and check on **avalanche conditions** (Bridger Teton Avalanche Center, 307/733-2664, http://jhavalanche.org) before you go.

Cross-Country Skiing and Snowshoeing

Unfortunately, housing and hotel developments have usurped the groomed Nordic centers in Jackson Hole and Teton Village, but some of the pathways around town are groomed for skate or classic skiing. Check current grooming conditions (307/739-6789) and download online maps of groomed trails (www.friendsofpathways.org).

Any summer trail around Jackson Hole can turn into a snowshoe trail in winter. One of the most scenic places to snowshoe is on the summit of **Teton Pass.** Follow Forest Road 019 south for about three-quarters of a mile (1.5 miles round-trip); it's short but big on scenery. A trail continues from the end of the road, but you'll need avalanche gear to proceed.

GUIDES AND RENTALS

Skinny Skis (65 W. Deloney, Jackson, 307/733-6094 or 888/733-7205, www.skinnyskis.com, 9am-6pm Mon.-Sat., 10am-5pm Sun., hours vary seasonally, $15-25/day) rents snowshoes and general touring, metal-edge touring, and skate-ski packages. The shop also waxes and tunes skis.

Hole Hiking Experience (Jackson, 866/733-4453, www.holehike.com, daily in winter, $75-175/person) guides half-day to full-day cross-country ski trips and snowshoe tours (2-6 hours), plus combination programs of hikes mixed with wildlife-watching or other activities.

Snowmobiling

Snowmobile routes tour the Gros Ventre Mountains. A unique trip goes to the **Granite Hot Springs** (20 miles round-trip, early Dec.-early Apr.) in Bridger-Teton National Forest. The tour follows snow-buried Granite Creek Road (Forest Rd. 30500) up Granite Creek to the hot springs. The route is suitable for beginning snowmobilers. **Togwotee Adventures** (1050 S. Hwy. 89, Jackson, 307/733-8800, www.togwoteesnowmobile.com) guides snowmobile tours to the Gros Ventre Mountains, Togwotee Pass, Granite Hot Springs, and Yellowstone.

Snowmobile rentals are available at **Leisure Sports** (1075 S. Hwy. 89, Jackson, 307/733-3040, www.jacksonholefun.com, 8am-5:30pm daily) and **Jackson Hole Adventure Rentals** (1060 S. Hwy. 89, Jackson, 307/733-5678 or 877/773-5678, http://jhadventure.com, 8am-5pm daily Nov.-Mar., 9am-6pm daily Apr.-Oct.). Snowmobiles run about $135-175 per day; winter gear costs $5-20 per item. Trailers are also available.

Ice-Skating

A free outdoor ice rink operates at the Town Square in Jackson. **Grand Teton Skating Association** (noon-8pm daily mid-Dec.-Feb.) runs the rink. Skate rentals ($5) are available. **Snow King Sports** (100 E. Snow King Ave., 307/201/1633, https://snowkingsec.com, daily mid-Oct.-Mar., $8 adults, $6 kids) has indoor public skating (noon-2pm) and open hockey (10:15am-11:30am, $10).

Tubing

King Tubes (Snow King Mountain, 100 E. Snow King Ave., Jackson, 307/734-9442, http://snowkingmountain.com, 2pm-7pm Tues.-Fri., 11am-7pm Sat.-Sun. early

Dec.-Mar., $20 adults, $15 kids for one hour, $5 each hour thereafter) requires no skill on the snow to have some fun sliding. A rope tow pulls you and your tube up a hill where you can then sail downhill.

Winter Sleigh Rides

In Teton Village, **Teton Village Sleigh Rides** (307/733-2674, www.tetonvillagetrail-rides.com, daily in winter, $35/person) operates horse-drawn sleigh rides from the corral across the street from Snake River Lodge. Rides depart three times each evening (5pm, 6pm, and 7pm). Reservations are a good idea.

Dogsledding

Dogsled tours (late Nov.-early Apr.) take place on the fringes of Jackson Hole and require longer drives or shuttles to reach their locations. Reservations are required, with pickups available in Jackson.

Jackson Hole Iditarod Sled Dog Tours (307/733-7388 or 800/554-7388, http://jhsled-dog.com) runs full-day and half-day trips up Granite Canyon in Bridger-Teton National Forest. The company is owned by eight-time Iditarod veteran Frank Teasley.

Entertainment and Shopping

NIGHTLIFE
Jackson

Most of the nightlife in Jackson takes place in venues surrounding Jackson Town Square. Top stop is the **Million Dollar Cowboy Bar** (25 N. Cache St., 307/733-2207, www.mil-liondollarcowboybar.com, 11am-2am daily year-round), crowned with its neon cowboy on a horse. The bar is decked out with knobbled-pine trim, silver coins inlaid in the bar, saddles with saddle blankets as stools, cowboy murals, wildlife mounts, and western artifacts. It's a place to shoot pool, and live music makes patrons take to the dance floor. The beer is made by Grand Teton Brewing Company; Jack Daniel's whiskey comes by the barrel. The Million Dollar Cowboy Steakhouse (307/733-4790, www.cowboyste-akhouse.net) downstairs serves western food.

The **Rose** (50 W. Broadway, 307/733-1500, http://therosejh.com, 5pm-2am daily), a partner of the Pink Garter Theatre, serves specialty cocktails, modern drinks, and upscale versions of well drinks. A menu of small plates complements the cocktails, as does the swanky vibe.

The **Silver Dollar Bar** (50 N. Glenwood St., 307/733-2190 or 800/322-2727, www.worthotel.com, 11am-2am), at the landmark Wort Hotel, mixes an authentic historic western ambience of oil paintings, murals, and bronzes with live entertainment. The bar counter is inlaid with 2,032 uncirculated silver dollars from 1921. Music plays four nights weekly on Tuesday (with bluegrass from local One Ton Pig), Thursday, Friday, and Saturday.

Part of the nightlife buzz around Jackson Town Square, the **Pink Garter Theatre** (50 W. Broadway Ave., 307/733-1500, www.pink-gartertheatre.com) hosts visiting bands—from hip-hop to string—in the standing-room-only venue, as well as films with full seating. The **Jackson Hole Center for the Arts** (265 Cache St., 307/734-8956, www.jhcenterforth-earts.org) houses a 500-seat theater that hosts concerts, plays, ballets, film tours, and other performances.

Located near the Jackson Town Square, the **Jackson Hole Playhouse and Saddle Rock Saloon** (145 W. Deloney Ave., 307/733-6994, www.jacksonplayhouse.com, $20-33 shows, $38-60 with dinner) puts on nightly theater performances in summer, fall, and late winter; summer usually features classic Broadway musicals. **Off Square Theatre Company** (240 S. Glenwood St., 307/733-4900, www.offsquare.org) stages four musicals and plays annually, put on by local actors at the Jackson Hole Center for the Arts and other locales in town.

Jackson Hole Cinemas (307/733-2939, www.jacksonholecinemas.com) runs three theaters in Jackson. Flicks show year-round at **Jackson Hole Twin Cinema** (295 W. Pearl St.) and **Movieworks Cinema** (860 S. Hwy. 89). The historic **Teton Theatre** (120 N. Cache St., 307/733-4393) shows movies in summer only.

Teton Village

The **Mangy Moose Saloon** (3200 W. McCollister Dr., 307/733-4913, http://mangymoose.com, 11am-close daily late May-early Oct. and Nov.-mid-Apr.) has an après-ski saloon vibe. Drink local microbrews next to the namesake mangy moose, order a spicy margarita made with jalapeños, and rock to live music. Loud, and at times raucous, the bar frequently makes the list of top après-ski bars in the country. It's located at the base of Jackson Hole Mountain Resort.

Jackson Hole Mountain Resort (3265 W. Village Dr., 307/733-2292 or 888/333-7766, www.jacksonhole.com) sponsors free family concerts around 5pm on Sunday in summer. Food and drink from local vendors is sold.

FESTIVALS AND EVENTS
Spring

In the early 1950s, elk antlers were used to build the first arch in the Jackson Town Square. Boy Scouts began collecting the antlers in the late 1950s; a decade later, they started the annual **Boy Scout Antler Auction** (Jackson Town Square, www.fws.gov/refuge/National_Elk_Refuge, May). Commonly known as Elkfest, the event takes place the Saturday before Memorial Day weekend. Registered bidders can purchase elk antlers collected from the National Elk Refuge; 75 percent of the proceeds go back to the refuge.

Summer

The **Jackson Hole Rodeo** (Teton County Fairgrounds, 447 Snow King Ave., Jackson, 307/733-7927, www.jhrodeo.com, 8pm-10pm Wed. and Fri.-Sat. late May-early Sept., $15-30) offers a chance to see local cowboys and cowgirls in action; events include bronc and bull riding, roping, and barrel racing. Kids can participant in a calf scramble to nab a ribbon off the tail of a calf. Three types of seating are available in the grandstands: reserved, general admission that is covered, and general admission that is not covered. Be prepared for rain, or book a covered seat. Tickets are available online (discounts in advance); print the tickets or put them on your cell phone to avoid the ticket lines at the rodeo grounds. Arrive at 7:15pm to claim a seat in the general admission zones.

For 10 days, the **Teton County Fair** (Teton County Fairgrounds, 447 Snow King Ave., Jackson, 307/733-5289, www.tetonwyo.org/fair, 8pm-midnight mid-July) hosts carnival rides, rodeos, farm animal shows, pig wrestling, food booths, and other county fair fun.

The **Grand Teton Music Festival** (Walk Festival Hall, 3330 Cody Ln., Teton Village, 307/733-1128, http://gtmf.org, July-mid-Aug., $10-55) draws musicians and conductors from top symphonies across the country and soloists from around the world. Concerts run five nights weekly. Single tickets go on sale in March (online or by phone) and are available in person at the box office (10am-5pm Mon.-Sat.) in late June.

Fall

For 11 days, Jackson is home to the **Jackson Hole Fall Arts Festival** (locations vary, Jackson, 307/733-3316, www.jacksonholechamber.com, mid-Sept.), which features about 50 events that highlight western, wildlife, Native American, and landscape works from nationally and internationally known artists. Music, food, and wine events take place throughout town and at local ranches; gallery walks tour downtown exhibitions. Some events are free; others charge a fee.

Winter

As Wyoming's Iditarod, the **International**

the International Pedigree Stage Stop Sled Dog Race

Mountain, 100 E. Snow King Ave., Jackson, 307/734-9653, www.snowdevils.org, 8am-6pm late Mar., $15). Crowds show up to watch the carnage as snowmobiles race up 1,500 vertical feet that steepens to 45 degrees. Those who fail roll back down the slope.

SHOPPING
Jackson

Shopping ranges from art galleries and outdoor shops to bookstores. More than 25 art galleries cluster in town, providing a combination of fine, western, Native American, and modern art in a variety of mediums. Most of the galleries are located in the few downtown blocks surrounding the Jackson Town Square. **Jackson Hole Gallery Association** (http://jacksonholegalleries.com) organizes art walks and has a list of the galleries online with a map.

Several galleries around Jackson Town Square sell handmade jewelry, woodcarvings, furniture, bronze sculptures, photography, and crafts from local artisans and internationally acclaimed artists. For traditional and innovative regional Western art, visit **Horizon Fine Art Gallery** (30 King St., 307/739-1540, www.horizonfineartgallery.com, 10am-6pm Mon.-Sat., 11am-5pm Sun.), **Mountain Trails Gallery** (155 North Center St., 307/734-8150, www.mtntrails.net, 10am-9pm daily, shorter hours in winter), **West Lives On Gallery** (75 N. Glenwood St., 307/734-2888, www.westliveson.com, 9am-6pm Mon.-Sat., 10am-6pm Sun.), and **Wild Hands** (265 W. Pearl Ave., 307/733-4619, www.wildhands.com, 10am-8pm Mon.-Fri., 10am-6pm Sun.). **Cayuse Western Americana** (255 N. Glenwood St., 307/739-1940, www.cayusewa.com, 10am-6pm Mon.-Wed., 10am-7pm Thurs.-Sat., 10am-4pm Sun.) is the place to go for antique cowboy items and Native American art.

Valley Book Store (125 N. Cache Dr., 307/733-4533, www.valleybookstore.com, 9am-8pm Mon.-Sat., 10am-6pm Sun.) is an independent bookstore that carries a good collection of field guides, trail guides, and

Pedigree Stage Stop Sled Dog Race (Jackson Town Square, Jackson, www.wyomingstagestop.org, late Jan.-Feb.) pits sled dogs and mushers in an eight-stage race across 350 miles through several states. Starting in downtown Jackson, this two-mile race leads through town as dogs pull mushers on sleds through streets lined with onlookers. The public can meet teams in the morning; festivities launch the event and take place around Jackson Town Square. The party continues at Snow King Mountain, with fireworks and a torchlight parade.

Jackson Hole Winterfest (locations vary, 307/733-3316, www.jacksonholechamber.com, mid-Feb.) is a 10-day festival that pulls together all kinds of winter activities: cutter races, ski joring, snowmobile races, Nordic races, ski and snowboard events, and concerts.

The whine of snowmobiles fills Jackson for four days in late March when the Jackson Hole Snow Devils put on their annual **Snowmobile Hillclimb** (Snow King books about the region, national parks, natural history, and recreation. The store also carries books by local authors.

Jackson has multiple outdoor shops. **Skinny Skis** (65 W. Deloney Ave., 307/733-6094 or 888/733-7205, www.skinnyskis.com, 9am-7pm Mon.-Sat., 9am-6pm Sun.) sells cross-country skate and classic ski gear, snowshoes, clothing, wax, and accessories. **Hoback Sports** (520 W. Broadway, 307/733-5335, www.hobacksports.com, 10am-6pm daily) carries downhill skis, snowboards, mountain bikes, and accessories. For hiking, fishing, skiing, snowboarding, and camping gear, go to **JD High Country Outfitters** (50 E. Broadway, 307/733-3270, http://jdhcoutfitters.com, 10am-6pm daily). **Stio** (10 E. Broadway, 307/201-1890, www.stio.com, 10am-7pm daily) carries outdoor mountain clothing for hiking, climbing, skiing, snowboarding, or bicycling. You can also buy recycled gear through **Headwall Recycle Sports**

(520 S. Hwy. 89, 307/734-8022, http://headwallsports.com, 9am-6pm Mon.-Sat.); they carry outdoor gear for hiking, camping, skiing, snowboarding, and biking. **Teton Mountaineering** (170 N. Cache St., 307/733-3595 or 800/850-3595, http://tetonmountaineering.com, 9am-6pm Sun.-Thurs., 9am-7pm Fri.-Sat.) is one of the oldest mountaineering shops in Jackson.

Wilson

Wilson Backcountry Sports (1230 Ida Ln., 307/733-5228, www.wilsonbackcountry.com, 10am-6pm Mon.-Fri., 10am-pm Sat.) is the place to go for backcountry skis and mountain, hybrid, and road bicycles.

Teton Village

In Teton Village, stores are geared toward ski and snowboard shops in winter and hiking in summer. **Teton Village Sports** (3285 W. Village Dr., 307/733-2181, www.

Cowboy Attire

While photos of Jackson Hole show plenty of cowboy hats, you don't have to own a cowboy hat to visit Wyoming, attend a rodeo, or walk into the Million Dollar Cowboy Bar. In fact, you don't even have to buy one as a souvenir. But if you want to go cowboy or cowgirl, check out the hats at **Jackson Hole Hat Company** (45 W. Deloney St., Jackson, 307/733-7687, www.jhhatco.com, 10am-6pm Mon.-Sat., noon-5pm Sun.). The company hand-makes custom hats and sells other famous brands. If you want the total cowboy look with hat and boots, head to **Stone's Mercantile** (80 W. Broadway, Jackson, 307/733-3392, www.stonesmercantile.com, 10am-6pm Mon.-Sat., 11am-5pm Sun.), where you can also tack on a belt buckle and other western accessories. The **Boot Barn** (840 W. Broadway, Jackson, 307/733-0247, www.bootbarn.com, 9am-8pm Mon.-Sat., 11am-6pm Sun.) has the biggest selection of boots, hats, and western garb, but it's also a chain store found in about half the states in the United States.

Cowboy culture flavors Jackson Hole, but most people wear casual modern outdoor clothing with a few plaid flannel shirts thrown in here and there. With the exception of upscale restaurants, you'll see people walk into cafés, brewpubs, restaurants, and bars while wearing ski clothing and snow boots in winter and hiking boots and gear in summer. After all, Jackson Hole is all about the mountain outdoors.

Folks dress in layers to adapt to the changeable weather that can happen during one day. Rain shells double as wind protection, especially in spring and fall. Gloves and hats protect extremities from frostbite or just getting cold. Even in summer, rain shells, layers, hats, and gloves may be necessary when a cold front blows in. That gear can also work in winter with the addition of warmer layers underneath. Jeans or Carhartts are also ubiquitous, especially for indoor activities, dining, and some outdoor activities such as horseback riding. But jeans soak up water from rain or snow like a sponge. For the wetter, colder seasons and summer hiking, quick-dry layers and rain pants will better protect you from the elements.

tetonvillagesports.com, 8am-6pm daily) carries high-quality outdoor clothing, Jackson Hole Mountain Resort logo wear, and outdoor gear for skiing, snowboarding, and hiking. MADE (Hotel Terra, 3335 Village Rd., 307/690-2896, www.madejacksonhole.com, 10am-6pm daily) carries the handcrafted art of 125 local and regional artists.

Accommodations

Visitors to Jackson Hole have considerable lodging choices. Jackson has moderate to inexpensive lodging, chain hotels, historic inns, and a handful of higher-end properties. Teton Village has the only remaining hostel in the valley, but mostly offers upscale and luxury lodges. In Jackson, rates are highest in summer, second-highest in winter; lower-priced seasons are spring and fall. Teton Village has the highest rates in winter, with summer the second-highest.

Most lodging in Jackson Hole is open year-round. Lodging in Teton Village generally has two seasons: late November-early April and early May-October. Guest ranches are only open in summer. Count on more amenities: Air-conditioning, wireless Internet, and televisions are common.

Two booking agencies are available for all kinds of lodging. **Jackson Hole Central Reservations** (888/838-6605, www.jacksonholewy.com) books hotels, condos, and inns in Jackson, Teton Village, and Jackson Hole. They often have seasonal travel packages that bundle up airfare, lodging, and sometimes activities. **Jackson Hole Resort Lodging** (307/733-3990, www.jhrl.com) rents condos, townhomes, and vacation homes. For vacation rentals, check on www.VRBO.com or **Jackson Hole Reservations Company** (800/329-9205, www.jacksonhole.net) for condos and luxury homes.

JACKSON

Staying in downtown Jackson offers a compact town where you can walk from lodging to restaurants, shopping, activities, and nightlife. To the west of town is a strip with motels that are beyond walking distance for many, but you can hop the START bus to downtown. Prices for familiar chains will be higher due to the resort nature of the town. Rates listed are from the lowest off-season to highest summer prices.

Hotels

Two boutique hotels offer unique lodging. ★ **Rusty Parrot Lodge** (175 N. Jackson St, 307/733-2000 or 888/739-1749 or 800/458-2004, www.rustyparrot.com, $300-760) has 32 luxury rooms. Rooms with a king bed or two queen beds feature high-end linens and amenities; some come with fireplaces, two-person whirlpool tubs, and sitting areas. The lodge is home to the full-service Body Sage Spa and offers fine dining in the Wild Sage Restaurant. The historic ★ **Wort Hotel** (50 N. Glenwood St, 307/733-2190 or 800/322-2727, www.worthotel.com, dates vary seasonally, $180-700) is the place to stay if you like character. The 59 rooms come in nine different styles with one king or two queen beds (or a mix of beds). Suites include sitting areas, two rooms, or theme decor. The Wort is also home the famous Silver Dollar Bar, which rocks with live music Tuesday, Friday, and Saturday nights.

Two other upscale hotels come with extras. **The Lodge at Jackson Hole** (80 Scott Ln., 307/739-9703 or 800/458-3866, www.lodgeatjh.com, $130-380) has 154 mini-suites. Large suites feature one king or two queen beds, plus sitting areas with sofa sleepers, rain showers in the bathrooms, and electronic hubs. The hotel includes the Jackson Hole Spa, indoor and outdoor heated pools, hot tubs, sauna, fitness center, and restaurant. The three-story **Wyoming Inn of Jackson Hole** (930 W. Broadway, 307/734-0035,

the Wort Hotel

www.wyominginn.com, $130-350) conveys Wyoming style with a stone fireplace, wood carvings of bighorn sheep at the check-in desk, saddle-leather couches, and a moose paddle chandelier in the lobby. Rooms have one king or two queen beds and custom window seats; some have fireplaces. The hotel has an on-site restaurant that serves organic, locally sourced breakfasts, as well as a fitness room and guest laundry.

Located on the strip away from downtown, the **Pony Express** (1075 W. Broadway, 307/733-3835, www.ponyexpresswest.com, $80-280) has 24 motel rooms and condos. Rooms include one queen bed, plus a kitchen or a twin bunk; some rooms allow pets. An outdoor heated pool is open in summer, and a guest laundry is available year-round. One block south of Jackson Town Square, the **Antler Inn** (43 W. Pearl Ave., 307/733-2535 or 800/522-2406, www.townsquareinns.com, $62-300) is a two-story hotel with outdoor stairs to the 2nd floor. Their 110 rooms have two double beds, two queen beds, or one king; some have fireplaces. The motel has a 25-person indoor hot tub, sauna, guest laundry, and fitness room.

Cabins

★ **Cowboy Village Resort** (120 S. Flat Creek Dr., 307/733-3121 or 800/962-4988, www.townsquareinns.com, $95-290) has 82 log cabins and kitchenettes. Cabins have one or two queen beds (some in bunks) plus a sofa bed and small porches with picnic tables and barbecue grills. The resort has an indoor pool, hot tub, laundry, fitness center, and business center. The same owners also run the **Elk Country Inn** (480 W. Pearl Ave., 307/733-2364 or 800/483-8667, www.townsquare-inns.com, $64-280), which has 25 log cabins with pine walls. The cabins have two rooms and kitchenettes. The complex also has eight family units that have three queen beds (one in a loft).

Resort and Condos

Located within seven blocks of Jackson Town Square, Snow King Resort and Grand View Lodge are operated by the same owners and offer a resort atmosphere. Winter activities include skiing, snowboarding, tubing, ice-skating, ice climbing, and a mountain coaster, while summer has alpine slides, climbing walls, hiking, a mountain coaster, horseback riding, and kids' activities. Due to their location, both are a notch quieter than hotels in the downtown core.

The older, but revamped **Snow King Resort** (400 E. Snow King Ave., 307/733-5200, www.snowking.com, $) has hotel rooms with two queen beds and condos (1-4 bedrooms), with an outdoor pool (heated year-round), hot tub, spa, salon, fitness center, and lounge. Rooms were redecorated in 2013, but still retain older fixtures. An on-site restaurant features large windows with decks looking out at Snow King Mountain. In summer, outdoor fire pits around the pool feature lounging couches.

Located on the hill above Snow King Resort, the newer **Grand View Lodge** (537 Snow King Loop Rd., 307/734-3000 or 800/522-5464, www.grandviewjacksonhole. com, $) has one- or three-bedroom upscale condos units with access to all the resort amenities.

Bed-and-Breakfast

Sitting adjacent to Flat Creek, the **Inn on the Creek** (295 N. Millward St., 307/739-1565, www.innonthecreek.com, $140-350) has two types of rooms. Jacuzzi Fireplace Rooms have a king or queen bed, while Creek Side Rooms have a queen bed and sitting area. A full breakfast is served in the breakfast room, in bed, or to-go for hitting the road early. Summer guests can lounge on the creek-side patio.

TETON VILLAGE

Teton Village is the resort complex at the base of Jackson Hole Mountain Resort. It is home to upscale and luxury hotels, a hostel, and a couple of mid-range hotels. Most hotels cluster around the base of the chairlifts, gondola, and Aerial Tram; for summer travelers, the lure is the village's one-mile proximity to Grand Teton National Park.

Peak season includes July, August, and winter holidays, when prices are highest and reservations are necessary 6-12 months in advance. Some hotels offer seasonal lodging

and activity packages. Most offer ski-and-stay packages in winter and summer activity packages.

Resorts and Lodges

The ★ **Four Seasons Resort** (7680 Granite Loop Rd., 307/732-5000, www.fourseasons.com/jacksonhole, May-Oct. and late Nov.-early Apr., $490-800) is the only Five Diamond, Five Star resort in Wyoming. It's a classy place with a professional, friendly atmosphere where casual outdoor attire is the norm. The layout of the resort's 156 guest rooms follows the contours of the mountain, yielding the atmosphere of a smaller, more intimate hotel.

Spacious guest rooms face the mountain, valley, or resort; most rooms have mountain or valley views. Rooms feature a gas fireplace, sitting area, and two double beds or one king; one-bedroom suites have a king and sofa bed. Concierge and valet services deliver seamless experiences for skiing and snowboarding in winter (they'll even put your ski boots on for you) and biking and hiking in summer. Naturalist activities take place in summer and winter. Outdoor pools and three hot pools offer fun for kids and adults. Clusters of outdoor fire pits complement the mountain scenery.

The Four Seasons houses the Westbank Grill, The Handle Bar, a spa, and a fitness facility with yoga classes, and offers ski and bike rentals. Guests can walk out the back door to the ski lifts (it's the closest hotel to the lifts). The hotel also caters to families, with child care, baby amenities, and a Kids Club.

Two hotels, owned by Noble House, sit adjacent to each other within a few minutes' walk from the Aerial Tram. Both have rooftop pools and hot tubs with big mountain scenery. They also manage multiple private luxury residences that have access to the hotel amenities.

★ **Teton Mountain Lodge** (3385 Cody Ln., 307/732-6865 or 855/318-6669, www.tetonlodge.com, $220-590 rooms, $1,300-2,400 residences, open year-round) turns mountain-style modern in its high-ceiling lobby. Hotel rooms include one king or queen bed or two double beds. Alpine Studios feature kitchens and gas fireplaces and have a Murphy queen bed; one-, two-, and three-bedroom suites have a king or queen bed or two double beds in separate bedrooms and a Murphy queen bed or sofa bed in the living room. On-site amenities include concierge services, Solitude Spa, Spur Restaurant, a fitness center with yoga classes, and indoor and outdoor pools.

Hotel Terra (3335 W. Village Dr., 307/739-4055 or 855/318-8707, www.hotelterrajack-sonhole.com, $250-600 rooms, $650-3,000 residences, open year-round) combines an urban indoor look with eco-features. The LEED-certified construction uses recycled products, water conservation, and low energy use systems. Hotel rooms have one king bed or two queens. Studios feature wall beds, and one-, two-, or three-bedroom suites come with full kitchens and gas fireplaces. All bathrooms have rain showers and air tubs. The hotel houses the Chill Spa, Terra Cafe, Il Villaggio Osteria, two hot tubs, and an outdoor infinity pool.

Wooden bear sculptures greet guests at the **Snake River Lodge** (7710 Granite Loop Rd., 307/732-6070 or 855/342-4712, www.snakeriverlodge.com, May-Oct. and late Nov.-early Apr., $200-700 rooms, residences $1,800-2,300), which has hotel rooms, one-bedroom suites, 2-3-bedroom residences with kitchens, and penthouse units. Some rooms have fireplaces and balconies, but few have mountain views. Most rooms have one king or two queen beds; some residences and penthouses have rooms with two twin beds for kids. The lodge has a restaurant, ski valet, spa, fitness room, and the Backcountry Adventure Center concierge for wildlife safaris, the Junior Ranger Program, stargazing, gear rentals, evening naturalist programs, and reservations for outdoor recreation. The heated pool is swim-through indoor-outdoor; indoor and outdoor hot tubs are landscaped with waterfalls.

Teton Club (3340 W. Cody Ln., 307/734-9777, www.tetonclub.com, year-round, $450-2,000) has two- and three-bedroom luxury residences with gas fireplaces, balconies, laundry machines, and gourmet kitchens. Minimum stays of 4-5 days are required, but you don't have to be a member to stay here.

Four Seasons Resort

stairs. Amenities include a heated outdoor pool, hot tub, and breakfast.

Hostel

The Hostel (3315 Village Dr., 307/733-3415, www.thehostel.us, year-round) has guest rooms that were renovated in 2011 and include private king or quad rooms ($80-120 summer and winter, $45-70 spring and fall) and male, female, or co-ed bunkrooms ($34-40 summer and winter, $20-28 spring and fall). Each room has a private bathroom and shower. Amenities include a washer, dryer, ski wax room, ski and board storage, and recreation room with refrigerator, microwave, freezer, and toaster. Pets are permitted for a fee.

JACKSON HOLE

Scattered across the valley floor of Jackson Hole are guest ranches, resorts, and cabins. Some sit between Teton Village and Jackson; others claim unique viewpoints.

Resort

Perched on East Gros Ventre Butte, the **Amangani** (1535 NE Butte Rd., Jackson, 307/734-7333, www.amanresorts.com, year-round, $900-1,800) offers prime views of the Tetons from floor-to-ceiling windows in common areas and outdoor decks, pools, and patios. Sumptuous guest suites feature stone and wood styling, king beds, sitting areas, spacious bathrooms, and balconies to enjoy the views of the Tetons or Jackson Hole. The dining room serves breakfast, lunch, and dinner with a commanding view of the mountains. There is also a lounge, art gallery, library, and outdoor pool and hot tub.

Cabins

Located between Teton Village and Wilson, **Fireside Resort** (2780 N. Moose Wilson Rd./ Hwy. 390, Wilson, 307/733-1177 or 877/660-1177, www.firesidejacksonhole.com, year-round, $225-500) has 23 modern and compact cabins with fireplaces, kitchenettes, private decks, and bathrooms with glass showers. Rather than the traditional log cabin look,

The Hostel in Teton Village

Hotels

Sitting adjacent to the Aerial Tram, **Alpenhof Lodge** (3255 W. Village Dr., 307/733-3242, www.alpenhoflodge.com, mid-May-Oct. and late Nov.-early Apr., $200-600) is one of the original hotels at Jackson Hole Mountain Resort. The 42-room hotel was modeled after Swiss chalets in the alps, with small and cozy rooms featuring one queen bed, mid-size rooms with a king or two doubles, or large spacious suites that have fireplaces, decks, or Jacuzzi tubs. The hotel has a heated outdoor pool, hot tub, bistro, bar, and the Alpenrose restaurant, which specializes in traditional fondues. Breakfast is included in the rates.

In a revamp of what was once a chain hotel, **The Inn at Jackson Hole** (3345 W. Village Dr., 307/733-2311 or 800/842-7666, www.innatjh.com, mid-May-Oct. and late Nov.-early Apr., $210-310) offers a combination of hotel rooms and suites. Rooms include one king or two queen beds; suites feature kitchenettes, fireplaces, sofa beds, and one and two bedrooms or loft bedrooms accessed by circular these modular cabins look like mini Frank Lloyd Wright structures and are sided with barn wood. Two cabin styles sleep 4-6 people: The basic one-bedroom has a king or queen bed, plus a sofa bed sleeper or an additional loft for twin beds. Front decks have picnic tables, grills, and fire pits. Three-night minimum stays are required. Pets are allowed for a fee.

Bed-and-Breakfasts

Three B&Bs are located in Wilson, where you may see a moose saunter through the yard. Two-night minimum stays are usually required, especially in peak season; check out options for shorter stays. Most charge additional fees for more than two people in a room.

Tucked into aspens, conifers, and native gardens, the **Wildflower Inn** (3725 Shooting Star Ln., Wilson, 307/733-4710, www.jacksonholewildflower.com, year-round, $280-410) is a romantic log inn on three acres. The inn has five guest rooms, each named after native wildflowers, with private baths and a queen or king bed. Some rooms can accommodate a child with a day bed. Common rooms include a living room, solarium, dining room, and several decks. Breakfast includes fresh fruits, baked breads, and hot entrées.

The **Bentwood Inn** (4250 Raven Haven Rd., Wilson, 307/739-1411, www.bentwood-inn.com, year-round, $275-400) is a rustic log inn with five guest rooms in a wooded setting. Western decor fills the inn and guest rooms. Four rooms have king beds; the Bunkhouse works for families, with a queen bed, a nook bed, and a ladder-accessed loft with twin beds and a skylight. The inn serves a full hot breakfast and evening hors d'oeuvres with wine.

With a covered deck soaking up views of the Tetons, the **Teton View B & B** (2136 Coyote Loop, Wilson, 307/733-7954, www.tetonview.com, late May-Oct., $200-350) offers four guest rooms, an indoor whirlpool tub, and a large outdoor hot tub. Three rooms have queen beds; two of the larger rooms include queen futon couches for additional

guests. A one-bedroom cabin includes a kitchen, one queen bed, a double futon couch, and twin trundle beds. Breakfast features a hot entrée, fresh fruit, and sides.

Guest Ranches

Jackson Hole is home to oodles of guest ranches, all of which are centered around horseback riding. Activities also include fishing, rafting, hiking, and kids' stuff.

With panoramic views of the Teton Mountains from its perch 1,000 feet above the valley floor, **Spring Creek Ranch** (1800 Spirit Dance Rd., Jackson, 307/733-8833 or 800/443-6139, www.springcreekranch.com, year-round, $200-720/night rooms, townhomes, and cabins; $1,800-2,600/night mountain villas) offers an upscale cowboy experience. Lodging is in rooms in rustic cabins, townhomes, or four-bedroom and four-bath mountain villas. Amenities notch the resort up with an indoor hot tub, outdoor heated swimming pool, tennis courts, full-service spa, and the four-star Granary Restaurant. Wildlife safaris provided by the ranch staff depart year-round; ranch naturalist programs run all season. In summer, the ranch leads horseback trail rides and dinner rides. Activities cost extra.

At the 325-acre **R Lazy S Ranch** (7800 Moose Wilson Rd., Teton Village, 307/733-2655, http://rlazys.com, mid-June-late Sept., $1,670-2,460/person/week) on Grand Teton National Park's southern boundary, you feel like you're off in your own world. The ranch accommodates up to 45 guests in 12 log cabins; most sleep 2-4 people, but a few can sleep six. Rates include lodging, meals, and activities such as horseback riding and instruction, waterskiing on Jackson Lake, and fishing. Meals are a combination of dining in the lodge, cookouts, and buffets. The ranch also provides quick access to neighboring Teton Village.

Remote **Flat Creek Ranch** (1 Upper Flat Creek Rd., Jackson, 307/733-0603, www.flatcreekranch.com, June-early Oct., $2,400-6,300/person/stay) requires a four-wheel-drive vehicle to handle the 15 miles of bumpy back road across the National Elk Refuge to get there. Or take the optional ranch shuttle and get dropped off to hike in to the ranch. Five renovated, historic log cabins each has a bedroom, living room, private bath with clawfoot tub, wood-burning stove, and porch. Solar rays power the electricity. Activities include horseback riding, fishing, hiking, canoeing, and kayaking. Meals feature gourmet meats and fresh produce from the ranch garden. Inclusive packages are for three, four, or seven nights, with summer stays at peak rates.

Camping

Jackson Hole has only a few private campgrounds, but national forest campgrounds are in the surrounding mountains. In midsummer, reservations are a must for campgrounds that accept them. While many of the national forest campgrounds are attractions in their own right, they can also serve as backup when the national park campgrounds fill up.

JACKSON AND VICINITY

There are three private campgrounds in and around Jackson; each has sites with full hookups (water, sewer, electricity), picnic tables, flush toilets, showers, drinking water, laundries, camp stores, and wireless Internet. Rates are usually for 2-4 people ($8 each extra person, kids under 6 free).

The **Virginian RV Park** (750 W. Broadway, Jackson, 307/733-7189 or 800/321-6982, http://virginianlodge.com, May-mid-Oct., $80) offers RVers a place to stay one mile from downtown. The campground is part of the Virginian Lodge, a motel complex with a restaurant, saloon, liquor store, hair salon, and heated outdoor pool and hot tub. The parking-lot-style campground has 103 sites; RVs are limited to 40 feet. Reservations are in demand since this is the only campground in town.

Located five miles south of Teton Village, **Jackson Hole Campground** (behind Fireside Resort, 2780 N. Moose-Wilson Rd., Wilson, 307/732-2267, www.jacksonhole-campground.com, mid-Apr.-Nov., $80-125 RVs, $50-60 tents) squeezes 63 grassy sites under mature cottonwoods and conifers; larger RVs may feel cramped by low branches and narrow slots. Open campsites grab prime views of the Tetons. Facilities include a disposal station. During the ski season, the resort also can accommodate small RVs (by reservation).

Located 12 miles south of Jackson on U.S. Highway 26/89/189/191 (almost to Hoback Junction), the **Snake River Park KOA** (9705 S. Hwy. 89, Jackson, 307/733-7078 or 800/562-1878, www.srpkoa.com, mid-Apr.-Nov., $40-90 RVs, $28-45 tents) is a combination campground and white-water rafting outfitter on the Snake River. Tucked into a deep and narrow canyon, the campground squeezes between the busy two-lane highway (rumbling with commercial haul trucks) and the Snake River. The 10 tent sites sit along Horse Creek and the river, and are held for river rafters in midsummer. The 47 back-in RV sites line up in parking-lot fashion, with mowed lawns between sites; RVs are limited to 30 feet. Stairs lead from the campground to the sandy riverbank. Amenities include fire rings with grills, a game room, firewood for sale, playground, and pet walk. Campers get 10 percent off white-water rafting trips or saddle and paddle trips. A corral is across the street from the campground.

Bridger-Teton National Forest

In **Bridger-Teton National Forest** (Jackson Ranger District, 25 Rosencrans Ln., Jackson, 307/739-5400, www.fs.usda.gov/btnf, late May-Sept.), several **first-come, first-served** national forest campgrounds are located in the Gros Ventre Mountains, east of Grand

Teton National Park or south of Jackson. Facilities typically include picnic tables, fire rings with grills, drinking water, bear boxes, and vault toilets.

For boaters, **Atherton Creek Campground** (20 sites, $12) is the place to go. Sites are strung around interconnected loops on a sunny hillside of aspens and conifers above Lower Slide Lake. Sites 16 and 17 sit on the water, while sites 18 and 20 overlook the water; other campsites have no lake views. A boat dock and ramp aids launching onto the lake for fishing, paddling, windsurfing, waterskiing, or boating. Amenities include tent platforms and campground hosts. To reach the campground, take the Gros Ventre River Road north of Kelly. Turn east onto Gros Ventre Road for 5.5 miles of bumpy, but paved road to the campground entrance on the right. If Atherton fills up, you can continue another 4.5 miles up Gros Ventre Road to **Crystal Creek Campground** (7 sites, $10), tucked on a trout-fishing stream. The quiet, older campground rarely fills and only fits smaller RVs.

The drive to **Curtis Canyon Campground** (1 site, $12) takes advantage of million-dollar views. At 7,000 feet on the east side of Jackson Hole, an overlook takes in the Jackson Hole valley, National Elk Refuge, and the Teton Mountains. The campground sits across the road in a small forest with one campsite (small RVs only) claiming the million-dollar view. To find the campground, drive the gravel National Elk Refuge Road north for 4.6 miles. Turn right onto Curtis Canyon Road for 2.6 miles to climb to the campground entrance on the right. Curtis Canyon Road is narrow, rocky, and has one sharp hairpin turn.

South of Jackson at Hoback Junction, multiple Forest Service campgrounds line the Snake River. **East Table** (20 sites, $15), **Station Creek** (16 sites, $15), and **Wolf Creek** (20 sites, $15) Campgrounds flank the white-water rafting section of the river. Eastward from Hoback Junction, along U.S. Highway 191 up the Wild and Scenic Hoback River, are **Hoback** (14 sites, $15) and **Kozy** (8 sites, $12) Campgrounds, highway roadside camps with fishing. **Granite Creek Campground** (51 sites, $15), near Granite Hot Springs, is 11 miles north of U.S. Highway 191 on Granite Creek Road (Forest Rd. 30500).

Food

Jackson Hole is a culinary treat. While many restaurants lean heavily toward Wyoming bison, game, and fish, innovative cuisine is common. Even the meat-heavy menus have yummy vegan, vegetarian, or gluten-free alternatives. In summer and winter, make reservations for dinner or you may have a very long wait.

JACKSON

Most restaurants and cafés are open year-round; some shorten hours or days in spring, fall, and winter. Expect meal prices to be high (due to Jackson's resort town status), but not as high as in Teton Village.

Cafés

★ **Persephone Bakery** (145 E. Broadway, 307/200-6708, http://persephonebakery. com, 7am-6pm Mon.-Sat., 7am-5pm Sun., $3-12) churns out rustic artisan breads and crispy pastries—classic croissants, brioche, and scones. Stop in for a baked treat with an espresso or unique meals such as the small herbed omelets with sweet potato and Brussels sprout hash. Breakfast toast and lunch sandwiches come on their bread. Soups include a coq au vin stew. The tiny bakery café serves breakfast until 3pm and lunch 10:30am-3pm.

Tucked into a historic log cabin with indoor and outdoor seating, **Café Genevieve** (135 E.

Persephone Bakery

Broadway, 307/732-1910, https://genevievejh.com, 8am-close daily) serves up southern- and south-of-the-border-influenced foods such as fried chicken and crawfish. Breakfast (8am-3pm, $8-14) includes waffles or eggs Benedict with house-made Cajun sausage or smoked salmon. Lunch (11am-3pm, $11-15) features sandwiches, burgers, and salads. Happy hour drinks (3pm-5:30pm) and appetizers fill in before dinner (5pm-close, $22-38) brings on an eclectic mix of meats, noodle bowls, fish, and Italian dishes.

American

People drive miles to get **MacPhail's Burgers** (399 W. Broadway, 307/733-8744, http://macphailsburgers.com, 11:30am-9pm Mon.-Sat., $13-30). The restaurant builds burgers with ingredients created fresh daily. They grind their own beef, bake their own buns, and cut their own fries. Burgers include buffalo burgers and beef burgers in lettuce wraps

for those who don't want the buns. Top it off with a shake, malt, beer, or wine.

Fine Dining

In a small old house, the **Blue Lion** (160 N. Millward St., 307/733-3912, http://bluelion-restaurant.com, 5:30pm-10pm daily, $22-40) specializes in fish, meats, and wine. It's the place to get an elk tenderloin, rack of lamb, or rainbow trout. It also has chicken and pasta dishes, some of which can be made vegetarian or vegan. Finish off the feast with the house mud pie. In a modern sleek restaurant, the **Kitchen** (155 Glenwood St., 307/734-1633, www.thekitchenjacksonhole.com, 5:30pm-close daily, $16-32) has modern plates with a twist of comfort food. The menu mixes highbrow foods with unique twists on fish, duck, pork and sides; or simply order pot roast and cheeseburgers. The Crudo Bar has unique fish appetizers.

At Spring Creek Ranch outside town, **The Granary** (1800 Spirit Dance Rd., 307/732-8112, www.springcreekranch.com, 7am-9pm daily year-round) has one of the best dining locations in the valley from on top of Gros Ventre Butte. High-ceiling windows take in the Teton Mountains, which make the best times for dining around sunrise or sunset. The seasonal menu revolves around eggs Benedict for breakfast (7am-11am, $12-20) and elk, bison, or fish for dinner (5pm-9pm, $27-45).

International

For classic Indian cuisine with tandoori chicken, curries, masalas, and lamb vindaloo, head to **The Indian** (165 Center St., 307/733-4111, www.theindianjh.com, noon-3pm and 5pm-9:30pm Mon.-Fri., 5pm-9:30pm Sat., $11-22). Some dishes can be made vegan; others are gluten-free. Lunch has an abbreviated menu, while dinner expands with more entrées plus starters of daal, raita, naan, and appetizers. Indian cocktails are made, too. **Lotus Café** (145 Glenwood St., 307/734-0882, www.tetonlotuscafe.com, 8am-9pm daily, $7-12) serves vegan, gluten-free, dairy-free, organic, all-natural, and local foods for breakfast (8am-2:30pm), lunch, and dinner. Get smoothies, extracted juices, house-baked breads, egg-white breakfasts, organic tofu, kale, fresh greens, grass-fed beef, Asian soups, tacos, and noodle or rice bowls. Ten-inch pizzas come out after 4pm, and you can get a kids' menu, beer, wine, and cocktails. **Thai Me Up** (75 E. Pearl, 307/733-0005, www.thaijh.com, 5pm-10pm daily, $10-15) combines a nano-brewery with noodles, curry, and rice dishes.

Steakhouse

Across the street from the Jackson Town Square, **Local** (55 N. Cache St., 307/201-1717, http://localjh.com, 11:30am-close daily) opened in 2012. Lunch ($10-17) is served until 2:30pm, and dinner ($18-44) starts at 5:30pm, but you can get appetizers and small plates in between. This chef-owned restaurant serves up local and regional fare: beer, wine, spirits, cheeses, steaks, lamb, and baked goods. Creative steaks and fish are one of the hallmarks of the **Snake River Grill** (84 E. Broadway, 307/733-0557, http://snakeriver-grill.com, 5:30pm-10pm daily, $22-40), artfully presented and cooked to perfection. For a lighter dinner, share several of their small plates, Kobe beef first course, or Alaskan crab claws.

Tapas and Small Plates

At ★ **Bin 22** (200 W. Broadway, 307/739-9463, www.bin22jacksonhole.com, 11:30am-10pm Mon.-Sat., 3pm-10pm Sun., $8-15), you'll think you're in a wine shop . . . which you are. Walk through the cases of wine to the back where delightful tapas and small plates are served with wines and craft beers. Choose a spot at the bar, outside on the patio, or at one of several big, shareable tables with stools that foster conversations between strangers. Tasty small-plate entrées are made to share: pancetta-wrapped dates, house-pulled mozzarella, and several Spanish dishes, with enough variety and substance to turn the whole dining

Bin 22

adventure into a full long, leisurely meal over wine.

Cookouts

Reservations are required for all cookouts. Reaching the **Bar T 5 Cookout** (812 Cache Creek Dr., 307/733-5386 or 800/772-5386, www.bart5.com, 4:30pm-5pm or 6pm-6:30pm departures Mon.-Sat. mid-May-Sept., $45 adults, $37 kids) requires riding two miles in a covered wagon from Jackson to Cache Creek. Once there, cowhands cook the all-you-can-eat meal of Dutch-oven roast beef under an outdoor pavilion. After dinner, the Bar T 5 band plays western music before guests ride the covered wagons back to town.

Located in Wilson (about 10 minutes from downtown Jackson), the **Bar J Chuckwagon** (4200 W. Bar J Chuckwagon, 307/733-3370 or 800/905-2275, www.barjchuckwagon.com, 7pm daily Memorial weekend-Labor Day, 7pm Mon.-Sat. Labor Day-late Sept., $24-30 adults, $12 kids) serves a mass western dinner for 750 people in cattle-call fashion. The gates open at 5:30pm with pre-dinner wagon rides, shopping in the western village, and Dutch-oven biscuits. Claim your own seat for the barbecued beef, chicken, ribs, or steak dinner with sides. The Bar J Wranglers do a western show with a combo of twangy music and cowboy stories.

Groceries

Jackson has multiple supermarkets. **Jackson Whole Grocer** (1155 S. Hwy. 89, 307/733-0450, http://jacksonwholegrocer.com, 7am-10pm daily) has the biggest selection of fresh, local, and organic produce. For upscale market items, check out the **Pearl Street Market** (40 W. Pearl St., 307/733-1300, www.pearlstmarketjh.com, 7am-7pm Mon.-Fri., 8am-7pm sat.-Sun.). Heading north out of Jackson toward Grand Teton National Park, you can stop at **Creekside Market** (545 N. Cache Dr., 307/733-7926, 7am-8pm Mon.-Fri., 7am-5pm Sat.-Sun.).

TETON VILLAGE

Most restaurants in Teton Village are open **late November-early April** and **mid-May-late September** in conjunction with Jackson Hole Mountain Resort lift operations. Only a few are open year-round. Make reservations for dinner; otherwise, you are guaranteed a long wait.

Café

Stop in the **Terra Cafe** (Hotel Terra, 3335 W. Village Dr., 307/739-4100, www.hotel-terrajacksonhole.com, 7am-11am daily) for espresso drinks with to-go breakfasts and pastries.

American

Steaks, meat, fish, burgers, and bison (this is Wyoming, after all) are served at several casual and family-friendly Teton Village restaurants that also have broad menus for light dining or multi-course meals. In summer, restaurants offer patio seating. The **Spur Restaurant and Bar** (Teton Mountain Lodge, 3385 Cody Ln., 307/732-6932, www.

tetonlodge.com, 7am-10pm daily year-round, hours shorten in spring and fall) serves a breakfast buffet (7am-10am, $17 adults, $10 kids), lunch (11:30am-5:30pm, $13-30), dinner (5:30pm-10pm, $15-42), and has a kids' menu. House specialties include charcuterie of local cheeses and meats, buffalo short ribs braised in the locally brewed Zonker Stout, and Snake River Farms Kobe steaks. The cocktail menu has fun finds and innovative shared plates for après-ski or hiking.

A longtime ski area classic, the **Mangy Moose Restaurant** (3295 Village Dr., 307/733-4913, www.mangymoose.com, 5:30pm-10pm daily mid-May-Oct. and late Nov.-early Apr., $15-40) has grown over the years from its roots next to the party-hard après-ski bar (the famous saloon across the hall in the same building). The two-story restaurant is adorned with funky ski and western relics. The menu serves up steaks, prime rib, Idaho rainbow trout, and elk chops. Go to the saloon for lunch (11am-5pm) and its signature spicy margarita; live music cranks up most evenings.

In a casual beer-hall atmosphere with outdoor terrace seating in summer and winter, **The Handle Bar** (Four Seasons, 7680 Granite Loop Rd., 307/732-5000, www.fourseasons.com/jacksonhole, 11am-11pm daily May-Oct. and late Nov.-early Apr., $12-40) is a modern take on an American pub. Sit in the restaurant, at the bar, or on the terrace flanked with gas flames in winter and enjoy views up to the summit of Rendezvous Mountain. The diverse menu features fish and chips, burgers, and sammies for lunch and steaks and fish for dinner. If you aren't walking or skiing to the pub, complimentary valet parking is available from the front of the Four Seasons.

International

An expansion from the original restaurant in Driggs, Idaho, ★ **Teton Thai** (7342 Granite Loop Rd., 307/733-0022, http://tetonthaivillage.com, 11:30am-9:30pm Mon.-Sat. summer, 11:30am-9pm Mon.-Sat. winter, closed spring and fall, $10-18) serves classic recipes

A Guide to Local Goodies

Snake River Brewing

For tasty local brews, try:

- **Snake River Brewing** (265 S. Millward, Jackson, 307/739-2337, www.snakeriverbrewing.com): This brewpub staple whips up award-winning pale ale, lager, and Zonker Stout along with a host of specialty brews.

- **Roadhouse Brewing** (2550 Moose-Wilson Rd., Wilson, 307/739-0700, www.roadhouse-brewery.com): The brewery and restaurant offers with hefty tastes of their Sweet Potato Porter, Brain Dead Double IPA, and Beautiful Buzz Espresso Stout.

- **Jackson Hole Brewing** (307/413-5459, www.jacksonholebrewingco.com): Find the few beers, such as Static Peak Stout, crafted by this brewery in local watering holes.

- **Grand Teton Brewing** (430 Old Jackson Hwy., Victor, ID, 888/899-1656, www.grandteton-brewing.com): Grand Teton Brewing's signature year-round brews include Old Faithful Ale, Howling Wolf hefeweizen, and Bitch Creek ESB, named for the creek on the Teton's west side.

- **Wildlife Brewing** (145 S. Main St., Victor, ID, 208/787-2623, http://wildlifebrewing.com): This Teton Valley staple puts out the Mighty Bison Brown Ale, Buckwild Double Blonde, and Ale Slinger IPA.

Espresso shops abound, as do cafés that serve lattes and cappuccinos. Local roasters include:

- **Jackson Hole Roasters** (50 S. Broadway, Jackson, 307/200-6099, www.jacksonholeroasters.com)

- **Cowboy Coffee Company** (125 N. Cache St., Jackson, 307/733-7392, http://cowboycoffee.com)

- **Elevated Grounds** (3445 N. Pines Way #102, Wilson, 307/734-1343, http://elevatedgroundscoffeehouse.com)

- **Snake River Roasting** (3610 S. Park Dr., Jackson, 307/734-9446, www.snakeriverroastingco.com, online only)

Satisfy that sweet tooth with these local faves in Jackson.

- **Moo's Gourmet Ice Cream** (110 Center St., Jackson, 307/733-1998, www.moosjacksonhole.com)

- **Cocolove** (55 N. Glenwood, Jackson, 307/733-3253) sells gelato and boutique chocolates.

from Bangkok—from pad Thai to roasted duck curry. Many dishes can be made vegan or vegetarian, and multiple curries can be customized for spiciness (and they can do HOT!). Beer, wine, sake, and specialty cocktails are available. The restaurant is located near Ranch Lot. Locals avoid waiting in lines by ordering take-out.

★ **Il Villaggio Osteria** (Hotel Terra, 3335 W. Village Dr., 307/739-4100, www.jhosteria. com, 5:30pm-close daily year-round, $8-32/ course) brings Italy to the Wyoming slopes with house-made pastas and an atmosphere that rings true to a bustling Italian eatery. The menu contains classic, but fresh takes on antipasti, seasonal ensalata, primi pastas, secondi, and wood-fired pizza. The salumi bar serves up imported hand-sliced meats and cheeses, and the wine list fills with flavors from the Italian countryside, plus American vineyards.

The **Alpenrose** (Alpenhof Lodge, 3255 W. Village Dr., 307/733-3242, www.alpenhoflodge.com, 5:30pm-close daily mid-May-Oct. and late Nov.-early Apr., $21-34) serves Swiss-German specialties that include raclette, schnitzel, sauerbraten, and strudel. Fondues serve multiple courses: meats, seafood, cheese, and chocolate. For a more casual version, try lunch (11:30am-3pm, $10-20) or dinner (6pm-9pm, $12-24) in the **Alpenhof Bistro,** with deck dining in summer.

Fine Dining

For gourmet dining overlooking the ski slopes, the ★ **Westbank Grill** (Four Seasons, 7680 Granite Loop Rd., 307/732-5000 or 307/732-5156, www.fourseasons.com/jacksonhole, 7am-11am and 6pm-10pm daily May-Oct. and late Nov.-early Apr., $34-56) combines professional service and knowledgeable sommeliers who can advise wine pairings with dinner. It's a romantic place for sinking into a leisurely multi-course dinner: appetizers, wine, entrées, and finishing with dessert. As a steakhouse, the grill serves regional Waygu beef and succulent game such as buffalo, elk, wild boar, and duck, all with choices of sauces. For diners coming by car, the resort has complimentary valet service. Breakfast and a children's menu are available.

Jackson Hole Mountain Resort

Jackson Hole Mountain Resort (307/739-2675, www.jacksonhole.com) operates several on-mountain eateries accessed via lifts. Reached via Aerial Tram at the top of Rendezvous Mountain, tiny **Corbet's Cabin**

Corbet's Cabin

(9am-4pm daily late May-early Oct. and late Nov.-early Apr., $7) serves waffles. (It's more about the fun of eating waffles at 10,440 feet rather than views or exceptional food.) The **Couloir Restaurant and Bar** (seatings at 5:45pm-6:15pm and 7:45pm-8:15pm daily late June-early Sept., Fri.-Sun. only in winter, $95-155) takes advantage of the views from 9,095 feet with huge windows overlooking Jackson Hole and the Gros Ventre Mountains. Dining is a four-course affair, or you can opt for drink specials, shared plates, and appetizers on the summer-only deck (starting at 4:30pm). Reach the Couloir via the Bridger Gondola.

The **Jackson Hole General Store** (307/732-4090, www.jacksonhole.com, 8am-5pm daily late May-early Oct. and late Nov.-early Apr.), located adjacent to the Aerial Tram, has coffee and ice cream.

Groceries

Teton Village has several small markets, but prepare for resort prices that are higher than at home. The cheaper markets are in Jackson. The **Mangy Moose Market and Cellars** (3200 W. McCollister Dr., 307/734-0090 or 307/734-0070, www.mangymoose.com, 10am-10pm daily late May-early Oct. and late Nov.-early Apr.) is the largest in Teton Village.

Transportation and Services

DRIVING

Driving in Jackson Hole is all on two-lane roads, with a handful of short stretches with four lanes around Jackson. From Jackson, it's 7 miles west to Wilson and 12 miles northwest to Teton Village. Highway 26/89/191 runs from Jackson north to Grand Teton National park, reaching the Moose Entrance in 13 miles and the Moran Entrance in 30 miles. From Jackson, Highway 189 travels 13 miles south to Hoback Junction while Highway 22 crosses Teton Pass to Teton Valley, Idaho. The town of Victor appears in 25 miles; Driggs is in 33 miles (Hwy. 33 in Idaho).

Access to the Gros Ventre Mountains is via Forest Service roads around Jackson. Most are two-lane dirt or gravel roads; no one road tours the Gros Ventres.

Parking in Jackson is difficult. To head downtown to the Town Square, shopping, restaurants, and nightlife, walk from your hotel or hop the START bus. It's far easier, especially if you drive a big RV. Parking at Teton Village is in four pay lots (late Nov.-early Apr., $10-15/day) during the winter ski season. Overnight guests get free parking through their lodges. **Gas** stations are located in Jackson, Wilson, and Teton Village.

Car Rental

Car rentals are available through three agencies at Jackson Hole Airport: **Avis** (307/733-3422 or 800/831-2847, www.avis.com), **Hertz** (307/733-2272 or 800/654-3131, www.hertz.com), and **Enterprise** (307/733-7066 or 800/261-7331, www.enterprise.com). Five more rental agencies are in Jackson: **Dollar** (307/733-9224, www.dollar.com), **Thrifty** (307/734-8312 or 800/367-2277, www.thrifty.com), **National** (307/733-0671 or 800/227-7368, www.nationalcar.com), **Alamo** (307/733-0671 or 800/327-9633, www.alamo.com), and **Leisure Sports** (307/733-3040, www.leisuresportsadventure.com).

AIR

Jackson Hole Airport (JAC, 1250 E. Airport Rd, Jackson, 307/733-7682, www.jacksonhole-airport.com) is actually inside Grand Teton National Park, just north of Jackson. If the Tetons and Jackson Hole are your destination, fly in here. The airport also is easy for accessing Yellowstone's South Entrance. Three airlines service Jackson Hole: United, Delta, and American. Fifteen flights or more have direct service to the airport from Washington DC, Newark, Atlanta, Chicago, Minneapolis, Salt Lake City, Denver, Dallas-Fort Worth, Houston, Seattle, Los Angeles, and San Francisco. Many flights run seasonally in winter or summer, and flights to Jackson Hole are usually more expensive than to other area airports. Taxis meet all flights.

Airport Transportation

AllTrans shuttles (307/733-3135 or 800/443-6133, www.jacksonholealltrans.com, daily June-Sept. and Dec.-Mar., $16-29/person one-way) meet all incoming and outgoing flights at Jackson Hole Airport. Shuttles link the airport to the town of Jackson or Teton Village. Round-trip tickets can save a few dollars. In spring and fall, shuttles are by reservation only (7pm on the day before your arrival or departure). If you make reservations earlier, call 24 hours ahead to reconfirm your reservations. A winter shuttle (by reservation only) runs from Jackson Hole Airport to Grand Targhee Resort. In summer, AllTrans runs daily shuttles from the Jackson Hole Airport to all lodges in Grand Teton National Park ($35-50/person).

Mountain States Express (800/652-9510, www.mountainstatesexpress.com, $75/person) also runs daily shuttles to and from the Salt Lake City, Utah, airport. The connection between Salt Lake City and the town of Jackson takes about five hours. **Salt Lake Express** (800/356-9796 or 208/656-8824, www.saltlakeexpress.com) services go between Salt Lake City Airport and Jackson, Wyoming, or West Yellowstone, Montana. Some of the destinations on this service are limited to summer months.

More than 15 taxi companies operate in southern Jackson Hole. Costs vary depending on distance; for 1-2 people from the airport to Jackson costs $35-40 and to Teton Village costs $60. Add on $7-10 per person for extra riders. Four limo services also operate around Jackson. Find a complete list of taxi and limo companies online (www.jacksonholeairport.com).

BUS

Teton County runs a public bus system that allows visitors to travel around southern Jackson Hole. The Southern Teton Area Rapid Transit, or **START** (www.startbus.com, daily year-round), schedules change seasonally. Buses within the downtown core of Jackson run about every 30 minutes (6am-10pm daily, free). Buses connections between Jackson, Wilson, and Teton Village run at varied intervals (5am-11:30pm daily, $1-8 one-way). Be sure to have the exact fare in cash; drivers do not carry change. Maps and route schedules are available online.

Save yourself the nasty winter drive over Teton Pass with the **Targhee Express** (AllTrans, 307/733-3135 or 800/443-6133, www.jacksonholealltrans.com, daily in winter, $54 round-trip), the express bus from Jackson and Teton Village to Grand Targhee Resort in the Teton Valley. Departure times vary (7am-7:50am) depending on pickup location. The bus arrives in Grand Targhee around 9:15am and departs the ski resort at 4pm with arrival back in Teton Village or Jackson by 5:30pm-6pm. Skiers and snowboarders can buy a combination round-trip bus ticket with a lift ticket for the day ($100). Make reservations at least one day in advance.

SERVICES

Post offices are located in **Jackson** (220 W. Pearl St., 7:30am-5pm Mon.-Fri.; 1070 Maple Way, 8:30am-5pm Mon.-Fri., 10am-1pm Sat.), **Wilson** (5605 W. Hwy. 22, 8:30am-5pm Mon.-Fri., 10am-noon Sat.), and **Teton Village** (3230 McCollister Dr., 9:30am-12:30pm and 1pm-4pm Mon.-Fri., 9:30am-12:30pm Sat.).

ATMs are common in Jackson and Teton Village, available in many hotels and at banks in Jackson. In Jackson, the **Broadway Laundry** (850 W. Broadway, 307/734-7627, daily year-round) has coin-op machines. For showers in Jackson, head to the **Teton County Recreation Center** (155 E. Gill St.,

307/739-9025, www.tetonparksandrec.org, 6am-8pm Mon.-Fri., noon-8pm Sat., noon-7pm Sun. year-round, $7 adults, $5-6 kids and seniors). The center has a swimming pool, fitness facilities, and locker rooms with showers; a day fee gets you access to all of it. In Teton Village, The Hostel (3315 Village Dr., 307/733-3415, www.thehostel.us, year-round, $5) allows non-lodgers to stop in for showers.

Media and Communications

Cell phone service is ubiquitous in Teton Village, Jackson, and Teton Valley. However, service will be interrupted in the surrounding mountains. Most hotels in Jackson and Teton Village have wireless Internet. Jackson also has several coffee shops and cafés with Internet access. In Jackson, Teton County Library (125 Virginian Ln., 307/733-2164, http://tclib.org) has free Internet access.

The local newspaper is the *Jackson Hole News and Guide* (www.jhnewsandguide.com). *Planet Jackson Hole Weekly* (http://planetjh.com) contains events, music, art, and entertainment around town.

Emergency Services

The closest medical facility is St. John's Medical Center (625 E. Broadway, Jackson, 307/733-3636, www.tetonhospital.org). For other emergencies, contact the Jackson Police Department (150 E. Pearl Ave., Jackson, 307/733-2331, http://townofjackson.com) or Teton County Sheriff Office (180 S. King St., Jackson, 307/733-4052, www.tetonsheriff.org). For national forests, contact Jackson Ranger District, Bridger-Teton National Forest (25 Rosencrans Ln., Jackson, 307/739-5400, www.fs.usda.gov/btnf).

Teton Valley

Many people visiting Grand Teton National Park and Jackson Hole assume that the Teton Valley is just another name for Jackson Hole. After all, the valley sits below the Tetons. But Teton Valley is on the less-traveled west side of the Teton Mountains. Dotted with tiny towns like Victor and Driggs in Idaho (bedroom communities for the high-priced Jackson Hole), Teton Valley accesses wilderness areas and Caribou-Targhee National Forest, which flanks the west side of the Teton Mountains and Grand Teton National Park. Teton Pass connects Jackson Hole to the Teton Valley.

SIGHTS
★ Teton Pass

Driving up Teton Pass is one of the steepest climbs in the country, ascending at a 10 percent grade in places. The road curls around the 8,431-foot summit at the southern tip of the Teton Mountains. From Jackson, the curvy route to the summit ascends 11 miles west along Highway 22, then drops about 12

miles to Victor, Idaho. On the east side, a few pullouts offer views that span Jackson Hole with the Snake River curving through its bowels and backdropped by the Gros Ventre Mountains. On the west side of the pass, the road (now Highway 33) follows the headwaters of the Teton River through a forested canyon of Caribou-Targhee National Forest. While the road is open year-round, it frequently closes in early mornings in winter for avalanche control work. Drive Teton Pass both directions, as the views are different.

Teton Valley Geotourism Center

The Teton Valley Geotourism Center (60 S. Main St., Driggs, ID, 208/354-2607, http://tetongeotourism.us, 9am-5pm Thurs.-Tues. summer; hours vary seasonally; free) has interpretive and interactive displays on winter activities, snow science, cultural history, Native American heritage, and summer activities. Information is available on camping,

Teton Valley

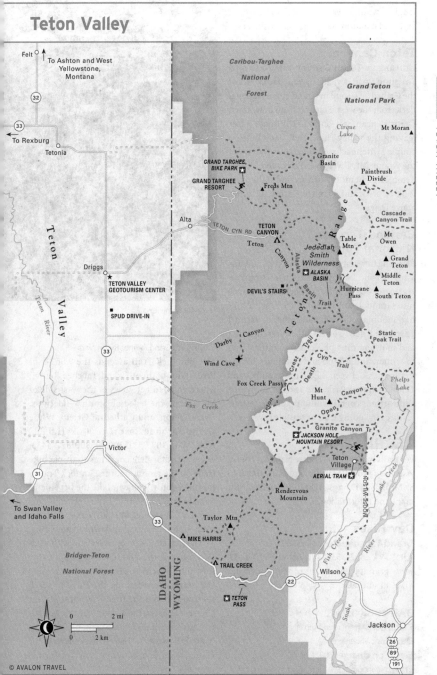

Felt

To Ashton and West Yellowstone, Montana

32

33

To Rexburg

Tetonia

Caribou-Targhee

National

Forest

Grand Teton

National Park

Cirque Lake

Mt Moran

Granite Basin

Paintbrush Divide

GRAND TARGHEE BIKE PARK

GRAND TARGHEE RESORT

Freds Mtn

Alta

TETON CYN RD

TETON CANYON

Teton

Cascade Canyon Trail

Table Mtn

Mt Owen

Grand Teton

Middle Teton

South Teton

Jedediah Smith Wilderness

ALASKA BASIN

DEVIL'S STAIRS

Hurricane Pass

Teton

Valley

Teton River

Driggs

TETON VALLEY GEOTOURISM CENTER

SPUD DRIVE-IN

33

Darby

Canyon

Wind Cave

Fox Creek Pass

Fox Creek

Canyon

Alaska Basin Trail

Teton Range

Static Peak Trail

Crest Trail

Death

Cyn

Trail

Teton

Canyon Tr

Mt Hunt

Open

Phelps Lake

Victor

Granite Canyon Tr

JACKSON HOLE MOUNTAIN RESORT

Teton Village

AERIAL TRAM

Rendezvous Mountain

MOOSE WILSON RD

Lake Creek

31

To Swan Valley and Idaho Falls

Taylor Mtn

MIKE HARRIS

TRAIL CREEK

33

Bridger-Teton

National Forest

IDAHO

WYOMING

22

Fish Creek

Wilson

TETON PASS

Snake

River

Jackson

26

89

191

0   2 mi

0   2 km

© AVALON TRAVEL

lodging, wildlife-watching, activities, events, and road conditions.

Teton Canyon

Cruising up **Teton Canyon** toward **Grand Targhee Resort** yields in-your-face views of the Cathedral Group in Grand Teton National Park from the west. Starting from downtown **Driggs,** head east on Ski Hill Road. After leaving the valley floor, the road climbs a couple switchbacks with eastward views of the Grand, Mt. Owen, Nez Perce, and Middle Teton. In eight miles, turn around at the overlook or at Grand Targhee Resort, 12 miles above Driggs.

Caribou-Targhee National Forest

Flanking the west side of the Teton Mountains and Teton Valley, **Caribou-Targhee National Forest** offers a backside entrance into Grand Teton National Park, with hiking, mountain biking, and camping. **Grand Targhee Resort** offers lift-accessed skiing and snowboarding plus cross-country skiing in winter, and hiking and mountain biking in summer. Between the ski resort and Grand Teton National Park, the **Jedediah Smith Wilderness** contains unique karst limestone features including trail-accessible caves.

RECREATION

For trails in Caribou-Targhee National Forest, visit the **Teton Basin Ranger District** (515 S. Main St., Driggs, ID, 208/354-2312) for maps and information.

Day Hikes

Grand Targhee Resort (3300 Ski Hill Rd., Alta, WY, 307/353-2300 or 800/827-4433, www.grandtarghee.com) offers guided day hikes in summer.

BANNOCK TRAIL
Distance: 6.4 miles round-trip
Duration: 4 hours
Elevation change: 2,002 feet
Effort: strenuous

Teton Canyon views

Trailhead: Grand Targhee Resort plaza

The Bannock Trail ascends the 9,862-foot Fred's Mountain at Grand Targhee Resort, where you can get views of the west side of Mt. Moran, the Jedediah Smith Wilderness, Grand Teton, and Cathedral Group. While **Grand Targhee Resort** (3300 Ski Hill Rd., Alta, WY, 307/353-2300 or 800/827-4433, www.grandtarghee.com) has multiple bike trails on the mountain, the Bannock Trail is for hikers only. You can take the lift (10am-5pm daily late June-mid-Sept, weekends only late Sept., $15 adults, $10 kids) either direction to cut uphill climbing or downhill pounding.

The trail climbs up open ski runs with wildflower meadows and broken forests to swing west into **Blackfoot Basin.** After crossing the basin, ascend along the ridge to reach the summit and the top of **Dreamcatcher Chairlift.** From the lift, a five-mile round-trip walk with 500 feet of climbing goes to **Mary's Saddle** for in-your-face views of the Grand Teton. Snow can cover parts of the trail into July.

Alaska Basin

★ **ALASKA BASIN**

Distance: 16.6 miles round-trip
Duration: 9-10 hours
Elevation change: 2,635 feet
Effort: strenuous
Trailhead: South Teton Canyon Trailhead at the end of Teton Canyon Road

This is the most popular hike in Caribou-Targhee National Forest, on the west side of the Tetons. The lure is Basin Lakes at 9,500 feet in elevation in Jedediah Smith Wilderness, a collection of small alpine lakes surrounded by stunning wildflower shows in August and blocky glaciated peaks along the Teton Crest. Afternoon thunderstorms are common, and the crest can often see high winds. Parts of the trail require following cairns across rock and rock-hopping to cross streams. Snow lingers until early July in the basin. No permits are required for backpacking in the wilderness.

The trail starts off deceptively easy, wandering along the **South Fork of Teton Creek** through conifers that give way to meadows, gaining 500 feet in Teton Canyon. At the junction with the **Devils Stairs Trail/Teton Shelf Trail** at 2.8 miles, the pitch catapults upward. The next miles ascend steeply to gain the remaining elevation above treeline before cresting into Alaska Basin. At the junction with the **Teton Crest Trail,** turn south and continue 0.1 mile to a junction; two forks diverge around **Basin Lakes** within 0.3 mile. These idyllic lakes have views of Mt. Meek, Buck Mountain, Veiled Peak, and Battleship Mountain. Mirror Lake is the largest of the Basin Lakes.

DARBY WIND CAVE

Distance: 5.2 miles round-trip
Duration: 4 hours
Elevation change: 1,800 feet
Effort: strenuous
Trailhead: Darby Canyon Trailhead
Directions: Go 3 miles south of Driggs on Highway 33. At 0.7 mile past the Spud Drive In, turn east onto Darby Canyon Road. Drive 3.2 miles east, turning south on Stateline Road for 0.1 mile, and then swinging left into Darby Canyon for 4.4 miles to the trailhead.

Wind Cave, tucked into 350 million-year-old dolomite, is a large cave on the west side of the Tetons. Its ceiling stretches up hundreds of feet in places, but exploring corners may force you to crawl through tight constrictions. Bring a headlamp for lighting. This trailhead is also an access for the **Teton Crest Trail**. Just above Wind Cave, Darby Ice Cave requires technical climbing gear to explore.

From the trailhead, the trail turns south to ascend the forested draw of **Darby Canyon** toward Fossil Mountain. After about one mile, the trail breaks into open meadows with views of the steep canyon walls. At the junction at 2.4 miles, continue straight on the right fork to climb up the west canyon wall to the cave.

Backpacking
ALASKA BASIN

In **Alaska Basin** (23-39 miles), backpackers can camp without a permit in the Jedediah Smith Wilderness. Make a base camp for several nights at 9,568-foot Basin Lakes. Most of the campsites (no fires allowed) tuck back from the lakeshores in spotty clumps of trees for wind protection. Plan at least three days for this trip, which allows time for a day trip north on the Teton Crest Trail to 10,338-foot Hurricane Pass (6.5 miles round-trip) in Grand Teton National Park. Schoolroom Glacier below the pass is only one of the views; for the biggest, you will stare straight at the west side of Grand Teton, Middle Teton, and South Teton peaks. Tack on another night at Basin Lakes to hike a 16.3-mile loop in the national park south via Static Peak Ridge, Death Canyon, Fox Creek Pass, Death Canyon Shelf, and Mount Meek Pass.

For shorter excursions from Basin Lakes, hike east to Static Peak Ridge (6.2-mile round-trip) or south over Meek Pass to walk Death Canyon Shelf to Fox Creek Pass (10.4 miles round-trip). Bear canisters aren't required in the wilderness, but bring them anyway; they provide easier food storage than tree hangs.

Grand Targhee Bike Park

Biking

A paved bike path runs on the old rail line between Victor and Driggs. Maps of Teton Valley biking routes and pathways are available from **Teton Valley Trails and Pathways** (http://tvtap.org).

The 104-mile **Yellowstone-Grand Teton Rail Trail** (http://tvtap.org) is a gravel and dirt old railroad bed that runs from Victor, Idaho, to West Yellowstone, Montana. As a rail trail, the riding is flat and easy, but a few sections are missing where you'll need to jump onto roads.

Habitat High Altitude Provisions (18 N. Main St., Driggs, ID, 208/354-7669, http://ridethetetons.com) carries demo and rental bikes, plus they do tune-ups. The shop also has rentals at Grand Targhee Resort.

★ GRAND TARGHEE BIKE PARK

At Grand Targhee Resort, the **Grand Targhee Bike Park** (3300 Ski Hill Rd., Alta, WY, 307/353-2300 or 800/827-4433, www.grandtarghee.com, mid-May-mid-Sept.) is becoming one of the most-lauded places to mountain bike in the Northern Rockies. Lifts service 13 miles of downhill trails, and 47 miles of cross-country multiuse single-track trails cruise through Caribou-Targhee National Forest. Targhee also has flow trails and a skills park. The park has a bike school, guided tours, women's camps, events, and rentals ($60-80). Combo bike park and lift passes cost $35 for adults and $30 for juniors. The annual **WYDAHO Rendezvous Teton Mountain Bike Festival** (http://tetonbike-fest.org, Sept.), a three-day event on Labor Day weekend, attracts about 500 riders and caps the summer ride season with group rides, clinics, trials, demos, music, food, and beer.

Golf

Targhee Village Golf Course (530 Perimeter Dr., Alta, WY, 307/353-8577, www.targheevillage.com, May-Sept., $18-24) is a nine-hole community golf course. Amenities include a small clubhouse serving food, cart rentals, and club rentals.

Winter Sports

Teton Valley Trails and Pathways (http://tvtap.org) grooms cross-country trails multiple times weekly at several locations. Maps and grooming reports are online. Use of the trails is free, but donations are appreciated.

GRAND TARGHEE RESORT

Less crowded **Grand Targhee Resort** (3300 Ski Hill Rd., Alta, WY, 307/353-2300 or 800/827-4433, www.grandtarghee.com, late Nov.-late Apr.) skis like a much bigger mountain and gains big backside views of the Grand Teton when weather permits. The resort has five lifts spread across 2,602 acres and 2,176 feet of vertical, but much of its terrain is open glade skiing, prime on powder days. Targhee is known for dry, light powder snow; the average snowfall tops 500 inches. Intermediate skiers relish the long groomer runs, and the kids' learning terrain has special kid-zone tree trails that help improve skills while having fun. **Lift tickets** ($75-80 adults, $32-37 juniors, $53-58 seniors) are more affordable. The resort also has terrain parks, rentals, lessons, naturalist programs, restaurants, hotels, and cat skiing.

Grand Targhee also has the biggest groomed Nordic ski area. Fifteen kilometers (9.3 miles) of scenic trails loop through open meadows, aspen groves, and forest. The resort has lessons in skate or classic skiing, and the ski shop rents the gear.

Snowcat Adventures (307/353-2300 ext. 1355, www.grandtarghee.com, $230-385/person) runs half-day and full-day trips where you can get 12,000-15,000 feet of vertical per day in glades and open bowls outside the lift-served terrain.

ENTERTAINMENT AND EVENTS

In a throwback to the 1950s, the **Spud Drive In** (2175 S. Hwy. 33, Driggs, ID, 208/354-2727, http://spuddrivein.com, summer) is recognizable with a huge potato on the bed of a 1946 Chevy truck. The outdoor theater is located between Victor and Driggs, and shows movies in double-feature format where you'll finish the second film around 2am. The snack bar is also a throwback to the 1950s with burgers, popcorn, and malts.

Festivals and Events

Grand Targhee Resort (3300 Ski Hill Rd., Alta, WY, 307/353-2300 or 800/827-4433, www.grandtarghee.com, $70 single day, $120-200 festival) hosts two long-running

the Spud Drive In theater in Teton Valley

music festivals each summer. The three-day **Targhee Fest** (times vary Fri.-Sun. mid-July) brings together folk musicians from across the country. For three days, the **Targhee Bluegrass Festival** (noon-11pm Fri.-Sun. mid-Aug.) attracts well-known bluegrass bands from North America. Bring a lawn chair to enjoy the outdoor venue; camping for tents or RVs is available in several parking lots. Food, drink, and retail vendors are on-site. Free buses run from Driggs to the festival site at the resort. Purchase tickets in advance for single days, all three days, for parking, and for all three days with camping.

ACCOMMODATIONS

Teton Valley offers reasonably priced, although limited, lodging and access to the west side of the Tetons through Caribou-Targhee National Forest. Some people prefer it for its less trammeled feel with more breathing space. Guest ranches, cabins, and vacation rentals range up and down Teton Valley. There are even a few chain motels (Super 8, Best Western) in Driggs.

For a quiet mountain atmosphere with expansive scenery and access to viewpoints of the Grand Teton, **Grand Targhee Resort** (3300 Ski Hill Rd., Alta, WY, 307/353-2300 or 800/827-4433, www.grandtarghee.com, mid-May-mid-Sept. and late Nov.-late Apr., $110-580) has four lodging options: economy rooms in Teton Lodge, large basic hotel rooms in Teewinot Lodge, larger studio, loft, and two-bedroom suites in Sioux Lodge, and one two-bedroom tower condo. The resort also has a restaurant, bar, fitness center, heated outdoor saltwater pool, outdoor hot tub, and activities. In winter, activities include skiing, snowboarding, cat skiing, cross-country skiing, snowshoeing, and sleigh rides. In summer, there are scenic lift rides, mountain biking, hiking, and horseback riding. Both seasons have naturalist programs.

In Driggs, **Teton Valley Cabins** (1 Mountain Vista Dr., 208/354-8153, www.tetonvalleycabins.com, year-round $70-105) takes advantage of the setting with cottonwoods and Teton views. Six small log cabins have 1-2 queen beds or bunks, and come with kitchenettes and private bathrooms. One cabin allows pets. The cabins are one mile up the road to Grand Targhee Resort.

Linn Canyon Ranch (1300 E. 6000 S., 208/787-5466, http://linncanyonranch.com, $99-185) is located in the western Teton foothills, between Driggs and Victor. A timber-frame cabin sleeps two adults or a small family and is available year round. In summer, large canvas tents (queen or king bed) have a carpeted floor with bathroom facilities in the nearby lodge. The ranch has horseback riding and pack trips in summer and sleigh ride dinners in winter.

CAMPING

On the west side of the Teton Mountains, **Caribou-Targhee National Forest** (Teton Basin Ranger District, 515 S. Main, Driggs, ID, 208/354-2312, www.fs.usda.gov/ctnf, late May-late Sept.) has four campgrounds with picnic tables, fire pits with grills, bear boxes, and vault toilets. **Reservations** (877/444-6777, www.recreation.gov) are accepted.

Two popular destination campgrounds sit east of Driggs, below the Grand Teton in Teton Canyon. A nearby trailhead serves as a leap-off point for hiking in the Jedediah Smith Wilderness and Grand Teton National Park. Located on Teton Creek 1.5 miles apart, **Reunion Flats Campground** ($12, $6 extra vehicle) has five individual sites in between large group sites, but can fit larger RVs. **Teton Canyon Campground** ($12, $6 extra vehicle) has 20 campsites, but can fit only smaller RVs. Both have drinking water.

On the west side of the Teton Mountains, climb up Teton Pass on Highway 22 from Victor to reach two roadside campgrounds. **Mike Harris Campground** (10 sites, $12, $6 extra vehicle) is 3.8 miles south of Victor, and **Trail Creek Campground** (10 sites, $10, $5 extra vehicle) is 5.6 miles south of Victor. Mike Harris has drinking water, but Trail Creek does not.

FOOD

In a cozy red house tucked off Main Street, **Pendl's Bakery Café** (40 Depot St., Driggs, ID, 208/354-5623, 7am-3pm Mon.-Fri. year-round, shorter hours Sat.-Sun., $4-12) serves espresso, crisp pastries, breakfast, and lunch. Sit indoors at the few tables in front of the wood stove, or outdoors in summer on the deck or in the yard around the fire pit.

Even in remote locations in Idaho, you can find an ethnic treat. **Teton Thai** (18 N. Main St., Ste. 100, Driggs, ID, 208/787-8424, http://tetonthai.com, 11:30am-2:30pm and 5pm-9pm Mon.-Fri., 5pm-9pm Sat. year-round, $10-18) specializes in classic dishes like pad Thai, stir-fry rice, and spicy hot curries. On the road heading up to Grand Targhee Resort, the small **Forage Bistro** (285 E. Little Ave., Driggs, ID, 208/345-2858, www.forageandlounge.com, 11am-9pm Tues.-Sun., $12-32) has a diverse menu in a European setting, with appetizers, small plates, fresh and unique salads, charcuterie, burgers, steaks, and prime rib on Sunday nights. Wine, beer, and cocktails round out the drinks.

Almost every small town in Teton Valley has a grocery. As the largest, **Broulim's Supermarket** (240 S. Main St., Driggs, ID, 208/354-2350, www.broulims.com, 7am-11pm Mon.-Sat.) carries fresh meats, produce, dairy, and baked goods, and has a deli. **Barrels & Bins Community Market** (36 S. Main St., Driggs, ID, 208/354-2307, 9am-7pm daily) is a deli and natural foods store that carries local and organic produce.

TRANSPORTATION AND SERVICES

Driving

Driggs, Idaho, is 33 miles northwest of the town of Jackson via Highway 22 (in Wyoming) and Highway 33 (in Idaho). The route from Jackson crosses the scenic **Teton Pass** (open year-round, weather dependent), reaching Victor, Idaho, in about 22 miles. From Highway 33 in Victor, Driggs is a straight shot north in about eight miles. To reach Grand Targhee in Alta, Wyoming, follow Ski Hill Road another 13 miles east. Allow at least one hour for the drive from Jackson to Driggs, and another 20 minutes if continuing to Alta, Wyoming. You can also reach Driggs from the west. The 73-mile route from Idaho Falls takes about 80 minutes. Head north on Highway 20 to Rexburg. North of Rexburg, take Exit 339 onto Highway 33 heading east. At Tetonia, the two-lane highway heads south to Driggs.

Bus

The Southern Teton Area Rapid Transit, or **START** (www.startbus.com, Mon.-Fri. year-round, schedules change seasonally, $8 exact cash fare) connects Driggs and Victor in Teton Valley with Jackson, Wyoming. Maps and route schedules are available online. Riders to Teton Village will need to debark in Wilson at the Village Road Transit Center and change to a bus going north. Two buses leave in the early morning and return in late afternoon.

Services

A **post office** (70 S. Main St., 8:30am-4:30pm Mon.-Fri., 10am-noon Sat.) is in Driggs. For emergencies, contact **Caribou-Targhee National Forest** (Teton Basin Ranger District, 515 S. Main St., Driggs, 208/354-2312, www.fs.usda.gov/ctnf, late May-late Sept.). Victor and Driggs have gas stations. The *Teton Valley News* (www.tetonvalleynews.net) is the weekly paper in Teton Valley.

Gateways

Several distinct gateways lead to Yellowstone and Grand Teton National Parks.

Big Sky, Montana, is the closest gateway to Yellowstone, with year-round access. A quick drive south reaches uncrowded trails in the park's northwest corner or the West Yellowstone entrance. In winter, the sprawling resort town attracts skiers. In summer, its upscale lodging lures vacationers.

Red Lodge, Montana serves as the eastern springboard for the most scenic drive to Yellowstone. With gray granite peaks, purple lupine, and clear shallow lakes, the Beartooth Highway climbs across high plateau to Yellowstone's northeast corner. Due to snow burying the road in winter, it is only a Yellowstone gateway late May-mid-October.

Cody, Wyoming, relishes its cowboy heritage with everything related to founder Buffalo Bill Cody. In summer, nightly rodeos and staged gunfights erupt from its Wild West roots. Seasonal routes through Shoshone National Forest reach the East Entrance of Yellowstone or the Northeast Entrance of the park. But both routes are only viable May through early November, due to snow-buried roads in winter.

In Wyoming, the Wind River Valley contains small gateway towns below the Wind River Mountains. Popping year-round over Togwotee Pass delivers stunning first images of the Teton Mountains and entrances to both national parks.

While all of the gateway towns are open year-round, heavy snow closes down access roads between some of them and the national parks in winter.

Previous: Beartooth Plateau; Rock Creek Vista Point on the Beartooth Highway. **Above:** Mesa Falls in Island Park.

Look for ★ to find recommended sights, activities, dining, and lodging.

Highlights

★ **Lone Mountain:** Ride a tram to the summit of this 11,166-foot peak, looming above Big Sky Resort (page 299).

★ **Big Sky Skiing:** Big Sky Resort offers more than 5,800 acres of skiing and snowboarding, while historic Lone Mountain grooms more than 85 kilometers (page 304).

★ **Downtown Red Lodge Historic District:** Browse this historic downtown's western storefronts (page 312).

★ **Beartooth Highway:** Drive far above tree line into alpine meadows with rugged scenery (page 312).

★ **Buffalo Bill Center of the West:** Visitors are catapulted back to the Wild West with five museums of exhibits on Native Americans, artists, natural history—and Buffalo Bill himself (page 324).

★ **Buffalo Bill Dam:** This National Civil Engineering Landmark squeezes into Shoshone Canyon (page 327).

★ **Cody Rodeo:** Experience rodeo thrills every summer night in this cowboy capital (page 332).

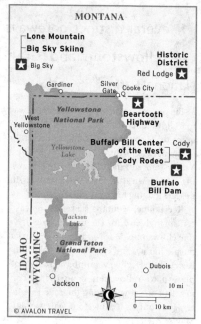

Big Sky, Montana

While Big Sky started with old Montana ranching homesteads, today it is a huge, bustling, and upscale resort below Lone Peak. Summer and winter bring on the crowds, rocketing the population from 2,500 to 10,000. Due to the proximity to Yellowstone, some visitors prefer staying at Big Sky rather than the closer West Yellowstone simply because of the ambience, luxury accommodations, and breathing room. Big Sky draws the rich and famous with lodges, vacation homes, and shopping hubs sprawled across several miles. Big Sky links to Yellowstone via U.S. Highway 191 south.

SIGHTS
★ Lone Mountain

For Montana, the 11,166-foot **Lone Mountain** isn't one of the highest peaks, but its prominence gives it stature. The old volcano that blew out its side rises more than 4,000 feet from the Big Sky valley surrounding it. From several sides, you can see its alpine zone sweep up rugged, cliff-ridden ridges to its pointed summit. Skiers and snowboarders at Big Sky Resort take the tram to the summit to ski three sides. In summer, golfers can see it while teeing off, mountain bikers can ride on it, hikers can tour its trails, photographers try to catch its sunrise light, and sightseers can ride lifts to the summit.

For adventurous sightseers, the 2.5-hour **Lone Peak Expedition** (Big Sky Resort, 406/995-5769, www.bigskyresort.com, summer, $85) takes visitors to the 11,166-foot summit of Lone Peak. The guided expedition

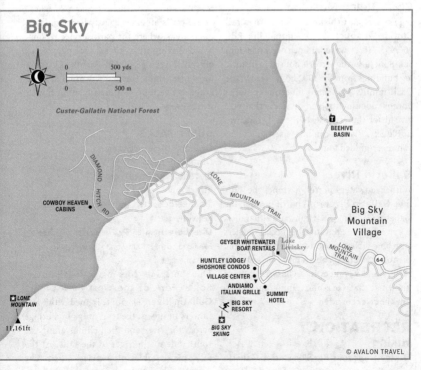

Big Sky

0   500 yds
0   500 m

Custer-Gallatin National Forest

DIAMOND HITCH RD

COWBOY HEAVEN CABINS

LONE MOUNTAIN TRAIL

BEEHIVE BASIN

Big Sky Mountain Village

LONE MOUNTAIN TRAIL

64

GEYSER WHITEWATER BOAT RENTALS

Lake Levinksy

HUNTLEY LODGE/ SHOSHONE CONDOS

VILLAGE CENTER

ANDIAMO ITALIAN GRILLE

SUMMIT HOTEL

BIG SKY RESORT

BIG SKY SKIING

LONE MOUNTAIN
11,161ft

© AVALON TRAVEL

Lone Mountain towers above Big Sky.

goes by chairlift, safari vehicle, and tram to reach the summit, where views take in three states and two national parks.

Crail Ranch Museum

Big Sky is home to historic ranches. The **Crail Ranch Museum** (2110 Spotted Elk Rd., 406/993-2112, www.crailranch.org, noon-3pm Sat.-Sun. July-Aug., free) is housed in historic log buildings from the 1902 homestead of the Crail family. The small museum contains photos, documents, and artifacts that will give history buffs a taste of the early ranchers in Big Sky. Visitors can take a self-guided or volunteer-guided tour.

Gallatin River

With headwaters in Yellowstone, the 120-mile **Gallatin River** runs north through the Gallatin Canyon. U.S. Highway 191 parallels the river, where calm stretches beckon anglers with blue-ribbon trout fishing. In the canyon, the rocky riverbed churns up white water for rafters and kayakers in a Class IV section known as the Mad Mile. Campgrounds also line the river corridor.

RECREATION
Hiking

Hiking trails tour Big Sky, Custer-Gallatin National Forest, and Yellowstone National Park. While the Big Sky hikes are heavily traveled, the Yellowstone trails see very few hikers due to the lengthy walks needed to reach destinations such as passes or lakes. These trails all enter grizzly bear management areas, where the park service recommends hiking with at least four people; no off-trail travel is permitted. For hikers looking for shorter trails, the first few miles of these are enjoyable, especially in early summer with wildflowers.

OUSEL FALLS

Distance: 1.6 miles round-trip
Duration: 1 hour
Elevation change: 80 feet
Effort: easy
Trailhead: Ousel Falls Trailhead in Custer-Gallatin National Forest
Directions: From Big Sky Town Center, take Ousel Falls Road 1.6 miles southwest to the trailhead parking lot on the right.

This short walk goes to a waterfall on the **South Fork of the West Fork of the Gallatin River.** The route is lined with wildflowers in July as the trail drops to a bridge across the river and then climbs along the south side of the river to the falls. At the falls, picnic tables offer places to sit. The falls, named for the American dipper, tumbles down stair steps, which toss up a cool mist. Pick up an interpretive trail guide at the trailhead.

BEEHIVE BASIN

Distance: 6 miles round-trip
Duration: 3-4 hours
Elevation change: 1,364 feet
Effort: moderate
Trailhead: Beehive Basin Trailhead in Custer-Gallatin National Forest
Directions: From Lone Mountain Trail 1.4 miles north of the Big Sky Resort turnoff, turn right onto Beehive Basin Road for 1.7 miles to the trailhead parking lot on the left.

Trail #40 goes to scenic Beehive Basin, a bit of a grunt after the deceptively easy start. But the scenery more than makes up for it. In early June, you may encounter snow on the trail and ankle-deep streams to cross. But by July, wildflowers cover the meadows in rampant color. Later in summer, the meadow grasses turn gold. In the basin a small, narrow, shallow lake at 9,285 feet surrounded by meadows tucks below rugged Beehive Peak in the Spanish Peaks.

From the trailhead, cross the creek and ascend north through meadows with intermittent trees. After climbing several switchbacks, the trail enters the upper basin and works north to **Beehive Lake** at the base of **Beehive Peak.**

SPECIMEN CREEK

Distance: 15.8 miles round-trip
Duration: 9 hours
Elevation change: 2,280 feet
Effort: strenuous
Trailhead: Specimen Creek Trailhead on U.S. Highway 191 in Yellowstone National Park

This level, mostly forested trail follows Specimen Creek up valley to a small alpine lake surrounded by meadows. En route, it passes plenty of trees that have been clawed by grizzlies. At two miles, just after entering the 2007 Owl Creek Fire burn, the trail reaches a **fork.** Hikers out just to enjoy the creek with meadows of early summer wildflowers can turn around at this junction. To continue up the **Sportsman Lake Trail,** take the left trail up the **East Fork.** At 4.1 miles, the trail reaches a meadow where hikers must ford **Specimen Creek.** At 5.9 miles, the trail reaches a second **junction.** The left fork begins the steep climb 1,400 feet up switchbacks to the **Sky Rim Trail** and **Shelf Lake** at 9,194 feet. Sheep and Bighorn

Specimen Creek Trail in winter

Peaks become visible as the trail breaks out of the trees.

FAWN PASS

Distance: 18 miles round-trip
Duration: 9-11 hours
Elevation change: 1,176 feet
Effort: moderate but long
Trailhead: Fawn Pass Trailhead on U.S. Highway 191 in Yellowstone National Park

This Gallatin Range trail is a sun-soaker. Between broad mosquito meadows and silvered blowdowns from forest fires, the trail can be a scorcher in midsummer and thick with black biting flies. It's also smack in the middle of a grizzly bear management area. In early summer, expect wildflowers galore in the huge sagebrush meadows. Shortly after starting, the trail reaches a couple of junctions. Stay right at both. About five miles in, a cutoff trail departs for the **Bighorn Pass Trail.** Head eastward, passing intermittent tiny ponds; before the pass, patchy forests appear. The final slope to the pass hikes straight toward Gray Peak. A sign marks the pass, which has a small lake for lunch just beyond and views of Crowfoot Ridge to the south.

BIGHORN PASS TRAIL

Distance: 21 miles round-trip
Duration: 12-13 hours
Elevation change: 1,885 feet
Effort: strenuous due to length
Trailhead: Bighorn Pass Trailhead on U.S. Highway 191 in Yellowstone National Park

The Bighorn Pass Trail follows the Gallatin River for a short distance, which makes the route a favorite for anglers going after cutthroat, rainbow, and brook trout in the stretches close to the highway. Because the route requires **fording rivers** at the start where bridges have been temporarily removed, you may need to wait until high runoff dissipates for safe crossing. The trail also traverses a heavy bear area. The hike up valley hits intermittent forest, but for much of it has broad open views of Crowfoot Ridge.

At 4.2 miles, the trail reaches the junction with the **Fawn Pass Cutoff Trail.** Continue up valley instead, ascending through meadows and past **backcountry campsites.** Just before **Bighorn Pass,** the trail switchbacks up into bighorn sheep terrain. From the pass, at 9,110 feet, you can look down into Yellowstone's interior at Swan Lake and Bunsen Peak.

Biking

With more than 40 miles of mountain biking trails, **Big Sky Resort** (406/995-5769, www.bigskyresort.com, summer only, $35) has 14 lift-accessed downhill trails for advanced riders. Wear full helmets and pads to handle the obstacles. In addition, nine cross-country single- and double-track trails for beginners and intermediate riders lead from Big Sky Village on loops across Andesite Mountain and through Moonlight Basin north of Lone Peak.

Through Big Sky, a **paved bike trail** (9.5 miles round-trip) goes from Ousel Falls Trailhead to U.S. Highway 191. From Big Sky Town Center, take Ousel Falls Road 1.6 miles southwest to the trailhead parking lot on the south side of the road.

Located in the Big Sky Village Snowcrest Building, **Different Spokes Bike Shop** (50 Big Sky Resort Rd., 406/995-5849, www.bigskyresort.com, 9am-4pm daily early June-late Sept., $30-95) rents downhill and cross-country bikes (helmets and full pads included). Tours, lessons, and coaching are available.

Horseback Riding

Jake's Horses (200 Beaver Creek Rd., 406/995-4630 or 800/352-5956, www.jakeshorses.com, year-round, $40-150) guides horseback trail rides in Gallatin Canyon, the national forest, and Yellowstone. Rides last 1-4 hours or all day. They also offer winter rides; a two-hour dinner ride adds in a steak fry.

Water Sports

Tiny **Lake Levinsky** at Big Sky Resort (800/548-4486, www.bigskyresort.com, early Dec.-mid-Apr. and early June-Sept.) offers a tame place for boating. **Geyser Whitewater**

Expeditions (46651 Gallatin Rd., 406/995-4989, www.raftmontana.com, $15/hour) rents pedal boats, canoes, kayaks, and paddleboards from the shore. Day passes and Family Adventure Cards offer more economical rates.

FISHING

The **Gallatin River** ranks as one of the prime rivers to fish for trout in Montana. The waters hold brown and rainbow trout, and anglers are not permitted to float much of it, making wading the way to fish.

Four fishing guide services operate out of Big Sky: **Grizzly Outfitters** (11 Lone Peak Dr., 406/579-7094 or 888/807-9452, www.grizzlyoutfitters.com), **Gallatin River Guides** (47430 Gallatin Rd., 406/995-2290, wwwmontanaflyfishing.com), **Lone Mountain Ranch** (750 Lone Mountain Ranch Rd., 406/995-4734, www.lonemountainranch.com), and **Wild Trout Outfitters** (47520 Gallatin Rd., 406/995-2975, www.wildtroutoutfitters.com). All fish the Gallatin River but offer a variety of trips, gear rentals, and instruction. Rates run $250-350 for a half day and $350-450 for a full day for two people. Tip 15 percent for an average day of fishing, but if you catch lots of fish, tip 20 percent. Montana fishing licenses (http://fwp.mt.gov, residents: $13-26; nonresidents: $25 for two days, $54 for 10 days, $70 season) are extra.

RAFTING

The **Gallatin River** meanders and crashes through the Gallatin Canyon, creating prime white-water rafting. Through the canyon, the river goes from slow swirly pools to thundering wave trains of almost continuous Class II-IV rapids. Most of the rafting is north of Big Sky in the 13 miles between Greek Creek and Spanish Creek. Expert boaters hit House Rock rapid and bash through the rocky, rough current of the Mad Mile. The best water runs May-mid-July. Self-guided canyon rafting on the Gallatin is only for those skilled in strong currents, rapids, and obstacles.

Two companies guide half- and full-day trips on calm, scenic float sections or the white water. **Geyser Whitewater Expeditions** (46651 Gallatin Rd., 406/995-4989, www.raftmontana.com) is based in Big Sky. **Montana Whitewater Raft Company** (63960 Gallatin Rd., 406/995-4613, www.montanawhitewater.com) is based in Gallatin Gateway, at the north end of the canyon about 16 miles north of Big Sky. Boats go out multiple times daily. Half-day trips run $45-58; full-day trips run $75-94. Plan to tip about 15 percent.

mountain bike trails at Big Sky Resort

Golf

Golfing at Big Sky can be a challenge between the views of Lone Mountain and the wildlife that saunters out on the course. **Big Sky Golf Course** (2100 Black Otter Rd., 406/995-5780, www.bigskyresort.com, dawn-dusk daily late May-early Oct.) is an 18-hole links-style par 72 Arnold Palmer course at 6,500 feet in elevation. The clubhouse has rentals, instruction, and the Bunker Bar and Grill. Rates run $48 for clubs and $50-80 for greens fees. Tee times are available online.

Spa

Located in the Huntley/Shoshone Lobby in Big Sky Village, the **Solace Spa** (50 Big Sky Resort Rd., 406/995-5803, www.bigsky-resort.com, 9am-5pm daily Nov.-mid-Apr. and June-mid-Sept., $55-395) offers face and body treatments, massages, manicures, pedicures, waxing, tinting, and scrubs. The spa also houses a salon.

Thrill Sports

In summer, **Big Sky Resort** (406/995-5769, www.bigskyresort.com, 9am-4pm daily mid-June-mid-Sept., rates vary) brings on the thrill sports. You can fly through the air on ziplines, feel the rush of a giant swing, monkey around on a high ropes course or climbing wall, fling around on the bungee trampoline, or hop on a tamer scenic lift ride. Reservations are advised for ziplines and the high ropes course.

Winter Sports

★ SKIING

In 2013, **Big Sky Resort** (50 Big Sky Resort Rd., 800/548-4486, www.bigskyresort.com, 9am-4pm daily late Nov.-mid-Apr.) acquired neighboring Moonlight Basin and Spanish Peaks to become one of the biggest ski areas in North America with 5,800 acres of terrain across four mountains. With its summit at 11,166 feet on Lone Mountain Peak, the ski area has more than 4,000 vertical feet with a reputation for broad groomers, gladed tree runs, and challenging steeps. It has 22 lifts, eight surface lifts, and 300 named runs. Lift

Big Sky Resort

tickets cost $103 for adults, $83 for seniors, juniors, and college students, and $53 for youth. Youth often can ski for free with lodging through Big Sky Resort.

With one of the largest Nordic ski trail systems, **Lone Mountain Ranch** (750 Lone Mountain Ranch Rd., 406/995-4734, www.lonemountainranch.com, dawn-dusk daily late Nov.-mid-Apr.) grooms 85 kilometers (53 miles) of trails for skate and classic skiing. Even though the trail system spans 2,200 feet in elevation, routes are designed on different loops for beginners, experts, and skill levels in between. The outdoor ski shop (8am-9pm) offers lessons, rentals, repairs, and guided cross-country ski trips into Yellowstone. Rentals cost $9-45 per day, and trail passes cost $10-20.

Snowshoeing

The trails at **Lone Mountain Ranch** (750 Lone Mountain Ranch Rd., 406/995-4734, www.lonemountainranch.com, dawn-dusk daily late Nov.-mid-Apr.) give snowshoers extensive touring options. The trails are separate from the Nordic ski trails. An outdoor shop (8am-9pm) offers guided tours on the ranch trails and in Yellowstone. Rentals cost $9-20 per day, and trail passes cost $10-20.

Ice-Skating

A full-size hockey and ice-skating outdoor rink, plus a kids' rink, are available at the **Town Center** (Ousel Falls Rd. and Aspen Leaf Dr., http://bssha.org, hours vary daily in winter, $5/person donation). Ice skate and helmet rentals ($7-8) are available from **Grizzly Outfitters** (11 Lone Peak Dr., 406/579-7094 or 888/807-9452, www.grizzlyoutfitters.com).

ENTERTAINMENT AND SHOPPING

With so much outdoor activity, nightlife consists mostly of restaurants, but there a handful of places to knock back a drink. In the village at Big Sky Resort, the Arrowhead Mall houses **Scissorbills** (406/995-4933, www.scissorbills.com, 11am-12:30am daily winter and summer only), a local's hangout that hops with DJ tunes and dancing, plus live music on the weekends. For movies, head to **Lone Peak Cinema** (50 Ousel Falls Rd., 406/995-7827, www.lonepeakcinema.com), where two theaters show a revolving lineup of new releases.

The **Big Sky Classical Music Festival** (406/995-2742, www.bigskyarts.org, Aug.) invites guest soloists and ensembles to perform with the Big Sky Festival Orchestra. Big Sky Arts also sponsors the free summer **Music in the Mountains** weekly series at the Town Center stage, usually on Thursdays July-August.

Shopping at Big Sky is separated into several different locations: **Town Center** (Ousel Falls Rd. and Aspen Leaf Dr., year-round), **Meadow Village** (Meadow Village Dr., Center Lane, and Little Coyote Rd., year-round), and **Big Sky Resort** (800/548-4486, www.bigskyresort.com, early Dec.-mid-Apr. and early June-Sept.). Shops carry upscale art, regional crafts, jewelry, furniture, and boutique and trendy clothing, but you can also find T-shirts, souvenirs, and sporting goods.

ACCOMMODATIONS

Big Sky is an upscale resort community with more than 3,000 rooms, condos, townhomes, and vacation homes with modern conveniences such as wireless Internet. It has accommodations across the spectrum, from family hotels to ultra-pricey luxury vacation

skiing from the top of Lone Mountain at Big Sky

homes, but lacks chain hotels. Several property management companies rent condos, townhomes, and vacation homes. **Big Sky Luxury Rentals** (406/995-4148, www.vacationbigsky.com) has upscale vacation homes and a concierge service. **Big Sky Vacation Rentals** (406/599-8850, www.bookbigsky.com) has about 80 vacation homes across price ranges.

Big Sky Resort

For the largest number of hotels, condos, cabins, and townhomes and especially slopeside options for winter and summer, check the listings with **Big Sky Resort** (50 Big Sky Resort Rd., 800/548-4486, www.bigskyresort.com, early Dec.-mid-Apr. and early June-Sept.) The resort offers lodging and activity packages during summer and winter, and summer lodging often includes free scenic lift rides. Lodging is in hotels, condos, townhomes, upscale cabins, and vacation homes. Many of the lodging properties have access to the outdoor swimming pool and fitness room at Huntley Lodge or have their own. Rates are highest in winter during the ski season and lower in summer. Book holiday lodging six months in advance. Hefty resort fees will add 17 percent to rates.

Quiet and with views of Lone Mountain from a slopeside perch, the ★ **Cowboy Heaven Cabins** ($275-810, three nights or 4-5 holiday nights minimum) are modern two-bedroom log cabins with full kitchens, fireplaces, two small bathrooms, living and dining area, and private outdoor hot tubs. They flank the Moonlight Basin side of Lone Mountain, and most have impressive views from their decks. The cabins sleep 4-8 people with one bedroom having a queen or king and the other twins or bunks. Some cabins also have a loft.

Big Sky Village slopeside hotels cluster around shops, restaurants, and lifts. The three-story ★ **Village Center** ($240-1,240) has luxury suites and condos to sleep 2-10 people with plush designer mountain decor. Studios have a queen wall bed, a sofa bed, and kitchen appliances. The one-, two-, and three-bedroom condos have a king or queen in the bedrooms. Some rooms also have sofa beds and wall beds. Each unit has 2-3 full bathrooms with tubs and showers. The center has an outdoor pool, hot tub, and fitness room, and the rates usually include breakfast in neighboring Huntley Lodge. The high-rise luxury **Summit Hotel** ($260-3,655) has studios, hotel rooms with two queens or a king,

Cowboy Heaven Cabins

condos, and penthouses. Rates usually include breakfast. Studios have queen wall beds. Condo suites have one, two, or three bedrooms, plus kitchens and 1-3 bathrooms. Penthouses, which have 2-4 bedrooms, have housed political notables such as the Obamas and Bidens. Some of the rooms have windows that frame Lone Peak. **Huntley Lodge** ($225-590) and **Shoshone Condominiums** ($360-1,175) were some of the early resort mainstays, but have seen several upgrades. Dining, shopping, the Solace Spa, an outdoor swimming pool and hot tubs, fitness center, sauna, and tennis courts are in the complex. Huntley Lodge rooms have 2-3 queen beds with mountain views or lofts as options. The seven-story Shoshone Condominiums come with one bedroom with or without a loft. They contain various combinations of queens, kings, wall beds, or sofa sleepers.

Located on U.S. Highway 191 just south of the turnoff to the ski resort, about 15 minutes from the ski area parking lots, **Whitewater Inn** ($136-185) is the least expensive place to stay in Big Sky and one of the few open year-round. Converted from a chain motel, rooms have 2-3 queens or a king, and some allow pets. The hotel includes a continental breakfast, fitness room, hot tub, and indoor swimming pool with a 90-foot slide.

Guest Ranches

Historic ranches are one of the mainstays of Big Sky. They offer a way to experience the Old West with modern amenities. Secluded at Big Sky in a side canyon with a wilderness feel, ★ **Lone Mountain Ranch** (750 Lone Mountain Ranch Rd., 406/995-4644, www.lonemountainranch.com, late Nov.-mid-Apr. and early June-Sept., $525-830 per person in summer, $300-500 per person in winter) has lodging in quaint log cabins with no televisions, air-conditioning, or phones. Woodstoves ward off the chill on cold days. In winter, Nordic ski trails wind between the cabins, which scatter on both sides of the burbling creek, and sleigh-ride dinners head to a cozy remote cabin. Ranch programs include horseback riding, fishing, hiking, kids' programs, Yellowstone tours, and skiing (seasonal). Package rates include activities and meals. Single-night to weeklong stays are available, and the dining room serves outstanding meals.

Located 12 miles south of Big Sky, the historic **320 Guest Ranch** (205 Buffalo Horn Creek, 406/995-4283, www.320ranch.com, year-round, $130-350 winter, $180-440

log cabins at Lone Mountain Ranch

summer and Christmas) flanks the Gallatin River. Lodging is in 29 small one-room duplex cabins, 12 two-bedroom cabins with efficiency kitchens, and seven three-bedroom luxury log homes. Summer stays include horseback riding, fly-fishing, and rodeos; winter offers sleigh rides. The restaurant is open in summer and winter only.

Motel

An independent motel and a longtime Big Sky roadside staple, **Buck's T-4 Lodging** (46625 Gallatin Rd./Hwy. 191, 406/995-4111 or 800/822-4484, www.buckst4.com, late May-mid-Oct. and late Nov.-mid-Apr., $180-200) is located on the highway. It has 72 motel rooms remodeled in 2012. Rooms have two queens or one king bed, and stays include a hot breakfast.

CAMPING

Custer-Gallatin National Forest (Bozeman Ranger District, 3710 Fallon St., Bozeman, 406/522-2520, www.fs.usda.gov/gallatin) RV and tent campgrounds line the Gallatin Canyon. They are popular with locals as quick getaways from Bozeman for fishing, river rafting and kayaking, and hiking. The campgrounds, open mid-May-late September, take **reservations** (877/444-6777, www.recreation.gov), mandatory in July and August. Facilities include picnic tables, fire rings with grills, vault toilets, drinking water, bear boxes, garbage service, firewood for sale, and wheelchair-accessible toilets and campsites. Campsites cost $10-15; extra vehicles cost $6.

The three most popular sit right on the highway and the Gallatin River, the first two located just north of Big Sky. In a loop around a sunny meadow, **Greek Creek Campground** packs out first with 14 campsites with RVs limited to 60 feet. Unfortunately, some campsites have views of the road, but campsites 14 and 15 overlook the river. **Moose Creek Flat Campground**, the closest campground to Big Sky, has 13 campsites with RVs limited to 60 feet. Located south of Big Sky in the Upper Gallatin Canyon,

Andiamo Italian Grille at Big Sky Resort

Red Cliff Campground is the closest to Yellowstone. Tucked in a young Douglas fir forest, the campground has 65 campsites with RVs limited to 50 feet and electrical hookups at half the sites.

Two quieter campgrounds tuck up side canyons north of Big Sky. **Spire Rock Campground** huddles below Storm Castle Mountain with 19 campsites in clusters surrounded by lush undergrowth of thimbleberries, wild roses, and vine maples. RVs are limited to 50 feet. **Swan Creek Campground** is in the steep-walled Swan Creek Canyon. In grassy meadows with sun and views of the forested canyon walls, the campground has 14 campsites with RVs limited to 45 feet.

FOOD

★ **Andiamo Italian Grille** (Big Sky Resort, 50 Big Sky Resort Rd., 406/995-8041, www.bigskyresort.com, 3pm-10pm daily early June-Sept. and early Dec.-mid-Apr., $18-42) serves antipasti, Tuscan specialties, Italian wines, and drool-worthy desserts that look more like artistry than food. A Montana flare puts a twist on the pastas that are house made, and the osso bucco is bison. Reservations, which can be made online, are advisable. Tucked into Huntley Lodge at Big Sky Resort, the **Fondue Stube** (50 Big Sky Resort Rd., 406/995-5733, www.bigskyresort.com, 5pm-9pm daily early Dec.-mid-Apr., $10-14/person) remakes the intimate Swiss tradition of huddling around a pot in a shared dinner. You can order the fondues separately: cheese, broth with meat or seafood, traditional oil with meat, and chocolate. But it's easier to do it all in the Lone Peak Experience ($38).

Lone Peak Brewery & Taphouse (Meadow Village, 48 Marketplace Dr., 406/995-3939, www.lonepeakbrewery.com, 11am-10pm daily year-round, hours shorten in spring and fall, $10-22) pours 12-14 craft beers on tap, including seasonal specialties, plus cocktails from the full bar. Burgers, tacos, fajitas, salads, fish and chips, sandwiches, nachos, and wings are served all day; dinner is added starting at 5:30pm with ribs, steaks, and lobster mac and cheese with bacon.

Olive B's Big Sky Bistro (151 Center Ln., 406/995-3355, www.olivebsbigsky.com, 11am-9pm Mon.-Sat. late May-mid-Oct. and early Dec.-mid-Apr., $27-35) serves up classic French fare such as French onion soup and blue cheese crème brûlée, but also has seafood choices, including a lobster mac and cheese. Lunch has salads, burgers, sandwiches, and appetizers. Dinner includes steaks, pasta, duck, pheasant, and lamb. Go here for a huckleberry martini, whiskeys, and wine.

Ousel and Spur Pizza Company (Big Sky Town Center, 50 Ousel Falls Rd., 406/995-7175, www.ouselandspurpizza.com, 5pm-close daily year-round, $14-25) specializes in elk sausage pizza. In addition to classic pizzas, you can get fresh salads, gnocchi, ravioli, polenta, other Italian goodies, and takeout. The **Lotus Pad** (3090 Big Pine Dr., 406/995-2728, www.lotuspadbigsky.com, 5pm-close daily year-round, shorter hours fall and spring, $14-30) serves vegetarian, gluten-free, and

spicy Asian meals. The menu lists multiple curries, stir-fries, noodle dishes, and seafood, plus specialty cocktails, sake, and beers from Japan.

Tucked by itself in a side canyon at Big Sky, ★ **Lone Mountain Ranch** (750 Lone Mountain Ranch Rd., 406/995-4644, www.lonemountainranch.com, late Nov.-mid-Apr. and early June-Sept.) has a dining room and saloon. Dinner (6:30pm-10pm daily, $22-40) is open to the public; reservations are highly recommended. The chef serves artistic plates of farm-to-table meals with fresh, lively flavors. Two menus are available nightly: traditional Montana ranch fare and a revolving selection of innovative entrées, including vegetarian. Appetizers are a must, and the desserts are exquisite. The ranch's **saloon** (4pm-9pm Mon.-Sat.) is a place to experience old Montana, with cocktails made from fresh, house-made infusions, and small plates.

On U.S. Highway 191, **Gallatin Riverhouse Grill** (45130 Gallatin Rd., 406/995-7427, http://gallatinriverhousegrill.com, 3pm-close daily year-round, $10-30) pumps out the barbecue—burgers, chicken, sandwiches, brisket, sausage, and ribs—and throws in live music for evening fun. Sampler platters serve 2-4 people and pile on the barbecue with traditional sides. **Buck's T-4 Lodging** (46625 Gallatin Rd., 406/995-4111 or 800/822-4484, www.buckst4.com, 5:30pm-9pm daily late May-mid-Oct. and late Nov.-mid-Apr., $11-42) serves burgers topped with duck bacon, sandwiches, shared plates, and full dinners with sides additional as well as a large wine menu. Dinner entrées focus on bison, meatloaf, duck, venison, rainbow trout, fish, ribs, and steaks. Vegetarians go for the pan-seared cauliflower.

Cookouts

In winter, Big Sky Resort's Summit Hotel transports groups by snowcat to the **Montana Dinner Yurt** (1 Lone Mountain Trail, 406/995-3880, www.skimba.com, 6:30pm-10pm daily late Nov.-mid-Apr., $87-97). After arriving at the yurt (a huge round tent heated by a woodstove), guests can sled outside or drink cocoa around the fire before a three-course dinner is served. Musical entertainment is part of the gig.

From **Lone Mountain Ranch** (750 Lone Mountain Ranch Rd., 406/995-2783, www. lonemountainranch.com, 6:30pm-10pm daily mid-Dec.-early Apr., $81-98), a horse-drawn sleigh slides through the snowy woods to the cozy North Fork Cabin for dinner. Dress for the cold with hat and gloves; wranglers will also supply blankets for the 20-minute ride. A woodstove heated in the cabin glows by the light of oil lanterns. Prime rib with all the trimmings and sides is served family-style, and live music and storytelling provides the entertainment.

In summer, dinner adventures turn western. At the **320 Guest Ranch** (205 Buffalo Horn Creek, 406/995-4283, www.320ranch. com, Wed. mid-June-mid-Sept., horseback $85 adults, $75 children; wagon $55 adults, $35 children), opt for dinner via wagon (two hours) or horseback ride. Dinner takes place by the Gallatin River and centers around steaks and barbecue chicken. The ranch also does a pig roast on their front porch on Monday nights in summer. The ranch is located about 12 miles south of Big Sky.

Most outfitters offer vegetarian alternatives to the main meal; request these when making your reservations. Most do not serve alcohol, but some permit BYOB. Reservations are required.

Groceries

Big Sky has several markets for groceries, deli items, meats, fruits, veggies, beer, wine, and baked goods. Two outlets of **Hungry Moose Market and Deli** (209 Aspen Leaf Dr., 406/995-3045, 6:30am-10pm daily; Mountain Mall at Big Sky Resort, 406/995-3075, winter and summer only; www.hungrymoose.com) sells meals to go and premade grab-and-go items: espresso, breakfast sandwiches, salads, sandwiches, wraps, ice cream, and baked goods. They also deliver groceries. The newest grocery in Town Center, the larger **Roxy's**

Hungry Moose Market and Deli

Market (20 Huntley Dr., 406/995-2295, http://roxysmarket.com, 7am-10pm daily), carries specialty items, too.

TRANSPORTATION AND SERVICES
Car

From Big Sky, **U.S. Highway 191** travels 20 miles south through several historic ranches before entering Yellowstone National Park. This 20-mile section of the park (no entrance station) is a good place to see bison, bears, or moose. After exiting the park, the road passes through Custer-Gallatin National Forest as it descends south into West Yellowstone and the **West Entrance** (47 miles south of Big Sky).

From the north, Big Sky is accessed via **Bozeman** and the Gallatin Gateway down U.S. Highway 191. The two-lane road can be a nightmare: It's narrow and curvy, and locals who know all its turns drive it fast. It's also the most-crowded access road to Yellowstone, with nonstop traffic in July and August. Because the road parallels the Gallatin River, scads of river rafters and anglers add to the traffic. If you pull off to let traffic pass, you may wait for quite a while to be able to pull back on. Winter can douse the road in snow or ice, which adds to the white-knuckle driving.

PARKING

Most first-time visitors to Big Sky expect a compact resort, but Big Sky is a sprawling unincorporated resort area that requires 20 minutes of driving from the highway through developments and forests to get to lodging sites at Big Sky Resort and parking for the lifts. Most lodges have specified parking areas. Parking areas for day visitors to Big Sky Resort are located in the Mountain Village and Madison Village areas, both marked on road junction signs.

Bus

The **Skyline Bus** (406/995-6287, www.sky-linebus.com, hours vary seasonally year-round, free) connects the various base areas of Big Sky Resort with businesses on the highway, including motels. It makes about 15 stops around the Big Sky area. A bus also runs between Bozeman and Big Sky ($5 cash, purchase tickets at Base Camp in Big Sky Resort). Buses run daily in summer and winter, but only Monday-Friday in fall and spring.

Services

Located at the junction of U.S. Highway 191 and Lone Mountain Trail, the **Big Sky and Greater Yellowstone Visitor Information Center** (55 Lone Mountain Trail, 406/996-3000, 8:30am-5:30pm daily summer, 8:30am-5:30pm Mon.-Fri. winter) is a place to get oriented before driving up through Big Sky. Operated by the Big Sky Chamber of Commerce, the center has brochures, maps, and information for both Big Sky and Yellowstone.

Find **ATMs** at Big Sky Resort, Town Center, and Meadow Village. Meadow Village has the **post office** (5 Meadow Center Dr. #2, 406/995-4540), and Town Center has **The Wash House** (3415 Cedar Dr., 406/993-2822, www.thewashhousebigsky.com) with coin-op washers and dryers. No public shower facility is available.

MEDIA AND COMMUNICATIONS

Big Sky has all the modern services: wireless Internet in hotels and ubiquitous cell phone service. The **Big Sky Community Library** (45465 Gallatin Rd., 406/995-4281, www.big-skylibrary.org, hours vary Sun.-Thurs.) has computers available for public use, but call first to check on changeable hours.

The Big Sky newspaper is the free weekly *Lone Peak Lookout* (www.lonepeaklookout.com), but the daily news comes from the *Bozeman Daily Chronicle* (www.bozeman-dailychronicle.com).

MEDICAL SERVICES

In Big Sky, call 911 for emergencies. The **Medical Clinic of Big Sky** (www.docsky.us) operates in two locations, depending on the season. The year-round clinic (11 Lone Peak Dr., 406/993-2797, 10am-5pm Mon.-Fri. mid-Apr.-late Nov. and Mon., Wed., Fri. during ski season) is in the Town Center. During the ski season, the mountain clinic (406/995-2797, 10am-5pm daily late Nov.-mid-Apr.) serves as the main location. The nearest hospital is more than an hour north in Bozeman: **Bozeman Deaconess Hospital** (915 Highland Blvd., 406/585-5000, www.boz-emandeaconess.org).

Red Lodge, Montana

Red Lodge is a throwback to the Old West, but with a modern mountain vibe. It attracts visitors from the upper Midwest and the Canadian plains for skiing in winter at Red Lodge Mountain and driving the Beartooth Highway in summer. Downtown shops and hotel and restaurant fronts retain the look of the Old West with two-story brick facades, but cater to tourists rather than horses. Part of the town's attraction is the mix of western tradition with outdoor sports. Ski joring (where a horse and rider pull a skier) is an annual competition as well as a recreational pastime. Red Lodge only serves as a gateway to Yellowstone **late May-mid-October,** when plowing opens the Beartooth Highway to the park's Northeast Entrance.

SIGHTS
★ Downtown Red Lodge Historic District

Downtown Red Lodge Historic District (Broadway Ave. between 8th and 4th Sts.) clusters in a few blocks along the main drag through town. Some of the two-story brick buildings go back to 1887, and retro signs from the 1950s convey another historical era. Shops cater now to tourists rather than the Old West, and restaurants have modern sensibilities. In the evening, walk between western saloons that ramp up a hefty and sometimes raucous nightlife scene with live music, dancing, live poker, gaming machines, cocktails, and local microbrews. Free **wagon rides** (7pm-9pm daily Memorial Day-Labor Day) travel Broadway Avenue, stopping at corners to pick up passengers.

Yellowstone Wildlife Sanctuary

In a wildlife-rich area such as the Greater Yellowstone Ecosystem, some animals need a little extra help. The **Yellowstone Wildlife Sanctuary** (612 2nd St. E., 406/446-1133, www.yellowstonewildlifesanctuary.org, noon-4pm Tues.-Fri., 10am-4pm Sat.-Sun., $3-6) offers a way to observe rehabilitating wildlife up close. Residents include wolves, bears, raptors, and even an elk. Entry fees help support the rescue efforts.

★ Beartooth Highway

The 68-mile **Beartooth Highway** (www.beartoothhighway.com, late May-mid-Oct.), also known as the All-American Highway, climbs over Beartooth Pass at 10,947 feet, the highest drivable pass in the Northern Rockies, in alpine tundra that runs for miles. Flanked by deep snowbanks in early summer and wildflowers in late August, the road yields 360-degree views of more than 20 peaks that

Historic brick buildings flank downtown Red Lodge.

Red Lodge

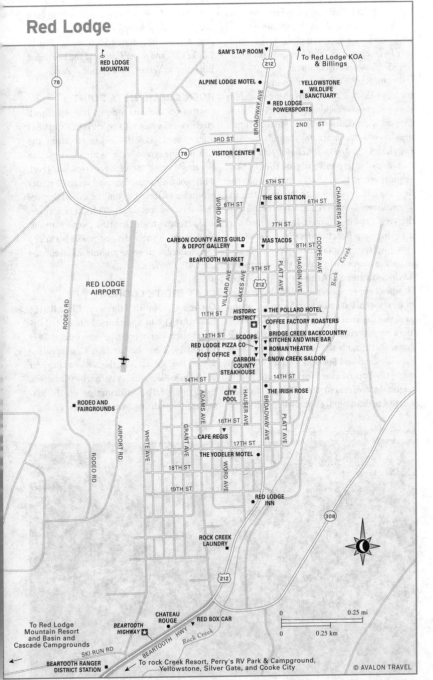

SAM'S TAP ROOM ▼

To Red Lodge KOA & Billings

212

RED LODGE MOUNTAIN

78

ALPINE LODGE MOTEL ●

YELLOWSTONE WILDLIFE SANCTUARY

● RED LODGE POWERSPORTS

BROADWAY AVE

2ND ST

3RD ST

78

VISITOR CENTER ■

5TH ST

THE SKI STATION ■   6TH ST

CHAMBERS AVE

6TH ST

WORD AVE

7TH ST

CARBON COUNTY ARTS GUILD & DEPOT GALLERY ■

MAS TACOS ▼   8TH ST

COOPER AVE

BEARTOOTH MARKET ■

9TH ST

PLATT AVE

HAGGIN AVE

Rock Creek

VILLARD AVE

OAKES AVE

212

RED LODGE AIRPORT

RODEO RD

11TH ST

HISTORIC DISTRICT ★

● THE POLLARD HOTEL
▼ COFFEE FACTORY ROASTERS

12TH ST   SCOOPS ▼
RED LODGE PIZZA CO ■
POST OFFICE ■

▼ BRIDGE CREEK BACKCOUNTRY KITCHEN AND WINE BAR
■ ROMAN THEATER
■ SNOW CREEK SALOON

CARBON COUNTY STEAKHOUSE ■

14TH ST   14TH ST

ADAMS AVE

CITY POOL ■

HAUSER AVE

● THE IRISH ROSE

BROADWAY AVE

PLATT AVE

16TH ST

RODEO AND FAIRGROUNDS ■

AIRPORT RD

RODEO RD

WHITE AVE

GRANT AVE

CAFE REGIS ▼

17TH ST

WORD AVE

THE YODELER MOTEL ●

18TH ST

19TH ST

RED LODGE INN ●

308

ROCK CREEK LAUNDRY ■

212

0   0.25 mi

0   0.25 km

To Red Lodge Mountain Resort and Basin and Cascade Campgrounds

CHATEAU ROUGE ▼   ● RED BOX CAR

BEARTOOTH HIGHWAY ✪

BEARTOOTH HWY

Rock Creek

BEARTOOTH RANGER DISTRICT STATION ■

SKI RUN RD

To rock Creek Resort, Perry's RV Park & Campground, Yellowstone, Silver Gate, and Cooke City

© AVALON TRAVEL

top 12,000 feet. Red Lodge anchors the route on the northeast end and Yellowstone on the southwest. The road can close during summer for snowstorms, and frequent afternoon thundershowers are common.

From Red Lodge, the road squeezes through Rock Creek Canyon as it climbs slowly southwest following the creek. As the canyon widens, its walls heighten. From a meadow at a cluster of campgrounds, the road switchbacks up to **Rock Creek Vista Point,** a developed interpretive stop on the highway. From there, it switchbacks higher onto the Beartooth Plateau, rife with lupine in August. The road winds around the plateau's edge with the view growing to include more peaks in the Absaroka-Beartooth Wilderness. After crossing from Montana into Wyoming and rounding above Twin Lakes, the **Beartooth Basin Summer Ski Area** on the Twin Lakes Headwall appears. Scenic overlooks en route to Beartooth Pass are worthy stops; at the pass, you can spot the Beartooth Peak looking like a narrow cuspid. From the pass, the road descends through alpine meadows and bogs to pass Island and Beartooth Lakes. Between them sits **Top of the World,** a funky little seasonal store. A spur dirt road goes to **Clay Butte Lookout** (only open when staffed by

volunteers). The road continues to drop via a couple switchbacks before reaching the Clarks Fork of the Yellowstone and climbing again to Cooke City and Silver Gate, and the Northeast Entrance to Yellowstone National Park.

ROCK CREEK VISTA POINT

A stop on the east side of the Beartooth Highway, the **Rock Creek Vista Point** has a giant view. At 9,190 feet in elevation, the five-minute paved walk to the overlook can be lung-taxing for visitors from sea level, while golden-mantled ground squirrels skitter around unaffected. From the overlook, peer thousands of feet down Rock Creek Canyon and across to high-elevation alpine plateaus. Gray granite snow-draped peaks backdrop the scenery with some mountains stretching above 12,000 feet.

CLAY BUTTE LOOKOUT

On the Beartooth Highway, **Clay Butte Lookout** (10am-5pm Tues.-Sun. early July-Aug.) offers one impressive view. Built at 9,811 feet in 1942 by the Civilian Conservation Corps, the lookout is on the National Register of Historic Places and is staffed by volunteers. Find interpretive information on the history of firefighting, the 1988 fires, geology,

Beartooth Plateau on the Beartooth Highway

BASIN LAKES NATIONAL RECREATION TRAIL

Distance: 8 miles round-trip

Duration: 4 hours

Elevation change: 2,065 feet

Effort: moderately strenuous

Trailhead: Basin Lakes Trailhead in Custer-Gallatin National Forest

Directions: South of Red Lodge, turn west onto West Fork Road for 2.8 miles. At the junction with the ski area road, stay left on West Fork Road for 4.1 miles to the trailhead.

The trail to Basin Lakes tops out at 8,995 feet in elevation, which is actually low altitude for the Beartooth Mountains. Still, it's high enough that some flatlanders and sea level residents will feel lightheadedness or labored breathing. The trail also has several scenic turnaround points for those who want a shorter walk. At 0.5 mile with minimal elevation gain, you first reach **Basin Creek Falls. Lower Basin Lake** is at 2.5 miles, and the **upper lake** is at four miles. Anglers usually have more luck fishing small brook trout in the upper lake rather than the lower lake.

The trail ascends through a lodgepole pine forest, some of it burned in a forest fire, on routes once originally used for logging by horses. The first part of the trail is an **old logging road.** Switchbacks then gain elevation along Basin Creek to reach the lower lake, a mosquito pond surrounded by lily pads. After the trail circles the south end of the lake, it climbs again along **Basin Creek** to the shallow upper lake with views of the cliff faces flanking Silver Run.

PARKSIDE NATIONAL RECREATION TRAIL

Distance: 2.5 miles round-trip

Duration: 1.5 hours

Elevation change: 200 feet

Effort: easy

Trailhead: Parkside Picnic Area in Custer-Gallatin National Forest

Directions: On the Beartooth Highway 10.7 miles south of Red Lodge, turn right onto the Main Fork Rock

Rock Creek Vista Point

Beartooth Plateau wildlife, and local flora. But the view is so huge that your vision is constantly pulled away to the panorama of peaks. To reach the lookout, turn north onto the dirt and gravel Forest Road 142 (between Beartooth Lake and the junction with Chief Joseph Scenic Highway 296) and climb three miles.

RECREATION
Hiking

Hikers in the Beartooth Mountains need to be prepared for frequent afternoon thundershowers, copious mosquitoes, and altitude. Prepare to enter the backcountry, even on short hikes. For trail descriptions and directions, contact the **Beartooth Recreational Trails Association, Inc.** (www.beartooth-trails.org) or stop by the **Beartooth Ranger District Office** (Custer-Gallatin National Forest, 6811 Hwy. 212 S., 406/446-2103, www.fs.usda.gov/custer).

Creek Road (Forest Rd. #2421). Turn right again in 0.25 mile and park in the first lot.

Starting from the **Parkside Picnic Area,** this gentle trail parallels **Rock Creek** to reach **Greenough Lake,** a tiny lake stocked with rainbow trout for fishing, especially good for kids. A small peninsula, almost like a dock, extends into the lake's north end. The lake sits in a deep, scooped-out glacial basin between immense high plateaus of the Beartooth Mountains. The trail alternates between conifers and meadows, crossing back and forth over Rock Creek. It connects **Parkside, Limber Pine,** and **M-K Campgrounds.** A spur trail links **Greenough Campground** to the lake.

GLACIER LAKE

Distance: 4.2 miles round-trip
Duration: 3-4 hours
Elevation change: 1,400 feet
Effort: strenuous
Trailhead: Glacier Lake Trailhead in Custer-Gallatin National Forest
Directions: From the Beartooth Highway 10.7 miles south of Red Lodge, turn right onto the Main Fork Rock Creek Road (Forest Rd. #2421). Drive past the three campground entrances, crossing the bridge over Rock Creek and continuing to follow the creek 7.7 miles to where it dead-ends at the trailhead.

After turning off the Beartooth Highway and crossing Rock Creek, a slow-going bumpy, washboarded, and potholed dirt road leads to the trailhead. Vehicles should have high clearance. The trailhead also has a reputation for animal vandalism with marmots chewing car wires. Consult with the Forest Service on current road and trailhead issues before driving up. The parking lot fills up fast, so go early. At 9,709 feet, Glacier Lake is a two-state affair; it straddles Wyoming and Montana and is surrounded by immense gray granite cliffs. While the trail is short, the altitude and climb up the difficulty. For anglers, the lake is stocked with Yellowstone cutthroat trout, and wildlife-watchers should see pika.

From the trailhead, the route switchbacks on a rocky trail up to a point where it crosses **Moon Creek** and climbs a side drainage. It works over the top of a rocky ridge before dropping to the **lake.** Once at the lake, you can explore shoreline trails, including adding on a walk to **Little Glacier Lake.**

BEARTOOTH HIGH LAKES

Distance: 6-8.4 miles round-trip
Duration: 4-7 hours
Elevation change: 200-2,130 feet
Effort: moderate to strenuous
Trailhead: Beartooth Lake Trailhead (in Beartooth Campground) or Island Lake Trailhead (at Island Lake Campground)

Starting from Beartooth or Island Lakes, trails loop back to countless lakes, from small ponds to larger scenic pools tucked into gray granite. The route in August is full of pink paintbrush and lush bluebells. But several things add to the challenge: altitude of 9,020-11,150 feet, swarms of mosquitoes and blackflies, soggy wetlands (your feet may get wet), and many stream crossings without bridges. The route from Beartooth Lake gains 2,130 feet during the 8.4-mile loop, while Island Lake, which starts at higher elevation, climbs 200 feet out and back to Beauty and Claw Lakes. Take a map, as side trails cut off to multiple small lakes on the Beartooth Plateau.

From **Beartooth Lake,** curve around through the wetlands at the head of Beartooth Lake and ascend the long meadow along **Beartooth Butte** to a junction with the **Island Lake Trail.** Head toward Island Lake, passing a string of small lakes and **Claw Lake.** At **Beauty Lake,** turn right at the junction to walk along the east shore and past **Crane Lake** to loop back to Beartooth Lake.

From **Island Lake,** the hike is better as an out-and-back to Beauty Lake (six miles) or Claw Lake (eight miles). It starts along the west shore of Island Lake, pops over a hill to **Night Lake,** and then traverses meadows, broken forest, and granite outcroppings to reach the junction at **Beauty Lake.** Continue around north of the lake to reach **Claw Lake.**

hiking to Island Lake in the Absaroka-Beartooth Wilderness

Biking

The coup for hard-core road cyclists is the Beartooth Highway. From Red Lodge to Beartooth Pass, the route climbs 5,379 feet in 31 miles. The best time for pedaling is late May, in the few days after road crews have plowed the road and before it is open to vehicles. Those days attract riders from across Montana, and it is a social event. After that, you do have to contend with cars and no shoulders on the road. Prepare for rapidly changing weather, wind, squalls, hail, and lightning, but despite the conditions, most riders chalk the route high in lifetime achievements, and it's been heralded as one of the top five rides in the country.

The Beartooth Mountains are loaded with trails for mountain biking, but many of them require at least intermediate single-track skills. For families, the best ride is the Rocky Fork Trail (three miles), built by the Beartooth Recreational Trails Association,

bicycling the Beartooth Highway

Inc. (www.beartoothtrails.org). The flat trail loops around the rodeo grounds, fairgrounds, and the airport. Park at the rodeo grounds entrance located on Highway 78.

Red Lodge mountain bikers tackle tough trails in the Beartooth Mountains of Custer-Gallatin National Forest, but be prepared for fast-changing weather and afternoon thundershowers. The **Silver Run Trails** (West Fork Rd.) have a variety of loops, steep, lung-busting climbs, and white-knuckle descents. Trails along the **West Fork Creek** are easier, with loops ranging 2.4-5.1 miles; the **Ingles Creek Trail** departs and connects with these. The **Basin Lakes National Recreation Trail** (eight miles round-trip) is also a popular ride. For trail descriptions, directions, and a map of the Silver Run Trails, contact the **Beartooth Ranger District Office** (6811 Hwy. 212 S., 406/446-2103, www.fs.usda.gov/custer). Note that bikes are not allowed in the Absaroka-Beartooth Wilderness.

The Beartooth Highway provides a paved downhill ride from **Top of the World,** (27 miles one-way). **The Ski Station** (510 N. Broadway, 406/446-1086, www.theskistation.com, 11am-4pm Tues.-Sat. May-Sept., $60) shuttles riders to the summit and provides rentals ($35) for the unguided trip. Reservations are required.

Horseback Riding

Elk River Outfitters (406/860-3698 or 406/860-3699, http://elkriveradventures.com, May-Sept., $35-60) guides 1-, 1.5-, and 2-hour trail rides along Rock Creek. For longer adventures, wranglers guide half-day and full-day trips.

Fishing

Flowing from the Beartooth Mountains, **Rock Creek** (Montana fishing license required, http://fwp.mt.gov, $13-26 for residents, $25-54 for nonresidents, $70 per season) harbors rainbow, brown, and brook trout—these are the fish to go after rather than the tiny ones in high-elevation lakes along the Beartooth Highway. Wade-fishing is best.

Lakes west of Beartooth Pass require a Wyoming fishing license (residents: $3 youth, $6 adult daily, $24 adult annual; nonresident: $15 youth, $14 adult daily, $92 adult annual). Wyoming fishing licenses are available at **Top of the World Resort** (307/587-5368, www.topoftheworldresort.com), between Island Lake and Beartooth Lake Campgrounds.

Golf

Located on the north end of town, **Red Lodge Mountain Golf Course** (828 Upper Continental Dr., 406/446-3344, www.redlodgemountain.com, dawn-dusk daily mid-May-mid-Oct.) is an 18-hole course with one island green on the back nine. Mt. Maurice and the Red Lodge Mountain ski area dominate the views. Greens fees vary $34-49. Discounts are available for golfers with Montana or Wyoming identification. Clubs rent for $15; carts cost $16.

Summer Skiing and Snowboarding

Due to the 10,900-foot elevation, the **Beartooth Basin Summer Ski Area** (23 miles west of Red Lodge on Beartooth Highway, 307/250-3767, www.beartoothbasin.com, 9am-3pm daily late May-early July, $20 for one hour, $35 for half day, $45 for full day) operates two poma lifts for early summer skiing or snowboarding near the summit of the Beartooth Highway. For advanced skiers and snowboarders, the steep, corniced Twin Lakes Headwall has runs with 1,000 vertical feet, moguls, and an air and rails park. Operations depend on weather and snow; the few groomed runs are rough due to above-freezing conditions. Pay cash at the trailer in the parking lot.

Winter Sports

While Red Lodge may be cut off from Yellowstone in winter, it still is a destination for downhill skiing and snowboarding, cross-country skiing, snowshoeing, and snowmobiling. **Red Lodge Mountain Resort** (305 Ski Run Rd., 406/446-2610, www.

redlodgemountainresort.com, 9am-pm daily late Nov.-early Apr.) has six lifts for hauling skiers and snowboarders up the slopes and 65 trails. The resort has a reputation for getting storms that dump 1-2 feet of snow and steep chutes that attract diehards. Family-friendly prices include an adult lift ticket around $52, lessons, and a rental shop.

Run by volunteers, the **Red Lodge Nordic Center** (Aspen Ridge Equestrian Ranch, Hwy. 78, www.beartoothtrails.org, dawn-dusk daily Dec.-Mar., $5 adults, kids and seniors free) grooms 15 kilometers of trails for skate and classic skiing west of Red Lodge. Rentals are available at **Sylvan Peak Mountain Shop** (9 S. Broadway, 406/446-1770 or 800/249-2563, 9am-6pm Mon.-Sat., $15-20).

Lions Park (5th St. and Villard, early Dec.-early Mar.) usually has an outdoor ice rink. Snowshoe and ice skate rentals are available at **The Ski Station** (510 N. Broadway, 406/446-1086, www.theskistation.com, 8am-5pm daily Nov.-Apr., $20-40).

Snowmobilers take to the Beartooth Highway when it gets buried in snow. **Red Lodge PowerSports** (1002 N. Broadway, 406/446-3199, www.redlodgepowersports.com, 8am-5pm Mon.-Fri., 8am-1pm Sat.) guides custom tours and rents snowmobiles.

ENTERTAINMENT AND SHOPPING
Nightlife

Red Lodge nightlife is all about barhopping downtown. Since the bars fit within a several-block strip on Broadway Avenue, you can park and walk between them. Find live music and dancing at the **Snow Creek Saloon** (124 S. Broadway Ave., 406/446-2542, www.snowcreeksaloon.com, 11am-2pm daily), along with log stools at the bar and cold beer. The **Roman Theater** (120 S. Broadway Ave., 406/446-2233), built in 1917, shows movies nightly at 7:15pm.

Festivals and Events

In summer, the **Red Lodge Music Festival** (www.redlodgemusicfestival.org, early June)

brings young classical musicians to town for a week. Faculty and student recitals for the public happen nightly. Cowboys and cowgirls compete in the **Home of Champions Rodeo** (www.redlodgerodeo.com, early July) for three days. The rodeo brings on all the classic western competitions, from bull riding to steer wrestling. A parade marches through downtown each day at noon.

Harley-Davidson bikers congregate to ride the Beartooth Highway during the annual three-day **Beartooth Rally** (www.beartoothrally.com, late July). Events include the Iron Horse Rodeo (a rodeo competitions with motorcycles instead of horses), and black leathers are the clothing of choice at the rally's street dance. For cyclists, the **Beartooth Blitz** (www.usacycling.org, late June) is a two-day stage race up the Beartooth Highway.

Two March events celebrate activities on snow. Winter Carnival brings a parade to town followed by cardboard-box derby races on the slopes at **Red Lodge Mountain Resort** (305 Ski Run Rd., 406/446-2610, www.redlodgemountainresort.com, free). Horses pull skiers in the **National Finals Ski Joring Races** (101 Rodeo Dr., www.redlodgeskijoring.com, $5 adults, children free), a competition on the rodeo grounds that combines the Old and New West.

Shopping

Downtown Red Lodge has a few shops for souvenirs, art and photography galleries, and outdoor gear stores. The **Carbon County Arts Guild and Depot Gallery** (11 W. 8th St., 406/446-1370, http://carboncountydepotgallery.com, 10am-5pm Mon.-Sat., noon-5pm Sun., free) shows the works of local and regional artists. **Sylvan Peak Mountain Shop** (9 S. Broadway, 406/446-1770 or 800/249-2563, 9am-6pm Mon.-Sat.) carries hiking, backpacking, outdoor, and ski gear.

ACCOMMODATIONS

Red Lodge has a few chain motels, but mostly independent hotels that are open year-round. Summer sees the most visitors and the highest prices. Reservations are highly recommended for July and August. Hunting season in fall and the winter ski season also bring in the visitors, but fewer than in summer. Spring usually has the lowest rates.

For vacation home rentals, visit **AAA Red Lodge Rentals** (406/425-2125, www.aaaredlodgerentals.com) or **Red Lodge Reservations** (406/446-4700 or 877/733-5634, www.redlodgereservations.com).

Several historic hotels and bed-and-breakfasts are in Red Lodge, where you can walk to restaurants and be in the middle of nightlife hotspots. ★ **The Pollard Hotel** (2 N. Broadway, 406/446-0001, www.thepollard.com, $100-250) is a three-story brick affair that looks like a bank on the outside but retains restored historical Victorian features inside, including a triple-story gallery. The hotel has 39 rooms of several types. Standard hotel rooms have 1-2 queen beds; some queen rooms include small sitting areas. Queen and king suites feature one bed with a sitting area, jetted tubs, and a private indoor balcony overlooking the gallery. The hotel has an elevator, restaurant, pub, and fitness center, and breakfast is included.

Three blocks from downtown, **The Yodeler Motel** (601 S. Broadway, 406/446-1435 or 866/446-1435, www.yodelermotel.com,

$80-140) is a historic two-story Bavarian lodge with 23 rooms, an outdoor hot tub, and a ski waxing room. Exterior stairs lead to downstairs and upstairs rooms. The rooms have 1-2 queen beds or one king; downstairs rooms are smaller and cheaper.

Red Lodge also has two basic, but clean motels with bicycle or motorcycle washing stations. Away from the downtown hubbub, **Alpine Lodge Motel** (1105 N. Broadway, 406/446-2213, www.alpineredlodge.com, $80-160) has simple lodge rooms and cabins, kitchenettes, picnic tables, a grill, and laundry facility. Within walking distance to restaurants, **Red Lodge Inn** (811 S. Broadway, 406/446-2030, www.theredlodgeinn.com, $70-130) has rooms with 1-2 queens or one king, two-room suites for families, a hot tub, continental breakfast, and a picnic area with grills.

The Irish Rose (302 S. Broadway, 406/446-0303, www.irishrosehost.com, $135-165) is a bed-and-breakfast with three rooms in a historic 1910 home run by an artist. Families will love **Chateau Rouge** (1505 S. Broadway, 406/446-1601 or 800/926-1601, www.chateaurouge.com, $65-160), which has eight studio rooms with kitchenettes and 16 two-bedroom condos in a funky A-frame retro lodge. Amenities include an indoor pool and

The Pollard Hotel

hot tub. Located five miles south of town on the Beartooth Highway, **Rock Creek Resort** (6380 Hwy. 212, 406/446-1111, www.rock-creekresort.com, $130-400) offers a variety of lodging options: lodge rooms, condos, town-homes, and a log cabin. Some rooms over-look Rock Creek and include kitchenettes. The complex also has an indoor pool, hot tub, sauna, fitness room, and restaurant.

CAMPING

Red Lodge has two private campgrounds, one on each end of town. Each has hookups for water and electricity, picnic tables, flush toilets, showers, drinking water, camp stores, and disposal stations. Make reservations for July and August. Rates are for two people; add on $3-5 for each extra person. Located four miles north of town under cottonwoods and aspens, the **Red Lodge KOA** (7464 Hwy. 212, 406/446-2364 or 800/562-7540, www.koa.com, early May-Sept., $38-60 RVs, $28-38 tents) has 68 RV and 19 tent campsites with sewer hookups for RVs, a laundry, playground, swimming pool (summer only), dog walk, and wireless Internet. On the south end of town, **Perry's RV Park and Campground** (6664 S. Hwy. 212, 406/446-2722, www.perrysrv.us, late May-Sept., $35 RVs, $20 tents, cash or check only) crams 30 RV campsites close to-gether on a large, sunny, and open parking lot with 13 tent campsites under cottonwoods. A few campsites sit on Rock Creek. RVs are lim-ited to 45 feet.

National Forest Campgrounds

Numerous national forest campgrounds are located between Red Lodge and Yellowstone; many are right on the Beartooth Highway. Facilities include picnic tables, fire rings with grills, drinking water, bear boxes, vault toilets, and firewood for sale. Many have campground hosts on-site. No hookups are available for RVs.

CUSTER-GALLATIN NATIONAL FOREST

Campgrounds in **Custer-Gallatin National Forest** (Beartooth Ranger District, 6811 Hwy. 212 S., Red Lodge, 406/446-2103, www.fs.usda.gov/gallatin) are between Red Lodge and Beartooth Pass. **Reservations** (877/444-6777, www.recreation.gov) are highly recom-mended for July and August. Rates are $12-16 for one rig; extra vehicles cost $8.

West Fork Rock Creek canyon is seven miles off the Beartooth Highway. It contains both the 30-site **Basin Campground** (mid-May-Sept.), popular for its paved access, na-ture trail around Wild Bill Lake, fishing, and national recreation trails; and the 30-site **Cascade Campground** (late May-early Sept.), overlooking the creek. RVs are limited to 30 feet. Along the Beartooth Highway's east side, campgrounds line up on spur roads with easy access. At 6,282 feet, **Sheridan** and **Rattin** (Ratine) **Campgrounds** (mid-May-Sept., 30-foot RV limit) sit one mile apart on the dirt and potholed East Side Road, flank-ing Rock Creek.

Farther along Rock Creek at 7,150 feet, three campgrounds cluster close together in Rock Creek Canyon: **Parkside, Greenough Lake,** and **Limber Pine** (mid-May-Sept., 40-45-foot RV limit) have 64 campsites straddling Rock Creek. They hide in the trees where the Beartooth Highway begins its 4,000-foot switchback ascent to Vista Point, Beartooth Plateau, and Beartooth Pass. If these camp-grounds fill, free primitive first-come, first-served campsites (open as long as they are snow-free) line the rough, potholed dirt road following Rock Creek upstream.

SHOSHONE NATIONAL FOREST

On the west side of the Beartooth Pass, **Shoshone National Forest** (Clarks Fork Ranger District, 203A Yellowstone Ave., Cody, WY, 307/527-6921, www.fs.usda.gov/sho-shone, July-mid-Sept., $15, 32-foot RV limit) runs two ultra-scenic campgrounds. All sites are **first-come, first-served;** no reserva-tions are available. While in high demand, the campgrounds are also at high elevation, where breathing can be labored and sleeping fitful. Boat ramps access both of the lakes for fish-ing small trout that grow in the short ice-free season; voracious mosquitoes breed thick. Regular afternoon thunderstorms can pelt rain, hail, or snow even in August. At 9,600 feet, **Island Lake Campground** is the highest. The campground loops 21 sites around a hillside of windblown pines and firs adjacent to a lake rimmed with fuchsia paintbrush and bluebells. **Beartooth Lake Campground** clusters 21 campsites at 9,000 feet in a lakeside forest with peek-a-boo views of the orange-streaked Beartooth Butte.

FOOD

Many of the Red Lodge restaurants cluster in the historic downtown area. Hours shorten in spring, winter, and fall.

★ **Café Regis** (501 Word Ave., 406/446-1941, www.caferegis.com, 6am-2pm Wed.-Sun., $7-12) serves meals indoors or out on a patio surrounded by organic gardens and greenhouses. They dish up fresh meals and house-baked goodies, and can handle vegan, vegetarian, gluten-free, and food allergies. Breakfast (served all day) includes scrambles, omelets, and Mexican dishes. Lunch sees wraps, salads, and grilled or cold sandwiches on the menu.

The **Carbon County Steakhouse** (121 S. Broadway Ave., www.redlodgerestaurants.com, 4:30pm-9pm daily, $23-44) serves wild game and hand-cut steaks. It's the place to go for bison meatloaf, rib eye, elk medallions, and Montana Wagyu Cattle Company American Kobe strip. An extensive wine menu includes worldwide vintners. **The Pollard** (2 N. Broadway, 406/446-0001, www.thepollard.com, 4pm-close daily, $14-25) pulls live music into their pub on weekends. Find classic pub fare of burgers, pot pies, bratwurst, steak, and fish and chips with lighter meals like Thai lettuce wraps. Drinks include beer from Red Lodge Ales, wine, or cocktails. The hotel also serves meals in its dining room: Breakfast (7am-10am Mon.-Fri., 7am-11am Sat.-Sun., $7-14) includes omelets, burritos, and eggs Benedict. Dinner (5:30pm-9pm Fri.-Sat., $16-28) rolls out osso bucco and Italian specialties. **Bridge Creek**

Red Lodge Pizza Company

Backcountry Kitchen and Wine Bar (116 S. Broadway, 406/446-9900, www.eatfood-drinkwine.com, 11am-9pm daily) serves lunch ($11-20) until 3pm, a bar menu 3pm-5pm ($8-21), and dinner 5pm-close ($19-35). Appetizers, sandwiches, salads, soups, burgers, pasta, steaks, seafood, and wild game comprise the menu. An extensive wine list helps pair vintages with any meal.

For lighter dining, Red Lodge has two local faves. **Sam's Tap Room** (1445 N. Broadway, 406/446-0243, www.redlodgeales.com, daily 11am-9pm, kitchen closes at 7pm, $8-10) serves salads, soups, and hot or cold sandwiches with indoor and outdoor dining. Mix dishes with Red Lodge Ales seasonal brews, classic Beartooth Pale Ale, or Glacier Ale. **Red Lodge Pizza Company** (115 S. Broadway Ave., 406/446-3333, www.redlodgerestaurants.com, daily 11am-9pm, $10-24) offers a diverse menu of pizzas, salads, burgers, sandwiches, Italian dishes, and Montana rolls. They also have a create-your-own pizza, gluten-free crusts, and takeout.

For takeout and fast food, stop by **Mas Taco** (304 N. Broadway, 406/446-3636, 11am-9pm Tues.-Sat., 11am-4pm Sun., $4-10), a local Mexican eatery that serves fresh fare. Choose from pork, chicken, or beef tacos, empanadas, quesadillas, burritos, or taco salad. The taqueria also serves chiles rellenos, but they fly out the door fast. Housed in a century-old train car, the **Red Box Car** (1300 S. Broadway, 406/446-2152, 11am-9pm daily Apr.-Sept., $4-7) is the place to go for burgers, fries, and ice cream. Crowds on their outside picnic tables attest to its popularity.

Red Lodge even has its own coffee roaster. Drop in for a pick-me-up espresso at **Coffee Factory Roasters** (22 S. Broadway Ave., 406/446-3200, http://coffeefactoryroasters.com, 6:30am-6pm daily) and then take some beans home, too: Beartooth Mountain Blend or Moose Joose. For old-fashioned ice cream, **Scoops** (205 S. Broadway Ave., 406/446-0160, 11am-9pm daily) serves sundaes, floats, and ice cream from its 1919 soda fountain.

Groceries

Beartooth Market (201 N. Oakes Ave., 406/446-2684, daily 7am-8pm) carries fresh produce and meats, beer and wine, and packaged groceries. It also has a deli.

TRANSPORTATION AND SERVICES

Car

Red Lodge is 60 miles (1.15 hrs.) southwest of Billings, Montana and 68 miles (2 hrs.) northeast of Yellowstone's Northeast Entrance via the Beartooth Highway (closed mid-Oct.-late May). Two-lane highways are the norm in Red Lodge. In summer, both the town and the Beartooth Highway are clogged with motorcycle clubs and road rallies jockeying for position. Throw in bicyclists and no shoulders on the road, and drivers need to pay attention.

Parking in downtown Red Lodge is mainly on the street on Broadway Avenue (between 8th St. and 13th St.), but it gets cramped. Campers driving large RVs should park at the visitors center (701 N. Broadway Ave.) or Lions Park (between 5th and 8th Sts.) to walk downtown.

Red Lodge Tour and Taxi (406/425-3091, www.redlodgetaxi.com) provides the town taxi service, but also runs shuttles on demand to Billings.

Services

The **Red Lodge Visitor Center** (701 N. Broadway Ave., 406/446-1718, www.red-lodge.com, 9am-5pm Mon.-Fri., 10am-2pm

Liver-eating Johnston's cabin at the Red Lodge Visitor Center

Sat.-Sun.) is a small information center run by the Red Lodge Chamber of Commerce. Guides and maps on Red Lodge, Beartooth Highway, and the Absaroka-Beartooth Wilderness, Yellowstone National Park information, and a self-guided historic tour are available. The building has restrooms indoors and picnic tables, water, and an RV dump station outside, plus the historic log cabin of Liver-eating Johnston. For more Forest Service maps, road conditions, and trail information, visit the **Beartooth Ranger District Station** (Custer-Gallatin National Forest, 6811 Hwy. 212 S., Red Lodge, 406/446-2103, www.fs.usda.gov/gallatin).

Red Lodge has a **post office** (119 S. Hauser Ave., 406/446-2629, 8am-4pm Mon.-Fri., 10am-1pm Sat.), an **RV dump** station at the visitors center (Hwy. 78 and U.S. 212), and showers available at the **Red Lodge City Pool** (14th St. and Hauser Ave., 406/446-3727, daily June-Aug., hours are weather dependent). The **Rock Creek Laundry** (1101 S. Broadway Ave., 406/446-9890) has coin-op machines and wireless Internet in the waiting area. A public laundry is also at the **Alpine Lodge Motel** (1105 N. Broadway, 406/446-2213, www.alpineredlodge.com).

MEDIA AND COMMUNICATIONS

Cell service is available in Red Lodge. Verizon phones work the best; other services get spotty reception. Reception (both cell and Wi-Fi) disappears entirely up the Beartooth Highway. Most hotels and campgrounds in town have wireless Internet. Public computers are available at the **Red Lodge Carnegie Library** (8th St. and Broadway Ave., 406/446-1905, 10am-6pm Tues.-Fri., noon-6pm Sat.). Several cafés in town also have wireless Internet.

The Red Lodge newspaper is the weekly *Carbon County News* (www.carboncountynews.com), but the daily newspaper is the *Billings Gazette* (http://billingsgazette.com).

MEDICAL SERVICES

The **Beartooth Billings Clinic** (2525 N. Broadway, 406/446-2345 or 877/404-9442, www.beartoothbillingsclinc.org) has a 24/7 emergency department. The nearest hospitals are both about 60 miles away: **St. Vincent Healthcare** (1233 N. 30th St., Billings, MT, 406/657-7000, www.svh-mt.org) and **West Park Hospital** (707 Sheridan Ave., Cody, WY, 307/527-7501, www.westparkhospital.org).

Cody, Wyoming

Cody, Wyoming, is a cowboy relic on the western slopes of the Rocky Mountains. Designed and founded by Buffalo Bill Cody in 1895, the town hangs on to its Wild West heritage, which distinguishes it from towns that lost their sense of history in the evolution to modern day. Cody serves as a gateway to Yellowstone National Park most of the year. Two routes link into Yellowstone, but they are only open **May-early November.** During winter, access to Yellowstone is only by snowmobile.

Many visitors prefer using Cody as an airline gateway for Yellowstone. Though limited, fights can be cheaper than those into Jackson Hole. The **Buffalo Bill Scenic Byway** (U.S. Hwy. 14/16/20) connects Cody to the East Entrance of Yellowstone on a route than climbs through spires and crags of Shoshone Canyon and the Absaroka Mountains.

SIGHTS
★ Buffalo Bill Center of the West

The **Buffalo Bill Center of the West** (720 Sheridan Ave., 307/587-4771, 8am-6pm daily May-mid-Sept., hours shorten mid-Sept.-May, $19 adults, $17 seniors, $11-15 kids) includes admission to five museums at the complex. It's a lot to take in (passes are good for two

Cody

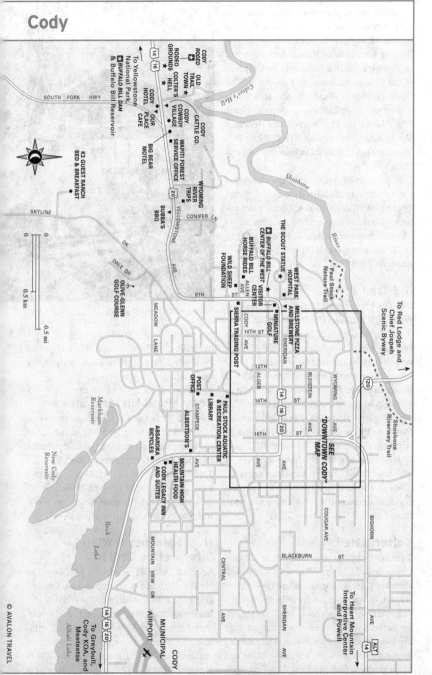

© AVALON TRAVEL

days), but provides a broad background. The **Whitney Gallery of Western Art** houses famous artwork of the American West. The **Draper Museum of Natural History** has exhibits on wildlife, ecology, and raptors of the Greater Yellowstone Ecosystem. The **Cody Firearms Museum** contains a collection of American and European guns. The **Plains Indian Museum** celebrates Native American heritage. The **Buffalo Bill Museum** has memorabilia from Buffalo Bill Cody's life.

Exhibits even spill outdoors with several wildlife sculptures. Listed on the National Register of Historic Places, *The Scout* (between Sheridan Ave. and Monument St.) is a bronze statue of Buffalo Bill Cody. Built in 1924, the statue was designed by Gertrude Vanderbilt Whitney.

Buffalo Bill Center of the West

Old Trail Town

Old Trail Town and Museum of the Old West (1831 Demaris Dr., 307/587-5302, www.oldtrailtown.org, 8am-7pm daily mid-May-Sept., $9 adults, $8 seniors, $5 kids 6-12) conveys the visual ambience of a western ghost town—but it's not a true ghost town. A local historian and archaeologist built the town as a replica of the original town of Cody. The buildings and artifacts are real, but were all moved to this location. The site contains 26 buildings that date from 1879 to 1901. Strewn around the town are 100 horse-drawn rigs plus frontier and Native American artifacts. The site also contains the graves of several regional personalities, but those too were moved here.

Colter's Hell

Tucked between the Stampede Rodeo Grounds and Old Trail Town, **Colter's Hell** (U.S. Hwy. 14) is a barren, sunny, 0.5-mile interpretive loop that circles a field where the original town of Cody sat in 1897. Rock-cairn lot markers, wagon wheel ruts, and tepee rings are identified. Interpretive signs are named for geothermals on the Shoshone River and cover geology, flora, and wildlife. Parking is in a pullout on the north side of U.S. Highway 14. On hot days, walk this trail only in the morning.

Cody Mural Historic Site

Edward T. Grigware's 36-foot mural of Mormon pioneers fills the rotunda ceiling of the visitors center at the **Cody Mural Historic Site** (1719 Wyoming Ave., 307/587-3290, http://codymural.com, 9am-7pm Mon.-Sat., 3pm-7pm Sun. June-mid-Sept., free). Also on-site, the **Pioneer Museum** (free) includes exhibits of Mormon pioneers.

Heart Mountain WWII Interpretive Center

Located 14 miles northwest of Cody, the **Heart Mountain Interpretive Center** (1539 Road 19, Powell, 307/754-8000, www.heartmountain.org, 10am-5pm daily mid-May-Sept., 10am-5pm Wed.-Sat. Oct.-mid-May, $7 adults, $5 seniors and students, children under 12 free) records the life of Japanese Americans during their internment

Downtown Cody

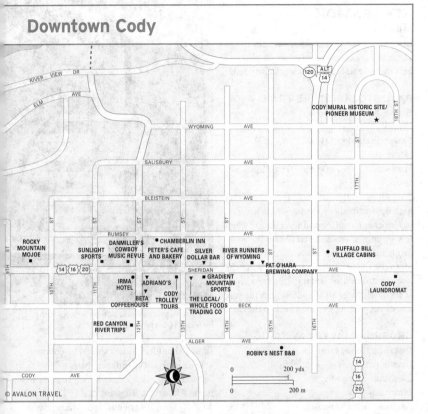

© AVALON TRAVEL

in World War II. In the three years of its existence, the Heart Mountain Relocation Center housed more than 14,000 people in 500 buildings. Only three buildings and a chimney remain, along with the colossal embarrassment of a country for such treatment of its citizens. The center uses replicas of barracks, a scale model of the camp, photographs, films, recorded oral histories, and interactive exhibits to convey what happened.

Buffalo Bill State Park

Buffalo Bill State Park (47 Lakeside Rd., Cody, 307/587-9227, http://wyoparks. state.wy.us) encompasses the Buffalo Bill Reservoir, the lower few miles of the North Fork of the Shoshone River, two campgrounds, Buffalo Bill Dam, and a few more miles of the Shoshone River. It's a place to camp, boat, fish, kayak, canoe, paddleboard, and windsurf.

★ BUFFALO BILL DAM

At 325 feet, the historic **Buffalo Bill Dam** (307/527-6076, www.bbdvc.com, 8am-7pm Mon.-Fri., 9am-5pm Sat.-Sun. June-Aug., shorter hours May and Sept., free) was the highest dam in the country when it was built in 1910. Today it houses a visitors center with indoor and outdoor interpretive exhibits about local history and wildlife. It is also a National Civil Engineering Landmark due to how it squeezes into Shoshone Canyon.

From Cody, drive the North Fork Highway (Hwy. 14/16/20) 4.5 miles west. As the road climbs along the cliffs of Shoshone Canyon, it passes through three tunnels, popping out of the third tunnel at the dam.

RECREATION

Hiking

In Cody, trails run along the Shoshone River. These two are close enough that you can connect them by walking a few blocks between.

PAUL STOCK NATURE TRAIL

Distance: 2.6 miles round-trip
Duration: 1.5 hours
Elevation change: 52 feet
Effort: easy
Trailhead: 801 Spruce Drive (west end of Spruce Street)

This sunny interpretive trail follows a gravel path upstream above the Shoshone River. It has benches for sitting and several short spurs to viewpoints. From the trailhead, the route drops to the river, where a short loop peels off to the right through a few trees. After the loop, continue upstream until the gravel ends at an overlook of an island. Return the way you came, gaining elevation back to the car.

SHOSHONE RIVERWAY TRAIL

Distance: 2.6 miles round-trip
Duration: 1.5 hours
Elevation change: flat
Effort: easy
Trailhead: end of 12th Street

A paved trail runs south along the Shoshone River for walkers and cyclists. The trail starts by crossing under the Belfry Bridge and then goes east for 1.3 miles through wetlands until it hits its lollypop-loop end. Return the same way.

Biking

Classic road rides are out-and-back trips on the Buffalo Bill Scenic Byway and the Chief Joseph Scenic Byway. **Buffalo Bill Scenic Byway** (Hwy. 14/16/20) is a century ride (100 miles round-trip) from Cody to the East Entrance of Yellowstone. It does not require as much climbing as the **Chief Joseph Scenic Byway** (Hwy. 296), which starts 17 miles north of Cody on Highway 120 and ends at the Beartooth Highway (Hwy. 212). Both routes require riding narrow two-lane roads with

This ball plug was used to stop up flow out of the Buffalo Bill Dam power conduit.

skinny shoulders; riders should be comfortable with large RVs whizzing past.

Mountain bikers have two resources in town: **Absaroka Bicycles** (2201 17th St. #7, 307/527-5566, 10am-6pm Mon.-Thurs., closes earlier Fri.-Sat.) and local bike club **Park County Pedalers** (http://parkcountypedalers.org). Park County Pedalers has been developing the **Beck Lake Bike Park** (2401 14th St.). Mountain bikers can ride free on the single-track, pump track, skills features, flow trail, and jumps. Trails extend into adjoining BLM land. The **Outlaw Trails**, about four miles north of town, have classic single-track and slickrock trails. Directions, maps, and trail descriptions are available from Absaroka Bicycles. The bike shop also rents mountains bikes ($40 with helmet) and guides bike tours.

Horseback Riding

Cody has trail riding in town. Most of the wranglers rely on tips; plan to tip 15 percent. Wear sturdy shoes and long pants for safety and comfort. **Buffalo Bill Horse Rides** (720

Sheridan Ave., 307/250-7660, http://centerof-thewest.org, daily June-Aug., $40) has one-hour trail rides from the Buffalo Bill Center of the West that circle the Paul Stock Nature Trail adjacent to the Shoshone River. Children under age five can enjoy pony rides ($20). **Cedar Mountain Trail Rides** (12 Spirit Mountain Dr., 307/527-4966, 8am-5pm daily June-Aug., from $35, cash only) offers one-hour, two-hour, or full-day rides from two locations: one mile west of the rodeo grounds in Cody or the Cody KOA Campground, one mile east of the airport. Children too young to ride alone can join their parents. The trip to the rodeo grounds is on a steep, rocky trail, and is more for those with a sense of adventure.

Ranches and other wranglers lead trail rides outside of Cody on the Buffalo Bill Scenic Byway. Located 26 miles west of Cody, **Bill Cody Ranch** (2604 North Fork Hwy., 307/587-2097 or 800/615-2934, http://billcodyranch.com, daily mid-May-late Sept., $55-265) leads two-hour horseback rides, four-hour lunch rides, all-day cookouts, and overnight pack trips. At Pahaska Tepee Resort, located 50 miles west of Cody, wranglers at **Real McCoy Horses** (183 North Fork Hwy., 307/527-7701, $40-165) lead one-hour, two-hour, half-day, and full-day rides.

Water Sports

Many days around Cody have calm air in the morning, but winds whip up in the afternoon, especially up on the Buffalo Bill Reservoir, located at 5,500 feet in the arid high-desert valley between raw mountains. Plan what you want to do on the water around what the winds deliver. It can be calm for paddleboarding in the morning, but perfect for windsurfing in the afternoon.

All boats, canoes, and kayaks require current **registration** for Wyoming residents or nonresidents (Wyoming Game and Fish, https://wgfd.wyo.gov, residents: $10 motorized, $5 nonmotorized; nonresidents: $30 motorized, $15 nonmotorized), and an Aquatic Invasive Species (AIS) sticker. The only exemption is for inflatable boats less than 10 feet long, paddleboards, and windsurfers.

BOATING

The reservoir at **Buffalo Bill State Park** (47 Lakeside Rd., Cody, 307/587-9227, http://wyoparks.state.wy.us) has boat launches easily accessible from U.S. Highway 14/16/20. The easiest and biggest launch is at North Shore Bay Campground (May-Sept., $4-6 day use), which has ample trailer parking, fish cleaning stations, cement ramps, restrooms, and

Real McCoy Horses at Pahaska Tepee

water. You can also launch from the South Shore Boat Launch, accessed via Gibbs Bridge (same turnoff as the campground at the west end of the reservoir) and a dirt road.

Rentals are available from **Gradient Mountain Sports** (1390 Sheridan Ave., 307/587-4659, www.gradientmountainsports.com, $30-50). The shop rents touring kayaks, sit-on-top kayaks, canoes, paddleboards, and white-water kayaks. Rates are good for 24 hours and include paddles, spray skirts, life jackets, roof pads, and straps.

FISHING

Anglers with boats can fish for rainbow, rainbow-cutthroat hybrids, Yellowstone cutthroat trout, brown trout, and lake trout in **Buffalo Bill Reservoir** (Buffalo Bill State Park, 47 Lakeside Rd., Cody, 307/587-9227, http://wyoparks.state.wy.us). Fly-fishing aficionados head for the North Fork of the Shoshone River (access is via Shoshone National Forest campgrounds and BLM campsites) after rainbow, brown, and Yellowstone cutthroat trout. Wade-fishing or float-fishing works in the river, and its tributaries also offer decent fishing. Anglers will need a **Wyoming fishing license** (Wyoming Game and Fish, https://wgfd.wyo.gov, residents: $6 day, $24 annual, $3 youth; nonresidents: $14 day, $92 annual, $15 youth) for the North Fork of the Shoshone River.

North Fork Anglers (1107 Sheridan Ave., 307/527-7274, www.northforkanglers.com, 9am-6pm daily May-Oct., 8am-9pm Mon.-Sat. Nov.-Apr.) guide floating trips ($350 half day or $450 full day for two people) or wading ($300 half day or $400 full day for two people) trips on the North Fork River. (Tip guides 10-20 percent.) The outfit also rents reels, rods, waders, and boots.

RAFTING

The Class I-III **Shoshone River** floats through **Shoshone Canyon** below Cody. Families can take a splashy 5-12-mile ride during rafting season (May-Sept.). Longer trips start with Red Rock Canyon, named for the dramatic red cliffs on both sides of the river, and work down through Lower Shoshone Canyon; shorter trips put in for the lower canyon only.

West of Cody, the **North Fork of the Shoshone River** (Wapiti Valley, above Buffalo Bill Reservoir) has Class II-III white water. Most rafting floats 11-13 miles of river starting from Shoshone National Forest's east boundary through Wapiti Valley, or from river accesses just east of Pahaska Tepee Resort. Rafting season here runs May-mid-July, before the water drops too low.

Guided trips run daily on both rivers. Companies provide transportation to and from the river, as well as life jackets and gear for nasty weather. Two-hour trips on the Shoshone River and Shoshone Canyon run $35-45 for adults. Half-day trips on the North Fork cost $70-80 for adults and include lunch. When available, inflatable kayak trips cost $35-85. Make reservations to guarantee slots, and plan to tip your guide 15 percent.

Three rafting companies guide daily trips on both rivers; two companies rent gear.

- **Red Canyon River Trips** (1119 12th St., 307/587-6988 or 800/293-0148, www.codywyomingadventures.com) guides three trips daily through Lower Shoshone Canyon and one trip on the North Fork. The company also rents inflatable kayaks, canoes, kayaks, and paddleboards ($20-80 plus $10-15/item for helmets, paddles, life jackets) for self-guided floaters.

- **Wyoming River Trips** (233 Yellowstone Hwy., 307/587-6661 or 800/586-6661, http://wyomingrivertrips.com) guides two trips daily through Red Rock Canyon and Shoshone Canyon, plus one trip on the North Fork. Inflatable kayak trips go through Red Rock Canyon.

- **River Runners of Wyoming** (1491 Sheridan Ave., 307/527-7238 or 800/535-7238, www.riverrunnersofwyoming.com) takes three trips daily down the Shoshone Canyon and one on the North Fork.

- **Gradient Mountain Sports** (1390 Sheridan Ave., 307/587-4659, www.gradientmountainsports.com) rents white-water and inflatable kayaks ($30-50) and helmets, car-top carriers, paddles, and wetsuits ($5-8).

SWIMMING
Paul Stock Aquatic and Recreation Center (1402 Heart Mountain St., 307/587-0400, www.cityofcody-wy.gov, 5:30am-10pm Mon.-Thurs., 5:30am-8pm Fri., 8am-6pm Sat., noon-6pm Sun. year-round, $12 adults, $6 students and youth, children under 4 free) has a lap swimming pool, leisure pool, therapy pool, aquatic climbing wall, diving board, and waterslide. Fitness equipment, a suspended track, a gymnasium, and racquetball courts are also on-site.

Golf
Olive Glenn Golf and Country Club (802 Meadow Ln., 307/587-5551, http://golfoliveglen.com, dawn-dusk daily Apr.-Oct.) is an 18-hole, par 72 public course with a pro shop, driving range, putting green, and restaurant. Greens fees are $60 with a cart, $50 without; club rentals are $20. An 18-hole **miniature golf course** (corner of 9th St. and Sheridan Ave., mid-May-mid-Sept.) is at Cody City Park.

Winter Sports
SKIING
Sleeping Giant Ski Area (348 North Fork Hwy., 307/587-3125, http://skisg.net, 9:30am-4pm Fri.-Sun. mid-Dec.-Mar.) is a small, resurrected community ski area with two lifts, a conveyer carpet, terrain parks, rentals, lessons, and a cafeteria. Lift tickets cost $34 for adults, $26 for juniors, and $16 for kids. To get there, take Highway 12/14/20 west for 47 miles to Cody. Turn south at the signed entrance.

CROSS-COUNTRY SKIING AND SNOWSHOEING
Volunteers groom the **Park County Nordic Ski Association** (307/272-1509, www.

nordicskiclub.com, Dec.-Mar., free, donations accepted) trails at **Pahaska Tepee Resort** (183 North Fork Hwy., 307/527-7701, www.pahaska.com). More than 19 kilometers (12 miles) are groomed for skate and classic skiing. Some trails permit snowshoers and dogs. To reach Pahaska Tepee, drive 49 miles (1 hour) west of Cody on Highway 12/14/20 and turn west into the parking lot.

Cross-country ski and snowshoe rentals are at **Sunlight Sports** (1131 Sheridan Ave., Cody, 307/587-9517 or 888/889-2463, www.sunlightsports.com, 9am-8pm Mon.-Sat., 9am-6pm Sun.).

SNOWMOBILING
Guided snowmobile tours enter Yellowstone through the East Entrance and over Sylvan Pass. **Rimrock Ranch** (2768 North Fork Hwy., 307/587-3970, www.rimrockranch.com, late Dec.-early Mar., $350 for two people on one machine) guides full-day tours that stop at Old Faithful, the geyser basins, Lower Yellowstone Falls, and Yellowstone Lake. Reservations are required.

ENTERTAINMENT AND SHOPPING
Nightlife
Summer nightlife in Cody is at the rodeo—period. If you want to check out a few bars, sidle up to a stool in the Silver Saddle Saloon at the historic **Irma Hotel** (1192 Sheridan Ave., 307/587-4221 or 800/745-4762, 11am-2pm daily) to admire the ornate wood-carved backboard. Shoot pool after ordering some burgers in the iconic **Silver Dollar Bar** (1313 Sheridan Ave., 307/527-7666, 11am-2pm daily), which has live rock-and-roll music on Friday and Saturday nights.

Guitars and fiddles boost the foot-stomping with live western music. For **Cody Cattle Company** (1910 Demaris St., 307/272-5770, http://thecodycattlecompany.com, 5:30pm-7:30pm daily June-late Sept., $28 adults, $14 kids) features music from Ryan Martin and the Triple C Cowboys Band accompanied by a western all-you-can-eat chuck wagon buffet. The cowboy show ends in time to see the rodeo, about a block away. For western music without the food, **Dan Miller's Cowboy Music Revue** (1171 Sheridan Ave., 307/272-7855, http://cowboymusicrevue.com, 8pm Mon.-Sat. mid-May-Sept., $16) gets the foot-stomping going in the Cody Theater. The family entertainment show mixes cowboy poetry, stories, humor, and well-known tunes. The **Irma Hotel** (1192 Sheridan Ave., 307/587-4221 or 800/745-4762, www.irmahotel.com, $28-35 adults, $11-16 kids) sells a dinner-ticket package for Miller's show.

The City of Cody puts on **free music concerts** in the downtown City Park (corner of 9th St. and Beck Ave., 6pm-8pm Thurs. July-Aug.), where musical talent spans the gamut.

Festivals and Events
CODY GUNFIGHT
A **Cody gunfight** (www.codygunfighters. com, 6pm Mon.-Sat. June-mid-Sept., free) bursts out in summer. Actors take to the street in front of the historic Irma Hotel (1192 Sheridan Ave.) with a 30-minute shoot-'em-up performance. Four different shows rotate throughout summer. Crowds pack the curbs with standing room only, so you'll want to nab

your spot around 5:45pm. Reserve chairs from **Cody Trolley Tours** (307/527-7043, www.codytrolleytours.com, $2) at the trolley station or from their ticket booth at the Irma Hotel.

★ CODY RODEO
Opening nightly with traditional flag pageantry, the **Cody Rodeo** (519 W. Yellowstone Ave., 307/587-5155, www.codystampederodeo.com, 8pm-10pm daily June-Aug., gates open at 7pm, $20 adults, $10 children 7-12) whoops it up with bronc and bull riding, barrel racing, and a kids' calf scramble. Late June usually has one night of extreme bull riding, featuring top riders and top kicking bulls. The week of July 4th ups the rider caliber to PRCA heavyweights (reserved seats for July 4th finals cost $25). The stands are covered, but if the weather looks foreboding, bring layers—the rodeo goes on even in rain. **Tickets** are available in advance online (www.codystampederodeo.com) or at the ticket office (1031 12th St.) and visitors center (836 Sheridan Ave.).

Cody Cowboy Stages (307/272-5573 or 307/272-0616, www.codytransportation. com, $5 adults, $3 children 9-14, children under 8 free) runs a nightly shuttle to the rodeo grounds, stopping for pickups at most

Cody Cattle Company

The Cody Rodeo occurs at Stampede Park.

Nordic skiing. The shop also rents camping gear ($3-30/day, discounts for multiple days) and skis, snowboards, Nordic skis, and snowshoes. The discount outdoor mail-order store **Sierra Trading Post** (1402 8th St., 307/578-5802, www.sierratradingpost.com, 9am-8pm Mon.-Sat., 10am-6pm Sun. year-round) has an outlet in Cody, right across from the Buffalo Bill Center of the West.

ACCOMMODATIONS

Summer is high season in Cody, when hotels pack out and prices are highest. To guarantee you can stay where you want, **make reservations 3-4 months in advance in summer.** In fall, winter, and spring, reservations are not needed. Cody has several moderate hotel chains, plus a few of the budget variety, although budget rates in summer may be higher than average. Lodging is available year-round, except for guest ranches.

For a full list of hotels and lodges, contact the **Park County Travel Council** (www.yellowstonecountry.org); for vacation rentals, contact **Cody Lodging Company** (307/587-6000 or 800/587-6560, www.codylodgingcompany.com).

Hotels

Cody is full of history, and its hotels are part of that. ★ **Chamberlin Inn** (1032 12th St., 888/587-0202, www.chamberlininn.com, $120-550) once served as the courthouse. Today it's a boutique hotel with fresh flowers, chocolates, and luxury linens in the rooms. The two-story redbrick building has 21 guest rooms; all are different and some have kitchenettes. Specialty rooms include the garden and historic courthouse residence. A library, sunroom, and enclosed lawn courtyard serve as communal spaces.

On the National Register of Historic Places, the **Irma Hotel** (1192 Sheridan Ave., 307/587-4221 or 800/745-4762, www.irmahotel.com, $132-200 summer, $70-100 winter) is a historical experience, even down to the cigarette-scented front porch and saloon. Built by Buffalo Bill Cody in 1902 and named for

hotels and campgrounds. No reservations are needed; pay cash when boarding.

Shopping

Western art and clothing shops abound in Cody. For cowboy hats, boots, bandanas, buckles, jeans, and jewelry, stop by **Custom Cowboy Shop** (1286 Sheridan Ave., 307/527-7300, http://customcowboyshop.com, 9am-6pm Mon.-Sat.) or **Boot Barn** (1625 Stampede Ave., 307/587-4493, www.bootbarn.com, 9am-8pm Mon.-Fri., 9am-7pm Sat.). For western art, peruse **Big Horn Galleries** (1167 Sheridan Ave., 307/527-7587, www.bighorn-galleries.com, 9:30am-5:30pm Mon.-Sat.) and **Simpson Gallagher Gallery** (1161 Sheridan Ave., 307/587-4022, www.simpsongallagher-gallery.com, 10am-5:30pm Mon.-Sat.).

Cody also has art galleries, crafts and artisans, and sporting goods stores. **Sunlight Sports** (1131 Sheridan Ave., 307/587-9517 or 888/889-2463, 9am-8pm Mon.-Sat., 9am-6pm Sun.) sells gear for climbing, hiking, backpacking, skiing, snowboarding, and his daughter, the hotel has historic and modern rooms in an old two-story brick building. Between the carpet, bedspread, and wallpaper, some rooms look like a patchwork of discordant styles. Bed configurations include doubles, queens, or a king, with some rooms adding 1-2 single beds. All rooms come with private bathrooms and air-conditioning. The hotel includes a restaurant and a bar, where you can watch the famous gunfight six nights a week from the front porch.

Motels and Cabins

A few lodging options flank the highway close to the rodeo grounds and Old Trail Town. Rooms at the **Cody Hotel** (232 W. Yellowstone Ave., 307/213-4481, http://thecody1-px.rtrk.com, $120-310) come in standard or deluxe versions with patios or balconies and feature 1-2 queens or a king bed; king suites have jet tubs and fireplaces. Breakfast is included. In the evening, the lobby serves treats and someone plays the baby grand piano.

Cody Cowboy Village (203 W. Yellowstone Ave., 307/587-7555, www.thecodycowboyvillage.com, May-mid-Oct., $90-200) is a collection of one- and two-story log buildings that house rooms and suites. The 40 cabin rooms include one king bed or two queens and bathrooms with tile showers. The 10 luxury suites feature two rooms with two queens and a queen-size sofa sleeper; bathrooms have tub-shower combos. The property has a giant hot tub fed by a small waterfall and offers concierge service, continental breakfast, and ADA rooms.

Big Bear Motel (139 W. Yellowstone Ave., 307/587-3117 or 800/325-7163, www.codywyomingbigbear.com, $60-120) has rooms in combos of queens, doubles, or one king, and a summer outdoor pool.

Located on the downtown strip and within walking distance to the nightly gunfight, **Buffalo Bill Village Cabins** (1701 Sheridan Ave., 307/587-5544, www.blairhotels.com, May-Sept., $175-200) includes 83 log-sided cabins built in the 1920s, but with updated pine-walled interiors. The one- and two-bedroom cabins with private bathrooms feature various combinations of king, queen, double, and twin beds. The cabins are part of the Buffalo Bill Village Resort, which also has a Holiday Inn, Comfort Inn, summer outdoor heated pool, and restaurant.

On the south end of town, **Cody Legacy Inn and Suites** (1801 Mountain View Dr., 307/587-6067, www.codylegacyinn.com,

the historic Irma Hotel

Pahaska Tepee

$80-160) offers lodgepole-pine-furnished rooms with two queens or one king, and family suites that can sleep 5-6 people. The complex also has a summer outdoor pool, hot tub, and sauna.

Bed-and-Breakfasts

Cody has plenty of B&Bs, but the best ones are 10 minutes from downtown. The **K3 Guest Ranch Bed and Breakfast** (30 Nielson Trail, 307/587-2080 or 888/587-2080, www.k3guestranch.com, May-early Oct., $120-210) offers a western take on the usual B&B. Five guest rooms sleep 2-6 people each and include a private bath. Each is unique—one room has a bed in a 19th-century chuck wagon, while another bed is located inside a hay wagon. The Teton Room features a mural of its namesake mountains and a log bed. Other accommodations are located in a small house made from canvas tenting and an 1897 sheepherders wagon with a cabin tent. A western-style breakfast is cooked on a campfire and served outdoors on a patio, or in the indoor dining

room when the weather sours. Outdoor activities include hiking, fishing, rifle target shooting, and sitting around a campfire.

Located on a small ranch, the **Southfork Bed and Breakfast** (797 Southfork Rd., 307/587-8311, http://southforkbb.com, June-Sept., $130-200) has three rooms in a large home with common areas that include a kitchen, dining room, bar, great room, and theater. Two rooms feature a queen bed, sitting area, and private bath. The Shoshone Room has a queen bed, but is only rented in tandem with the neighboring Teton room; families or friends must share a bathroom. Breakfast is a large affair with a menu that changes daily.

Lodges and Guest Ranches

A lineup of historic lodges flanks the Buffalo Bill Scenic Byway (U.S. Hwy. 14/16/20) between Cody and Yellowstone's East Entrance. Located 18 miles west of Cody, historic **Wapiti Lodge** (3189 North Fork Hwy., 307/763-5880, www.wapitilodge.com, late May-Oct., $170-250) overlooks the North Fork of the Shoshone River. The 1904 lodge was renovated in 2012 and has six suites, two cabins, and kitchenettes or full kitchens. Amenities include a continental breakfast and fishing on the river.

In Shoshone National Forest, halfway between Cody and Yellowstone, the 1925 **Bill Cody Ranch** (2604 North Fork Hwy., 307/587-2097 or 800/615-2934, http://billcodyranch.com, early May-late Sept., $120-225) features 17 rustic log cabins (no kitchens) on Nameit Creek below Ptarmigan Mountain. A restaurant and horseback riding are on-site.

Located three miles from Yellowstone's East Entrance, **Shoshone Lodge and Guest Ranch** (349 North Fork Hwy., 307/587-4044, www.shoshonelodge.com, May-early Oct., $120-330) centers 18 cabins around a 1920s rustic log lodge that includes a restaurant, bar, and horseback riding. Acquiring its fame as the 1904 lodge built by Buffalo Bill Cody, **Pahaska Tepee Resort** (183 North Fork Hwy., 307/527-7701 or 800/628-7791, www.

pahaska.com, May-mid-Oct., $100-230) is a funky mountain resort with a main log lodge on the National Register of Historic Places. A mix of rustic A-frame motel-style cabins and two-story log cabins accommodate guests.

CAMPING

Cody's sunny campgrounds are the place for RVers (even the big rigs) looking for full hookups (water, sewer, electricity, and cable TV) and action close to town. Amenities include flush toilets, showers, drinking water, picnic tables, camp stores, playgrounds, laundries, dump stations, and wireless Internet. Make summer reservations one month in advance. Rates include two people ($3-6 for each additional person; children under 6 free).

Located near the airport, the **Cody KOA** (5561 Greybull Hwy., 307/587-2369 or 800/562-8507, www.codykoa.com, May-Sept., $45-60 RVs, $25 tents, $6 each additional person) has 161 RV sites and 12 tent sites. Amenities include a swimming pool, hot tub, wading pool, game room, dog playground, and a shuttle to the nightly rodeo. Located on the west end of town, the **Ponderosa Campground** (1815 8th St., 307/587-9203, http://codyponderosa.com, mid-Apr.-mid-Oct., $35-50 RVs, $30 tents, $31 tepees) has half of its sites under the shade of big trees and half in open sun. In addition to the usual amenities, the campground has a cappuccino bar, six tepees, several cabins, and pickups for trolley tours, rodeos, and river rafting.

Located 9 and 13 miles west of Cody are two sunny campgrounds in **Buffalo Bill State Park** (47 Lakeside Rd., 307/587-9227, http://wyoparks.state.wy.us, May-Sept., $10 primitive, $22 hookups, $7 fee for nonresidents). Together, they comprise 99 campsites. Sites include those with hookups (water and electricity), primitive sites, ADA sites, and walk-in tent sites. Picnic tables, fire rings with grills, vault toilets, drinking water, disposal stations, coin-op showers, and campground hosts are available. The **North Shore Bay Campground** has a boat launch and overlooks Buffalo Bill Reservoir from a windblown arid slope between the highway and the water; some sites have windbreak fences. The **North Fork Campground** sits west of the reservoir and flanks the North Fork River. Sites are spread around a mowed green lawn. **Reservations** (877/996-7275, http://travel.wyo-park.com) are recommended for July and August.

Shoshone National Forest

From Cody, campgrounds flank routes into Yellowstone in **Shoshone National Forest** (Wapiti Ranger District, 203A Yellowstone Ave., Cody, 307/527-6921, www.fs.usda.gov/shoshone, mid-May-Sept., $10-15 primitive, $20 hookups). **Reservations** (877/444-6777, www.recreation.gov) are accepted for Big Game, Wapiti, Rex Hale, Threemile, and Hunter Peak.

BUFFALO BILL SCENIC BYWAY

A string of eight campgrounds line the Buffalo Bill Scenic Byway (Hwy. 14/16/20) 28-48 miles west of Cody. Sites sit along or near the North Fork of the Shoshone River with access to fishing and floating. Two campgrounds sit 29 miles west of Cody on U.S. Highway 14. Located a half mile apart, brushy **Big Game Campground** (no water) and **Wapiti Campground** have 56 campsites between them. Wapiti can fit larger RVs and has electrical hookups; it stays open through hunting season until late November. Yellowstone's East Entrance is 23 miles west.

Four campgrounds cluster in sagebrush, junipers, and pines about midway between Cody and Yellowstone, with 85 campsites between them. Located 30 miles west of Cody, **Elk Fork Campground** (no water) has river access. **Clearwater Campground** (43 miles west of Cody, no water) is popular with tent campers for its scenic walk-in sites on the river. Near Mummy Cave, **Rex Hale Campground** (35 miles west of Cody) has sites with electrical hookups, while sites at **Newton Creek Campground** (38 miles west of Cody) have views of dramatic pinnacles. Yellowstone's East Entrance is due west.

Shoshone National Forest

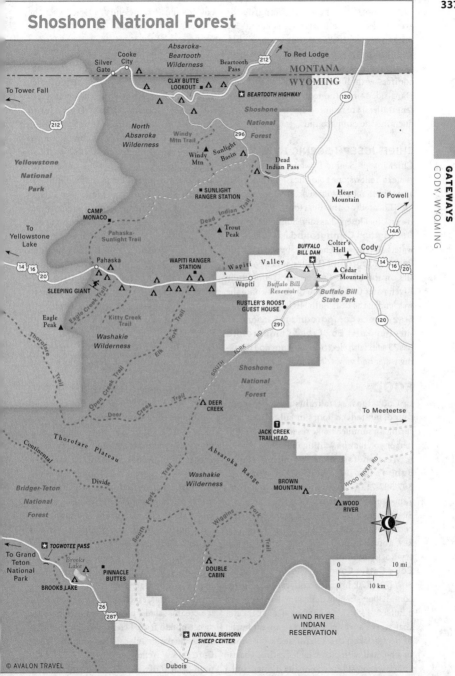

GATEWAYS
CODY, WYOMING

© AVALON TRAVEL

The more sought-after campgrounds are closest to Yellowstone, located 3-7 miles west of the East Entrance. **Eagle Creek Campground** and **Threemile Campground** scatter in cow parsnips and conifers with 40 campsites between them. Hard-sided units (no tents, tent pop-ups, or tent trailers) are required due to grizzlies frequenting the campgrounds.

CHIEF JOSEPH SCENIC BYWAY

Chief Joseph Scenic Byway (Hwy. 296), en route to Yellowstone's Northeast Entrance, has a few Shoshone National Forest campgrounds, too. Located on the Beartooth Plateau between Chief Joseph Pass and Sunlight Canyon, **Dead Indian Campground** has 10 sites (no water). On the west end of the byway, **Hunter Peak Campground** (10 sites, water available) sits on the Clarks Fork of the Yellowstone River. After turning from the byway onto the west end of the Beartooth Highway (Hwy. 12), **Crazy Creek Campground** has 16 forested sites (no water). **Fox Creek Campground** has 33 sites with electrical hookups and drinking water and views of Index and Pilot Peaks.

FOOD

In Cody, most restaurants are open year-round, but reduce hours in fall, winter, and spring. In summer, make reservations for dinner, or you may be waiting in lines.

Western fare is a Wyoming staple. **Bubba's Bar-B-Que** (512 Yellowstone Ave., 307/587-7427, www.bubbasbar-b-que.com, 7am-8pm Sun.-Thurs., 7am-9pm Fri.-Sat., $9-26) uses a hickory-fired smoker to slow cook ribs, sausage, brisket, pulled pork, turkey, and chicken. This is one place you can try Rocky Mountain oysters (bull testicles). **Cody Cattle Company** (1910 Demaris St., 307/272-5770, http://thecodycattlecompany.com, 5:30pm-7:30pm daily June-late Sept., $28 adults, $14 kids) is a cowboy dinner theater that serves a western all-you-can-eat buffet of beef brisket, chicken, or steak ($8 more) in a big hall with picnic table seating. Classic chuck wagon sides accompany dinner, and a

cowboy music show ends in time to see the rodeo. Also available is a dinner show-rodeo package.

Fine-dining restaurants offer something other than western food. ★ **The Local** (1134 13th St., 307/586-4262, http://thelocalcody.com, 8:30am-9pm Tues.-Sat., $10-40) serves espresso (8:30am-11am), lunch (11am-2pm), and dinner (5pm-9pm) using fresh ingredients in unique combinations. Choose from in-house breads and pastries; vegan and vegetarian options made with local organic ingredients are the hallmarks of their small and large plates. An imaginative, upscale menu spans broad seasonal choices, from scallops, crab cakes, and ceviche to pork porterhouse, bison, and Wagyu striploin. **Adriano's Italian** (1244 Sheridan Ave., 307/527-7320, http://adrianositalian-restaurant.com, 11am-close daily, $9-27) serves what the owners term as "spaghetti western" food—steaks with pasta sides or burgers and subs with Italian toppings. Both lunch (11am-3pm) and dinner (5pm-close) include Italian pastas and thin-crust pizza, but dinner adds on veal, steak, chicken, sausage, and seafood.

Rocky Mountain Mojoe (1001 Sheridan Ave., 307/578-8295, htttp://rockymountainmojoe.com, daily 6am-7pm, $4-10) is a local espresso stop that serves huge cinnamon rolls and grab-and-go breakfast sandwiches for those looking to hit the road early to Yellowstone. Breakfasts feature scrambles, burritos, and stuffed hash browns, while lunch offers gourmet sandwiches, paninis, and wraps. The restaurant is cramped inside, but has outdoor seating in summer. **Peter's Café and Bakery** (1219 Sheridan Ave., 307/527-5040, 6:45am-8pm Mon.-Sat., 6:45am-5pm Sun., $5-10) offers sandwiches to go and food made with fresh ingredients—breakfast items, espresso, scones, sticky buns, ice cream, salads, burgers, sandwiches, and sweet-potato fries. Peter's also doubles as an ice cream parlor. A local's hangout, **Our Place Cafe** (148 W. Yellowstone Ave., 307/527-4420, 6am-2pm daily, $6-12, cash only) serves

Sunlight Gorge on the Chief Joseph Scenic Byway

organic, local, GMO-free, sustainable foods along with specialty gluten- or dairy-free items. Find specialty health foods at **Mountain High Health Foods** (1902 17th St., Ste. A, 307/587-1700, 9:30am-6pm Mon.-Fri., 9:30am-5pm Sat.) and traditional groceries at **Albertson's Supermarket** (1825 17th St., 307/527-7007, 6am-11pm daily).

TRANSPORTATION AND SERVICES
Car
The main highway cuts right through downtown Cody, and driving becomes clogged in summer. Street parking is minimal; explore side streets to find a spot. Those driving large RVs should head to the back lots at the Buffalo Bill Center of the West (720 Sheridan Ave.) and walk into town from there.

Two scenic driving tours enter Yellowstone from Cody.

CHIEF JOSEPH SCENIC BYWAY
The 80-mile route to the **Northeast Entrance** of Yellowstone travels the **Chief Joseph Scenic Byway** (Hwy. 296) over 8,076-foot Dead Indian Pass. To reach Chief Joseph Scenic Byway, drive north on Highway 120 for 17 miles and turn left, where the climb begins past red rock cuts and bluffs. At the pass, the view opens up to the **Clarks Fork of the Yellowstone River** dividing the Absaroka and Beartooth Mountains. Stop at the viewpoint to read about the **flight of the Nez Perce** who took this route while being chased by the U.S. Army. Drop down the switchbacks past Dead Indian Campground to **Sunlight Gorge** for another stop, looking down 300 feet into the dizzying narrow slot to Sunlight Creek. Continue heading northwest toward the distinctive toothy peak of **Pilot Butte.** When, you reach the Beartooth Highway (U.S. Hwy. 212), turn left to go through Cooke City and Silver Gate to reach the Northeast Entrance to Yellowstone. While the Chief Joseph Scenic Byway stays open year-round (except for temporary closures in heavy snowstorms), the eight-mile section of

traditional breakfast and lunch; think biscuits and gravy or chicken-fried steak.

Pat O'Hara Brewing Company (1019 15th St., 307/586-5410, 11am-10pm Mon. and Wed.-Sat., $10-20) is a classic Irish brewpub with fish and chips, shepherd's pie, bangers, and corned beef the backbone of the menu. Beers on tap include their own craft brews, plus other regional ales. **Millstone Pizza Company and Brewery** (1057 Sheridan Ave., 307/586-4131, 11am-9pm Sun.-Thurs., 11am-10pm Fri.-Sat., $7-20) has a menu that goes far beyond pizza, with burgers, hot dogs, oven-baked subs, soups, salads, and appetizers. Sixteen beers are on tap, including the company's own seasonal and mainstay brews.

For espresso drinks, stop in at **Beta Coffeehouse** (1132 12th St., 307/587-7707, 6am-6pm Mon.-Sat.).

Groceries
In downtown Cody, **Whole Foods Trading Company** (1134 13th St., 307/587-3213, 10am-6pm Mon.-Sat.) has fresh, healthy,

the Beartooth Highway—from Pilot Creek, Wyoming, to Cooke City, Montana—**closes in winter** (early Nov.-early May).

BUFFALO BILL SCENIC BYWAY

The more direct route from Cody follows the 52-mile **Buffalo Bill Scenic Byway** (North Fork Highway, U.S. Hwy. 14/16/20) west up the Wapiti Valley to the **East Entrance** of Yellowstone. The road begins by climbing narrow Shoshone Canyon via three tunnels to pop out at **Buffalo Bill Dam** and Reservoir. Walk to the top of the dam, which is listed on the National Register of Historic Places, and tour the **visitors center** (307/527-6076, www. bbdvc.com, 8am-7pm Mon.-Fri., 9am-5pm Sat.-Sun. June-Aug., shorter hours May and Sept.). Continue driving west through the arid high desert flanking the reservoir and then follow the **North Fork of the Shoshone River** upstream as the terrain changes into pine forests alternating with fields. In **Shoshone National Forest**, campgrounds line the route to the park entrance. While you can drive the North Fork Road in winter, the **East Entrance of Yellowstone is closed early November-April.**

Bus and Taxi

Greyhound (800/231-2222, www.greyhound. com) buses reach Cody, but do not travel into the park. Two taxi companies operate in Cody: **Cody Cab** (307/272-8364) and **Cody's Town Taxi** (307/250-8090).

Tours

Cody Trolley Tours (1192 Sheridan Ave., 307/527-7043, http://codytrolleytours.com, daily late May-late Sept., $27 adults, $25 seniors, $15 kids) carts visitors for a one-hour historical tour around town on a bus that has been converted to look like a trolley. The tours include stories of the Wild West, heroes, and renegades. Tours go out at 11am and 3pm, but 9am and 1pm tours add on in midsummer when needed. Make reservations. Purchase tickets at the trolley station, Cody Country Visitor Center (836 Sheridan Ave.), and other

locations. The Buffalo Bill Center of the West (720 Sheridan Ave.) sells a combo ticket for the trolley and the center ($41 adults/seniors, $24 kids). The trolley company will pick you up at your hotel with a free shuttle to the trolley station.

Day tours lasting about 10 hours go to Yellowstone National Park early May-late October for sightseeing and wildlife-watching. Reservations are required, and companies do hotel pickups. Lunches are usually included. Rates run about $175-275 per person. Clarify whether park entrance fees are included. Tip your guide at least 15 percent. **Cody Wyoming Adventures** (307/587-6988 or 800/293-0148, www.codywyoming-adventures.com) takes 15-passenger vans for touring the park. **Yellowstone Tours** (307/527-6316, www.tourtoyellowstone.com) uses SUVs for touring.

Air

Cody's **Yellowstone Regional Airport** (COD, 2101 Roger Sedam Dr., 307/587-5096, http://flyyra.com) has service through United, Delta, and SkyWest from Denver and Salt Lake City. Flying through Cody is convenient for reaching the East or Northeast Entrances to Yellowstone May-October when roads are open for driving. It is not a winter option.

Rental cars are available at the Yellowstone Regional Airport: **Budget** (307/587-6066 or 800/527-0700, www.budget.com), **Hertz** (307/587-2914 or 800/654-3131, www.hertz. com), and **Thrifty** (307/587-8855 or 800/367-2277, www.thrifty.com).

Services

The **Cody Country Visitor Center** (836 Sheridan Ave., 307/587-2777, www. codychamber.org, 8am-7pm daily late May-late Sept., 8am-5pm Mon.-Fri. late Sept.-late May) has information, maps, brochures, and road conditions. The center also sells tickets to most summer events and attractions. For Shoshone National Forest information, stop by the **Clarks Fork, Greybull,** and **Wapiti Ranger Districts Office** (203A

Yellowstone Ave., 307/527-6921, www.fs.usda.gov/shoshone).

Cody has a **post office** (1301 Stampede Ave., 307/527-7161, 8:30am-5pm Mon.-Fri., 9am-noon Sat.). **ATMs** are ubiquitous around town. For showers, go to the **Paul Stock Aquatic and Recreation Center** (1402 Heart Mountain St., 307/587-0400, www.cityofcody-wy.gov, 5:30am-10pm Mon.-Thurs., 5:30am-8pm Fri., 8am-6pm Sat., noon-6pm Sun. year-round, $12 adults, $6 students and youth, kids 4 and under free). The **Cody Laundromat** (1728 Beck Ave., 307/587-8500, 24/7 daily) has coin-op washers and dryers.

For emergencies, go to **West Park Hospital** (707 Sheriden Ave., 307/527-7501, www.westparkhospital.org).

MEDIA AND COMMUNICATIONS

Cell service is available in Cody and part of the Wapiti Valley toward Yellowstone. As the mountains close in, cell service becomes spotty to nonexistent. Do not expect service in the last 30 miles before Yellowstone's East Entrance.

Wireless Internet is common in Cody hotels. The **Park County Library** (1500 Heart Mountain St., 307/527-1880, http://parkcountylibrary.org, 9am-8pm Mon.-Thurs., 9am-5:30pm Fri., 9am-5pm Sat., 1pm-4pm Sun.) has public computers. **Rocky Mountain Mojoe** (1001 Sheridan Ave., 307/578-8295, daily 6am-7pm) has wireless Internet.

Founded by Buffalo Bill Cody, the Cody newspaper is the *Cody Enterprise* (www.cody-enterprise.com), published twice weekly.

Lander and Dubois, Wyoming

Lander and Dubois are on one of the dramatic entrances to Yellowstone and Grand Teton National Parks. U.S. Highway 26/287 cuts between the Wind River Mountains and Absaroka Mountains to cross the Continental Divide at Togwotee Pass. The western descent faces the implacable wall of the toothy Tetons to enter Grand Teton through the **Moran entrance** with access to the **South Entrance** of Yellowstone. Most travelers whip past Lander and Dubois to get into the parks.

LANDER

Lander has grown from its cow town roots into a center for outdoor training. It is the home of **Northwest Outdoor Leadership School** (NOLS, 284 Lincoln St., 307/332-5300 or 800/710-6657, www.nols.edu), founded by mountaineer Paul Petzoldt.

The **Museum of the American West** (1445 W. Main St., 307/335-8778, http://museumoftheamericanwest.com, 9am-4pm Mon.-Sat. Mar.-Nov., free) preserves the cultural heritage of the Wind River area and central Wyoming, including pioneers, Native

Americans, and cowboys. The Pioneer Village (mid-May-Oct.) preserves 10 buildings, including a chapel, cabins, stables, carpentry shop, plus tepees. Some of the buildings are historic; others are replicas. Donations are appreciated.

Lander is 130 miles southwest of the Moran entrance to Grand Teton (158 miles from Yellowstone).

Accommodations and Food

Holiday Inn Express Suites (1002 11th St., 877/859-5095, www.ihg.com, $) has a pool, fitness center, wireless Internet, and continental breakfast. **Sleeping Bear RV Park and Campground** (515 E. Main St., 307/332-5159 or 888/757-2327, www.sleepingbearrvpark.com, year-round) has 45 RV sites ($30-44) and 10 tent sites ($25) with full hookups for RVs, electrical and water hookups at tent sites, flush toilets, showers, wireless Internet, and barbecue facilities.

On the west edge of town, Sinks Canyon contains the Popo Agie River disappearing into a limestone cave, sinking underground, and emerging downstream in The Rise. In the canyon, **Sinks Canyon State Park** (3079 Sinks Canyon Rd., 307/332-6333 or 307/332-3077, http://wyoparks.state.wy.us, Memorial Day-Labor Day, $10 Wyoming residents, $17 nonresidents) has two first-come, first-served campgrounds—Sawmill and Popo Agie—with drinking water, restrooms, and picnic tables. The park has a visitors center, fishing, and hiking trails.

The **Lander Bake Shop and Cafe** (259 Main St., www.landerbakeshop.com, 307/438-4305, 6:30am-5pm Mon.-Fri., 8am-2pm Sat.-Sun., $4-9) goes beyond pastries, cupcakes, scones, cinnamon rolls, and espresso. Breakfast includes burritos and bagels, while lunch features sandwiches, paninis, and soup. For dinner, try the **Cowfish** (148 Main St., 307/332-8227, www.cowfishlander.com, 5pm-9pm Mon.-Thurs., 5pm-10pm Fri.-Sat., $11-33). Yes, it's a silly name for a Wyoming locale, and the restaurant can be noisy, but they serve steaks, trout, salmon, and ribs, plus a lighter pub menu to accompany brews from Lander Brewing Company.

Camping

On the northeast side of the Wind River Mountains are six first-come, first-served campgrounds in **Shoshone National Forest** (Washakie Ranger District, 333 E. Main St., Lander, 307/332-5460, www.fs.usda.gov/shoshone) outside Lander. **Sinks Canyon** (on Hwy. 131, 14 sites, $15), **Worthen Meadow** (off Hwy. 131, 28 sites, $15), and **Fiddlers Lake** (off Hwy. 131, 20 sites, $15) have drinking water. **Dickenson Creek** (via U.S. 26/287, 15 sites, free), **Louis Lake** (off Hwy. 28, 9 sites, $10), and **Little Popo Agie** (off Hwy. 131, 4 sites, free) do not have drinking water.

Services

ATMs, gas, cell service, wireless Internet (in motels and cafés) are available in town, as is a **post office** (230 Grandview Dr.). Lander's newspaper is the *Daily Ranger* (www.daily-ranger.com). For Forest Service maps and current information, contact **Washakie Ranger District** (333 E. Main St., 307/332-5460, www.fs.usda.gov/shoshone). For emergencies, head to **SageWest Health Care** (1320 Bishop Randall Dr., 307/332-4420, http://sagewesthealthcare.com).

DUBOIS

Dubois has a distinction as a real cowboy town. Dubois is 55 miles southeast of the Moran entrance to Grand Teton (83 miles from Yellowstone).

The **National Bighorn Sheep Interpretive Center** (10 Bighorn Ln., 307/455-3429, www.bighorn.org, 9am-6pm daily late May-early Sept., 10am-4pm Mon.-Sat. early Sept.-late May, $3 adults, kids free) has information about the four species of wild sheep in North America. Exhibits include mounts, films, and interactive activities. Bighorns winter in the vicinity in one of the largest herds in the Lower 48.

Accommodations and Food

On 40 acres, the **Longhorn Ranch Lodge and RV Resort** (5810 Hwy. 26, 307/455-2337, www.thelonghornranch.com, early May-mid-Oct.) is a big complex with motel rooms, cabins, and an RV campground. Motel rooms and cabins ($90-180) have private bathrooms, and some include kitchenettes. Surrounded by cottonwoods, ponds, and a river, the campground has 42 RV sites ($36-45) with full hookups. The complex includes a store, coin-op laundries, fishing, kennels, massage services, and wireless Internet. In town, the **Stagecoach Inn** (103 Ramshorn St., 307/455-2303, www.stagecoachmotel-dubois.com, $60-175) has rooms with 1-2 queens, king suites, and rooms with kitchenettes. The inn also has a hot tub, outdoor heated pool, laundry, and wireless Internet.

On the Wind River, the **Dubois/Wind River KOA** (225 Welty St., 307/445-2238, www.koa.com, mid-May-Sept.) has 43 RV campsites ($48-60) with full hookups and 14 tent campsites ($28-35), plus showers, flush toilets, wireless Internet, fishing, and an indoor pool.

For dining in Dubois, the cafés are best. The older, homestyle **Cowboy Café** (115 E. Ramshorn, 307/455-2595, 7am-9pm daily, $10-25) serves up pecan pancakes, elk skillets, bison burgers, sandwiches, and steaks. Their claim to fame is pie baked from scratch daily. **Nostalgia Bistro** (202 E. Ramshorn, 307/455-3528, www.nostalgiabistro.com, 11am-3pm and 5pm-9pm Tues.-Sat., $10-30) does a mix of Asian fusion meals and western food: smoked trout, beef stir-fry, tempura or sweet chili chicken, eclectic burgers, Jenga-stacked pork ribs, braised kale, homemade soups, and fresh salads. Make reservations for dinner in summer.

Services

Dubois has gas, ATMs, cell service, wireless Internet, and a **post office** (804 Ramshorn St.). For Forest Service information, contact **Wind River Ranger District** (1403 W. Ramshorn St., 307/455-2466, www.fs.usda.gov/shoshone).

TOGWOTEE PASS

From Dubois, two-lane U.S. Highway 26/287 ascends 30 miles to 9,658-foot Togwotee Pass (pronounced TOE-ga-tee), with broad views of the valley and the eroded escarpment of **Sublette Peak** rising to the north during the climb. You'll barely know when you reach the summit, which has no significant pullout. But at the pass, the road crosses the **Continental Divide,** slicing between the summits of 11,010-foot **Breccia Peak** and 10,724-foot **Two Oceans Mountain.** On the westward descent to reach the national parks, the Teton Mountains rise up with their toothy spires, lit up by morning sunlight or backlit at sunset. The route is

open year-round, but closes during blizzards in winter.

Seventeen miles east of Grand Teton National Park near Togwotee Pass, **Togwotee Mountain Lodge** (27655 Hwy 26-287, 866/278-4245, www.togwoteelodge.com, late May-mid-Oct. and Dec.-Mar., $135-270) has 28 lodge rooms with two queens, six family bunk suites, 54 cabins, a restaurant, a saloon (11:30am-10pm daily), and a hot tub. The on-site **Grizzly Grill** (7am-10am, 11:30pm-2pm, and 5:30pm-9pm daily, $10-24) serves breakfast, lunch (winter only), and dinner.

In the Absaroka Mountains north of Togwotee Pass, **Shoshone National Forest** (Wind River Ranger District, 1403 W. Ramshorn, Dubois, 307/455-2466, www.fs.usda.gov/shoshone, late June-mid-Sept., $10-15) has two coveted, ultra-scenic campgrounds: **Brooks Lake** (13 sites) and **Pinnacles** (21 sites). At 9,100 feet on the Continental Divide, sunrises and sunsets cast orange glows on the surrounding escarpments and pinnacles, yielding *National Geographic*-caliber photos. You can hike on the Continental Divide, or boat, paddle, and fish in Brooks Lake. The first-come, first-served campgrounds can accommodate hard-sided vehicles only (no tents) and have picnic tables, fire rings, vault toilets, and bear boxes; only Pinnacles has drinking water. They are located on Brooks Lake Road (Forest Rd. 515), about 28 miles north of Dubois and 30 miles east of the Moran entrance to Grand Teton.

Continental Divide Dog Sled Adventures (307/222-0421, www.dogsledadventures.com) leads dog sled tours around the Continental Divide—from Togwotee Pass to Brooks Lake Lodge. The company also runs overnight dog sled tours to yurts.

Background

The Landscape

GEOLOGY
Yellowstone

Why does Yellowstone National Park attract 3.5 million visitors a year? It is one of the few places on earth where people can watch volcanic activity. Instead of eyeing only the aftermath of geological processes, visitors can gape at volcanism in action with erupting geysers, bubbling mud pots, fuming vents, and steaming hot pools. All the action is due to Yellowstone's hot spot, a place where the molten magma rises near to the earth's surface.

SUPERVOLCANO

Volcanic activity in Yellowstone started with a supervolcano—far more than an ordinary volcano. The U.S. Geological Survey uses "supervolcano" for any eruption flinging more than 1,000 cubic kilometers of magma, ash, and pumice in one big eruption. Yellowstone's supervolcano qualifies with the Lava Creek eruption that took place 640,000 years ago. It left a caldera 34 by 45 miles, one of the largest calderas in the world, and shot ash to the Canadian and Mexican borders. See the tuff ash from that explosion at the Tuff Cliff Picnic Area.

The Lava Creek eruption was the last in a string of major eruptions on the Yellowstone Plateau. To Yellowstone's southwest, the Island Park Caldera formed from an eruption 2.1 million years ago, and then the Mesa Falls eruption created the Henry's Fork Caldera 1.3 million years ago. The Lava Creek eruption may not be the last one. In fact, the Island Park, Henry's Fork, and Lava Creek eruptions are the last three in a long arc of volcanoes created by the Yellowstone hot spot as it moved northeastwardly across southern Idaho over the past 16 million years, similar to the Hawaiian Island arc.

The action from Yellowstone's supervolcano changes constantly. Old Faithful has shifted from erupting about every hour before the 1959 Hebgen Earthquake to erupting on average every 92 minutes. Then in 2013, the average dropped to 88 minutes. In some of the geyser basins, boardwalks around thermal features have been moved as the action shifted. Even Firehole Drive west of Old Faithful closed temporarily in 2014 when a new hot spot started melting the road.

The supervolcano still has the potential to erupt again, but scientists don't know when. The Yellowstone Volcano Observatory (http://volcanoes.usgs.gov/observatories/yvo) monitors activity to keep tabs on heat, movement, and shifting thermals. Just think about something other than supervolcanoes erupting when you try to fall asleep at night.

TWIN CHAMBERS AND THE CALDERA

After eruptions, huge calderas, or cauldrons, remain at the volcano's site. In Yellowstone's case, two magma chambers pushed like oversize pimples toward the surface of the earth. As they hoisted the earth's crust upward into the monstrous supervolcano, giant circular fractures grew around the mountain's apex. When the pressure became too much, the twin chambers exploded through the crust along the fracture rings, sending ash and pumice into the air and lava flowing down mountainsides. As magma depleted in the chambers, the roofs collapsed along the circular fractures, forming the rounded caldera. As smaller eruptions continued, lava flows dammed up places where streams drained from the caldera. The dams created

Nature at Work

Yellowstone is a testament to the power of nature. In addition to geothermal features, geological upthrusts, and glaciation, other factors are still shaping the landscape.

Erosion: Wind, water, and ice conspire to whittle rocks and mountains. Winds tears particles off softer features. Water washes boulders downstream, and flooding reshapes water channels in the landscape. On lakes, wave action wears away shorelines. The freezing and thawing of ice pries shards of rock from cliffs.

Look for evidence of these forces at the **Grand Canyon of the Yellowstone.** While the first scouring of the canyon started when lava flows dammed up lakes that overflowed, glacial lakes bursting their ice dams carved the canyon deeper and deeper until about 10,000 years ago when the dams melted. Winds carve away at the canyon sides, creating hoodoos, or pointed spires.

Earthquakes: Each year, the park has 1,000-3,000 quakes, most of which occur along faults in the earth's crust. The earthquakes help keep the plumbing systems of geysers and hydrothermal features operational, while the shaking breaks up sinter that may clog water routes to the surface. Earthquake swarms, a series of quakes localized in an area in a short amount of time, occurred in **Lake Village** in 2009. Many faults converge at **Mud Volcano,** making earthquake swarms common.

Exhibits at the **Canyon Visitor Education Center** (307/344-2550, www.nps.gov/yell, 8am-8pm daily late May-mid-Oct., shorter hours in fall) show real-time earthquake data. The University of Utah Seismograph Station (www.seis.utah.edu) records earthquakes in Yellowstone; their online map shows earthquakes park-wide in the last hour, day, or week.

Fire: Every summer, lightning causes an average of 22 forest fires in Yellowstone. Most go out naturally before reaching an acre in size. Since 1988, the annual number of fires has ranged from 1 to 77. The fires are key in creating wildlife habitat, diversifying vegetation, preserving grassland communities, and eradicating bug infestations. After a fire, the nutrients from ash added to the soil contributes to a burst of new plant life. Dead standing trees provide places for woodpeckers to chip holes, creating homes for cavity-dwelling birds and wildlife.

In 1988, Yellowstone experienced below normal precipitation, which led to wildfires that burned 1.1 million acres in the Greater Yellowstone Ecosystem, including 36 percent of the park. Today, you can see stands of burned, silvered timber from the fire fast being replaced by a new forest of lodgepoles. **Grant Visitor Center** (307/344-2650, www.nps.gov/yell, 8am-7pm daily late May-Sept.) was evacuated twice during the fires and now hosts an exhibit on fire ecology.

Yellowstone's lakes: Shoshone, Lewis, and Yellowstone.

Since the supervolcano eruption, the twin chambers have refueled themselves with magma, bulging upward again. Today, these two bulges, called resurgent domes, are near Old Faithful and Hayden Valley. Magma continues to push to the earth's crust, sometimes producing uplifts. Over a six-year period ending in 2010, instruments recorded a large vertical push inside the eastern rim of the caldera. The land rose 11 inches, but then dropped more than 2 inches. Frequent earthquakes release pressure to let the uplifts ebb.

RECENT ERUPTIONS

Soon after the Lava Creek eruption 640,000 years ago, volcanic activity continued on a smaller scale. Magma flowed through labyrinths of underground cracks to ooze out over the caldera floor. The most recent lava flows occurred 60,000-75,000 years ago. Many contained rhyolite, the predominant rock inside the caldera. In a few places, lava flows crested the caldera rim. Others surfaced along small fault lines outside the caldera, such as 180,000 years ago at Obsidian Cliff. Many of Yellowstone's trails are dotted with obsidian from these more recent eruptions, formed from rapidly cooling lava.

Smaller eruptions have also occurred since the supervolcano. West Thumb Geyser Basin erupted 150,000 years ago. After the eruption, the volcano collapsed, creating the caldera. Water flowed into the caldera, turning it into a bay off Yellowstone Lake.

EARTHQUAKES

Yellowstone is active with earthquakes, caused when the crust slips against itself along fault lines. Each year, 1,000- 3,000 earthquakes shake across the park; these brittle failures are daily occurrences, although most cannot be felt. The University of Utah Seismograph Station (www.seis.utah. edu) monitors the earthquakes. Check out recent earthquakes on the Yellowstone Volcano Observatory website (http://volcanoes.usgs. gov/observatories/yvo). Sometimes, swarms of earthquakes occur when numbers of quakes spike far above normal. A 2009 swarm tallied 900 quakes in 14 days. The largest recorded swarm in 1985 produced 3,000 quakes over three months.

Earthquakes perform an essential function in letting thermals release pressure. Thermals use heat, water, and a plumbing system that constricts gas bubbles to produce geyser eruptions. Earthquakes take the place of Drāno in keeping the underground pipes open. Shaking unseals cracks from minerals that are solidifying them closed. Between earthquakes and hydrothermal features, pressure releases to keep the caldera operating at a slow boil rather than building into a catastrophic eruption.

VOLCANIC SCULPTURES

Hydrothermal activity creates fantastical sculptures. But some sculptures are built from different components. Within the caldera, the landscape is built on rhyolite, formed from thick, liquid flows of the Lava Creek eruption 640,000 years ago. Light beige-colored silicate minerals and silica solidified in the rhyolite. Since rhyolite is the underlying bedrock, many of the fountains and cones in the geyser basins are created from silica gushing up with water and clinging as building-block crystals on the sculptures. Castle and Grotto Geysers are two of these in the Upper Geyser Basin.

But the Mammoth Hot Spring terraces are different. They are made from calcium carbonate that comes from limestone underground. As the water comes to the surface, it brings calcium carbonate with it to spill out over the terraces. That's what creates the smooth-sculpted features that look more like frozen water.

BACKGROUND
THE LANDSCAPE

Obsidian is found in the sand on many of Yellowstone's trails.

Hydrothermal Features

Of Yellowstone's 13,000 thermal features that have been mapped in the park, only four types exist.

GEYSERS

Geysers blow super-hot water into the air. Some erupt nonstop, while others blow on schedule, intermittently, or after long hiatuses of years. Eruptions result from big clogs of boiling water. After surface water percolates to a hot spot, it then boils toward the earth's surface. When boiling, gas bubbles get trapped in channels below heavy water above. Increasing bubbles push the water upward to make it overflow just enough to crank up fierce boiling that shoves water skyward. Eruptions finish when the gas bubbles reach air. Yellowstone's 300 geysers come in two types: Fountain geysers spray water in multiple directions, while cone geysers blast water upward in a narrow stream. More than half the earth's active geysers are in Yellowstone.

HOT SPRINGS

Hot springs, the most numerous thermal feature in Yellowstone, are created from underground channels just like geysers. But they behave differently due to larger channels that don't clog up with steam bubbles and cooler water exchanged back down. Those factors prevent eruptions. At 199°F, most hot springs don't exceed the boiling point. Yellowstone's hot springs exhibit vibrant colors from two sources: Blues (the hottest on the color spectrum), come from the refraction of sunlight on the water, and other colors often fringing the pool are from thermophiles, or heat-loving life forms.

MUD POTS

Mud pots form in depressions when hot water saturates clay-like sediments. Below the mud pot, as steam pushes upward into the saturated sediments, gaseous bubbles surface to pop and gurgle. Mud pots often have hydrogen sulfide gases that produce a rotten egg smell. Minerals tint mud pots different colors.

FUMAROLES

Just like a hot spring, fumaroles are holes or vents in the ground. But instead of filling with hot water, they are drier, transforming the small amount of water into super-hot steam. Some can heat to 238°F. Black Growler has reached 300°F. Often the steam creates noise as it rushes through the vent. It roars, hisses, or whistles.

PETRIFIED TREES AND BOBBY SOX TREES

A series of volcanic eruptions 40-50 million years ago petrified trees in Yellowstone. They were ancient redwoods, some up to four feet in width and 40 feet tall. They were swept along in lahars, flows of volcanic debris. Silica in the debris soaked into the living trees, petrifying them into rock. While redwoods no longer populate the park, their presence in petrified form indicates that Yellowstone once had a wetter, more tropical climate. Yellowstone's forest of petrified trees may be the largest in the world. To see them, stop at Petrified Tree or hike Specimen Ridge.

Lodgepole pines that populate the Yellowstone caldera today grow well in the sand-like sediments. But shifting thermal areas affect forests, killing the trees. Dead tree trunks stand erect in pools of hot water. Because many of the dead lodgepoles turn white around the base of their trunk, due to soaking up silica in the water, they have garnered the name "bobby sox trees." Look for the bottom foot or two of trunks appearing like they were painted white.

GLACIERS

Glaciers covered Yellowstone many times, starting two million years ago when the

Erosion carved the Grand Canyon of the Yellowstone.

YELLOWSTONE LAKE

Yellowstone Lake, the largest lake in the park, resulted from geologic forces. Part of the lake lies within the caldera and part outside. When lava flows dammed up caldera outlet streams, the lake formed. The portion inside the caldera still has active hydrothermal features, such as West Thumb Geyser Basin and Steamboat Point. But glaciers also reshaped the landscape on the southern half of the lake, in particular gouging out the South and Southeast Arms.

A five-year mapping project that ended in 2003 gave scientists a sneak peek at the lake's floor. Sonar and an ROV (remotely operated vehicle) recorded unknown features: explosion craters, fissures and faults, vents, and siliceous spires. They make up the lake-bottom landscape in the north where volcanic processes are still active. But in the southeast, the lake lacks volcanic features. Instead, the lake basin contains glacial debris such as erratics.

In the lake's north, hydrothermic vents created underwater spires, discovered in the late 1990s. One spire collected for study was dated at 11,000 years old, its age revealing its formation after the glacier that created the lake retreated. The spire also revealed a network of conduits—tubes for releasing steam and gases.

GRAND CANYON OF THE YELLOWSTONE

While fire and ice shaped most of the park with volcanism and glaciation, erosion also lent its artistry. The handiwork of wind erosion is evident in spires and hoodoos, while freeze-thaw cycles dislodged mountainsides into colossal talus piles. But water erosion is to thank for the Grand Canyon of the Yellowstone. While the canyon contains rusty oxidized rhyolite for a splash of color and steam escaping hydrothermic vents, its narrow V-shaped slot resulted from river cutting rather than glacial carving.

The canyon's formation is attributed to the ice damming that formed Yellowstone Lake 14,000-18,000 years ago. Ice dams typically melt and refreeze. During melt phases,

earth descended into a cooling phase in the Pleistocene Ice Age. While ice appeared and melted between bouts of volcanic spitfire, two late ice ages left evidence. The Bull Lake glaciation buried the park about 150,000 years ago, but due to more recent glaciation, not much record is left from it. Beginning about 50,000 years ago, the Pinedale glacial era buried the park under 4,000 feet of ice. Yellowstone's high elevation and ice flowing down from the Beartooth Plateau created a localized island of ice disconnected from the continental ice sheet shoving south from Canada. Ice filled Yellowstone's caldera, forming an ice cap. Most of the ice in the Yellowstone ice cap melted 13,000-14,000 years ago.

Find evidence of glaciers across the park. Moraines marked their sizes, and they left large boulders called erratics strewn about. The oldest evidence of glaciers is at Tower Fall in a sediment layer that is 1.3 million years old. Despite the evidence of glaciers, Yellowstone has no active glaciers today.

torrents of water gushed downstream from the lake. The force of those repeated flash floods cut the canyon. Even today, the Yellowstone River continues to eat away at the canyon's depth.

Grand Teton

While Yellowstone represents ancient geologic forces, by comparison Grand Teton National Park is a young pup. The park hides ancient sea sediments, but its peaks are some of the newest in the Rocky Mountains. The wow factor comes from the extreme contrast between the flat plain of Jackson Hole and the Teton's sky-scratching teeth. A dose of faulting, glaciers, and erosion added the final brush strokes to the scene.

ANCIENT SEAS

Long before faulting shoved the Teton Mountains into existence, ancient shallow seas flooded portions of Wyoming. More than 2.7 billion years ago, their shorelines shifted over millennia eastward and westward from where the Tetons now stand. As gravel, limey mud, clay, and sand washed into the sea basins, the debris settled to the bottom in layers. Over eons, the sedimentary layers compressed, and between the seabed layers,

magma seeped in, adding volcanic rocks. Heat and pressure converted the sedimentary layers to gneiss, a metamorphic rock. The colorful rocks in Jackson Lake are from various sedimentary sea layers.

As recent as 510 million years ago, inland seas flooded the region. However, this time the sediment layers included fossils of plants and animals of seabed origins. Sea creatures such as trilobites, brachiopods, corals, and algae fossilized into layers of shales, limestones, and sandstones. Today, these ancient layers of sedimentary sea rock are exposed from fault thrusting. More than 1,000 feet of seabed layering is visible, particularly on the Teton's west side.

MOUNTAIN UPLIFT

Massive tectonic forces created the Rocky Mountains, starting 120 million years ago. When a Pacific Ocean plate slammed into North America, the resulting uplift of land shoved the Rocky Mountains upward. To the east of Grand Teton National Park, pressure from the tectonic movement created the Gros Ventre Mountains about 70 million years ago. In comparison, they are much more weathered and rounded than the younger, jagged Tetons. As the mountain-building repercussions of

colorful sedimentary rocks on the bottom of Jackson Lake

the tectonic collision waned, volcanic activity kicked into action, including Yellowstone's supervolcano. Lava and volcanic debris built up to form the Absaroka Range opposite the north end of the Tetons.

TETON FAULT

The Tetons came late into the Rocky Mountains. It just took awhile for the Teton Fault to wake up. About 10 million years ago, the fault's alarms went off, right where Jackson Hole abuts the Tetons today. As the two sides of the fault stretched apart, daring the other to tear away, massive 7.5 magnitude earthquakes rumbled. The fault's west side rose upward while Jackson Hole on the east side sank into a valley. Each violent earthquake shoved the mountains up about 10 feet while dropping Jackson Hole 30-40 feet, each time creating a new exposed scarp of almost 50 feet.

The Teton Fault is responsible for creating the prominence of the Teton Mountains. While the Grand Teton reaches 13,770 feet in elevation, it stretches 7,000 feet above Jackson Hole. Because the Jackson Hole side of the fault sank lower, no foothills formed. That vertical disparity, or prominence, between the peaks and Jackson Hole adds wow-worthiness. Geologists have also used the height of the Grand Teton to estimate the offset of the Teton Fault at 30,000 feet.

The last two major mountain-building earthquakes occurred 8,000 and 4,800 years ago. Today, very few earthquakes shake along the Teton Fault. Since Yellowstone's supervolcano erupted late in the Teton mountain-building process, gaseous lava clouds hit the north end of the range, where the mountains diverted them down Jackson Hole and Teton Valley. The summit of Signal Mountain has deposits from Yellowstone's explosions.

GLACIATION

As the earth's climate cooled two million years ago into the Pleistocene Ice Age, ice chewed on the landscape of the Tetons. The Bull Lake advance of ice that covered Yellowstone also buried the lower elevations of the Tetons. The ice stretched south in Jackson Hole nearly to Hoback Junction, burying the town of Jackson with 1,500 feet of glacier. The Pinedale glaciation filled Jackson Hole, creating Jackson Lake but leaving the summit of Signal Mountain exposed. The melting of these glaciers flooded Jackson Hole with sand, gravel, and glacial debris to form the flat plain.

As the Tetons sat above the ice, the cooler temperatures piled up snow to compress over time into alpine glaciers. These glaciers are responsible for the artistic sculpting of cirques, horns, arêtes, and U-shaped valleys in the Tetons. Some of the glaciers descended to the valley floor where they deposited debris in moraines. These terminal moraines dammed up creeks to create lakes right at the base of the mountains: Leigh, Jenny, Bradley, Taggart, and Phelps Lakes are the handiwork of ice.

Grand Teton National Park still has about 10 named glaciers, but they are minuscule. From a recent ice age that plunged temperatures starting in 1400, they are responsible for carving cirques and hanging valleys. Known as the Little Ice Age, this glacier-building period was confined to higher elevations. In 1850, when warming began, the glaciers began to shrink. The annual new accumulation of snow could not keep up with the amount of ice lost to summer melting. The past four decades has reduced the glaciers by 20-25 percent despite the annual 450 inches of snowfall. From different locations on the floor of Jackson Hole, you can see Skillet and Falling Ice Glaciers on Mt. Moran and the Teton Glacier on the Grand Teton. Plenty of static snowfields persist all summer, but due to their size and depth, they no longer move like glaciers.

EROSION

Wind, water, freeze-thaw cycles, and ice erode Grand Teton National Park. From high elevations surrounding Jackson Hole, streams descend to the Snake River. Cutting through glacial till, the river gradually carved a twisted trough through Jackson Hole. As it dug deeper, it left exposed terraces where channels ran in the past. The erosion continues slowly today as the river moves sediments downstream and digs lower.

CLIMATE

Yellowstone and Grand Teton National Park experience four distinct seasons, but despite snowfall, the area surprises many with its semi-arid climate, forcing more water intake than at home. Higher elevations cling to winter longer, and weather can swing wildly during even one day. Be prepared in all seasons for unpredictability. Skies may be blue and sunny in the morning only to turn into raging thunder or snowstorms by the afternoon. Hats, gloves, layers, and shells are needed year-round, and they need to go in your day pack regardless of blue morning skies.

Northwest Wyoming is a land of extremes, with annual highs and lows separated by more than 100 degrees. Record highs range 93-99°F across both parks. The coldest temperature ever recorded was -66°F in Yellowstone near the West Entrance. Each summer swelters with several warm bouts of 90-degree heat, while each winter freezes with several periods of subzero temperatures made colder by windchill.

Spring

Springtime is moody in northwest Wyoming. Mild days with cool nights can ricochet with little warning into spitting rain and snowstorms. Sometimes a foot of snow can fall during a stormy cold front. Winds often accompany storms, which can make the temperatures seem colder. During April, May, and early June, daytime temperatures push into the 50-60°F range, but may barely top 30°F during storms. Overnight lows can sink to 5-20°F. June is mosquito season.

Summer

Summer is short, usually limited to July and August, with bugs prevalent in the early part of summer. Afternoons frequently see sporadic thundershowers, especially in the mountains. Likewise, winds tend to blow in the afternoons, turning lakes from placid flat water to raging whitecaps. Blue-sky days hang mostly around 70-85°F with a few spikes into the 90s. Nights are cool, dropping to lows of 35-45°F. High elevations may have below-freezing nights with frost in the early morning on trails.

Fall

While fall can be pleasant with warm bug-free days and cool nights, it can also be schizophrenic with snow or rainstorms. Days of blue skies can alternate with several days of a wintry mix, dusting the higher elevations with snow. Winds accompany the arrival and departure of storms. Daytime warm-weather temperatures stay in the 50s-60s, but cold fronts can plummet the thermometer into the 30s. Overnight lows often drop into the teens or single digits.

Winter

White is the color of winter. From early November to late April, snow blankets the ground at all elevations. When the sun pokes out between storms, days are cold, and nights sink into frigid zones. Daytime temperatures range from zero to 20°F. Snowfall is common but varies from windy blizzards to lilting flakes. Nighttime lows often dive below zero. In winter, four-wheel- or all-wheel-drive vehicles handle snow better, and all-weather or studded snow tires are helpful.

Mountain Effects

Elevation plays a huge game with the weather, too. At higher elevations in the Tetons, for instance, temperatures can be 5-20 degrees cooler than on the valley floor of Jackson Hole. Winds can also amp up in strength. Frequent afternoon thundershowers douse hikers, and freezing temperatures, snow, and frost can show up on trails even in July and August. Heavy snowfall descends in November through April. While lower

cross-country skiing in winter

Humans are one of the biggest threats to Yellowstone's thermal features. Recent studies of some of Yellowstone's hot springs such as Grand Prismatic, Sapphire, and Morning Glory have shown that the color of the pools has changed due to the interference from humans. Spectrometer evaluations revealed that water hues have altered. What once was deep blue is now a rainbow of greens to golds due to visitors tossing coins and trash into the hot pools. The foreign objects partially block the water flow, which lowered the temperatures of the pools and changed the spectrum of color to what is visible today. It is impossible for the park service to remove the object without causing further damage.

Air pollution is also affecting Yellowstone and Grand Teton. Both parks experience periods of air pollution that turn sharp, far-reaching mountain panoramas into hazy landscapes. Aspens, one species impacted by air pollution, are showing signs of decline. While anyone driving a vehicle into the parks contributes to emissions in the air, some of the pollution also comes from industry or forest fires in the surrounding states. In the past decade, Yellowstone has made strides in reducing the smelly clouds of pollution along the road to Old Faithful during winter. By limiting numbers of snowmobiles and snowcoaches plus requiring machines to have lower emissions, the winter air is now cleaner for visitors. During the other three seasons, all visitors can help reduce air pollution by turning off vehicles instead of idling, taking shuttles where available, and walking or riding bicycles for short-distance trips.

The acoustic environment is also important to protect in the park—for two reasons. Visitors can hone in on the sounds of nature, and wildlife can continue to communicate with each other and hear predators. While the parks are studying noise levels, especially with motorcycles, visitors can minimize noise

elevations may see 170 inches of snowfall in winter, upper elevations in the Tetons can accumulate 450 inches of snow.

Microclimates

Due to thermal activity in Yellowstone and extreme elevation differences in the Tetons, microclimates produce weather incongruities. In spring and fall, thermal areas often create intermittent fog that can roll out across nearby Grand Loop Road. On temperamental days, it's common to drive through a snow squall, fog, and sun within 10 minutes. In winter, cross-country skiers in Yellowstone's Upper Geyser Basin may encounter melt-outs in microclimates near hot features. Sometimes in shoulder seasons, Yellowstone and Jackson Lakes create their own wild squalls. No matter what season, higher elevations in the Tetons always have more extreme conditions than Jackson Hole.

by turning vehicles off and opting for headphones to listen to music.

Climate Change

The current increase in global temperatures affects the Greater Yellowstone Ecosystem. Glaciers in Grand Teton National Park have shrunk in number and size since 1850 and will continue to melt into oblivion in the next few decades. Spring snowpack is melting earlier across both parks. In the 21st century, average annual temperatures have risen 1.4 degrees, while summers have been 2.3 degrees warmer.

These warming temperatures are already causing shifts in the ecosystem. Whitebark pines that grow at high elevations and play an important role in the grizzly bear diet have historically been protected by frigid beetle-killing winters. But no longer. Warmer temperatures have released tree-killing beetles in epidemic droves. Cutthroat trout numbers are also declining due in part to climate change. With the reduction of both of these food sources, bears are shifting toward a more meat-based diet.

Researchers are predicting warmer and drier conditions for Yellowstone and Grand Teton in upcoming decades. That will result in less mountain snow, more catastrophic wildfires, and the reduction of native trees such as aspens, spruce, and pines. In turn, the Greater Yellowstone Ecosystem may shift from forest lands to desert shrublands. Animals requiring forested cover will see their habitat stripped.

With warming temperatures shifting floral habitats, wildlife may be forced to change elevation or latitude in search of food sources. Species such as the heat-intolerant pika may suffer extinction, and animals adapted to cold, such as mountain goats, bighorn sheep, lynx, and wolverines, may decline. Ptarmigan, short-tailed weasels, and snowshoe hares that molt with the amount of daylight to white in winter and brown in summer become easier prey when their colors fail to camouflage them on the ground. Melting glaciers, earlier snowmelts, fewer frost days, and hotter summers also contribute to rising stream temperatures that threaten the ability of cold-loving cutthroat trout to spawn.

Endangered Species and Species of Concern

GRAY WOLVES

Now delisted as an endangered species in the Greater Yellowstone Ecosystem, gray wolves have seen a recovery in population. Once ranging throughout most of North America, gray wolves disappeared from the Yellowstone region in the early 1900s due to predator-control programs and loss of habitat. In the 1970s they were placed on the Endangered Species List. Two decades later, the federal government transplanted 41 wolves from Canada and northwest Montana to Yellowstone. While the return of the wolf helps keep the elk population in check, the introduction program met with resistance from ranchers and some landowners outside the national park. Wolf packs require huge territories, many of which range outside park boundaries. Today, 400-450 wolves populate the Greater Yellowstone Ecosystem. Winter counts inside Yellowstone National Park usually tally around 100 wolves, with counts waffling based on the elk population. While no hunting is permitted inside the park, wolves cross park boundaries and can be hunted outside the park. Biologists keep radio and GPS collars on 25-30 wolves each year for tracking.

GRIZZLY BEARS

In the 1800s, more than 100,000 grizzly bears roamed grasslands and foothills in the Lower 48, but loss of habitat and predator extermination programs whittled their numbers down to a handful of small populations in the Northern Rockies. Greater Yellowstone's grizzly bears represented their southernmost stronghold, but the island population reduced genetic viability. In the 1970s, the isolated region's 136 grizzlies were listed as threatened on the Endangered Species List. With a recovery plan in place, biologists managed the rebound of grizzlies with the goal of sustaining the Greater

Yellowstone population at 500. They have now expanded into surrounding ecosystem mountains: the Wind River, Gallatin, Absaroka, and Grand Tetons. Today, more than 700 grizzlies populate the Greater Yellowstone Ecosystem. As of 2016, wildlife agencies are preparing to remove the bear from the Endangered Species List. In Yellowstone, for instance, seasonal trail and backcountry campsite closures protect feeding zones, particularly where sows take cubs in spring. A few times the Moose-Wilson Road in Grand Teton has closed for bears feeding on berries. While hunting grizzlies is allowed by permit in specific locations outside the national parks, no one can hunt bears inside the parks.

Humans cause grizzly mortalities through poaching, traffic, and improper storage of livestock grain, garbage, and bird feeders. In 2015, annual grizzly deaths in Greater Yellowstone topped a record 59. Biologists continue to monitor grizzlies by radio and GPS collaring.

CANADA LYNX

Recorded sightings of the Canada lynx have declined substantially in the Greater Yellowstone Ecosystem, prompting it to be listed in 2000 as threatened on the Endangered Species List. Found in coniferous forests above 7,700 feet, the lynx follows its primary prey, the snowshoe hare, and the cat's cyclical population mirrors the ups and downs of hare numbers. Lynx habitat is threatened by intermittent fragmented forests. Snowshoe hare populations are often so small and dispersed that they cannot support the lynx well enough for it to consistently inhabit the region, give birth, and rear kits. With such scattered habitat, home ranges are huge, requiring lynx to travel long distances between sites to find prey. DNA studies based on samples of scat and hair snags have revealed only a handful of lynx in the Greater Yellowstone Ecosystem. The road to recovery for the lynx relies on minimizing human effects on the habitat and species.

WOLVERINES

In 2015, the federal government declined proposals to place wolverines on the Endangered Species List, citing the need for more studies. In the Greater Yellowstone Ecosystem, they live above 8,000 feet with huge home ranges. Known as voracious eaters, the gluttonous weasels require deep and long spring snowpack for denning and rearing kits. Many biologists fear a warming climate threatens their survival. Since 2001, a study has radiotagged wolverines and located denning sites. It discovered the extreme distances wolverines travel: One walked 550 miles in less than six weeks, while another traveled from Togwotee Pass to Rocky Mountain National Park. Between that study and other hair snag studies, biologists estimate the Greater Yellowstone Ecosystem houses 60 wolverines.

BIGHORN SHEEP

Other species not officially listed as endangered are species of concern. Of all the ungulates, bighorn sheep face the greatest risk. Once widely scattered across most western mountain ranges, the sheep today live in fragmented pockets. Around the Greater Yellowstone Ecosystem, bighorns pick up disease from domestic sheep, which can decimate wild herds. A disease outbreak in 2009-2010 reduced populations by 50 percent. Fragmented habitat poses concerns for the sheep's future.

BISON

Bison herds have rebounded from the small herd of 23 that remained in Yellowstone by the late 1800s. Today, the parks have some of the largest bison herds in the world, and their numbers are of concern. Due to fear of brucellosis infecting cattle, ranchers surrounding the parks want to keep bison numbers down so fewer migrate out of the park in winter to lower elevations and limited locations. Testing programs are in place to help with the brucellosis issue, but managing the herd number has required hunting. Wildlife managers have determined to keep the Yellowstone bison at 5,000 animals maximum. For winter migrations, the northern herd, which number about 3,500 bison, spills out of the park near Gardiner. The central herd, which tallies about 1,500 bison, heads toward West Yellowstone. Not all bison leave the park in winter, but many of those that do are subject to licensed hunts as a method to cull herd numbers. In Jackson Hole, hunting the Grand Teton herd resulted in 300 bison killed during the 2014-2015 hunt; another 500 were killed north of Yellowstone in an annual slaughter as a way to limit herd size. Recent changes in policy have allowed for transferring some bison to Native American reservations, to keep the heritage animal on their lands, rather than using hunts or slaughters. State and federal wildlife managers are in the process of revamping the Greater Yellowstone bison plan to change how the animals are managed when they roam outside the parks.

Invasive Species

Yellowstone and Grand Teton's waters hold native cutthroat trout, one of the most sought-after fish for anglers. But the introduction of two species has reduced trout numbers. In Yellowstone and Jackson Lakes, lake trout have significantly reduced native

Bighorn sheep are threatened by habitat fragmentation.

trout populations. While lake trout were introduced as a sport fish, they out-compete native trout for food. Lake trout populations are kept in check by fishing creel limits to keep

Bison give birth to calves in spring.

them from decimating trout populations into oblivion.

Aquatic invasive species such as the whirling disease parasite and New Zealand mudsnails have now found their way into park waters in certain locations. By cleaning their gear, anglers can avoid transporting these creatures to uninfected waters. Boater permits require rigs to be cleaned before entering park waters.

Invasive plants can displace native vegetation. In fact, some introduced species even inhibit the growth of native plants that are vital to wildlife. Yellowstone has 218 species of invasive plants that include Canada thistle, toadflax, leafy spurge, ox-eye daisy, and spotted knapweed. The parks use targeted spraying programs to control the spread of these, especially along roadways.

Fire

Fires are part of the natural rejuvenation of the landscape, ensuring a patchwork of foliage to support a variety of wildlife and maintain biodiversity of plant species. Every summer sees lightning start small fires across the Greater Yellowstone Ecosystem. Nearly 75 percent of the annual fires in Yellowstone burn less than a quarter of an acre. They keep bug infestations in check, restore nutrients to the soil, open up forest understories, maintain grasslands, and improve wildlife habitat. But the amount and severity of fires are increasing.

Up until the 1990s, lightning ignited about 22 fires each summer. Since then, the average has been increasing due to warmer temperatures and drought—drying factors that reduce the moisture in fallen trees and dead limbs while increasing the fuel content. Severe drought can lead to catastrophic fires that burn a huge amount of acreage and pump smoke thousands of feet into the air. The drought-stricken summer of 1988 conflagrated into 250 fires across the region that burned 1.2 million acres. Inside Yellowstone National Park, about 36 percent (793,880 acres) of the landscape burned. While wildlife populations survived the fires, 67 buildings did not.

In general, most lightning fires are allowed to burn, while those near human structures are handled on a case-by-case basis. Check online (http://inciweb.nwcg.gov) to follow fires in Yellowstone and Grand Teton National Parks.

Historical Protection

Yellowstone National Park has more than 1,800 Native American and European American archaeological sites, more than 900 historic buildings, one National Historic Trail, and 25 sites listed on the National Register of Historic Places. Grand Teton National Park likewise has historical resources that include homesteads, working ranches, and park service buildings, with 36 structures listed on the National Register of Historic Places. While the park service is charged with overseeing the preservation of these historical assets, it's up to visitors to treat them with respect to preserve them, too.

Plants and Animals

PLANTS

With its tremendous diversity, the Greater Yellowstone Ecosystem contains a mosaic of flora that in turn supports a broad spectrum of wildlife. Due to Yellowstone's thermal features, the park contains extremely unique flora, and because of Grand Teton's vertical relief, multiple elevations of plant communities are represented. The ecosystem houses more than 1,300 native plants, including seven conifers and 1,150 flowering species. Yet for those big numbers, only a few species are endemic, or found only in the region.

Geothermal Plants

A few plants can tolerate Yellowstone's geothermal zones. Mosses, for one, can endure the hot soil because they lack roots. The endemic Ross's bentgrass, which grows only in Shoshone Geyser Basin and the Firehole River geyser basins, clings to places that collect moisture, such as cracks, and takes advantage of a short growing season enhanced by hot temperatures that preclude other plants competing with it. It also accomplishes seed dispersal by hitching rides on the hooves of bison and elk. Tweedy's rush can grow in acidic hydrothermal zones that usually prove destructive to other vascular plants.

Wetlands

Eleven percent of Yellowstone's plants grow in wetlands. Some are unusual species. Due to thermally heated waters, warm spring spikerush proliferates in streams. Usually found in tropical and subtropical zones, it can survive the harsh cold winters because of the thermally heated water. One red-flowering paintbrush usually found in the Southwest grows in two wetlands in Yellowstone, due to warm springs. Many of the wetlands also contain plants more commonly found in the boreal regions of Alaska and northern Canada.

Grasslands and Sagebrush Plains

Thousands of acres of grasslands and sagebrush steppes occupy Yellowstone and Jackson Hole. Receiving low moisture, they harbor grasses, wildflowers, and small shrubs that can tolerate arid, treeless environments and trampling from bison. Idaho fescue is one of the more dominant grass species, and mountain big sagebrush blooms with tiny yellow flowers in August. As snow melts, wildflowers start to bloom. Spring beauties and glacier lilies are the first to appear, sometimes even rushing to grow through lingering snow. As summer progresses, large arrowleaf balsamroot splash yellow across drier slopes, and more color comes from blue lupine and red or orange paintbrush. In August, purple asters and goldenrod dry into stiff yellow stalks.

Forests

The forests consist of seven conifers and several leafy deciduous species. In Yellowstone, 80 percent of the forest is lodgepole pine, one of the first tree species to grow after a fire. Its cones need the heat from fire to reseed. The species grows well in Yellowstone's rhyolitic soil because it can tolerate the poor sand-like conditions. Other conifers include Engelmann spruce, subalpine fir, limber pine, whitebark pine, Douglas fir, and Rocky Mountain juniper. All of them grow 75-100 feet tall, with the exception of junipers, which max out at 30 feet. Whitebark pine and subalpine fir grow at higher elevations. Deciduous species are birches, cottonwoods, and aspens. Because quaking aspen are joined underground with connected roots, entire groves in fall change to yellow or orange in unison. Their "quaking" name denotes their flat-leaf petioles, or stems, enabling them to quiver at the slightest breeze.

Subalpine

In the high-elevation subalpine around tree line, wetter meadows become lush oases that support rabid wildflowers. The short growing season forces them to bloom and disperse their seeds fast. Prairie smoke, yellow fritillary, yellow columbine, paintbrush, mountain heather, bluebells, gentian, and harebells are just a few of the subalpine wildflowers. In this upper elevation zone, conifers are stunted due to high winds and brutal conditions. Dwarfed, they often twist into contorted, low-to-the-ground shapes called krummholz. When firmly established, the krummholz can serve as an anchor for stunted subalpine firs to grow upright.

Alpine Tundra

Dry winds, extreme cold, lack of soil, no shade, and burning sunlight impede flora in the alpine tundra above tree line. From a distance the ground looks like bare rock, but

Sky pilot grows in sub-alpine meadows.

tiny flowers cling low to the ground to survive, soaking up what moisture collects under rocks. Sky pilot, alpine forget-me-nots, and Parry's primrose bloom shortly after snowmelt to finish seed dispersal before snows return. Moss campion, which blooms with tiny pink flowers, grows in mats that can be a couple hundred years old.

Wild Berries

Succulent berries grow in the wild. Bears favor them, and so do humans. Thimbleberries, wild raspberries, and elderberries are just a few that bears and humans eat. But the huckleberry is the favorite, a small purple orb resembling a blueberry, but much sweeter. Other berries, such as serviceberry, chokecherry, buffaloberry, and twinberry, are food for mammals and birds. Berries may be on the upswing due to the reintroduction of wolves. Since the return of wolves to the ecosystem, berry bushes have been rebounding because the wolves keep elk populations in check, reducing herd sizes that used to decimate berry crops. Berries have now become a bigger part of the grizzly bear diet. Find lowland berries in late July, but mid-August-early September is known as huck season.

ANIMALS

The Greater Yellowstone Ecosystem houses one of the greatest concentrations of mammals in the Lower 48 with 67 species. In addition, the region harbors 300 species of birds, 16 species of fish, four species of amphibians, and five species of reptiles.

Megafauna

Megafauna, the big animals everyone wants to see, populate the Greater Yellowstone Ecosystem. **Black bears** and **grizzly bears** top the big carnivore list along with members of the dog and cat families. Three elusive members of the cat family, **mountain lions, bobcats,** and **Canada lynx,** are quiet nocturnal hunters. With keen eyesight and hearing, they may see you while you can't see them. For mountain lions, deer tops the menu, while lynx favor snowshoe hares. Both cat populations rise and fall with their prey populations. At the top of the dog family is the **gray wolf** with packs that inhabit fairly large ranges of 100-300 square miles. In Yellowstone, the wolf diet is 92 percent elk and 8 percent bison, deer, and pronghorn. Each wolf eats about 22 elk per year. Wolf pups, born in April, weigh one pound and are blind. **Coyotes** are the biggest

Wildlife Facts

BISON

How can a 2,000-pound bison walk through deep snow? Herds walk in winter on groomed roads to avoid sinking in deep snow, and when they do travel in deep snow, they walk single file, allowing the bison in front to break trail. Although they seem docile, they can run up to 40 mph (more than three times faster than humans) and jump six-foot fences.

Bison cluster in smaller herds in winter, with about 20 members as opposed to 200 or more in summer. Because they feed mostly on grasses, geyser basins provide a refuge, as heat from geothermal activity keeps the snow thin or melted with patches of dry grasses. Bison also migrate in winter to lower elevations outside the park, where feeding is more readily attainable. Herds winter in the Lamar, Hayden, Firehole River, and Pelican Valleys.

BEARS

Grizzly bears have a unique mechanism called delayed implantation. After mating in spring, the female's uterus hangs onto the fertilized eggs rather than letting them implant. The eggs wait until her body is ready in November. If she has not gained enough fat to survive feeding the cubs through winter, no implantation will occur. Grizzlies usually have 1-3 cubs; the number of eggs that implant correlates to the mother's health.

In winter, bears opt for denning. After bulking up on calories during hyperphasia in fall, grizzly bears dig dens on the north sides of slopes where deeper accumulating snows will insulate them from winter temperatures dropping below zero. While respiration, heart rate, and body temperature drop during winter sleep, bears do not eat, drink, urinate, or defecate. But females give birth while denning.

WOLVES

Wolf rules are strict. Packs of 5-10 animals form hierarchies led by the alpha male and female, the only breeders. After the alpha female gives birth to the pups, the other adults in the pack aid in caring for the young. They bring the pups pre-chewed food, which they regurgitate from their stomachs. Wolves are active year-round with mating usually occurring in February. Ninety percent of their winter diet consists of elk—especially the young, elderly, and injured. Because of their dependence on elk, they often follow the herds.

WOLVERINES

Eating machines in the wild, wolverines have the Latin name *Gulo gulo*. Literally, it translates as "glutton, glutton," reinforcing their voracious appetites. They prey upon much larger animals such

predator of wolf pups, but have lessened in numbers since the return of wolves. As their numbers diminished, **fox** populations rebounded. Less often seen large carnivores are **wolverines** and **badgers.**

Ungulates crowd both national parks and spill outside their boundaries. **Bison** are the biggest, weighing in at 2,000 pounds for males and 1,000 pounds for females. **Elk** produce the largest antlers of the ungulates and provide a bigger food source than bison for wolves. Since wolf reintroduction reduced

elk populations, aspens, willows, and cottonwoods have bounced back, bringing the return of beaver and moose. With a diet that is 60 percent water and 40 percent plants, **moose** browse mostly on willows around streambeds and lakes. **Mule** and **white-tailed deer** live throughout the parks in forests, while **mountain goats** and **bighorn sheep** cling to higher rocky slopes that have cliffs for protection. One herd of about 200 **pronghorn** populates the northern section of Yellowstone. As the second-fastest animal

Bison herds walk single file in snow.

as elk. With powerful jaws and teeth, they can chomp right through bones. They eat everything, including teeth and bones.

ELK

What's all the bugling about? During fall when elk breed, bulls bugle to attract cows into their harems. A bugle starts with a bellow that rises into a squeal and finishes with grunts. The bugle also shows the bull's prowess to other bulls, a statement that he's ready to fight for the harem and a warning for other bulls to steer clear.

Elk retreat to lower elevations for winter and limit movement to preserve energy. Some migrate south to the National Elk Refuge in Jackson Hole where they are fed during winter. Smaller herds hang along the Madison and Firehole Rivers or head into Gardiner, Montana.

BIGHORN SHEEP

Bighorn sheep opt to winter in lower elevations of the northern valleys of the Gardner, Lamar, and Yellowstone Rivers. November-April, they feed on dry grasses exposed in the thin snowpack of windblown slopes. Breeding typically happens in November-December.

in the world, pronghorn can run 35 mph for 5-6 miles.

BEARS

Two bear species roam the Greater Yellowstone Ecosystem: the black bear and the grizzly bear. Omnivores and opportunistic feeders, bears will eat anything. Spending most of their waking time eating to gain 100-150 pounds before winter, bears feed on a protein-heavy diet of army cutworm moths, whitebark pine nuts, ungulates, and cutthroat trout. These foods supply the greatest nutrition for the least foraging effort. They also rely on seasonal supplemental foods: bulbs, roots, berries, shoots, flowers, ants, insects, carrion, and ground squirrels. Due to the waning of two of their traditional foods, whitebark pine seeds and cutthroat trout, bears are shifting toward meat from elk, bison, moose, and carrion. Contrary to popular opinion, humans are not on their menu of favorite foods.

Because bears learn fast, they adapt quickly to new food sources, be it a pack dropped by

Safety in Bear Country

Even though colors are used to name the bears, black and grizzly bears display a variety of hues. For instance, a reddish-black bear can give birth to three cubs of different colors: blond, black, and brown. Grizzlies, named for silvered hair, appear in all colors of the spectrum. Don't be fooled by color; look instead for body size and shape.

Grizzlies are bigger than black bears, standing on all fours at 3-4 feet tall and weighing in at 300-600 pounds. Black bears average 12-18 inches shorter on all fours. Adult females weigh around 140 pounds, while males bulk up to 220 pounds.

In profile, the grizzly has one notable feature: a hump on its shoulders. The solid muscle mass provides the grizzly's forelegs with power for digging and running. Black bears lack this hump. Their face profiles are also different. On the grizzly, look for a scooped or dished forehead-to-nose silhouette; the black bear's nose will appear straighter in line with its forehead. Note the ears: Grizzly ears look too small for their heads, while black bear ears seem big, standing straight up. Paw prints in mud reveal a difference in their claws and foot structure. Grizzly claws are four inches long with pads in a relatively straight line, while black bear claws are 1.5 inches long with pads arced across the top of the foot.

With a few precautions, you can eliminate bear scares. Although both bears have mediocre vision, they are fast runners. In three seconds, a grizzly bear can cover 180 feet.

- **Make noise.** To avoid surprising a bear, use your voice—sing loudly, hoot, or holler—and clap your hands. Bears tend to recognize human sounds as ones to avoid; they'll usually wander off if they hear people approaching. Make loud noise in thick brushy areas, around blind corners, near babbling streams, and against the wind.

- **Hike with other people.** Avoid hiking alone. Keep children near. Very few bear attacks happen to groups of four or more.

the side of the trail or dog food left out in a campground. For this reason, strict rules for handling food and garbage are enforced inside and outside the parks. All garbage cans and dumpsters are bear resistant. Bears that eat human foods and garbage often become more aggressive in repeating the behavior. As a result, bear managers are forced to move them to new habitat or, worse, destroy them.

Because grizzly and black bears are integral to the ecosystem, the National Park Service employs several bear rangers whose jobs entail monitoring and deterring bears from trouble. To discourage bruins from lingering near roadways and front-country campgrounds, bear teams uses hazing methods: loud noises, gunshots, pellet beanbags, and sometimes Karelian bear dogs. Nuisance bears are transplanted to remote park drainages or destroyed if their offenses warrant. "A fed bear is a dead bear," the truism goes. A bear that dabbles in human food often aggressively seeks more.

Bears are one of the least fertile mammals. Females must reach about seven years old to be fertile, and then they only give birth once every two or three years. Each birth usually results in 2-3 cubs born during winter's deep sleep.

Bears don't actually hibernate, as their respiration and pulse remain close to normal. Instead, they enter a deep sleep in which the body temperature drops slightly. Before crawling into their dens, they scarf down mountain ash berries, rough grasses, and twigs to form an anal plug, which inhibits eating, urinating, or defecating during winter. Bears emerge in the spring ravenously hungry, immediately heading out to rummage for snow-buried carcasses.

Small Mammals

Members of the weasel family—fishers, pine martens, minks, and weasels—inhabit forests and waterways. The short-tailed weasel

- **Avoid bear feeding areas.** If you stumble across an animal carcass, leave the area immediately and notify a ranger. Toward summer's end, be cautious around huckleberry patches.

- **Hike in broad daylight.** Avoid early morning, late evening, and night.

- **Never approach a bear.** Head swaying, teeth clacking, laid-back ears, a lowered head, and huffing or woofing are signs of agitation: Clear out slowly.

- **If you do surprise a bear, back away.** Contrary to all inclinations, do not run. Instead, back away slowly, talking quietly and turning sideways or bending your knees to appear smaller and nonthreatening. Avoid direct eye contact. Leave your pack on; it can protect you if the bear attacks.

- **Use pepper spray or play dead.** If you surprise a bear that attacks in defense, aim pepper spray at the bear's eyes. Protect yourself and your vulnerable parts by assuming a fetal position on the ground with your hands around the back of your neck. Play dead. Move again only when you are sure the bear has vacated the area.

- **If a bear stalks you as food, or attacks at night, fight back.** Bears rarely stalk humans as prey. If one does, use any means at hand, such as pepper spray, shouting, sticks, or rocks, to tell the bear you are not an easy food source. Try to escape up something, like a building or a tree.

- **Respect trail closures.** Trail and backcountry campsite closures are usually in heavy bear feeding areas. Staying out of these areas guarantees hikers a safer experience.

Two books have accurate information on bears: Bill Schneider's *Bear Aware* and Stephen Herrero's *Bear Attacks: Their Causes and Avoidances.*

changes color in winter: Its fur becomes white, except for the small black tip of its tail. Snowshoe hares also change to white in winter, their large feet providing extra flotation on snow. In subalpine country, a chorus of eeks, screams, and squeaks bounce through rockfalls. The noisemakers are pikas, which look like tailless mice, and the ubiquitous Columbian ground squirrel, recognized by its reddish tint. Looking like fat fur balls, yellow bellied marmots splay on rocks, sunning themselves. Scampering between high alpine rocks, golden-mantled ground squirrels look like oversize chipmunks with golden stripes.

Fish

Yellowstone and Grand Teton are home to 16 species of fish. Eleven are native, including mountain whitefish, arctic grayling, westslope cutthroat trout, and Yellowstone cutthroat trout. Nonnative rainbow, brook, brown, and lake trout were introduced to enhance sport fishing. Historically, about 40 percent of Yellowstone's rivers and lakes were barren of fish. Stocking programs converted many of those to fisheries with nonnative species. Those nonnative species now threaten native fish through predation, competition, and hybridization. In order to protect native fish, the park service has adopted stringent fishing guidelines.

Birds

The Greater Yellowstone Ecosystem has almost 300 species of birds: songbirds, waterfowl, shorebirds, and raptors. About 150 species nest in Yellowstone National Park. Two species of concern are the common loon and trumpeter swan. Yellowstone has about 28 loons, equating to 75 percent of the breeding and nesting loons in Wyoming. The trumpeter swan is more rare. Only about 20 resident birds populate the park year-round, which includes two pairs of breeders. The

Trumpeter swans winter in Yellowstone around thermally heated streams.

swan is North America's largest bird, with a wingspan of eight feet.

Songbirds show up in spring, and the trees liven with their songs during breeding and nesting season. By August, the forests quiet as many begin migrating south. Mountain chickadees, gray jays, red-breasted nuthatches, and American dippers are year-round residents.

Waterfowl and shorebirds are common due to the big lakes, wetlands, and rivers. Visitors can see American pelicans, sandhill cranes, great blue herons, and a variety of ducks and geese.

Nineteen raptors nest in the Greater Yellowstone. These include golden eagles, bald eagles, osprey, peregrine falcons, and owls. The park service monitors nests, keeping tabs on 21 bald eagle nests in Yellowstone. Recoveries of bald eagles and peregrine falcons have removed them from the Endangered Species List.

Snakes

While several snakes inhabit the region, the prairie rattlesnake is the only venomous one. It is only found in the Black Canyon of the Yellowstone; most of Yellowstone and Grand Teton are too high and too cold for its survival.

History

NATIVE AMERICANS

Archaeological evidence in Yellowstone and Grand Teton National Parks shows that Native Americans appeared around 11,000 years ago after the Yellowstone Ice Cap melted. A few stone tools indicate their presence. One was an obsidian Clovis point. The obsidian matches the rock in Obsidian Cliff, which has an ancient quarry on top. Other points and projectiles were found around Yellowstone Lake in what was probably a summer camp.

Increased use of the Yellowstone area spiked about 3,000 years ago as many tribes found hospitable summer environments, wildlife for hunting, fish, and edible or usable vegetation. Some tribes used geothermal areas for ceremonies and medicine rites. Popular trade and travel routes brought multiple tribes through the area in the 1800s: Shoshone,

Crow, Blackfeet, Flathead, and Nez Perce. The Bannock Trail, a route used by western tribes crossing the Rockies to hunt bison, traverses the northern part of the park.

The Sheep Eaters, or Tukudika, members of the Shoshone, were assumed to be permanent residents of Yellowstone. They relied on bighorn sheep for survival. But their residential presence in the park may be myth. While conical timber lodges, wickiups, drive lines with sheep traps, and rustic structures are attributed to the Sheep Eaters, little evidence ties the constructions solely to this tribe. By the time Yellowstone became a national park, the Sheep Eaters had mysteriously disappeared.

Shortly after Yellowstone became a national park, it served as a temporary haven for the Nez Perce in 1877 on their flight toward Canada to escape the U.S. Army. The Nee-Me-Poo spent nearly two weeks in the park, bumping into a few visitors. The 1,170-mile Nez Perce National Historic Trail (http://www.nps.gov/nepe), which commemorates their flight, traverses the central part of Yellowstone.

TRAPPERS, EXPLORERS, AND HOMESTEADERS

In the late 1700s, European American fur trappers arrived in Yellowstone and Jackson Hole to trade with Native Americans and acquire beaver pelts. Shortly after, Lewis and Clark bypassed the Yellowstone area 50 miles to the north. On their return trip, one of their members departed the expedition to hook up with fur trappers. John Colter explored parts of Yellowstone including Yellowstone Lake in 1807-1808 and may have visited Jackson Hole and seen the Tetons. With only word of mouth, his stories amazed people but left little concrete documentation of his travels. Only the unverified Colter Stone bears his name and the 1808 date.

As the decline of beavers shifted fur trapping on to other pursuits, a small unofficial expedition in 1869 succeeded in documenting the Tower Fall, Mud Volcano, West Thumb, Shoshone Lake, and Firehole River geyser basins. The expedition's reports sparked the first official organized explorations. The 1870 Washburn-Langford-Doane expedition surveyed some of the same places as the previous exploration, climbed peaks, toured down the Grand Canyon of the Yellowstone, and tried to measure some of the natural features. This expedition named Old Faithful. A year later, the Hayden expedition ran concurrent with a U.S. Army Corps of Engineer survey. It served as the first scientific expedition with experts in botany, zoology, meteorology, ornithology, entomology, and mineralogy. Artists, a topographer, and a photographer came along to document the sites and terrain.

The Homestead Act of 1862 sent droves of settlers out West. But settlers avoided Jackson Hole with its sand and cobble soil, arid summers, and frigid winters. The first homesteaders who finally put down roots in 1884 struggled with farming and ranching.

CREATING THE FIRST NATIONAL PARK

The expeditions fueled fervor in the nation's capital, and explorers submitted a bill to preserve Yellowstone. Thomas Moran's paintings, William Henry Jackson's photographs, and Henry W. Elliot's sketches gave visual clarity to the written expedition reports. Even though Congressional legislation of the era supported westward expansion and resource exploitation, Congress agreed with the value of preservation, partially in the wake of preserving Yosemite as a California state park eight years earlier. In 1872, Yellowstone became the nation's, and the world's, first national park.

Legislating the creation of Yellowstone was one thing. But creating a park for people to visit was quite another. No park service existed to run Yellowstone, and the bill setting aside the land as a park included no government funding. No one really knew what a national park was, except that it was for people to enjoy rather than develop. No legislation protected its natural features and wildlife, and the park's first superintendent—who was unpaid—visited it only twice, the first time in 1872 with the second Hayden expedition. Several expeditions surveyed Yellowstone for science, mapping, and exploration, but the park floundered, unfunded and directionless.

Six years after the park's inception, Congress finally appropriated money to "protect, preserve, and improve" Yellowstone. The park's second superintendent, Philetus Norris, tackled the job. He built a few primitive roads and designed the Grand Loop Road. For headquarters, he constructed a rudimentary station at Mammoth Hot Springs. He hired the park's first gamekeeper to battle poachers. But political machinations swapped in a series of useless superintendents, and in its second decade, Yellowstone ran wild. Vandals destroyed natural features, poachers slaughtered wildlife, loggers harvested timber, squatters threw up shelters and camps for tourists, and hot springs facilities were erected as laundries and baths.

When Yellowstone was created, it looked like a big square on the map with no accommodation for topographical features. The northwest boundary was expanded in 1929 to include petrified trees, and the east boundary was reconfigured to match watersheds in 1932.

U.S. ARMY AND BISON

The public loved the idea of Yellowstone, but Congress trashed annual funding in 1886 due to ineffective management of the park. The solution to Yellowstone's management was the U.S. Army, already operating out of several forts in the territories of Montana, Idaho, and Wyoming. That year, the army took up residence in the park to enforce regulations. In 1891, Fort Yellowstone was erected at Mammoth Hot Springs, including the headquarters, officers' quarters, a guardhouse, and barracks. Many of the buildings were constructed of sandstone from a quarry located between Mammoth Campground and the Gardner River.

Outside the park, bison slaughters fed the booming fur and meat business. The federal government even encouraged them, especially as a means to subdue Native American tribes that relied on bison for food and force them to move onto reservations. Inside Yellowstone, poachers likewise jeopardized the survival of bison. With eviction from the park as the maximum punishment, the army had no strong clout. After a journalistic outcry at one bison slaughter in Pelican Valley, Congress passed the National Park Protection Act in 1894 to protect birds, animals, and natural features in Yellowstone. Guilty violators faced fines and jail.

By 1910, the army stationed 324 soldiers at Fort Yellowstone. Soldiers were sent out on details to various outposts throughout the park. The army managed Yellowstone until 1918 when the two-year-old National Park Service took over.

EARLY VISITORS

When Yellowstone first opened as a national park with no services, roads, or lodging, only the hearty visited. To reach the park required riding a stagecoach. At the park, some visitors hired unsanctioned guides to sightsee via long hours on horseback and overnighting in canvas tents. Yellowstone's first year as a park logged 300 visitors.

In the park's fifth year, the Nez Perce came through en route to Canada while fleeing from the U.S. Army. In their two weeks in the park, they met up with 25 visitors and ended up killing two. Stories of wild Indians kept some would-be visitors away. Philetus Norris, the park's second superintendent, countered with fabricated stories that the Native Americans stayed away in fear of the geysers.

In the early 1880s, the Northern Pacific Railway added a train station at Livingston, Montana, 52 miles north of the park boundary. A rail spur to Gardiner opened in 1883, increasing visitation to 5,000. By 1908, when park visitation pushed toward 20,000 annual visitors, the Union Pacific Railroad wanted in on the action, so the company built a line to West Yellowstone.

The World's First National Park

On March 1, 1872, the U.S. Congress made Yellowstone the first national park in the country. The park marked the first time that the federal government set aside land for the "pleasure of the people." Parkhood for Yellowstone came even before statehood for Montana and Wyoming. In addition to being the first national park in the United States, Yellowstone was also the first national park in the world.

On the tail of the Lewis and Clark expedition in 1806, exploration of the Northern Rockies put Yellowstone country on the map. Although the first descriptions of huge bubbling mud cauldrons and hot water shooting into the sky were dismissed as too fantastical, multiple expeditions began to document the landscape.

While the concept of a national park got its foothold when Yosemite was deeded to the State of California to preserve for people to enjoy, Yellowstone benefitted from champions of preservation such as John Muir and George Bird Grinnell, who laid the groundwork. When the government deployed Ferdinand Hayden in 1871 with a cadre of artists and photographers to document Yellowstone, he filed a recommendation to make the area a national park, an idea suggested to him by Northern Pacific Railway lobbyist A. B. Nettleton, who saw the benefit to train ridership.

Hayden's report to Congress included details of Yellowstone's uniqueness, but also pointed out that the land was unsuitable for farming or mining, rendering it not valuable for development. With Hayden's recommendations also came a warning: to avoid the fate of Niagara Falls, a national treasure surrounded by private development.

At inception, Yellowstone had no funding, no staff, and no services. Refinement of the national park concept took several more decades. In the meantime, the U.S. Cavalry oversaw the park from Fort Yellowstone, today known as Mammoth. Finally, in 1916, the federal government created the National Park Service to operate the parks, a concept first enacted by Canada.

When Yellowstone first became a national park, 300 people visited during its first year, challenged with sightseeing on horseback and camping. A decade later when trains delivered visitors to Gardiner, that number climbed to 5,000. Today, Yellowstone sees about four million annual visitors.

As the first national park, Yellowstone paved the way for 58 other U.S. national parks. Worldwide, almost 100 countries have set aside more than 6,000 national parks as places for protection of wildlife, landscapes, and resources plus the enjoyment of people.

BUILDING LODGES

Immediately following the park's establishment, requests poured in from entrepreneurs who wanted to build hotels. A few rustic lodging facilities were constructed in the park's first decade, mostly on temporary 10-year leases. But the pressure to add more lodging came from the railroads, which needed facilities for their passengers. Nine small hotels were built in the early 1890s at the Lower Geyser Basin, Norris, and Canyon. The Fountain Hotel introduced feeding bears for guest entertainment, a practice that was picked up later at garbage dumps in the park until 1970.

The Northern Pacific Railway bankrolled the biggest hotel venture. In 1891, the Lake Yellowstone Hotel opened on the shore of Yellowstone Lake. While the hotel boasted scenery and elegance, its boxy architecture was bland. Within 12 years, Robert Reamer, the architect of Old Faithful Inn, gave the hotel old colonial character with Ionic columns, false balconies, extended rooflines.

Reamer's Old Faithful Inn, built in 1903-1904, has the rustic log-and-wood appearance that defines vintage parkitecture. The foundation is built from rhyolite from the caldera, and lodgepoles harvested nearby were used for the log walls. Posts, rails, and other details were crafted from knobby wood. The inn's shingles were painted with a red mineral thought to reduce flammability. Electric lights and steam heat made it modern, and elegance came from dining to the music of a string quartet. Later renovations added the east and west wings.

In 1897, the town site of Jackson was laid out around the town square, its central location selected for ease of access from ranches at all ends of Jackson Hole. By the early 1900s, homesteaders fed up with the toil required for farming such poor soil and managing cattle through long winters shifted to tourism, aiming to cash in on the desire of wealthy easterners to ride horses and experience the West. By 1920, dude ranches became vogue, piggybacking off the allure of Yellowstone National Park and Teton grandeur.

HISTORIC YELLOW VEHICLES

With the advent of the automobile, America grew infatuated with road travel, but the railroad and park transportation company dug in hard to maintain inside-park travel by horse-drawn surreys and painted yellow stagecoaches. When the political pressure boiled, Yellowstone admitted its first automobiles in 1915, with a Ford Model T as the first one, followed by 50 cars that summer. Drivers paid an exorbitant entrance fee of $5-10 ($116-232 in today's dollars) to take on the challenge of rough dirt roads at a maximum speed of 20 mph. Within two years, the park banned horse-drawn vehicles.

For summer 1917, the Yellowstone Park Transportation Company drove 116 snazzy new seven-passenger touring cars and 11-passenger sedans for toting affluent visitors around the sights. White Motor Company had leapt into the national park business of creating touring vehicles designed specifically for sightseeing. In addition to Yellowstone, their vehicles became iconic fleets in Glacier, Zion, and other national parks. Canvas tops allowed visitors to stand up to see wildlife and grab grander views. The fleet of 11-passenger touring sedans grew to more than 300 by the mid-1920s.

The touring sedans were replaced over the decades by updated White Motor Company models, all painted yellow and some holding 13 passengers. As private auto traffic increased in the wake of World War II, only 124 vehicles remained in service. The company sold off the vehicles in the 1950s. In 2007, Xanterra bought eight of the original White Motor Company Model 706 rigs, revamping them to modern safety standards for guided summer sightseeing tours of Yellowstone.

GRAND TETON NATIONAL PARK

As Jackson Hole attracted development in the early 1900s, the Teton Mountains became a backdrop for enterprises such as dancehalls, billboards, and racetracks thrown up in open fields. That horrified some longtime locals, who favored conservation and wilderness. Talk favored an extension of Yellowstone or a new park. In the mid-1920s, Yellowstone superintendent Horace Albright brought John D. Rockefeller to Jackson Hole. The scenery of the Tetons captured Rockefeller, who purchased 35,000 acres of land tracts under his Snake River Land Company with the aim of donating the land to the national park. Some locals, however, feared the loss of tax revenue if those valley land tracts became part of a national park. The battle over conservation landed in a Congressional hearing.

The process of making Grand Teton National Park sprawled across several decades. In 1929, Congress created Grand Teton National Park, but it consisted only of the mountains of the Teton Range and several moraine lakes along the base. In its first year, 51,500 people visited the park. In the 1940s, the federal government gained two large pieces of acreage in Jackson Hole: Franklin Delano Roosevelt converted the federal land in the valley into Jackson Hole National Monument, and John D. Rockefeller donated his land to the national park. In 1950, Congress combined the three into Grand Teton National Park. Later, Rockefeller's name was put on his donated land to honor his philanthropy.

Today, the John D. Rockefeller, Jr. Memorial Parkway sits between Yellowstone and Grand Teton National Parks.

TOURISM TODAY

Following World War II, tourism skyrocketed. But travel patterns had changed. Train travel and the desire for elegant hotels waned in favor of private cars and camping, cabins, or moderate motels. In 1948, Yellowstone surpassed one million annual visitors; so did Grand Teton six years later. With visitation escalating every year, the parks needed more facilities. The National Park Service's Mission 66 program provided the answer. The 10-year program was designed to get park facilities nationwide up to snuff by the 50th anniversary of the park service in 1966.

In Yellowstone, Mission 66 intended to revamp older park developments and, in some cases, move them away from sensitive geothermal zones. The old Canyon Hotel was razed and replaced by Canyon Village. Grant Village was built two miles south of West Thumb to protect the geyser basin, which had encroaching development and a proposal for accommodations to house 2,500 visitors.

Firehole Village was intended to replace Old Faithful Inn and Old Faithful Lodge, but that village project never materialized. In Grand Teton, Mission 66 built Jackson Lake Lodge and Colter Bay Visitor Center in the mid-1950s. John D. Rockefeller financially supported construction of the lodge and Colter Bay Cabins.

New facilities came just in time. By the 1960s, both parks hit the two million mark for annual visitation. The popularity of Yellowstone and Grand Teton continue to grow. In 2015, both parks saw record-breaking attendance: Grand Teton hit three million visitors and Yellowstone topped four million.

WINTER TOURISM

Official organized winter tourism launched in Yellowstone in 1949 when snowplanes delivered passengers to the park's interior. By 1955, snowcoach trips started, carrying 500 people in winter to see Old Faithful. But overnight winter lodging did not open until 1971. Following the 1988 fires, the Snow Lodge was constructed at Old Faithful especially to accommodate winter visitors. Today, more than 30,000 people stay overnight in winter

Yellow touring sedans are still used in Yellowstone.

inside the park either at Old Faithful Snow Lodge or Mammoth Hot Springs Hotel. In winter, 5,000-6,000 visitors per month pass through the Roosevelt Arch, Yellowstone's North Entrance gate at Gardiner. The road from Gardiner to Mammoth and Cooke City is open year-round for private vehicles.

In Jackson Hole, the Snow King Ski Area launched on a hill cleared by a forest fire adjacent to the town of Jackson. Skiers hiked the hill to ski down until a cable tow powered by an old Ford tractor engine was installed in 1939. It was Wyoming's first ski lift. In the 1960s, Jackson Hole and Grand Targhee opened for skiing on opposite sides of the Teton Mountains, where some years they have received more than 500 inches of snowfall. Today, they are icons in the ski industry.

LANDMARKS AND DESIGNATIONS
National Historic Landmarks

Yellowstone has eight National Historic Landmarks. They are Old Faithful Inn, Fort Yellowstone District, Northeast Entrance Station, Obsidian Cliff, Lake Yellowstone Hotel, and the museums at Fishing Bridge, Madison, and Norris. Grand Teton National Park has two National Historic Landmarks: the Murie Ranch Historic District and Jackson Lake Lodge.

National Register of Historic Places

The National Register of Historic Places protects many sites in Yellowstone and Grand Teton. Walking tours are available in larger historic locations.

In Yellowstone, some of the 25 sites include districts: Mammoth Hot Springs, Old Faithful, and North Entrance Road including Roosevelt Arch, Roosevelt Lodge, and Lake Fish Hatchery. As districts they contain multiple buildings or structures that warrant preservation, and five of them influenced rustic park architecture. Other places on the national register include the Lake Hotel, Lamar Buffalo Ranch, Obsidian Cliff interpretive

kiosk, Queen's Laundry Bathhouse, and Mammoth Post Office. Yellowstone has more than 900 historic buildings.

Grand Teton National Park has 36 sites listed on the National Register of Historic Places. Some are districts with many buildings such as Mormon Row, Murie Ranch, Menors Ferry, Jenny Lake Ranger Station, and several ranch areas. Other sites are individual cabins, barns, and lodges.

Wilderness Designations

Since the creation of the Wilderness Act in 1964, huge swaths of the 20 million acres of the Greater Yellowstone Ecosystem have become part of the wilderness system. Two million of Yellowstone's 2.2 million acres are managed as wilderness. Much of the mountainous terrain in Grand Teton National Park has been recommended as wilderness. Despite lacking official designation, it is managed as de facto wilderness.

The Greater Yellowstone Ecosystem also contains multiple designated wilderness areas in the national forests surrounding and bordering the parks. These wilderness areas include the Absaroka-Beartooth, North Absaroka, Lee Metcalf, Washakie, Teton, Jedediah Smith, and Gros Ventre. The Wind River Mountains, a southeast spur of the ecosystem, contain the Bridger, Fitzpatrick, and Popo Agie Wilderness Areas. These wilderness areas are key to the survival of many species, including wolves and grizzly bears.

Wild and Scenic River Designations

In 2009, Congress added the Snake River Headwaters to its list of federally recognized Wild and Scenic rivers. The designated river distance totals 387.5 miles, but that includes multiple tributaries. More than half is designated as wild with the remaining miles as scenic or recreational. Snake River Headwaters encompasses waterways in Yellowstone and Grand Teton National Parks, John D. Rockefeller, Jr. Memorial Parkway, National Elk Refuge, and Bridger-Teton National

Forest. The Wild and Scenic designation covers the Lewis River, the Snake River above and below Jackson Lake, and multiple tributaries including Granite Creek, Pacific Creek, Buffalo Creek, and the Gros Ventre River.

Yellowstone Biosphere Reserve

In 1976, Yellowstone was designated as a UNESCO Biosphere Reserve. Because it was created as the first national park in the world, it was one of the first places chosen to be a Biosphere Reserve. It gained the recognition due to its hydrothermal features, diversity of plant communities, wildlife, and outstanding opportunities for research on geology, fire ecology, vegetation, mammals, and fisheries.

Yellowstone World Heritage Site

In 1988, UNESCO also named Yellowstone as a World Heritage Site. It gained this designation because it contains the world's largest concentration of geysers and is one of the few large intact northern temperate ecosystems. Many of the park's features contributed to its status as a World Heritage Site: scenery, evidence of natural history in fossils and geothermal activity, wild flora, and wildlife.

Local Culture

INDIGENOUS CULTURE

Located between Native American cultures from the Great Basin, Great Plains, and Plateau Indians, Yellowstone has 26 associated tribes with historical connections to the land. Since Yellowstone began its ethnographic program in 2000, the park service and the sovereign Native American nations have consulted together on mutual issues. Two concerns for Native Americans are the bison that leave the park and wickiup preservation. Four tribes have treaty rights to hunt Yellowstone bison. Collaborative work developed interpretation on the Yellowstone portion of the Nez Perce National Historic Trail, and the park service inventories culturally important and sacred sites. The Heritage and Research Center in Gardiner houses the immense Yellowstone collection of cultural and historical artifacts, including Native American items.

Three of the tribes that hunted, camped, fished, and held ceremonies in Yellowstone and Grand Teton National Parks have reservations nearby. None of the Shoshone, Crow, or Cheyenne reservations share boundaries with the national parks, but they are close enough for frequent visits. Some members still visit for religious, ceremonial, or medicinal purposes, and each celebrates their culture every summer with a powwow and rodeo.

Shoshone

East of Grand Teton National Park sits the 2.2-million-acre Wind River Reservation. It is home to the Eastern Shoshone (www.shoshonebannocktribes.com) and the Bannock, who stayed because their reservation in Idaho never was established. While historically the Shoshone tribes named themselves after their foods (sheep eaters, salmon eaters, seed eaters, buffalo eaters, deer eaters), today the Shoshone-Bannock call themselves Newe, meaning "The People." One of the largest powwows in the region, Eastern Shoshone Indian Days, takes place the last week of June. The grave and a memorial for Sacagawea, the guide for the Lewis and Clark Corps of Discovery expedition, are located on the reservation.

Crow

The Crow Nation (www.crow-nsn.gov) concentrates on the 2.3-million-acre reservation northeast of Yellowstone in Montana. The reservation is home to Little Bighorn Battlefield National Monument, which commemorates the Native American victory over Custer and the 7th Cavalry. The Crow Fair Powwow and Rodeo takes place during the third week of August to celebrate the heritage of the Apsaalooké, or "Children of the Large Beaked Bird."

Cheyenne

To Yellowstone's northeast, a 444,000-acre reservation sits adjacent to the Crow Reservation in Montana. It is home to the Northern Cheyenne Nation (www.cheyennenation.com), two merged tribes known as the Tsitsistas and the Só'taeo'o. The Northern Cheyenne Powwow and Rodeo happens over Memorial Day weekend.

MODERN COWBOYS

Cowboy life in Montana, Wyoming, and Idaho has strong roots. Wyoming snagged the "Cowboy State" moniker for its 1890 statehood, and William "Buffalo Bill" Cody took his Wild West show on the road in the late 1800s to celebrate the lifestyle. But modern cowboy life is more than pulling on a pair of jeans, chaps, boots, hat, bandanna, and deerskin gloves. Being a real cowboy is physically demanding. It requires riding long hours in the saddle, wrangling cows, repairing fences, bucking wood, slinging hay bales, and putting up with arbitrary weather.

While many working ranches still operate in Jackson Hole, guest ranches have continued to meet the tourism desire to play cowboy for a week. As the popularity of Jackson Hole grew as a vacation paradise, developers began to buy up ranch lands for millionaire second and third homes. Cowboys and cowgirls can no longer afford to buy a home in Jackson Hole where the average price is over $1 million.

Yet the cowboy way of life persists, in part thanks to tourism. The world's longest-running shoot-out happens six nights a week in summer in Jackson. It keeps alive the lawless West in a theatrical performance, and rodeos give local cowboys and cowgirls a chance to show off their skills in summer. The Million Dollar Cowboy Bar even teaches country-western dancing to keep traditions alive.

Essentials

Getting There

SUGGESTED DRIVING ROUTES

Getting to Yellowstone and Grand Teton requires navigating wild country where gas stations are few and far between. In places, gas stations sit 75 miles apart. Schedule gas fill-ups at major towns. Winter blizzards and icy roads can turn a two-hour drive into a four-hour nightmare. All times given below are for dry roads in summer. To get current road conditions, call 511 or consult state highway agency websites: Idaho (http://lb.511.idaho.gov/idlb), Montana (www.mdt.mt.gov/travinfo), and Wyoming (www.wyoroad.info). All driving routes are open year-round except where winter closures are mentioned.

I-90 to North and West Entrances

I-90 takes a latitudinal cross through Montana north of Yellowstone. From the freeway between Billings and Butte, multiple routes drop south to reach the park's West, North, and Northeast Entrances.

FROM BOZEMAN, MONTANA

To reach West Yellowstone, drivers have two options: via the Madison River or Gallatin River, both north-south roads with the Madison Range separating them. Drivers of large RVs prefer Madison over Gallatin due to the straighter roadway and fewer vehicles. Both routes take longer in snow.

For the Madison Valley route (117 miles, 2.25 hours), leave I-90 at Exit 274 west of Three Forks between Butte and Bozeman. Head south on U.S. Highway 287. The two-lane route goes through several blink-and-you-miss-it towns and Ennis, a fishing mecca with multiple fly-fishing outfitters, guide

services, fly-fishing schools, and gear shops. Past Ennis, the highway parallels the Madison River, a headwater tributary of the Missouri River. Follow the river eastward up a canyon to Quake Lake, the site of the 1959 earthquake that caused a landslide. Earthquake Lake Visitor Center (206/682-7620, http://fs.usda.gov/gallatin, 10am-6pm daily late May-mid-Sept., free) is worth the stop. After passing Hebgen Lake, turn south onto U.S. Highway 191 to reach West Yellowstone. Once at West Yellowstone, U.S. Highway 191 becomes Canyon Street; follow it seven blocks to Yellowstone Avenue and turn left to reach the West Entrance.

The Gallatin Valley route (90 miles, two hours) clogs with more traffic as the most heavily traveled road to Yellowstone. From I-90 at Belgrade, take Exit 298 and drive south on Highway 85 (Jackrabbit Ln., Gallatin Rd.) through strip malls toward Gallatin Gateway. En route, U.S. Highway 191 from Bozeman joins the road. From then on, the road is U.S. Highway 191, squeezing between the Madison and Gallatin Ranges. Between Gallatin Gateway and Big Sky, locals speed along the narrow two-lane curves. After passing Big Sky and historic ranches, the road enters Yellowstone's northwest corner, which has no entrance station. After exiting the park, the highway drops straight south into West Yellowstone.

To reach Yellowstone's North Entrance at Gardiner, use Paradise Valley (53 miles, one hour) from Livingston, east of Bozeman. From I-90, take Exit 333 to head south on U.S. Highway 89. The two-lane highway follows the Yellowstone River, with outstanding fishing, upstream through bucolic valley ranch lands tucked between the Gallatin and

---

Previous: hiking in Grand Teton; the Grand Loop Road in Yellowstone.

Absaroka Ranges. Watch out for pronghorn, bighorn sheep, and elk that frequently cross the road, especially in winter. About 20 miles south of Livingston, Chico Hot Springs (163 Chico Rd., Pray, MT, 406/333-49333, www.chicohotsprings.com, 8am-11pm daily year-round, $8 adults, $4 kids 3-6) has two outdoor hot pools for soaking, as well as showers, changing rooms, a restaurant, saloon, lodge rooms, and cabins.

After entering Gardiner, stay on the highway, which becomes the main road through town, curving right onto the bridge over the Yellowstone River. At the T intersection, turn right. Smaller vehicles can curve left around a 180-degree turn to drive through the narrow Roosevelt Arch, while RVs can take the shortcut to reach the North Entrance Station, less than a half mile from the arch.

FROM BILLINGS, MONTANA

The most scenic approach to Yellowstone is the **Beartooth Highway** (http://beartooth-highway.com, late May-mid-Oct., weather depending, 111 miles, three hours without stops) to the **Northeast Entrance.** At Laurel west of Billings, cut off I-90 at Exit 434 going south onto U.S. Highway 212. Drive 43 miles south to Red Lodge. If you are coming on I-90 from the west, leave the freeway in Columbus (Exit 408) to take Highway 78 instead to Red Lodge. Gas up in Red Lodge. Stay on U.S. Highway 212 through town, which becomes the 68-mile Beartooth Highway (All-American Highway). The climbing begins as the road gains elevation along Rock Creek. As the canyon opens up into a huge glacier-carved valley, the switchbacks begin. The highway climbs via switchbacks and curves to 10,977 feet at Beartooth Pass. Sightseeing stops and weather will add time. If snowstorms hit, which can be common in June or fall, the road may close until plowed. Driving in the morning will reduce the glare from the sun in your eyes as you cross the Beartooth Plateau. This route has multiple campgrounds en route, making it popular with RVers and tent campers.

I-15 to West and South Entrances

In Idaho, I-15 runs north-south along the west side of Yellowstone, Grand Teton, and Jackson Hole. This is the route to use when coming from Boise, Pocatello, Idaho Falls, and Salt Lake City. On I-15 in Idaho Falls is where the choices begin.

The Beartooth Highway is one of the most dramatic roads to Yellowstone.

FROM IDAHO FALLS, IDAHO

To head to **West Yellowstone**, the most direct route to Yellowstone National Park, take the **Targhee Pass Highway** (80 miles, 1.75 hours). From I-15, use Exit 119 onto U.S. Highway 20. Go through Rexburg to head north, climbing on the two-lane road into the **Island Park** caldera and then pass Henrys Lake, both with many places to camp. After Henrys Lake, the route tops the Continental Divide at Targhee Pass at 7,105 feet to cross into Montana. The highway ends in West Yellowstone where it becomes Firehole Avenue. Turn right onto Canyon Street and left onto Yellowstone Avenue to reach the West Entrance Station.

As an alternative from Ashton on U.S. Highway 20, fans of going remote on dirt roads can sneak in to Cave Falls, Bechler Trailhead, and the Bechler River Ranger Station in Yellowstone. Turn off U.S. Highway 20 onto the Mesa Falls Scenic Byway (Hwy. 47) for six miles, passing through Ashton and Marysville, then turn right onto Marysville Road, which becomes the dirt Cave Falls Road (Forest Rd. 5820). Follow that to its terminus at Cave Falls or its junction for the Bechler River.

To head to **Jackson Hole** and **Grand Teton National Park**, go via Teton Pass or Alpine-Hoback. The latter, often a preferred route for large RVs, avoids climbing the steep pass. They both start on the same route from Idaho Falls. From I-15, take Exit 115 to head east on U.S. Highway 26 through the Swan Valley. At Swan Valley, make your choice. The shorter **Teton Pass** (87 miles, 1.75 hours) connects Teton Valley with Jackson Hole, but on a steep 10-percent-grade climb and descent. Be sure to use lower gears for descending Teton Pass, and check road conditions before you go. From Swan Valley, turn north onto Highway 31 to cross over the Big Hole Mountains into Victor, where a right turn puts you on the Teton Pass Highway (Hwy. 33) over the Teton Mountains into Jackson Hole.

For **Alpine-Hoback** (109 miles, two hours), stay on U.S. Highway 26 through Swan Valley, passing Palisades Reservoir to reach Alpine Junction. Turn left onto U.S. Highway 26/89 through the Grand Canyon of the Snake River to Hoback Junction to continue north on U.S. Highway 26/89/189/191, paralleling the Snake River to reach Jackson.

VIA ASHTON-FLAGG RANCH ROAD

From Ashton on U.S. Highway 20, adventurous drivers with high-clearance vehicles can enter both parks via the **Ashton-Flagg Ranch Road** (a.k.a. Grassy Lake Road, 43 miles, 3-4 hours, snow-free June-Oct.), a narrow, rough cobble road through Caribou-Targhee National Forest in Wyoming with primitive campsites and solitude. Bumps, potholes, and washboards reduce speeds to 15-20 mph. It's not for large RVs or big trailers, but RVs can handle the road most of the time. Drivers must be comfortable meeting oncoming vehicles in narrow stretches and backing up. Before driving, get current conditions from the **Ashton-Island Park Ranger District** (46 S. Hwy. 20, Ashton, ID, 208/652-7442, www.fs.usda.gov/ctnf). From Ashton, turn right onto the Mesa Falls Scenic Byway (Hwy. 47) and turn right after seven blocks onto Highway 32. Drive one mile and turn left onto the Ashton-Flagg Ranch Road. After 12 miles of pavement, the fun begins. The route ends in John D. Rockefeller, Jr. Memorial Parkway at the intersection with U.S. Highway 89/191/287. Turn left to Yellowstone's South Entrance or right for Grand Teton National Park.

FROM SALT LAKE CITY, UTAH

From **Salt Lake City** (288 miles, five hours), the fastest route to drive heads north on I-15 to U.S. Highway 89. Exit at Brigham City to take U.S. Highway 89 north to connect with the Alpine-Hoback route at Alpine Junction to reach Jackson, Wyoming.

I-25 and I-90 to East Entrances

I-25 running north from Denver meets up with I-90 in north-central Wyoming. These

Island Park

On U.S. Highway 20 from Ashton, Idaho, drivers climb the southern rim to drop inside the Island Park caldera en route to West Yellowstone. Sandwiched between the Craters of the Moon lava flows and the Yellowstone supervolcano, Island Park erupted 2.1 million years ago and the resulting 58-mile by 40-mile caldera sits partly inside Yellowstone. The smaller Henry's Fork caldera formed inside the Island Park caldera 1.3 million years ago, sharing a western rim. The residual heat produces warm springs that make for a rich habitat for wildlife and aquatic animals in Caribou-Targhee National Forest (208/558-7301, www.fs.usda.gov/ctnf).

- Highlights include roaring Mesa Falls, a 300-foot-wide drop of 114 feet, and Big Springs, an idyllic natural pool that stays 52°F year-round and provides wildlife habitat.

- The historic Mesa Falls Visitor Center (9:30am-5:30pm daily summer, 9:30am-5:30pm Sat.-Sun. winter, $5/vehicle) has exhibits on history, geology, plants, and wildlife.

- Float the Warm River on a tube at Warm River Campground (nine miles north of Ashton on Warm River Road off the Mesa Falls Scenic Byway), or wet a line fly-fishing on the Henry's Fork in Harriman State Park (3489 Green Canyon Rd., Island Park, 208/558-7368, http://parksandrecreation.idaho.gov, year-round).

- Stay at one of 11 campgrounds (877/444-6777, www.recreation.gov, late May-Sept., $13-15 first vehicle, $7 second vehicle). Several campgrounds have hookups and accept reservations.

interstates connect to the east entrances for Yellowstone and Grand Teton National Parks. They are the routes to use coming from Cheyenne, Casper, and Sheridan in Wyoming plus I-90 in South Dakota. Drivers from Denver should use this route for Yellowstone, but not for the Moran Entrance to Grand Teton, as the I-80 route is more direct. To get to Yellowstone's East Entrance requires going through Cody. To get to Grand Teton's east entrance at Moran requires driving through Wind River Indian Reservation and over Togwotee Pass. Check on road conditions (call 511, www.wyoroad.info) for driving over the passes. Be cautious of relying on a GPS, as it can select a more direct route through curvy byways or dirt backroads.

FROM CODY, WYOMING

Cody is accessed from the junction of I-90 and I-25 at Buffalo (169 miles, three hours). Follow U.S. Highway 16 west through Ten Sleep to Worland, U.S. Highway 16/20 north to Basin and Greybull, and then U.S. Highway 14/16/20 west to Cody.

From Cody, the Buffalo Bill Scenic Byway (U.S. Hwy. 14/16/20, 56 miles, 1.25 hours) passes Buffalo Bill Reservoir and goes along the North Fork of the Shoshone River through Shoshone National Forest with campgrounds right off the highway. A few minutes after Pahaska Tepee Resort, the highway reaches the East Entrance to Yellowstone.

From Cody, Chief Joseph Scenic Byway (80 miles, 1.75 hours) accesses the Northeast Entrance of Yellowstone. Take Highway 120 north from Cody for 16 miles, turn left on Wyoming 296 for 46 miles, and turn left onto U.S. Highway 212 (closed mid-Oct.-late May) for 16 miles to reach Yellowstone's Northeast Entrance.

FROM CASPER, WYOMING

To go to Grand Teton's east entrance at Moran via Togwotee Pass (256 miles, five hours), head on I-25 to Casper. Take Exit 189 onto U.S. Highway 20/26 to Shoshoni. Turn left, staying on U.S. Highway 26 to Riverton, where the highway turns right toward Dubois. After U.S. Highway 20 joins U.S. Highway 287 from Lander, continue northwest through the Wind River Indian Reservation and Dubois to climb over the Continental Divide at 9,658-foot Togwotee Pass. The ultra-scenic route yields outstanding views of the Teton Mountains on the descent into Jackson Hole to Grand Teton's east entrance at Moran.

I-80 to Grand Teton

I-80 across the southern part of Wyoming provides the best access to get to the south entrances of Yellowstone and Grand Teton National Parks and Jackson Hole. From Denver (550 miles, 9-10 hours), routes go to the Moran Entrance of Grand Teton via Lander and Togwotee Pass or Jackson via Pinedale.

From Rawlins on I-80, Togwotee Pass (248 miles, five hours) leads to the Moran Entrance of Grand Teton, which connects to the Yellowstone's South Entrance. Take U.S. Highway 287/Highway 789 northwest to Lander. From Lander, continue northwest through the Wind River Indian Reservation and Dubois to climb over the Continental Divide at 9,658-foot Togwotee Pass. Prepare for big views of the Teton Mountains descending the west side of Togwotee Pass into Jackson Hole to reach Grand Teton's east entrance at Moran.

To go to Jackson, Jackson Hole, and the south entrances to Grand Teton (177 miles, 3.5 hours) drive I-80 to Rock Springs. From there, take U.S. Highway 191 north along the Wind River Mountains to Pinedale. After Pinedale, stay on U.S. Highway 191 until U.S. Highway 189 joins it and swings north. Follow U.S. Highway 189/191 northwest through Bridger-Teton National Forest and along the Hoback River through Hoback Canyon, with a few roadside campgrounds. At Hoback Junction, turn north on U.S. Highway 26/89/189/191 to reach Jackson, Jackson Hole, and the south entrances of Grand Teton National Park.

TRAVEL HUB: BOZEMAN, MONTANA

Bozeman, Montana, a year-round hub for Yellowstone, has grown far beyond its cow town roots. As a college town, home of Montana State University, it has a young vibrancy, and hiking, skiing, snowboarding, mountain biking, and fishing are imbued in the culture. With the Bridger Mountains to the north and Gallatin Range to the south, accessing mountain activities is quick. The town is known for the Museum of the Rockies (600 W. Kagy Blvd., 406/994-2251, www.museumoftherockies.com), home of one of the largest dinosaur collections in the world and Dr. Jack Horner, whose legendary

the Buffalo Bill Scenic Byway

paleontology work garnered him fame as a character in the *Jurassic Park* books and movies. The town also serves as a base for skiing and snowboarding at **Big Sky Resort** (800/548-4486, www.bigskyresort.com) and **Bridger Bowl** (800/223-9609, www.bridgerbowl.com) and cross-country skiing on groomed trails at **Bohart Ranch** (406/586-9070, www.bohartranchxcski.com). From Bozeman, year-round roads go to Yellowstone.

Air

Bozeman Yellowstone International Airport (BZN, 406/388-8321, 850 Gallatin Field Rd, Belgrade, MT, www.bozemanairport.com) is the closest for reaching Yellowstone's entrances at West Yellowstone and Gardiner. Winter travelers planning to base out of Mammoth, Gardiner, Big Sky, and West Yellowstone should fly into Bozeman, and most visitors heading to Old Faithful to overnight use this airport. Arrivals by midafternoon can drive into the park in the same day. Five airlines serve Bozeman: Alaska, Allegiant, Delta, Frontier, and United. The airport sees almost 30 flights per day from Newark, Atlanta, Chicago, Minneapolis, Denver, Salt Lake City, Houston, Las Vegas, Phoenix, Seattle, Portland, and Los Angeles.

(The airport gets its international designation from charter flights to Canada.) Some service is seasonal: Flights correlate with the winter ski season or summer high season in the parks.

Bus and Shuttles

Greyhound (800/231-2222, www.greyhound.com) has whistle stops at Bozeman/Belgrade and Livingston. **Trailways** (www.trailways.com) offers service to Bozeman, but not to Yellowstone. **Karst Stage** (406/556-3540 or 800/287-4759, www.karststage.com) operates shuttles or buses daily year-round to Big Sky and West Yellowstone and daily in winter and summer to Mammoth Hot Springs and Gardiner. The **Skyline Bus** (406/995-6287, www.skylinebus.com) to Big Sky runs multiple times daily summer and winter, but weekdays only in fall and spring. For skiers and snowboarders, free buses run weekends in winter to Bridger Bowl. **Bozeman Limo** (406/585-5466, http://bozemanlimo.com) also goes to Big Sky.

Tours

In summer, **Karst Stage** (406/556-3540 or 800/287-4759, www.karststage.com, daily May-Oct., $109/person) runs one-day

Bozeman is known for dinosaur exhibits in the Museum of the Rockies.

loop tours of Yellowstone. The company picks riders up at their hotels in Bozeman or Livingston. The tour goes through the Gallatin Canyon to West Yellowstone and then into the park to Old Faithful, West Thumb Geyser Basin, Lake Yellowstone, Grand Canyon of the Yellowstone, and Mammoth Hot Springs. The final link of the loop goes up Paradise Valley to return to Livingston and Bozeman. Rates do not include meals, park entrance fees, or driver tips. At least four people are needed for the tours to go.

For wildlife-watching or sightseeing in Yellowstone, the Bozeman-based **Yellowstone Safari Company** (406/586-1155, http://yellowstonesafari.com, year-round) guides full-day and multiday trips. They supply binoculars, spotting scopes, and lunch.

Car Rental

Several car rental companies have desks in the airport: **Alamo** (406/388-6694 or 800/227-7368, www.alamo.com), **Avis** (406/388-4091 or 800/352-7900, www.avis.com), **Budget** (406/388-4091 or 800/527-0700, www.budget.com), **Enterprise** (406/388-7420 or 800/261-7331, www.enterprise.com), **Dollar** (406/388-3484 or 800/800-5252, www.dollar.com), **Hertz** (406/388-6939 or 800/654-3131, www.hertz.com), **Thrifty** (406/388-3484 or 800/847-4389, www.thrifty.com), and **National** (406/388-6694 or 888/868-6204, www.nationalcar.com).

Bozeman also has several other rental car companies around town and in the area: **Journey Rentacar** (30 Homestake Dr., Bozeman, 406/551-2277, www.journeyrentacar.com), **Phasmid Rentals** (32 Dollar Dr., Belgrade, 406/922-0179, www.phasmidrentals.com), and **Toyota Rent-a-Car** (8472 Huffine Ln., Bozeman, 406/585-2010, www.resslermotors.com).

RV Rental

For those flying in, **Montana RV Rentals** (65 Woodbury Ave., Belgrade, 406/534-9349, www.sarpyrv.com) is closest to the airport.

Cruise America (80675-b Gallatin Rd., Bozeman, 800/671-8042, www.cruiseamerica.com) is located about 11 miles from the airport on U.S. Highway 191, which heads straight south to Big Sky and West Yellowstone. **C and T RV Rentals** (501 N. 3rd, Bozeman, 306/587-0351 or 800/481-8610, www.ctrvrentals.com) is located in downtown Bozeman, about 10 miles east of the airport.

Equipment Rental

For outdoor gear, **Phasmid Rentals** (32 Dollar Dr., Belgrade, 406/922-0179, www.phasmidrentals.com) rents camping gear, sleeping bags and pads, camp cook gear and furniture, coolers, tents, fly-fishing rods and reels, binoculars, bear spray, bear canisters, baby car seats and cribs, car racks, GPS, and maps. Most items cost $2-12 per day. With two locations, **Northern Lights Trading Company** (1716 W. Babcock or 83 Rowland Rd., Bozeman, 406/585-2090 or 406/586-6029, http://northernlightstrading.com) rents backpacks, tents, sleeping bags, bear canisters, skis for alpine touring or cross-country, snowshoes, mountain climbing gear, kayaks, canoes, paddleboards, rafts, and drift boats. Most gear costs $2-25 per day; boats cost $40-250 per day.

Accommodations

Bozeman has loads of chain hotels. Some in town grouse about the lack of upscale hotels, but no one has built one yet. Lodging is open year-round, with the highest rates in summer and around the college home football games. Winter sees the lowest rates.

Opened in 2015, **The Lark Bozeman** (122 W. Main St., 866/464-1000, www.larkbozeman.com, $120-250) has modern rooms crafted of leather, metal, and wood and spiffed up with individual pieces from local artists. **Gallatin River Lodge** (9105 Thorpe Rd., 406/338-0148 or 888/387-0148, www.bozemanbedandbreakfast.com, $170-500) is an upscale lodge with nightly B&B lodging or all-inclusive packages on a ranch 12 miles outside town with guided fly-fishing on the

Gallatin River. Run by two ex-park rangers in Yellowstone, **Bozeman Lehrkind Mansion** (719 N. Wallace Ave., 406/585-6932, www.bozemanbedandbreakfast.com, $150-250) has nine rooms, three in the mansion and six in the garden house, all decked out with antiques. The bed-and-breakfast is in a colorful 1897 Queen Anne-style Victorian mansion listed on the National Register of Historic Places.

In downtown Bozeman, the **Treasure State Hostel** (27 E. Main St., 406/624-6244, www.treasurestatehostel.com, $28-38) opened in late 2015. It has small dorm rooms with 3-5 twin/bunk combos and private rooms with double beds. Rates include sheets, blanket, towel, Wi-Fi and breakfast. Parking costs $5 per day.

Food

Bozeman's classic restaurants are downtown. In an old railroad freight house, **Montana Ale Works** (611 E. Main St., 406/587-7700, www.montanaaleworks.com, 4pm-11pm daily, $11-23) carries 40 beers on tap, many of them regional craft brews, and house cocktails and wine to accompany locally sourced beef and bison burgers, steaks, sandwiches, small plates, and salads. You can even get a gluten-free beer and meal. **Starky's Authentic Americana** (24 N. Tracy Ave., 406/556-1111, http://starkysonline.com, 11am-9pm daily, $10-22) serves burgers, sandwiches, soups, big salads, comfort foods like mac and cheese, and classic dinner meat and pasta entrées that change daily. Many of their dishes can be dairy- or gluten-free, and the Starky interpretation of Americana includes Mexican, Italian, and Asian flavors. Founded by media mogul Ted Turner, who has a bison ranch in the area, **Ted's Montana Grill** (105 W. Main St., Ste. B, 406/587-6000, www.tedsmontanagrill.com, 11am-10pm daily, $11-33) specializes in bison: burgers, meatloaf, pot roast, and steaks. The menu has 18 burgers that can either be beef or bison. For casual upscale dining, the **Emerson Grill** (207 W. Olive St., 406/586-5247, 5pm-10pm Mon.-Sat., $13-37)

goes Italian: antipasto, insalata, pizza, pasta, and entrées of meats or eggplant Parmesan.

TRAVEL HUB: BILLINGS, MONTANA

As Montana's largest and fastest-growing city, Billings serves as a gateway hub to the parks. Connecting with Yellowstone requires driving over the **Beartooth Highway** (3-4 hours minimum, mid-May-mid-Oct.). Billings is only a viable travel hub for the parks while the highway is open.

If you have a few hours to kill, take in the **Yellowstone Art Museum** (401 N. 27th St., 406/256-6804, www.artmuseum.org), where you can see traveling exhibits and some of their permanent collection of modern art from the Northern Rockies and Plains.

Air

While the **Billings Logan International Airport** (BIL, 1901 Terminal Circle, Billings, MT, 406/657-8495, www.flybillings.com) is open year-round, the route from Billings over the Beartooth Highway to Yellowstone's Northeast Entrance is only open late May-mid-October. For summer travelers, it's an outstanding option due to the utterly scenic drive. The airport is serviced by Alaska, Allegiant, Delta, Cape Air, and United with more than 30 flights per day from Minneapolis, Salt Lake City, Denver, Las Vegas, Phoenix, Seattle, Portland, and several towns in eastern Montana. If you fly into Billings in the morning, you can make it to Yellowstone by dark, but otherwise, spend the night in Billings or Red Lodge to be able to drive the Beartooth Highway in daylight without rushing.

Bus and Shuttles

Trailways (www.trailways.com) services Billings from the Midwest, but buses and shuttles do not run from Billings to Yellowstone. Bus travelers are better off going to Bozeman to get connections into the park. **Greyhound** (800/231-2222, www.greyhound.com) has a depot stop at Billings.

Car Rental

Eight car rental companies have desks in the airport: **Alamo** (406/252-7626 or 877/222-9075, www.alamo.com), **Avis** (406/252-8007 or 800/331-1212, www.avis.com), **Budget** (406/259-4168 or 800/527-0700, www.budget.com), **Enterprise** (406/294-2930 or 800/736-8222, www.enterprise.com), **Dollar** (406/248-9993 or 800/800-4000, www.dollar.com), **Hertz** (406/248-9151 or 800/654-3131, www.hertz.com), **Thrifty** (406/248-9993 or 800/847-4389, www.thrifty.com), and **National** (406/252-7626 or 800/227-7368, www.nationalcar.com).

RV Rental

Montana Happy Campers (2110 1st Ave. N., 406/245-9008, www.montanahappycampers.com) and **Sarpy RV** (831 Cerise Rd., 406/534-9349, www.sarpyrv.com) are located 3-6 miles from the airport. **Pierce RV Supercenter** (3800 Pierce Pkwy., 406/655-8000, www.pierceRV.com) and **Cruise America RV** (720 Central Ave., 406/245-9800, www.cruiseamerica.com) are nine miles west of the airport, but right on I-90 in the direction you need to go to get to Yellowstone.

Equipment Rental

Sunshine Sports (304 Moore Ln, 406/252-3724 or 800/773-3723, www.sunshine-sports.com) rents inflatable rafts, canoes, touring and river kayaks, paddleboards, and all the accessories to go with them. Rentals for camping gear are not available.

Accommodations and Food

Billings is a hub of chain motels and small conference center hotels. Contact the **Billings Chamber of Commerce** (www.visitbillings.com) for options. The historic **Northern Hotel** (19 N. Broadway, 406/867-6767 or 855/782-9589, www.northernhotel.com, $90-270) has renovated upscale rooms and suites with 24-hour room service, a diner, and a fine-dining restaurant. **Ledgestone Hotel** (4863 King Ave. E., 406/259-9454, http://ledgestonehotel.com, $85-120) is one of the newer hotels in town with hotel rooms, suites, and kitchenettes. For families, the **Big Horn Resort** (1801 Majestic Ln., 406/839-9300, http://thebighornresort.com, $115-250) has a hot breakfast buffet included and an indoor water park.

Brewpubs have been sprouting up in Billings to show off craft beers. Go to **Montana Brewing Company** (113 N. Broadway, 406/252-9200, www.montanabrewingcompany.com, 11am-2am Mon.-Sat., noon-10pm Sun., $8-10) for wood-fired flatbread pizzas and local beer, or **Uberbrew** (2305 Montana Ave., 406/534-6960, http://uberbrewmt.com, 11am-9pm daily, $7-11) for burgers, sandwiches, and brats or healthy salads.

TRAVEL HUB: IDAHO FALLS, IDAHO

Idaho Falls, the largest city in eastern Idaho, sits on a high desert plateau about two hours from Grand Teton National Park and Jackson Hole. Most visitors using this hub head straight to their destination, but if you have time to spare in downtown Idaho Falls, take a walk along the **Snake River Greenbelt** (www.idahofallsidaho.gov) to explore where the Snake River goes after Grand Teton. Walking paths along both sides of the river go past a 600-foot-wide waterfall and historic downtown buildings to make a six-mile loop.

Air

The **Idaho Falls Regional Airport** (IDA, 2140 N. Skyline Dr., Idaho Falls, 208/612-8224, www.idahofallsidaho.gov) has flights via SkyWest/Delta from Salt Lake City and Minneapolis-St. Paul, United Express from Denver, and Allegiant Air from Las Vegas, Phoenix, Los Angeles, and Oakland. Some flights are daily, while others are weekly or summer only. The airport is still a two-plus-hour drive to Jackson Hole and Grand Teton National Park, but you can reach the park in the same day you fly in, unless winter snowstorms impede driving. Some people prefer flying into Idaho Falls as the flights are often cheaper than to Jackson Hole.

Bus and Shuttles

Greyhound (800/231-2222, www.greyhound.com) buses service Idaho Falls. The **Salt Lake Express** (800/356-9796 or 208/656-8824, www.saltlakeexpress.com) bus service runs between the Idaho Falls Airport and Jackson, Wyoming, twice a day for about $52 one-way.

Car and RV Rental

Four rental car companies are located in the airport terminal: **Avis** (208/522-4225 or 888/897-8848, www.avis.com), **Budget** (208/522/8800 or 800/527-0700, www.budget.com), **Hertz** (208/529-3101 or 800/654-3131, www.hertz.com), and **National** (208/522/5276 or 800/227-7368, www.nationalcar.com). Elsewhere in town are **Thrifty Rent-A-Car** (208/227-0444 or 877/283-0898, www.thrifty.com) and **Enterprise** (208/523-8111 or 855/266-9289, www.enterprise.com).

Two RV rental companies operate in Idaho Falls: **Smith RV** (1523 N. 25th E., 208/535-2500, www.smithrvidaho.com) and **American Carriage Rentals** (208/529-5535, www.rv-rentals-yellowstone.com).

Equipment Rental

Idaho Mountain Trading (474 Shoup Ave., 208/523-6679, www.idahomountaintrading.com) rents tents, sleeping bags, packs, bikes, kayaks, downhill skis, cross-country skis, snowboards, and snowshoes. Rates run $2-30 per item.

Accommodations and Food

Due to its placement on the interstate, Idaho Falls is the land of chain hotels, budget to mid-range. The **Residence Inn** (65 W. Broadway, 208/542-0000, www.marriott.com) sits at the falls, and **Hilton Garden Inn** (700 Lindsay Blvd., 208/522-9500, http://hiltongardeninn3.hilton.com) is right on the river. Find other options through the **Idaho Falls Chamber of Commerce** (http://visitidahofalls.com). For uniqueness, the **Destinations Inn** (295 Broadway St., 208/528-8222, www.destinationsinn.com, $150-240) bed-and-breakfast has 14 upscale rooms, each themed from a different location around the world. Think Thailand, Morocco, Paris, Athens, and Alaska, for starters, tucked into a 1905 building.

Despite the town's location in Idaho's high desert, you can find ethnic dining. **Tandoori Oven** (3204 S. 25th E., 208/522-8263, www.tandoorovenif.com, 11am-2:30pm and 4:30pm-9:30pm Mon.-Sat., $9-25) can continue the travel theme with Indian specialties cooked in a tandoor, vegetarian dishes, and traditional Indian breads. You can choose your own spiciness. For American fare, the **SnakeBite Restaurant** (401 Park Ave., 208/525-2522, www.snake-bite-restaurant.com, 11am-3pm Mon., 11am-3pm and 5pm-9pm Tues.-Sat., $10-29, cash or check only) serves a large menu of stacked burgers (go for the Teton burger), steaks, fish, pasta, and salads. Eighteen beers are on tap, including local and regional brews.

Getting Around

DRIVING

Yellowstone and Grand Teton National Parks have two-lane roads that are easy to drive. However, several factors escalate concerns. Wildlife uses the roads: Bison back up traffic as they walk down the yellow line, and traffic jams clog the road when bears feed nearby. Deer, elk, and coyotes run out in front of cars, and they are especially difficult to see around dawn or dusk. For RV drivers, sections of curvy road demand more attention, especially climbing Dunraven Pass. Sections of road can be narrow with minimal shoulders. Due to wildlife, car jams, traffic, weather, and maximum speed limits of 35-45 mph, national park miles take longer to cover than the same miles at home. Watch for wildlife at all times: Both

Driving Tips

Driving in Yellowstone and Grand Teton demands fortitude, especially around the congested geyser basins. Crowds of vehicles in summer, wildlife, and seasonal road construction put drivers in a precarious position. Adapt by settling into a slower mode. For trip planning and updates, consult the parks for road construction, seasonal closures, and other road issues (307/344-2117, www.nps.gov/yell).

- **Mileage, signage, and GPS:** The national parks do not have mileage markers. Use the park map received at the entrance for figuring out your location. Road junctions have directional signage with mileages. GPS will work except in deep canyons, but it will not show seasonal road closures.

- **Wildlife on the road:** Fences? Not here. Bison, elk, bears, deer, bighorn sheep, wolves, and moose cross roads anywhere. Wildlife crossings are not marked. Sometimes bison and bears walk straight down the yellow line in the middle of the road. Give them room (25 yards for most wildlife, but 100 yards for wolves and bears), drive slowly, and avoid honking at them. Just enjoy the show. You may be able to inch by them if they seem calm. Bison may look docile, but one kick can dent your vehicle.

- **Wildlife jams:** Wildlife jams are one of the biggest clogs on the park roads. Bear jams, wolf jams, elk jams, moose jams, and bison jams. When most of us see wildlife, we want to stop to watch as it's such a rare treat to see animals cruising the wilds. Jams occur all over the park, in any season, but are particularly bad during July and August when so many vehicles clog the roads. Whenever possible, use pullouts for wildlife viewing and sightseeing.

- **Speeds:** The speed limit on most park roads is 35-45 mph in Yellowstone and 35-55 mph in Grand Teton. Traffic congestion, wildlife, or road construction often makes driving slower. Plan for longer than usual driving time to cover even short distances.

- **Road construction:** Perennial road construction happens every summer. Long winters force road repairs and reconstruction to take place in the same season as high visitation. Look online before your trip to see where construction is planned and how it may affect your travel.

- **Road closures:** Although roads may close temporarily in summer for various reasons, the National Park Service aims to keep all roads open May-early November. Some roads can open mid-April. Winter road closure for wheeled vehicles is November-mid-April.

- **Weather:** Due to high elevation, snow can show up every month of the year, even in summer. Sudden snowstorms, whiteouts, or fog can reduce visibility and slicken road surfaces. Adjust your speed accordingly.

Yellowstone and Grand Teton see more than 100 animal deaths each year due to vehicles.

Junctions in Yellowstone can clog with cars. With each upcoming lane dividing into two lanes, each four-way junction has 11-12 lanes with stop signs, not lights, controlling the flow. First-time visitors can find the crowded junctions intimidating, and lines of RVs and cars can cover up the directional markers painted on the lanes. To turn right, get into the right lanes. To go straight or turn left, stay in the middle or left lane. When you reach the front of the line, use the rule, yield to the right.

GPS and Mobile Apps

Visitors can get around the parks with the use of GPS and map apps on phones. Be aware that you will have dead zones for phones, and the programs don't account for seasonal road closures. You'll still need to find out about these the old-fashioned way by inquiring at visitors centers or looking on the park websites (www.nps.gov/yell or www.nps.gov/grte).

Maps and Planners

While you can get USGS topographical maps of Yellowstone and Grand Teton National Parks, the **National Geographic Trails Illustrated** maps of both parks are more suited to most park visitors. They are a cross between a topographical map and a more detailed version of the National Park Service maps. You can buy them in park bookstores, or order them ahead for trip planning through **Yellowstone Association** (406/848-2400, www.yellowstoneassociation.org) or **Grand Teton Association** (307/739-3403, www.grandtetonpark.org). Both parks also have trip planners available online (www.nps.gov/yell or www.nps.gov/grte).

SHUTTLES
Bus

Yellowstone does not have a shuttle bus system inside the park, but Grand Teton has **AllTrans, Inc.** (307/733-3135 or 800/443-6133, www.jacksonholealltrans.com, $14/day) that runs between Jackson and Flagg Ranch with stops in between. It operates multiple times daily in summer with stops at Jenny Lake, Signal Mountain, Jackson Lake Lodge, and Colter Bay. In winter, the daily shuttle goes between Jackson, Teton Village, and Flagg Ranch. Rates cover unlimited use in one day. Park entrance fees are extra.

Boat

In Yellowstone, the only boat shuttle in summer is by reservation for hauling backcountry campers and kayakers from Bridge Bay to **Yellowstone Lake's southern arms** (Xanterra, 307/242-3893). In Grand Teton, a summer boat shuttle runs every 15 minutes all day long to convey hikers across **Jenny Lake** (Jenny Lake Boating, 307/734-9227, www.jennylakeboating.com).

TOURS
Bus

Sightseeing tours operated by multiple companies go out daily in summer in both parks. In Yellowstone, they depart from park lodges

and West Yellowstone. In Grand Teton, they depart mostly from Jackson, but some will pick up riders at lodges. Some tours are sightseeing, making loops to take in the scenery, lodges, thermal hot spots, and natural wonders. Because both parks have substantial wildlife-watching opportunities, many companies guide wildlife-watching tours, some year-round. Find lists online (www.nps.gov/yell or www.nps.gov/grte) of all companies licensed to operate in the parks.

Boat

Daily summer boat tours operate on Yellowstone Lake in Yellowstone and Jackson Lake and Jenny Lake in Grand Teton. **Xanterra** (307/344-7311 or 866/439-7375, www.yellowstonenationalparklodges.com) runs the Yellowstone Lake tours. On Jackson Lake, **boat tours** (307/543-2811, www.gtlc.com) go out from Colter Bay. **Jenny Lake** (307/734-9227, www.jennylakeboating.com) also has boat tours.

Snowcoach and Snowmobile

In winter, the only way to tour the interior of Yellowstone is by snowcoach or snowmobile, mid-December-early March. Launch points for day tours are from Flagg Ranch, West Yellowstone, and Mammoth Hot Springs. Multiple companies operate tours, and lists of licensed operators are online (www.nps.gov/yell). Grand Teton does not permit snowcoach tours or snowmobiling.

RVS

Traveling Yellowstone and Grand Teton by RV is a fun way to go. Most roads are easy to drive, although they are narrow and sometimes shoulder-less. In Yellowstone, Grand Loop Road in one section requires caution for RV drivers: For 19 miles, the road between Tower Fall and Dunraven Pass is steep, curvy, narrow, and along cliffs.

Restrictions

Unfortunately, RVs are not permitted everywhere. In Yellowstone, RVs, buses, and

In winter, buses convert to tracks or oversized tires for touring on snow.

trailers are not permitted in some parking lots (Midway and Lower Geyser Basins) due to sharp, tight turnarounds or short-length parking stalls. They also are not allowed on Upper Terrace, Blacktail Plateau, Virginia Cascade, and Firehole Lake Drives. In Grand Teton, the Moose-Wilson Road is closed to RVs including trailers due to the narrow, curvy road. Trailers are also not permitted on Signal Mountain Road.

Campgrounds

Most of the campgrounds inside Yellowstone and Grand Teton do not have hookups. However, a few do. In Yellowstone, Fishing Bridge Campground has hookups. In John D. Rockefeller, Jr. Memorial Parkway at Flagg Ranch, Headwaters Campground has hookups. In Grand Teton, hookups are at Colter Bay Campground and Signal Mountain. Outside of the parks, you'll find private campgrounds with hookups in Gardiner, West Yellowstone, Moran, and Jackson.

Many of the campgrounds have campsites that are limited in the RV lengths they can fit. Check on these when making reservations. More options are available for 30-foot RVs rather than 40-foot RVs.

Rentals and Repairs

Two mobile RV repair services can come fix your rig, although it may be costly to cover the distance to where you are. **Mobile RV Tech** (406/682-4100) and **RV Fixit Pro** (801/831-8111) are based in West Yellowstone, Montana. **Mobile RV Repair** (307/699-1225) is based in Jackson, Wyoming. RV rentals are available in Billings and Bozeman in Montana, and Idaho Falls.

BICYCLES

Road cyclists in Wyoming's national parks must contend with huge RVs at their elbows and drivers gawking at scenery or wildlife instead of the road. For that reason, bikers should wear helmets, bright colors, and lights at dawn or dusk. Roads in Grand Teton tend to have paved shoulders, which make cycling easier. But Yellowstone's narrower roads lack shoulders in many stretches. Throw in blind curves, high snowbanks in spring, and heavy traffic in summer, and visibility of cyclists diminishes. Wildlife poses its own dilemmas with two-ton bison standing in the road. Maintain your distance, or use cars as shields when confronting them.

Most cyclists ride early in the day before traffic clogs roads. Afternoons often bring hefty winds or thunderstorms, another reason to ride early in the day. Most campgrounds in both parks reserve a few designated campsites for hikers and cyclists to share. Per person

Paved bike trails parallel roads between Jenny Lake and Jackson.

paved bike trail parallels roads between Jenny Lake, Moose, Antelope Flats, and Jackson. In spring, after plowing is completed in both parks, some roads become prime cycling trails sans vehicles until they officially open for the season. Plowing and opening dates vary in different locations. Top roads to ride in early spring are the Teton Park Road (Inside Road) and Yellowstone roads between West Yellowstone and Mammoth.

MOTORCYCLES

Motorcyclists enjoy the scenery of the Wyoming national parks. But riding in the parks is not like riding at home. You can round a blind corner into a bison or grizzly bear. Animals can speed across the road in front of you, and traffic clogs the road midday. Riding shortly after sunup and in the evening will be less harried, but you also may encounter more animals. Since weather can mutate fast from a warm sunny day into a snowstorm, be prepared with the appropriate riding gear to handle these wild swings. Higher elevations can have icy roads in spring and fall, and unseasonable snowstorms can hit in August. Wyoming law requires helmets, but Montana and Idaho do not for anyone older than 18. Motorcycle rentals are available in Jackson Hole in Wyoming, Bozeman and Billings in Montana, and Idaho Falls.

rates run $5-10. Bear boxes are available for storing food.

Bike Trails

In Yellowstone, several old roadbeds provide biking trails: Old Gardiner Freight Road, Fountain Flat Drive, Lone Star Geyser Road, and Natural Bridge Road. In Grand Teton, a

Recreation

CAMPING

Camping in the national parks requires a bit of savvy. In summer, you cannot waltz in around sunset to claim a campsite. Campsites are filled up long before that.

In Yellowstone, you can make **reservations** (Xanterra, 307/344-7311 or 866/439-7375, www.yellowstonenationalpark-lodges.com) for five campgrounds one year in advance. These are Fishing Bridge, Bridge Bay, Madison, Canyon, and Grant Village. Fishing

Bridge, which allows only hard-sided rigs (no tent trailers), is the only one with hookups for RVs. Seven campgrounds in Yellowstone are first-come, first-served: Mammoth, Slough Creek, Pebble Creek, Indian Creek, Tower, Norris, and Lewis Lake.

In Grand Teton, six campgrounds (Headwaters/Flagg Ranch, Lizard Creek, Colter Bay, Signal Mountain, Jenny Lake, and Gros Ventre) have first-come, first-served campsites. Full-hookup RV campsites, which should be reserved one year in advance, are at Colter Bay (800/628-9988, www.gtlc.com) and Headwaters at Flagg Ranch (307/543-2861 or 800/443-2311, www.gtlc.com). You can also reserve tent sites at Headwaters. Jenny Lake is for tents only.

HIKING

Miles of hiking trails tour the Greater Yellowstone Ecosystem. Yellowstone National Park has 900 miles (1,449 kilometers) of trails; Grand Teton National Park has 200 miles (320 kilometers) of trails. Surrounding the

Reservation Tips

Yellowstone is the fourth most visited national park in the country, and Grand Teton is the eighth. The onslaught of summer campers means that campgrounds fill up fast. Don't have reservations for camping? Here are a few tips to snagging a campsite in summer.

- Make a base camp and stay put rather than shuffling campgrounds every day or so. You'll spend a little more time driving to some destinations, but you'll experience the park more with the time you save from searching campground after campground only to be confronted with full signs.

- On any day you plan to move camp, change locations in early morning to get a campsite before campgrounds fill up. Make getting your next campsite the first priority rather than sightseeing.

- At campgrounds that allow self-selection of campsites, plan to begin prowling to nab a site when someone departs an hour or more before the fill times mentioned below.

YELLOWSTONE

- For a central location, claim a spot before 9am at **Norris Campground.** For **Slough Creek** or **Pebble Creek,** claim a campsite before 9am. For **Indian Creek, Mammoth,** or **Lewis Lake,** claim your campsite by 10am or earlier. These campgrounds have self-selection of campsites. Check online (www.nps.gov/yell) for campground fill times and daily availability.

- Unfortunately, most of the centrally located campgrounds in Yellowstone book full months in advance. Do not bother trying to get in line for a potential opening at the reserved campgrounds at Madison, Canyon, Fishing Bridge, Bridge Bay, and Grant Village. Instead, call to check for **last-minute cancellations** (Xanterra, 307/344-7311 or 866/439-7375, www.yellowstonenationalparklodges.com). They do not take names on a waiting list, so it's sheer luck that scores a campsite.

- Camp outside the park in **West Yellowstone,** Shoshone National Forest west of **Cody,** or in Custer-Gallatin National Forest near **Big Sky, Gardiner,** or **Cooke City** the night before entering the park. Then head in early to claim a campsite before going adventuring for the day.

GRAND TETON

- **Jenny Lake** (tents only) campground fills by 9am.

- **Colter Bay Campground** rarely fills up, but it can in July-August. If you arrive after the check-in station closes for the night, a sign usually lists open campsites and directions.

- At **Signal Mountain, Colter Bay,** and **Headwaters,** campsites are assigned at the entrance office rather than self-selection.

- Camp outside the park in **Shoshone National Forest** around Togwotee Pass, in **Bridger-Teton National Forest** on the west side of Teton Pass, or along U.S. Highway 26/89/191 or Highway 189 the night before entering the park. Then head in early to claim a campsite.

national parks are national forest trails, some of which connect with park trails. The 3,300-mile Continental Divide Trail goes northward through Bridger-Teton National Forest and Yellowstone.

Yellowstone has two types of trails: traditional dirt trails and boardwalk trails. The short boardwalk trails are designed for protecting visitors and sensitive features in high-traffic geothermal areas. In geothermal areas without boardwalks, stick to the trail to avoid scalding by boiling water. Grand Teton trails are traditional dirt trails, with the exception of the paved Multi-Use Pathway. In both parks, bridges do not span all streams. You may need to ford creeks. In June, melting snow can raise water levels, making hiking poles helpful for stream crossings. Streams tend to be at their highest levels in the afternoon and lowest levels in the morning. Consult visitors centers on trail conditions before you go.

Hiking trails ban mountain bikes or motorized trail bikes in the parks, but many are open to horse travel. If you meet up with horses while hiking, step off the trail on the downhill side, if possible, to let them pass. Trail etiquette dictates that uphill hikers have the right of way; downhill hikers should step aside to let them pass, unless the uphill hikers opt to take a breather to rest. When planning hikes, consider the higher altitude. You may hike less far or more slowly than at lower elevations. Many trailhead parking lots pack out midsummer; plan for early starts to claim a parking space.

In winter, when snow buries trails, hikers travel by snowshoes or cross-country skis. Most trails are not marked with tree tags or other route-finding devices; navigation skills are required. Some trails also cross avalanche zones: Take beacons, probes, and shovels. Know how to use them and assess snow stability. Be aware of travel etiquette: On roads where snowcoaches and snowmobiles travel, skiers and snowshoers should travel on the right side to allow vehicles to pass. With skier-set tracks, snowshoers should blaze their own trails.

Hiking with kids can either be a nightmare or a hoot. To make it more fun, take water and snacks along to prevent hunger and thirst from zapping their energy. Take extra layers to keep kids warm if the weather turns. Help them connect with the environment while hiking by asking them about what they see and why things are the way they are. If you make hiking a fun experience for them, they'll want to do it again.

Boardwalks protect the fragile ecosystems from trampling.

Hiking Essentials

Hiking, especially in the Teton Mountains, demands preparedness. Unpredictable, fast-changing weather can mutate a warm summer day into wintry conditions in hours. Different elevations vary in temperature, wind, and visibility: Sun on the shore of Jenny Lake may hide knock-over winds barreling over Paintbrush Divide 5,000 feet higher. To be prepared in the backcountry, take the following:

- **Extra clothing:** Rain pants and jackets can double as wind protection, while gloves and a lightweight warm hat will save fingers and ears. Carry at least one extra water-wicking layer for warmth. Avoid cotton fabrics, which stay soggy and fail to retain body heat.

- **Extra food and water:** Depending on the hike's length, take a lunch and snacks, like compact high-energy food bars. Low-odor foods will not attract animals. Always carry extra water: Heat, wind, and elevation lead quickly to dehydration, and most visitors find they drink more than they do at home. Avoid drinking directly from streams or lakes. Due to the possibility of illness-inducing bacteria, filter or treat water sources before drinking.

- **Map and compass or GPS:** Although national park trails are well signed, take a map for ascertaining distance traveled and location. A compass or GPS will also help, but only if you know how to use it. In the deep, heavily forested canyons of the Tetons, a GPS may not pick up satellites.

- **Flashlight:** Carry a small flashlight or headlamp for after-dark emergencies. Take extra batteries, too.

- **First-aid kit:** Two bandages aren't enough. Carry a fully equipped standard first-aid kit with blister remedies. Many outdoor stores sell suitably prepared kits for hiking. Don't forget to add personal items like bee-sting kits and allergy medications.

- **Sun protection:** Altitude, snow, ice, and lakes all increase ultraviolet radiation. Protect yourself with SPF 30 sunscreen, sunglasses, and a sun hat or baseball cap.

- **Emergency toilet supplies:** Not every hike conveniently places a pit toilet at its destination. To accommodate an alfresco toilet stop, carry a small trowel, plastic baggies, and toilet paper, and move at least 200 feet away from water sources. For urinating, aim for a durable surface, such as rocks, logs, gravel, or snow. "Watering" fragile plants, campsites, or trails attracts animals that dig up the area. Bury feces 6-8 inches deep in soil. Do not bury toilet paper; use a baggie to pack it out.

- **Feminine hygiene:** Carry heavy-duty zippered baggies to pack out tampons, pads, and toilet paper.

- **Insect repellent:** Summer can be abuzz at any elevation with mosquitoes and blackflies. Insect repellents that contain 50 percent DEET work best. Purchase applications that rub or spray at close range rather than aerosols that go airborne onto other people, plants, and animals.

- **Pepper spray:** If you want to carry pepper spray, purchase an eight-ounce can, as nothing smaller will be effective; however, do not bother unless you know how to use it and what influences its effectiveness. Do not use it like bug repellent.

- **Miscellaneous:** A knife may come in handy, as can a few feet of nylon cord and a bit of duct tape (wrap a few feet around something small like a flashlight handle or water bottle). Many hikers have repaired boots and packs with duct tape and a little ingenuity.

Trail Signs

All in-park trailheads and junctions have good signage. Some signs are just directional pointers with destination names. Others have multiple destinations with distances. Distances, when included, are listed in miles. Some signs add distances in kilometers, too. Geyser basin trailheads have large maps of thermal features and boardwalks posted, and Upper Geyser Basin adds "you are here" signs at every junction. Trail closures for seasonal bear management are permanently signed with the closure dates.

Bear Closures

With a high density of grizzly and black bears in the Greater Yellowstone Ecosystem, Yellowstone National Park has implemented Bear Management Areas to prevent human-bear conflicts. During certain seasons of high bear use in these areas, the park service closes trails or does not permit off-trail hiking. Backcountry campsites close, too. Some trails require hiking with four or more people or during daylight hours only. These restrictions affect day hiker trails, paddle destinations on Yellowstone Lake, and backpacker routes.

Most of the Bear Management Areas are located around Yellowstone Lake, Hayden Valley, Pelican Valley, Tower-Roosevelt, the Firehole River geyser basin areas, and northwest Yellowstone. All restrictions are seasonal, but the seasons vary depending on the region. Lists of Bear Management Areas, seasonal dates of impacts, and a map of the regions are in the *Backcountry Trip Planner* (www.nps.gov/yell) or in visitors centers or permit centers. Grand Teton National Park and Jackson Hole also have annual seasonal closures (www.nps.gov/grte), such as Hermitage Point and Willow Flats in early summer.

BEAR BELLS AND PEPPER SPRAY

On trails, you'll hear sporadic jingle bells, sold in gift shops as bear bells. Locals call them "dinner bells," and many hikers hate them. While making noise best prevents surprising a bear, bells fail to carry sound the way a human voice does. To check their minimal effectiveness, see how close you get to hikers before you hear the ringing. Bear bells are best as a souvenir, not as a substitute for human noise on the trail in the form of talking, singing, hooting, and hollering. You may feel silly at first, but everyone does it.

Most hikers carry pepper spray with a capsicum derivative to deter bear attacks. Unlike insect repellents, do not use bear sprays on your body, in tents, or on gear; spray it directly into a bear's face, aiming for the eyes and nose. Wind and rain may reduce its effectiveness. Small purse-size pepper sprays are too small to deter bears; buy or rent an eight-ounce can. Practice how to use it, but still make noise on the trail.

Weather Concerns

Weather in Yellowstone and Grand Teton is unpredictable. Warm summer days can disintegrate into rainy squalls or snowstorms. Afternoons see hefty wind gusts, bringing with them thundershowers and lightning. If lightning approaches, descend from peak tops, high ridges, and open meadows into forest for more protection. Hikers should plan on early starts in order to descend in elevation by the time afternoon storms hit. Pack layers and always take rain gear, even when the weather looks like a blue-sky day.

Guides

Yellowstone licenses companies to guide hikes and backpacking trips; Grand Teton permits no guided hiking. Lists of approved concessionaires for Yellowstone are available online (www.nps.gov/yell). National Park Service naturalists guide free day hikes in both parks. Consult the park newspapers for schedules and locations.

BACKPACKING

Yellowstone and Grand Teton National Parks have backcountry campsites that offer solitude, scenery, and unique experiences. Backcountry trip planners detail campsite

Winter Safety Tips

Visiting the parks in winter is a whole different game than in summer. Frigid temperatures, strong winds, snow, blizzards, ice, and avalanches conspire to change a walk in the park into a life-threatening adventure.

- Be in shape: Know your skills, abilities, and limitations.

- Ski and snowshoe with other people.

- Prepare for changing weather conditions. Storms can move in fast, plummeting temperatures and bringing blizzards.

- Always leave a trip plan with a responsible person and check in upon your return.

- Plan to handle emergencies. Cell phones may not have service, and batteries can go dead in the cold.

- Watch for signs of hypothermia: slurred speech, stumbling, and uncontrolled shivering. Hypothermia can cause fatalities. Treat hypothermic victims by getting them out of the elements, adding clothing, administering warm liquids, and seeking help if incapacitated.

- Pack winter travel gear: first-aid kit with blister kit; headlamp; high-energy snacks, bars, and drink additives; map and compass or GPS; ski or snowshoe and pole repair kit; sunglasses and sunscreen. Bring water in an insulated bottle (water hoses often freeze).

- Always carry extra clothing: wind protection, waterproof, and extra hat and gloves.

- Packets of hand warmers can aid in preventing and treating hypothermia.

- Only venture into potential avalanche terrain if you have the appropriate skills, knowledge, and gear. Carry a beacon, probe, and shovel, and know how to use them.

- Check on current avalanche conditions before you go; contact **Bridger-Teton National Forest Avalanche Center** (307/733-2664, www.jhavalanche.org) for Grand Teton and read the **climbing ranger blog** (http://tetonclimbing.blogspot.com).

locations, regulations, permits, and safety concerns. Only Yellowstone permits concessionaires to guide backpacking trips.

Permits

Both national parks require permits for backcountry camping. A percentage of backcountry campsites may be reserved in advance in Yellowstone ($25, with submission of form available online) and Grand Teton ($35, www.recreation.gov, early Jan.-mid-May). Permits are also available first-come, first-served. In Yellowstone, they are available 48 hours before departure ($3/person/night, $15/party maximum, children 8 and younger free). For more information, access the online *Backcountry Trip Planner* (www.nps.gov/yell) for route and plan options. It

also contains lists of areas that are closed annually in spring, early summer, or fall due to heavy bear concentrations.

In Grand Teton, Backcountry camping permits are required and are available in advance online (www.recreation.gov, apply early Jan.-mid-May, $35/trip). Walk-in permits ($25/trip) are available first-come, first-served in person 24 hours before departure. Competition for walk-in permits is high in July and August; a waiting line usually forms at the Jenny Lake Ranger Station one hour before opening at 8am. Permits are also available at the Craig Thomas Discovery & Visitor Center in Moose. You may need an ice ax into early August for steep snowfields. Bear-proof canisters are required for food storage; the permit office has loaners.

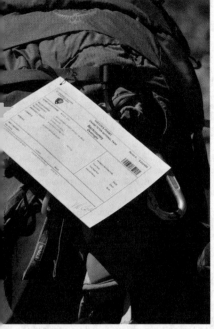

Backcountry permits are required in both parks.

Food Storage

Proper food storage while backpacking is essential in bear country. In Yellowstone, bear boxes are provided at a few backcountry campsites for storing food. In other places, hang food from bars or poles. Pack along a 35-foot rope and stuff sack to hang food. In Grand Teton, bear canisters are required for storing food. Permit offices have loaners, and rental gear shops in surrounding towns have them, too.

CLIMBING AND MOUNTAINEERING

If you want to stand on top of the Grand Teton, you can. Permits are not needed for mountaineering and climbing in the parks. But if trips require overnighting, then backcountry camping permits are needed. Several companies offer instruction and guide climbs in Grand Teton National Park. Two companies with worldwide reputations are **Exum Mountain Guides** (307/733-2297, http://exumguides.com) and **Jackson Hole Mountain Guides** (307/733-4979, www.jhmg.com).

FISHING

In Yellowstone National Park, more than 16 percent of the park's four million annual visitors go fishing. That high percentage compared to other parks speaks to the clean quality of the streams and lakes.

The epitome of Yellowstone fishing is fly-fishing. Hit up local fly shops to gain the best information on where the fish are biting, what flies are hatching, and what the fish are eating; then, purchase flies to match that scenario.

Anglers can fish sunrise to sunset, Memorial Day weekend through the first weekend in November. Park fishing regulations are strict: catch-and-release only of native trout, no fishing from docks or bridges, no bait, no barbs on hooks, and no lead. Seasonal closures occur for bears, low water levels, or high water temperatures. Consult the nearest ranger station or visitors center for specifics regarding where you want to fish, as catch-and-release rules and creel limits vary between waters.

Inside Yellowstone, a **fishing permit** is required for anglers 16 years and older ($18 for three days, $25 seven days, $40 season). Kids under 16 can fish on their parent's permit or get their own free permit signed by a parent or guardian. Kids must be supervised fishing under a parental license, but can fish by themselves with the free permit. Purchase fishing permits and pick up regulations at park visitors centers.

Outside Yellowstone, you'll need a **Montana fishing license** (http://fwp.mt.gov, $13-26 for residents, $25-70 for nonresidents). East of Cooke City, you'll need a **Wyoming fishing license** (residents: $3 youth, $6 adults daily, $24 adults annual; nonresidents: $15 youth, $14 adults daily, $92 adults annual). When purchasing your license, pick up a list of current regulations for the state and the waters you plan to fish.

In Grand Teton, you'll need multiple permits for boating or paddling excursions.

Leave No Trace

To keep the national parks pristine, visitors to these parks need to take an active role in maintaining them.

- **Plan ahead and prepare.** Hiking in the backcountry is inherently risky. Three miles at the high elevations in Wyoming may be much harder than three miles through your neighborhood park back home. Choose appropriate routes for mileage and elevation gain with this in mind, and carry hiking essentials.

- **Travel and camp on durable surfaces.** In front-country and backcountry campgrounds, camp in designated sites. Protect fragile plants by staying on trails even in mud, refusing to cut switchbacks, and walking single file. If you must walk off the trail, step on rocks, snow, or dry grasses rather than wet soil and delicate plants.

- **Leave what you find.** Flowers, rocks, and fur tufts on shrubs are protected park resources, as are historical cultural items. For lunch stops and camping, sit on rocks or logs where you find them rather than moving them to accommodate comfort.

- **Properly dispose of waste.** Pack out whatever you bring, including all garbage. If toilets are not available, pack out toilet paper. Urinate on rocks, logs, gravel, or snow to protect soils and plants from salt-starved wildlife, and bury feces 6-8 inches deep at least 200 feet from water.

- **Minimize campfire impacts.** Make fires in designated fire pits only, not on beaches (except by permit at Jackson Lake). Use small wrist-size dead and downed wood, not live branches. Be aware: Fires and collecting firewood are not permitted in some places in the parks.

- **Respect wildlife.** Bring along binoculars, spotting scopes, and telephoto lenses to aid in watching wildlife. Keep your distance. Do not feed any wildlife, even ground squirrels. Once fed, they become more aggressive.

- **Be considerate of other visitors.** Particularly be aware of cell phones and how their use or noise cuts into the natural soundscapes of the parks.

For more Leave No Trace information, visit www.LNT.org.

Purchase a Wyoming Aquatic Invasive Species (AIS) sticker and then successfully pass an AIS inspection in order to get a Grand Teton National Park boating permit. You will need additional permits if you plan to build a beach fire or camp overnight on Jackson Lake, or fish any lake or river while floating.

Native Species

National park fishing regulations enforce protection of native species through selected area closures and limits or bans on taking native species. Native trout include mountain whitefish, arctic grayling, and two cutthroat trout: the westslope and Yellowstone. Conserving these native species means relying on catch-and-release methods with barbless hooks and learning to recognize the fish. In particular with cutthroat, if you see a red slash along the throat, release it back into the water. You can also help protect these pristine fisheries by avoiding the use of lead and bait. By protecting native fish, you will also be aiding those animals such as bears and osprey that rely on them as food sources.

Nonnative fish were introduced into Yellowstone to help populate some of the once fishless waters and boost recreational fishing. While no longer stocked, they now pose a threat to native species through competition, predation, and hybridization. Fishing regulations encourage the taking of nonnative species. In some areas, anglers are asked to kill nonnative fish even if they do not plan to consume them. Nonnative species include rainbow, brown, lake, and brook trout. Fisheries managers are considering plans to remove nonnative trout and hybridized cutthroat from Soda Butte Creek in order to restock with native Yellowstone cutthroat.

Bear Concerns

Bears pose special considerations. Since smells attract bears that travel waterways, lessen your bear encounter chances by keeping fishy scents away from clothing. Catch-and-release fishing minimizes attracting bears.

For cleaning fish in the front country, dispose of the entrails in bear-resistant garbage cans. In the backcountry, do not bury or burn the innards, as that may attract bears. Instead, puncture the air bladder and throw the entrails into deep water where caught at least 100 feet away from a campsite, dock, or boat launch.

HORSEBACK RIDING

Dude ranches lines the perimeters of the parks and offer a modern cowboy and cowgirl approach to exploring the sights. Cowboy hats are optional for horseback riding, which was the traditional way of touring the park in its early days. But wear long pants rather than shorts to prevent chafing, and hiking boots, cowboy boots, or tennis shoes rather than sandals. Make reservations for these trips, and tip guides 15 percent.

WINTER SPORTS

Be mindful of skier and snowshoer etiquette. On roads where snowcoaches and snowmobiles travel, skiers and snowshoers should travel on the right side to allow vehicles to pass. On groomed trails, snowshoers should stay off the parallel skier tracks. With skier-set tracks, snowshoers should blaze their own trails. Winter trail maps are available online (www.nps.gov/yell) and at visitors centers.

New regulations for quieter, cleaner snowmobiles and limits on numbers of winter rigs mean vehicles are not the ambience wreckers they once were. To snowmobile on your own, you'll need a permit acquired in the annual **lottery** (www.recreation.gov, early Sept.-early Oct.). If you miss the lottery, you can pick up remaining or cancelled permits in November. If you bring your own snowmobile, it must be an approved BAT (Best Available Technology) snowmobile. All participants in your group must complete the **Yellowstone Snowmobile Education Certification** (www.nps.gov/yell) online training course, have driver's licenses, and be of certain ages to rent machines.

Visas and Officialdom

INTERNATIONAL TRAVELERS

Yellowstone has trip planning information in 10 different languages. Grand Teton has a selection of brochures in six languages. Ask for copies at visitors centers or online (www.nps.gov/yell or www.nps.gov/grte).

Entering the United States

International travelers entering the United States must have passports. One exception applies to travelers from Canada and countries in the Western Hemisphere Travel Initiative, who may use a U.S. passport card, enhanced driver's license, or acceptable alternate border crossing cards. In addition, visas are required except for countries with visa waivers (http://state.travel.gov). Except Canadians, international travelers entering the United States must have a current I-94 form ($6). You'll only need to show documentation at your international port of entry. Once in the United States, you will not need to show documentation when traveling between states except for commercial flights.

Money and Currency Exchange

International travelers should exchange currency at their major port of entry. As you travel, use ATM cards to get more cash. Smaller denominations ($50 and under) work best. Canadians who commonly use Canadian dollars in northern Montana should plan to convert to U.S. dollars instead. Businesses around Yellowstone are not prepared to handle other currency. Using a credit card while traveling will give you the best exchange rates.

Restricted Items

In general, the United States does not allow plants, drugs, firewood, or live bait to cross borders. Some fresh meats, poultry products, fruits, and vegetables are restricted, as are firearms. Pets are permitted to cross the border with a certificate of rabies vaccination dated within 30 days prior to crossing. Bear sprays are not allowed on airplanes in checked or carry-on luggage.

Travel Tips

TOURIST INFORMATION
Cell Phones

Cell phone coverage in Yellowstone and Grand Teton is not comprehensive, but around many of the larger developed areas, cell phones will work. Verizon is the predominant service. Cell phones using other services may have dropped calls. While hiking in remote terrain, canyons, or mountainous areas, you may not have coverage, so plan on self-rescuing rather than relying on a 911 call.

When using cell phones, be considerate. Turn off ringers, as phone noise catapults park visitors from a natural experience back into the hubbub of modern life. If you must make a call, move away from campsites and other visitors to avoid disrupting their experience. On trails, refrain from using phones in the presence of other hikers. Be considerate of other people in the backcountry and their desire to get away from it all.

Internet Access

Some of the park hotels have wireless Internet available, but not all. None of the visitors centers or campgrounds have wireless Internet, with the exception of the Craig Thomas Discovery & Visitor Center in Grand Teton National Park. Most hotels and private campgrounds outside the park have wireless Internet.

ACCESS FOR TRAVELERS WITH DISABILITIES

Yellowstone and Grand Teton National Parks offer accessibility brochures (www.nps.gov/yell or www.nps.gov/grte) at visitors center and online. Both parks have TDD (Yellowstone: 307/344-2386; Grand Teton: 307/739-3400) and ADA facilities, although they are not ubiquitous. All lodging facilities have a few rooms or cabins that are accessible. Inquire about these through the individual concessionaires that run the lodging properties. Most campgrounds have a few wheelchair-accessible sites and restrooms. These are listed in the accessibility brochures for both parks.

Yellowstone and Grand Teton have some paved and hard-surface trails that are wheelchair-accessible. While some of the boardwalk trails at the geothermal areas in Yellowstone are wheelchair-accessible, many of the boardwalks have steps at some point. All accessible trails are listed in the accessibility brochures. Both parks also offer some interpretive activities that are accessible. Locate these in the seasonal park newspapers. While pet dogs are not permitted on backcountry trails, service dogs are allowed, although due to bears, they are discouraged. With service dogs, be safe by sticking to well-traveled trails during midday.

Enhance Your Park Experience

With expert instructors, **Yellowstone Association Institute** (406/848-2400, www.yellowstoneassociation.com) offers trips for wildlife-watching, bird-watching, hiking, cross-country skiing, snowshoeing, sightseeing, and natural history exploration. The institute runs single-day and multiday field seminars, learning programs, private tours, and programs for kids, youth, teens, college students, and families. In-park transportation is in 14-passenger buses. Lodging at the institute's Lamar Buffalo Ranch inside Yellowstone is sometimes included.

With three campuses, two in Grand Teton National Park and one in Jackson, the **Teton Science School** (877/404-6626, www.tetonscience.org) runs programs in Grand Teton, Jackson Hole, National Elk Refuge, and Yellowstone. They offer wildlife-watching trips, summer camps, and programs for kids, teens, adults, and families. Programs can be half day, full day, or multiday. Some programs add hiking, cross-country skiing, or snowshoeing.

Both Yellowstone and Grand Teton use volunteers to help out on a variety of projects with their **Volunteer-in-Parks** programs (www.volunteer.gov/gov). Projects can be working in visitors centers, doing maintenance, helping with office and clerical work, and rehabilitating abused campsites and trails.

Blind or permanently disabled U.S. citizens and permanent residents can get a free lifetime National Parks and Federal Recreational Lands **Access Pass** (https://store.usgs.gov/pass/access.html). The pass admits the pass holder plus three other adults in the same vehicle; children under age 16 are free. Pass holders also get 50 percent discounts on federally run tours and campgrounds. Passes are available in person at entrance stations (proof of medical disability or eligibility for receiving federal benefits is required).

TRAVELING WITH CHILDREN

Yellowstone and Grand Teton were made for kids. Geysers, sputtering mud pots, fishing, and rampant wildlife are natural kid attractions. The National Park Service has designed ways to pique the interest of kids through educational activities online (www.nps.gov/yell or www.nps.gov/grte under "Learn About the Park"), in-park activities, and visitors center hands-on activities.

Junior Ranger Programs (www.nps.gov/kids/jrRangers.cfm) mix educational activities with experiences for families to do in the park. Pick up Junior Ranger activity guides ($3) at any visitors center. Kids complete the activities

and receive a Junior Ranger badge after stopping at a visitors center to get sworn in.

Yellowstone offers some **ranger programs** specifically geared toward kids. At the Madison Junior Ranger Station, 30-minute programs for families run multiple times daily during summer; 20-minute kids programs take place daily at Old Faithful Visitor Education Center. Check with visitors centers, campground bulletin boards, hotel activity desks, and park newspapers for other seasonal park schedules.

Yellowstone also has a **Young Scientist** program. Kids can become a Yellowstone Young Scientist with booklets ($5) full of self-guided science activities sold at Old Faithful Visitor Education Center. Different booklets on volcanic activity are geared to specific age groups. Check out a Young Scientist Toolkit for the gear to do the science study. When finished, return to the visitors center for a Young Scientist patch or key chain. Grand Teton's Jenny Lake has a **Young Naturalist Program** (307/739-3392, 1:30pm Mon., Wed., Fri. June-Aug., free) for self-guided outdoor exploration that the whole family can do together. The online **WebRangers** (www.nps.gov/webrangers) program offers games, coloring pages, and quizzes that can help kids learn about wildlife, plants, geysers, and ecology in both parks.

Other park programs include **Wildlife Olympics,** where kids test their physical skills against wildlife skills. Summer drop-in programs happen several days each week throughout the summer at Old Faithful Visitor Education Center (www.nps.gov/yell). In West Yellowstone, kids can learn about being smokejumpers through the **Junior Smokejumper Program** (Yellowstone Nature Connection, 10 Yellowstone Ave., 406/646-7557, http://yellowstonenatureconnection.org, 10am or 3pm daily mid-June-Sept. and Mon.-Fri. mid-May-mid-June, $5). Kids get to jump out of a plane and be sworn in as smokejumpers. Reservations by phone or online are recommended; parents can join in, too.

TRAVELING WITH PETS

Pets are allowed in the national parks, but only in limited areas: campgrounds, parking lots, and roadsides. They are not allowed on trails, boardwalks, beaches, in the backcountry, or on the Multi-Use Pathway in Grand Teton. Preventing conflicts with wildlife is the main reason; bears and bison provide their own class of reasons. To hike with your pooch, go to surrounding national forests.

While outside a vehicle or in a campground, pets must be caged or on a leash six feet or shorter. Be kind enough to avoid leaving them unattended in a car anywhere. Be considerate of wildlife and other visitors by keeping your pet under control and disposing of waste in garbage cans.

Inside Yellowstone, several of the cabin complexes permit pets for a fee ($25). Check for additional restrictions when you make reservations. In general, lodging in Grand Teton does not permit pets, but many outside-park locales in Jackson do. For kenneling pets, Jackson Hole has **DogJax** (3590 Southpark Dr., Jackson, 307/733-3647, http://dogjax.com).

SENIOR TRAVELERS

National parks, as well as lands run by the U.S. Fish and Wildlife Service, U.S. Forest Service, and Bureau of Land Management, offer a great bargain for U.S. citizens or permanent residents who are ages 62 and older: the National Parks and Federal Recreational Lands Pass ($10), which is valid for life. To purchase one, bring proof of age (state driver's license, birth certificate, or passport) in person to any national park entrance station. In a private vehicle, the card admits four adults in the vehicle, plus all children under age 16. The lifetime park pass also grants 50 percent discounts on fees for federally run tours and campgrounds; however, discounts do not apply to park concessionaire services like hotels, boat tours, and bus tours.

SOLO TRAVELERS

Plenty of people travel solo to national parks, but hiking alone in the Greater Yellowstone Ecosystem is not recommended due to bears and mountain lions. Nevertheless, some hikers still venture into the backcountry alone. If you're one of them, make lots of noise while hiking, carry pepper spray, and brush up on your bear skills. Solo travelers looking for trail companions can join park naturalist hikes. For times and dates, check with visitors centers, in park newspapers, or online. You can also connect with the Bozeman Adventure Club or Teton Sierra Club (www.meetup.com) for hikes. At popular trailheads, you can just hang out at the start and follow a larger group, staying close to them, or ask if you can join another few hikers. Many are happy to include additional hikers.

Health and Safety

WILDLIFE

Safe behavior can deter bear attacks. With strict food and garbage rules, the Greater Yellowstone Ecosystem has minimized aggressive bear encounters, attacks, and deaths, for both humans and bears. Bears are dangerous around food, be it a carcass in the woods, a pack left on a trail, or a cooler left in a campsite. Protecting bears and protecting yourself starts with being conscious of food, including wrappers and crumbs. Snack-mix tidbits dropped along trails attract wildlife, as do biodegradable apple cores chucked into the forest. Pick up what you drop, and pack out all garbage; don't leave a Hansel-and-Gretel trail for the bears.

Camp safely: Use low-odor foods, keep food and cooking gear out of sleeping sites in the backcountry, and store it inside your vehicle or inside bear boxes in front-country campgrounds. In front-country campgrounds, you'll find detailed explanations of how to camp safely in bear country stapled to your picnic table.

While hiking, make noise, go in groups of at least four people, stay on the trail, and carry and know how to use pepper spray. Be alert. If you come across a carcass, depart immediately. Avoid hiking at dawn or dusk, which are prime animal times. If you encounter a bear, remain calm. Back away slowly rather than running away like prey. Lower your eyes in deference and talk quietly. If a bear charges, use pepper spray in its eyes. Pepper spray should be sprayed directly at the sensitive facial tissues, not on people like bug repellent. If attacked, drop face down onto the ground and play dead, leaving your pack on to protect your back.

Mountain lions rarely prey on humans, but they can with small kids. Making noise for bears will also help you avoid surprising a lion. Hike with others, and keep kids close. If you stumble upon a lion, above all, do not run. Be calm, and group together to appear bigger. Look at the cat with peripheral vision rather than staring straight on, and back away slowly. If the lion attacks, fight back with everything: rocks, sticks, or kicking.

While **bison** appear docile, they are speedier than they look. They can head-butt or gore people.

LAND AND WATER HAZARDS

Drowning from falling into swift water is one of the top causes of death in the Greater Yellowstone Ecosystem. Be extremely cautious around lakes, fast-moving streams, and waterfalls. Rivers can be swift, frigid, clogged with submerged obstacles, unforgiving, and sometimes lethal. A second cause of injuries and death is falling while climbing off-trail on steep, cliffy terrain.

It's really cool to see geysers and mud pots, but they are dangerous in several ways. **Boiling geothermal waters** have scalded people stupid enough to think of them as hot tubs. They've even caused death. **Breakable crusts** surrounding features can hide boiling waters. Thermals can contain infectious organisms that can be fatal, and can emit toxic gases. To protect yourself, stay on boardwalks and trails. If gases make you feel sick, leave the area.

While **ice** often looks solid to step on, it harbors unseen caverns beneath. Buried crevasses (large vertical cracks) are difficult to see, and snow bridges can collapse as a person crosses. **Steep-angled snowfields** also pose a danger from falling. Use an ice ax and caution, or stay off them. If you want to slide on the snow for fun, slide only where you have a safe run out away from rocks and trees.

Inhaling dust from deer mice droppings can lead to **hantavirus** infections, with

Wildlife Safety Tips

While there are no guarantees of spotting wildlife, huge broad meadows in the parks make it easy to see wildlife. You may get to see bison, elk, moose, deer, pronghorn, wolves, coyotes, foxes, raptors, or bears. Remember that wildlife is just that....WILD. Though bison, elk, or even bears may appear tame, they are not and gorings are common. Here are a few hints to remain safe.

- Do not approach wildlife. Although our inclinations tell us to scoot in for a closer look, crowding wildlife puts you at risk and endangers the animal, often scaring it off. Seemingly docile bison and elk have suddenly gored people crowding too close. Sometimes simply the presence of people can habituate an animal to hanging around people; with bears, this can lead to more aggressive behavior. Maintain at least **100 yards away** (the length of a football field) from bears and wolves. For all other wildlife, stay at least **25 yards away**.

- Safety is important when watching wildlife—safety for you and safety for the wildlife. For spying wildlife up close, use a good pair of binoculars or a spotting scope.

- Use telephoto lenses for photography rather than scooting in too close. Bison gorings have been getting more prevalent, all related to taking photos, especially selfies with tablets or cell phones. Since 2000, bison have injured 25 people, at least half when taking photos.

- Do not feed any animal. Feeding can amp up their aggression. Because human food is not part of their natural diet, they may suffer at foraging on their own. If you see a carcass on a trail, move away and report it to park rangers. No doubt an animal is nearby protecting it.

- Follow instructions for food storage. They are designed to protect you and wildlife. Bears, wolves, and coyotes may become more aggressive when acquiring food, and ravens can strew food and garbage, making it more available to other wildlife. Your actions may affect the next camper staying at your campsite.

- Let the animal's or bird's behavior guide your behavior. If the animal appears twitchy, nervous, or points eyes and ears directly at you, back off: You're too close. The goal is to watch wild animals go about their normal business, rather than to see how they react to disruption. If you behave like a predator stalking an animal, the creature will assume you are one. Use binoculars and telephoto lenses for moving in close, rather than approaching an animal.

- If you see wildlife along a road, use pullouts or broad shoulders to drive completely off the road. Do not block the middle of the road. Use the car as a blind to watch wildlife, and keep pets inside. If you see a bear, you're better off just driving by slowly. Bear jams tend to condition the bruin to become accustomed to vehicles, one step toward getting into more trouble.

accompanying flu-like symptoms. Avoid burrows and woodpiles thick with rodents. Store all food in rodent-proof containers. If you find rodent dust in your gear, disinfect it with water and bleach (1.5 cups bleach to one gallon water). If you contract the virus, get immediate medical attention.

Lakes and streams can carry parasites like *Giardia lamblia.* If ingested, it causes cramping, nausea, and severe diarrhea for up to six weeks. Avoid giardia by boiling water (for one minute, plus one minute for each 1,000 feet of elevation above sea level) or using a one-micron filter. Bleach also works (add two drops per quart and wait 30 minutes). Tap water in campgrounds, hotels, and picnic areas has been treated.

Bugs can carry diseases such as **West Nile virus** and **Rocky Mountain spotted fever**. Protect yourself by wearing long sleeves and pants, plus using insect repellent in spring and summer when mosquitoes and ticks are common. If you are bitten by a tick, remove it, disinfect the bite, and see a doctor if lesions or a rash appears.

PERSONAL SAFETY

Due to the high elevation and arid climate, winds, altitude, and lower humidity can add up to a fast case of **dehydration**—which often manifests first as a headache. While in the Greater Yellowstone Ecosystem and especially while hiking, drink lots of water. Carry enough water to consume more than you normally would. With children, monitor their fluid intake.

Some visitors from sea level feel lightheadedness, headaches, or shortness of breath at the **high altitudes** of Yellowstone and Grand Teton. To acclimatize, slow down the pace of hiking and drink lots of fluids. If symptoms spike, descend in elevation as soon as possible. Altitude also increases UV radiation exposure: To prevent sunburn, use a strong sunscreen and wear sunglasses and a hat.

Insidious and subtle, **hypothermia** sneaks up on exhausted and physically unprepared hikers. The body's inner core loses heat, reducing mental and physical functions. Watch for uncontrolled shivering, incoherence, poor judgment, fumbling, mumbling, and slurred speech. Avoid becoming hypothermic by staying dry. Don rain gear and warm moisture-wicking layers, rather than cottons that won't dry and fail to retain heat. Get hypothermic hikers into dry clothing and shelter. Give warm, nonalcoholic and non-caffeinated liquids. If the victim cannot regain body heat, strip and use skin-to-skin contact with another person in a sleeping bag.

Incorrect socks and ill-fitting shoes cause most **blisters.** Cotton socks absorb water from the feet while you're hiking and hold onto it, providing a surface for friction. Synthetic or wool-blend socks wick water away from the skin. To prevent blisters, recognize "hot spots" or rubs, applying moleskin, blister pads, or New-Skin to sensitive areas. In a pinch, slap duct tape on trouble spots. Once a blister occurs, apply blister bandages or Second Skin, a product developed for burns that cools blisters and cushions them. Cover Second Skin with moleskin to absorb future rubbing and secure it in place.

Resources

Suggested Reading

GEOLOGY

Bryan, T. Scott, *The Geysers of Yellowstone*. Boulder, CO: University Press of Colorado, 2008. A guidebook for geyser fans, the work has maps, photos, and cultural and historical information on visiting the park's 500 thermal features, including geysers.

Craighead, Charles, *Geology of Grand Teton National Park: How the Mountains Came to Be*. Windsor, CO: Paragon Press, 2006. This 55-page book covers the geology behind the Tetons and Jackson Hole and details the peaks and major features.

Good, J. M. M., and Kenneth L. Pierce, *Interpreting the Landscape: Recent and Ongoing Geology of Grand Teton and Yellowstone National Parks*. Moose, WY: Grand Teton Association, 1997. This 58-page book with photos and diagrams covers the basics for both parks, but does not include more recent geologic discoveries.

Love, J. David, John C. Reed Jr., and Kenneth L. Pierce, *A Geological Chronicle of Jackson Hole & the Teton Range*. Moose, WY: Grand Teton Natural History Association, 2003. Maps, photos, charts, and elevation graphs add to the discussion of the sinking valley and youngest peaks in the Rockies.

Smith, Robert B., and Lee J. Siegel, *Windows into the Earth: The Geologic Story of Yellowstone and Grand Teton National Parks*. New York, NY: Oxford University Press, 2000.

The authors detail the volcanic and tectonic past of Yellowstone-Teton country with an emphasis on dynamic processes.

Thomas, Robert, and William Fritz, *Roadside Geology of Yellowstone Country*. Missoula, MT: Mountain Press Publishing Co., 2011. With color photos, diagrams, and maps, this classic geology guide covers Yellowstone and surrounding regions, including the Beartooth Mountains, Quake Lake, and the valleys of Gardiner, Wapiti, and Paradise.

GUIDEBOOKS

Schmidt, Jeremy, and Steven Fuller, *National Geographic Yellowstone and Grand Teton National Parks Road Guide: The Essential Guide for Motorists*. National Geographic, 2010. A handy 93-page guide to driving the roads in both parks. Each section has maps with roadside stops identified and detailed.

Walker, Carter, *Moon Montana & Wyoming: Including Yellowstone, Grand Teton & Glacier National Parks*. Berkeley, CA: Avalon Travel Publishing, 2014. A guidebook for traveling in Montana and Wyoming.

Yellowstone Association, *Yellowstone: The Official Guide to Touring the World's First National Park*. Yellowstone Association, 2014. The Yellowstone Association annually updates this cross between a top highlights guide to the park and a color photo book. It describes road tours, sights, hikes, wildlife, and flora.

HIKING AND CLIMBING

Anderson, Roger, and Carol Shively Anderson, *A Ranger's Guide to Yellowstone Day Hikes*. Helena, MT: Farcountry Press, updated 2013. Written by two park rangers, this guide covers 29 hikes, with details about geology, plants, and history.

Duffy, Katy, and Darwin Wile, *Teton Trails: A Guide to the Trails of Grand Teton National Park*. Moose, WY: Grand Teton Natural History Association, 1995. Very detailed descriptions including natural history on trails in the park. Covers short hikes to overnighters.

Ortenburger, Leigh, and Reynold Jackson, *A Climber's Guide to the Teton Range*. Seattle, WA: The Mountaineers, 1996. This climbing guide details 800 routes on 200 peaks.

Rossiter, Richard, *Best Climbs Grand Teton National Park*. Guilford, CT: Falcon Guides, 2012. This new version of his 1994 Teton Classics book covers popular climbing routes on the Teton peaks, from easier ascents to technically challenging summits.

Schneider, Bill, *Best Easy Day Hikes in Grand Teton National Park*. Guilford, CT: Falcon Guides, 2012. Descriptions of day hikes for the park, including family-friendly options.

Schneider, Bill, *Best Easy Day Hikes in Yellowstone*. Guilford, CT: Falcon Guides, 2011. A trail guide covering 30 day hikes in Yellowstone for families. Includes geyser basin walks.

Schneider, Bill, *Hiking the Absaroka-Beartooth Wilderness*. Guilford, CT: Falcon Guides, 2015. For travelers on the Beartooth Highway, this is the hiking guide for the trails along the way.

Schneider, Bill, *Hiking Grand Teton National Park*. Guilford, CT: Falcon Guides, 2012. A comprehensive guide on trails in Grand Teton—from short jaunts to long ascents, including backpacking routes.

Schneider, Bill, *Hiking Yellowstone National Park*. Guilford, CT: Falcon Guides, 2012. A comprehensive hiking guide covering more than 100 hikes, from short flat trails to long traverses, including backpacking trips.

Woods, Rebecca, *Jackson Hole Hikes*. Jackson, WY: White Willow Publishing, 2009. A hiking guide for Grand Teton National Park, Gros Ventre Wilderness, Teton Wilderness, Snow King, and Teton Pass.

HISTORY

Barnes, Christine, *Old Faithful Inn: 100th Anniversary*. WW West, 2003. From the author of the Great Lodges books, this book celebrates the history of Yellowstone's historic lodge in photos and text.

Black, George, *Empire of Shadows: The Epic Story of Yellowstone*. New York, NY: St. Martin's Griffin, 2013. The story of the early explorations of Yellowstone until the establishment of the park and the flight of Chief Joseph and the Nez Perce.

Miller, M. Mark, *Adventures in Yellowstone: Early Travelers Tell Their Tales*. Guilford, CT: TwoDot, 2009. A narrated collection of stories from early park travelers with historical photos.

Miller, M. Mark, *The Stories of Yellowstone: Adventure Tales from the World's First National Park*. Guilford, CT: TwoDot, 2014. A collection of writing from early park visitors from 1807 to the 1920s.

Nabokov, Peter, and Lawrence Loendorf, *Restoring a Presence: American Indians and Yellowstone National Park*. Norman, OK: University of Oklahoma Press, 2004.

Identifies Native American archaeology and ethnography in Yellowstone National Park.

Nerburn, Kent, *Chief Joseph & the Flight of the Nez Perce: The Untold Story of an American Tragedy*. San Francisco, CA: Harper One, 2006. Chronicles the 1,800-mile journey made by Chief Joseph and 800 Nez Perce from Oregon to northern Montana while fleeing the U.S. Army.

Righter, Robert W. *Crucible For Conservation: The Struggle For Grand Teton National Park* and *Peaks, Politics, and Passion: Grand Teton National Park Comes of Age*. Moose, WY: Grand Teton Natural History Association, 1982 and 2014. The first work recounts the history behind the creation of the park, a battle that stretched over 50 years. The second book, a continuation of the first, covers parkhood to the present day.

Whittlesey, Lee H., *Yellowstone Place Names*. Wonderland Publishing Co., 2006. Gives the background and trivia on about 1,000 names of places in Yellowstone.

NATURAL HISTORY

Living Colors: Microbes of Yellowstone National Park. Yellowstone Association, Montana State University Biology Institute, and Montana Institute Ecosystems, 2013. A 52-page book with color photos of the park's geothermal microbes and information on where to see them.

Johnson, Kurt F., *A Field Guide to Yellowstone and Grand Teton National Parks*. Helena, MT: Farcountry Press, 2013. Written by a Jackson Hole naturalist and photographer, this broad and well-rounded field guide gives details on rocks, minerals, plants, animals, birds, and fish.

Kershaw, Linda, Andy MacKinnon, and Jim Pojar. *Plants of the Rocky Mountains*. Auburn, WA: Lone Pine Publishing, 1998. A Lone Pine Field Guide for eight types of flora found in the Rocky Mountains: trees, shrubs, wildflowers, aquatics, grasses, ferns, mosses, and lichens. Although the pictures are small, the detailed descriptions of appearance, season, and habitat help in identification. Notes on each of the 1,300 species in the book include fun tidbits on the origin of names and Native American uses.

Shaw, Richard, and Marian A. Shaw, *Plants of Yellowstone and Grand Teton National Parks*. Helena, MT: Wheelwright Publishing, 2008. Written by botanists and veterans of 31 years as naturalists in Yellowstone, the book identifies wildflowers, shrubs, and trees.

Yellowstone National Park, Yellowstone Resources and Issues Handbook. Washington, DC: National Park Service, U.S. Department of the Interior, annually published. Heavy on current information, this 268-page compendium is produced and reviewed annually by the staff of Yellowstone. Covers current research on history, cultural resources, Greater Yellowstone Ecosystem, geology, thermal life, vegetation, fire, and wildlife.

RECREATION

Gollin Evans, Lisa, *Outdoor Family Guide to Yellowstone & Grand Teton National Parks*. Mountaineers Books, second edition, 2006. Contains 50 family outings including hiking, biking, paddling, and horseback riding.

Harrison, Melynda, *Ski Trails of Southwest Montana: 30 of the Best Cross Country & Snowshoe Trails Near Big Sky, Bozeman & Paradise Valley*. Bozeman, MT: First Ascent Press, 2007. Covers cross-country ski and snowshoe trails surrounding northern Yellowstone. As of 2015, planned sequels for the Greater Yellowstone Ecosystem to take in West Yellowstone, Yellowstone, the Tetons, and Jackson Hole have not been published.

Lomax, Becky, *Moon Montana, Wyoming & Idaho Camping: Including Yellowstone, Grand Teton, and Glacier National Parks.* Berkeley, CA: Avalon Travel Publishing, third edition, 2014. A camping guide for the northern Rocky Mountains, especially the national park corridor.

Nelson, Don, *Paddling Yellowstone and Grand Teton National Parks.* Guilford, CT: Falcon Guides, 1999. For kayakers and canoers, 38 paddle routes cover day trips to overnighters on park lakes. Some of the permit information is out of date, but routes are still doable.

Parks, Richard, *Fishing Yellowstone National Park: An Angler's Complete Guide to More than 100 Streams, Rivers, and Lakes.* Guilford, CT: Lyons Press, 2007. Written by a Montana fishing guide, the book tells you where and when to fish, plus tips on lures and tackle.

Retallic, Ken, *Flyfisher's Guide to Wyoming: Including Grand Teton and Yellowstone National Parks.* Belgrade, MT: Wilderness Adventures Press, revised edition 2012. Written by a local angler, this guide covers iconic rivers in Yellowstone and Grand Teton, plus famous rivers surrounding the parks.

Verderber, Gustav W., *Photographing Yellowstone National Park: Where to Find Perfect Shots and How to Take Them.* Woodstock, VT: Countryman Press, 2007. Part of The Photographer's Guide series, this 88-page book provides advice on where, when, and how to get stellar wildlife and scenery shots.

WILDLIFE

Fisher, Chris, *Birds of the Rocky Mountains.* Auburn, WA: Lone Pine Publishing, 1997. A Lone Pine Field Guide for birds found in the Rocky Mountains, from raptors to waterfowl, songbirds to woodpeckers. Large drawings help with identification, and descriptions include details on size, range, habitat, nesting, and feeding.

Fisher, Chris, Don Pattie, and Tamara Hartson, *Mammals of the Rocky Mountains.* Auburn, WA: Lone Pine Publishing, 2000. A Lone Pine Field Guide for 91 species of animals found in the Rocky Mountains. Each animal has details on physical description, behavior, habitat, food, denning, range, and young.

McMillion, Scott, *Mark of the Grizzly.* Guilford, CT: Lyons Press, 2011. This second edition of McMillion's top-selling book adds more recent stories on bear attacks to his original collection and digs deeper into why they happened.

Schneider, Bill. *Bear Aware.* Guilford, CT: Falcon Press, 2004. This handy little 96-page book is packed with advice on how to hike safely in bear country, debunking bear myths with facts.

Smith, Douglas, and Gary Ferguson, *Decade of the Wolf, Revised and Updated: Returning the Wild to Yellowstone.* Guilford, CT: Lyons Press, 2012. Written by a wolf biologist and nature writer, this book tells the story of the restoration of wolves to Yellowstone.

Steinhart, Peter, *The Company of Wolves.* New York, NY: Vintage Books, 1996. An analysis of wolf behavior: familial relationships, social ties, and predation.

Wilkinson, Todd, and Michael H. Francis, *Watching Yellowstone and Grand Teton Wildlife: The Best Places to Look from Roads and Trails.* Helena, MT: Riverbend Publishing, 2004. This 96-page book describes the best places to spot 45 different species of wildlife in the parks.

Internet Resources

YELLOWSTONE NATIONAL PARK

Yellowstone National Park
www.nps.gov/yell
Official National Park Service website for the park.

Yellowstone Association
www.yellowstoneassociation.org
Home of the Yellowstone Association Institute educational programs and Yellowstone Association bookstores.

Trail Guides Yellowstone
www.trailguidesyellowstone.com
A Yellowstone National Park concessionaire that guides hiking and backpacking trips, but also offers detailed trail descriptions with photos on their website.

GRAND TETON NATIONAL PARK

Grand Teton National Park
www.nps.gov/grte
Official National Park Service website for the park.

Teton Association
www.grandtetonpark.org
Information and bookstore for Grand Teton.

Teton Science School
www.tetonscience.org
Educational programs for Grand Teton, Yellowstone, and Jackson Hole.

Teton Hiking Trails
www.tetonhikingtrails.com
A new source of detailed information on hiking trails in Grand Teton National Park.

JACKSON HOLE

National Elk Refuge
www.fws.gov/nationalelkrefuge
Information on visitor activities and wildlife on the National Elk Refuge.

Jackson Hole Chamber of Commerce
www.jacksonholechamber.com
Businesses, activities, entertainment, lodging, and restaurants for Jackson Hole.

NATIONAL FORESTS

Recreation.gov
www.recreation.gov
Official site for campground reservations in the national forests surrounding Yellowstone and Grand Teton. Also, the website for Grand Teton backcountry campsite reservations.

Bridger-Teton National Forest
www.fs.usda.gov/btnf
Official site for national forest land east and south of Grand Teton National Park and Jackson Hole.

Caribou-Targhee National Forest
www.fs.usda.gov/ctnf
Official site for national forest land west of Grand Teton and southwest of Yellowstone.

Custer-Gallatin National Forest
www.fs.usda.gov/gallatin
Official site for national forest land on the north end of Yellowstone.

Shoshone National Forest
www.fs.usda.gov/shoshone
Official site for national forest land on the east side of Yellowstone and Grand Teton.

IDAHO

Idaho Department of Commerce
www.visitidaho.org

Idaho Transportation Department
http://511.idaho.gov
For road conditions, construction disruptions, webcams, and travel information.

MONTANA

Montana Office of Tourism
www.visitmt.com

Montana Department of Transportation
www.mdt.mt.gov/travinfo
For road conditions, construction disruptions, webcams, and travel information.

WYOMING

Wyoming Travel and Tourism
www.wyomingtourism.org

Wyoming Department of Transportation
www.wyoroad.info
For road conditions, construction disruptions, webcams, and travel information.

Index

XYZ

List of Maps

Also Available

MONTANA

JUDY JEWELL & W. C. McRAE

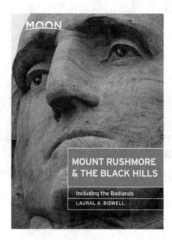

MOUNT RUSHMORE
& THE BLACK HILLS

Including the Badlands

LAURAL A. BIDWELL

WYOMING

CARTER G. WALKER

DENVER
BOULDER &
COLORADO SPRINGS

MINDY SINK

MAP SYMBOLS

≡≡≡ Expressway	○ City/Town	✈ Airport	⛳ Golf Course
≡≡≡ Primary Road	◉ State Capital	✈ Airfield	🅿 Parking Area
≡≡≡ Secondary Road	⊛ National Capital	▲ Mountain	⛬ Archaeological Site
⁃⁃⁃⁃ Unpaved Road	★ Point of Interest	✛ Unique Natural Feature	⛪ Church
—— Feature Trail	• Accommodation		⛽ Gas Station
- - - Other Trail	▾ Restaurant/Bar	☈ Waterfall	Glacier
·········· Ferry	▪ Other Location	▲ Park	Mangrove
≡≡≡ Pedestrian Walkway	Λ Campground	❶ Trailhead	Reef
▪▪▪▪ Stairs		🎿 Skiing Area	Swamp

CONVERSION TABLES

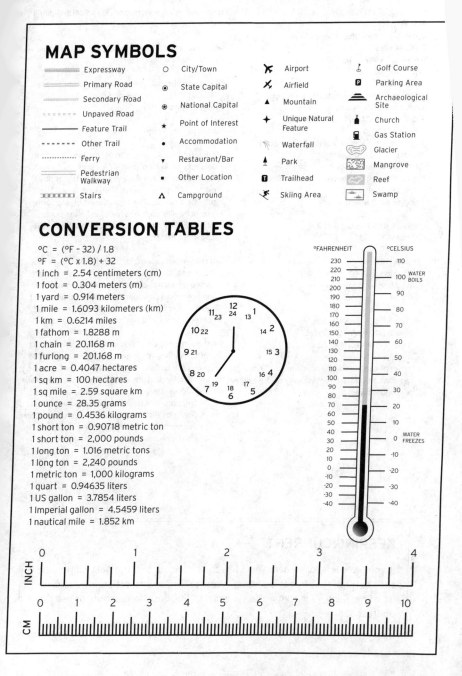

°C = (°F - 32) / 1.8
°F = (°C x 1.8) + 32
1 inch = 2.54 centimeters (cm)
1 foot = 0.304 meters (m)
1 yard = 0.914 meters
1 mile = 1.6093 kilometers (km)
1 km = 0.6214 miles
1 fathom = 1.8288 m
1 chain = 20.1168 m
1 furlong = 201.168 m
1 acre = 0.4047 hectares
1 sq km = 100 hectares
1 sq mile = 2.59 square km
1 ounce = 28.35 grams
1 pound = 0.4536 kilograms
1 short ton = 0.90718 metric ton
1 short ton = 2,000 pounds
1 long ton = 1.016 metric tons
1 long ton = 2,240 pounds
1 metric ton = 1,000 kilograms
1 quart = 0.94635 liters
1 US gallon = 3.7854 liters
1 Imperial gallon = 4.5459 liters
1 nautical mile = 1.852 km

ΟΝ YELLOWSTONE & GRAND TETON
)n Travel
ember of the Perseus Books Group
0 Fourth Street
keley, CA 94710, USA
ww.moon.com

ditor and Series Manager: Sabrina Young
Copy Editor: Ann Seifert
Production and Graphics Coordinator:
  Elizabeth Jang
Cover Design: Faceout Studios, Charles Brock
Moon Logo: Tim McGrath
Map Editor: Kat Bennett
Cartographers: Kat Bennett, Lohnes + Wright,
  Chris Henrick
Indexer: Greg Jewett

ISBN-13: 978-1-63121-264-2
ISSN: 1542-8850

Printing History
1st Edition — 2000
7th Edition — May 2016
5 4 3 2 1

Text © 2016 by Becky Lomax.
Maps © 2016 by Avalon Travel.
All rights reserved.

Some photos and illustrations are used by
  permission and are the property of the original
  copyright owners.

Front cover photo: Yellowstone's Black Pool © Vadim
  Balakin/Getty Images

Back cover photo: biking along the base of the
  South Tetons © Becky Lomax

All interior photos © Becky Lomax except pages
  248, 291 © Steve Penner, and page 292 © Grand
  Targhee Resort

Printed in Canada by Friesens

KEEPING CURRENT

If you have a favorite gem you'd like to see included in the next edition, or
see anything that needs updating, clarification, or correction, please drop
us a line. Send your comments via email to feedback@moon.com, or use the
address above.